REAL
ESTATE

SECOND EDITION

REAL ESTATE

Larry E. Wofford
University of Tulsa

With legal assistance provided by
John Forrester Hicks
College of Law
University of Tulsa

JOHN WILEY & SONS
New York Chichester Brisbane Toronto Singapore

Library of Congress Cataloging in Publication Data:

Wofford, Larry E. (Larry Eugene)
  Real estate.

  1. Real estate business.   I. Title.
HD1375.W63 1986   333.33   85-26462
ISBN 0-471-83885-3

Printed in the United States of America

10 9 8 7 6 5 4 3 2 1

Dedicated to the memory of
Martha Kennett Wofford,
friend, wife, inspiration

PREFACE

This book is written for students. It is designed to take advantage of the innate curiosity that real estate students have about the field. Whether this curiosity is the result of a fascination with how the buildings around them are created, bought, and sold, or a more practical concern with being prepared for the real estate dealings they will be making throughout their lifetimes, the curiosity is there. To harness this curiosity and effectively channel it into an interesting and productive learning experience, *Real Estate* has been carefully organized and made highly readable. It holds attention and generates interest by actively involving the reader in the fascinating field of real estate.

Real Estate is also written for instructors. The coverage is broad enough and the organization flexible enough to complement a wide range of personal preferences for course organization and emphasis. The instructor can easily and conveniently tailor virtually any type of course imaginable. In addition, such customizing can occur without affecting the organizational aspects of the book.

How does *Real Estate* provide these benefits for both the reader and the instructor? It does the job with special features that deserve brief mention.

Mentor Approach

Real Estate is written directly to the reader. It is a step-by-step introduction to the fundamental concepts and practices of real estate by a personal mentor. This direct, "mentor style" of writing provides a level of continuity and involvement not found in other textbooks. The continuity is enhanced by an example found throughout the book: a 30-acre farm named Blackacre. Blackacre is woven into many chapters to provide a consistent theme and frame of reference, and to maintain reader interest. Numerous other examples are used to further enhance understanding.

Organization and Coverage

Real Estate is organized around the integrative Real Estate Environment Model. This model organizes all of the activities and areas of study associated with real estate into three major categories. The model highlights the fact that each real estate activity and area of knowledge is related to all other such areas. The three major categories in the model are real estate fundamentals, real estate decision areas, and real estate decision support areas. Each of the three major categories in the model then becomes the focal point of a major section of the book. When combined with introductory and closing sections, the result is a cohesive, organized, and integrated learning package. Such organization provides the reader with a perspective and a sense of order concerning fundamental real estate knowledge.

The organization of the book is quite straightforward. Part One is an introduction to real estate and the real estate business using the Real Estate Environment Model. Part Two, Real Estate Fundamentals, develops an understanding of basic knowledge common to all areas of real estate activity. In Part Three, the decision areas of lending, equity investment, and development are examined. The need for assistance in making and executing these decisions leads to the consideration of real estate decision support areas. Therefore, Part Four deals with the areas of marketing, management, appraisal, and counseling. The book concludes with a consideration of the outlook for real estate in Part Five.

Within this organizational framework is a coverage broad enough to provide material for many different teaching emphases. All traditional and many less traditional topics are included. Representative of the less traditional chapters are real estate counseling and real estate markets. In addition, the coverage of certain topics is spread between two or more chapters to enhance flexibility. For example, in the area of fundamentals are two chapters on federal income taxation. The first chapter covers basic tax concepts and the tax consequences of single family home ownership. The second taxation chapter considers the taxation of real estate investments. For an instructor choosing not to emphasize investments, the second chapter may be skipped or given only cursory treatment. Chapters on brokerage, real estate investment, and appraisal fall into this same category.

Other Features

Each chapter of the book is designed to maximize the reader's learning. Chapter objectives clearly identify the critical concepts to be covered by the chapter. At the conclusion of each chapter a "Quick Quiz" provides instant feedback about the level of understanding of basic concepts. A "Questions and Exercises" section provides additional insights. "Key Terminology" summarizes the particular words and phrases necessary to speak the language of real estate. Additional sources of information on the subject of the chapter are suggested in the "If You Want to Read More" feature at the end of each chapter.

Within the body of the chapters, extensive use is made of tables and charts. All of these items illustrate or reinforce an important real estate point or concept. This reinforcement is crucial to learning. With respect to reinforcement, frequent cross references clearly convey the interdependencies between the various areas of study in real estate.

Instructor's Resource Manual

For instructors, a complete resource manual containing numerous planning and teaching aids is available. This manual contains course outlines for courses with various emphases, chapter outlines, tips on teaching adult students, answers to all questions and exercises in the text, key terminology definitions, additional suggested assignments, and a test bank containing over 1000 questions. The manual is designed to make the instructor's teaching as efficient and effective as possible.

A Final Word

Real Estate is a flexible, up-to-date introduction to the fascinating world of real estate. It is organized and readable for students and teachable for instructors. The package of *Real Estate* and *Instructor's Resource Manual* is a comprehensive and usable educational system.

As you use *Real Estate,* please make notes of any changes you think would improve the package and send them to me through my publisher at this address:

Larry E. Wofford
c/o Real Estate Editor
John Wiley & Sons, Inc.
605 Third Avenue
New York, New York 10158

Your help in making the third edition more effective is appreciated.

I sincerely hope you enjoy using this book and the Instructor's Resource Manual. Real estate is simply too much fun not to enjoy learning about it *or* teaching it.

Larry E. Wofford

ACKNOWLEDGMENTS

Although this book has only my name on the cover, many other people made substantial contributions to its development and ultimate completion. For their efforts, these individuals deserve special recognition and a public expression of my appreciation.

Two individuals shared some of the writing duties with me. John Forrester Hicks, Professor in the College of Law at the University of Tulsa, prepared the initial drafts of Chapters 4, 5, 6, and 14. John also acted as a consultant on many other legal questions that arose in the course of writing the book, and always made time to deal with my problems. Stephen A. Pyhrr, Partner, Davis and Associates, Austin, Texas, wrote the first draft of the material that later became Chapters 18 and 19. Their work was outstanding and made my job much easier.

In writing the first edition of this book I was fortunate to have a publisher and a group of true professionals eager to provide any necessary assistance. Among that group was Rick Leyh, who sweated along with me for much of the entire gestation period. In preparing the second edition Rick Leyh performed many of the very early duties. Frank Burrows then provided outstanding assistance for the remainder of this edition, and his direction and support are genuinely appreciated. Other members of the Wiley staff who played key roles in producing the final product are Scott Klein and Jane Hanley, copyediting supervisors; Debora Fratello, production supervisor; and Dawn Stanley, the designer of this edition. Each of them has my thanks.

During the writing of the first edition, many useful comments were received from reviewers. These comments led to revisions that substantially improved the text. I appreciate the willingness of these professionals to share their expertise. In alphabetical order these reviewers are:

David Barnett, Southwestern Oklahoma State University
Donald Bodley, Eastern Kentucky University

Ken Combs, Del Mar College
Lawrence Danks, Stockton State College
Richard Duce, North Seattle Community College
Stephan Hamilton, Willamette Consulting, Inc.
Vincent Hubin, Fairleigh Dickinson University
Hans Isakson, University of Texas at Arlington
Joseph Isert, Lexington Technical Institute/University of Kentucky
Vance Johnson, Florida International University
Robert Lyon, Texas A & M University
Jerry Prock, Pan American University
Terry Robertson, University of Oklahoma
Anthony Sanders, Ohio State University
David Schurger, South Oklahoma City Junior College
John Selling, Property Factors
Martha Troxell, Indiana University of Pennsylvania
Bill Weaver, North Texas State University
James Webb, University of Akron
Wayne Weeks, Eastern Michigan University

A smaller group of reviewers provided welcome criticism for the second edition. These comments were quite helpful in honing and shaping the revision effort. These reviewers and their affiliations are (in alphabetical order).

James Earle, Southwest Missouri State University
George C. Potter, Western Illinois University
Edward Prill, Colorado State University
Herbert Roth, Shippensburg University
H. Joe Story, Pacific University

Other individuals making significant contributions to this book are John D. Dorchester, Jr. and Joseph J. Vella, both of Real Estate Research Corporation. Donald Bodley of Eastern Kentucky University, provided many useful suggestions. Jack Friedman and Jack Harris of the Texas Real Estate Research Center provided needed assistance at critical times. Others providing useful comments for the second edition are Larry Robertson, Executive Officer of the Metropolitan Tulsa Board of Realtors; James Webb, University of Akron; Christopher Manning, Long Beach State University; Donald C. Guy, East Carolina University; and Vincent Harrington, Boston College. The late Donald W. Bell of the

ACKNOWLEDGMENTS

University of Hawaii at Manoa provided many useful suggestions for the first and second editions before his death in 1984.

Three individuals provided very special assistance in performing the many tasks associated with preparation of the manuscript. For the second edition, Scott Cooper provided outstanding assistance ranging from computer systems design to research to word processing. Scott performed every task in a competent and exacting manner. In preparing the first edition, Ralph Nakamoto and Kati Rau performed above and beyond the call of duty. Scott, Ralph, and Kati have contributed a great deal to this book.

Finally, my wife, Livvie, provided encouragement and a cheerful attitude throughout the entire project. For her support, I am most grateful.

To my friends and colleagues who would always ask about the book even when they were tired of hearing about it, I extend a warm thank-you.

Larry E. Wofford

A SPECIAL NOTE TO THE READER

This book is written for *you*. Everything in it has been put there with you and your learning in mind. *Real Estate* is written to be like visiting with your own personal "mentor" dedicated to teaching you the fundamentals necessary to understand real estate. Within each chapter are several features you should use. For example, at the start of each chapter, the objectives of that chapter are presented. At the end of each chapter is a "Quick Quiz" to provide a painless test of your understanding. "Key Terminology" is listed and additional sources of information are provided. All of these items are there to improve your learning. You are encouraged to use them.

One final thought. Real estate is a subject in which you can actively participate. Take note of the real estate activity around you and try to apply the concepts you are learning to that activity. Also, try to be an active participant in this book. In many portions of the book you will be asked to mentally place yourself in a particular situation. If you will go along with this approach and think about the situation, the information in this book will be much more interesting and your learning more complete. In short, participate in real estate *and* this book. I hope that participation makes real estate an enjoyable experience for you. Good luck!

CONTENTS

PART ONE

DEVELOPING A PERSPECTIVE

This part of the book is designed to provide you with a perspective for studying real estate. Such an understanding will make learning easier and more complete for you, as well as make your study of real estate more logical. Keep this objective in mind as you read the book and, if necessary, refer back to this first section often to refresh your perspective and fit any particular topic into its proper place.

This section is brief; it contains only two short chapters. Chapter 1 considers the basic nature of real estate and its role in the world and the United States, as well as its importance to individuals. Chapter 2 introduces the real estate business. Areas of specialization within the real estate business and the relationships between them are considered. Since the book is organized around the real estate business, an organizational model for the book is also presented in this chapter.

So get ready for the "big picture." This section is your opportunity to develop a perspective on real estate for use throughout the entire book. The remainder of the book examines the material introduced in these first two chapters in more detail.

1

Real Estate in the Overall Scheme of Things

PREVIEW

It is quite natural for you to wonder about the nature and relevance of any subject you are about to spend a good bit of time studying. Developing answers to questions such as "What is real estate?" and "How does it affect your life and the lives of others?" will not only satisfy your natural curiosity; it will also help form a foundation for learning. If you can develop a "feel" for real estate—what it is, what it does, and how it affects and is affected by the world in general—everything that follows in this book will make more sense, be easier to understand, and likely be retained longer than if such a feel is not developed. This chapter helps you develop this feel for what you are about to study. In it, you will learn:

1. What real estate is, what it does, and how it has affected and continues to affect our lives.
2. How real estate has influenced the development of the United States.
3. How real estate has adapted to new demands and how that adaptive process continues today.

EARTH — THE FOCUS OF ATTENTION

Real estate deals with the Earth. **Real estate** is defined as land and everything, natural or man-made, attached to it. When real estate is viewed as dealing with the Earth itself, there is little question about its basic importance to mankind. Throughout history it has provided humanity the essentials of life: food, clothing, and shelter. Those nations blessed with fertile or mineral-rich land have tended to prosper and enjoy relatively high standards of living. On the other hand, nations with less productive lands have had more difficult times.

Real Estate and the World

Given the importance of real estate to a nation's economic well-being, it is not surprising that it has a prominent place in history. Some of our most exciting and brightest adventures involve explorers searching for new lands to increase their personal wealth and the wealth of their country or patron. The voyages of Columbus, Balboa, and Captain Cook are examples of such efforts. Unfortunately, some of the darkest chapters in history also involve efforts to acquire, control, or conquer land and the resources it contains. Numerous armed conflicts, costing many lives, have resulted from these efforts. In recent history, these conflicts have resulted in two world wars and other military actions in Korea, Vietnam, the Middle East, Afghanistan, and the Falkland Islands.

Today, real estate continues to be an important factor in the economic, political, and social development of nations. Many developing countries are finding their lands simply not capable of providing enough food and resources to support an escape from starvation and economic chaos. More highly developed societies are realizing that they are not as independent as they once thought. Because of need, economic advantage, or both, many nations are becoming increasingly dependent on the real estate resources of other nations. Russia, for instance, is dependent on other countries with more fertile lands and better climates for food. The United States depends on other countries for real estate-related resources such as minerals and petroleum.

The pattern of mutual dependence has evolved with changes in politics, weather, and technology, among other factors. Politics affects the pattern by affecting alliances and preferential economic terms between nations. As politics have changed, so have patterns of reliance on real estate resources. Long-run and short-run changes in weather dramatically affect the agricultural productivity of land. A short period of bad weather can move a country from food self-sufficiency to widespread shortages. Droughts or changes in rainfall patterns can create more permanent disruptions in food production. In the somewhat longer run, the deterioration of the ozone layer and the changing of rainfall patterns created by clearing rain forests promise to further alter the relative abilities of land to produce food. Finally, changes in technology can either reduce or increase interdependence on land resources. New technology can reduce dependence on others by allowing the conversion of existing resources into other resources or the substitution of one resource for another. The conversion of oil shale into oil is an example of this process. However, new technology can also increase interdependence by creating a need for real estate-related resources possessed by other nations.

As the pattern of dependence changes, those countries with particularly valuable resources will become richer and more influential. On the other hand, countries depending on foreign sources of raw materials will become more dependent on other countries and must produce materials and products demanded by others in order to remain economically viable. Countries rich in resources demanded by new technologies may someday reap tremendous economic bonanzas. Others with developing agricultural abilities will also improve their economic situation. Thus, real estate will continue to affect you and others on a global basis.

Individual Ownership of Real Estate

Just as real estate has affected nations, it has also affected individuals. Those owning land that is rich in minerals, extraordinarily fertile, or in a choice location have tended to prosper. These benefits have made the desire to own land a persistent theme throughout history, although historically land was owned only by royalty. This desire to own land, coupled with economic considerations, led to the development of the **feudal system,** in which the monarchy gave nobles the right to use land in return for their promises to be loyal, pay taxes, and defend the monarchy. Eventually, poor economic conditions forced the monarchy to transfer ownership, not just use, to the nobles. The same sort of economic conditions ultimately forced the nobles to transfer ownership to the peasants actually working the land. These transfers were the beginning of the **allodial system,** which provides for private ownership of land.

Real Estate and the Development of the United States

Real estate, especially the desire for private ownership of it, has greatly affected the development of the United States. The significance of real estate's role is found in the very document outlining many of our rights as citizens, the United States Constitution. Because of the concern of its authors about land ownership rights, you have the right to own real estate and receive the benefits of that ownership. Those benefits may be in the form of your personal enjoyment or income from others willing to pay you for the right to use your real estate. You also have Constitutional protection against having your rights in land taken away without due process of law and the payment of just compensation. Today, private real estate ownership in the United States is common, with almost two-thirds of all homes being owner-occupied.

The collective national appetite to control real estate has had a strong influence on the history and development of the United States. Some felt it was our "manifest destiny" to have borders stretching from coast to coast. Explorers, settlers, and those simply seeking to get rich quick pushed westward and found much fertile, mineral-rich land. Our "manifest destiny" quickly became a reality. From a land area of 864,746 square miles in 1790, the United States grew to a coast-to-coast nation of 2,940,042 square miles in 1850. Since 1850, this land area has increased to over 3,500,000 square miles. Figure 1.1 summarizes U.S. land acquisitions.

While the United States was busy expanding its borders, its people were busy developing the land. Americans began a relentless western migration motivated by the lure of quick fortunes from gold and silver, free federal government land, and other business opportunities. To encourage development, the federal government granted railroads large parcels of land, some of which the railroads sold to raise the money necessary to build the rails and purchase rolling stock and to develop markets for their transportation services. Figure 1.2 is an example of the

Figure 1.1 Acquisition of the territory of the United States and origin of the public domain, exclusive of Alaska and Island Possessions. (Source: Peter Wolf, *Land in America.* New York: Pantheon Books, 1981, p. 37.)

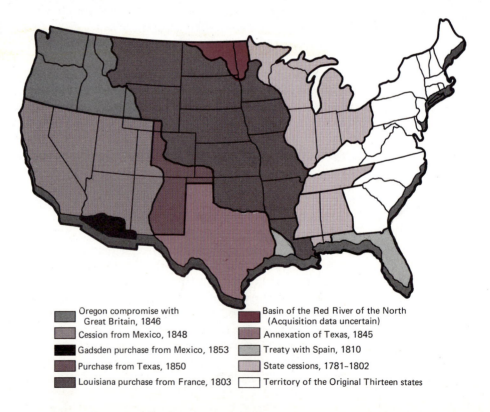

Oregon compromise with Great Britain, 1846

Cession from Mexico, 1848

Gadsden purchase from Mexico, 1853

Purchase from Texas, 1850

Louisiana purchase from France, 1803

Basin of the Red River of the North (Acquisition data uncertain)

Annexation of Texas, 1845

Treaty with Spain, 1810

State cessions, 1781–1802

Territory of the Original Thirteen states

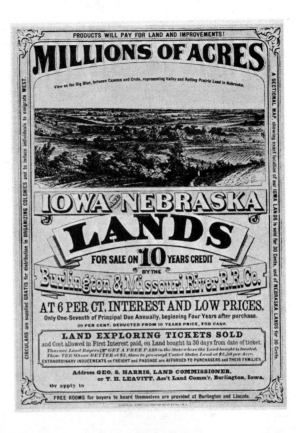

Figure 1.2 Example of advertising to sell western lands. (Source: "Government and Land Use Regulation," *Real Estate Today,* September 1976, p. 45.)

advertising efforts of the railroads to attract buyers for their land. Cities and towns sprang up around deposits of natural resources; along rivers, railroads, and seaports; and at the edge of "civilization" as "jumping-off points" for those going west. These cities developed to serve the needs of the new and growing populations around them. Some of these new cities grew from existing small towns, such as St. Louis. Others were created by private real estate companies. These companies laid out entire cities and sold lots to investors.

Within these new cities, those in the real estate business were working to provide places for people to live, shop, work, and be entertained. The same process was being repeated in eastern cities, which were also experiencing substantial growth from industrial development. Then, as it has been throughout history, the basic job of the real estate business was to provide space for people to perform the tasks of living.

In order to provide this space, the real estate industry has had to adapt to changing demands. Improvements in transportation and the desire to escape the city led to the development of suburban housing. Not too far behind were suburban shopping centers and suburban office space. Other uses of the land have developed over time. Spurred on by the demands of large numbers of people to work and live in certain locations, creative real estate people combined technology with limited amounts of available land to produce the skyscraper. Gradually, mixed-use skyscrapers were developed such as Water Tower Place in Chicago, which contains eight levels of shopping, a luxury hotel, and private residences all in one building. Garden apartments, covered-mall shopping centers, and condominiums all represent attempts to satisfy the demand for space.

Real Estate Today

The process of providing space continues. As the U.S. population continues to grow, space must be provided for these Americans to live, work, and play. Additionally, as our population shifts from one part of the country to another, additional space must be provided. For instance, the area known as the Sunbelt, essentially the southern and southwestern states, is expected to experience a growth rate substantially above that of the rest of the nation. Another important movement predicted for the 1980s is the movement of an increasing number of people from large cities to rural areas and small towns. The needs of these people must also

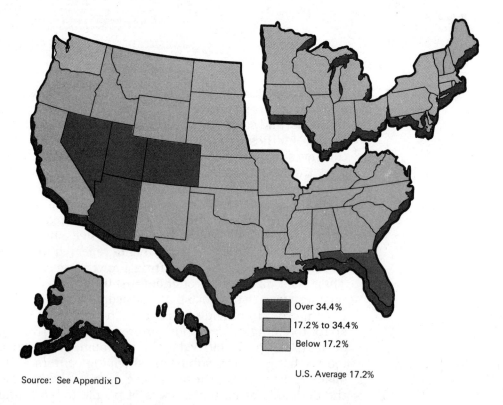

Figure 1.3 Projected population changes 1980–2000. (Source: "Sun Belt/Frost Belt: The Realignment of America," *Real Estate Today*, May 1981, p. 36.

Over 34.4%

17.2% to 34.4%

Below 17.2%

U.S. Average 17.2%

Source: See Appendix D

be satisfied by the real estate business. All of this means the process of adapting to change must continue. This adaptation process has been and will be a fascinating one to observe. It is an even more fascinating one in which to participate.

SUMMARY

This chapter has provided you with an overview of real estate with the goal of developing a perspective on real estate. You now know that real estate deals with land and everything attached to it. Land has had an impact on world development as nations have sought to control land rich in minerals or fertile enough to grow food. Nations controlling such lands have generally developed to a greater degree than those not having such lands. A growing awareness has developed of the dependence of all nations on the real estate resources of other countries. Patterns of interdependence shifts with changes in politics, weather, and technology.

Private ownership of land evolved from ownership by the king to the feudal system to the allodial system. Private ownership rights were so important to our nation's founders that guarantees of the right to private ownership of real property are in the U.S. Constitution.

This importance is appropriate because real estate played an important role in the development of the United States. This country quickly went from a small, Atlantic seaboard nation to one that stretched all the way to the Pacific. The land was then developed by pioneers pushing westward.

Throughout history, the real estate business has been concerned with providing space for people to live, work, and play. This mission continues today. The real estate business has had to adapt to the changing demands for space. New types of space such as the skyscraper, enclosed shopping malls, and garden apartments have been developed to satisfy these demands. This adaptation process makes real estate a dynamic and fascinating field in which to participate.

QUICK QUIZ

1. The right of individuals to own land is a part of the _____ .

    a. allodial system   c. Constitutional system
    b. feudal system   d. gentry system

2. Today, the United States has a land area of about _____ .

    a. 4,000,000 square miles   c. 3,500,000 square miles
    b. 3,000,000 square miles   d. 5,000,000 square miles

3. The primary function of the real estate business is —————— .

  I. providing space for people
II. buying and selling land

  a. I only   c. Both I and II
  b. II only   d. Neither I nor II

4. As people have demanded and technology has allowed, —————— have developed.

5. Today, about —————— percent of all homes in the United States are owner-occupied.

6. —————— led to the development of the feudal and allodial systems.

QUESTIONS AND EXERCISES

1. List three recent examples of how real estate has adapted to the need to provide new kinds of space in your town or a nearby town.

2. What kinds of change do you foresee in the types of space provided in the future?

3. See if you can identify any parcels of land in your town that have likely substantially increased in value recently because of location.

4. Many cities are experiencing increased rehabilitation of older or close-in residential areas; what factors contribute to this phenomenon?

KEY TERMINOLOGY

allodial system
feudal system
real estate

IF YOU WANT TO READ MORE

JOHN MCMAHAN, *Property Development* (New York: McGraw-Hill Book Company, 1976), Chapters 1 and 2.

PETER WOLF, *Land in America* (New York: Pantheon Books, 1981), Chapters 1 and 2.

"Land in the New World," *Real Estate Today*, January 1976, pp. 6–11.

"The Frontier and the American Character," *Real Estate Today*, March 1976, pp. 38–40.

2
Real Estate
Business Environment

PREVIEW   From Chapter 1 you know that the real estate business is concerned with
providing space for people. Providing that space requires many different
business and professional activities, all of which are related to one another in some manner. This chapter introduces you to the activities in
the real estate business and their organization. After reading it you
should have developed an understanding of:

1. The basic real estate decisions to be made and who makes them.
2. The support available to those making real estate decisions.
3. The kinds of careers available in real estate.
4. The necessity of understanding real estate fundamentals.
5. The interdependencies between real estate fundamentals, decision
   areas, and decision support areas.
6. The general organization of this book.

Before you continue reading this chapter, jot down your answer to the
question, "What is the real estate business?" Be honest; do not continue
until you have answered. If you were to ask this question of 50 people on
the street, the majority of the responses would involve "brokerage" or
"selling homes." Put another way, the majority of people equate the real
estate business with marketing. This answer, like many answers, is

correct, but only partially. Marketing *is* an important aspect of the real estate business, but it is not the only one.

This answer should be expected since marketing is the most visible portion of the real estate business, with yard signs and offices virtually everywhere. Also, for many people, buying or selling a home or renting an apartment is their only participation in the real estate business. People with other exposure to the real estate business, for example an uncle who manages a shopping center, may give answers other than marketing. However, since brokerage experiences dominate, brokerage is the most common response.

The point is that the real estate business cannot be accurately summarized by one or two areas of activity any more than any other industry. For example, the automobile industry cannot be adequately described as "selling automobiles." It involves the production of automobiles and all the problems of design and engineering associated with that production: financing the production, marketing the production, and managing or coordinating the entire process. The real estate business involves the same activities of producing, financing, marketing, and managing as any other industry or business; the product is just different.

In real estate the basic product is *space.* The real estate business is concerned with providing space for people to use for living, working, and playing. People are willing to pay for the right to use space tailored to their particular needs. This space may involve extensive man-made improvements or virtually none. For example, some people will pay for the opportunity to camp in completely natural areas, while others will pay for the natural beauty of woods and mountains from the patio of a luxury resort hotel. People will also pay for office space, apartment space, warehouse space, and so on. The idea that people will pay for the right to control and use space over some period of time is one of the fundamental concepts of real estate. All facets of the business exist, in the final analysis, to help people satisfy this need for space. It is this need that creates demand for the products and services provided by those in the real estate business.

If the real estate business involves many general areas of activity, how shall we define it? We know that it involves land and improvements to land and we know it involves providing space. We could define the real estate business as all of those activities associated with land and improvements to land with the intention of providing usable space. You probably already realize that this definition is of limited usefulness. It simply does not provide adequate detail about the real estate business.

For example, recognition that the real estate business is concerned with land and involves producing, financing, managing, and marketing does not provide you with a clear understanding of who performs these functions. It would be easy to say that developers produce usable space, lenders finance it, property managers handle its day-to-day operation, and brokers market it. But that would ignore the roles played by others in the real estate business such as appraisers, counselors, and investors who purchase space to use or for the income it will produce. Also ignored to this point is the extent to which these areas are related and the dependencies among them. Further, since you are just starting your study of real estate, it would be useful to consider the areas of knowledge important to each of these aspects of the real estate business.

ORGANIZATION OF THE REAL ESTATE BUSINESS

The activity areas in the real estate business may appear to be a disorganized hodgepodge. Actually, they are quite well organized. If you think of the real estate business as a machine, such as a watch, each activity area is a vital cog in its operation. It is important to realize that none of the activities, or cogs, operate independently of the others; they are all interdependent. A clear comprehension of these relationships will be valuable to your overall understanding of the real estate business.

Virtually nothing happens in the real estate business until someone considers making or actually makes a decision to build, buy, sell, or lend. These decisions are much like the mainspring of a watch; they activate the rest of the real estate business. For sales to occur, a broker must find someone who has decided to sell and someone else who has decided to buy. Property managers manage properties for investors called equity investors, who at one time decided to buy the property. Counselors provide advice and research for those considering or who have made a real estate decision. Appraisers are often asked to value real estate as support for a lending decision. Truly, those making building, buying, selling, and lending decisions form the core of the real estate business.

How shall we categorize these real estate activity areas? We might start by asking what these categories have in common. In the category containing lending, development, and equity investment, it seems that a common element is decision making. Decisions to develop, invest, and lend are the basic real estate decisions. Given their decision orientation, this group of activities is labeled **real estate decision areas.** Common to the remaining activity areas of marketing, appraisal, counseling, and property management is the provision of services to decision makers. Essentially they perform a support function for developers, equity investors, and lenders. For this reason, these activity areas are labeled **real estate decision support areas.**

To help develop a better perspective for reading and studying the remainder of the book, each activity area mentioned earlier is now briefly considered. Each of them is also the subject of one or more later chapters, which will supply much detail not provided here.

REAL ESTATE DECISION AREAS

Development

Development is the production end of the real estate business. Developers combine the familiar factors of production—land, labor, capital, and entrepreneurial ability—to produce improvements on land. Improvements are any permanent addition to the land. They may or may not actually improve the land in the sense that it is "better" after the improvement than before. Improvements may range from sewer pipes in a single family home building lot to more spectacular projects such as the 70-story Peachtree Plaza Hotel in Atlanta and the Transamerica "Pyramid" in San Francisco.

Motivations for development are varied. It has been suggested that some developers have an "edifice complex." That is, some individuals and corporations develop real estate to immortalize themselves. A more common motivator is likely to be *profit*. Just like any other producer, the developer hopes to realize a profit by producing a product that can be sold for more in the marketplace than it cost to produce.

Developers use the services of many other people. For example, architects and land planners may be used to design an attractive, functional project. Real estate counselors skilled in market research may be used to develop information about features desired by those who will use the space and to suggest possible rents for the project. Lenders will be used as a source of money for much of the construction. An appraiser may be retained to estimate the value of the project when completed. Tax specialists and financial counselors may provide valuable information about the possible after-tax profitability of the project. A broker may be used to find an investor to purchase the project either during construction or upon completion. As you can see, the development decision creates a demand for all kinds of services and makes very clear the extent to which decision makers depend on the services of others in the real estate business.

Equity Investment

Equity investment involves the ownership and operation or use of real estate. This activity is called equity investment because it is the amount investors are actually putting into the project. The lender puts in the rest. The **equity** in a real estate investment is the difference between the value of the investment and any outstanding obligations on the property. Equity investors purchase real estate for the benefits it produces. For example, single family homeowners are equity investors and receive benefits from the use of the property and from any price appreciation that may occur. Equity investors in real estate rented to others, such as apartments, usually invest for the potential profit involved, not to use the property themselves.

Conceptually, profitable equity investment is simple—buy at a reasonable price, receive benefits from use or rents while the property is owned, and sell the property for a substantial gain. The trick is not in knowing what to do, but doing it consistently. If everything associated with equity investment were simple, unchanging, and known with certainty, consistency would be easy to achieve. However, this is not the case. Equity investment takes place in a complex, dynamic, and uncertain environment.

Equity investors depend on many of the same real estate activity areas as developers for support services. Lenders, brokers, tax experts, attorneys, property managers, and others are invaluable to the equity investor. Certainly not all of these experts are consulted on every investment decision, but their help *is* needed often.

Lending

Few development projects or equity investments could occur without the use of borrowed money. Imagine trying to buy a new home without borrowing any money! It is common for single family home buyers to be able to borrow a high percentage of the appraised value or purchase price of a home. For income-producing real estate, it is not uncommon to borrow 75 to 80 percent of the purchase price. It is not surprising that at the end of 1985 Americans owed over $2 trillion ($2,000,000,000,000) on mortgage loans!

Lenders will make a loan when they feel the risks and returns from that loan are favorable compared to other investment opportunities. Assessing the risks and returns and making the lending decision is called **underwriting.** Lenders often rely on other real estate activity areas for information used in the underwriting process. For example, an appraiser is usually asked to value the property since it is going to be pledged as security for the loan. That is, if the loan is not repaid according to the loan agreement, the lender may ask the courts to order the property sold and the proceeds used to pay off the note. The work of financial consultants, market researchers, and attorneys is also often used. Once again, the interdependent nature of the real estate business is made apparent.

REAL ESTATE DECISION SUPPORT AREAS

Marketing

One of the most important services provided to developers, equity investors, and lenders is marketing. Marketing services are provided by real estate brokers and their sales forces made up of salespersons. Brokers and salespersons usually work for the seller on a commission basis: that is, they receive a percentage of the sales price as their fee. The marketer's primary job is to find a buyer who is ready, willing, and able to purchase a property on terms acceptable to the seller. Brokers and salespersons provide other services to buyers and sellers and guide all parties through a transaction as efficiently as possible.

Acting as a broker or salesperson requires more than office space and desire. All 50 states and the District of Columbia have enacted laws requiring brokers and salespersons to be licensed. These laws were enacted to protect the public by establishing minimum standards of education and experience for licensees. Over the years, many states have made these standards more stringent, and the trend continues today.

Appraisal

Imagine yourself as a lender considering a home mortgage loan application. If the home is going to serve as security for the loan, you will likely consider a reliable estimate of its value in the marketplace a necessary part of your decision. Real estate appraisal deals with making reliable estimates of market value supported by market data. The appraiser performing the appraisal may be an employee of your institution or a third party, called an independent fee appraiser, performing appraisals for a fee.

Real estate appraisers are real estate market experts. They gather, organize, and analyze market data on real estate sales, new construction, rents for various types of properties, costs of construction, and many other variables. They then rely on this data, combined with their judgment, to estimate the market value of a parcel of real estate.

Market value estimates are also used by people other than lenders underwriting mortgage loans. Buyers and sellers may use appraisals as an aid in pricing real estate or in negotiations. Developers planning new projects are always interested in what the project will likely bring in the marketplace when completed. Thus, real estate appraisers, like others in decision support areas, provide valuable assistance to real estate decision makers.

Counseling

Suppose you were considering purchasing an office building as an investment. Whom would you see to help you perform a financial analysis of the property under consideration? For legal advice? For tax advice? The answer, in the broadest sense, is a real estate counselor. Real estate counselors may be attorneys, accountants, market researchers, financial analysts, appraisers, brokers, or any number of other specialists. The term **real estate counselor** is often used to indicate anyone providing services for a fee not fitting strictly into the categories of brokerage, appraisal, or property management.

In many situations more than one counselor may be needed. In such instances the coordination of counselors may itself be a major undertaking. Some counselors provide a service in which they coordinate other counselors for the client, and this service can be quite valuable.

Property Management

Many real estate projects have been successfully developed only to become financial disasters and bitter disappointments to the equity investor. In some cases this unpleasant result is caused by poor design, poor construction, or poor location. However, in many cases the culprit is bad management. Few properties can survive the curse of bad property management no matter how bright the prospects before purchase. Good property management is a critical factor in making forecasted and actual performance coincide.

Property management includes many activities such as leasing space, collecting rents, and maintaining the property. For example, property managers may help developers make decisions about which features to include in a project and which to exclude. They help answer questions such as, "Do tennis courts in apartment complexes really pay for themselves by producing higher rents?" They also help developers and equity investors choose a target market for their project and develop a profile of likely tenants. Property managers also are responsible for maintaining the property and preparing, or overseeing, the preparation of budgets and operating reports for property owners. Thus, there is much more to property management than answering the telephone, showing apartments, and making sure the swimming pool is clean.

RELATIONSHIP AMONG ACTIVITY AREAS

It should be emphasized that all of the activity areas in the real estate business are related. They are not only related, they are *dependent* on one another. In Figure 2.1 these relationships and dependencies are illustrated in the "Real Estate Business Environment Model." In this figure, the decision support areas and decision areas are each grouped to indicate that they are related to and somewhat dependent on the activity areas grouped with them. For example, developers are dependent on lenders and equity investors for their ultimate success. Brokers often depend on appraisers to help establish a reasonable value for properties on the market. Other activity areas within each group are similarly related and dependent. The arrows between the decision support areas and the decision areas indicate the dependency between these general areas.

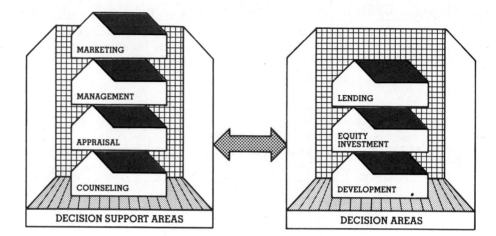

Figure 2.1 Real estate business environment.

Throughout the real estate business you will find specialists. Few real estate people go to the office and wait for a phone call from a client to see whether they are going to perform appraisal, property management, or brokerage duties that day. This is not to say that people perform only one function, but rather that most people in the real estate business choose to concentrate their efforts in one specialization as much as possible. Among the reasons for specialization is personal preference. For example, you may enjoy very structured activities, meeting people, and using quantitative skills while someone else may enjoy exactly the opposite situations. Another reason for reducing the scope of your activities is the vast amount of time required to stay current in a number of areas. To remain competent in any real estate area requires that you continually read, attend courses and seminars, and study the market. Time simply does not allow you the luxury of staying truly current in a number of areas. This situation can be frustrating if you're the type of person who enjoys staying up-to-date.

Exactly which areas you specialize in depends on your preference and abilities. You will tend to study and learn more about those things you find interesting. If your interests and abilities coincide, then it is easy to choose the activity area for you. If they do not, it may be a little more difficult to find the best fit. As a result, you probably will find the one activity area you enjoy most or do best, and specialize in it. As you become more specialized you become more dependent on others.

Just because you may specialize does not mean that you need know nothing about other activity areas. You should have a working knowledge of other areas in order to develop a perspective about where your skills best fit. Only when you know your role and the role of others in the real estate business are you likely to be aware of potential problems and the best persons to help you avoid or solve them.

NEED TO UNDERSTAND FUNDAMENTALS

Just as you cannot play a game without knowing the rules, you cannot learn about specialized areas of real estate without knowing the fundamentals. Fundamentals are the common foundation of knowledge for all the specialty areas in the real estate business. They represent the essential information you need to understand the nature of real estate and what makes it different than other areas of business. Fundamental areas of knowledge include: real property law, real estate markets, taxes affecting real estate, the pertinent aspects of physical environment, characteristics of urban areas, and basic financial math. If you have a strong understanding of fundamentals, your study of specialty areas will be much easier.

Thus, your strategy should be to learn the fundamentals of real estate and then tackle the body of specialized knowledge associated with each decision and decision support area. The relationship between fundamentals and specialized areas is illustrated in Figure 2.2, the "Real

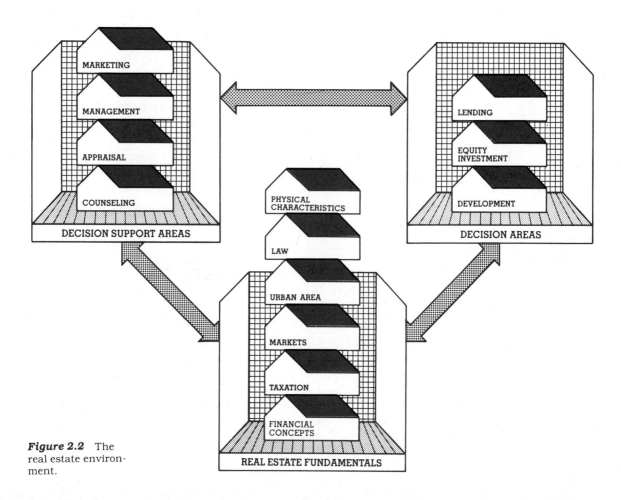

Figure 2.2 The real estate environment.

Estate Environment.'' In this figure, fundamentals have been added to the decision and decision support areas of Figure 2.1. If you think of the specialty areas as also representing areas of real estate knowledge, the Real Estate Environment represents both areas of business activity and study. Once again, the arrows indicate that each of the various components is related to, and dependent on, the others. This model should help you visualize the organization and relationships present in your study of real estate.

PREVIEW OF BOOK

This book is designed to help you achieve your goal of learning about real estate. By reading and studying it, you will develop a working knowledge of real estate. This knowledge will be sufficient to help you better understand many of the real estate decisions you must make in your personal and business life. If you choose to pursue a career in real estate, this book provides you with a firm foundation on which to build and to make the most of your business experiences.

This book is organized around the Real Estate Environment of Figure 2.2. It is organized into parts with each of the next three parts dealing with one of the major portions of the Real Estate Environment. First, fundamentals are covered, followed by decision areas, and then decision support areas. This organization provides you with an orderly introduction to real estate. To help you keep your perspective, the Real Estate Environment model will be used at the beginning of each new part of the book to pinpoint the area about to be studied and its relationship to other real estate knowledge and business specialties.

A FEW FINAL WORDS
ABOUT REAL ESTATE CAREERS

You likely have more than a passing interest in real estate or else you would not be reading this book. This interest may stem from an interest in a real estate career or a desire to learn more about a subject that is of economic importance to you throughout your life. Regardless of your motivation for reading this book, take a few minutes to consider real estate careers.

Many people have found satisfying careers in the real estate business. This satisfaction has been in the form of economic and psychological returns. Since each activity area discussed earlier represents one or more career possibilities, finding the best real estate career for you may be a trial-and-error process. This seems to be the approach that has worked for many persons in the real estate business. Many started in one area and switched areas as their interests changed.

With respect to income, real estate careers offer the potential for economic security. Some real estate careers, such as brokerage, offer commission-type compensation schemes in which your income is directly related to your productivity. This arrangement is attractive to some persons and not to others. Other career areas, such as appraising, offer salaried positions or some combination of salary and production-related income. You must consider your disposition toward different ways of receiving your income when considering areas of employment in the real estate business.

Real estate also provides you the opportunity to operate your own business. Many successful real estate people ultimately start their own firms. This decision is a difficult one because it often means that you reduce your direct participation in real estate and spend more time managing others. Starting a business also involves taking some substantial risks. In short, real estate offers attractive opportunities no matter what your interests and abilities. It also offers substantial income potential for those willing to take the necessary risks.

QUICK QUIZ

1. The basic real estate product is _____ .

    I. land
   II. space

    a. I only   c. Both I and II
    b. II only   d. Neither I nor II

2. Real estate decision areas include _____ .

    a. development   c. lending
    b. equity investment   d. all of the above

3. Real estate decision support areas include _____ .

    a. math, real estate markets, real property law
    b. appraisal, lending, property management
    c. counseling, appraisal, marketing
    d. marketing, property management, urban economics

4. Real estate decision and decision support areas _____ .

    I. are related and interdependent
   II. contain various areas of specialization within the real estate business.

    a. I only   c. Both I and II
    b. II only   d. Neither I nor II

5. The major areas of the Real Estate Environment Model are
_____ , _____ , and _____ .

6. All fifty states require real estate brokers and salespersons to be
_____ .

7. The knowledge that forms a common background for all real estate
specialties is collectively called _____ .

QUESTIONS AND EXERCISES

1. Make a list of the things you want a career to provide you.

2. What kind of compensation scheme do appraisal firms in your area
offer? Property management firms? Brokerage firms?

3. Why are lending, development, and equity investment decisions so
important to the real estate business?

4. What real estate careers require a license in your state?

5. What are the basic requirements for obtaining the license(s) in
Question 4?

KEY TERMINOLOGY

appraising
counseling
development
equity
equity investment
marketing

property management
real estate counselor
real estate decision areas
real estate decision support areas
underwriting

IF YOU WANT TO READ MORE

National Association of License Law Officials, *Guide to Examinations and Careers in Real Estate* (Reston, Va.: Reston Publishing Co., 1979).

HERBERT D. WEITZMAN and ROBERT W. EICHINGER, "The Statistics Behind Success," *Real Estate Today,* April 1978, pp. 11–17.

Economics and Research Division, National Association of Realtors, "The State of the Membership: 1981," *Real Estate Today,* November/December 1981, pp. 45–51.

PART TWO

REAL ESTATE FUNDAMENTALS

Nobody likes to lose. Nobody likes to be embarrassed. Many people in the real estate business suffer these fates every day. Homebuyers, brokers, developers, and others in real estate have deals elude them, make poor decisions, lose their own money, lose the money of a client, or simply embarrass themselves because they do not understand the basic ground rules of the real estate business. These ground rules are the "fundamentals" of real estate. As in many other endeavors, you cannot expect to become a polished performer in real estate until you know them. This section of the text acquaints you with these fundamental concepts, practices, and principles.

There are 11 chapters in this section. The first chapter considers the physical and economic characteristics of real estate, including how real estate is legally described. The next three chapters develop an essential legal foundation for your study. Following this are two chapters devoted to urban areas: how and why they develop and how cities plan for and control growth and development. Chapter 9 provides an overview of the operation of the urban real estate market. The next three chapters introduce the area of taxation. Both property taxes and income taxes are covered. The final chapter covers the basic logic and calculations of finance.

The knowledge contained in these chapters will not ensure your success in the real estate business; nothing can do that for you. Judgment and blind luck are still too important for any book to guarantee success. Part 2 provides a knowledge of real estate fundamentals to help you avoid mistakes caused by a lack of understanding of basic real estate concepts, to develop your judgment, and to take advantage of whatever good fortune comes your way.

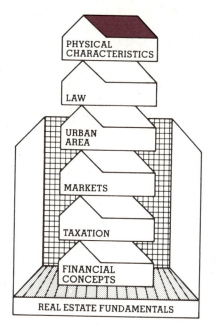

PHYSICAL
CHARACTERISTICS

LAW

URBAN
AREA

MARKETS

TAXATION

FINANCIAL
CONCEPTS

REAL ESTATE FUNDAMENTALS

3

Real Estate: physical characteristics and description

PREVIEW   Real estate has some important physical characteristics that make it different from other assets and that also determine the use made of each parcel of land. These characteristics make it necessary to develop methods for describing the exact location and boundaries of each parcel. Your study of this chapter will allow you to:

1. Understand the general physical characteristics of real estate and their impacts on the use and value of real estate.
2. Be able to define and identify site-specific characteristics of real estate and explain their impacts on the use and value of a parcel of real estate.
3. Be able to explain the need for legal descriptions of real estate and the techniques for producing such descriptions.

You now know that real estate is defined as land and those things permanently attached to it. This connection to land is important, for it gives real estate some characteristics that make it physically different from all other assets not associated with land. That real estate differs from nonreal estate assets may seem obvious to you, but the economic and legal significances of the differences are so important that we must carefully examine them and their implications for those in the real estate business. For example, the physical characteristics of real estate create the need for an entire body of law relating to legal rights in land that is distinct from the body of law dealing with all other property. These characteristics also affect the economics of using land and are therefore important to those making decisions to develop or invest in real estate in any form. Characteristics common to all real estate that serve to differentiate it from all other assets are called **general physical characteristics.**

In addition to the general physical characteristics, each parcel of real estate also contains **site-specific characteristics** that differentiate one parcel from all others. Examples of site-specific characteristics include soil type, topography, availability of utilities, size and shape of the tract, vegetation, and accessibility. These characteristics impact the type and quantity of improvements built on a parcel. For example, a small hillside parcel may be quite desirable for a single family home but not for a shopping center because of size and the construction costs associated with building on a hillside. Also, certain soil types require expensive site preparation and foundation work to support structures. These added costs may mean the difference between making a profit and sustaining a loss or between a large building and a small building that may be less expensive per square foot to construct.

Both general and site-specific physical characteristics of real estate affect a parcel's ability to provide satisfaction or income, which ultimately affects its value. Consider two equal-sized parcels of agricultural land. All other things being equal, the more fertile tract will have a greater value because it can produce more product and more income for the farmer. You may be willing to pay more for a home building lot where the topography provides a view than for one without such a view. As you learn more about the physical characteristics of the real estate commodity, always keep in mind the impact of these characteristics on land use and value.

The physical attributes of real estate are important legally as well as economically. Since each parcel of real estate is unique with respect to location, it is important that each be identified, or described, in such a way that no confusion exists about its location and boundaries. If the physical location and boundaries of land could not be sufficiently described to avoid disagreements between property owners, countless court battles would develop. In this chapter, a number of methods for describing the location and boundaries of real estate are presented.

Think of this chapter as an introduction to the physical characteristics *and* their implications. Much of the real estate business involves understanding, assessing, and interpreting the physical characteristics of particular parcels of real estate. Consequently, much of the remainder of this book is concerned, directly or indirectly, with these physical characteristics.

GENERAL PHYSICAL CHARACTERISTICS
OF REAL ESTATE

Real estate has a number of general physical characteristics common to all parcels whether in downtown Detroit or the wilderness areas of Alaska. These characteristics distinguish real estate from other assets. As you will see later, they also affect the use and value of real estate and the operation of the real estate market.

Immobility

Land cannot be moved from place to place. While this observation comes as no surprise to you, its economic impact may. The demand for a particular parcel of land is for the land right where it is, not one block east or 10 miles north. To be valuable, land must be able to satisfy demand without being moved. Sometimes even slight differences in location may make a big difference in the demand for land for a particular use. To illustrate, if you owned a large tract of land at the intersection of two major thoroughfares in an area that is developing as a major residential area, your land may be quite valuable because of the present and future demand for shopping space and its accessibility by shoppers. However, if you owned a tract just a quarter of a mile down one of the thoroughfares it may not be as suitable for shopping and may be worth a great deal less than the corner tract unless it is demanded for some other use that may increase its value.

Let's continue with this example to illustrate another aspect of the importance of land being fixed in location. Suppose that you own the corner tract, and someone builds a large shopping center on one of the three remaining corners of the intersection. What happens to the value of your land? If the new center satisfies all or most of the shopping demand likely to exist over the next 5 to 10 years, then your parcel is no longer worth as much as it was. On the other hand, with the passage of time, additional shopping demand may develop and the value of your property may increase.

This example illustrates the dynamic nature of land values when the surrounding area is changing. Increases and decreases in value occur constantly because of changes in supply-and-demand conditions surrounding a parcel of land. Investors buying land in anticipation of future development are always hopeful that development around their site will increase the value of their holdings. Many investors have become rich by correctly anticipating the pattern of development and demand and making land investments accordingly. Many other investors have lost fortunes doing the same thing.

The dynamic nature of land values and the impact on value of activity surrounding a particular parcel can be made clearer if you will visualize a relief map of your city on which the height of the peaks is determined by land values. Your city then will look like a mountain range with tall peaks in the downtown area where land values are high and other peaks and valleys throughout the city. Now imagine how this map changes over time as new areas of the city develop and older areas either rejuvenate or decay. New peaks and valleys are constantly being formed. The changes in this price landscape illustrate the dynamic nature of land values and the fact that a parcel is dramatically affected by what goes on around it since it cannot be moved.

Heterogeneity

Each parcel of real estate is unique. No two parcels are just alike, even if they differ only in location. It is the unique aspects of a parcel that often create value by creating a monopolistic ability to satisfy the demand for a particular type of space in a particular location. Uniqueness creates a need to analyze carefully the factors that contribute to that uniqueness and how they affect the possible uses of the site and its value.

Heterogeneity also has some interesting legal implications for real estate. Because the law recognizes that parcels are not perfect substitutes, it often protects the interests of buyers by requiring that a specific parcel be conveyed rather than merely a similar one. Thus, if you are purchasing a particular parcel and the buyer wishes to substitute a parcel of equal value or back out of the transaction altogether, the law will frequently require that he convey the particular parcel to you. This is called **specific performance** in legal terminology. This situation should be contrasted with other commodities, such as wheat and sand, in which similar products may be perfect substitutes.

Limited Supply

Will Rogers was once supposed to have advised investing in land because they weren't making any more of it. Will Rogers was right; there is only a set amount of land in the United States — a little over 2.25 billion acres of it! That amounts to over 10 acres for each person now living in the United States — not a critical shortage of land by most standards. Furthermore, almost 75 percent of our people live in metropolitan areas as defined by the Bureau of the Census and occupy only a little over 14 percent of the total land in the United States.

While on a national basis there is not a shortage of land, there are often shortages of land suitable for certain uses in certain locations. For example, in some cities many people want to live closer to the downtown area and sufficiently large undeveloped parcels of land are difficult to find. Thus, there is a shortage of land for this particular use in a particular place. Since in large urban areas many people want to be near the same activities — jobs, shopping and entertainment, for example — shortages of suitable land develop. When this happens land prices tend to increase as developers realize they can build larger and taller buildings based on the rents they can charge those wanting to be close to particular activities. The order here is important. The demand to be close to something creates the potential to collect higher rents or charge higher purchase prices, say for living units, which in turn leads to higher land prices. Many people erroneously believe that high land prices force developers to build larger and taller buildings. You now know that the chain of causation runs the other way; land prices are high *because* developers are able to rent or sell enough space at sufficiently high prices to justify the higher land prices. This is simply the idea that land use determines land values.

Indestructibility

Land cannot be destroyed. No matter what you do to it, a parcel of land will continue to exist. The usefulness and value of the land may be reduced, but the physical space still exists. The same cannot be said of a cassette tape recorder, a desk, or the pen you may be holding in your hand as you read this page. Drastic alterations may be made to a parcel's appearance, say by strip mining, but the parcel still exists, and if you owned it before the mining, you still have an ownership interest in it.

Three Dimensionality

Real estate includes more than just the surface of the earth. It also includes the areas above (airspace) and below (subsurface or subterranean areas), as may be seen in Figure 3.1. Legally, you may "own" any or all of these areas. (The legal meaning of ownership is explored in Chapter

Figure 3.1 Three physical dimensions of real estate.

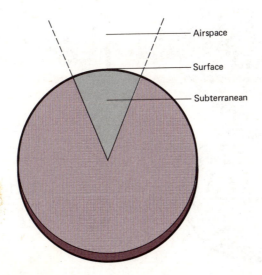

Airspace

Surface

Subterranean

4.) The airspace and subsurface area may be more valuable than the surface in many instances. For example, in areas of Oklahoma, Texas, Louisiana, Colorado, and Wyoming, oil and natural gas make the subsurface rights quite valuable. Many farmers and ranchers in these areas have sold or leased the subsurface rights to recover petroleum to oil companies for large amounts of money. In large cities, airspace may be quite valuable as a building site. In New York, the 59-story Pan Am Building is built in airspace over railroad tracks formerly owned by the Penn Central Railroad. The surface is now owned by Conrail and trains still use the tracks. In Chicago, the Illinois Center is being built over Illinois Central railroad tracks.

SITE-SPECIFIC PHYSICAL CHARACTERISTICS

While real estate's general physical characteristics distinguish it from other assets, they do not physically distinguish one parcel of real estate from another since every parcel possesses these characteristics to the same degree. Site-specific physical characteristics create such distinctions since they are not possessed to the same extent by every parcel. Particular to each parcel of real estate are certain physical characteristics such as topography, soil types, accessibility, size and shape of the parcel, and the availability of utilities. Together these characteristics determine the physical potential of a parcel to be developed or, conversely, they determine the physical limitations to development. These concepts are highlighted in Figure 3.2.

Figure 3.2 General and site-specific physical characteristics and their impacts.

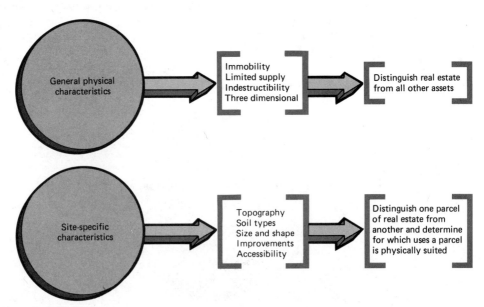

General physical characteristics → Immobility / Limited supply / Indestructibility / Three dimensional → Distinguish real estate from all other assets

Site-specific characteristics → Topography / Soil types / Size and shape / Improvements / Accessibility → Distinguish one parcel of real estate from another and determine for which uses a parcel is physically suited

Topography

Topography, or "the lay of the land," refers to the surface characteristics of a tract of land. Is it hilly, flat, or rolling? For some land uses, your home for example, a hilly site may be quite desirable. For other land uses such as a manufacturing plant, a flat site is preferred. Topography can greatly affect the costs of development by requiring earth work, provisions for storm water drainage, and other extra expense. Topographical maps, such as in Figure 3.3, may be used to analyze a parcel. Whether the topography of a particular site is good or bad depends on the land use being considered.

Soil Types

If you are a developer considering a site for a new development, the types of soil may be a decision factor. Several aspects of the soil are important —load-bearing capability, percolation (absorption) ability, depth of bedrock, and corrosiveness. Some soils can support heavy loads better than others and require less preparation for building. If pilings must be driven, the depth of bedrock will affect construction costs. If rock is too near the surface, it can also increase building costs by making it expensive to install utilities.

Percolation is the ability of soil to absorb moisture. It impacts development by affecting water runoff and the ability of a parcel to accommodate septic tank sewerage systems. A septic tank is a buried chamber in which sewage is decomposed by bacteria. The decomposed sewage then drains into a system of pipes, called laterals, where it is allowed to seep into the ground. If a parcel of real estate cannot absorb enough effluent, health regulations will limit or prohibit development that depends on a septic tank sewerage system. Percolation also affects runoff from rainfall. In areas where storm water drainage is a problem, regulations may restrict development or require the developer to reduce the runoff from the site by building retention ponds to collect excess storm waters and release them at a slower rate.

Size and Shape of Parcel

In pursuing the ideal site, developers seek one that is the correct size and shape—correct in the sense it allows them to do what they want to do. For example, assume a shopping center development company planning a large, enclosed shopping mall knows that they need a minimum of 30 to 50 acres. Not just any 30 to 50 acres, but 30 to 50 acres that will allow them to build the center and sufficient, convenient parking. Finding a site that perfectly fits preconceived ideas is often not an easy task. Land owned by more than one owner must often be purchased and combined to form a larger tract. This process is called **plottage** or **assemblage.** Aerial photographs, like the one in Figure 3.4, are often used to locate a

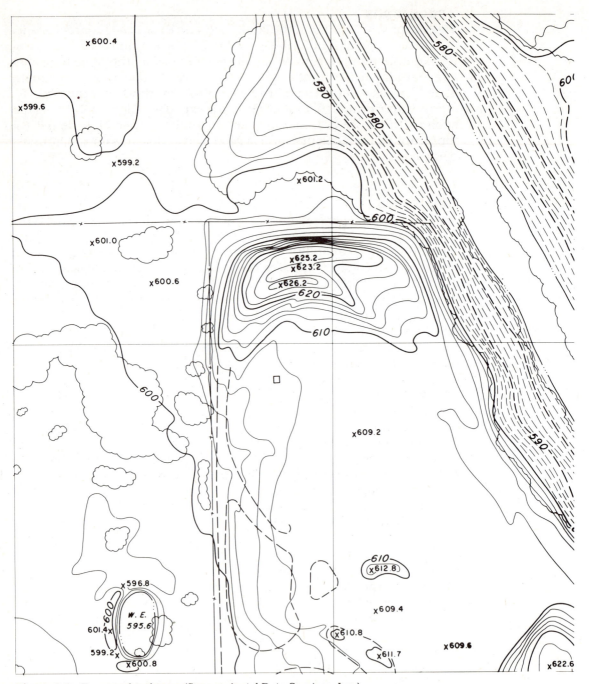

Figure 3.3 Topographical map. (Source: Aerial Data Services, Inc.)

Figure 3.4 Aerial photographs are often used to assess the physical characteristics of a parcel or parcels of land. (Source: Aerial Data Services, Inc.)

parcel of suitable size and shape. Problems can result if all owners do not want to sell or if one owner becomes aware of the effort to assemble a tract and holds out for an exorbitant price.

For a developer already owning a parcel of land, its size and shape affect the decision on how to use it. As you will learn in Chapter 8, zoning laws dictate the types of improvements allowed on a site and the minimum lot sizes necessary for particular kinds of development. They also establish the maximum number of square feet of improvements that can be developed on a given site. Parcels with irregular shapes often do not legally allow developers to build as many square feet of improvements per square foot of land as square or rectangular parcels. This means fewer square feet of improvements to generate rents or sales revenue to pay for the land. Thus, such parcels are worth less than those allowing more intensive development.

Improvements

Natural physical features of real estate are not the only ones influencing its use and value. An otherwise ideal site will not be desirable for development without certain man-made physical improvements such as utilities. Sewerage, drinking water, natural gas, electricity, and storm water drainage are absolutely necessary for a successful development. If these facilities are not already provided to the land, they must be extended to it before development can occur. If the developer must pay for extending these services to the site, the development may not be economically attractive. If you are going to develop, invest in land for price appreciation, or just try to predict where development is likely to occur, the location of existing utilities and the timetable for extending them is a critical factor to consider.

Obviously, buildings on a parcel also affect its use and value. When buildings represent the best use of a site in terms of the type of use and the quantity of space provided, given the market, the value of the parcel is maximized. In such a situation, the buildings are called the *highest and best use* for the site. However, many times you will face a situation in which a building was constructed some time ago and the deterioration of the buildings or changes in the surrounding area have caused it to no longer be the most profitable use of the site. Perhaps a four-story suburban office building was built 10 years ago on what was then the edge of town. As the city developed, the parcel became one of the prime office locations and now could profitably be used for a much larger building. This larger building will be developed only if the land and existing building can be purchased and the building demolished for a cost that will still allow the larger building to be sufficiently profitable. You can probably see situations in or near your town where buildings have been demolished long before they were worn out to make way for a more profitable, or higher and better, use. You can probably also identify properties that are likely targets for such a situation in the future.

Accessibility

Accessibility refers to the cost in time and money of getting to desired destinations from a parcel or to the parcel from specified origins. Generally the lower the cost in time and money of these trips, the more valuable the parcel. As a simple example, consider the situation around a major hospital. Since time is precious for doctors practicing at the hospital, office space built on land providing lower time and money costs for getting to and from the hospital will receive premium rents. Such land can capture at least a portion of the cost savings it provides physicians in the form of higher rents, and these higher rents will produce a land value greater than less accessible sites. The same reasoning applies to land used for other purposes. This concept explains why certain land uses are located where they are and why more intensive developments occur at particularly desirable locations.

DESCRIBING REAL ESTATE

If you purchase a new automobile there are few problems in identifying exactly what you have purchased — a "Belchfire Custom" has a certain appearance and a serial number to identify your particular automobile. Manufacturer's specifications can be used to verify that your car is exactly what it is supposed to be. Not long ago some court cases resulted when an automobile manufacturer used engines from one line of cars they produce in another line. In this case the purchasers contended the cars they had received were not exactly what they had ordered. However, if you purchase a parcel of real estate it is often difficult to know exactly what you have purchased. Unlike other commodities, the boundaries of a parcel of real estate are not generally visible or even identifiable. To avoid conflicts with adjoining property owners and for your own peace of mind you will want to know the exact location and boundaries of your property.

Legally, there is also a need for establishing the physical boundaries of a parcel of real estate. In Chapters 4, 5, and 6, which consider the legal aspects of real estate ownership, you will learn that legal documents pertaining to real estate require what is called a **legal description** of the real estate involved. A legal description may be thought of as one which will stand up in a court of law. Such a description must be complete and precise enough to identify the subject property in such a way that it is not confused with any other parcel in the world. There are four methods commonly used to describe real estate:

Metes and bounds	Rectangular survey
Monuments	Lot and block

To assure the accuracy of a legal description, you should engage a registered surveyor to conduct a survey. Such a survey will establish the corners and boundaries of the property. You can then consult with the owners of adjoining properties to see whether any disagreement exists over the boundaries of the tract. For example, a neighbor may have part of a building on property about to be sold by your client. When improvements are placed on the land of another, it is called an **encroachment.** Figure 3.5 shows some typical encroachments. If material differences of opinion exist among adjoining landowners, you will want to settle them before continuing with the transaction.

While allowing you to physically inspect the perimeter of a property, the survey also reduces the description to writing — writing that may be used in documents dealing with the land. Surveyors produce very precise and accurate descriptions. You should not attempt to produce a legal description without the aid of a qualified surveyor. To do so may expose you to a legal liability you do not wish to have. However, you should understand the basics of how a surveyor will describe land that unambiguously distinguishes it from all other parcels and will be accepted by the courts as being a sufficient legal description. Therefore,

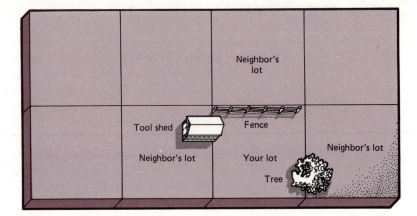

Figure 3.5 Examples of some common encroachments. (Source: Adapted from Bruce Harwood, *Real Estate Principles*. Reston, Virginia: Reston Publishing Company, Inc., 1977, p. 51.)

what follows is a consideration of the basic methods for legally describing land and how to interpret them, not a discussion of how to operate a tape measure and transit or how to manage a survey team.

Metes and Bounds

The metes and bounds method of describing real estate is one of the oldest available. Metes are popularly defined as distances, whereas bounds are directions. Starting from an identifiable point of beginning, a metes and bounds description verbally walks the reader around the boundaries of the parcel by providing a direction and the distance to be traveled in that direction, followed by another direction and associated distance, and so on until the reader is brought back to the point of beginning. A lack of care used in preparing these descriptions creates many disputes.

Professional surveyors can produce accurate descriptions using the metes and bounds method. Surveyors can measure bearings (angles) and distances very precisely. Bearings are measured in *degrees, minutes,* and *seconds*. Distances are measured to 1/100th of a foot. The following description illustrates the metes and bounds type of description:

Beginning at a point, thence N 45° 0'0" E 400.00 feet to a point; thence S 45° 0'0" E 200.00 feet to a point; thence S 45° 0'0" W 400.00 feet to a point; thence N 45° 0'0" W 200.00 feet to the point of beginning.

The distances in this description are easily understood, but the bearings may not be clear. The first bearing is read as 45 degrees, zero minutes, and zero seconds. Other bearings are read in a similar manner. There are 360 degrees in a circle, 60 minutes in each degree, and 60 seconds in each minute. All bearings will start with either north or south to let you know whether the angle is measured from due north or due south. The direction that follows the number of degrees, minutes, and seconds tells you whether the angle is east or west of due north or due south. For example, the bearing, S 45° 0'0" E, is 45 degrees east of due south, as shown in Figure 3.6. Likewise, the bearing, N 45° 0'0" E, produces a line that is 45 degrees east of due north.

In Figure 3.6, look at the line labeled, N 45° 0'0" E, and you will notice that this line also can be described using the set of axes on its other end. Coming from the other direction, the bearing is S 45° 0'0" W. These two bearings are identical. They are called reciprocals of one another. Surveyors will sometimes use the reciprocal bearing, which means you must be alert in reading descriptions.

It is important that the lines described by the bearings and distances completely enclose an area. Failure to do so will mean that a property is effectively unbounded. For this reason, metes and bounds

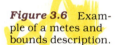

Figure 3.6 Example of a metes and bounds description.

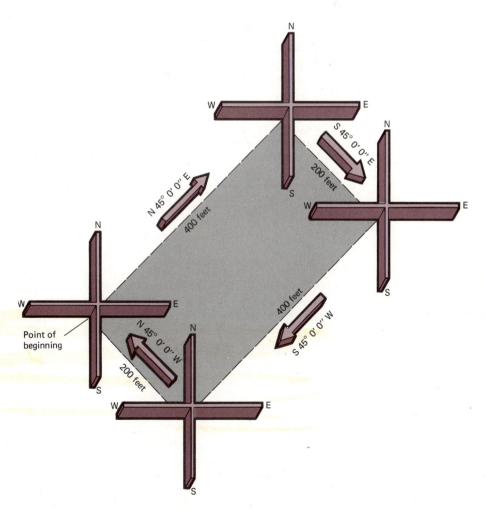

descriptions will often end with the phrase "back to the point of beginning." The starting point in a metes and bounds description is called the point of beginning. It is established precisely by professional surveyors in such a way that it can be located again and again if necessary.

To summarize, surveyors establish a point of beginning, measure bearings and distances precisely, and make sure the description returns to the point of beginning to fully enclose a parcel of land. Metes and bounds descriptions are widely used today, especially to describe parcels with odd, or otherwise unique, shapes.

Monuments

Before professional surveyors were generally available, property owners would develop a very informal land description using natural and man-made objects, such as concrete posts, trees, roads, and streams. In these descriptions, these objects would be used to identify corners and even boundary lines of parcels. Objects used in such descriptions are called **monuments,** and this method of describing land is called the **monuments method.**

Monuments descriptions generally suffer from two maladies. First, they were often carelessly prepared, which introduced many errors. Second, many of the monuments eventually were destroyed or moved. For example, streams changed course, trees were cut and stumps cleared, and concrete posts were removed. Such situations created problems between adjoining landowners. For these reasons, monuments descriptions have been steadily replaced by other methods for describing land.

Rectangular Survey

The vast quantities of land made a part of the United States through the Northwest Territories and Louisiana Purchase effectively doubled the land area of this country. This land also created some problems for the young nation, one of which was its surveying and effective cataloging. The need was great for a uniform system for describing these and other lands that may be acquired later. The system that was selected and adopted by the government was called the **rectangular survey method,** or alternatively, the **government survey method.** It has proven to be an effective and widely used description method. Thirty states make use of it to describe land within their boundaries as indicated by shaded states in Figure 3.7.

Essentially, the rectangular survey uses a graph paper, or grid, concept to describe land. The basic idea is simple: given two axes as references, any point can be precisely located by referring to its position on each axis. Of course, parcels of land are larger than points and this basic concept must be modified a bit to describe these larger areas. However, the logic remains intact. Of interest now is how the axes are

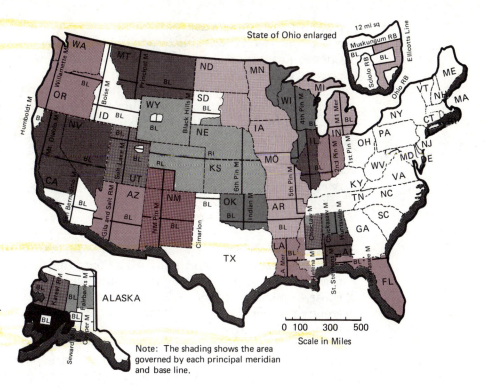

Figure 3.7 Rectangular survey system. (Source: Bureau of Land Management, Department of the Interior.)

Note: The shading shows the area governed by each principal meridian and base line.

identified, how locations are expressed relative to them, and how parcels of different size are handled—in other words, the mechanics of the process.

The axes in the system are called **base lines** and **principal meridians.** Base lines run due east and west, while principal meridians run due north and south. Rather than one "grand" base line and principal meridian used for the entire country, there are 33 sets of them. In many cases these axes were positioned to expedite the work of the survey crews. Figure 3.7 indicates the location of each of the sets and the area affected by it. Principal meridians have names. For example, land in Idaho is described using the Boise Meridian, while next door in Oregon and Washington, land is described using the Willamette Meridian. Base lines are not named, probably because each principal meridian is named and has only one base line associated with it. If you have not done so, you should check Figure 3.7 to see whether the rectangular survey is used in your state and, if so, which principal meridian is used and where it and the base line are located.

Checks The rectangular survey works by progressively dividing an area into a number of smaller and smaller areas. Starting from the entire area affected by a particular principal meridian and base line, areas 24 miles by 24 miles, called **checks,** are developed. Checks are set by establishing **guide meridians** parallel to the principal meridian every 24 miles and **correction lines** parallel to the base line every 24 miles. Checks are important because they provide a way to solve a problem created by the fact that all north-south lines converge at the two poles. This means that, in the northern hemisphere, parallel lines running north and south get closer together as you go north, eventually intersecting at the North Pole. Thus, two guide meridians that are exactly 24 miles apart at one point will not be 24 miles apart farther north or south. To solve this problem, surveyors make corrections every 24 miles north and south of the base line by re-establishing the 24-mile distance between the guide meridians. If you were able to see a guide meridian, it would be a series of 24-mile long segments, each segment slightly offset from the ones north and south of it.

Townships The next smaller division is the **township,** a 6-mile square area. Running north and south of the base line and east and west of the principal meridian are imaginary, parallel lines 6 miles apart forming these 6-mile square areas. Simply imagine graph paper on which each square represents an area 6 miles on each side. The rows of townships running east and west are called *townships,* or **tiers,** while the columns of townships running north and south are called **ranges.** The tiers are numbered according to their direction from the base line. For example, the third tier or row of townships north of the base line is labeled Township 3 North, abbreviated as T3N. Ranges are similarly labeled. The second range west of the principal meridian is called Range 2 West,

Figure 3.8 Tiers and ranges in the rectangular survey.

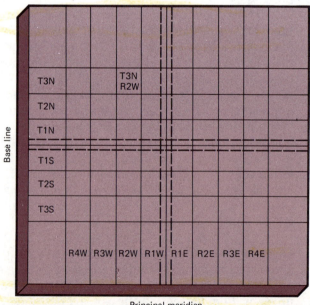

R2W. With the ability to identify tiers and ranges we can now label individual townships by identifying the tier and range the township occupies. For example the township formed by the intersection of the third tier north of the base line and the second range west of the principal meridian is simply identified as T3N, R2W, as shown in Figure 3.8.

The 36 square miles contained in a township is still not small enough to be useful for most parcels. Accordingly, townships are divided into **sections,** areas one mile square. Each section contains 640 **acres,** and each acre contains 43,560 square feet. The 36 sections within a township are numbered starting in the northeast corner going west across the first row and then dropping down to the second row and numbering east and so on as seen in Figure 3.9. Section 36 is in the southeast corner of the township. If you were buying Section 14 of the township just described earlier, the legal description would be Section 14, T3N, R2W.

Even the 640 acres contained in a section is not a small enough unit to accommodate most transactions. Smaller tracts are described by dividing the section into halves, quarters, halves of quarters, quarters of quarters, and so on. For example, if you were buying the 160 acres located in the northeast corner of Section 14 it would be described as the northeast quarter, abbreviated NE$\frac{1}{4}$ or NE/4, of Section 14. When combined with the township, the description becomes: NE$\frac{1}{4}$ of Section 14, T3N, R2W. This parcel is illustrated in Figure 3.10. For smaller tracts the process of using fractions to break the section into smaller pieces is continued. For example, the 40-acre tract located in the southwest corner of the section would be described as the SW$\frac{1}{4}$ of the SW$\frac{1}{4}$ of Section

Figure 3.9 Numbering the sections in a township.

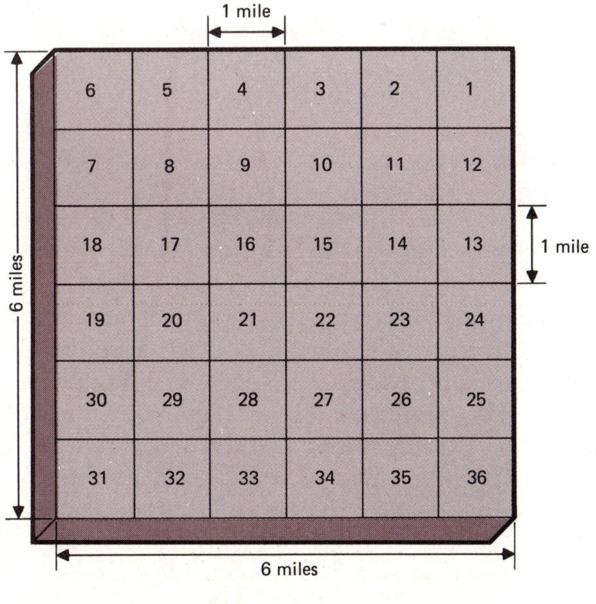

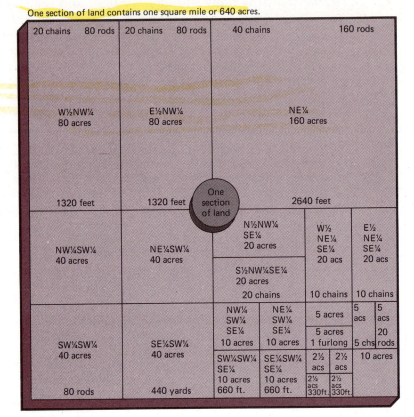

One section of land contains one square mile or 640 acres.

Figure 3.10 Fractions of a section. (Source: *Dimensions: A Guide to Describing Real Property*. Santa Ana: First American Title Insurance Company, 1979, p. 9.)

14, T3N, R2W. Descriptions for various sized parcels are illustrated in Figure 3.10.

To find the number of acres in a parcel you can apply a simple reduction approach using the property description. For example, a quarter section contains $\frac{640}{4} = 160$ acres. A quarter of that quarter would contain 40 acres. A half of that 40 acres would contain 20 acres. Thus, you can start with the last fraction in a description and work backwards dividing the parcel into smaller pieces. You could also simply multiply all the fractions together and then multiply the result by the 640 acres in a section. To illustrate, the N$\frac{1}{2}$ of the SW$\frac{1}{4}$ of the NE$\frac{1}{4}$ of a section has 20 acres in it: $\frac{1}{2} \times \frac{1}{4} \times \frac{1}{4} = \frac{1}{32}$; $\frac{1}{32} \times 640$ acres = 20 acres.

As you probably suspect, people do not always buy and sell land that corresponds exactly with quarters and halves of sections. For example, your grandfather may have left you his farm, called Blackacre, in his will. Blackacre may have 40 acres as illustrated in Figure 3.11. To describe Blackacre, areas A and B must be described. Area A is the SW$\frac{1}{4}$ of the SE$\frac{1}{4}$ of the SE$\frac{1}{4}$ of Section 14 whereas area B is the E$\frac{1}{2}$ of the SE$\frac{1}{4}$ of the SE$\frac{1}{4}$ of Section 14. The full rectangular description of Blackacre would be

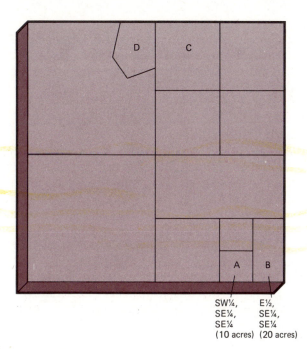

Figure 3.11 Describing two parcels of land.

SW¼,
SE¼,
SE¼
(10 acres)

E½,
SE¼,
SE¼
(20 acres)

The SW¼ of the SE¼ of the SE¼ and the E½ of the SE¼ of the SE¼ of Section 14, T3N, R2W, County of College, State of Euphoria.

Note that this description adds the county and state to complete the description.

Irregularly Shaped Parcels Some parcels do not have straight boundaries or shapes that can readily be described using the rectangular survey method. For such parcels, a combination of rectangular survey and metes and bounds descriptions may be used. Any portion that can be described using the rectangular survey will be so described, and the remainder of the parcel will be described using the metes and bounds method with the rectangular survey method providing a point of beginning. In Figure 3.11, the areas labeled C and D comprise a parcel of land. Area C is the NW¼ of the NE¼ of Section 14. Area D must be described using metes and bounds techniques. For that description, a convenient point of beginning is the NW corner of the NE¼. Starting from this point the rest of the metes and bounds description would follow as discussed earlier.

Combining metes and bounds and rectangular survey methods is quite common. It is also quite common to use the rectangular survey to establish the point of beginning even when the parcel is to be described entirely with the metes and bounds method. When the point of beginning does not coincide with an easily identified point in the rectangular survey, the surveyor will locate the nearest such point and provide the bearings and distance to the point of beginning. For example, a surveyor may describe the point of beginning as being 245.50 feet S 46°, 07′, 53″ E of the SW corner of the SE¼ as the starting point for a metes and bounds description.

Lot and Block

If you buy a lot in a subdivision, that lot will probably be described using the lot and block method. This method is used for subdivisions to make the numerous descriptions easier and less subject to error. Essentially, the lot and block method begins with a detailed legal description of a larger tract (the entire subdivision) using the metes and bounds or the rectangular survey method. This larger tract is then divided into blocks and the blocks are divided into lots. The blocks and lots are numbered starting with one. When you purchase a lot, its legal description is simply the lot and block number assigned to it.

Mechanically, the process is more involved and detailed than this brief overview. The person developing the subdivision must prepare a detailed map of the subdivision showing the exact location and dimensions of each lot along with the location and dimensions of streets, areas where the city and power companies have the right to run pipes and cables, park land, and any other item of physical relevance in the subdivision. This map, called a **plat map,** must be approved by the city or county government in whose jurisdiction the subdivision is located. Whether or not the plat is approved depends on whether the subdivision meets all the *subdivision requirements* established by the city or county. Critical elements in producing the final, approved plat are a legal description of the entire subdivision and detailed dimensions of all lots. Once approved, the plat is presented to the proper public official for recording and, when recorded, becomes part of the state's official public land records. Documents in public land records are organized into books and pages. Each document is assigned a page number and certain numbers of pages are organized into books. Indexes are available for finding documents pertaining to a particular parcel. Public land records are open to inspection by anyone; this means that you or anyone else can examine the recorded plat map for your subdivision and from that plat map determine the exact legal description of the subdivision and the exact dimensions of your lot.

Plat maps must be filed any time a parcel of land is divided into more than a specified number of smaller parcels. While the requirements a developer must meet with respect to specifications for streets, sewers, and other matters differ between industrial, office, and residential subdivisions, they must all be approved and recorded. Many subdivision regulations require that a plat map be filed if a tract is subdivided into four or more lots for any purpose. Figure 3.12 is an industrial subdivi-

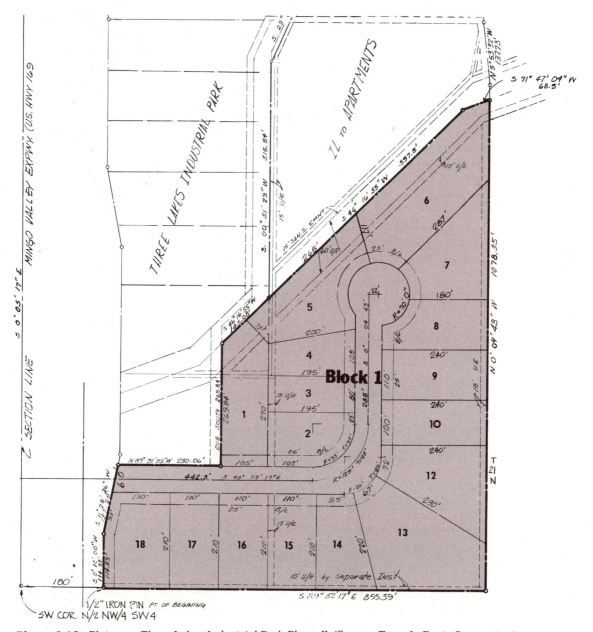

Figure 3.12 Plat map: Three Lakes Industrial Park Phase II. (Source: Terry L. Davis Companies.)

sion plat map in which the subdivision contains only one block. A **block** is a series of lots, all of which can be reached without crossing a street. All 18 of the lots in the Three Lakes Industrial Park Phase II can be reached without crossing a street and are, therefore, in one block.

There are several interesting things you should note about this plat.

First, each lot is numbered and its dimensions are given. You should also note that the overall boundaries of the subdivision are described using a metes and bounds description from a point of beginning based on the rectangular survey method. By looking in the lower left-hand corner you can find the point of beginning for the description. This point was established by referencing the SW Corner of the $N\frac{1}{2}$ of the $NW\frac{1}{4}$ of the $SW\frac{1}{4}$ of Section 29, T21N, R14W, Tulsa County, Oklahoma, and following the bearing S 89°, 52′, 17″ E exactly 180.00 feet. As you can see, the rectangular survey provides an excellent means of establishing the point of beginning for a metes and bounds description.

Any lot in Three Lakes Industrial Park Phase II can be described using the plat map recorded in the county land records office. The plat details every lot in the subdivision and also contains a legal description of the subdivided land. Lot and block descriptions may follow different forms in different areas. For example, a lot and block description may take the following form:

Lot 6, Block 1 of Three Lakes Industrial Park Phase II according to the plat recorded on February 21, 1986, as Plat Number 4020, Book 4504, Page 1019, Tulsa County, State of Oklahoma.

The same lot may also be described in some areas as:

Lot 6, Block 1, Three Lakes Industrial Park Phase II, an addition to the City of Owasso, County of Tulsa, State of Oklahoma, according to the recorded plat thereof.

Lot and block descriptions provide a brief, effective way to describe land that has been subdivided and platted.

Describing Condominiums

A condominium is an ownership arrangement in which an individual or firm has exclusive ownership of a unit and shares ownership in the land and common, or nonprivate, areas of the improvements. Common areas include swimming pools, tennis courts, lawns, and other areas open to all residents. This raises the question of how individual units are described. That is, if you buy a unit on the 14th floor, or even the first floor since you do not own the land, how is that unit legally described? As in the lot and block method, the answer is found in the documents the developer must file in the public records. To form a condominium, a developer must file a number of documents (discussed later in the book), including plat maps and building plans containing the legal description of the entire tract of land and the location and dimensions of each unit. Each unit is then described referencing the unit number and recorded documents. Any interested person can then access the public records to find the exact dimensions of the unit.

CAVEATS ON PREPARING LEGAL DESCRIPTIONS

Preparing legal descriptions requires a great deal of care. Incorrect legal descriptions can create legal complications for buyers, sellers, and the party preparing the description. Unless you are an attorney or surveyor, you should refrain from preparing legal descriptions. While you should know how to read such descriptions, you should carefully consider the possible legal and financial penalties associated with preparing incorrect descriptions. If you have any questions about a legal description, you should consult an experienced real estate attorney.

SUMMARY

In this chapter you learned about the physical aspects of real estate. First, you learned that all real estate has some physical characteristics that distinguish it from nonreal estate assets. These general physical characteristics include immobility, limited supply, indestructibility, and three dimensionality. In addition, each parcel of real estate has a set of site-specific characteristics that distinguish it from all other parcels of real estate. Site-specific characteristics include topography, soil types, size and shape, improvements, and accessibility. These characteristics collectively determine the physical ability of the parcel to be used for different purposes and its value.

Next, the chapter considered how land can be described in such a manner that a parcel's boundaries are unambiguous and capable of being defended in court. Such descriptions are called legal descriptions. Four methods for legally describing real estate were discussed: metes and bounds, monuments, rectangular survey, and lot and block. Each of these methods requires a great deal of care to produce an accurate legal description.

QUICK QUIZ

1. General physical characteristics _____ .

  I. physically distinguish real estate from all other commodities
 II. are common to all parcels of real estate

    a. I only   c. Both I and II
    b. II only   d. Neither I nor II

2. Site-specific characteristics include _____ .

    a. industructibility, topography, soil types
    b. size and shape of parcel, soil types, topography
    c. indestructibility, improvements, soil types
    d. topography, availability of utilities, immobility

3. Which of the following is not a method for legally describing real estate?

a. lot and block   c. rectangular survey
b. metes and bounds   d .boundary line

4. An acre _____ .

I. contains 43,560 square feet
II. is 1/600th of a square mile

a. I only   c. Both I and II
b. II only   d. Neither I nor II

5. In the rectangular survey, land is divided into areas measuring six miles by six miles called _____ .

a. checks   c. sections
b. ranges   d. townships

6. The $S\frac{1}{2}$ of the $SE\frac{1}{4}$ of the $NE\frac{1}{4}$ contains _____ acres.

7. Physically, the area above the surface of a parcel of land is called _____ .

8. The cost in time and money of getting to and from a site is a measure of that site's _____ .

9. Using the metes and bounds method, a description begins with the _____ .

10. All bearings in a metes and bounds description begin with either the direction _____ or _____ .

QUESTIONS AND EXERCISES

1. Select a parcel of land that has either an office building, apartment complex, or shopping center on it and assess, as best possible, how its site-specific characteristics affected the development.

2. Find a parcel with no buildings on it and, based on its site-specific characteristics, identify an appropriate use for it. Detail the reasoning behind your decision.

3. What information about soils in your area is available publicly? If you owned a parcel of land and were considering development, how would you find out about its soil characteristics?

4. Select a residential subdivision and analyze how well it incorporates site-specific characteristics into its design and construction.

5. What site-specific characteristics do more expensive home building lots in your area possess? What about less expensive lots? Compare the two.

6. See if you can find an improved parcel that is experiencing negative changes in its immediate neighborhood and identify what the negative influences are. Identify a parcel experiencing positive changes and the sources of that change.

7. Identify a shortage of land for a specific land use somewhere in your town.

8. Identify a cluster or node of office buildings and assess how accessibility contributed to the development of that node. Accessibility to what activities is important to office building development?

9. For each of the following portions of a section of land, indicate the number of acres it contains and its dimensions and also draw a figure showing it within the section.

    a. $NE\frac{1}{4}$
    b. $SW\frac{1}{4}$ of the $SW\frac{1}{4}$ of the $SW\frac{1}{4}$
    c. $S\frac{1}{2}$ of the $SE\frac{1}{4}$ of the $NW\frac{1}{4}$ of the $NW\frac{1}{4}$
    d. $E\frac{1}{2}$ of the $N\frac{1}{2}$ of the $SE\frac{1}{4}$ of the $SW\frac{1}{4}$ of the $SE\frac{1}{4}$

KEY TERMINOLOGY

accessibility	percolation
acre	plat map
air space	plottage
base line	point of beginning
bearing	principal meridian
check	range
correction line	rectangular survey method
encroachment	section
general physical characteristics	site specific physical characteristics
government survey method	soil types
guide meridian	specific performance
immobility	subterranean
indestructibility	three dimensional
legal description	tier
limited supply	topography
lot and block	township
metes and bounds	

IF YOU WANT TO READ MORE

Dimensions: A Guide to Describing Real Property (Santa Ana, Calif.: First American Title Insurance Company).

JOHN MCMAHON, *Property Development* (New York: McGraw-Hill Book Company, 1976), Chapter 13.

Residential Development Handbook (Washington, D.C.: Urban Land Institute, 1978), Chapters 2–4.

Office Development Handbook (Washington, D.C.: Urban Land Institute, 1982), Chapter 3.

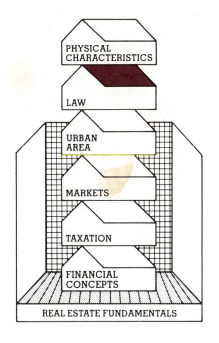

PHYSICAL CHARACTERISTICS

LAW

URBAN AREA

MARKETS

TAXATION

FINANCIAL CONCEPTS

REAL ESTATE FUNDAMENTALS

4

Legal Fundamentals: interests in real property

PREVIEW   Most of us are fascinated with "property" throughout our lives. From interest in toys as youngsters we turn to clothes and cars as teenagers, and to homes, businesses, bank accounts, and stocks as adults. These "things" are what we consider to be property. However, the law looks at property in a different light. This chapter introduces you to the legal concept of real property by answering the following questions:

1. What is property?
2. What are the different types of property?
3. What is an interest in real property and what forms of interests exist?
4. How may real property be owned by more than one person?
5. If you own real property, are there any limitations to your rights?

LEGAL NATURE OF PROPERTY

Many of the most important forces in life are unseen. You cannot see or touch intangibles such as political ideas or religious beliefs, yet they shape many aspects of our lives. Law is another intangible of great importance. Law exists in the realm of the mind, but affects your daily life in many ways. In your study of real estate, an important legal concept affecting your daily life is that of **property.** Take note of the fact that property is a concept, not a physical object — that is, it is an *intangible* rather than a *tangible* item. On the other hand, real estate is a tangible item, the earth and everything permanently attached to it.

The legal concept of property is composed of various interests in objects that the law recognizes and protects. An **interest** is a right or privilege such as the rights of possession, enjoyment, and disposal of a particular asset. You may have interests in items that are tangible, such as land, or intangible, such as the copyright on this book. The owner of the copyright to this book has interests that the law protects by punishing those who reproduce its pages without permission. To illustrate and expand the concepts of property and interests, let's assume that your grandfather, at his death, conveyed to you in his will a tract of land called "Blackacre" located on the urban fringe of your hometown. To help you understand what it is you own, let's ask some questions about the legal aspects of your ownership of Blackacre.

Question 1. Is the "property" you own the physical assets, such as the soil and trees?

The law's answer is no. Legally, what you have, as owner, are various interests or rights in connection with Blackacre. For example, you have the right to make a wide variety of uses of Blackacre. You may live on it, farm it, or conduct a business on it. You have the right to transfer your interests to another person outright (by sale or gift) or the right to transfer to a lender the power to transfer your interests if you fail to repay a loan owed to the lender (a mortgage). You may also lease the property to another. This collection of interests you have in connection with Blackacre is often called a "bundle of rights." This "bundle" comprises ownership; you, as the holder of the "bundle," are the owner of Blackacre.

Question 2. Must you own all the rights in Blackacre?

The law's answer is no. Because the interests constituting property are multiple, you can own less than all of the rights, with the other rights being owned by other persons. If you think in terms of all the rights in a property constituting the complete bundle, then it should be easy to visualize owning only some of the rights. You have a bundle of rights, it is just not complete. One or more other persons own the remaining rights in the complete bundle. The fact that there are outstanding interests in other persons will place limitations on what you can do with your rights in Blackacre in order to protect the rights of other owners. The various rights constituting the "bundle" may be divided among people in different ways, as you will see shortly.

Question 3. Assuming you own all of the rights in Blackacre, is your ownership absolute?

The law's answer is no, because the state ("state," as used here means any level of government) may still claim rights in Blackacre. We will examine what these claims may be later.

So, who owns Blackacre? The concept of property ownership being a bundle of rights instead of an all or nothing proposition makes it apparent that you cannot glibly say that you alone own Blackacre, even though you acquired it from your grandfather by his will. Our task now is to define the nature of your interests and the nature of the interests of any other persons in Blackacre in more detail and unravel the mystery of "What do you own?"

TYPES OF PROPERTY

When your grandfather left Blackacre to you there may have been a house on it in which he was living at the time of his death. Did you acquire ownership of both the land and the house? Yes, because you acquired ownership in **real property,** which is defined as interests in land and *all* permanent attachments to land. The house qualifies as a permanent attachment; so do trees, fences, and outbuildings. You should take note of the fact that real property involves interests in real estate. Real estate was earlier defined as land and all permanent attachments to it. Many people use the phrases "real property" and "real estate" to mean the same thing. Technically, such usage is incorrect, but it remains very common.

If your grandfather's pickup truck was on the land at the time of his death, you would not have acquired ownership of it unless he had left it to you in another provision of his will. This is because it is classified as **personal property,** which is defined as interests in all things other than land and permanent attachments to land. Many other items on Blackacre could be similarly classified as personal property: your grandfather's clothes in the house, the cattle in the field, and the surveyor's instruments he used in his job before retirement. These items are called **chattels.**

In some instances, classifying items as either real or personal property is not easy. What constitutes permanent attachment is subject to different interpretations. For example, wooden paneling is usually nailed to a wall, and few people would argue that nailing is not a permanent attachment. However, a window air-conditioning unit may be installed using bolts and other permanent attaching devices or simply slid into a window in a very temporary manner, or anywhere between these two extremes.

Whether something is real or personal property is very important to you. When you acquired Blackacre you acquired interests in all the real property. So even if an item was once personal property, but is now permanently attached to the land, you became the owner. The same thing would be true if you had purchased Blackacre. Items that were originally personal property but are now considered real property are called **fixtures.** Disputes over whether an item is fixture are often not easily settled because much judgment is required. Three tests which can be used to determine if an item is fixture are these:

1. *Manner of attachment.* This test asks the question, "Is the item attached in a permanent manner or in a manner such that removal would cause significant damage?" Burying, planting, nailing, bolting, gluing, and so on generally produce a permanent attachment. For example, a washer and dryer will not likely be considered a fixture by virtue of being plugged into an outlet and connected to water and gas pipes. But if the washer and dryer are built into a custom cabinet, they may be considered fixtures.

2. *Intent of the parties.* An agreement between the parties clarifies the situation. For example, if the sellers wish to take a particular chandelier with them, they should ask the buyer to sign an agreement allowing them to do so. Such an agreement removes any doubt

Figure 4.1 Relationship between real property, personal property, and fixtures.

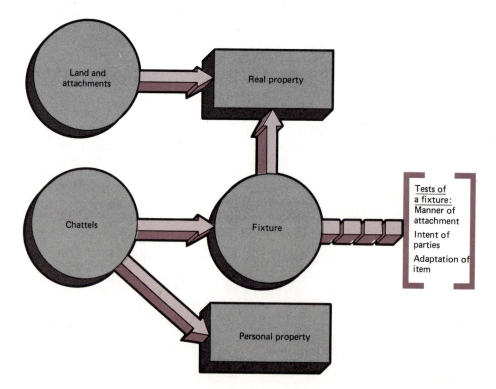

about the status of the chandelier. In the absence of an agreement, the intent of the parties can still be useful. If the buyer and seller act as if they intended to make a certain item part of the real property, that may be sufficient evidence to cause that item to be considered a fixture. Certainly, intent is very difficult to prove.

3. *Adaptation of the item.* If an item is such an integral component of a building that its removal would reduce the building's usefulness or if an item was made specifically for a particular building, it is likely a fixture. For example, a custom-made awning covering an odd-shaped patio may be a fixture, whereas a standard awning bought off the shelf may not.

Figure 4.1 summarizes the relationship between personal property, real property, and fixtures, and the tests used to determine an asset's status. If disputes over which assets are considered fixtures and which are considered personal property cannot be resolved by the parties involved, they will be resolved by the courts using the above tests.

FORMS OF OWNERSHIP OF REAL PROPERTY

As was mentioned earlier, because "ownership" is a collection of interests in real (or personal) property, it is possible to divide these interests among different people in various ways. To expand your understanding of the legal nature of real property, we now examine the ways in which the interests in Blackacre could be divided. These interests in real property are summarized in Figure 4.2.

Figure 4.2 Interests in real property.

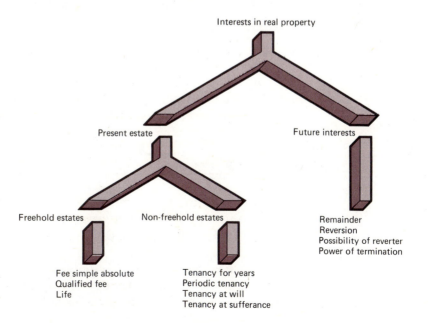

Interests in real property

Present estate

Future interests

Freehold estates

Non-freehold estates

Remainder
Reversion
Possibility of reverter
Power of termination

Fee simple absolute
Qualified fee
Life

Tenancy for years
Periodic tenancy
Tenancy at will
Tenancy at sufferance

Present and Future Interests

First, the property interests in Blackacre could have been divided on a time basis by your grandfather. He could have created a present interest only, or both present and future interests. A **present interest** is one in which you, as owner, have a current right to possession of the land. Possession means some degree of physical control over the land with the right to make an "unlimited" number of uses of it. (As you will see later, there may be limits on your uses of Blackacre but there are no uses to which you *must* put Blackacre.) This is what your grandfather conveyed to you. Suppose, however, that your grandfather's will had conveyed Blackacre to you for your life, with your younger sister receiving it upon your death. You would now own the present interest in Blackacre, with your sister owning a **future interest:** an interest that may become possessory at some future date.

The present interests in real property are called **estates.** These estates are divided into various categories based on the rights involved. The two most general categories of present estates are freehold and non-freehold estates. Property laws are enacted by each state, and, while much of our property law comes from English law, variations exist among the states. The following description of basic property law concepts conveys generally accepted principles of property law. You should always consult an attorney for your state's specific laws.

Freehold Estates

Freehold estates involve the ownership of real property. These estates last for an indefinite period of time. They are considered of indefinite duration because they do not last for a specified period of time such as 10 months, 12 years, and so on. For example, your interest in Blackacre will continue until your death. You may choose the new owner by using a will or, if you have no will, the state will choose the new owner by the laws of succession. Of course, you may sell or give your interest away any time you wish. The point is that the duration of the estate is not known in advance. There are three types of freehold estates:

Fee simple absolute

Qualified fee

Life

These estates all involve ownership of real property, but differ with respect to the duration of your interests and your right to choose who will own the property in the future.

Fee Simple Absolute The most complete bundle of rights is contained in the **fee simple absolute** estate. Theoretically, this estate will last forever. If your grandfather has conveyed this estate to you, it can last throughout your life, and upon your death, it will pass to your successors either through a will or, in the absence of a will, by state statutes of descent and distribution. You can, however, transfer your fee simple absolute during your life to a transferee by gift or purchase. That transferee will have exactly the same interest in Blackacre as you had. That is, the purchaser will own Blackacre for the rest of his life, with it passing at death by will or descent, unless he transfers it away during his lifetime. Because this estate lasts for an infinite length of time, there can be no future interest following it. This estate is often referred to by other names such as fee or fee simple. These terms generally mean the same as fee simple absolute.

Qualified Fee Simple The second type of freehold estate your grandfather could have willed to you is a qualified fee simple. A **qualified fee simple** estate ends upon the occurrence of some specified event. For example, your grandfather could have conveyed Blackacre to you so long as the land is operated as a farm. Although your estate can last for an infinite length of time, just as will a fee simple absolute, if you ever cease to farm the land, your estate automatically comes to an end and ownership automatically reverts back to your grandfather or, in this case, his heirs. This means there is a future interest, called a **possibility of reverter,** that will become possessory if (but only if) the condition is ever violated. Present and future interests are summarized in Figure 4.3. What has just been described is sometimes called a **qualified fee determinable.**

Another type of qualified fee simple estate requires that the grantor (or his heirs) go to court to end your ownership should you fail to comply with the conditions stipulated by the grantor (your grandfather). Such an estate is called a **qualified fee conditional,** also frequently called **qualified fee subsequent.** The future interest is called a **power of termination** or **right of reentry.** Because of the complex and somewhat messy nature of qualified fee estates they are not used extensively. If you should ever become involved in a situation involving qualified fee estates you should consult an attorney.

Life Estate The third type of freehold estate your grandfather could have willed you is a life estate. A **life estate** creates an ownership interest that ends with the death of a designated person, usually the person owning the life estate. Suppose you had received a life estate in Blackacre, with your younger sister designated as the person to receive your interest upon your death. Your life estate is of indefinite, but not infinite, duration. Unfortunately for you, your estate must come to an end some day. The future interest your sister owns is a **remainder;** that is, what ''remains'' of your grandfather's fee simple absolute after your death. Your sister is called a **remainderman.** If the remainderman is known and no other conditions must be met for the interest to become possess-

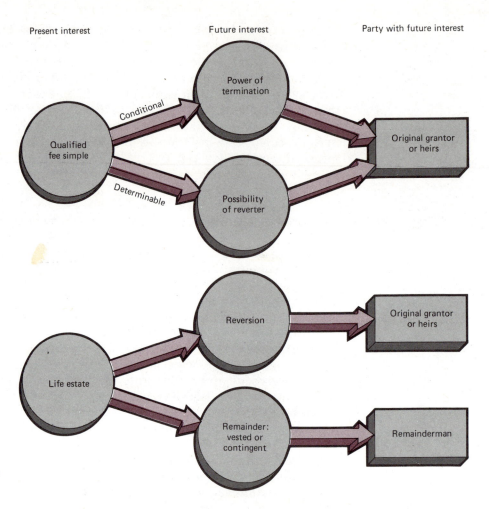

Figure 4.3 Present and future interests.

ory, the remainder is a **vested remainder.** If either condition is not met, the remainder is called a **contingent remainder.** For instance, if Blackacre had been left to you, with the remainder going to your spouse, the remainder remains a contingent remainder until you marry, at which time it becomes a vested remainder.

Had your grandfather not created a remainder in your sister, but only a life estate in you, the future interest automatically created would be called a **reversion;** that is, the estate would revert to the grantor (your grandfather). Since he is dead, it would revert to his successors in interest under his will or under the statutes of descent and distribution. This is a popular use of the life estate. To illustrate its use, suppose you wanted to provide a home for your parents, but because you were supplying all the money, you did not want the home to be divided among your brothers and sisters when your parents die. You could purchase the home and create a life estate for your parents with a reversionary interest to bring ownership back to you.

You can sell or give away your life estate in Blackacre during your lifetime, but you cannot do so at your death because your estate automatically comes to an end by operation of law. However, the person purchasing or receiving the life estate as a gift will have only a life estate tied to your life. When you die their interest ends and the appropriate person receives either the remainder or reversion and becomes the new owner of the property.

Note the existence of a "time equation" in this example. Your grandfather's fee simple absolute, which theoretically runs to infinity, has been divided into a life estate and a remainder (or reversion) that runs forever from the end of the life estate. There is also a "rights equation," since all the rights in Blackacre must be owned by someone, though not necessarily the same person, and all these rights must add up to a fee simple absolute estate. These time and rights equations are summarized in Table 4.1.

In some states, life estates in some portion of real property owned by the family are created by law when a spouse dies and the other spouse is still living. These laws were passed in an attempt to ensure that the spouse will not be denied all interest in real property. The right of the wife to a portion, usually one third to one half, of the family's real property is called **dower**, whereas the right of the husband is called **curtesy**. Curtesy rights generally provide less protection for the husband and in many states husbands have been given dower rights. Dower and curtesy are treated in more detail later in the chapter.

Table 4.1. Real Property Equations

Time		
All Interests	=	Infinity
Fee Simple Absolute	=	Infinity
Present Interests + Future Interests	=	Infinity
For Example:		
Qualified Fee + Possibility of Reverter	=	Infinity
Life Estate + Remainder or Reversion	=	Infinity

Rights		
Fee Simple Absolute	=	All Rights
Fee Simple Subject to Conveyed Rights + Rights Conveyed to Others[a]	=	All Rights

[a] Leases, mortgages, easements, etc.

NON-FREEHOLD ESTATES

Non-freehold estates involve rights of possession and use of real estate. We commonly call a non-freehold estate a lease, although this term actually refers to the document used to create a non-freehold (leasehold) estate. Leases allow one party to possess and use the property of another for a rental fee. The parties involved are the tenant (lessee) and landlord (lessor). The tenant has the present estate and the landlord has a future interest. In discussing the non-freehold estates, let's leave Blackacre temporarily and focus on another tract of land, Whiteacre, on which are located 20 apartment units. Let's assume you are considering leasing a unit in the Whiteacre Apartments for the balance of the school year.

What kinds of leasehold estates can exist between you and the landlord or his agent, the apartment manager? There are four types of leasehold interests, called tenancies. A *tenancy* refers to the conditions under which the leasehold is created and operates. Tenancies are classified according to the period of time covered by the lease and the provisions relating to continuing or terminating the lease.

Since both parties have interests in the property that continue through time, each party's rights should be clearly defined. These agreements as to the rights enjoyed by each party are called **covenants** or **conditions** and are included in the lease document. In addition to these agreements, each state will have landlord/tenant laws that provide guidance in many areas of the relationship between the parties to a lease. You should become familiar with the basics of landlord/tenant laws in your state.

Tenancy for Years The **tenancy for years** is a leasehold that has a specified duration and automatically ends at the end of that period. Although the term *years* is used in its name, the period of time can be less than or more than 1 year. Neither the landlord nor the tenant must give notice to the other that the tenancy will terminate at the end of the period.

Periodic Tenancy A second type of leasehold estate is a **periodic tenancy,** also called **tenancy from period-to-period.** In contrast to the tenancy for years, this estate has an indefinite duration because, rather than terminating at the end of a specified period of time, it is automatically renewed for additional periods unless the tenant or landlord gives the other appropriate notice of intent to terminate the tenancy. The period can be of any length—1 week, 1 month, 1 quarter, or 1 year.

This type of tenancy can be created expressly by the parties, but often it is implied by the law because of the conduct of the parties. Assume that you originally entered into a lease of a unit in the Whiteacre Apartments for 6 months and, at the end of that time, rather than moving out, you stayed, paying the rent each month to the landlord as before.

The conduct of you and your landlord of paying and accepting rent each month would normally raise a presumption that both of you intended to continue some type of tenancy relationship. A common conclusion would be that you and your landlord have now entered into a periodic tenancy for a period equal to the periodic rental payments, in this case a month-to-month tenancy.

This tenancy keeps being renewed at the end of each period unless either you or the landlord gives the other appropriate notice of termination. What notice is appropriate? The notice must generally meet two requirements. First, the notice must attempt to terminate the tenancy at the end of a period, not at any time during a period. Second, you or the landlord must give the notice an appropriate length of time prior to the end of a period. What an appropriate period is may be determined by statute. In your Whiteacre Apartments lease it would be common for your periodic tenancy to begin on the first of each month and for there to be a 1 month's advance notice requirement to terminate. Therefore, if you want to terminate your lease as of June 1, you must notify the landlord before May 1.

Tenancy at Will Like the periodic tenancy, the **tenancy at will** has no specific length when created. However, unlike the periodic tenancy, the tenancy at will does not automatically renew for a given period of time at certain intervals. For example, in the periodic tenancy, the lessor and lessee may agree that unless one party cancels before the first of the month the lease will automatically renew for another month. The tenancy at will has no such provisions. Once started it continues until either the landlord or the tenant gives notice of termination. Either party can terminate the tenancy at any time, although it is common to find a requirement that notice of termination must be given a certain length of time in advance of the termination date.

Tenancy at Sufferance The last type of leasehold, the **tenancy at sufferance,** masquerades as an estate but is not. Rather, it is a status a tenant occupies under certain circumstances. To understand the tenancy at sufferance we need to discuss the rights of the landlord when the tenant remains in possession of the land after his leasehold estate has come to an end.

Assume once again that you have entered into a 6-month lease of a unit in Whiteacre Apartments on September 1. Your lease, because it is a tenancy for years, will end automatically on March 1 of the following year. If you remain in possession on and after March 1 without the owner's permisson, you are a tenant at sufferance because you no longer have a legal right to be in possession. You are called a "tenant" only because of your past association with the landlord. You are actually a wrongful possessor who has given the landlord the right to take one of two possible legal courses of action.

First, the landlord could treat you as a trespasser and bring legal action to remove you from possession of the apartment unit. This action is normally in the form of a summary legal action called **forcible entry and detainer.** This legal action is the most common type of "eviction" and results in some public official, such as a sheriff, physically removing you and your possessions from the apartment unit.

Second, however, the landlord has the right to unilaterally decide to treat you as a tenant for a new term and hold you responsible for all the obligations, including rent, of the original lease. The tenancy at sufferance, then, is not a true estate at all. Rather, it is merely a status a former tenant occupies that serves as the basis for the landlord's legal right to unilaterally decide whether to remove the tenant from possession as a trespasser or hold the tenant to continued responsibility under an extended lease. The extended lease will often be viewed as a periodic tenancy.

The essential legal elements of the lease document are considered in Chapter 6. Other aspects of leases and leasing, such as rental payment schemes and landlord/tenant relations, are considered in Chapter 22, which deals with property management.

Airspace, Surface, and Subsurface Interests

So far, you may have been thinking of real estate as being only the surface of the Earth and, consequently, limited your thinking about freehold and non-freehold interests to interests in this surface. If this is so, you should change your concept of real estate to include the area above (airspace) and below (subterranean or subsurface) the surface of the Earth. Once you consider that the physical commodity of real estate may be divided into three components, it is not difficult to understand that each of these physical components may have their own freehold and non-freehold estates, which may be held by different individuals.

That is, one person may have a freehold or leasehold interest in the subsurface (subsurface rights) whereas another individual has a freehold or leasehold interest in the airspace (air rights) and still another has a freehold or leasehold interest in the surface (surface rights). For example, in Oklahoma, Texas, and certain other states, it is common for oil and gas companies to lease or purchase subsurface rights in order to drill for oil and natural gas. In larger cities, such as New York and Chicago, it is common for air rights to be sold or leased to allow the construction of large projects. Multistory condominiums, which allow ownership of individual units, are also examples of ownership interests in airspace. Of course, situations involving interests in the various physical dimensions of real estate require a clear definition of each party's rights to have access to and make use of its interest. When a building is constructed in air rights, the air rights owner will have certain rights to place pillars on the surface and underground. Likewise, a party with subsurface interests will have certain rights to set up drilling platforms on the surface. The party with an interest in the surface will not be strictly confined to the surface, but rather, will have rights above and below the surface within established limits. These rights must be carefully balanced so that each party with an interest can still make adequate use of the real estate.

This possible division of interests means that even if you are obtaining a fee simple estate, you must be very careful to determine in which physical portions of the parcel you are obtaining interests. For those portions in which you are obtaining a fee simple interest, you will want to know whether any leasehold interests exist. For instance, you may be obtaining a fee interest to the airspace, surface, and subsurface, but the subsurface may have been leased to an oil company. In such a case, you will be obtaining a fee simple interest *subject to* an existing lease. A competent attorney can help you in this process.

Interests in Water

If Blackacre has a stream running through it or by it or contains or adjoins a lake or other body of water, you may be wondering what rights you have to use that water. Because water, and the ability to use it, have literally meant the difference between survival and prosperity, the question of water rights, called **riparian rights,** has received a great deal of attention. Water presents a particularly thorny question because the rights of all parties bordering the stream must be considered. The use one landowner makes of water may affect all the other owners. This issue has been treated differently by various states, making generalization most difficult.

However, two general doctrines to the problem exist. You should remember that the implementation of these doctrines varies substantially from state to state. The first approach is that of riparian rights and is followed by many eastern states and selected other states. In this approach, an owner of land adjoining a stream has the right to access and use the water so long as that use does not significantly reduce the quality or quantity of water available to other riparian owners. What constitutes a significant reduction in quality and quantity is a crucial question. The second approach is the **appropriation doctrine,** also called the **doctrine of prior appropriation.** In this doctrine, those first to use the water develop a water right and may continue this use even though a later user may have more urgent needs. Needless to say, many disputes arise over how much water a user is entitled to and the priority of water rights. In many instances, claims of water rights may exceed the total amount of water in the stream. State regulatory bodies and the courts must decide such cases. The appropriation doctrine is used primarily in certain western states. Some states have combined elements of both doctrines in developing water rights law.

Rights to water in the ground, called *ground water,* also differ from state to state. Ground water that flows is treated essentially the same as flowing surface water. Nonflowing ground water, called percolating ground water, is generally considered to be the property of the landowner and may be used accordingly. Some states stipulate that this usage must be reasonable so as not to deprive surrounding landowners of ground water.

So far, we have considered the rights you may have to the water on Blackacre, but what about the land under that water? Once again, there are tremendous variations in state laws on this subject. Usually, for nonnavigable streams and lakes, riparian owners' property goes to the center of the body of water. Thus, you can build piers and other structures on your land under the water. If the body of water is navigable, the boundaries of your property are the shoreline or some predetermined water level such as the flood level of the stream. Your property boundaries are limited to protect the public's use of that stream. This means that if a stream forming a boundary for Blackacre is navigable, you must obtain a permit to build a swimming pier or boat dock. Usually such permits are obtained from the U.S. Army Corps of Engineers.

Being on the water creates another situation of importance to you: the gain or loss of land. Gradual changes caused by the water can change the amount of land you own through erosion and accretion. **Erosion** is the loss of land as it is washed away by water. **Accretion** is an increase in land area as a stream gradually builds up an area of land by depositing dirt and rock. However, quick or violent changes in the stream's course will not generally change land boundaries.

CONCURRENT VERSUS INDIVIDUAL OWNERSHIP OF REAL PROPERTY

Thus far we have assumed that only one person, you, has a present interest in Blackacre. Ownership by one person is called **ownership in severalty.** Do not confuse severalty with the usual meaning of "several." Here it means "standing alone." However, it would have been possible for your grandfather to convey a present estate in Blackacre to both you and your sister. When two or more persons have a right to possession of real estate together, they have *concurrent estates.* Concurrent estates can be created either intentionally by choice, as in the case of your grandfather, or unintentionally by the operation of law.

Concurrent Ownership Intentionally Created
Concurrent ownership can be intentionally created in three forms: tenancy in common, joint tenancy, and tenancy by the entirety.

Tenancy in Common In a **tenancy in common,** the concurrent owners, called tenants in common, own undivided interests in a parcel of real estate. An **undivided interest** is one in which each tenant in common has an interest in all of a parcel. For example, if Blackacre is a 30-acre tract and you and your sister own equal interests as tenants in common, each of you has an equal interest in the entire 30 acres rather than an exclusive interest in 15 acres. This equal right of possession, known as **unity of possession,** means that each of you has a right to possess the entire 30 acres, but not a right to exclude the other.

The equal right of possession points up the fact that cooperation among tenants in common is necessary if the relationship is to work successfully. If you and your sister cannot agree on your mutual rights to possession, then the tenancy should be terminated, with each person receiving exclusive ownership of a portion of Blackacre. The procedure used to accomplish this purpose is known as **partition.** Each tenant in common has an absolute right to partition at any time.

In a tenancy in common it is not necessary for each tenant in common to own the same percentage of the property. You could own a 75 percent interest in Blackacre while your sister owned the remaining 25 percent. In the absence of any agreement specifying the ownership percentages, it is generally assumed that each tenant in common has an equal interest in the property. For example, if there are five tenants in common, each is assumed to have a 20 percent interest in the property.

Other Ownership Characteristics Your undivided ownership in Blackacre can have many of the characteristics of ownership we have already discussed. Our example above assumes that your grandfather conveyed your undivided interest in fee simple absolute. However, he could have conveyed this one-half interest to you in another type of freehold estate, such as a life estate, or as a non-freehold estate (although this would be rare). Also, you may convey your one-half interest to another during your life or (assuming it is a fee estate) pass it at your death by will or by the statutes of descent and distribution.

However, the fact that your ownership is concurrent with that of your sister creates some duties between the two of you that do not exist in nonconcurrent ownership situations. For example, if you were to farm Blackacre or rent it to someone else to farm, any rents or profits you receive may have to be shared with your sister, if she demands an accounting. An **accounting** is the process by which rights and responsibilities between concurrent owners are determined and adjusted. However, you would not have to account to your sister for your personal use of Blackacre because, as a concurrent owner, you have a right to possess it, so long as you recognize her equal right to possession.

Joint Tenancy A second way your grandfather could have left Blackacre to you and your sister is as joint tenants. Although **joint tenancy**

has many characteristics of a tenancy in common, there is one important difference: when a joint tenant dies, rather than his interest passing under his will or by the statutes of descent and distribution, the surviving joint tenant(s) automatically acquires ownership of the interest by a **right of survivorship** that the law recognizes. So if you were the first to die, your sister would automatically acquire your interest and own Blackacre in fee simple absolute. This feature makes joint tenancy attractive to married couples who want the surviving spouse to have the property upon the other's death.

It is important to understand, however, that this right of survivorship exists only among the original joint tenants. Any conveyance of a joint tenant's interest during his lifetime destroys the survivorship right. What kinds of conveyances could you or your sister make that would defeat the survivorship right? First, you could voluntarily convey your undivided one-half interest to your brother. Thereafter, he would hold that one-half interest as a tenant in common with your sister. Second, a creditor of yours who had received a judgment against you for a debt owed could institute legal action to force a sale of your one-half interest. Third, you and your sister could partition Blackacre. The partition could be "in kind," that is, each of you taking exclusive ownership of a portion of the land, or "by sale," in which case Blackacre would be sold and the proceeds divided.

Because of the important consequences of joint tenancies, the intention to create a joint tenancy must be made very clear and meet prescribed conditions. The requirements for creating a joint tenancy are often referred to as the **four unities.** For a joint tenancy there must be the unities of:

Time	Interest
Title	Possession

The unity of time means a joint tenancy must be created in each joint tenant at the same time. Unity of title means that each joint tenant must have the same quality of title. For example, one joint tenant cannot have a fee simple estate and another a qualified fee simple estate. The third unity, interest, means that each joint tenant has an equal ownership interest in the property. That is, if five joint tenants are involved each will have a one-fifth, or 20 percent, interest in the property. The unity of possession means that each tenant has an equal right to possess the entire parcel.

Tenancy by the Entirety The ability to convey freely an interest to a third party by a sale or gift distinguishes the joint tenancy from the third type of concurrent estate, **tenancy by the entirety.** This concurrent estate can be held only by husband and wife. Thus, although your grandfather could not convey Blackacre to you and your sister this way, he could have conveyed Blackacre to your father and mother as tenants by the entirety. This estate also has a right of survivorship, just as the joint tenancy does. Thus, if your father were to die first, your mother would thereafter own Blackacre entirely as surviving tenant by the entirety.

The law protects this right of survivorship in a tenancy by the entirety in a way not found in joint tenancy. Neither spouse may convey his or her interest away without the other's consent. Thus, neither your father nor mother could voluntarily convey away their interest; a creditor of one of them could not force a sale of the interest; and neither could partition Blackacre without the other's consent. However, your father and mother, by joint action, could sell Blackacre or partition it. Also, the divorce of your parents would cause the tenancy by the entirety to automatically be transformed into a tenancy in common, assuming they continued co-ownership of Blackacre. The limitations on the ability of one tenant by the entirety to convey his or her interest has been viewed by many states as undesirable. This attitude has caused the estate to be modified or no longer recognized at all in these states.

Concurrent Ownership
Unintentionally Created

All of the types of concurrent ownership we have discussed so far have been intentionally created. That is, your grandfather deliberately created one of these estates in you, in you and your sister, or in your parents. In other situations buyers themselves create them. There is a situation, however, in which the law may recognize concurrent ownership even where it has not intentionally been created. This one situation involves a married couple where one spouse acquires ownership of real or personal property. Our society strongly supports the institution of marriage. One evidence of this is the property rights given to one spouse when the other acquires title to property. These interests are called **marital property rights.** Two different types of marital property rights exist and each is recognized in a different part of the country. You should find out if your state recognizes either of them.

Community Property In eight states, Spanish or French heritage has caused a recognition of a type of property interest called community property. These states are Arizona, California, Idaho, Louisiana, Nevada, New Mexico, Texas, and Washington. **Community property** is real or personal property acquired by either a husband or a wife during their marriage by any method other than a gift from a living person, a gift from a dead person by his will, or an inheritance from a dead relative by the statutes of descent and distribution. Community property is owned equally by the husband and wife, regardless of who takes legal title. Assume Blackacre is located in Texas and your father purchased it with money saved from his salary earned after his marriage to your mother. Your mother would own one half of Blackacre, even if he took title in his name alone.

However, if Blackacre was acquired by your father prior to his marriage to your mother or was acquired by your father after marriage by gift, devise, or descent (as discussed above), it would be classified as separate property, and your father alone would have title, your mother taking no interest in it. Notice that your father and mother take equal ownership only if the property is acquired while they are married, that is, while they are a "community."

Dower, Curtesy and Homestead The second type of marital property rights recognized in many other states, the so-called **common law property states,** acknowledges interests in a spouse that are more contingent than community property interests. These interests arise only upon the death of one party, rather than during the existence of the marriage. The wife's interest is known as dower and gives the wife a right to a life estate in a portion of her husband's real property upon his death. The husband has a similar right to a life estate in all or a portion of his wife's real property upon her death. This interest was originally called curtesy, but now is commonly called dower also.

Some common law property states have abolished dower and curtesy and adopted an even more limited marital property right called **homestead,** applicable only to the family residence. A homestead right, although limited to the family residence, may be protected in a number of ways. First, the homestead may be exempt from forced sale by creditors of the husband or wife. This protection normally extends to all debts of the husband and wife except (1) a mortgage loan used to buy the homestead, (2) debts for the physical improvement of the homestead, and (3) property taxes on the homestead. Second, it may be necessary for both husband and wife to join in signing a deed to the homestead in order to convey it away. This protects each party from the unilateral action of the other. And, third, upon the death of either party, the survivor may be given a continuing interest in the homestead, such as a life estate, regardless of who otherwise inherits it.

Investment Settings for Concurrent Ownership

Most of the types of concurrent ownership discussed so far are mainly used in a noninvestment setting, although it is possible for any of them to involve investment property. Investment property is more commonly owned as a partnership; to a more limited degree, as a corporation; and also in the form of a real estate investment trust (REIT). These three ownership arrangements are now examined to see how they differ from other concurrent ownership arrangements.

With the exception of the traditional partnership, which will be explained shortly, the partnership, corporation, and REIT do not represent concurrent ownership of real estate in the strictest sense. This is so because the real property is owned by one entity, the partnership, corporation, or REIT. These entities are, in turn, owned concurrently by any number of shareholders or partners as illustrated in Figure 4.4. Thus, the partnership, corporation, or REIT is concurrently owned, not the real property. The discussion of each of these entities begins with partnerships, one form of which is contrary to the concept presented in this paragraph.

Partnership A partnership involves a situation in which two or more parties agree to undertake business efforts pursuant to a written or oral agreement and not in the form of a corporation or trust. The agreement creating the partnership is called the **partnership agreement** and specifies the purposes of the partnership and the rights and responsibilities of each party. In the **traditional partnership,** the partnership is not recognized as an entity, and thus the partners are required to own all property as individuals. If you formed a traditional partnership and wanted to purchase land, you and the other partners would have to purchase the land as tenants in common or joint tenants and then use the land for partnership purposes. For example, assuming your grandfather conveyed Blackacre to you and your sister as tenants in common or joint tenants, the two of you could then agree to conduct a landscape and nursery business on Blackacre as partners in a traditional partnership. Technically, you and your sister are operating a partnership and contributing your concurrently owned real property to that endeavor. If the

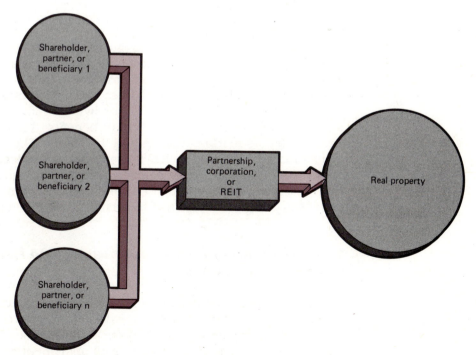

Figure 4.4 Concurrent ownership in investment settings.

partnership is dissolved, your tenancy in common or joint tenancy will not be affected. To dissolve that ownership one of you must go to court to have the property partitioned.

Now, it is possible in most states for the partnership itself to hold title to Blackacre in an estate known as **tenancy in partnership.** This arrangement recognizes the partnership as an "entity" capable of holding title to land. If the partnership is dissolved, the land must be sold since the land is owned by the partnership.

Corporation The corporate form of ownership goes much farther than the tenancy in partnership in recognizing a separate entity as owner of Blackacre. You and your sister may decide, for legal and tax reasons, to incorporate your landscape and nursery business. Incorporation involves filing the proper documents with the appropriate state office, usually the Secretary of State. In this case title to Blackacre could be transferred to the corporation, which is recognized as a separate entity, a type of "artificial person," by the law. You and your sister would own stock in the corporation that now owns Blackacre. Notice that there is no true concurrent ownership of Blackacre any longer. Rather, the corporation alone owns Blackacre and your ownership is in shares of stock in the corporation.

Real Estate Investment Trusts (REITs) A trust is an arrangement in which one party holds property for the benefit of another party. Such arrangements have been allowed by law for some time. Blackacre, for instance, may have been held in a personal trust for you until you reached an age specified by your grandfather in his will. Changes in federal income tax laws that became effective in 1961 made the trust vehicle very attractive from a tax standpoint, if it met certain stringent requirements such as having at least 100 investors and distributing a high percentage of its earnings to its owners. Many REITs were organized to take advantage of these tax benefits. These unincorporated REITs acted as mortgage and equity investors. The real property was owned in the name of the REIT for its **beneficiaries,** the people who owned its certificates of beneficial interest (the equivalent of shareholders). Thus, the real property was owned by a single entity that, in turn, was concurrently owned by any number of beneficiaries.

Condominiums and Cooperatives: Hybrid Forms of Concurrent Ownership

Condominiums When you purchase a **condominium,** you purchase a package of interests in a parcel of real estate. To better understand this concept, it is helpful to think of a property large enough to provide space for more than one occupant, such as an apartment or office building. If you were renting in such a situation, you would be paying rent to have exclusive use of certain space, such as an office or apartment, and to share other space, such as tennis courts, lobbies, and hallways, with fellow tenants. In a condominium you do not rent space; rather, you own it. You own the space you use exclusively in fee simple. Further, you own the space you share in a tenancy in common with other fee simple space owners. This means that when you buy a condominium you are getting both a fee simple interest and an undivided interest in real property. The condominium form of ownership is authorized by state governments in laws that are usually called *Horizontal Property Acts*.

As the fee simple owner of certain space, you are responsible for the maintenance of that space. You and the other tenants in common are responsible for the maintenance and operation of the shared areas, which are called *common areas*. These items include such things as painting the exterior of the building, resurfacing parking lots, maintaining elevators, cleaning the swimming pool, and so on. Also, to promote a harmonious use of all space and to minimize what, in legal terms, is called nuisance, certain ground rules outlining accepted behavior and the responsibilities of all owners must be developed and implemented. To facilitate and coordinate these tasks, an *owners association* will be established, with all owners being voting members. Association members will elect a board of directors to oversee the management of the property and to establish necessary policies. The board of directors will either hire management and maintenance staff as employees or contract with a property management firm to handle the day-to-day operation of the property. To pay for all these activities, you and other owners will pay an *owners association fee.*

The condominium is a form of ownership, and like any other form of ownership, it can be applied to virtually any type of real estate. Not surprisingly, then, condominiums can be, and are, quite varied. Condominiums can be created for space used for virtually any purpose. Office space, living space, shopping space, hotel space, and industrial space have all been sold as condominiums. Physically, any style of building or buildings can be a condominium. High rises, low rises, and detached buildings have all been used as condominiums. Finally, the age of a building does not affect its ability to be used as a condominium. Condominiums do not have to be built from scratch. Many properties have been converted into condominiums after they were constructed. Your thinking about condominiums should not be limited with respect to age of building, type of space, or style.

Time-Share Condominiums While Blackacre is an attractive parcel of land, you may desire to have a place where you can vacation and relax each year. You could sell Blackacre and purchase a property, such as a residential condominium, in your favorite vacation spot, say the island of Maui in Hawaii. However, this may not be feasible because Blackacre cannot be sold for enough to cover the cost of such a condominium or because you feel that purchasing a condominium that you will use only 2 weeks a year is foolish. Developers aware of this problem conceived the idea of selling interests giving you the right to use a condominium unit a given number of days each year. The right to use it during the remainder of the year is sold to other people interested in such an arrangement. Your interest in the unit will run for a stated number of years, usually related to the expected life of the building. Such a concept adds another element to the concept of property ownership—time. This arrangement is called **time-share** or **fractional time period ownership.**

Although there are variations on this basic theme, the concept is the same in all of them—you are buying the right to use a unit for a specified period of time each year for a given number of years. Purchasers find this arrangement attractive because they do not have to make as large an investment as they would in buying an entire unit and do not have to worry about renting the unit when they are not using it. Developers find it attractive because the prices paid for a unit by all the people owning a part of it may be 150 to 300 percent of the price they could get from selling the unit to one buyer. Problems exist with respect to pricing and selling the non-prime time periods and allocating the maintenance and operating expenses fairly among buyers paying very different prices for time periods in the same unit. Buyers face an uncertain resale market, especially for non-prime time periods and may find that sales commissions create substantial losses in selling time-share interests. Finally, state laws in this area are generally vague or nonexistent. You should analyze any time-share arrangement very carefully and consult with an attorney familiar with the laws of the state in which the property is located.

Cooperatives The cooperative form of real property ownership is most popular in cities in the North and Northeast, particularly New York. However, they can be found all around the country. A **cooperative** is a not-for-profit corporation that owns and operates a property. By purchasing a specified amount of the cooperative's stock, you are allowed to rent an apartment in the property. Your rental payment goes to maintain the building, pay any mortgage on the property, and pay operating expenses. In theory, the cooperative eliminates the profit a landlord would earn and allows the tenant/owner to obtain living space at a lower price than would otherwise be possible. When you decide to move, you sell your cooperative stock to another person, who will then rent your space.

LIMITATIONS OF OWNERSHIP

Let's return to our original illustration. Your grandfather has conveyed Blackacre to you alone in fee simple absolute. Is this "absolute" ownership really absolute? The answer must be no; you have to take the term

Table 4.2. Limitations to Ownership Rights

Public
Police Power
Eminent Domain
Taxation
Escheat

Private
Liens
Easements
Restrictive Covenants

"absolute" with a grain of salt because there will inevitably be various public and private limitations on your ownership. These are outlined in Table 4.2.

Public Limitations

The public limitations stem from the fact that all land ownership is originally derived from the State. This concept is rooted in our strong historical ties with England. In England all land was owned by the king, who distributed it to various nobles, subject to a variety of conditions. Although the types of conditions imposed by the State on ownership have changed dramatically over the centuries, the basic idea of the State's paramount authority is still with us. In the United States, the State's paramount authority is controlled by the United States Constitution and the various state constitutions. At the present time there are four types of public interests that the State may exert in Blackacre:

Police Power	Taxation
Eminent Domain	Escheat

Police Power The **police power** is the inherent power of government to control the activities of private individuals to protect certain public interests such as health, safety, morals, or general welfare. For example, your hometown may have city ordinances (laws) prohibiting landowners from storing dynamite or other explosives dangerous to life and property. These ordinances would limit your right to store dynamite to be used for blasting tree stumps from a portion of Blackacre your grandfather cleared several years ago. Building codes specifying material and workmanship standards and environmental protection laws are also exercises of the police power. The exercise of the police power by government does not require compensation to private landowners.

Another form of police power is the **zoning code,** a law that controls the use and development of land, which places Blackacre in an "agricul-

tural'' zone (since it is on the outskirts of town). This zoning classification may allow you to live and farm on Blackacre, but not to operate a
landscape and nursery business, or to construct an apartment complex
(such as the Whiteacre Apartments) or a service station. You would have
to consult the zoning code to determine the allowable uses of Blackacre.
Before you could make other uses of the land, you would have to obtain a
change in the zoning classification from your hometown city council.

Eminent Domain A second public limitation your ownership interest
will be subject to is the right of **eminent domain,** the right of the State to
force you to sell your land to the State if the land is needed for some public
purpose. If Blackacre is in the path of a proposed state highway, the State
can require you to convey to it the amount of land necessary to build the
highway across Blackacre. The State must pay just compensation for
that portion taken, but you have no choice whether or not to sell, as you
would with a private buyer.

Taxation A third public interest you will be subject to is a particularly
inevitable one, **ad valorem property taxation.** The tax on your property
and that of other landowners in the community may be used to finance a
variety of public needs such as the local school system and local government operations. If you fail to pay the yearly tax assessed against Blackacre, the State is allowed to sell your property at a tax foreclosure sale
and use the proceeds to satisfy the tax liability. Taxation can limit your
rights by causing you to lose title if you fail to pay your tax obligation.

Escheat The fourth public interest that the State might assert is **escheat,** the right to assert ownership of Blackacre at your death if you die
without conveying Blackacre to anyone by will and without leaving any
heirs (relatives) who can take ownership under the statutes of descent
and distribution. In other words, in the absence of any private person's
right to acquire ownership of Blackacre at your death, the State can
assert ownership. Usually the State will conduct a public sale of property
acquired through escheat to return it to private ownership. Actual
transfer of ownership to the State seldom occurs because most people
will have heirs.

Private Limitations

Not only will Blackacre be subject to these public interests, but chances
are excellent that there will be a variety of private interests in other
persons that will limit your fee simple absolute ownership. These private
interests may have been created by your grandfather, or an owner prior
to him, and remain when you acquire ownership, or they may be created
by you after you acquire ownership.

Liens Your grandfather may have created a lien on the title to Blackacre. A **lien** is a claim on property for the payment of some debt or obligation. The most common lien is a mortgage. Let's assume that when your grandfather purchased Blackacre, he did not have the entire purchase price, so he borrowed money from the bank and gave the bank an interest in the property called a **mortgage,** which would allow the bank to cause Blackacre to be sold in case he failed to repay the obligation (defaulted). When your grandfather conveyed Blackacre to you, the mortgage was not affected and you now hold title encumbered with the bank's mortgage. This lien can be removed only by the bank, and of course, the bank will do this only when the debt is completely paid.

Another type of lien is the **mechanic's and materialman's lien.** Assume your grandfather hired a carpenter to enclose the back porch of his house on Blackacre and convert it into a bedroom, and that he purchased lumber and other materials from a lumber company to be used by the carpenter. The carpenter who supplied the labor and the lumber company that supplied the materials, if unpaid, could each assert a lien on Blackacre and force its sale to receive the money owed them.

Easements A second type of private interest that may encumber your title to Blackacre is an easement. An **easement** is the right of one person to use the land of another. The telephone company may have a utility easement to place poles and stretch wires across Blackacre. The gas company may have a utility easement to place pipelines under the surface of Blackacre. Your grandfather may have given his neighbor, Jed, a right to use a road across Blackacre, a **right of way** easement, in reaching his adjoining land, Greenacre. Rights of way may also exist in conjunction with the utility easements above to provide access necessary to make repairs.

All of these interests must have one thing in common. In order to be valid, easements must have been created by written document. If they were created orally, they would be considered licenses. A **license** is revocable permission to use land. For example, when you buy a ticket to a football game or a movie, you are actually obtaining a license to use the property of another. These licenses are revocable by the issuer. If you examine a ticket to an NCAA football game it will contain wording indicating that consuming alcoholic beverages in the stadium may cause your ticket to be revoked and you to be ejected from the stadium. An easement, by contrast, is an irrevocable interest in land.

Creation of Easements The utility easement and the right of way easement described above were created expressly by a written document and deed. Such an easement is said to be created by **express grant.** Easements can be created in other ways, however. An easement may be created by *implication.* That is, the law may imply the creation of an easement by the conduct of the parties, even if no easement is expressly created. For example, assume your grandfather at one time owned both Blackacre and Greenacre. Also assume he had regularly used a road across Blackacre to reach Greenacre. Upon the sale of Greenacre to Jed, the law may imply an easement that would allow Jed to continue to use the road across Blackacre.

Long continued use of land can also result in an easement by *prescription*. Had Jed never been given an express or implied easement in Blackacre, but after purchasing Greenacre regularly crossed Blackacre for a long period of time, the law may recognize that his action, although originally wrongful, is now legally protected and may continue. The reasoning behind this startling result is explained in Chapter 5 in the discussion of adverse possession.

Easements can be created by necessity and reservation. Consider the situation in which land is sold that does not have access to a road. In such a situation the law generally requires that an easement for access to the parcel be provided. If the seller has adjoining lands over which such an easement can be provided, an easement by *necessity* will be created over those lands. In this instance the document creating the easement will be a court decree. A **court decree** is a legal document stating the court's decision in a case signed by the judge presiding at the proceedings. An easement may also be created by *reservation* when a seller reserves the right to use the land being sold for a specific purpose. For example, the seller may ask for the right of access to a lake on the property for fishing.

What Happens to Easements When Land is Sold? If you sell a portion of Blackacre and are required to provide access through an easement by necessity over your remaining land, what happens if that buyer later sells the land to another person? Does the easement stay in effect or is it ended? The answers to these questions depend on whether the easement is held to benefit a parcel of land or an individual. In the case of the easement by necessity for access, the benefits accrue to the land. If, as above, you request an easement by reservation to access a lake for fishing, that right is a personal one for you alone. An easement providing benefits for a parcel of land is called an **easement appurtenant** whereas one benefiting a particular individual is an **easement in gross.** Easements appurtenant are assumed to attach to the land and pass from owner to owner. When something attaches to or accrues to the land it is said to "run with the land," also called "pass with the land" or "follow the land." The legal word, "appurtenant," means that something is automatically transferred to any new owner. The access you were required to give the buyer of part of Blackacre will pass to any new buyer. However, easements in gross cannot usually be sold or transferred to another. Your right as owner of Greenacre to fish in the Blackacre lake cannot be transferred to another.

Restrictive Covenants

A third type of private interest that may encumber your title to Blackacre is a restrictive covenant or deed restriction. **Restrictive covenants** are limitations on the use of land created at the time the real property is conveyed from one owner to another. The instrument used to convey ownership interests is the deed. Restrictive covenants are placed in the deed, and for this reason are often called **deed restrictions.** The new covenants included in a deed are a matter of negotiation between buyer and seller. However, once the covenants are included in the deed, they become appurtenances and will remain in effect forever unless removed by the party creating them or his heirs or by the courts.

To illustrate, assume that after you finish school you want to live in your grandfather's house on Blackacre, but do not want the entire 30 acres. This area of your hometown is becoming the newest residential area and you decide to sell 25 acres to a developer to finance the rest of your education. You naturally want those 25 acres to be developed in a way that will not detract from the residential qualities of the five acres you have retained. You can, by agreement with the purchaser, restrict the use of the 25 acres sold to residential uses. Covenants in past deeds would also restrict the actions of the new buyer since they attach to the land and not the particular buyer. The final result of all this is that the developer cannot defeat your intent by selling the land to someone else and then buying it back in attempt to eliminate the covenants.

Violations of covenants are not crimes and, therefore, are not enforced by crack police SWAT teams or other law enforcement agencies. If the developer should violate the covenants you agreed to, you must bring court action to force him to stop. Restrictive covenants are extensively used in subdivisions to ensure that all homes meet certain standards.

SUMMARY

In this chapter you have learned that property is a collection of legally recognized and protected interests in objects. If the object is land and permanent additions to land, the interests are considered real property. Interests in real property can be divided on a time basis between present estates and future interests. The present estates are the freehold estates of fee simple absolute, qualified fee simple, and life estate, and the non-freehold estates of tenancy for years, periodic tenancy, tenancy at will, or tenancy at sufferance. The future interests of possibility of reverter, remainder, power of termination, and reversion are rights that may become possessory in the future because the present interest is less than absolute.

These various present and future interests can be owned by one person or by two or more persons concurrently as tenants in common, joint tenants, or tenants by the entirety. Concurrent ownership between husband and wife can also take the form of community property, dower, curtesy, or homestead. Business entities such as partnerships, corporations, and REITs may be utilized as an indirect form of concurrent ownership. Landowners may be restricted in their rights by public limitations such as the police power, eminent domain, taxation, and escheat, as well as by private restrictions created by liens, easements, and restrictive covenants.

QUICK QUIZ

1. If you "own" Blackacre in fee simple

   I. you have the right to sell or give it away
  II. the period of your ownership may run forever

  a. I only   c. Both I and II
  b. II only   d. Neither I nor II

2. A qualified fee estate

   I. ends on the occurrence of a specified event
  II. requires that a future interest exist

  a. I only   c. Both I and II
  b. II only   d. Neither I nor II

3. Which of the following is a freehold estate?

  a. periodic tenancy   c. unwanted tenancy
  b. tenancy at will   d. tenancy for a period of time

4. A joint tenancy differs from a tenancy in common in that

   I. upon the death of a joint tenant, his interest is allocated to surviving joint tenants
  II. a joint tenancy is easier to create than a tenancy in common

  a. I only   c. Both I and II
  b. II only   d. Neither I nor II

5. An easement appurtenant

   I. attaches to the land
  II. is conveyed to new purchasers

  a. I only   c. Both I and II
  b. II only   d. Neither I nor II

6. _____ were once personal property but are now considered real property because of being attached to land.

7. In case of a dispute, the courts will determine whether an item is a fixture by examining _____, _____, and _____.

8. Because land is not limited to just the surface of the Earth, owner-ship interests may exist in the _____ and _____.

9. For a joint tenancy to be created the unities of _____, _____, _____, and _____ must be present.

10. Interests in land and everything attached to it describes _____.

QUESTIONS AND EXERCISES

1. Try to identify a use of airspace by someone other than the owner of the land's surface.

2. For each of the items listed below, describe circumstances that would tend to cause them to be treated as fixtures.

   a. window air conditioner
   b. refrigerator
   c. above-ground swimming pool

3. Examine an apartment lease and identify the type(s) of tenancy(ies) it creates.

4. Try to find three instances where public limitations have signifi-cantly limited the rights of private landowners in your community.

5. Where would you go to find the current zoning of a parcel of land near your home?

6. If you live in a subdivision, try to obtain a copy of the restrictive covenants that apply to its lots. How would you categorize the re-strictions? Do the covenants have any positive benefits for lot owners?

KEY TERMINOLOGY

accounting
accretion
ad valorem property taxation

air rights
appropriation doctrine
appurtenant

beneficiaries

chattel

common law property states

community property

concurrent ownership

conditions

condominium

contingent remainder

cooperative

corporation

court decree

covenants

curtesy

deed restrictions

doctrine of prior appropriation

dower

easement

easement in gross

eminent domain

erosion

escheat

estate

express grant

fee simple absolute

fixture

forcible entry and detainer

four unities

fractional time period ownership

freehold estate

future interest

interest

license

lien

life estate

marital property rights

mechanic's and materialman's
   lien

mortgage

non-freehold estate

ownership in severalty

partition

partnership

periodic tenancy

personal property

police power

possibility of reverter

power of termination

present interest

property

qualified fee conditional

qualified fee determinable

qualified fee simple

qualified fee subsequent

real property

remainder

remainderman

restrictive covenant

reversion

right

right of reentry

right of survivorship

right of way

riparian rights

taxation

tenancy at sufferance

tenancy at will

tenancy by the entirety

tenancy for years

tenancy from period-to-period

tenancy in common

tenancy in partnership

time share

traditional partnership

undivided interest

unity of possession

vested remainder

zoning code

**IF YOU WANT
TO READ MORE**   The books listed below are real estate law books with the exception of the
book on condominiums. Each of them provides an excellent source of
additional information on real estate law. The chapters indicated after
each are the chapters dealing with the legal concepts discussed in this
chapter.

PHILIP B. BERGFIELD, *Principles of Real Estate Law* (New York: McGraw-Hill Book Company, 1979), Chapters 1–8.

DAVID CLURMAN and EDNA L. HEBARD, *Condominiums and Cooperatives* (New York: John Wiley & Sons, 1970).

ROBERT N. CORLEY, PETER J. SHEDD, and CHARLES F. FLOYD, *Real Estate and the Law* (New York: Random House, Inc., 1982), Chapters 1–3.

WILLIAM B. FRENCH and HAROLD F. LUSK, *Law of the Real Estate Business,* 4th ed. (Homewood, IL: Richard D. Irwin, Inc., 1979), Chapters 1 and 3–5.

BENJAMIN N. HENSZEY and RONALD M. FRIEDMAN, *Real Estate Law* (Boston: Warren, Gorham & Lamont, 1979), Chapters 1–4.

ROBERT KRATOVIL and RAYMOND J. WERNER, *Real Estate Law,* 7th ed. (Englewood Cliffs: Prentice-Hall, Inc., 1979), Chapters 1–4 and 6.

5

Legal Fundamentals: conveying and protecting title to real property

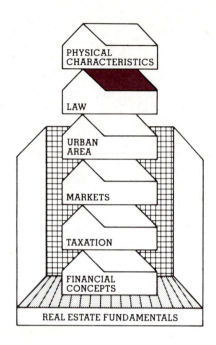

PHYSICAL CHARACTERISTICS

LAW

URBAN AREA

MARKETS

TAXATION

FINANCIAL CONCEPTS

REAL ESTATE FUNDAMENTALS

PREVIEW   Because of the importance of property interests, they are generally created and transferred by some type of written document, rather than by a mere oral transaction. Indeed, the law requires that many types of property interests be transferred only by a written document. How ownership, or title, is conveyed from one person to another is the subject of this chapter. In it you will learn:

1. What title is and the situations leading to its conveyance.
2. The documents used to convey title.
3. The process of recording interests in real property in a public office.
4. The need to protect your ownership interest by examining recorded documents affecting title.
5. How title is protected.

As used in real estate, title has three closely related meanings. First, title means ownership. To have title in real property is to have an ownership interest in land. Title also refers to a collection of documents evidencing ownership from the origination of the interest down to the present time. As successive owners (grantors) transfer ownership to new owners (grantees), a series of documents such as deeds, leases, and mortgages relating to the property interest involved comes into existence. This series of documents is also called the title to the property interest. Finally, title is sometimes used to describe the written document that transfers property interests from one party to another. Thus, title can refer to ownership or an individual document or collection of documents evidencing ownership. This chapter focuses on the individual document and the collection of documents and explains their nature, functions, and place in the law of real estate.

TITLE TRANSFER SETTINGS

The situations in which title to Blackacre can be transferred can be quite varied. Let's briefly examine these various settings, dividing them into situations where an owner voluntarily transfers title to a grantee and situations where an owner involuntarily transfers title to a grantee. Blackacre, the farm you inherited from your grandfather in the last chapter, is once again used to illustrate title transfer.

Voluntary Transfer Situations

When you, acting on your own free will, transfer your interests in real property to another, you have been involved in a **voluntary transfer.** Voluntary transfers involve not only private individuals and companies but transfers by government as well. Three types of voluntary transfers are examined in this section: the patent, the deed, and the will. These are summarized in Table 5.1.

Patent Have you ever wondered how title to Blackacre first started? Title probably did not start with your grandfather. He may have been only one of many owners stretching many years into the past. Some titles in the east and southwest go back for hundreds of years. But no matter how old or young a title is, it was originated by a transfer from a sovereign. In the United States, title to all real estate begins with the State as sovereign. The term *State* is used here quite generally to refer to many possible current or historical sovereigns such as the federal government, a state government, the King of Spain, or an Indian nation. Title originates then, in a **public transfer** from the State to a private individual. The document typically used to transfer title from the State to the first private grantee is known as a **patent.**

Deed The second voluntary transfer setting involves the transfer of title from a private owner during his lifetime to a grantee. This **private transfer** from one party to another is the most common type of all the transfers we discuss. The transfer can be by way of *gift,* wherein the grantee pays nothing for the transaction. Your grandfather could have

Table 5.1. Title Transfer Settings

Voluntary Transfers	
Patent	Transfer from public body to private owner using a patent
Deed	Transfer from private owner to either another private owner or a public owner
Will	Transfer from deceased individual to another private owner or public owner using a will and court decree

Involuntary Transfers	
Eminent Domain	Transfer from private owner to public body using either a deed or a court decree
Adverse Possession	Transfer from private owner to another private owner by court decree
Public Sale	Transfer from private owner to private owner using a special deed
Intestate Succession	Transfer from deceased individual to legally determined heirs using a court decree
Bankruptcy	Transfer from private owner to another private owner using a deed or court decree
Erosion	Loss of land caused by water washing it away, may or may not be transferred to another landowner

transferred Blackacre to you this way during his lifetime but chose not to. Or the transfer can be a *purchase* in which the grantee pays an agreed price. This is the most common real estate transaction in the United States. Both the gift and purchase transactions have one thing in common — a written document is used to transfer title. That document is a **deed.** Deeds are examined in greater detail later in the chapter.

Will The third voluntary transfer setting involves the transfer of title from an owner at time of death to a grantee. This is the method by which you acquired title to Blackacre from your grandfather. He could have conveyed Blackacre to anyone he chose. He indicated the fact that he had chosen you to receive title to Blackacre by a written document called a **will.** Notice that the will transaction is a gift transaction since you have paid nothing to receive title to Blackacre. Wills are considered again later in the chapter.

Involuntary Transfer Settings
In all the previous situations the owner willingly transferred title to someone else. However, there are a number of settings where the owner will be forced or deemed to have transferred title to another, even though the owner does not desire this result. So can you ever lose title to Black-acre involuntarily? Yes you can — now let's see how. (See Table 5.1.)

Eminent Domain Eminent domain is the right of the state to acquire private property for public use in return for just compensation. As was discussed in Chapter 4, eminent domain is one of the public limitations to private ownership. You may not want to sell Blackacre, but if it is needed to build a highway, a park, a lake, or for other public use, the State can require you to sell to it upon the payment of just compensation. The process of filing suit and forcing the sale of private real property so it can be used for an appropriate public purpose is called **condemnation.** Just compensation is usually considered to be market value, the value of property in the marketplace.

If you agree to transfer title to the State in this situation, the document used will be a deed and the transaction will proceed much as a normal private sale does. However, if you protest, the State must file a lawsuit against you in an appropriate court in order to force you to transfer title. You will, of course, be paid just compensation for your property. The document used to transfer title will be the court's decree determining the right of the State to acquire title.

Adverse Possession Blackacre, as you recall, is a 30-acre tract of land on the edge of your hometown. Assume that 20 years ago when a new owner of Blueacre, an adjoining parcel of land, built a fence on what he thought was the property line. He then began farming up to the fence. Could the title to Blackacre be affected if the owner of Blueacre had mistakenly enclosed one acre of Blackacre within the boundary of Blueacre and had been using that one acre as a part of Blueacre over the past 20 years? The answer is yes, if the doctrine of adverse possession applies. **Adverse possession** is a legal doctrine that can result in a transfer of ownership from the original owners to an "adverse possessor."

The law of *adverse possession* declares that if a non-owner has been in wrongful possession of the land of another under certain circumstances, he will acquire the title of the owner, even though the owner never intended such a result. What circumstances will allow such a result and what can possibly justify such a seemingly unjust result? The circumstances must show that the possessor has been possessing the land *continuously* for a stated period of time as the owner would possess it. The required period of time varies from state to state. The possessor must also be using the property *without the consent of the owner* with *no attempt made to hide* the use. If the property owner exercises his property rights and has the proper authorities remove the adverse possessor as a trespasser, the period of time starts all over.

Adverse possession is similar to the old concept of "squatter's rights." As you can imagine, the possibilities for adverse possession situations exist all the time in suburban neighborhoods where chain link or wooden fences are extensively used. In many instances such situations are not really that important, but adverse possession can have some very important results. It is important that you understand the concept and avoid the possibly unpleasant results of adverse possession by exercising your ownership rights, when necessary.

The doctrine of adverse possession differs from the previous methods of transferring title, whether voluntary or involuntary, in that transfer occurs automatically. No document is necessary. However, this creates a problem for the new owner because he has no evidence of ownership, which a document can provide. In this case, the new owner needs to bring a law suit against the former owner asking a court to determine and declare his ownership with a court decree. Such court decree will then be the document of title.

Public Sale The third setting for an involuntary transfer of title involves the enforcement of a lien on Blackacre. As discussed in Chapter 4, a lien is a claim on property for the payment of some debt or obligation. Mortgages and property taxes are the most common examples of liens. Since your grandfather left you Blackacre with a mortgage still on it, you have acquired title to Blackacre subject to his lien. If you default on any of your obligations under the mortgage, such as failing to pay the monthly installments of principal and interest, the lender can begin the process of having Blackacre sold at a public sale in order to use the sale proceeds to pay off the indebtedness. This process is called **foreclosure.** If the sale involves judicial proceedings, the court will order some public official, such as the county sheriff, to conduct the sale and convey your title to the purchaser using a special type of deed called a **sheriff's deed,** also called a **referee's deed,** or **master commissioner's deed.** Loss of the property through foreclosure is an inherent risk of mortgage financing, although happily, only a small percentage of mortgage loans are foreclosed. A similar circumstance can occur if you fail to pay the property taxes on Blackacre.

Other Involuntarily Transfers Involuntary transfers of ownership can also occur through bankruptcy and the actions of waters that physically change the boundaries of land. If you are declared bankrupt, the courts may force the sale of certain assets, some of which may be real property, with the proceeds going to creditors. Nature can also affect the quantity of land you own, as was discussed in Chapter 4. Erosion, the gradual loss of land caused by it being washed away by water, and accretion, an increase in land area caused by a stream gradually building up an area of dry land by depositing dirt and rock, effectively decrease and increase the quantity of land you own. However, quick or violent changes in the stream's course will not generally change the boundaries.

Intestate Succession All of the above settings for an involuntary transfer of title have one thing in common: they arise during the lifetime of the owner. The last setting for an involuntary transfer differs in that it arises upon the death of the owner. This setting involves the death of the owner who does not have a will. You will recall that a will is the document that transfers the owner's title to another at the owner's death. If the owner leaves such a document, properly executed, the law will honor it.

However, if the owner dies intestate, that is, without a will, the law dictates who among the owner's relatives takes title under the **statutes of descent and distribution.** These designated relatives are called heirs, or next of kin. The fact that your grandfather wanted you to have Black-acre is immaterial without a will. The law conclusively determines who inherits the title based on relationship to the deceased; the deceased's desires are not considered. This is another area in which a good attorney should be consulted for legal advice.

Although the relatives of your grandfather designated as heirs would immediately inherit Blackacre upon his death intestate, there once again would be no evidence of title. A legal action would have to be brought in the appropriate probate (or surrogate's) court, resulting in a court decree determining heirship. This decree would be the document serving as evidence of transfer of title from your grandfather to his heirs.

DOCUMENTS OF TRANSFER

Each transfer setting typically has its own type of document that transfers title. If ownership of Blackacre is being transferred in the typical purchase situation, a deed is used. If it is being transferred at death, a will may be used; if it is being transferred involuntarily, a court decree may be the document used. Why is a document so important? At least two reasons should be emphasized. First, the law makes such a document a requirement in most cases in order to have an effective transfer. Without it, only a license, a revocable right to use land, may be created. Second, the document has great practical importance because it gives evidence of the grantee's title. Later, when the grantee wants to transfer ownership to another, he or she will rely on the document and those of predecessors to prove ownership of the title to the land.

This means that all the prior documents used to transfer title to Blackacre will make it easier for you to be able to transfer title someday on the open market to a purchaser. Thus, documents of title affect the marketability of Blackacre. Title documents are necessary to a **market- able title,** that is, a title that a reasonably prudent purchaser, willing but not obligated to buy, will accept. The law places great emphasis on your having a marketable title to Blackacre at the time you want to transfer title to another.

Deeds

The deed is the most commonly used document of transfer. Every state has a statute, commonly known as the **Statute of Frauds,** which re- quires that most interests in land be transferred by a written document.

Generally, the only exception that Statutes of Frauds make to the requirement of a written document relates to leases of 1 year or less. Therefore, you could orally rent an apartment in the Whiteacre Apartments for 6 months (although it would not be advisable because it is best to reduce your agreement to writing for certainty and clarity). The Statute of Frauds is discussed in more detail in Chapter 6. What follows is a discussion of deeds and their functions.

Functions of a Deed What functions does a deed serve? Recall in the last chapter that we assumed that you have decided to sell 25 acres of Blackacre to finance the rest of your education, but want to retain 5 acres to live on later in life. A developer has contacted you and you have agreed to sell to him. Your deed to him will serve three functions.

1. The deed will serve the function of transferring title to the developer. This is the most fundamental and indispensable function a deed serves. The Statute of Frauds requires that you use a written document to validly transfer title to the developer.
2. The deed can serve the function of containing promises by you to the developer that you, in fact, do have title and that there are no outstanding interests in Blackacre. The developer may very well want the legal protection given by these promises. These promises, called **title warranties,** or covenants, are discussed later.
3. The deed can serve the functions of giving you, the developer, or both of you further rights in connection with this transaction beyond the transfer itself. You want to make sure the land is developed for residential use only because you want your retained 5 acres to be suitable for residential use. The developer would like a right of way easement across your retained 5 acres in order to reach a public highway. Both of these purposes could be accomplished in the deed through appropriate language.

Understanding these different functions a deed may serve will help you in comprehending the contents of a deed.

Elements of a Deed Let's now consider how these three functions are accomplished within a deed by examining the elements of a deed. Assume that your attorney has drafted the deed in Table 5.2 for you to execute in conveying title to Blackacre to the devloper. This deed contains language sufficient to accomplish the transfer, warranties, and additional rights you and the developer desire. Letters identify the relevant parts of the deed.

First, examine the parts of the deed related to transferring title. T1 identifies the grantor by name, county, and state. The term GRANTOR (person transferring title to another) is thereafter used to simplify and clarify the language of the deed. T2 identifies the grantee (person receiving title) by name, county, and state, and refers to him or her as GRAN-

Table 5.2. General Warranty Deed

THIS DEED between (T¹) _____ of _____ County, State of _____ , hereinafter called GRANTOR, and

(T²) _____ , of _____ County, State of _____ , hereinafter called GRANTEE.

WITNESSES, That in consideration of the sum of (T³) _____ dollars and other valuable consideration, paid by the GRANTEE to the GRANTOR, the (T⁴) GRANTOR does hereby convey unto the GRANTEE, his heirs and assigns the following described real estate, located in _____ County, State of _____

(T⁵) _____

_____

_____

together with all improvements thereon and all the estate and rights pertaining thereto.

(T⁶) TO HAVE AND TO HOLD the described real estate unto the GRANTOR, his heirs and assigns forever.

(R¹) The grantee, his heirs and assigns, hereby covenants with the grantor, his heirs and assigns, to develop and use the real estate conveyed for single family, detached dwelling residential purposes only.

(R²) The grantor hereby conveys to the grantee, his heirs and assigns, a right of way easement in the following described real estate, located in _____ County, State of _____

(W¹) The grantor, his heirs and assigns, hereby covenants with the grantee his heirs and assigns that the grantor is lawfully seized of an absolute estate in fee simple in the described real estate, (W²) that the grantor has good right to convey the described real estate, (W³) that the described real estate is free from all encumbrances except as stated herein:

(place exceptions here)

and (W⁴) that the grantor will warrant and forever defend the title to the described real estate.

IN WITNESS WHEREOF, the grantor has duly executed this deed on this _____ day of _____ , 19 ____

(T⁷) _____

ACKNOWLEDGMENT

State of _____)

County of _____) ss.

Before me, the undersigned, a Notary Public, in and for said County and State, on this _____ day of _____ , 19 _____ , personally appeared _____ to me known to be the identical person who executed the within and foregoing instrument, acknowledged to me that _____ executed the same as _____ free and voluntary act and deed for the uses and purposes therein set forth.

Given under my hand and seal of office the day and year above written.

_____
Notary Public

My Commission expires _____ .

TEE for the reasons just mentioned. T3 states the consideration for the conveyance. Normally, the full consideration, that is, the total purchase price, will not be listed; for confidentiality reasons only a nominal consideration such as $10 will be included. Some states require that full and actual purchase price be on the deed or an **affidavit,** a sworn statement, be filed in the appropriate county office. T4 identifies the words of conveyance used ("does hereby convey"). Although no particular word or words are necessary, a deed *must* contain language indicating the intent of the grantor to transfer an interest to the grantee.

T5 describes the property by county, state, and by one of the legally recognized methods of describing land considered in Chapter 3. T6 is the so-called **habendum clause,** which describes the estate being conveyed. Here the language indicates that a fee simple absolute is being transferred. T7 contains the signature of the grantor. The signing of a deed is part of the execution process that makes the deed legally effective to transfer title. The *execution process* consists of the signing of the document and its delivery. Delivery is the indication by the acts or words of the grantor that he or she intends the document to presently convey title and relinquish control to the grantee. The execution process is the last essential element of a deed that simply conveys title.

Next, examine the parts of the deed related to **warranties** as to the grantor's title. These warranties are also called covenants. They are promises that the grantor makes to the grantee concerning the title being conveyed. These warranties are identified with a "W" followed by a number. Common warranties or covenants include:

Covenant of seizen

Warranty of good right to convey

Warranty against encumbrances

Covenant of quiet enjoyment

W1 describes the covenant of seizen — the promise that the grantor does, in fact, own the fee simple absolute estate being transferred. W2 describes the warranty of good right to convey. This warranty is synonymous with the warranty of seizen. W3 describes the warranty against encumbrances. Encumbrances are interests that limit a fee simple, such as liens, easements and restrictive covenants. This warranty promises that there are no encumbrances except as set out in the deed. W4 describes the covenant of warranty, also known as the covenant of quiet enjoyment — the promise that the grantee will not have the title disturbed by another title holder. Each of these warranties, related to different aspects of the title, are important because they are what allow the grantee to sue the grantor in case the title proves to be defective.

The next section of the deed contains provisions related to additional rights given to the grantor and grantee. R1 describes a restrictive covenant (promise), also called a deed restriction that limits the grantee's use of the property being transferred to limited residential purposes. This promise gives you, as the owner of the five remaining acres in Blackacre, the protection you desire. R2 describes an easement that you as grantor are giving the grantee over a portion of your retained land. This is in addition to the fee simple absolute you have conveyed.

The **acknowledgment** is not a formal part of the deed; the deed is valid without it. It is certification by some designated person, such as a notary public, that the grantor appeared and stated that he or she did, in fact, voluntarily execute the deed. However, as a safeguard to the authenticity of a deed, all states require that a deed be acknowledged in order to be eligible for recording, also called recordation, in the public land records. The importance of recordation is discussed later.

Types of Deeds There are two basic types of deed, those that contain warranties of title and those that do not. Both are equally effective to convey title. The sample deed above is an example of the most common type of deed—the **warranty deed.** As explained above, it is a deed that, in addition to conveying title, also contains promises to the grantee as to the quality of title. If the title is not as represented, the purchaser can sue the seller on the warranties. This deed is advantageous to the purchaser.

Warranty deeds differ with respect to the period of time covered by the grantor's warranties. In a *special warranty deed,* the grantor warrants title only for the period during which he or she owned the property. Thus, if any claim should arise pertaining to that period, the grantor is obligated to defend (in court) the grantee's title and pay any judgments awarded by the court. In a general warranty deed, the grantor warrants title for his or her period of ownership and the entire period before obtaining title. Thus, if anyone should claim title in the future, the grantor must defend the grantee's title in court, if necessary, and pay any judgments.

The second type of deed is a **quit claim deed.** It differs from a warranty deed in two respects. First, it contains no warranties of title at all. If the title turns out to be defective, the purchaser has no legal recourse against the seller. Second, rather than conveying a defined estate, it merely conveys the grantor's "right, title, and interest" in the land, without specifically defining what that interest is. In essence, the grantor simply says, "Whatever interest I had, you now have," without defining that interest. Obviously, the deed is advantageous to the seller, since it makes no warranties and does not obligate the seller to defend the buyer's title. It should be emphasized that the quit claim deed conveys the grantor's interest in the property as effectively as any other deed.

Other Deeds In some states, such as California, for example, a grant deed is often used. By using a **grant deed,** the grantor promises that no interest was conveyed to any other party and that no encumbrances on the land were created during the grantor's period of ownership. The grantor also covenants that any interest acquired later will be conveyed to the grantee. As you can see, the net result of using a grant deed is similar to that of using a special warranty deed in that the grantee receives guarantees pertaining only to the period the grantor owned the property.

Another deed that is used in some states is the **bargain-and-sale deed.** This deed implies the grantor has a certain interest in the property, but does not contain any express covenants to this effect. Thus, this deed does not provide the grantee as much protection as the special warranty or grant deed, but may afford more protection than the quit claim deed.

Many special deeds are used in particular situations. Some of these deeds are sheriff's deed, referee's deed in foreclosure, and executor's deed. All of these deeds perform the same functions as the deeds discussed above and may or may not contain covenants. If you have any questions about any deed, you should see an attorney.

Will

Your grandfather has conveyed Blackacre to you in his will. Why do you suppose he chose this method, rather than utilizing a deed to accomplish his purposes? More than likely it is because of the characteristics of a will that differ from a deed. Both can effectively transfer title, but a deed transfers title immediately on its execution. Not so a will. A will is a document executed during a person's lifetime that conveys that person's property only at his death. Your grandfather may have executed his will 10 years ago. However, it had no legal effect during his lifetime, only at his death 6 months ago.

This characteristic points out other features of a will. Since it has no legal effect during the person's lifetime, it can be amended at any time or revoked entirely. A will, then, has much more flexibility than does a deed. Your grandfather probably chose a will as a device to convey Blackacre to you because he could retain ownership until his death, yet be sure you would own Blackacre at his death. This would hold true unless he decided to amend the will and convey Blackacre to your sister or revoke the will entirely. Since the testator (your grandfather) is no longer alive to tell us what his desires concerning his property are, the law places stringent requirements on the execution of a will to reduce the possibility of fraud or overreaching by those who might want to acquire the property. To insure that a will is valid an attorney should be consulted.

Court Decree—Substitute for Voluntary Transfer

When there is a voluntary transfer of title, there may be no need for any judicial action to make the conveyance effective. But when title is transferred involuntarily, as we discussed earlier, it is often necessary that a court hear the matter and issue a decree determining the title. The nature of the lawsuit can vary widely. It may be one brought by the State, as is the case in eminent domain proceedings, or by a private party, as is normally the case in lien enforcement proceedings. It may be wholly contested, as is often the case in adverse possession or it may be a noncontroversial affair, as is often the case with intestate succession proceedings.

Court Decree Combined with Voluntary Transfer In some situations both a voluntary transfer document and a court decree must be used. One of the most common is the will situation. For example, you have acquired title to Blackacre by your grandfather's will. But this assumes that the document was, in fact, executed by him and intended to serve as his will. These and other questions must be answered by an appropriate court before we can say with assurance that you now own Blackacre. This means it takes both the will and a court decree determining the validity of the will for you to acquire a "marketable" title to Blackacre.

Jurisdiction In order for a court to issue a decree affecting title to Blackacre, it must have jurisdiction over the subject matter of the lawsuit and over all of the parties who have any property interest in Blackacre. Subject matter jurisdiction means that the lawsuit must be brought in the appropriate court that has authority to deal with the type of suit involved. Personal jurisdiction means that all parties who have or claim an interest in Blackacre must be given notice of the lawsuit and an opportunity to appear and participate in the suit.

Recordation of Transfer Documents—
Public Land Records System

You now own Blackacre. In order for your ownership to be useful to you, however, other people must accept your ownership of Blackacre by being able to examine the documents creating your ownership. How can that be accomplished? One way would be for you to possess your grandfather's will that conveyed Blackacre to you. Then you could show it to any interested person, such as a lender or purchaser. But what if your grandfather had conveyed another tract of land, Pinkacre, to your sister. Wouldn't she also want to possess the will as evidence of her title? Also, you would need the documents showing that your grandfather and earlier owners also had rightful ownership of Blackacre. All of this could amount to a rather bulky packet of documents. Doesn't sound very efficient, does it? You are right; it isn't. This is why another system of evidencing ownership of land exists.

Rather than physically retaining all the documents evidencing ownership of Blackacre, if each document was recorded in a public place, then any interested person could check these records to determine ownership of Blackacre. This public office where the records were kept could serve as a sort of depository of documents concerning ownership of land. This office would serve as a permanent, official storehouse of information concerning land ownership. This is the system used throughout the United States.

In your state, you will find that public land records are kept in each county. All documents affecting ownership of land within the county can be recorded, or filed, in a designated office. The public office goes under different names in different states: the county clerk's office, the county registrar's office, the registrar of deeds, or the county recorder's office.

Recording a document is important because it constitutes **constructive notice** of an interest in real property. This is the first function of public land records. It is assumed that any person becoming involved with Blackacre has knowledge of all the recorded documents pertaining to Blackacre and, furthermore, that these recorded documents are the only ones recognized by the law for settling disputes concerning interests in Blackacre. For example, if you were dishonest and sold Blackacre to two people, each unaware of the other's purchase, who is the legal owner of Blackacre? The courts will generally hold that the owner is the first buyer to record his interest. This is sometimes called the **race notice concept.**

The second function of public land records is to provide a retrieval system that allows a person wishing to examine the title to Blackacre to locate only the documents related to Blackacre, and ignore all the others. Without an adequate retrieval system, trying to locate the documents relating to Blackacre would literally be like trying to find a needle in a haystack. There may be 100 documents related to Blackacre in an office that has millions of filed documents.

There are two retrieval systems currently in use. One is an index that is set up on a name basis, called **Grantor-Grantee index** (also called the Direct-Indirect Index in some states). Documents are indexed on the basis of grantor's names or on the basis of grantee's names. Knowing the names of the parties to transactions allows you to locate the relevant documents. The second retrieval system is set up on a property basis. It is named the **tract system.** Documents are indexed by the legal description of the property. Knowing the legal description allows you to locate all documents related to the described property. Recording and its impact are illustrated in Figure 5.1.

More efficient retrieval systems utilizing computers are presently being developed in some locations. Most land records systems are products of the 19th century. The use of computers may be the means of bringing these systems into the 20th century.

Requirements for Recording Documents The law requires that there be some minimum assurance that the document is valid before it can be

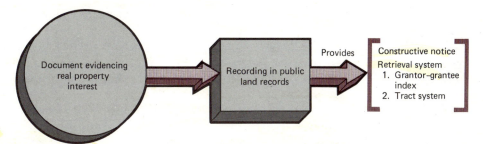

Figure 5.1 Recording and its impact.

recorded. The minimum assurance required by most states is that the document be acknowledged before some designated person, such as a notary public, who certifies to the acknowledgment on the document itself. The acknowledgment is an oral statement by the grantor to the public official that he or she intended to execute the document. The public official certifies that such acknowledgment has been given using written statement to that effect placed at the bottom of the document, accompanied by the official's signature and seal. See the acknowledgment at the end of the deed in Table 5.2. Some states accept the signatures of at least two witnesses to the signing of the document in place of notary public's statement.

In many states, another requirement for recording a deed is the payment of a **transfer tax.** Prior to 1968, the federal government required that documentary stamps be purchased and attached to deeds when recorded. Since the federal government discontinued this practice, many states have initiated a transfer tax, which is collected in land recording offices when deeds are recorded. Some states tax the entire purchase price, whereas others tax only the difference between the purchase price and any outstanding mortgages on which the buyer agrees to make payments. Thus, in these states, if a home is purchased for $80,000 and the buyer agrees to take over a $50,000 mortgage, transfer taxes will be collected on the difference, $30,000. While rates differ from state to state, the rate once used by the federal government, $.55 per $500 or fraction thereof, is the most widely used rate. At this rate, in a state taxing the entire price of a property, recording a deed for a $50,000 home would produce a tax of $55. This is found by multiplying the rate times the number of $500 tax units,

$$\text{Transfer tax} = \text{Tax rate} \times \text{Number of tax units}$$
$$= \$.55 \times \$50,000/\$500$$
$$= \$.55 \times 100$$
$$= \$55.00$$

If the sales price had been $50,001, another tax increment would have been created, and the tax would have been $55.55. Since deeds generally do not have to state the actual cash consideration being paid, recording offices will either simply ask for an oral statement of the amount of

Figure 5.2 Recording procedure.

actual consideration or require you to complete an affidavit stating the actual consideration.

Recording Procedure The usual format for recording a document is to take it to the public land records office and give it to the official for filing as can be seen in Figure 5.2. The official will stamp the exact time of filing on it, indicate where in the public records it will be reproduced, place an official seal on it, place tax stamps on it if there is a tax on the transaction, and collect a recording fee. This recording fee is to help cover the cost of maintaining the public land records. Then one or more copies will be made for recording purposes.

The office will record the documents and index it in the index system maintained, as described above. Photocopies of documents are organized in chronological order in *books* open to the public. Each document is assigned a *page* number. The book and page number are entered in the index system. Finally, the document will be returned to the person who filed it. But the original document has lost much of its legal significance. From now on, the record of it found in the public land records office will be the important evidence of title.

Title Examination and Protection

Title Examination We know you own Blackacre. But we also know now that the developer who is contemplating buying 25 acres from you wants evidence that you own Blackacre. This evidence will be found through an examination of the public records. This examination can take one of two forms. Which form is used is largely a matter of custom and practice in a community. The first form is direct examination of the public records. The developer could hire an attorney to go to the land records office and check on each document relating to Blackacre by using the appropriate indexes, tracing title from you, through your grandfather, all the way back to the State. The attorney is seeking to identify the **chain of title,** that series of claims to Blackacre which leads to you. But if the chain of title to Blackacre is very long and involved, this would be a time consuming and expensive process for the attorney and, hence, the developer. This is still done in some communities, but it is not practical for most transactions.

The second form of examination involves the application of classic American free enterprise principles to this area. If it is too time consuming for the developer or an attorney personally to check the public land records, what if a private business compiled land records and furnished a copy of all documents affecting title to Blackacre? The attorney could then examine this compilation of documents much more efficiently. Enter the abstract company. An **abstract company** is a concern that uses the public records to compile chronological histories of title to real property, called **abstracts,** and furnish these abstracts for a fee to inter- ested persons.

If there is an abstract company in your county, you or the developer could order an abstract of the title to Blackacre that the developer's attorney could examine. Better yet, if your grandfather had an abstract on Blackacre, you could have the abstract company update it by adding any documents recorded since the last one in the abstract and provide it to the developer. This updating is much cheaper than obtaining a completely new abstract since many abstract companies charge a set amount per page in the abstract.

Title Protection Always keep in mind that title examination is never an end in itself. Its purpose is to disclose the status of title to the examiner so as to render some type of title protection to the purchaser. The developer wants to be protected in buying a portion of Blackacre from you. The title examination provides the facts surrounding the status of title. How are these facts used to protect the purchaser in the transaction? Three different forms of protection are used, as summarized in Table 5.3. Which is used in your area will largely be determined by custom and practice.

One common form of title protection, used mainly in the Midwest, is the attorney's title opinion. If the developer uses this form of title protection, an attorney will examine the abstract of title and then write a letter to the developer describing the results of the examination: who currently owns Blackacre, what kind of ownership it is, whether there are any defects in title or outstanding encumbrances that must be removed, and whether there are any land use restrictions, such as restrictive cove-

Table 5.3. Protecting Title to Real Property

Type of Title Protection	Action	Protection
Attorney's Opinion (Title Opinion)	Attorney examines chain of title and reports any defects	Defects revealed and attorney liable for mistakes
Title Insurance	Title insurance company examines chain of title and notes any defects; issues policy covering title defects except those discovered in their analysis, if they are not cured	Financial indemnification should loss occur due to covered title defects
Torrens Title	State certifies title	State certified title precludes other valid claims to title

nants, that the developer needs to be aware of. If there are **defects,** or **clouds on the title,** the attorney will recommend that they be cured, or eliminated, before the transaction is completed. Perhaps a spouse failed to sign a deed conveying his or her interest in property owned jointly by the couple. Defects are often cured by asking the party, which may have an interest in the property, to execute a deed, usually a quit claim deed, transferring the interest to you or to file a quiet title suit in court asking the court to declare the outstanding interest extinguished. The title protection involved is the expert professional advice the attorney gives the purchaser. It is "preventive medicine," preventing the purchaser from acquiring a title that is defective.

However, the attorney's title opinion gives no financial protection to the purchaser in case title in fact turns out to be defective, except for the attorney's professional liability. Financial protection against title loss is the attribute of the second form of title protection — title insurance. The **title insurance** company issues a policy insuring the purchaser or a lender against a financial loss due to defects in the title.

Title insurance, however, operates quite differently from other forms of insurance. Most forms of insurance, such as fire, health, and life, compensate a person upon the occurrence of a future event. Title insurance insures against existing defects in title, but not against defects that arise in the future following the transaction. You can be sure, then, that a title insurance company carefully examines the title to the property to determine if there are any defects. If the company discovers defects, it either demands that they be cured or will except them from the policy. However, if there are existing defects not excepted from the policy which cause loss to the purchaser, then the company will indemnify, or pay, the insured for the loss. Title policies, called mortgagee's policies, are also available to protect a lender's interest in a property. The title protection that title insurance offers is financial indemnification against loss as well as advice concerning the quality of title. Title insurance is used throughout the United States, but particularly in the East and West.

The attorney's title opinion and title insurance share one characteristic — they both operate on private professional judgment that has no State authentication behind it. They operate on a private assessment of title. What would give the purchaser (or lender) greater title protection would be State authentication of the status of title. This is the third form of title protection. It is known as a **registered title** or **Torrens title.** It operates on a principle that the State makes an official determination of the status of title, records that determination on a title document, and, thereafter, only interests appearing on the title document have any legal validity. Under this form of protection, the registered title is the ownership of the property, not merely evidence of ownership, as are the public land records we have described. Theoretically, a registered title gives the greatest title protection because of its official status. However, the chances are great that title to Blackacre cannot be registered because it is a system in use in only a few areas of the country. Ironically, there is enough opposition to the registered title system from all sources, ranging from groups doubting its effectiveness to groups concerned about its economic impact on their title business, to ensure that it will not soon expand throughout the country and compete with the two dominant forms of title protection — the attorney's title opinion and title insurance.

SUMMARY

Property interests are created and transferred by written document. Both the individual document and the series of documents concerning a tract of land are evidence of ownership we call the title to the land. Most title transfers are voluntary and occur during the life of the owner by deed or at death by will. A few title transfers are involuntary: condemnation, adverse possession, foreclosure, and intestate succession to title at death. These utilize either a deed or court decree. The three documents used to transfer title are the deed, the will, and the court decree. The deed serves three functions: conveying title, giving promises concerning the status of title, and creating other rights for the transferor or transferee. A will, because it transfers title at a time when the landowner is no longer present, is surrounded by more stringent requirements to ensure its genuineness. A court decree, either alone or in conjunction with a deed, can transfer title to land. The principle consideration relates to the court's authority or jurisdiction to enter a decree affecting title. All documents affecting title may be recorded in a public land records office. This office serves as a library of information concerning land titles that interested persons can use. Examination of the public land records allows a prospective purchaser to determine the "marketability" of the seller's title. This determination can be made not only from an examination of the public land records directly, but also from copies of the public land records, called abstracts of title, supplied by private business. Three different methods of using these public or private land records give a purchaser information concerning the status of the title that can protect his or her position in the title transaction. One is the attorney's opinion, the second is the use of title insurance, and the third is the use of a state registered title.

QUICK QUIZ

1. A voluntary transfer from one living person to another is accomplished using:

a. a deed   c. a patient
b. a will   d. a court decree

2. Which of the following functions cannot be performed by a deed?

a. promise that grantor has title and will defend grantee against others' claims
b. give the grantor further rights in the property after it belongs to the grantee
c. convey ownership from government to an individual
d. transfer title from one person to another

3. An acknowledgment to a deed is necessary to:

a. have a valid deed   c. record the deed
b. deliver the deed   d. obtain a mortgage loan

4. The promise in a deed that the grantor owns the particular interest being transferred is the

a. covenant of seizen
b. warranty of defects
c. warranty against encumberances
d. covenant of quiet enjoyment

5. Adverse possession does not require

a. building an improvement on the land
b. occupying the land continuously for a specified period of time
c. using the land without the permission of the owner
d. using the land openly with no attempt to hide the use

6. The deed in which the grantor makes no warranties about the quality of title is a _____ deed.

7. When someone dies without leaving a will, his or her real property will be distributed according to the laws of _____.

8. The _____ requires that deeds be in writing.

9. Recording a document in the proper public office constitutes _____ to all third parties as to the interest of the party named in the document.

10. The three ways to protect your title are _____, _____, and _____.

QUESTIONS AND EXERCISES

1. Would you depend on the title protection given by a warranty deed? Why?

2. What is the name of the government official in your state who records documents relating to interests in land?

3. Name three possible encumberances to a clear title to real property.

4. If you secretly fish in the pond of a local farmer at night for the necessary number of years, can you claim ownership by adverse possession? Why?

5. What are the essential elements of a valid deed?

6. Name three functions of a deed.

KEY TERMINOLOGY

abstract
abstract company
accretion
acknowledgment
adverse possession
affidavit
bargain-and-sale deed
chain of title
cloud on the title
condemnation
constructive notice
court decree
covenants
deed
defects
erosion
escheat
foreclosure
grant deed
grantee
grantor
grantor-grantee index
habendum clause
intestate succession
involuntary transfer
license

marketable title
master commissioner's deed
patent
private transfer
public transfer
quit claim deed
race notice concept
recordation
referee's deed
registered title
sheriff's deed
statutes of descent and
    distribution
Statute of Frauds
title
title examination
title insurance
title opinion
title protection
Torrens title
tract system
transfer tax
voluntary transfer
warranty
warranty deed
will

**IF YOU WANT
TO READ MORE**

PHILIP B. BERGFIELD, *Principles of Real Estate Law* (New York: McGraw-Hill Book Company, 1979), Chapters 10–12 and 14.

ROBERT N. CORLEY, PETER J. SHEDD, and CHARLES F. FLOYD, *Real Estate and the Law* (New York: Random House, Inc., 1982), Chapters 4, 5, and 12.

Additional readings in other real estate law texts are listed at the end of Chapter 4.

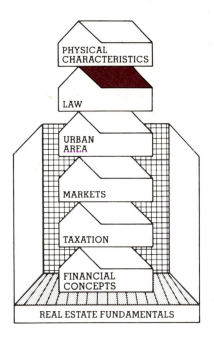

PHYSICAL CHARACTERISTICS

LAW

URBAN AREA

MARKETS

TAXATION

FINANCIAL CONCEPTS

REAL ESTATE FUNDAMENTALS

6

Legal Fundamentals: contracts

PREVIEW   Agreements between two or more parties to do or not to do certain things are essential to the operation of the real estate business. Such agreements are called contracts. Because of the legal and practical importance of contracts, you need a basic understanding of them and their creation. This chapter furnishes you with an understanding of the basic concepts involved in contracts by explaining:

1. Why contracts are necessary.
2. How contracts may be classified.
3. The elements of a valid and enforceable contract.
4. The ways in which a contract can be performed, discharged, and breached.
5. Real estate sales contracts.
6. Other common contracts related to real estate.

Your being in college right now is probably no accident. You and your family have planned (and perhaps sacrificed) so that you can attend. You are attending because you have some goals, specific or vague, that you hope college can help you attain. In other words, your college education is both the end product of and the stepping stone to planning for the future. We humans don't live just in the present; we think about the future a great deal. Understanding this idea can help you understand the concept of contracts.

NEED FOR CONTRACTS

The law of contracts helps people plan for the future. Blackacre, that 30-acre tract of land your grandfather willed to you, can help illustrate the function of contracts. Assume you decide to sell 25 acres in order to finance the balance of your education. It would be wonderful if a buyer magically appeared at your front door, cash in hand, ready to buy and you immediately executed a deed to the buyer. The transaction is completed and you are ready to invest your money! As we know all too well, however, life does not work that way. You will have to market the property, probably with a real estate agent. Even if a prospective buyer is located, the title will not be taken immediately. The buyer will want to examine the title and arrange financing. Will the real estate agent spend the time and money necessary to locate a buyer unless he or she has adequate assurance that you will pay the agreed-upon commission? Will you hold your property off the market while the buyer checks the title and secures financing unless you have adequate assurance that the buyer will, in fact, buy once title and financing are cleared? Will the buyer go to the effort and expense of checking the title and arranging financing unless there is adequate assurance you will, in fact, sell at the proper time? The answer to all the questions is obviously "no." Each party wants adequate assurance that the other party will perform his or her responsibilities at some point in the future.

Promises related to future actions and the assurance that the promises will be performed are what contracts are about. Any contract relates to:

1. A promise, commitment, or undertaking that something shall or shall not be done in the future, and
2. The sanctions that the law places behind the promise, commitment, or undertaking.

This idea is a hallmark of any advanced society. Society members need not act only in the present, but can plan for the future with the assurance that society will enforce agreements among members related to future conduct. A contract, then, is an exchange of promises that certain acts shall or shall not be done in the future that may or may not be enforceable by law.

CLASSIFICATION OF CONTRACTS

Contracts are not all alike; there are different varieties. This section discusses the different forms in which contracts may be classified (Figure 6.1).

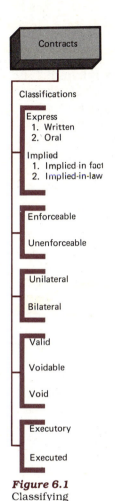

Classifications

Express
1. Written
2. Oral

Implied
1. Implied in fact
2. Implied-in-law

Enforceable

Unenforceable

Unilateral

Bilateral

Valid

Voidable

Void

Executory

Executed

Figure 6.1
Classifying
contracts.

Express Versus Implied Contracts

This distinction relates to whether language or conduct creates the obligation. If you promise orally or in writing to pay a real estate agent to locate a buyer for Blackacre, your promise would involve an **express contract.** However, assume that, prior to beginning the sales process, you conduct an auction to get rid of some old farm machinery located on the land. One person bids $100 on an item and then a second bidder holds up two fingers. It would be understood that he or she was bidding $200. If no one makes a higher bid and the gavel is struck on the second bid, that person's conduct would indicate a promise to pay $200 which was accepted by you. This contract has been created by the conduct of you and the bidder. This contract is known as an **implied-in-fact contract.** Although the express and implied-in-fact contracts are created by different means, they both share the common element of manifested promise or commitment to pay a sum of money in the future.

The express contract and the implied-in-fact contract differ from another type of contract, called the **implied-in-law contract** or quasi-contract. It is unfortunate that the term "contract" is applied because there is no underlying promise or commitment, as in the previous cases. Rather, where one person confers a benefit on another in the expectation of compensation, the law may allow the person conferring the benefit to recover its value in order to prevent the other person from being "unjustly enriched." For example, assume your sister lived with your grandfather during the last years of his life, providing housekeeping and nursing functions for him, in the belief that he would will Blackacre to her. If she received nothing in his will, she may be able to recover the value of her services from his estate. Notice the fundamental difference between the implied-in-law contract and the express or implied-in-fact contract. The function of the former is to return the parties to their original positions (as if there had been no unjust enrichment), whereas the function of the latter is to fulfill the reasonable expectations created by the making of a promise.

Bilateral Versus Unilateral Contracts

A **bilateral contract** is created when people exchange promises concerning future action. For example, assume you locate a buyer for Blackacre and both of you sign a written document in which you promise to sell Blackacre for $60,000 and the buyer promises to buy Blackacre for $60,000. It is bilateral, or two-sided, because the legal rights and duties are reciprocal; each of you has a right to enforce the other's promise and each of you is obligated to perform his or her own promise. You have a right to require that the buyer pay you $60,000 and are under a duty to convey title to the buyer. The buyer has a right to require that you convey title to him or her and is under a duty to pay you $60,000. Most contracts are bilateral.

A **unilateral contract,** in contrast, contains only one promise. Thus, only one right and one duty are created. The person making the promise wants the other person to engage in certain conduct, not make a mutual promise. The contract is formed only upon the completion of the requested conduct. For example, assume your grandfather had signed a written document promising to will Blackacre to your sister if she cared for him during the balance of his life. He would not be asking for a promise of care from your sister but performance of such care. Only if she, in fact, cared for him during the balance of his life would a contract be formed. There would be only one right, that of your sister to receive Blackacre; there would be only one duty, that of your grandfather to will Blackacre to her. Relatively few contracts are unilateral.

Valid, Voidable, and Void Contracts

A **valid** contract is one that is binding on all parties and cannot be nullified by any of the parties. A contract is classified as **voidable** if one of the parties to it has the power to terminate it by indicating an intention to do so. To illustrate, let's assume you enter into a contract to sell Blackacre to a buyer whom you believe to be 21 years old, but who is, in fact, only 17 years old. One of the reasons you contract with the buyer is that the person represents to you that he or she has the money necessary to purchase Blackacre, a representation he or she knows to be false. This person is a minor, one whom the state has specified is not fully legally responsible for his or her actions. For contractual purposes, a person is no longer a minor when they reach the age of majority. Minors can usually terminate, or avoid, contracts into which they enter; that is, they have the ability to void their contracts. Likewise, one who is induced to enter into a contract by untrue statements deliberately made by another (fraud) can avoid that contract. For you, the contract may be voidable. Thus, by deliberately making untrue statements to you, the minor gave you the ability to avoid the contract. But until one of you exercises the right to terminate the contract, it remains in effect.

A **void** contract, on the other hand, is really a contradiction in terms because it is no contract at all. In this type of contract the law refuses to recognize any duty of performance by the promisor. The most common illustration of a void contract is one made illegal by statute or public policy. Assume you contract with a real estate agent to pay him or her a commission if the agent locates a buyer for Blackacre. If the agent is not licensed by the state, the state real estate licensing law may dictate that the contract is void. You would have no obligation to pay the agent a commission even if a buyer was located. Here, unlike the voidable contract, there is no necessity for you to elect to terminate because a valid contract was never created.

Enforceable Versus Unenforceable Contracts

If you enter into a valid *written* contract to sell Blackacre, the buyer's refusal to honor his or her promise to buy would give you the right to go to court and recover money damages or seek specific performance that requires the buyer to pay the contract price and take title. Because you have these legal, court-imposed remedies, the contract is said to be *enforceable.* On the other hand, if the contract were oral, the buyer would be able to raise an effective defense to your court suit because the law requires contracts for the sale of land to be in writing, a point discussed later. This means that the contract is unenforceable by you. This is not to say that the contract is invalid; it is valid, but it cannot be enforced in court in its present condition.

Executory and Executed Contracts

Prior to the performance of all the obligations of a contract, the contract is said to be *executory.* When all obligations have been performed the contract is said to be executed. Thus, if you sign a contract giving a person the right to purchase Blackacre at a specified price within the next 90 days, that contract will be executory until either the person commits to purchase Blackacre or the 90 days elapse. When either of these events occurs the contract would be classified as executed.

ELEMENTS OF A VALID CONTRACT

Not every agreement related to future conduct will be enforced by the law. Assume that you locate a person, Ima Buyer, who agrees to purchase Blackacre for $60,000 and the two of you sign a written agreement. At the same time you invite Ima to your home for dinner to celebrate the agreement and she accepts your invitation. Thereafter, you have second thoughts about the deal, believing that you should have asked $75,000. You become so upset that you telephone Ima and state that you do not intend to sell Blackacre to her nor have her to dinner at your house. Ima may very well be able to enforce the contract, but certainly will not be able to enforce the dinner invitation. The former may be a valid legal agreement fully enforceable; the latter is merely a social agreement not legally enforceable. In order for an **agreement** to be a valid contract at law, certain elements must always be present, as listed in Table 6.1. This section discusses these crucial elements.

Reality of Assent

There must always be two or more parties who have, in fact, reached an agreement. There must be mutual assent, a true meeting of the minds,

Table 6.1. Elements of a Valid Contract

Reality of Assent
Competent Parties
Consideration
Lawful Objective
Proper Form

between them. This mutual assent normally takes the form of an offer and acceptance.

Offer The initial promise is called an offer. The person making it is the *offeror* and the person receiving it is the *offeree*. An **offer** is a promise to do something in return for a requested act or counterpromise. Assume that you have been negotiating with Ima Buyer over the sale of Blackacre, but the two of you have reached no definite agreement. Based on your conversations, your draft and sign a written document promising to sell Blackacre to Ima in exchange for her promise to pay $65,000. This document constitutes an offer. It is a promise on your part to do something in the future (convey title to Blackacre to Ima) *if* Ima also promises to do something in the future (pay you $65,000).

An offer must have certain characteristics. First, it must be communicated to the offeree. This would be accomplished by delivering the document to Ima. Second, the terms of the offer must be reasonably definite and certain; otherwise, there will be no promise complete enough for the law to reasonably enforce. Refer to the sample contract in Table 6.3 later in this chapter to see what terms should be included. Third, an offer must be outstanding at the time of the offeree's acceptance. If it is withdrawn by the offeror prior to acceptance, no contract is created. An offer can be withdrawn or terminated before acceptance in four different ways:

1. By the lapse of a stated time period or, if none is stated, after a reasonable time.
2. By a revocation of the offer that is communicated to the offeree prior to acceptance.
3. By the offeree making a counteroffer, that is, changing any term of the offer.
4. By certain changes in circumstances surrounding the parties, such as death or insanity of the offeror or offeree, or the destruction of the property.

Acceptance The effect of your offer to Ima is to create in her a power to cause a contract to come into existence by giving the requested promise (to pay $65,000) and agreeing to the offer (promising to buy Blackacre). The exercise of this power constitutes the **acceptance.** An acceptance must be made and communicated according to the manner, time, place, and terms specified in the offer. If there are no such specifications, then the acceptance must be made and communicated in a reasonable fashion. Let's assume that Ima made a counteroffer of $55,000 to you and, after negotiation, the two of you have agreed on a sales price of $60,000. The customary manner of indicating your mutual agreement is for both of you to sign a contract such as the sample contract found later in this chapter.

Defects to Assent Certain factors can prevent mutual assent even though there has been a formal offer and acceptance made. These defects are listed in Table 6.2. The assent must be *real*, not just *apparent*.

Fraud, misrepresentation, or mistake may preclude there being any actual assent. **Fraud** involves a deliberate misrepresentation of a material fact with the purpose of inducing action by another. For example, you tell Ima that Blackacre has utilities (electricity, gas, and water) as an inducement for her to buy when you know that no utilities have yet been extended to Blackacre. **Misrepresentation,** on the other hand, involves an innocent misstatement of fact. For example, Ima asks you if there is an ample water supply on Blackacre. Remembering your grandfather often saying that a water well could successfully be drilled on the property, you tell Ima, without actually knowing, that the water table under Blackacre is ample for a water well when, in fact, it is not.

Mistakes are errors made by one or both parties to a transaction and can be of many different types. Some mistakes have no effect on a contract. For example, a mistaken belief caused by a failure to inform oneself about the contract is of no legal consequence. The fact that Ima believes she can pay for Blackacre with a personal check because she did not read the contract clause requiring cash or a certified check is immaterial. But mistakes of the parties concerning the existence or identity of the subject matter of the contract can be crucial. For example, if Blackacre were an operating orange grove and both Ima and you had negotiated your agreement on this basis, a fire that sweeps through the area and destroys the orange grove on Blackacre at the moment you and Ima are signing could affect the contract. The sale and purchase of Blackacre without orange trees is not what you and Ima had in mind in making the

Table 6.2. Possible Defects to Assent

Fraud
Misrepresentation
Mistakes
Undue Influence
Duress
Menace

contract. This mutual mistake in the assumed continued existence of the orange grove on Blackacre prevents true assent.

Undue influence, duress, and menace may also preclude there being any actual assent. **Undue influence** consists of abusing the control or influence that one person has over another because of their relationship. This is a problem mainly involving the elderly, whose weakness in mind or body may make them susceptible to such influence by relatives or friends. **Duress** involves compelling a person by force to do or agree to do an act. **Menace** involves compelling a person by threat of force to do or agree to do an act. The latter two concepts involve the *Godfather* situation of "the offer you can't refuse."

Finally, mutual assent means that the parties be serious in their entry into a contract, thus precluding jokes. If one of your classmates learns you are interested in selling Blackacre and laughingly says "I'll take my student loan funds and buy Blackacre from you," you had better keep looking for a buyer!

Competent Parties

If the fundamental nature of a contract is the assent of two or more persons to be bound by an agreement, it is important that the person giving his or her assent have the competency to give it. The law assumes that any person is competent to enter into a contract with the exception of:

Minors

Mentally ill or mentally defective persons

Intoxicated or drugged persons

Persons under legal guardianship

A minor has historically been defined as one under the age of 21, although many states now define a minor as one under the age of 18. Some persons under the age of majority may be classified as **emancipated minors** with the right to contract and incur financial responsibility. Criteria for emancipated minor status often include marriage, self-support, and others. Mental illness involves conditions such as congenital deficiencies in intelligence, brain damage caused by disease or accident, deterioration caused by old age, and various mental defects causing hallucinations, delusions, confusion, and depression. Intoxication or drug abuse could destroy the ability of the afflicted person to understand fully the nature and consequences of the agreement to affect competency. Incompetency on any of these grounds renders the contract "voidable" by the incompetent party.

This means that the contract is valid, but can be either disaffirmed or ratified after regaining competency. Ratification can be express, by conduct or by failure to disaffirm within a reasonable time after regaining competency. Only the incompetent party has the power to disaffirm the contract; the other party is bound by it without the right to disaffirm. However, where a person has been declared incompetent by the court and had a guardian appointed, he or she has absolutely no capacity to contract. Therefore, any contract made by such a person is void, there is no contract in reality. The incompetent party has no power to ratify it because no valid agreement was ever created. Thus, no party to the contract is bound by it.

Consideration

Not only must an agreement be reached by competent parties, but the agreement must be supported by consideration. **Consideration** is the bargained-for exchange of something of legal value by two or more people; it is a promise that one person makes to another in exchange for a price. The "price" may be another promise, money, action, or forebearance from action. For example, in the illustration we have been using, you have promised Ima to sell Blackacre to her in exchange for her promise to pay you $60,000. As an alternative you could promise to sell Blackacre to Ima if she pays you (not merely promises to pay you) $60,000. Finally, you could promise Ima to sell Blackacre to her if she refrains from smoking and drinking for 1 year. Each of these examples illustrates a different kind of "price" that Ima has given for your promise. But all three contain the essential elements of consideration:

1. Something considered to be of legal value has been given (Ima's promise, money, or forebearance from certain acts).
2. Your promise (to convey) has induced the giving of Ima's promise, money, or forebearance, and likewise, Ima's promise, money, or forebearance has induced the giving of your promise; that is, there has been a bargained-for exchange of promise and "price" between you and Ima.

With respect to consideration, the law does not limit what constitutes legal value to what is called **valuable consideration,** that is, money, promises, or property. Another category of consideration, **good consideration,** is composed of love and affection and is deemed to have legal value. These seemingly technical, legal requirements serve the social function of controlling what kind of agreements are important enough to be backed by the sanctions of the law.

Lawful Objective

The requirement of a lawful objective also serves a social function — controlling what kinds of agreements are so detrimental to society as not to be backed by the sanctions of the law. An agreement may be found to be illegal for one of two reasons: (1) because it is prohibited by statute or

(2) because it violates some public policy. We have already mentioned one example falling into the first category: a contract with an unlicensed real estate agent to sell Blackacre. Such an agent could not enforce such a contract against you if the state requires licensing as a condition to recovery of a commission. An example falling into the second category would be a contract to sell Blackacre to Ima for the purpose of her growing some illegal substance such as marijuana on the land. Even though the contract standing by itself is perfectly lawful, the fact that it facilitates the accomplishment of an unlawful purpose by Ima makes it illegal on public policy grounds.

Proper Form

Many contracts, if they contain the elements just discussed, are valid and enforceable even though they are created orally or by conduct. Recalling two earlier examples, you may be able to enter into an oral listing agreement with a real estate agent to locate a buyer for Blackacre and you may conduct an auction of various items of personal property located on Blackacre whereby contracts of sale arise by the conduct of the auctioneer and the bidders. However, the law requires some types of contracts to be evidenced by a writing in order to be enforceable. Many agreements relating to real estate are subject to this requirement — sales contracts, installment sale contracts, option contracts, exchange contracts, and, in many states, listing agreements.

The laws imposing the requirement of a writing are generally known as the Statute of Frauds. As the name suggests, this statute is aimed at preventing fraudulent claims based on alleged oral contracts whose existence and terms may be subject to doubt and controversy. The purpose of this statute, then, is to require more definite and reliable proof of the existence and terms of a contract. For this reason this statute requires that certain contracts be *evidenced* by a writing, not that the contract itself be in writing. Obviously, if the contract has, in fact, been reduced to writing, this requirement has been met. But also, any writing, such as a memorandum, note, letter, or so on, drafted after the oral contract is made will also satisfy the Statute of Frauds requirements. To be effective the writing must:

1. Adequately identify the parties, subject matter and terms of the contract, and
2. Be signed by the party to be charged or the agent.

This last requirement means that before one party to a contract subject to the Statute of Frauds can have the contract enforced against him or her, either the party or his or her representative must have signed the writing evidencing the contract. Notice that the legal effect of not having the contract evidenced by a writing is that it is unenforceable — proper form is a prerequisite to enforcement of the agreement.

ENDING THE CONTRACT: PERFORMANCE, DISCHARGE, AND BREACH

Contracted relationships extend over some period of time as the parties carry out their promises. They can be terminated by either discharge or breach. The duties in a contract can be discharged by either completing all obligations or by the occurrence of certain events that legally end the contractual relationship. A contract can also be terminated by a failure of either party to perform as promised; a situation called breach. Thus, a contract may end by discharge or breach.

Discharge

Discharge by Performance The most common method by which a contract is completed is by each party performing his or her obligations under it. Your contract with Ima Buyer, for example, will normally be completed by your conveying title to Blackacre to Ima and by Ima paying you $60,000. As you remember, prior to the performance of these obligations the contract is said to be executory; after performance by you and Ima the contract is said to be executed.

Discharge Involving Nonperformance Obligations under a contract can be discharged in ways other than performance. First, obligations can be discharged by agreement of the parties. For example, you and Ima could terminate your contract by **mutual recision.** A document signed by each of you rescinding the contract would discharge each of you from your obligations under the contract. Sometimes the agreement involves a third person. Assume that Ima purchases Blackacre and finances the purchase by borrowing money from a bank. Ima will sign a note evidencing the debt and her promise to repay the loan. If Ima later wants to sell Blackacre to her sister Ura, the three parties (Ima, Ura, and the bank) may enter into an agreement whereby Ura promises to repay the note (i.e., become a substitute debtor) and the bank releases Ima from obligation on the note and agrees to look only to Ura for repayment. This type of agreement, which substitutes one promisor for another, is called a **novation.**

In some situations, it is not necessary for both parties to agree to terminate a contract. That is, the contract can be rescinded by one party acting alone. This situation is the result of legislation passed as a result of the consumer protection movement. One such example of the ability of a buyer to back out of a transaction is in interstate land sales. The Interstate Land Sales Act provides that buyers of such land have certain rights of recision.

Second, obligations under a contract can be discharged by circumstances beyond the control of the parties. For example, the contract may state a **condition precedent** to the obligation of one party to perform. A condition precedent is an event that must occur or a condition that must exist before an obligation for one of the parties is created. If the condition precedent does not occur, the obligation to perform is discharged. If your contract with Ima is conditioned on her ability to secure a loan of 90 percent of the purchase price from a lending institution, and if no lending institution will loan her this amount, then she is discharged from her obligation to buy Blackacre. Also, **destruction** of the subject matter of a contract through no fault of the parties may discharge their obligations. If you contract to sell some old farm machinery on Blackacre to a purchaser, destruction of the machinery by fire before its delivery to the purchaser will generally discharge his or her obligation to purchase and pay for it.

Breach

The failure of a contracting party to perform an obligation that has not been discharged results in a **breach** of the contract by that party. You would breach your contract with Ima by failing to convey title to Blackacre to her; she would breach the contract with you by failing to pay you the $60,000 purchase price. In either case the law gives remedies to the nonbreaching party against the breaching party.

The normal remedy available for breach of contract is money damages. The object of this remedy is to put the nonbreaching party in as good a position as he or she would have been in had the breach not occurred, that is, had the contract been performed. Remember that the law of contracts is to allow people to plan for the future and rely on promises related to future conduct. Law gives protection to this reliance through money damages in case of breach. So if you fail to convey title to Blackacre to Ima and force her to buy a similar tract of land, Whiteacre, for $70,000, Ima's expectations have been defeated to the extent of $10,000. But she can be put in the same position economically as she would have been in had you not breached the contract if she recovers $10,000 from you. Thus, Ima can bring a lawsuit against you to recover her monetary damages of $10,000.

But wait a minute! Has the law put Ima in the same position as she would have been in had you performed the contract? Had you performed, she would now own Blackacre, not Whiteacre. Most people would agree that no two tracts of land are exactly alike. If nothing else, their location is different. But, more fundamentally, each tract of land has an individual identity formed of many unique characteristics. Blackacre may have better quality soil than Whiteacre; Blackacre may have a better location for commercial development than Whiteacre; or Blackacre may have a better view esthetically than Whiteacre. Consequently, money damages alone have never been viewed as adequate for breach of a contract for the sale of real estate. The breach of this type of contract gives rise to the remedy of specific performance. Thus, if you fail to convey title to Blackacre to Ima, she can maintain a lawsuit against you for specific performance and compel you to convey title to her.

REAL ESTATE SALES CONTRACTS

Purpose

We purchase most items quickly once we have made the decision to do so. Once you decided to buy this book (although your professor effectively made the decision for you!), you took it to the bookstore cashier and immediately purchased it by paying with cash, check, or credit card. Some transactions are more complex, however, and therefore require more time to complete. Real estate sales transactions fall into this category.

Ima Buyer will not purchase Blackacre as rapidly as you purchased this book. There are two principal reasons why. First, Ima will want to be sure that you have title to Blackacre and will want you to provide her with proof of your ownership. Title is something you did not worry about when you purchased this book at the bookstore. You assumed that the bookstore had title. The law protects you in that assumption when you purchase personal property from a dealer. But different principles apply to the sale of real estate, making it unsafe for a purchaser to assume the seller has title. Therefore, the seller must provide proof of title. The process of providing proof of title and examining that proof is the title examination phase of the transaction, described in Chapter 5, and is time consuming. Second, Ima will probably not have the $60,000 purchase price, but will have to borrow it from a commercial lender. The process of arranging financing through the use of a note and mortgage, discussed in Chapter 14, is also time consuming.

But you do not want to hold Blackacre off the market while Ima checks title and arranges financing unless you are sure Ima is committed to buying once the arrangements are made. And Ima does not want to go to the trouble and expense of checking title and arranging financing unless she is sure you are committed to selling once the arrangements are made. Each of you needs a binding commitment from the other related to future conduct. One purpose of a real estate sales contract is to bind the parties to an agreement that will take some time to complete.

A second purpose also relates to the inherent complexity of a real estate sales transaction. Many details must be agreed upon. What kind of title must you prove you have? What kind of financing must Ima be willing to accept? What kind of deed must you use to convey Blackacre to Ima? Who bears the risk of loss if Blackacre is damaged by fire, flood, or tornado between the time you sign the contract and the time you convey title? The contract contains the agreement of you and Ima on these points. It serves as a ''blueprint'' of the agreement you and Ima have made. This is the second purpose of the contract—to serve as a blueprint that controls the terms of the transaction until its completion.

Elements of a Sales Contract

Let's examine how these two purposes are accomplished. Assume that your attorney has drafted the contract in Table 6.3 for you and Ima to sign. This contract contains language sufficient to bind you and Ima to sell and buy, respectively, and it also contains a blueprint for the most commonly found aspects of a real estate sales transaction.

Provision 1 contains the full legal name of the seller who, for simplicity, is thereafter referred to throughout the contract as the "Seller." There are similar provisions for the buyer.

Provision 2 contains a direct promise to sell by the seller followed by a direct promise to buy by the buyer. These mutual promises create a bilateral contract between the parties, enforceable by each, subject to the later provisions of the contract.

Provision 3 describes the property by county, state, and one of the legally recognized methods of describing land, the rectangular survey method. This description also contains a general description of the quantity of land involved. When two or more methods of description are used, care should be exercised to insure that they correspond to each other. Informal designations, such as "Blackacre," should be avoided.

Provision 4 describes that improvements, called fixtures, are included in the sale. It is not legally necessary that this clause be included because the law defines what fixtures are and holds that fixtures to real estate are included in the sale of the real estate unless specifically excluded. However, it is desirable for the parties to specify questionable items to be included in the sale in order to avoid misunderstanding. This is the "blueprint" function of the contract at work clarifying the details of the agreement.

Provision 5 states what the total purchase price is and how it is to be paid. Payment is often made in two installments: (1) at the execution of the contract and (2) at the closing of the contract when title is conveyed. Notice that the $5000 paid at the execution of the contract serves a dual function: it is not only part payment of the purchase price, but also earnest money that can be retained by the seller in case the buyer breaches the contract, as specified at 14. The paragraph specifies in what form the balance of the purchase price is to be presented to the seller at closing. A personal check is normally not acceptable.

Provision 6 contains the financing contingency, which protects the buyer. This paragraph should be read in conjunction with 13. Together, they allow the buyer to cancel the contract if she cannot obtain financing of a specified type within a specified time. These paragraphs prevent the buyer from going out on the "financial limb" of having to purchase whether financing is available or not and regardless of the terms of the available financing.

Table 6.3. Real Estate Sales Contract

(1) Alphonso Stuart Dent ("Seller") (2) agrees to sell and Ima Land Buyer ("Buyer") agrees to buy (3) the following described real estate ("Property") located in College County, State of Euphoria: E½ of SE¼ of SE¼ and E½ of SW¼ of SE¼ of SE¼ of Section 36, T1N, R2W, Hometown Meridian, containing 25 acres, more or less (4) together with the following improvements: all structures and all plumbing and lighting fixtures, heating and cooling systems, water heaters, built-in stoves and ranges, bathroom fixtures and window coverings contained therein, and all fences, trees, shrubbery, and plants.

(5) The total purchase price is $60,000.00 payable by Buyer as follows: $5000.00 on execution of this contract, receipt of which is acknowledged by Seller, as earnest money and part payment of purchase price; and the balance of the purchase price in cash or certified check upon delivery of the deed ("closing").

(6) This contract is contingent upon the Buyer obtaining a mortgage loan on this Property within 21 days of the execution date of this contract in an amount not less than $55,000.00 for a term not less than 30 years at an interest rate no higher than 14% and loan commitment fees not to exceed 2% of the loan amount.

(7) Seller shall furnish buyer at Seller's expense (a standard American Land Title Association title insurance policy issued by Euphoria Title Insurance Company) (an abstract of title certified at least to the date of this contract) showing title vested in (Buyer) (Seller) subject only to utility easements and building restrictions of record and no other interests.

(8) All taxes other than general ad valorem taxes for the current calendar year and all special assessments due upon the date of closing shall be paid by the Seller.

(9) Ad valorem taxes for the current calendar year, rents, and all income expenses related to ownership shall be prorated between the Seller and Buyer as of the date of closing.

(10) Seller shall furnish Buyer, at Seller's expense, a current report by a licensed exterminating company reflecting that buildings on the Property are free from visible termite infestation and visible termite damage.

(11) Until closing or transfer of possession, risk of loss to the Property, ordinary wear and tear excepted, shall be upon Seller; after closing or transfer of possession, such risks shall be upon Buyer.

(12) The closing shall be held on or before June 30, 198-. At the closing Seller shall deliver to Buyer a duly executed and acknowledged warranty deed conveying the Property to Buyer. Possession of the Property shall be transferred to Buyer at the closing.

(13) If the Buyer is unable to obtain a mortgage loan as specified above or if the Seller is unable to deliver title as specified above, or if the Property is destroyed or materially damaged prior to closing or transfer of possession, the Buyer may terminate this contract and recover the earnest money in full. If the Seller fails to fulfill any other obligation herein, the Buyer may terminate this contract and recover the earnest money in full, accept lesser performance, or sue for specific performance.

(14) If the Buyer fails to fulfill any obligation herein, the Seller may sue for specific performance, or, in the alternative, be released from all obligation under this contract and retain the earnest money as liquidated damages. The Seller and Buyer agree that it would be impractical and extremely difficult to determine actual damages.

(15) Time is of the essence in this contract.

(16) Seller has employed Terra Firma Realty Company as Broker and agrees to pay $2500.00 to Broker in accordance with the Listing Agreement between Seller and Broker. If this contract is not completed because of a breach by the Buyer, the Broker shall share equally the earnest money retained by Seller as liquidated damages, not to exceed the above-stated commission.

(continued)

Table 6.3. Real Estate Sales Contract (cont.)

⑰ This contract contains the complete agreement of the Seller and Buyer and supercedes all previous negotiations, representations, and agreements between them and their agents. This contract can be amended only by a written agreement signed by Seller and Buyer.

⑱ When executed by Seller and Buyer, this contract shall be binding upon and inure to the benefit of Seller and Buyer, their heirs, legal representative, successors, and assigns.

⑲ Unless all the parties whose names appear at the beginning of this contract sign it on or before the 5th day of June, 198-, this contract shall not become effective.

⑳

Seller	Date	Buyer	Date

Seller	Date	Buyer	Date

Provision 7 specifies what evidence of title the seller must furnish the buyer. This paragraph is for the buyer's protection because, without it, the seller would not have to furnish any evidence of title, although the law would imply an obligation on the seller to have a marketable title, one that a reasonably prudent purchaser would accept without any reduction in the purchase price. In many areas title insurance is used, in which case the language in the first set of parentheses would be included. In other areas of the country an abstract containing copies of the documents affecting title recorded in various public records is provided for the buyer's attorney to examine. After examination, the attorney will render an opinion to the buyer concerning whether the seller's title is marketable. If an abstract is to be provided, then the language in the second set of parentheses would be included. This paragraph should also be read in conjunction with 13. Together they allow the buyer to cancel the contract in case the seller cannot provide satisfactory evidence of title. Title examination and protection were covered in detail in the preceding chapter.

Every tract of land is invariably subject to interests held by third parties. It is very rare to find one person who owns the totality of interests in land. Blackacre is no exception. Therefore, these outstanding interests need to be excepted from the seller's obligation to furnish evidence of a marketable title. All exceptions agreed to by the seller and buyer should be included in the contract. This contract includes the most commonly found exceptions related to urban land — utility easements and building restrictions.

Certain monetary obligations related to the property are customarily payable entirely by either the seller or the buyer. Provision 8 provides that property taxes and any special assessments, due at the time of closing are to be paid by the seller.

On the other hand, there are other monetary rights and obligations that are customarily shared by both seller and buyer. For example, property taxes are paid in arrears in some areas. This means that if you sell Blackacre during the tax year, the new owner will receive the tax bill for the entire year at year end. Ordinarily you will be expected to pay the buyer your *pro rata* share of the taxes at closing. This sharing approach is called proration and is provided for at 9. Prorating income and expense items insures that each party receives the benefits and shares the burdens of ownership for that time when each held ownership. If ownership is transferred during the middle of an income or expense period, the income or expense is prorated as of the time of transfer.

Provision 10 relates to the physical condition of the property and requires the seller to furnish evidence that any structures on the property are free of visible termite infestation or damage. Real estate sales historically have been "as is" sales, with the buyer bearing the risk as to the quality of the real estate. Sales contracts today are increasingly placing greater responsibility on the seller concerning the quality of the real estate. This provision is a reflection of this trend. Some contracts go further and require that all electrical, mechanical, and plumbing systems be in good working order as of closing and give the buyer the right to inspect the premises in order to determine their condition.

Provision 11 also relates to the physical condition of the premises. Historically, the law placed the risk of loss due to natural disasters such as fire, flood, tornado, hurricane, or earthquake on the buyer during the executory period of the contract. Under this view, if Blackacre were damaged by fire prior to closing, Ima would still be required to purchase at the contract price of $60,000. This contract provision alters this result by placing the risk of loss on the person who has either title or possession of Blackacre. The theory of this clause is that the risk of loss should be on the person who has the beneficial incidents of ownership.

Provision 12 deals with the closing time when the sale will be completed by the seller delivering the deed to the buyer and the buyer paying the purchase price to the seller. This paragraph provides three important details. First, it specifies the time within which the closing must occur. This prevents the contract from being open-ended as to completion. But it is also a potentially risky clause to both parties because unforeseen difficulties could prevent either party from being able to close at the time specified. Second, it specifies what kind of deed the seller must deliver to the buyer. The deed must be a warranty deed and in a form fit for recording in the public land records. Third, it specifies that possession is to be transferred to the buyer at closing. If the parties want to transfer possession prior to or subsequent to closing, they should consider a separate lease agreement that sets out in detail the rights and responsibilities of the parties.

Provision 13 specifies the buyer's remedies in case the contract is not completed due to some event other than his or her own fault. First, the buyer is allowed to rescind the contract and recover the earnest money if the financing, title, or damage contingencies found in 6, 7, and 11 occur. Second, the buyer is given additional remedies in case the seller defaults on his or her obligations. For example, if you had a change of heart about wanting to sell Blackacre and refused to convey title, as an alternative to recision of the contract and return of the earnest money, Ima could sue to require you to specifically perform the contract by conveying title.

Provision 14 specifies the seller's remedies in case the contract is not completed due to the buyer's default. First, the seller is given the right to specific performance. But in case the seller does not want to go to the effort, time, and expense of forcing the buyer to complete the transaction, the contract also specifies that the seller may retain the earnest money as the damages suffered as a result of the buyer's breach. It is important that the contract reflect the fact that the parties have agreed in advance that the earnest money represents an estimation of the seller's damages and that actual damages would be difficult to ascertain. It is also important for the seller to consider what the potential damages might be at the time the parties agree on what the earnest money deposit will be. Costs such as real estate agent fees, attorney fees, title costs, and loss of profit should be considered in order for the earnest money deposit to be adequate from the seller's standpoint and yet not excessive.

Provision 15 is a clause that requires each party to perform obligations at the exact time specified in the contract. Without such a clause, the law allows each party a reasonable time within which to perform. Such an open-ended right can create problems when the parties are operating within a tight time frame. But this clause can also be a two-edged sword because it can cause a party to be in default when a short time delay would be all that is needed to solve a problem and allow performance to occur.

Provision 16 is a clause that protects all three parties when a real estate agent has been involved in the sale. It protects the seller by specifying the commission. It protects the buyer by specifying that the seller is responsible for paying the commission. And it protects the real estate agent by providing for the circumstances in which the commission is due.

Provision 17 is a protective clause for both parties that prevents any prior or subsequent informal agreements from altering the formal contract.

Provision 18 makes the contract enforceable by and against the successors in interest to the seller and buyer. For example, the death of you or Ima would have no effect on the contract. Each of you should be sure you want this result; otherwise, this clause could create an unintended hardship on your successors.

Provision 19 is a clause that allows either party to use this contract originally as an offer and require the other party to accept the terms contained within a specified period of time. If not accepted within the time specified, the offer would lapse automatically. The offer must be accepted in its entirety; any change in the terms of the offer would constitute a rejection of the offer and the advancement of a counteroffer.

At Provision 20 space is provided for the signatures of the parties and the dating of the signatures. The signatures are required by the Statute of Frauds for the contract to be enforceable against the contracting parties. The dating is necessary because of 6 and 19 of the contract; otherwise, dating would not be necessary.

One last point about this sample contract (or almost any contract) should be emphasized; it is a document subject to negotiation. Any and all of the terms can be changed by the parties by mutual agreement. Negotiating a contract is a give-and-take affair. The objective is to reach an agreement that is satisfactory to all parties.

OTHER COMMON REAL ESTATE CONTRACTS

The real estate sales contract is only one general type of real estate contract. Many others are commonly used, including listing contracts and installment sales contracts. The character and use of each of these contracts are now considered.

Listing Contracts

You may very well need help in locating a buyer for Blackacre. Of course, you could tell your friends and relatives and advertise in the newspaper, but often you need the help of a professional real estate agent who has the expertise to market your property. An agreement between you and an agent whereby you promise to pay the agent a fee for locating a buyer is another important contract relating to real estate.

The contract of employment between seller and agent is known as the listing agreement, that is, property is "listed" with the agent. In most states this contract can be oral, although some states require the contract to be in writing to be valid and enforceable. It should always be in writing for clarity to avoid misunderstandings between the parties and must contain the elements of any valid contract.

This contract creates a relationship between the parties known as a principal/agent relationship. The seller, as principal, authorizes the real estate agent, as agent, to act for him or her in locating a buyer. (In some cases, an agent is asked to find properties for a buyer.) This is the only action the agent can perform for the seller unless the contract provides for additional authority. Often, for example, the contract gives the agent authority to receive and hold a down payment from a prospective buyer who is making an offer to the seller. The listing contract is a unilateral one, since only the principal promises to do something, pay the agent a fee *if* a buyer is found for the property.

A real estate agent is a service-provider in the real estate transaction. In addition to performing the service of locating a buyer, the agent often helps a buyer obtain financing for the purchase and helps both parties in the details of closing the transaction. These services are typically provided for a fee, usually paid by the seller. Some agents, however, will provide only part or all of these services for a graduated fee.

In this principal/agent relationship, each party owes certain obligations to the other. The agent is obligated, among other functions: (1) to perform the contract by using reasonable efforts to locate a buyer, (2) to keep any down payment received from the buyer in a separate bank account from the agent's own account and to account for the money, and (3) to be loyal to the seller (principal) by communicating all offers to the seller, by not purchasing the property himself without full disclosure to the seller, and by not disclosing confidential information received from the seller.

These obligations can create problems, particularly in the area of loyalty to the seller. Some people argue that the agent actually renders services to both parties to the transaction and that the realities of the modern transaction are that the agent serves as a "middleman," facilitating the transfer of property between seller and buyer. For this reason, these individuals would not fully apply the principal/agent relationship between seller and agent. But, for the most part, the traditional rules of principal/agent law are applied to real estate agents.

The seller (principal) owes the duty to pay the agreed-upon commission to the agent when the agent has earned it under the listing contract. When the agent has earned his or her commission depends on the type of listing contract entered into by the parties. There are three main types of listing contracts.

One type of listing contract is the **open** or **non-exclusive listing**. Here the agent earns a commission only when he or she is the **procuring cause** of locating a buyer who is ready, willing, and able to purchase the property on terms stipulated or agreed to by the seller. The seller can hire more than one agent. Once one agent, or the seller himself, locates a buyer, the agency relationship with the other agents is terminated and they are not entitled to a commission. Notice that to earn a commission the agent must meet three requirements: (1) the agent must be the procuring cause, that is, be responsible for locating and motivating the buyer; (2) the buyer must be *ready and willing* to purchase and to enter into a contract to do so; and (3) the buyer must be *able,* in terms of financial ability, to purchase the property. Because of the uncertainty of ever earning a commission under these circumstances, even after expenditure of time and money, many agents do not like open listing contracts.

A second type of listing contract is the **exclusive agency.** Here the seller agrees not to hire other agents. If another agent locates a ready, willing, and able buyer, the listing broker is still entitled to a commission. This type of listing gives the agent greater protection in spending the time and money necessary to locate a buyer. However, the seller still has the right to attempt to locate a buyer and, if successful, the listing agent is not entitled to a commission.

A third type of listing contract is the **exclusive right to sell.** Here the listing broker is entitled to a commission if a ready, willing, and able buyer is located during the term of the listing agreement, regardless of whether the buyer is located by the agent, the seller, or a third party. This type of listing gives the greatest protection to agents and is favored by them.

There are two variations of these types of listing agreements. The first variation involves a **multiple listing service (MLS),** also known as multilist. This service involves a local organization of agents who share listings with each other in order to increase sales opportunities. Members of the organization agree to split a commission earned on such listings between the listing agent and the selling agent.

A second variation is known as a **net listing.** Here the seller specifies the net price he or she wants for the property and allows the agent to sell the property at any price possible over the net price. Rather than a stated commission, the agent's fee is the difference, if any, between the sales price and the net price. This form of listing is not recommended because experience shows that it leads to misunderstandings in agent/seller and agent/buyer relationships. This listing has been outlawed in many states. The important topics of agency and listing agreements are considered again in Chapters 20 and 21.

Leases

The rights of possession and use are frequently exchanged for consideration. The person giving up the rights of possession and use is called the lessor or landlord and the person receiving these rights in return for giving consideration, called rent, is the tenant or lessee. The document creating this landlord and tenant arrangement is a contract called a **lease.**

Under the Statute of Frauds, leases for more than one year must be in writing. It is a good idea to reduce all leases to writing to avoid misunderstandings and provide maximum legal protection to both parties. To be valid, a lease must meet the minimum standards of any contract:

Reality of assent   Lawful objective

Competent parties   Proper form

Consideration

From a practical standpoint, leases will contain much more detail than the minimum standards of legal acceptability. The lease will contain a description of the property being leased and any restrictions on the uses the lessee can make of the property. The lease will also specify the rental period, if and how the lease can be renewed, how rents will be determined, and when rents are due. Other items frequently included in the lease are conditions or covenants relating the habitability of the property, the ability of the tenant to sublease the property, how fixtures placed on the property by the tenant are to be treated when the lease terminates, and responsibility for maintenance and repairs. Most residential leases are relatively short, usually two to three pages. However, leases for office space, shopping center space, and other commercial uses are somewhat longer. It is not unusual for shopping center leases to be 20 to 30 pages long.

None of the provisions of the lease can be in violation of landlord/tenant laws enacted by the state. These laws, establishing the rights and obligations of landlords and tenants, have undergone significant change in recent years, generally in the direction of providing more protection for the tenant. The impact of these laws and the importance of various lease provisions to the landlord and tenant are considered in Chapter 22, dealing with property management.

Installment Sales Contracts

We have discussed the fact that the ordinary real estate sales contract has a dual purpose: to obligate the parties to fulfill their promises to sell and buy and to serve as a blueprint for the transaction. Once all the terms of the contract are met, the seller conveys title to the buyer and the contract comes to an end. This process usually takes only a matter of weeks or, at the most, a few months.

Notice that one function the ordinary sales contract does not serve is a financing function. It does not provide a financial method for the buyer to purchase the property. Rather, it merely provides for what kind of financing the buyer will obtain. The types of financing most often used are discussed in Chapters 14 through 16 and involves the use of a note and mortgage.

The installment sales contract, unlike the ordinary real estate sales contract, provides a financial method for the buyer to purchase the property. In fact, the contract is the financing tool used, rather than a note and mortgage. This type of contract provides for the buyer to have the right of possession and the obligation to pay the purchase price to the seller in installments over a period of months or years. Pending the completion of all the installments, the seller retains the title; upon completion the seller promises to convey title to the buyer. This contract remains in effect for a longer period than does the ordinary sales contract. For this reason, the ordinary real estate sales contract is sometimes referred to as a short-term contract and the installment sales contract as a **long-term contract, land contract,** or **contract for deed.**

The contract governs the rights of the parties during its term while the buyer is paying the purchase price in installments. The buyer is normally given the right to possession and the responsibility for paying taxes and property insurance and maintaining the property. In many ways the buyer acts as the owner would. But he or she is not yet the owner since the seller retains the title. A variety of problems can result from this arrangement. Who is to convey title if the seller dies before the buyer completes the installment payments? What right does the seller or buyer have to convey other interests in the property? The parties must carefully arrange the installment sales contract in order to avoid unexpected difficulties during its term.

The contract also governs the rights of the parties in case the buyer defaults on any obligations under the contract. The buyer's principal obligations will normally be to pay taxes and property insurance, maintain the property, and pay the installments on the purchase price when due. Typically, the contract provides that if the buyer defaults on any of these obligations, the seller has the right to declare the contract void, to retain all installments already paid such as liquidated damages and rent, and to regain possession of the property. This remedy is harsh compared to the remedy available to the financing party under a note and mortgage, as is explained in Chapter 14. For this reason, many states are beginning to protect the buyer in the installment sales contract from this type of forfeiture and give the seller no greater rights than he or she would have had if the sale was financed through the more traditional note and mortgage.

Option Contracts

If you, for a sum of money, were to give Ima Buyer the right to buy Blackacre for $60,000 if she exercised her right within one year, you and Ima would have entered into an **option contract.** Notice that this contract is different from a real estate sales contract in that Ima has no obligation to purchase Blackacre; rather, she has the privilege of exercising or not exercising her option to buy. Notice also that this contract is different from a mere offer to sell on your part, which could be revoked at any time before acceptance. The option, because it is based on consideration, is a valid contract that gives Ima the exclusive right to purchase Blackacre for a specified price within the prescribed period.

The option contract gives the option holder time within which to decide whether to purchase or not, with the assurance that the property will be available for purchase throughout the option period. If Ima exercises the option, a mutually enforceable contract of sale arises. If Ima does not exercise the option within the specified period, the option contract is discharged and she loses only the money paid for the option. The option contract should specify whether the consideration paid for the option applies to the purchase price if the option is exercised.

Exchange Contracts

We have been assuming throughout this chapter that you have wanted to sell Blackacre for cash in order to finance your schooling. Most real estate transactions are for monetary consideration. But in other circumstances, you might prefer to exchange Blackacre for another tract of land.

Parties usually exchange real estate rather than sell it for cash for two common reasons. First, it may be preferable to acquire other property without raising a large amount of cash. For example, if you were farming Blackacre and wanted to get out of farming and into the farm machinery business, you could sell Blackacre for cash and use that cash to buy other land on which to start a farm machinery business. But if you could trade directly for the land you want, it would be much more convenient. More important than convenience, however, is the fact that an exchange could help you and the other property owners arrange a deal if the money market is tight. If interest rates are high, it may be difficult or financially unwise for a prospective buyer to borrow the money necessary to buy Blackacre. A property exchange could sidestep or reduce the necessity for borrowing money.

A second reason for exchanging property is an income tax reason. Federal income tax law provides that no gain or loss is recognized if real estate held for trade, business, or investment purposes is exchanged solely for real estate of a *like kind* that is also going to be held for trade, business, or investment purposes. This provision could fit our illustration in the previous paragraph. This means that, in certain situations, any profit you make in the exchange of Blackacre with another property will not be taxed at the time of the transaction. Such a **tax-deferred exchange** between or among parties can be financially advantageous. However, you should understand that taxes will be due in the future when, and if, you ever sell instead of trade the property.

Exchanges can be entered into among three or more parties as well as between just two. For example, assume that you are farming Blackacre and Ima is operating a farm machinery business on Whiteacre. You would like to own Whiteacre but Ima does not want Blackacre. Assume that E.Z. Rest owns motel property, Greenacre, and wants to retire to the country. If you could interest Ima in acquiring Greenacre and E.Z. in acquiring Blackacre, then a three-way exchange could be worked out.

Real estate of equal value does not have to be exchanged. For example, if Blackacre is worth $60,000 and Whiteacre is worth $50,000, you could convey Blackacre to Ima in exchange for Whiteacre and $10,000. Or, alternatively, if Blackacre is worth $60,000 and Whiteacre is worth $100,000 and is subject to a $40,000 mortgage, you could convey your unmortgaged property to exchange for Ima's mortgaged property.

In the exchange transaction the exchange contract contains all of the terms and is subject to all of the considerations that we have already discussed relative to the real estate sales contract. But because of the nature of the transaction as an exchange, the exchange contract must be carefully drafted in certain respects. For example, care must be taken in describing the consideration (the properties) for the exchange in order to receive full tax benefits. Also, because several real estate agents are often involved, care must be taken in describing each agent, the commission each is entitled to, and who owes the commission.

SUMMARY

You have learned in this chapter that contracts help people plan for the future by making certain promises related to future actions legally enforceable. All contracts are not alike; they vary in many respects. These variations cause contracts to be classified according to: (1) how they are created (express, implied-in-fact, and implied-in-law contracts); (2) whether the contract calls for a promise in exchange for a promise or an act in exchange for a promise (bilateral versus unilateral contracts); (3) whether the contract contains a defect that does not invalidate the contract until raised or that automatically invalidates the contract (voidable versus void contracts); and (4) whether or not there are remedies available for breach of the contract (enforceable versus unenforceable contracts).

The elements necessary for the creation of a valid and enforceable contract are: (1) mutual agreement between the parties, expressed by an offer and acceptance, free from fraud, misrepresentation, mistake, undue influence, duress, menace, or jest; (2) the existence of competent parties who are not affected by minority, mental illness, intoxication, or guardianship; (3) the existence of consideration; (4) a lawful objective; and (5) a proper form, such as a writing, as to contracts involving real estate. The most common way in which a contract is completed is by each party performing his or her obligations. However, obligations imposed by a contract can also be discharged by mutual agreement and by certain conditions. The failure to perform a contractual obligation not otherwise discharged is a breach of the contract. The normal remedy for breach of contract is the recovery of money damages. However, the remedy of specific performance may also be available for the breach of a real estate sales contract.

The most important contract related to real estate is the real estate sales contract. It serves the dual functions of: (1) binding the parties to their agreement during the time-consuming process of arranging and completing the sale, and (2) creating the blueprint supplying all the necessary details of an innately complex transaction. Other common real estate contracts include: (1) the listing contract between a prospective seller and a real estate agent; (2) the lease contract creating a leasehold estate for the lessee; (3) the installment sales contract, which is a financing tool for purchasing real estate; (4) the option contract, giving one the exclusive right to purchase real estate for a specified period; and (5) the exchange contract, calling for the exchange of real estate between or among owners.

QUICK QUIZ

1. Which of the following is not a way in which contracts may be classified?

    a. bilateral versus unilateral
    b. voidable versus void
    c. fair versus unfair
    d. enforceable versus unenforceable

2. Which of the following are remedies for breach of contract?

    a. monetary damages and imprisonment
    b. specific performance and fines
    c. fines and imprisonment
    d. monetary damages and specific performance

3. A contractual relationship can end by

    a. performance   c. breach
    b. discharge   d. all of the above

4. Which of the following is not an essential element of a valid contract?

    a. must be typewritten   c. reality of assent
    b. competent parties   d. proper form

5. A contract signed by a minor is

    a. valid   c. void
    b. voidable   d. evidence of fraud

6. _____ is a legal term that means "a meeting of the minds."

7. A(n) _____ contract is created when both parties to a contract promise to perform or not perform certain acts.

8. Compelling a person by threat or force to do or agree to do an act is _____.

9. The contract between the seller and agent that creates the agency relationship is called a(n) _____.

10. A(n) _____ is an event that must occur or a condition that must exist before an obligation for one of the parties to a contract is created.

QUESTIONS AND EXERCISES

1. What is the difference between fraud and misrepresentation?

2. What may constitute "consideration" in a contract?

3. What two purposes does a real estate sales contract serve?

4. Why do people often seek a specific performance remedy in breaches of real estate sales contracts?

5. What characteristics must a valid offer have?

6. What are the essential elements of a valid contract?

KEY TERMINOLOGY

acceptance
agreement
breach
competent parties
condition precedent
consideration
  good
  valuable
contract
  bilateral
  enforceable
  exchange
  express
  for deed
  implied-in-fact
  implied-in-law
  installment sales
  land
  listing
  long-term
  option
  sales
  unilateral
  valid
  void
  voidable
destruction
discharge
duress

emancipated minors
exchange contract
exclusive agency listing
exclusive right to sell listing
executory
fraud
lawful objective
lease
marketable title
menace
misrepresentation
mistakes
money damages
multiple listing service
mutual recision
net listing
non-exclusive listing
novation
offer
open listing
performance
procuring cause
reality of assent
specific performance
undue influence

IF YOU WANT TO READ MORE

ROBERT N. CORLEY, PETER J. SHEDD, and CHARLES F. FLOYD, *Real Estate and the Law* (New York: Random House, Inc., 1982), Chapter 11.

BENJAMIN N. HENSZEY and RONALD M. FRIEDMAN, *Real Estate Law* (Boston: Warren, Gorham & Lamont, 1979), Chapter 5.

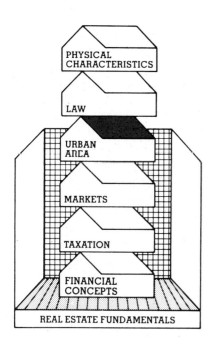

PHYSICAL CHARACTERISTICS

LAW

URBAN AREA

MARKETS

TAXATION

FINANCIAL CONCEPTS

REAL ESTATE FUNDAMENTALS

7

The Urban Area: real estate economics and location

PREVIEW   Your farm, Blackacre, is located on the edge of the developed area of your town. How the community develops economically and demographically, and how that economic development is translated into the need for space, will directly affect how Blackacre can best be used and its value. Your problem is to analyze the present situation, the changes likely to occur, and what they mean for the use and value of Blackacre. Fortunately, certain principles underly the economic growth and land use patterns found in urban areas of all sizes. In addition, certain principles affect all individual location decisions, whether urban or rural. This chapter examines the economic principles of urban development and the concepts underlying location decisions. You will learn about:

1. The historical development of urban areas in the United States.
2. How urban development is affected by national economic and demographic trends.
3. The concept of economic base and its importance to real estate.
4. Where to find urban economic and demographic information.
5. Patterns of urban land use, their causes, and their importance to you in the real estate business.
6. How location decisions are made.

Chances are good that you live in an urban area, since about 75 percent of all people in the United States do. Not surprisingly, a high percentage of all real estate activity occurs in urban areas to satisfy human needs for space in which to live, work, shop, and be entertained. For a particular community, the type, amount, and quality of space needed for these activities depends, in part, on its characteristics, such as the number of people employed, their occupations, their incomes, and their ages.

Different economic characteristics create demands for different kinds of space, and the types, quantity, and quality of space demanded affect all activity areas of the real estate business. For instance, a city with a concentration of industrial employment will need more industrial and warehouse space than a city of similar size that serves as an office center. Likewise, the income of the workers in a town influences the quantity and quality of homes demanded. Other characteristics of the population also affect real estate. The study of a population is called **demography,** and the specific population characteristics are called **demographic characteristics.** An example of a demographic characteristic affecting real estate is the increase in the number of unrelated couples forming households, which has increased the need for additional housing units. The increasing average age of the U.S. population is another demographic characteristic affecting the amount and types of space demanded. An understanding of how economic and demographic factors affect urban areas is an important tool for your bag of real estate skills.

DEVELOPMENT OF URBAN AREAS IN THE UNITED STATES

The United States has not always been an urbanized country, nor did it become one overnight. Urbanization has been going on throughout our history and continues today, although at a slower pace than in the recent past. Urbanization is not unique to the United States; much of the world has undergone the same transformation. Innovations coming out of the industrial revolution, which began in the eighteenth century, are at the heart of the development of cities as we now know them. This revolution of creativity generated tremendous advances in technology that influenced the structure and organization of the entire world.

Prior to the Industrial Revolution, cities were small by today's standards and were essentially trade and government centers. In this pre-Industrial Revolution setting, many people did not live in cities, for some good reasons. Agricultural techniques did not allow farmers and ranchers to produce enough food for large urban populations, nor were there means of getting it to urban areas. Few jobs were available in cities, as products were still handmade by artisans and transporting goods was so difficult and costly that products could not be shipped great distances to create larger markets. Not surprisingly, the lack of food and jobs severely limited the development of cities.

New technology introduced in the Industrial Revolution created a climate in which urban areas started to grow, and the primary catalyst for this growth was the development of the factory system. Factories, located in cities, required large numbers of workers and, since these workers had to live near their workplace, city populations began to swell. At the same time, improved agricultural techniques and transportation removed any remaining barriers to the growth of communities.

Urbanization created problems. Tenements were crowded and filthy. Poor sanitation facilities promoted the spread of disease, while the many factories produced massive amounts of air pollution. Ironically, the automobile, now a major source of pollution, was once hailed at the time as a solution to another urban pollution problem—the horse! In spite of these obstacles, cities continued to grow; large cities grew into metropolises, smaller cities grew into large ones, and new cities were established.

Different regions of the United States have experienced urbanization at different times and different rates. During the 1800s, cities developed in the East, Midwest, and West Coast areas in a manner that paralleled the development of the country as a whole. Eastern cities developed as manufacturing and financial centers for various reasons; one was the concentration of population that could be efficiently served from those cities. Midwestern cities developed as cattle centers, commodities centers, and "jumping off" points for pioneers and settlers heading west.

West Coast urban development was influenced by gold and other minerals located there. "Forty-niners" participating in the California Gold Rush of the mid-1800s, for example, had a great impact on the development of many California cities. Southern and southwestern cities have experienced much of their growth since World War II. Atlanta, Houston, Dallas, and Phoenix developed into cities of national importance during this period. Cities in the southern portion of the United States, called the "Sunbelt," are predicted to continue to grow at rates substantially above the national average, as seen in Figure 7.1.

Much of the movement from rural to urban areas which, along with overall population growth, fueled urban growth in the past is over. Smaller towns and rural areas are expected to receive substantial growth during the 1980s. Even so, urban growth should continue in the future because of overall U.S. population growth. From the current population of about 220 million, the U.S. population should reach 250 million by the year 2000. A significant portion of this growth will occur in urban areas. "Urban areas" as used in this chapter are not limited to large cities. They include virtually any concentration of people, from small towns of 2500 and up. Urban areas are not limited to the political boundaries of towns. Urban areas also include areas in which people do

Figure 7.1 Ten fastest growing cities in the 1980s. (Source: Chase Econometrics and Chicago Tribune Graphics.)

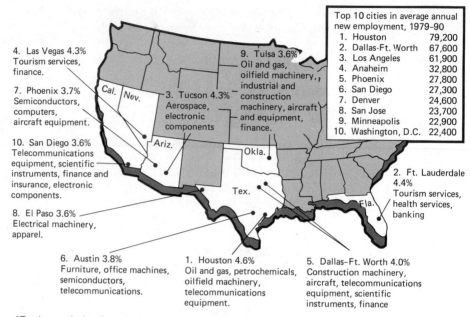

4. Las Vegas 4.3% Tourism services, finance.

7. Phoenix 3.7% Semiconductors, computers, aircraft equipment.

10. San Diego 3.6% Telecommunications equipment, scientific instruments, finance and insurance, electronic components.

8. El Paso 3.6% Electrical machinery, apparel.

3. Tucson 4.3% Aerospace, electronic components

9. Tulsa 3.6% Oil and gas, oilfield machinery, industrial and construction machinery, aircraft and equipment, finance.

2. Ft. Lauderdale 4.4% Tourism services, health services, banking

6. Austin 3.8% Furniture, office machines, semiconductors, telecommunications.

1. Houston 4.6% Oil and gas, petrochemicals, oilfield machinery, telecommunications equipment.

5. Dallas-Ft. Worth 4.0% Construction machinery, aircraft, telecommunications equipment, scientific instruments, finance

Top 10 cities in average annual new employment, 1979-90	
1. Houston	79,200
2. Dallas-Ft. Worth	67,600
3. Los Angeles	61,900
4. Anaheim	32,800
5. Phoenix	27,800
6. San Diego	27,300
7. Denver	24,600
8. San Jose	23,700
9. Minneapolis	22,900
10. Washington, D.C.	22,400

*Total nonagricultural employment
Chicago Tribune Graphic. Source: Chase Econometrics

not live in a community of 2500, but make regular trips for work, shopping, and other purposes to a nearby town or city. Using this larger concept of an urban area, a very large percentage of Americans are "urbanites."

The remarkable satellite photograph and map in Figure 7.2 show the results of urban development in the United States. The photograph is of lights from urban areas and, even though only urban areas of about 40,000 people or more are visible, it clearly illustrates several interesting aspects of urban development. First, you can see that urban areas occupy only a small percentage of the total U.S. land area. Second, you can see that the majority of urban areas are in the eastern half of the country. Of particular interest is the tremendous concentration of people along the Atlantic coast from Washington to Boston, which is clearly visible. This complex of cities and communities has been given the name "Megalopolis."

Size differences between cities are also highlighted by the photograph. If we took a series of photographs from the same vantage point over the next 30 years, the present urban areas would get larger and brighter and new urban areas would begin showing up. Not all urban areas will grow at the same rate during this period. Some will grow rapidly whereas others will grow more slowly or will lose population. To understand the reasons for differing growth rates, it is necessary to examine the economic process by which cities grow.

Figure 7.2 Satellite Photo and Population Density Map.

This composite satellite photo vividly illustrates the extent and location of urban concentrations in the United States. (Source: U.S. Air Force.)

Population densities, as seen in this density map, closely follow the light patterns in the satellite photo. (Source: Bureau of the Census, Department of Commerce.)

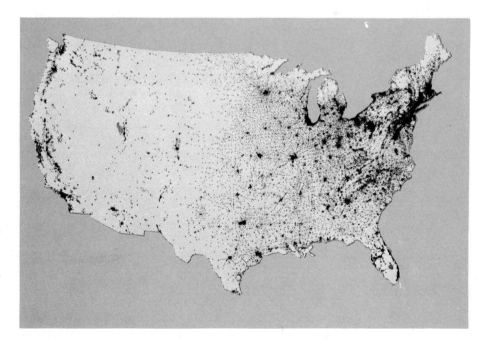

HOW DOES A CITY GROW?

What caused the recent growth experienced by cities such as Phoenix, Atlanta, Houston, Denver, and Dallas? What causes any city to gain or lose population? If you think about it, you can probably come up with a list of good causes for a city gaining or losing population. Changes in employment for any city are related to changes in the condition of the national and regional economies.

While some cities are more sensitive than others to changes in the national and regional economies, every urban economy is part of a larger economic system and is affected by that system. It is important to explore the magnitude and timing of the relationship between the local urban economy and larger areas. It is difficult for any city to have an economy that runs counter to a severe national or regional downturn or, conversely, it is difficult for any city not to benefit from a vibrant national or regional economy. National and regional economic changes account for only a portion of an urban area's economic development. Much of a city's development is a function of its attributes, some of which may be unique and valuable to firms already there and firms considering expanding or relocating. The relative attractiveness of a city and the resulting economic development process are of some interest.

Houston, for example, has experienced substantial growth partly because energy-related companies have located offices, research centers, and plants there to take advantage of skilled personnel and access to other firms with whom they do business on a regular basis. When Shell Oil decided to locate its corporate offices in Houston, it created many new jobs in the city. Some of these jobs were staffed by Shell employees transferred from other cities. Others were filled by persons already in Houston or attracted there by job opportunities. Thus, Shell had a direct impact on total employment in Houston.

However, Shell's employees were only a part of Shell's total impact on the city. Many other jobs were created in food stores, department stores, doctors' offices, insurance agencies, real estate offices, and other places to provide goods and services for new Shell employees. These "service" employees in turn required more service employees to satisfy their needs for goods and services. Thus, Shell's move created many other new jobs in the Houston economy. Put another way, the total number of new jobs created in the local economy by Shell's move greatly exceeded the number of new jobs at Shell.

In economic terms, Shell represents a **basic, or export, employer** in the Houston economy because it produces goods and services that are sold principally outside the immediate metropolitan area. That is, it exports its products. This is an important concept because the salaries of Shell employees and the purchases made by Shell in Houston, such as office supplies, are paid for with money earned from sales in other parts of the country. The more products Shell sells nationally, the more employment it will likely have in its Houston headquarters. Employment in firms producing goods and services that are sold within the Houston area is called **nonbasic, or service, employment.**

With these definitions in mind, let's consider how employment in your city can change. First, if the income of its citizens, adjusted for inflation, increases, spending will increase. This increase in local spending may create a need for additional nonbasic employment to satisfy the increased demand for goods and services. Second, basic employment can increase if local basic firms increase their sales outside your town. This would increase basic employment, which would, in turn, create an increase in nonbasic employment. Finally, a new basic firm could move to town, a situation that would increase basic and ultimately nonbasic employment. Of course, if these situations were reversed, employment would decrease.

How much total employment changes when basic employment changes depends on your town's **employment multiplier.** The employment multiplier is the ratio of total change in employment to the change in basic employment:

$$\text{Employment multiplier} = \frac{\text{Change in total employment}}{\text{Change in basic employment}}$$

If, in the earlier example, Shell had created 5000 basic jobs and the total change in employment was 15,000 jobs, the employment multiplier would be 3,

$$\text{Employment multiplier} = \frac{15,000}{5,000}$$
$$= 3$$

This means that for Houston, an increase or decrease of one basic job results in an increase or decrease of two nonbasic jobs, for a total of three jobs. As you can see, large changes in basic employment can dramatically affect your local economy. Problems in the aerospace industry had a multiplier effect on employment in Seattle during the late 1960s and early 1970s, causing substantial problems in that local economy. Likewise, Detroit and other cities with substantial automobile-related employment suffer substantial unemployment when automobile sales decrease.

Detroit and Seattle illustrate a very important idea — that the mix of industries in your town directly affects its short-term employment stability and its longer term prospects for employment changes. If your town has a high percentage of its basic employment in industries that experience frequent and pronounced fluctuations in employment, then your town as a whole will experience frequent fluctuations in employment. Over the longer run, changes in your town's employment will also be affected by the mix of industries in its economic base. The higher the percentage of basic employment in fast growing industries, the greater increases in employment that are likely. By looking again at Figure 7.1, you can see that the cities projected to have the highest growth rates in the 1980s will have that growth because they now have, or are expected to have, rapidly growing basic industries located there.

To avoid short-term fluctuations, many cities seek to diversify their economic base. They seek new industries different from those already in their economic base. Seattle, for example, has been able to reduce the importance of the aerospace industry in its economy. Certainly, aerospace is still important, but many new industries have helped Seattle diversify. This diversification process is especially important to communities faced with employment concentrations in industries expected to have little or no growth, or even decreases in employment. In considering the economy of your town, you will be interested in the diversity of its economy with respect to the short-term and long-term prospects for each industry.

You may be concerned that not all firms are purely basic or nonbasic since they sell their product both locally and outside the local area. For instance, Shell Oil sells some of its products in the Houston area. What about a large law firm that may perform half its services for clients outside the city? How is basic and nonbasic employment to be identified in these situations?

Before considering approaches to assigning industries to basic and nonbasic categories, it is useful to consider how employment and production data is gathered and organized. The Department of Commerce gathers and processes a variety of data about business activity. This data is classified according to the Standard Industrial Classification system, called simply the SIC code for short. The Department of Commerce provides data for industrial classification with up to four digits. This SIC code provides a consistent framework for classifying and gathering economic data.

Now to return to methods for identifying basic and nonbasic employment. One approach is to simply make assumptions about basic and nonbasic employment. This approach suffers from some obvious shortcomings. Another method is to ask each firm how many employees are necessary for their local sales and how many are necessary for sales outside the local area. Many employers would not be able to give you such details and even more would decline to do so, even if they knew.

Another approach to estimating basic employment involves using publicly available employment data. At the heart of this approach is a comparison of the percentage of an urban area's total employment in various industries (according to SIC codes) to the percentage of total employment in the same industry in the entire United States. If, for example, employment in energy represents 10 percent of total U.S. employment, then it is assumed that 10 percent of total employment is sufficient to provide all the energy needs of the nation. Extending this logic, the same percentage of employment in energy should be able to supply any state, city, or region of the nation with its needs. If Houston has 21 percent of its total employment in the energy industry, then it is more than providing for its own energy needs since, on average, it needs only 10 percent of its work force in energy to meet its needs. This means that the extra 11 percent must be producing products for export out of the Houston area. Thus, 11/21, or 52 percent, of Houston's energy employment is basic and 10/21, or 48 percent, is nonbasic. This same approach would be used on each industry to determine the proportions of employment in that industry that are basic and nonbasic.

Sometimes, to determine the extent to which an industry provides basic employment, a location quotient is calculated as follows:

$$\text{Location quotient} = \frac{\text{Industry's percentage of total employment in local economy}}{\text{Industry's percentage of total employment in United States}}$$

For our example in Houston, the location quotient for the energy industry is 2.1,

$$\text{Location quotient} = \frac{.21}{.10}$$
$$= 2.1$$

Obviously, if energy employment in Houston had been the same as energy employment in the United States, the location quotient would have been one. If the percentage in Houston is greater than the nation, the location quotient is greater than one, and if Houston's percentage is less than the nation's, the location quotient is less than one. Thus, industries with any basic employment will have a location quotient greater than one. The location quotient is a measure of employment concentration relative to a larger area, such as the United States.

The concept of economic base has been criticized for several shortcomings. First, it is contended that the multiplier is not constant over cities of different size. The larger a city becomes, the greater the multiplier. Of course, variations exist among cities of similar size. Another criticism is that in more complex economies it may be difficult or impossible to identify and measure basic and nonbasic employment. Another criticism is that all basic employment is generally assumed to have the same impact on the urban area, an assumption that is not true. However, in spite of these and other criticisms, economic base analysis still provides interesting and useful insights into the economic development of an urban area.

Employment Changes and Population Changes

Local population changes are directly related to changes in local employment. City planners and others interested in forecasting population often use estimates of employment change as the basis for their forecasts. They usually relate changes in employment to the number of new households such changes will necessitate. They then factor in changes in local unemployment to estimate the net number of required households. From the number of households, the net change in population is estimated using information about the average number of persons per household.

Consider, for instance, what change in population is likely to be caused by 900 new basic jobs in a community. If the employment multiplier is 3, then the total number of new basic jobs and nonbasic jobs is 2700 (3 × 900 = 2700). To begin, let's assume that all the jobs are filled by persons now living outside the city. The number of households supported by the new jobs can be estimated by dividing the number of new jobs by the average number of employed persons per household. If 1.5 persons per household are employed, then the 2700 jobs will provide employment for 1800 households:

$$\text{Number of households} = \frac{\text{Number of new jobs}}{\text{Number of jobs per household}}$$
$$= \frac{2700 \text{ Jobs}}{1.5 \text{ Jobs/household}}$$
$$= 1800 \text{ Households}$$

The total impact on population can be estimated by multiplying the number of households provided employment by the average number of persons per household. If there are 3.1 persons per household, then 5580 people can potentially be supported by the new employment:

$$1800 \text{ Households} \times 3.1 \text{ Persons/household} = 5580 \text{ Persons}$$

Actually, the impact on population will not be 5580 people since some unemployed persons already in the city will now be employed. For example, if 300 of the jobs are filled by such unemployed persons, then 2400 new jobs will be available for those not presently living in the area. The number of new households that can be supported is 1600, (2400/1.5), and the total increase in population is now 4960 people (1600 × 3.1 = 4960). From this example you can clearly see the significant impact a gain or loss of basic employment can have on the population of your town.

Importance of Demography

Sufficiently detailed information about current and expected economic activity and employment provides you with a basis for making some important forecasts about current and expected demand for workspace. If over the next 5 years 5000 new office jobs and 6000 new industrial jobs are expected to be created, you are in a position to estimate the amount of office and industrial space needed to satisfy this demand. By multiplying the number of office and industrial employees by the average square footage needed for each office or industrial employee respectively, you can produce a crude estimate of space demands. Then, by subtracting the amount of office and industrial space already in place or expected to be in place in the near future, the net new space demanded can be estimated. Further research into the amount of land used per square feet of space will allow you to estimate the amount of land demanded for office and industrial uses. These estimates can be refined if more detailed forecasts about the specific types of office and industrial employment are available because different types of employees require different amounts of space.

Information about expected population changes provides a basis for estimating the demand for housing. To estimate housing demand, population figures must be converted into households, because it is the number of households that determine the demand for housing units. To refine this overall estimate into rental versus owner-occupied, rental and price ranges, styles, condominium versus detached homes, and other categories, demographic information about the population must be analyzed. Income, age, marital status, and other variables affect the housing choices of the population. A skilled analyst can use demographic data to produce a more precise estimate of housing demand.

The demand for shopping space is a function of population and demographics. Research has shown that income, age, number of children, marital status, and other variables affect shopping patterns. Department of Commerce data provides a wealth of information about these variables and has been the object of research leading to the development of mathematical models for forecasting expenditures. A number of firms provide computerized retrieval systems for generating population and demographic data for virtually any portion of the United States. They also produce computer-generated forecasts of retail sales by product lines for a relatively small fee. As before, expenditure estimates can be converted into space demand using data on sales per square foot for various types of retailers.

URBAN INFORMATION—WHAT AND WHERE?

Employment and population forecasts, especially when coupled with income forecasts, are valuable to you in the real estate business since real estate provides places for people to live, work, shop, and play. If you have a good idea of changes in employment; what types of employment, manufacturing versus office employment for example; income levels associated with that employment; educational levels of new employees; ages; and other demographic information likely to occur in your town, you are in an excellent position to begin estimating what kinds of space will be needed during the forecast period. The value of such insights is obvious; the question is not whether to use this information, but where and how to find it.

To be in the real estate business, you do not have to be an urban economist. Much of the information you will need to know about the general economic and demographic situation in your town has been gathered and analyzed for you and is readily available from public and private sources. Public sources, such as federal, state, and local governments, all gather data and make it available to you. Private organizations — chambers of commerce, real estate boards, and home builders associations — also gather, analyze, and publish urban economic and demographic data. Universities frequently collect and analyze useful data as well.

Of all these sources, the federal government has more economic and demographic information than any other source. Through its many censuses and other data-collection efforts, it has information on just about every facet of business. Most libraries will have *some* volumes of government data. Special libraries, known as depositories, receive virtually every federal government report released to the public. The biggest problem with using census data and other government reports is locating the right information. If you are going to use federal government documents, ask your librarian to recommend a good published guide to federal documents. A good starting point for finding federal government data is the *Statistical Abstract of the United States,* published by the Department of Commerce. This inexpensive volume contains data on many aspects of life in the United States and gives the location of more extensive data on each subject.

Federal government data is organized for various sized units. Some of the data is available for relatively small geographic areas called blocks and census tracts. It is also aggregated for cities and counties. Another useful level of aggregation is the metropolitan statistical area, abbreviated as MSA, as defined by the Bureau of the Census of the Department of Commerce. An MSA is a county or group of adjoining counties representing an integrated economic and social unit and containing one or twin cities with a population of at least 50,000 or an urbanized area as defined by the Census Bureau with at least 50,000 inhabitants and a total MSA population of at least 100,000.

The MSA concept attempts to capture the larger meaning of an urban area by including not only the city, but also those areas in which people depend on the city for employment, entertainment, shopping, hospitals, and other services. For urban areas of one million or more population, separate component areas may be defined if specified criteria are met and statistics developed for it. Such a component area is called a primary metropolitan statistical area (PMSA). Further, any area containing a PMSA is designated a consolidated metropolitan statistical area (CMSA). Throughout the United States there are 257 MSAs, 20 CMSAs, and 71 PMSAs.

Economic and demographic information gathered and published by state governments varies greatly in quantity and quality. Some states regularly gather and publish such data. However, even within a given state, the availability and regularity of such information is difficult to predict. State reports are also often more difficult to locate since there is usually no coordinating body to organize and catalog all of the available reports. If you want to find information quickly, with a minimum of problems, state sources may not be the answer.

Local governments are often excellent sources of demographic information. Many cities have economic development departments performing demographic and economic studies that may be particularly valuable to you in the real estate business. Planning departments and councils of government (COGs) also perform such studies. Visits with local agencies and your librarian can provide useful information on the availability of local research reports and studies.

Economic Base Studies

If you gather enough demographic and economic data and carefully analyze it, you can develop a snapshot of a city's current economic situation and its outlook for the future. This do-it-yourself approach may be quite reasonable for answering very specific questions. However, for most purposes, an economic base study is the best source of information. An **economic base study** combines economic, demographic, and other data into a comprehensive examination of the current and likely future status of a local economy.

At the heart of an economic base study is an analysis of basic and nonbasic employment. Such an analysis provides insights into not only basic and nonbasic employment, but which industries are represented in each category. This analysis serves the same function as a personal physical examination; it establishes the city's current condition and provides a baseline for making a prognosis about its future health. Economic base studies are developed by city governments and private groups such as chambers of commerce. Universities often perform economic base studies and publish their results. If you can find such a study, it will provide much of the information you need on your local economy.

PATTERNS OF URBAN LAND USE

After developing estimates of expected economic development and its implications for the types and quantities of space demanded, you may become interested in where in your town this space is likely to be demanded. In other words, knowing that 1,500,000 square feet of additional office space will be needed over the next 5 years to satisfy demand in your town does not tell you whether office space is likely to be demanded in the area of Blackacre. The same question could be asked about other types of space. Where will new shopping space, manufacturing space, and living space of various types be located? Answering these questions concerns persons in the brokerage, development, lending, and investment areas of real estate. It concerns them because answering such questions can mean the difference between profits and losses, success and failure. It is of direct interest to you because it affects the likely use and value of Blackacre.

A good starting point for answering these questions is the analysis of existing land use patterns in your town. That is, if during the past 20 years expensive new homes have been constructed exclusively in its southern portion, why shouldn't this trend continue? If reasons cannot be found for expecting a change, then the southern portion of the urban area is a good bet for the location of additional construction of expensive new homes. Similar patterns for other types of real estate provide support for estimating the location of the general areas of new development within the urban area. Extended observations of development have produced some theories of urban land use patterns (see Figure 7.3). While any one of these theories may not completely describe the land use patterns of your town, each provides a rationale for explaining the location of at least some of its land uses. A combination of the theories can often explain the majority of land uses in a given urban area.

Concentric Ring Theory

Ernest W. Burgess developed the concentric ring theory in the 1920s by observing the development of Chicago.[1] In this theory Burgess contends that land uses develop in concentric rings around the central business district (CBD). Four other zones, or land use categories, are considered. The transition zone is immediately around the CBD and contains manufacturing and other businesses. Next is the low-income housing zone followed by middle- and upper-income housing zones. A basic premise of the theory is that new housing for upper-income families is added in the outside ring and older housing is *filtered*, or passed, down to lower-income groups.

Sector Theory

Another theory that suggests that similar land uses are grouped together is the sector theory developed by Homer Hoyt.[2] This theory posits that

[1] Ernest W. Burgess, "The Growth of the City," in R.E. Park et al., *The City* (Chicago: University of Chicago Press, 1925).

[2] Homer Hoyt, *The Structure and Growth of Residential Neighborhoods in American Cities* (Washington: Government Printing Office, 1939).

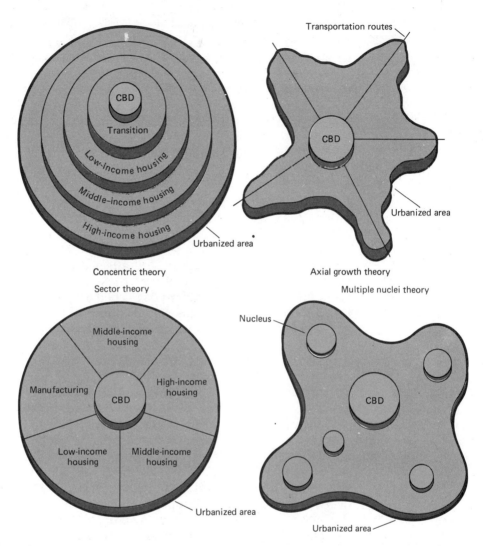

Figure 7.3
Patterns of land use.

land use is generally uniform as you travel away from the CBD in a straight line. That is, if expensive housing is found immediately east of the CBD then expensive housing would be found generally east of the CBD all the way to the edge of the urbanized area. This would hold true for other types of housing and manufacturing in other sections of the city. The rationale for this behavior is that cities grow by adding development at the edges, and the most likely development is more of the same since this is likely the most profitable use of that land. Thus, according to this theory, if you are trying to estimate where housing of a certain type will be developed in the near future, you should identify where this land use has occurred in the past and simply extend this trend beyond the currently developed area.

Axial Growth Theory

Richard Hurd incorporated the impact of transportation arteries on urban growth in this theory, developed in the 1930s.[3] Hurd contends that development tends to occur first along or very near transportation routes leading to the CBD. The savings in time and money afforded by these transportation arteries make sites close to them attractive. As a result, urban areas tend to develop in a "star" or "octopus" shape by first developing along, or close to, transportation routes. Later development occurs in the areas between the transportation routes.

Multiple Nuclei Theory

Later, Chauncy Harris and Edward Ullman questioned the idea of a single center for urban areas.[4] While recognizing the CBD as the most important focal point for the urban area, they suggested that other centers, or *nuclei*, may exist and affect the shape of the urban area. Harris and Ullman reasoned that these nuclei represented land uses other businesses and individuals needed or wanted to be near. Competition for sites near a nucleus would cause land values to increase near a nucleus and decrease as you move away from it.

The development of a major shopping center on the edge of an urbanized area provides an excellent example of a nucleus and the land uses surrounding it. Other developers wanting to take advantage of the potential customer traffic generated by such a center will attempt to develop other shopping centers. Free-standing retail stores, such as K-Mart and Woolco, will also try to locate close to the center in an attempt to cash in on the flow of customers ready to buy goods. Office buildings, movie theaters, banks, and eating establishments also realize the benefits of being close to the center. Likewise, many people want to live within a convenient distance of the center. The result of all this desire to be close to the shopping center can be seen by simply looking at the land uses surrounding such a center in your town. If sufficient time has passed since the center was constructed, you should see these different kinds of space positioned around it.

Exactly where around the center different types of space are developed depends on a number of factors such as automobile traffic patterns, available land, land use controls, and topography. After all these factors are taken into consideration, the land use that can generate the greatest profits on a site will tend to locate there. The reason is simple: the developer of that use can pay more for the site than other potential users. In many instances, the ability to pay for a site is related to the quantity of space that can be developed. The more intensive the use, the more that

---

[3] Richard Hurd, *Principles of City Land Values* (New York: The Record and Guide, 1924).

[4] Chauncy D. Harris and Edward L. Ullman, "The Nature of Cities," *The Annals of the American Academy of Political And Social Science,* Vol. 242, 1945.

can be paid for the site. For this reason, you will often find more intensive development nearer a nucleus than less intensive development. The desirability of a particular site for a particular type of space depends on the physical factors discussed in the next major section of this chapter. However, the basic concept here is quite clear — sites around the nucleus, the shopping center in this case, are allocated on the basis of the ability to pay. Thus, the type of space and quantity of that space likely to be developed on Blackacre depends on whether it is developed as a nucleus or, if not, whether it is near one or more nuclei.

Investment Theory of Urban Development[5]

None of the individual theories just considered fully explains all land use patterns in a given urban area. That is, every urban area contains elements of each theory. For example, in your town you can probably see evidence of upper-, middle-, and lower-income housing development occurring in about the same parts of the urban area as in the past, supporting the sector theory of development. You can also probably identify nuclei and surrounding development and observe development occurring first along transportation arteries. You should spend little time trying to fit only one theory to your urban area. Each theory should be used where appropriate to help you understand and predict your town's land use patterns and, in turn, make better real estate decisions. An understanding of urban development is made easier by yet another theory of land use, which integrates all of these theories into one, somewhat more cohesive theory.

The land use theories just considered share a common element, economics. Since the theories were developed by observing existing development, they represent the results and interpretations of past developer and investor decisions. This emphasis on developer and investor decisions forms the basis of another theory of urban development. Essentially, the **investment theory of urban development** suggests that the land use patterns in any urban area are the result of many public and private real estate development and investment decisions. Cities did not spring up fully developed, but were and continue to be developed piece by piece, with the pieces being real estate developments such as office buildings, shopping centers, and residential subdivisions. Where and in what form these developments occur determine the ultimate pattern of land use and the "character" of the city.

If we assume that developers are rational, then we can conclude that space will be developed where developers think it will produce the best combination of expected return and risk. For example, if you were a developer wishing to develop a subdivision of expensive single family

[5] Richard U. Ratcliff, *Real Estate Analysis* (New York: McGraw-Hill Book Company, 1961), pp. 306–331.

homes, you would seek a location that maximizes your chances of making a profit or, at least, that minimizes the chances of sustaining a loss. You might use market research to analyze what kind of homes and features potential buyers want, and *where* they want the homes to be located. You may also use your own knowledge of urban development and past development patterns in making the decision of exactly what to produce and where to produce it. Cost is another important consideration. The potential of a site to produce income must be tempered by the cost of producing that income in order to estimate profits and the risk involved. Put another way, you will proceed with the use that is the highest and best use of the site. (This is an oversimplified view but still captures the essence of what goes on.)

In short, profitability determines when, where, and what kind of urban land development occurs. To project land development in your urban area, you must estimate where each type of real estate can be most reasonably developed. This involves analyzing the supply of and demand for various types of space and determining the most desirable locations for each type of space. Determining the most desirable location for a particular type of space requires an understanding of the factors affecting location decisions. As you will learn in Chapter 8, legal limits on what may be constructed and the location of public real estate projects such as golf courses and sewerage treatment plants affect the location of some land uses.

LOCATION DECISIONS

How does McDonald's consistently make good location decisions? The same question can be asked about Hyatt Hotels, Sears, or any other service or retailing establishment. How do office developers, shopping center developers, and families choose good locations? On a personal level, how did you decide on the location of your present home? In answering, it would be easy to get bogged down in the detail of all the questions you or any location decision maker must address in making a location decision. However, such a detailed approach is not necessary. A small number of critical factors are common to all location decisions: convenience, favorable and unfavorable exposure, and price.[6]

Convenience
Convenience refers to the cost in terms of time and money associated with moving persons or goods to and from a given site. The convenience associated with a given site depends on the land use being considered. Different land uses have different costs because each requires the move-

[6] ibid. pp. 63–71.

ment of goods and persons from it to different destinations and to it from different origins. For example, McDonald's is interested in the time and cost required for customers to reach its restaurant as compared to reaching a competitor. If the same site was being considered for a medical office building, the time required for physicians to reach certain hospitals could be of critical importance.

To assess the convenience of a site, you must identify the frequent destinations of trips from the site and the frequent origins of trips to the site. These destinations and origins are said to be *linked* to the site (see Figure 7.4). A matched destination and origin comprise a **linkage.** For example, a home and the place of employment of one of the spouses constitute a linkage. Other common linkages for families include schools, shopping areas, entertainment centers, and the homes of friends. A linkage can have an outward or inward orientation. An **outward orientation** means that the primary concern is moving from the site to some particular destination. An **inward orientation** means the emphasis is on getting to the site from some origin.

A family making a home location decision will choose the location providing the best trade-off in the time and cost associated with the various linkages. The weighting placed on each linkage varies between families. For some families, access to schools is of primary importance whereas other families are more interested in the accessibility of work places. Maximum acceptable travel times from homes suggested by the Urban Land Institute are shown in Figure 7.5. Whatever particular linkages are considered more important, most home location decisions have linkages with an outward orientation.

Other location decisions emphasize linkages with inward orientations, in which the time and cost of getting to the site from other places is of prime importance. For example, location decisions involving retail

Figure 7.4
Examples of linkages for residential site. (Source: John McMahan, *Property Development,* McGraw-Hill Book Company, 1976, p. 115.)

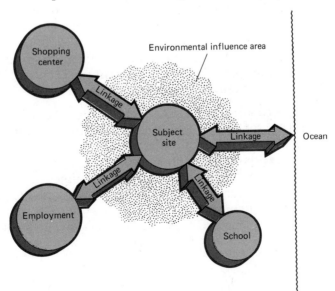

Figure 7.5
Maximum acceptable travel times. (Source: Reprinted with permission from *Residential Development Handbook* (1978), published by the Urban Land Institute, p. 36.)

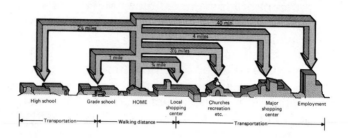

stores and shopping centers emphasize inward orientations. In these decisions the customers' ability to reach the site receives the most attention. For this reason, some developers spend a great deal of money and effort researching these linkages.

Consider the location decision facing the developer of a large shopping mall (regional shopping center). Developers know that the market for a shopping center is defined by **accessibility;** the time and cost associated with reaching the center. Customers will ordinarily shop at the most convenient shopping facilities available that meet their needs. Because of this desire for convenience, our developer must carefully analyze the ability of the proposed center to attract customers. That is, the market for the center must be defined. Actually, for a large shopping center, two or three markets will be defined:

1. Primary Market. The nearby (up to 10 to 15 minutes driving time) population from which the center should get a high percentage of retail sales and which should constitute 60 to 70 percent of center's sales volume.
2. Secondary Market. Population outside primary market but within 15 to 20 minutes of site with some shopping alternatives and providing 15 to 20 percent of total shopping center sales.
3. Tertiary or Fringe Market. Population outside secondary market but close enough to frequent the proposed center if it should have a competitive advantage.[7]

By estimating the maximum driving times associated with each market and actually driving to the site at various times of the day you can estimate the time boundaries of the primary, secondary, and tertiary markets and plot them on a map. Then, by considering the location of competing centers and any expected changes in accessibility, such as a new expressway, you can draw the final estimate of primary, secondary, and tertiary markets on the map. Whether the markets, as defined by this process, provide enough customers for the proposed center depends on

[7] *Shopping Center Development Handbook* (Washington: Urban Land Institute, 1977), pp. 22–31.

the demographic and economic characteristics of the persons in the markets. Many types of development must consider primary, secondary, and even tertiary markets in analyzing a location.

Favorable and Unfavorable Exposure

Another factor affecting location decisions is the extent to which a site provides psychological and esthetic satisfaction or dissatisfaction. Of particular importance is the **environmental influence area,** the area surrounding the site that the user perceives to influence the site's character.[8] The bounds of the environmental influence area will vary from one land use to another and from one person to another.

Favorable exposure is any attribute of the environmental influence area, not related to convenience, that enhances the desirability of a site. It includes attractive views, clean air, and proximity to expensive homes, among others. For example, two homesites of equal size and convenience to the same destinations may not be equally desirable. One site may provide a wooded, park-like setting in a neighborhood of nice homes, whereas the other site may possess no trees and be in a neighborhood of generally less expensive homes. The same principle applies to businesses as well. A retailer, such as a fine jewelry store, may find a location next to a Neiman-Marcus department store very prestigious. In Chicago, Michigan Avenue is *the* location for fine clothing stores and in New York, Fifth Avenue enjoys the same reputation.

Just as favorable exposure can enhance the desirability of a site, unfavorable exposure can reduce its appeal. **Unfavorable exposure** is any attribute of the environmental influence area, not related to convenience, that reduces the desirability of a site. Noise, air pollution, odors from factories, refineries, and paper mills, and proximity to unattractive and annoying land uses can make a site unattractive. Not only present but possible future problems must be considered in evaluating a site.

Price

Often the site considered best on the basis of convenience, favorable exposure, and unfavorable exposure is not the best site — it is too expensive. McDonald's can pay a premium price for a choice site because such a site will place its competition at a disadvantage and produce high sales volumes and profits; moreover, the premium represents only a small increase in total operating expenses. Price involves more than just the purchase price. Differences in development costs between sites must also be considered. For instance, if McDonald's is considering one site that is already zoned for an eating establishment and requires no special

[8] John McMahon, *Property Development* (New York: McGraw-Hill Book Company, 1976), p. 118.

earth moving or drainage work, the cost of building the new outlet may be $600,000. Another site likely to produce greater sales may require a zoning change and extensive grading and drainage work, making the cost of building the new outlet $700,000. This $100,000 difference in costs must be considered in deciding which parcel to purchase. There is a limit to how much any rational decision maker can pay for a site. If the price premium for the best site exceeds the value of the increased profits it can produce as compared to the next best, lower priced alternative site, that premium should not be paid.

Price acts as an allocator of sites. When a site is placed on the market, the user who can put it to the most profitable use can outbid others. Such a use is called the site's **highest and best use.** Others desiring the site but unable to pay must find a second best site. Therefore, you should be prepared to optimize your location decision rather than maximize it. ''Optimize'' means finding the best available location given your financial constraints. ''Maximize'' means finding the best location regardless of price.

Changing Nature of Locations

As an urban area changes so does the relative desirability of locations. The best shopping center sites of the 1950s may have little appeal as shopping sites today. Today's best office location may be more or less desirable five years from now. This process, called **land use succession,** becomes visible when a structure is demolished to make way for another use or is extensively renovated to take advantage of changing market conditions. Since real estate improvements will be around for a long time, the long-run success of any real estate project depends on a location that continues to be attractive through the years. Many developers and investors seek a location that is very good and improving, rather than one that is at its peak. No one can guarantee the future of a location, but by paying attention to the important factors affecting location decisions and possible changes in those factors, the best possible decisions can be made. Real estate is dynamic, and your decisions should not be limited to considerations of present conditions.

SUMMARY

Ours is an urban country in the sense that a high percentage of our people live in cities. Cities have not developed by accident; the Industrial Revolution provided the impetus for much of the current urbanization. Different regions of the country have urbanized at different times, and this trend continues with Sunbelt cities currently having the fastest growth rate, a trend that is expected to continue. Many small cities and essentially rural areas are also expected to have growth rates exceeding the national average in the near future.

Economically, a city's growth and stability are strongly affected by its economic base. Basic industries are those producing goods and services sold outside the area under consideration. By producing income from sales outside the area and paying wages and buying products locally, basic industries fuel the local economy. Firms producing or supplying goods and services for the local population are called nonbasic industries. The creation or elimination of basic jobs has a multiplier effect on total employment. How great this impact is depends on the community's employment multiplier.

Economic growth and the people ultimately employed in and moving to a city determine the demand for working, living, shopping, and being entertained. Analysis of urban areas has produced the concentric ring, sector, axial growth, and multiple nuclei theories of where different types of space are generally located in an urban area. The investment theory of urban growth explains existing urban land use patterns as being the result of many public and private investment decisions. Further, this theory suggests that future development patterns may be forecast by examining where different kinds of space can be most profitably developed.

On an individual level, location decisions are a function of convenience, favorable and unfavorable exposure, and cost. Convenience is the cost in terms of time and money of traveling to desired destinations from the site and from specific origins to the site. Favorable and unfavorable exposure are proximity to desirable and undesirable environmental features, respectively. Cost is the price that must be paid for a site. A decision maker must balance these factors in selecting the best location.

QUICK QUIZ

1. An industry whose products are sold outside the metropolitan area in which they are produced is a

   a. nonbasic industry   • c. basic industry
   b. outward industry   d. tertiary industry

2. The addition of 1000 new basic jobs will create how many nonbasic jobs if the employment multiplier is 3?

   a. 3000   c. 2000
   b. 1000   d. 4000

3. The growth theory that suggests that development occurs first along transportation routes is the

   a. concentric ring theory   c. multiple nuclei theory
   • b. axial growth theory   d. sector theory

4. Location decisions are based on

    a. accessibility   c. price
    b. unfavorable exposure   ⦁d. all of the above

5. Accessibility, favorable exposure, and unfavorable exposure are balanced against _____ in making a location decision.

6. The destinations and origins important to a particular land use are called _____ .

7. Accessibility is measured in terms of __*time*__ and __*cost*__ .

8. A snapshot of your local economy is called a(n) _____ .

QUESTIONS AND EXERCISES

1. If a real estate brokerage firm was thinking of finding a new location for their only office, what specific factors within the general areas of accessibility, favorable exposure, and unfavorable exposure should they consider? What factors should Hilton Hotels consider in locating a new convention hotel?

2. If your community's population is projected to grow a total of 18 percent over the next decade, what specific impacts would this growth have on the need for office, shopping, and living space?

3. What are the largest basic industries in your town? How rapidly are these growing on a national basis?

4. How do the employment and population forecasts in Questions 1 and 2 affect the need for office, shopping, and living space?

5. Where, in general, in your town is new office construction likely to occur? New shopping space? New houses of various prices? Why?

6. Identify a nucleus in your town. Rank the ability of different land uses to bid for land around that nucleus. Is this ranking logical to you? Why?

7. For which of the theories of land use patterns do you see evidence in your town? Be specific.

KEY TERMINOLOGY

accessibility
axial growth theory
basic employment

concentric ring theory
demographic characteristic
demography

economic base study
employment multiplier
environmental influence area
export employment
favorable exposure
highest and best use
investment theory of
   urban growth
inward orientation

land use succession
linkage
location quotient
multiple nuclei theory
nonbasic employment
outward orientation
sector theory
service employment
unfavorable exposure

IF YOU WANT TO READ MORE

MICHAEL GOLDBERG and PETER CHINLOY, *Urban Land Economics* (New York: John Wiley & Sons, Inc., 1984).

J. HARVEY, *The Economics of Real Property* (London: The Macmillian Press Ltd, 1981).

JOHN MCMAHON, *Property Development* (New York: McGraw-Hill Book Company, 1976), Chapters 4–6.

STEPHEN A. PYHRR, JAMES R. COOPER, LARRY E. WOFFORD, and STEVEN D. KAPPLIN, *Real Estate Investment: Strategy, Analysis, Decisions* (New York: John Wiley & Sons, 1986), Chapters 10, 11, and 12.

RICHARD U. RATCLIFF, *Real Estate Analysis* (New York: McGraw-Hill Book Company, 1961), Chapter 4.

Residential Development Handbook (Washington, D.C.: Urban Land Institute, 1978), Chapter 2.

THOMAS W. SHAFER, *Urban Growth and Economics* (Reston, Va.: Reston Publishing Company, Inc., 1977), Chapters 2–7.

8

The Urban Area: planning and land use controls

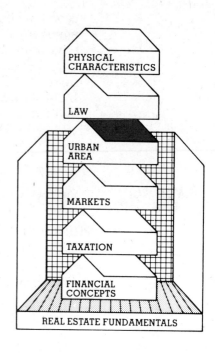

PHYSICAL CHARACTERISTICS

LAW

URBAN AREA

MARKETS

TAXATION

FINANCIAL CONCEPTS

REAL ESTATE FUNDAMENTALS

PREVIEW

The development of cities is usually not left to chance; government must plan to insure adequate public services for all citizens at a minimum cost. Planning directly affects the real estate business through actions designed to encourage, discourage, or otherwise shape development. All of these actions ultimately affect the land use patterns and the timing of development within a city. For a developer these actions may create or destroy many opportunities, while for others in the real estate business, they affect the supply of particular kinds of space available at any time. How you can develop Blackacre is going to be affected by planning efforts and land use controls. This chapter explains the basics of planning and land use controls and their impact on the real estate business. Specifically, after studying this chapter you should understand:

1. The need for growth planning.
2. The phases of the growth planning process.
3. The land use controls and incentives available to governments to influence growth and development, especially zoning and subdivision regulations.
4. The impact of growth planning and land use controls on real estate.

You have probably sat in bumper-to-bumper traffic during rush hour at some time or another and asked the question, "Why didn't someone do a better job of planning?" Or you may have noticed potholes in streets, low water pressure, poorly maintained parks, decaying and decrepit sections of the inner city, overcrowded schools, or periodic flooding in certain parts of your city and asked the same question. These and other problems are casually laid at the doorstep of the urban planner.

Urban planning is concerned with the quality of life in an urban area. Planners deal with the problem of providing services affecting every aspect of urban life: police and fire protection, drinking water, sewerage, transportation, recreation, health services, and so on. These services are important; they are the government services that most affect your daily life. Planners, through careful study, seek to provide these services in adequate quantity and quality at the lowest cost. For cities, as in your personal life, the ability to achieve a desired quality of life is constrained by the availability of money.

Financially, many cities are experiencing severe problems. The experiences of New York and Cleveland dramatically illustrate this point. But older cities such as these are not the only ones concerned about finances. Many younger cities experiencing rapid growth are also concerned about finances. While New York, Cleveland and other older cities are concerned with maintaining existing services, younger cities are concerned with how to pay the bills associated with providing basic services for new residents and the associated new real estate development.

It is common to envision a planner as a generalist hovering over maps and models of the "ideal city." In reality, much of the planner's time is spent dealing with details — often in such exotic areas as drinking water and storm drainage. However, these details are necessary parts of the comprehensive, or master, plan for the city. The master plan represents the overall game plan for the city. It identifies where the city would like to go, how it can get there, and how to determine when it has arrived. Just because these more mundane activities are not as visible as other planning activities does not diminish their impact on the quantity and quality of services you enjoy in your city.

The real estate development associated with growth — homes, apartments, offices, factories, and shopping centers — requires services from the city. Some services, such as water and sewerage systems, require large capital investments by government, and much long-range planning. For example, the expansion of sewerage capacity requires several years for planning, financing, and construction. A city simply cannot wait until the present system is operating at capacity to consider expansion. Other services such as police protection can be expanded within certain limits more readily and without large, lump-sum investments. However, these services also require long-range planning to produce this flexibility.

Given the impact of real estate development on the demand for services, planners are very interested in the type, quantity, timing, and location of new development. By analyzing the impact of these aspects of development, planners can affect the city's overall cost of providing services to all its citizens. Planners can also reduce the transportation time and costs to citizens by assuring necessary services such as shopping and office space are readily available. Additionally, they can stabilize property values by insuring orderly development while not reducing the quality and quantity of services supplied to existing residents. As you can see, planning for growth and change is important to the citizens of the urban area, especially those in the real estate business.

Growth planning can be a costly activity for a city's residents. If, by restricting development, planning reduces the supply of homes, office and shopping space, apartments, or any other type of space, below that demanded by people in the city, rents and prices for available space will increase. How much they increase will depend on the extent of the imbalance between the quantity of space supplied and demanded. For example, if office development in suburban areas is restricted, rents in existing buildings may increase as more office space is needed. Owners of existing office buildings benefit from these higher rents and values at the expense of renters and subsequent purchasers. These subsequent owners will also benefit if rents continue to be maintained at artificially high levels by growth controls.

To carry the office building example a little further, planning may also create costs for residents through increased driving times to work in office buildings and factories and in higher fees for the products and services of those occupying the expensive office space such as dentists, accountants, and real estate brokers. This is not to suggest that planning should not occur, but only that its costs and benefits should be evaluated as completely as possible when making planning decisions. Planners should also analyze *who* is paying the costs, for example renters in some cases, and *who* is receiving the benefits.

OVERVIEW OF GROWTH PLANNING PROCESS

Growth planning is the name given the process of planning, implementing, and monitoring orderly urban development. At the heart of growth planning is the objective of minimizing the costs of urban development while maintaining necessary services and the quality of life. Growth planning should not be confused with the concept of "nogrowth." Some urban areas, such as Boulder, Colorado, have decided for economic, environmental, and esthetic reasons, that future growth should be substantially curtailed. Other urban areas have chosen to seek growth rates ranging from very slow to fast. While a decision on growth rate preferences is part of the growth planning process, there is nothing inherent in the concept of growth planning that suggests what that rate should be. Growth planning is concerned with promoting the most efficient and economical handling of possible growth, whatever growth rate is selected.

While it is difficult to disagree with the idea of developing a city in the most efficient manner, the implementation of growth planning is not considered a cure-all without side effects. Within growth planning are the seeds of vigorous disagreement. This conflict is a fundamental one between the rights of property owners to use their land as they see fit and the police power — the ability of a governmental body to control the use of private land to protect the health and safety and promote the general welfare of the public *without compensating* land owners. Keep this conflict in mind as you read about the growth planning process. It is considered in more detail later in the chapter.

The growth planning process has three major phases: planning, implementing, and monitoring. Each phase, in turn, is comprised of a number of steps. An understanding of this process will acquaint you with many of the considerations of growth planning for the city and their implications for the real estate professional. The major phases of the growth planning process are illustrated in Figure 8.1.

Planning Phase

In the planning phase, information is generated to provide planners with a statistical snapshot of the urban area. This information is used to identify growth possibilities and problems. Once they have been identified, goals and objectives of growth planning are defined. The tools to be used and the plan for implementation complete this phase of the growth planning process. The planning phase is a necessary, and often under-emphasized, step in creating a workable growth planning program.

Implementation Phase

Once established, the growth plan must be implemented. Urban governments often must adopt ordinances and regulations and develop policies and procedures to implement these plans. The final step in the implementation phase is that of administering the ordinances and regulations. This, the individual parcel decision making phase of the growth planning process, often receives the most publicity. These decisions receive a great deal of media coverage because there is often sharp disagreement between those wanting to develop land and those opposing the development, often resulting in confrontations and legal maneuvers. There are often no "right" or "wrong" solutions to these disagreements; each decision is a subjective judgment about how well the proposed land use satisfies the goals and objectives identified in the growth plan.

Figure 8.1 The growth planning process. (Source: Eddie L. Schwertz, Jr., *The Local Growth Management Guidebook*, Stillwater, Ok: The Southern Growth Policies Board, 1979.)

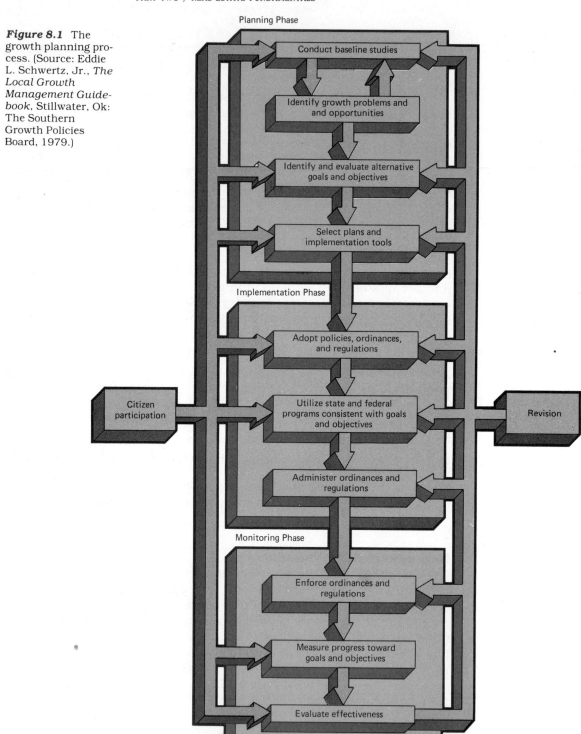

Monitoring Phase

Once decisions are made they must be enforced. Violations must be identified and corrected. Also, on a continuous basis, the extent to which the growth plan has achieved its original goals and objectives must be evaluated.

Implications of Growth Plans

For persons in the real estate business, the development and implementation of a growth plan offers potential benefits and problems. Among the benefits of such a plan are stability and consistency in government decision making, both critical for effective real estate business planning and decision making. On the negative side, the plan may not adequately represent the land use needs of the urban area, creating conflicts between land uses demanded by people and land uses provided in the plan. Developers are caught in the middle in such situations and may see many potentially useful and profitable opportunities evaporate because of a lack of planning approval. The growth plan represents a set of constraints within which development must occur. A thorough understanding of growth plans is a useful tool for persons in every real estate activity area.

LAND USE CONTROLS AND INCENTIVES

Implementing the growth management plan requires a set of controls and incentives that allows planners and urban governments to influence the types, quantities, location, and timing of real estate development. Not all approaches to growth management involve simply saying "no." Positive approaches involving incentives, such as reduced property taxes, are also used to achieve the goals and objectives of growth management programs. Whether planners and urban governments use controls to limit the use of land or incentives to encourage its use in a particular way, the days of a landowner acting independently of government are gone.

Land use controls and incentives (simply "controls" from here on) have not been created and implemented overnight. They have evolved over time and that evolution continues. New techniques continue to be developed to satisfy new needs. Table 8.1 lists some 68 techniques for influencing development. This listing is not intended to be exhaustive, nor are all the techniques used to an equal extent. It does illustrate the variety of available land use tools, old and new. The most popular of the regulatory mechanisms are zoning and subdivision controls.

The police power gives to government the power to enact and enforce laws necessary to protect the health and safety and promote the general welfare of the public. This is the same concept used to establish

Table 8.1. Techniques for Influencing Development

I. POLICY AND ASSESSMENT TOOLS
 1. Planning
 2. Carrying Capacity
 3. Fair Share Housing Allocation
 4. Cost-Revenue Analysis/ Fiscal Impact Analysis
 5. Environmental Assessment

II. REGULATORY MECHANISMS
 A. USE CONTROLS
  6. Zoning
  7. Special Permits/Special Exceptions/Conditional Use Permits
  8. Variances
  9. Floating Zones
  10. Conditional Zoning
  11. Contract Zoning
  12. Cyclical Rezoning
  13. Comprehensive Plan Consistency Requirements
  14. Zoning Referendum
  15. "Prohibitory" Zoning
  16. Agricultural Zoning/ Large Lot Zoning/Open Space Zoning
  17. Phased Zoning/Holding Zones/Short-term Service Area
  18. Performance Zoning/ Performance Standards
  19. Planned Unit Development (PUD)
 B. BULK CONTROLS
  20. Subdivision Regulations
  21. Minimum Lot Size
  22. Minimum Lot Size Per Dwelling Unit
  23. Minimum Lot Size Per Room
  24. Setback, Frontage, and Yard Regulations
  25. Minimum Floor Area
  26. Height Restriction
  27. Floor Area Ratio (FAR)
  28. Land Use Intensity Rating
  29. Flexible Zoning/Cluster Zoning/Density Zoning

 C. ALLOCATION CONTROLS
  30. Adequate Public Facilities Ordinance
  31. Permit Allocation System
  32. Facility Allocation System
  33. Development Moratorium/Interim Development Controls
 D. SPECIAL CONTROLS
  34. Special Protection Districts/Critical Areas/Environmentally Sensitive Areas
  35. Developments of Regional Impact
  36. Extraterritorial Zoning and Subdivision Powers
 E. COMPENSATORY CONTROLS
  37. Transferable Development Rights (TDR)
  38. Compensable Regulation
  39. Zoning by Special Assessment Financed Eminent Domain (ZSAFED)
 F. MISCELLANEOUS CONTROLS
  40. Official Mapping
  41. Timed Conditional Annexation
  42. Long-term Service Area/Long-term Limit Line/Urban-Rural Service Areas
  43. Total Population Limitation/Growth Cap
 G. PRIVATE MARKET INCENTIVES
  44. Restrictive Covenants
  45. Nonzoning
  46. Bonus and Incentive Zoning
  47. Land Acquisition Assistance
  48. Special Development Districts/Municipal Utility Districts

III. CAPITAL EXPENDITURES
 A. FACILITIES CONSTRUCTION
  49. Facility location
  50. Capital Improvements Programming
 B. LAND ACQUISITION
  51. Fee Simple Acquisition
  52. Advance Land Acquisition/Project Land Banking
  53. General Land Banking
  54. Less Than Fee Simple Acquisition

IV. REVENUE MECHANISMS
 A. PROPERTY TAXES
  55. Conventional Property Taxation
  56. Use-Value taxation
  57. Deferred Taxation
  58. Restricted-Use Taxation
  59. Differential Taxation
  60. Land-Value Taxation
  61. Tax Base Sharing
 B. SPECIAL TAXES AND FEES
  62. Land Gains Tax/ Special Capital and Real Estate Windfall Taxes (SCREWTS)/ Incremental Value Taxes
  63. Special Assessment
  64. Variable Service Fees/Marginal Cost Pricing
 C. EXACTIONS
  65. Mandatory Dedication
  66. Fees in Lieu of Mandatory Dedication
  67. Development Impact Fee
  68. Mandatory Low-cost Housing

SOURCE: Land Management: A Technical Report on Controls and Incentives for Use by State and Local Government. (Washington, D.C.: Public Technology, Inc., 1977.)

speed limits on streets and highways; public safety is more important than the individual automobile owner's right to use his or her private property (car) without any limitations. Many of the tools in Table 8.1 represent limitations on the fee simple ownership of land, insomuch as the urban government can regulate how land is used.

Zoning

Zoning is the most widely used land use control in the United States. Over 10,000 municipalities currently exercise zoning powers. Zoning establishes what can be built on a parcel of land, how much of it can be built, how tall the building can be, and where on the parcel the building can be located. This means that if you want to use a portion of Blackacre for an office building, the zoning code may dramatically affect your plans. If present zoning does not allow office buildings on the site and that zoning cannot be changed, you will not be able to build an office building at all. If the zoning allows office buildings, but does not allow you to build as many square feet of office space as you need to make a reasonable profit, the project may not be financially feasible. Likewise, if you simply wish to sell Blackacre to a developer, zoning will affect its value by defining what that developer can do with Blackacre and the resulting profits. Zoning and changes in zoning affect the use and value of real property. Fortunes have been made and lost gambling on obtaining the necessary zoning for real estate development.

Modern zoning has its legal roots in the United States Supreme Court case of *Euclid vs. Ambler Realty Co.*, decided in 1926. In this case, the Supreme Court upheld the rights of a municipality to zone as a part of the police power. Since 1926, every state has passed legislation enabling cities to zone. Most of this enabling legislation was patterned after the Standard Zoning Enabling Act developed by the United States Department of Commerce.

Zoning Basics Zoning ordinances define a number of zones, or districts, corresponding to possible land uses. The number of different zoning classifications varies from city to city but will usually include the general categories of residential, commercial, industrial, agricultural, and office. Within each of these general categories are subcategories, usually broken down by intensity, also called density, which is the amount of development per unit of land. The more square footage or units per acre or square foot of land, the higher the intensity of that development. A listing of representative zoning classifications and their abbreviations is contained in Table 8.2. Notice, for example, that the general classification of office zoning is broken down by density into four classifications or districts. If Blackacre is zoned as an "Office Low-Intensity District," you can build a low-intensity, garden-type office building like those you see in the suburban areas of most cities. However, if Blackacre is zoned for "Office High-Intensity District," you can build

Table 8.2. Representative Zoning Classifications

Abbreviation*	Zoning Classification*
AG	Agricultural District
RS-1	Residential Single-Family Low-Density District
RS-2	Residential Single-Family Medium-Density District
RS-3	Residential Single-Family High-Density District
RD	Residential Duplex District
RM-T	Residential Multifamily Townhouse District
RM-O	Residential Multifamily Lowest Density District
RM-1	Residential Multifamily Low Density District
RM-2	Residential Multifamily Medium-Density District
RM-3	Residential Multifamily High-Density District
RMH	Residential Mobile Home Park District
P	Parking District
OL	Office Low-Intensity District
OM	Office Medium-Intensity District
OMH	Office Medium to High-Intensity District
OH	Office High-Intensity District
CS	Commercial Shopping Center District
CG	Commercial General District
CH	Commercial High-Intensity District
CO	Corridor District
IR	Industrial Research and Development District
IL	Industrial Light District
IM	Industrial Moderate District
IH	Industrial Heavy District
FD	Floodway District
PUD	Planned Unit Development (Supplemental Zoning District)

* The specific names and abbreviations of the various classifications will vary from city to city.

much more office space on the same tract of land. Where the low-intensity zoning may allow only a two-story building on your site, the high-intensity zoning may have no height limitations.

To better understand the importance of zoning classifications and how zoning controls your use of Blackacre, let's consider the office zoning classifications in more detail. Table 8.3 contains a summary of some of the more important information about the office zoning districts in Table 8.2. Assume that you have selected a 200 foot by 200 foot parcel within Blackacre as the site for an office building and that the site is zoned as a medium-intensity office district (OM). First, OM zoning does not have a minimum lot size associated with it, as does OH zoning. Next, you can see that OM zoning requires a parcel fronting on an arterial (major) street or freeway service road to be at least 100 feet wide and one fronting a nonarterial street to be 50 feet wide. So far, nothing has acted as a contraint on your Blackacre parcel.

However, the next item, the maximum **floor area ratio (FAR),** defines how intensively you may use Blackacre. The FAR is the factor,

Table 8.3. Summary Information for Office Zoning Classification

	Districts			
	OL	OM	OMH	OH
Lot Area Minimum (sq. ft.)	NA	NA	NA	10,000
Frontage (min. ft.)				
Arterial and Freeway Service Road	75	100	100	NA
Not an Arterial	50	50	50	NA
Floor Area Ratio (Maximum)	.25	.50	2.0	8.0
Setback from Centerline of Abutting Street (min. ft.). Measured from centerline of abutting street; add, to the distance designated in the column to the right, $\frac{1}{2}$ of the right-of-way designated on the Major Street Plan or 25 feet if the street is not designated on the Major Street Plan.				
Arterial and Freeway Service Road	50	50	50	10
Not an Arterial	25	25	25	10
Setback from Abutting AG or R District				
Boundary Lines (min. ft.)	10	10*	10*	10
Building Height (max. ft.)	1-Story	NA	NA	NA

* Plus 2 feet of setback for each 1 foot of building height exceeding 15 feet, if the abutting property is within an RS or RD District.

which when multiplied by the area of parcel, determines the number of square feet of improvements that can be constructed. The OM zoning has a maximum FAR of .50, which means that to find the maximum square feet of office space you can build, you must multiply .50 by the number of square feet in your parcel. Since there are 40,000 square feet in your parcel (200 feet × 200 feet = 40,000 square feet), you can construct 20,000 square feet of office space (.50 × 40,000 square feet = 20,000 square feet). Notice that the FAR for the OH zoning is 8, which means you could have legally constructed 320,000 (8 × 40,000 square feet) square feet of office space on the same parcel.

So far, so good; you can construct a one-story office building covering half your site—or can you? The answer is maybe, because the code also establishes where on the site you can place improvements through a series of **setback requirements** establishing minimum distances from your improvements to the street and adjoining parcels. These setback requirements are sometimes called **bulk restrictions** because they limit the parcel's buildable area and the bulk of the completed building. Since the street by your parcel is an arterial, you must set your building 100 feet back from the centerline of the street. Fifty feet of the setback is dictated by number in the column under OM zoning and the other fifty feet is dictated by the requirement to set the building back an additional amount equal to half the width of the street right-of-way. Since your street has a 100-foot right-of-way, this adds another 50 feet of setback as seen in Figure 8.2. If any of the parcels around your site are zoned either for agricultural or residential use, you must set your improvements back 10 feet from such a property's boundaries. After all the setback requirements, the buildable area is found to be 115 by 180 feet and contains 20,700 square feet. This means you can build the allowed 20,000 square feet of space as a one-story building. However, if the OM zoning had allowed more than 20,700 square feet, you would have had to build more than one story because of the setback requirement.

Notice that OM zoning does not have a specific height limitation. You can build your allowed 20,000 square feet by covering half the parcel with a 1-story building or you could cover only one-fourth of the parcel with a 2-story building with 10,000 square feet per floor, or you could cover only one-eighth of the parcel by building a 4-story building with 5000 square feet per floor, and so on. However, notice that the asterisk next to the setback requirement in the OM column leads to another setback requirement. For every foot over 15 feet in height, you must set the building an additional 2 feet away from single family and duplex parcels. Thus, if you build a 2-story building that is 27 feet tall, that building exceeds the 15 foot limit by 12 feet. This means the building must be setback from RS and RD parcels an additional 24 feet.

Figure 8.2 Impact of setback requirements on buildable area (medium office zoning).

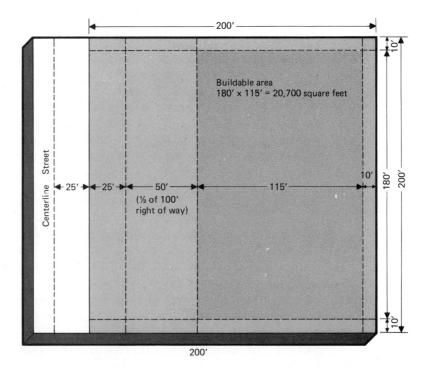

Depending on your Blackacre parcel, these additional setback requirements may or may not be desirable.

Exceptions to the provisions of a zoning district can be granted in special situations. For example, if you wanted to build a 4-story office building on the Blackacre parcel, but the added setback requirements would force you to construct the building too close to a high pressure natural gas pipeline, you may ask for permission to build closer to adjoining properties. You will be seeking a **variance,** special permission to override a specific portion of the zoning requirements. Needless to say, variances defeat some of the original intent of the zoning ordinance. However, they do provide property owners with a measure of flexibility a strict interpretation of the zoning code would not.

Zoning Administration Zoning is administered locally, usually by city government, but sometimes by a metropolitan or countywide body that cuts across municipal boundaries. Zoning administrators assign a zoning classification to all parcels of real estate within their jurisdiction. They also establish procedures for rezoning property as a result of either a reassessment of the urban area's goals and objectives or a request by the landowner.

A city's zoning jurisdiction may extend beyond its political boundaries in some states. Such power is called **extraterritorial jurisdiction.** In these states, some cities have the power to zone a specified number of miles beyond their city limits. The limits of extraterritorial jurisdiction vary from state to state. This power is based on the idea that development frequently occurs outside city limits. If cities did not have the ability to zone beyond their city limits, a high percentage of total development could occur outside their control. As cities extend their political boundaries through a process called **annexation,** they may inherit problems that could have been avoided by proper zoning.

Having zoning powers beyond its political boundaries does not solve all of a city's zoning problems. County government may claim that authority for areas outside city limits should be theirs. Smaller, suburban communities with zoning powers of their own can also create complications. First, these communities may virtually surround the developed area of the larger central city, as in the cases of Chicago and St. Louis. Second, these smaller communities may annex large amounts of undeveloped land and thereby control its zoning. Third, some of these communities may also be large enough to have zoning powers beyond their city limits. The net result of these three situations is a loss of zoning jurisdiction and control for the city even if it legally has zoning powers beyond its city limits.

The fact that more than one, and sometimes many, government bodies in an urban area may be making zoning decisions creates complications, not only for those administering zoning, but also for those seeking zoning changes. Different bodies administering zoning means that you must be aware of which body has jurisdiction, be able to assess the probability of success in rezoning, and know the proper rezoning procedures for that body. A good land use attorney is valuable in this process.

Decision Making Zoning decisions are usually made by the city commission or city council or its equivalent. Playing an advisory role to the city commission or council is the **planning commission.** This body is composed of citizens, usually either appointed by the mayor or selected by the city commission or city council, who serve without pay. Assisting and advising the planning commission is the planning commission staff, or planning staff, which conducts the commission's day-to-day business. Professional planners, statisticians, economists, and other support persons are on the planning staff.

If you are seeking a zoning change, you will deal initially with the planning staff. While rezoning procedures vary greatly, Figure 8.3 illustrates a representative zoning change procedure. As you can see, the procedure begins with you discussing preliminaries such as the application and fees with the planning staff. Next, you will file the rezoning application, pay a filing fee, and agree to pay for public notice. Public notice is accomplished by placing an ad conveying your intentions to rezone in a general circulation publication, usually a legal newspaper published to serve this purpose, and by placing a sign with the same information on the property to be rezoned, along with the date and place of public hearings on the rezoning. Additionally, the planning staff will send letters to all property owners within a specified distance from your property, notifying them of the proposed rezoning and public hearings. All of these measures are designed to make those affected by the rezoning aware of the proposed change.

Following these initial steps, public hearings before the planning commission will be scheduled. At the public hearing those supporting and opposing rezoning will have the opportunity to state their case. It is not uncommon for opposition to develop when persons fear the proposed rezoning will adversely affect them. These adverse effects can take many forms: flooding, increased traffic congestion, noise, school overcrowding, decreased property values, and so on. In San Francisco, for example, considerable controversy developed over zoning for high-rise buildings in the downtown area. The controversy led to a referendum election on the question of limiting the height of buildings.

After listening to all sides and considering the recommendations from the planning staff, the commission makes a decision. The planning commission can recommend complete approval, approval with modifications, or disapproval by the city commission or council.

Once the planning commission reaches a decision, the city commission will then consider the rezoning application in a public hearing at which proponents and opponents will be allowed to present their views. Since city commissioners are elected officials, political pressure

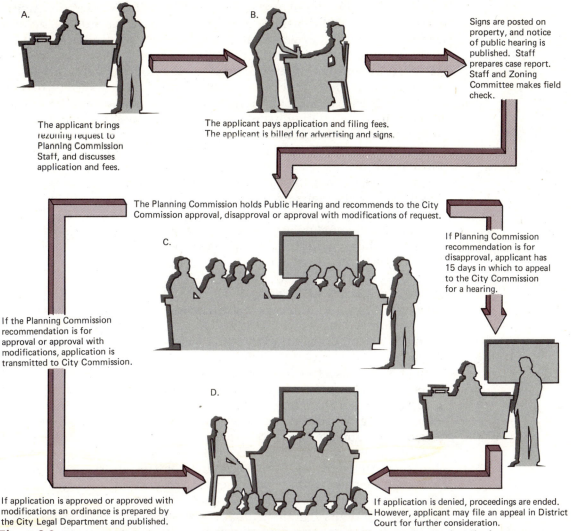

A.

The applicant brings rezoning request to Planning Commission Staff, and discusses application and fees.

B.

The applicant pays application and filing fees. The applicant is billed for advertising and signs.

Signs are posted on property, and notice of public hearing is published. Staff prepares case report. Staff and Zoning Committee makes field check.

The Planning Commission holds Public Hearing and recommends to the City Commission approval, disapproval or approval with modifications of request.

C.

If Planning Commission recommendation is for disapproval, applicant has 15 days in which to appeal to the City Commission for a hearing.

If the Planning Commission recommendation is for approval or approval with modifications, application is transmitted to City Commission.

D.

If application is approved or approved with modifications an ordinance is prepared by the City Legal Department and published.

If application is denied, proceedings are ended. However, applicant may file an appeal in District Court for further consideration.

Figure 8.3 Elements of a typical rezoning procedure. (Details will vary from city to city, but the basic concepts are similar.) (Source: Indian Nations Council of Governments.)

can more readily be brought to bear on them than on the appointed planning commission. The city commission weighs the arguments made by all sides and the planning commission recommendation before reaching a decision. The city commission can approve, approve with modifications, or disapprove the rezoning application.

Even the city commission isn't necessarily the final word. Its decision can be appealed to the courts by either the applicant or the opposition. Essentially, the courts must decide whether the rezoning decision was capricious and arbitrary. How far court appeals proceed depends on the financial commitment of those for and against the project, since court appeals are expensive.

Occasionally, the planning commission will change the zoning of parcels without being asked to by the landowner in order to achieve desired patterns of development. If improvements already exist on the site, they may no longer fit the parcel's zoning classification. They are called a **nonconforming use.** Generally, a landowner will be allowed to continue using such improvements, but cannot make additions to them and, in most cases, cannot even make extensive renovations. When the rezoning involves changing the zoning to a less intensive zoning classification, it is called **downzoning.** For instance, if Blackacre were rezoned from medium-intensity office to agricultural use only, it would have been downzoned.

Zoning decisions involve economic, social, psychological, and legal elements. Growth plans provide a basis for consistent decision making but individual rezoning decisions still require a great deal of judgment. Zoning officials must balance the possible benefits and costs to the public against the ownership rights of the property owner. Thus, zoning is, and likely will remain, a very subjective process.

Changing Nature of Zoning Variations on the basic zoning theme have been developed in recent years to provide greater flexibility to zoning boards and landowners. One of them is the **planned unit development (PUD).** Under traditional zoning you would have to obtain zoning for each parcel involving a different use. For example, earlier in this chapter you found that one parcel of Blackacre was zoned for office development. If you wanted to develop a shopping center you would have to designate a specific parcel and obtain the appropriate zoning for that tract, abiding by all the provisions of the zoning code. Planned unit development zoning allows you to develop a mixture and intensity of uses traditional zoning does not, by allowing you to develop an overall plan for Blackacre and obtain zoning for the entire development. Usually, the city will require promises with respect to the development in return for granting you the flexibility to develop in a manner that would be impossible under regular zoning. The rationale for PUD zoning is that a more cohesive development is possible than otherwise could be.

Cluster zoning allows developers to deviate from the usual side, front, and back yard requirements in return for providing open land that may be used by homeowners. Such a concept allows for higher density development while minimizing the feeling of being crowded.

Subdivision Regulations

When a developer wants to create a number of smaller lots from a larger tract, he must conform to a set of rules called **subdivision regulations.** These regulations are intended to protect the city from inheriting developed areas with inadequate streets, sewerage systems, storm water drainage, and other problems that may create future operating ex-

Figure 8.4 Final plat map. (Source: Terry L. Davis Companies.)

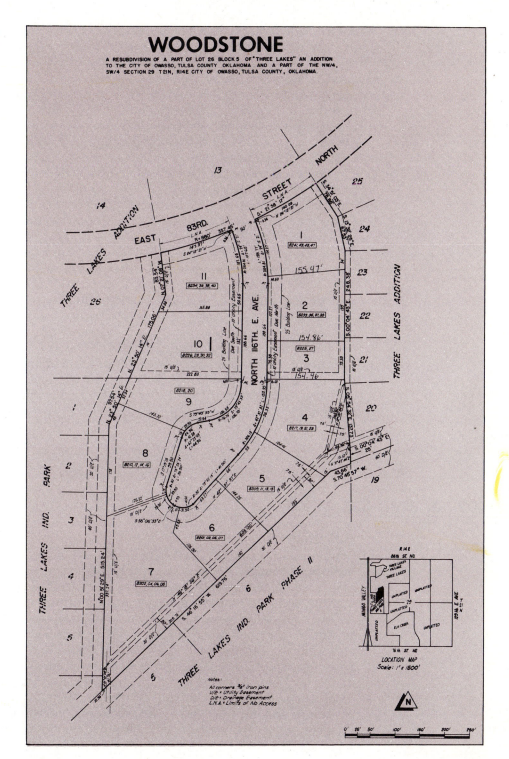

penses. Subdivision regulations also protect the purchasers of lots from unexpected expenses required to correct problems in sewerage, streets, or other areas. In addition to establishing minimum design and engineering standards for subdivisions, such regulations may require developers to **dedicate,** or give, land for schools and parks rather than the city or school having to purchase the land. The theory behind such regulations is that developers will pass the costs associated with meeting subdivision regulations on to those receiving the benefits from these facilities, the lot purchasers.

Subdivision regulations require the developer to file a **plat** of the proposed development showing the location and dimensions of streets, lots, utilities, park land, easements, and school sites. Plat maps were considered earlier in Chapter 3, in the section dealing with methods for legally describing real estate. A *preliminary plat* is required first from the developer. This plat is analyzed by the planning agency and interested city departments, such as water and sewerage, for compliance with objectives and standards and to determine whether the city can provide the necessary services. If the preliminary plat is approved or approved with modifications agreed to by the developer, construction can usually commence. A *final plat* is prepared and submitted reflecting the review and changes of the preliminary plat. A final plat is illustrated in Figure 8.4. The final plat review is the last opportunity the approval agency has to change the plat. When the final plat is approved, the developer and the city have reached agreement about obligations to one another.

OTHER LAND USE CONTROLS

Building Codes
Before constructing an improvement you must obtain a city or county **building permit.** The fee you pay for this permit is used to operate an inspection department to assure that your structure complies with the building code. The **building code** specifies minimum standards for materials and quality of work, and requires certain safety features such as sprinkler systems. In many instances, changes are made in building codes after a tragedy, such as the MGM Grand Hotel fire in Las Vegas. After this fire, Las Vegas instituted some stringent fire safety requirements for hotels. During construction, a property must pass periodic inspections for work to continue. When completed, a final inspection is performed and if the property is satisfactory, a **certificate of occupancy** is issued. This certificate must be obtained before the structure may be occupied.

Extension of Public Facilities

Land without drinking water, sewerage service, adequate streets, and storm water drainage is not suitable for development, even if the location is excellent. Raw land, or land in its natural state, requires a good deal of investment, on and off site, to make it useful for building. Some of this investment is public in nature and some is private. If the public chooses not to invest in extending public services necessary to support development, then private developers and builders must provide these services. This is often not economically feasible, and consequently, development does not occur. Ramapo, New York, a community about 60 miles from the city of New York, instituted a program in which the construction of new residences was limited to the number for which the city could economically provide necessary services. Other cities have since considered or enacted similar growth-control programs. A refusal to extend public facilities is called a **moratorium.**

Eminent Domain

Instead of regulating the use of privately owned land to achieve its objectives, a city could simply purchase the land. For example, if your city has a rapidly growing section, there may be some concern about it having enough open space. To insure adequate open space the city could rezone some of the land in the area to allow no building. Another option is for the city simply to buy enough land to provide the open space needed. Such a purchase would cost the city a tidy sum of money, whereas the zoning option would shift costs to owners of downzoned land through lower property values. Likewise, the city can use **eminent domain** to encourage development by purchasing land and constructing an improvement such as a park or golf course. Such developments increase the desirability of surrounding land and increase its chances of being developed.

Using the power of eminent domain, cities can purchase property for public purposes whether the private owners want to sell or not. The workings of eminent domain were considered in Chapter 5, but its use as a land use tool to either prevent or encourage development was not made clear. The biggest drawback to the use of eminent domain as a land use tool is the cost. Since the city must pay the private owner a fair market price, the cost is often prohibitive. The city could avoid some of these high costs by purchasing land in advance of development when it is cheaper. However, few cities have enough money to purchase and hold property for that period of time.

TAKINGS ISSUE

As you have read about the land use controls available to the city, you may have been wondering about the property rights of the landowner.

Exercise of the police power does not require compensation to the property owner, even though his or her ownership rights, or collection of property rights, are reduced. If you have been thinking about how far city, state, and federal governments can go in the use of the police power, you are not alone.

The slow-growth or no-growth policies adopted by some cities with growth problems, and others simply trying to avoid growth problems, have given rise to a new set of controls, such as in the Ramapo, New York, example, and new variations on old ones. Other municipalities have considered requiring developers to prepare and file a fiscal impact analysis showing the revenues a proposed project would contribute to the city and the costs it would impose. Refusals to extend sewers and water lines, rezoning land on the edge of the city to agricultural uses only, and large lot zoning requiring large, expensive lots, are other techniques used to discourage development.

Those contending that some of these techniques are violations of private property rights cite the Fifth and Fourteenth Amendments to the Constitution. The Fifth Amendment provides that private property shall not be taken without just compensation. The Fourteenth Amendment adds the provision that private property shall not be taken without due process of law. Some persons feel that private property is effectively taken without compensation or due process if its use is so limited by regulation that its value in the marketplace or its usefulness to the owner is substantially reduced. It is argued that the law guarantees certain private property rights.

Others, supporting the implementation of more stringent land use controls, contend that property rights are always changing and subject to being redefined by society from time to time. They contend that if society chooses not to protect certain property rights, then the definition of property rights changes; uncertainty about present and future property rights is no more of a problem than uncertainty about business conditions.

This entire issue is called the **takings issue.** When does a taking occur? Where is the line between the exercise of the police power requiring no compensation and eminent domain requiring compensation? There are no final answers to these questions. The courts have taken a case by case approach rather than making sweeping definitions. You will be hearing more about the takings issue during the coming years.

STATE AND FEDERAL LAND USE CONTROLS

Many state governments, as well as the federal government, are becoming increasingly active in land use planning and control. This increased activity is aimed primarily at rural lands presently not affected by local land use planning efforts. Much of this interest in rural lands has been prompted by increasing development activity in these areas and a growing concern about the environment. Many states and the federal government have simply decided that land resources are too important not to be managed in some manner.

At the state level, land planning agencies have been created to begin the job of land use planning on a statewide basis. Initially, these agencies perform the necessary task of compiling land use information — information about what land uses exist in the state, where they exist, and the extent of each type of land use. Of particular interest is identifying areas in which development may have profound effects that cannot be reversed. Developing an inventory of land uses with adequate detail is a big job. Many states have used a combination of field personnel, aerial and satellite sensing, and the work of the U.S. Geological Survey in developing this inventory.

Actual land use controls instituted at the state level are varied. Most states are in the early stages of considering or implementing such controls. Some states, such as California with its beautiful coastline, have enacted laws limiting coastal development. Others have simply attempted to identify existing and potential environmental problems. The exact form of future state land use planning activity and the resulting controls or regulations are not clear. One thing is certain, however; the increased awareness of the environment and the desire to protect rural lands not currently subject to planning efforts will lead to more active state land use planning.

Environmental issues have also received considerable attention at the federal level. In 1969, the National Environmental Policy Act was enacted. This act is administered by the Environmental Protection Agency (EPA) which seeks to develop, with each state, plans for controlling all types of pollution. Environmental concerns have also caused members of Congress to introduce legislation creating a national land use policy. As yet such a policy has not been adopted by Congress. As with the states, federal efforts in land use planning will likely increase in the future although the nature of those planning efforts and regulations is not known.

SUMMARY

In this chapter you have learned about the need for urban planning, the urban planning process, and how it affects the real estate business. Urban planning is necessary because the growth and development of a city places increased demands on it for services. Urban planning is concerned with providing the best level of services at a minimum cost. Planning for growth involves three phases: planning, implementing, and monitoring. Growth planning should not be confused with "no-growth". It is concerned with the most efficient and economical handling of growth, whatever its rate.

Urban areas can influence land use and development patterns in many ways. Positive approaches include reduced property taxes and the development of public amenities, such as parks and golf courses. Actual controls are also numerous, with the most widely used control being zoning. Zoning was approved by the Supreme Court in the case of *Euclid vs. Ambler Realty Co.*, decided in 1926. Zoning ordinances determine the use, intensity, bulk, and height of the improvements on a parcel of land. Variances can be granted that allow landowners to avoid compliance with specified provisions of the zoning code. New approaches to zoning have evolved over time to provide more flexibility to the city and landowner. Such changes include planned unit developments and cluster zoning.

Subdivision regulations cover the creation of a number of smaller parcels from a larger parcel of land. They insure that all improvements meet city or county specifications. Developers must file preliminary plats of their development, leading ultimately to the final plat showing the details of the subdivision. Building codes, the extension of public facilities, and eminent domain also are used to influence and control development.

The exercise of the police power is not without limits. Those limits are the subject of the takings issue. At issue is when the exercise of the police power so reduces ownership rights that the property is effectively taken. Definite answers are lacking on this issue, and it is not likely to be resolved in the near future.

Finally, state and federal land use planning and controls were seen to be in the early stages. Much of their activity is in the area of taking an inventory of land resources and protecting areas subject to irreversible damage from development. However, state and federal governments are likely to take a much more active role in land use planning and controls in the future.

QUICK QUIZ

1. The phases of the growth planning process do not include

a. implementation
b. planning
c. monitoring
d. assembling

2. Growth management, with respect to land use, is implemented using

I. controls
II. incentives

a. I only
b. Both I and II
c. Both I and II
d. Neither I nor II

3. The part of a zoning classification that establishes the maximum amount of space that can be erected on a site is called a(n)

    a. setback requirement   c. floor area ratio
    b. building code   d. intensity factor

4. The takings issue involves

    a. the balance between private property rights and the police power
    b. what price should be paid for land taken under eminent domain
    c. the ability of government to force a private land owner to sell land
    d. none of the above

5. The laws governing the creation of a number of smaller lots from a larger tract are called _____ .

6. Once a property is completed, the appropriate government body must issue a _____ before the building may be used.

7. The _____ allows government to enact and enforce laws necessary to protect the health and safety and promote the general welfare of the public.

8. The most widely used land control in the United States is _____ .

9. _____ is the power of a city to zone in areas outside its political boundaries.

QUESTIONS AND EXERCISES

1. Suppose that one year ago you purchased 160 acres on the edge of town with the intention of someday developing it as a residential subdivision, for which it was already zoned. Today you find out that the city council plans to rezone the land for agricultural use only in order to provide open space and control urban sprawl. Develop arguments supporting and opposing this action. Also develop arguments supporting and opposing the contention that this action constitutes a taking of your property without just compensation.

2. Discuss the pros and cons of a city having extraterritorial jurisdiction.

3. Discuss the idea that developable land is a manufactured product.

What are the implications of this concept for those investing in or developing land?

4. Discuss the relationship between zoning and land values.

5. What are the advantages and disadvantages of PUD zoning?

6. What incentives can a city offer to developers to encourage development in a particular section of the city? How effective do you think these incentives can be?

7. Find a copy of your town's comprehensive plan and identify its land use objectives.

KEY TERMINOLOGY

annexation
building code
building permit
bulk restrictions
certificate of
   occupancy
cluster zoning
dedication
density
downzoning
eminent domain
extraterritorial
   jurisdiction
floor area ratio
growth planning
intensity

land use controls
land use incentives
moratorium
no-growth
nonconforming use
planned unit
   development
planning commission
plat
setback requirement
subdivision
   regulations
takings issue
variance
zoning

IF YOU WANT TO READ MORE

F. STUART CHAPIN, JR. and EDWARD J. KAISER, *Urban Land Use Planning, Third Edition* (Urbana, IL: University of Illinois Press, 1979).

JOHN MCMAHON, *Property Development* (New York: McGraw-Hill Book Company, 1976), Chapter 2.

WILLIAM K. REILLY, ed., *The Use of Land: A Citizen's Policy Guide to Urban Growth* (New York: Thomas Y. Crowell, 1973).

EDDIE L. SCHWERTZ, JR., *The Local Growth Management Guidebook* (Stillwater, Okla.: The Southern Growth Policies Board, 1979).

HERBERT H. SMITH, *The Citizen's Guide to Planning, Revised Edition,* (Chicago: American Planning Association, 1979).

PETER WOLF, *Land in America* (New York: Pantheon Books, 1981), Chapters 3 and 5–8.

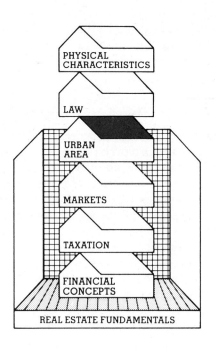

PHYSICAL CHARACTERISTICS

LAW

URBAN AREA

MARKETS

TAXATION

FINANCIAL CONCEPTS

REAL ESTATE FUNDAMENTALS

9

Real Estate Markets

PREVIEW

A television commercial for a leading tire maker boasted that their tires were best "where the rubber meets the road." Implied in this statement is the idea that "where the rubber meets the road" is the acid test for any tire — a difficult point to quarrel with. In real estate, the equivalent acid test for a property is "where the property meets the market." Real estate markets are where the efforts of everyone involved in real estate are evaluated; it's *the* final examination that every property and every potential transaction must pass. Successful real estate projects are those that have passed the market test by providing needed space and, by so doing, commanding competitive or above normal rents or prices. It is in markets that the real estate winners and losers are determined. This chapter explores real estate markets and their workings. After reading this chapter you should understand:

1. What a market is and what it does.
2. The different types of real estate markets and how they operate.
3. The importance of real estate markets to everyone in the real estate business.
4. Why supply and demand are so important and yet so difficult to estimate in many cases.
5. Why real estate appraisers are needed to estimate market value.

6. Basic approaches to analyzing real estate markets.
7. How well real estate markets operate and what this means to you.

WHAT ARE REAL ESTATE MARKETS?

When you are looking for a place to rent, you are involved with real estate markets. Developers are also involved with markets when they try to determine if more suburban office space is needed in a particular location. Real estate brokers are involved in real estate markets when they try to bring buyers and sellers together. You, the developer, and the broker have different perspectives on real estate markets and will define them accordingly. That is, the definition of "market" may vary with your perspective. For example, to you the market may consist of the homes or apartments fitting your needs and budget. The developer thinks of the market in terms of the amount of existing suburban office space and the amount of office space needed in that area by people and companies. From the point of view of the broker, the market is the number of properties for sale and the number of prospective buyers for those properties.

CLASSIFYING MARKETS

If you consider the above examples of what real estate markets may be, you will notice that two distinct areas of activity were being considered. You and the developer were concerned with renting space — you from the standpoint of a lessee and the developer from the standpoint of the lessor. Both of you were concerned with the **rental market** — the market in which space of all types is leased. The broker was concerned with people buying and selling ownership, or equity, interests in real estate. Equity, or ownership, interests are bought and sold in real estate **equity markets.** (The developer may also be concerned with equity markets if he is trying to sell a development.)

The division of real estate markets into rental and equity markets is for convenience — it is not intended to indicate that these markets function independently of one another. Just the opposite is true; these markets are closely related. It is the need for space and the willingness of people to pay for its use in the rental markets that create income flowing to equity investors.

The greater the income a property produces the more it is worth to an equity investor. You would usually be willing to pay more for an investment producing $100 per month than one producing $50 per month if all other aspects of the investment, such as risk, were the same. You may be thinking that the equity markets for homes are not affected by the rental markets since equity investors invest in homes to use and not for the rent dollars they generate. However, the rental and equity markets for homes are related since anyone buying a home could rent living space instead. If the overall cost of renting is less than the cost of owning, people will rent instead of buying and vice versa. Even the equity market for single family homes is affected by the condition of rental markets.

It is probably not surprising to you to learn that equity markets are affected by conditions in rental markets. However, you should be aware that rental markets are also affected by conditions in equity markets. For example, in periods of high interest rates, it is difficult for equity investors to find investments providing enough income to support the large loans necessary to purchase real estate. As a result, new equity investment slows dramatically, and as it does, so does development since developers now have no buyers for their projects. Thus, little or no new space is produced, causing rents to increase. Other conditions affecting the equity markets may also affect the space markets in a similar fashion. The important thing to remember is that the relationship between space and equity markets works both ways (Figure 9.1).

The division of real estate markets into rental and equity markets is only the first step in identifying the many submarkets that in total represent *the* real estate market. In both the equity and rental markets there are actually many **submarkets.** For example, there is not one rental market, but rather submarkets for apartments, office space, retail space, warehouse space, and so on. You may be looking for an apartment and having a terrible time finding a suitable vacant unit while a retail business may have many shopping centers to choose from because of overbuilding by shopping center developers. Under such conditions, apartment rents may be high in your city compared to other cities while retail space is a relative bargain!

Figure 9.1 Real estate markets.

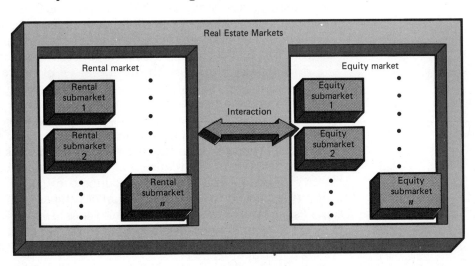

It may have occurred to you that not even all apartments compete with one another in either the rental or equity markets. This means that the apartment market may have submarkets within it, such as suburban and downtown, low-rise and high-rise, economy and luxury. Each of these submarkets may have differences just as was described above between apartment and retail rental markets. Exactly how many submarkets may exist in your city is a judgment call. How many submarkets you care to identify depends on your reasons for considering submarkets. The important thing to remember is that using the phrase "real estate market" in a general sense may be misleading. The overall real estate market is not often that interesting. It is the submarket(s) relating to a specific problem that is more exciting and relevant. Identifying a submarket with superior profit potential is a common objective of most everyone in the real estate business. An equity investor may find that one apartment submarket is quite a good investment while another is not. You may also find a similar situation when you buy a single family home.

BASIC MARKET ECONOMICS

All real estate submarkets perform basically the same task — establishing a price. Rental markets establish a price for the use of space over some period of time, whereas equity markets establish prices for ownership interests. Price is established by the interaction of buyers and sellers in the market. It is an historical number that represents the *result* of a transaction. Since it is in the best interest of both the buyer and seller to get the best possible deal, a good bit of negotiating accompanies most real estate transactions. Out of that negotiation a price is established. The **market** should be thought of as a mechanism or process that establishes price. It is not a particular building or place.

Price is very important in the operation of the real estate market. Consider your own housing situation; probably the only thing standing between you and a luxurious mansion is price. Price allocates existing space, such as mansions, based on the ability and desire to pay. It also determines what kinds of new space are produced by developers. If one submarket is capable of producing very high rents relative to other submarkets, developers will realize that these additional dollars will be attractive to equity investors and produce the highest prices when the property is sold. It is not surprising that developers will build more of that type of space than other, less profitable types of space. You should have a keen interest in how price is determined in real estate markets.

Supply + Demand = Price

So far, we have avoided the use of the economic terms **supply** and **demand.** These economic concepts determine that all important item, price.

Supply Supply can be defined as the quantity of a good or service that will be offered in the market at different prices. In other words, supply is a list, or schedule, of prices and the corresponding number of units offered for sale. Suppose you have surveyed homeowners in a selected neighborhood and estimated the number of three-bedroom homes likely to be offered for sale at different prices. Table 9.1 contains the results of your survey and estimates.

Usually, the higher the price, the more of a given good or service that will be supplied. This situation does not occur because some economist wants it to, but because human nature is such that most people will ultimately sell most assets for the right price. Consider a home. At very low prices the owners would not think of selling it. But if prices were to get high enough they may reconsider and offer it for sale, thus increasing the quantity of housing supplied. By expanding this logic to the entire market it is easy to see that greater quantities of goods and services will be supplied at higher prices than lower ones.

Demand Demand tends to work just the opposite way — as prices increase, the quantity of a good or service demanded decreases. Demand is a schedule of prices and the corresponding number of units demanded at each price. Once again this relationship appeals to our intuition — people will generally buy more of an item at lower prices than at higher prices. Table 9.2 contains the results of research into the demand for three-bedroom homes in the same neighborhood as above.

Determining Price

With the information in Tables 9.1 and 9.2, the price that will ultimately be achieved can be estimated. In Figure 9.2, the supply and demand estimates from Tables 9.1 and 9.2 have been plotted and lines drawn

Table 9.1. Number of Homes Supplied at Varying Prices

Price	Number of Homes Offered
$50,000	52
$55,000	64
$60,000	75
$65,000	86
$70,000	98

Table 9.2. Number of Homes
Demanded at Varying Prices

Price	Number of Homes Demanded
$50,000	92
$55,000	83
$60,000	75
$65,000	67
$70,000	60

between them. In this figure, the supply schedule is represented by the SS curve and the demand schedule by the DD curve. The two curves intersect at a price of $60,000 and at that price 75 homes will be supplied and demanded. This is the only point the two curves have in common and represents the point where the **quantity demanded** equals the **quantity supplied.** Since the quantities demanded and supplied are equal at this point, there are no unsold units and no unsatisfied demand — the market is cleared. At this point the market is in balance, or using the economic term for balance we can say it has achieved **equilibrium.** Markets generally move toward an equilibrium price, in this case $60,000.

What has just been described may sound very idealistic. You may be wondering why the market will move toward the price of $60,000 and equilibrium. The answer is found in the behavior of buyers and sellers. For example, look at Figure 9.2 and examine what would happen if we

Figure 9.2 Supply of and demand for housing in a particular neighborhood.

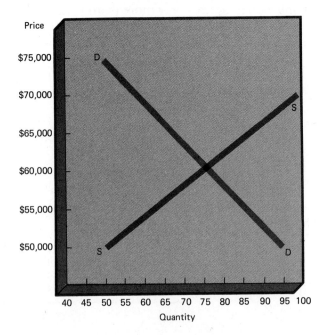

assume a price different than the $60,000 equilibrium price. For instance, at $70,000 only 60 homes are demanded while 98 are offered for sale. Sensing the oversupply of homes, buyers will offer less than $70,000 and sellers will realize that the only way they can sell their home is to lower the price. As prices start to fall, sellers will remove their homes from the market and new buyers will enter the market. This process will continue until buyers and sellers have equal bargaining strength at the $60,000 equilibrium price. If we had started at $50,000 the process would have just been reversed.

Real estate markets seldom achieve equilibrium. If they do, the condition will last only a short while. Real estate markets are dynamic and do not simply sit still once equilibrium is achieved. New buyers and sellers are entering and leaving the market all the time. Other factors, such as inflation and changes in income, constantly affect supply and demand schedules. As a result, markets are constantly moving toward equilibrium, but seldom if ever achieving it, and then only momentarily. A market's work is truly never done.

To illustrate the changing nature of markets, consider the three-bedroom homes above. What do you think would happen if the interest rate on home loans decreased by two percent the day after Figure 9.2 was drawn? It is likely that those interested in buying would now feel they can afford to spend more on a home because of the lower payments associated with the lower interest rates. If you think of demand as a list, or schedule, of units demanded at each and every price, the decrease in interest rates will cause an increase in the number of homes demanded at each price. As a result, the demand curve shifts out, indicating this

Figure 9.3 Change in demand for housing in a particular neighborhood.

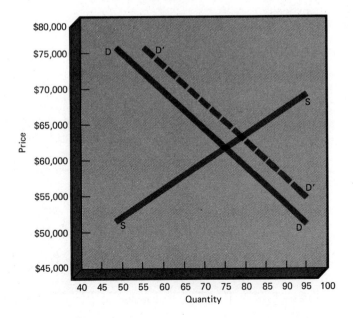

greater willingness to buy homes at each and every price. The new demand curve is the D'D' curve in Figure 9.3. The market will move toward a new and higher equilibrium price. Whether or not the new equilibrium price is achieved depends on how much time passes before other changes cause additional shifts in the supply or demand curve, or both.

The Short-Run Supply Problem

The discussion above dealt with the market for existing homes. When the subject is changed to the market for a particular type and quality of rental office space, the analysis changes. The fundamental change is the inability of office building owners and developers to produce additional space in the short run. The planning and production of additional office space require a substantial period of time. Thus, if demand increases, supply does does not adjust quickly and the result is an increase in rents.

Figure 9.4 illustrates this situation. In the graph, the supply curve is shown as a vertical line to highlight the fact that supply cannot be reduced or increased in the short run. When an increase in demand occurs, the only immediate impact is a new and higher level of rental rates. However, given time, the quantity of space supplied can be increased. The greater the amount of time allowed, the greater the possible change in the quantity of office space supplied as developers react to higher rental rates. Thus, the supply curves discussed earlier apply only to markets in which short-run changes in the quantity supplied are possible — a situation not descriptive of many real estate markets. You should keep the temporal aspects of adjustments in real estate markets in mind as you analyze them and consider the real estate development process.

Figure 9.4
Short-Term supply
and demand.

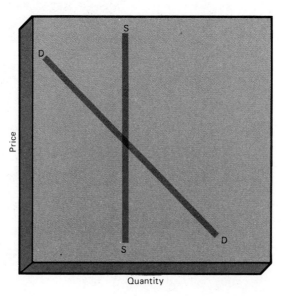

Supply, demand, and the determination of price are the most fundamental economic concepts affecting markets. Surprisingly, it is the simple concepts such as these that are often overlooked or taken for granted in making real estate decisions. As a result, well-designed, well-built projects are developed when and where they are not needed and cannot be rented or sold, except for disastrous amounts. Less apparent are the situations in which underdevelopment occurs; that is, a developer builds the right kind of space at the right time in the right place but fails to maximize profits by not building a project large enough to satisfy demand. In all that follows dealing with real estate markets, the simple concepts of supply and demand are critical to your overall understanding.

REAL ESTATE MARKET ORGANIZATION

Now that you understand the basics of supply and demand, attention can be shifted to the organization and operation of real estate markets. Who participates in real estate markets and who provides assistance to those participating in real estate markets? How are markets organized? These questions are now considered for equity and rental markets.

Real Estate Equity Markets

The purpose of real estate equity markets is to bring buyers and sellers together. Only when potential buyers know of properties for sale and potential sellers know of the needs of potential buyers can market transactions occur. Left on their own, many buyers and sellers will not find each other and many transactions attractive to both parties will not occur. In other instances, properties would simply remain on the market longer than necessary while buyers and sellers search for each other. To remedy this problem, real estate brokers are used. What follows is a simplified view of brokerage to allow you to concentrate on the role brokerage activity plays in real estate markets. Brokerage is discussed in greater detail in Chapters 20 and 21.

A real estate broker is someone who, for a fee, helps others sell, lease, or trade real estate. The broker is usually employed by the seller and receives a fee based on a percentage of the sales price, although any compensation scheme may be used. Legally, brokers are **agents** since they act on behalf of another individual called the *principal.* This agency relationship, along with its terms, are created by a contract called a listing agreement. The listing agreement contains provisions about the length of the agency relationship and the compensation the broker is to receive if the property is sold. Usually, the broker will receive no compensation unless a ready, willing, and able buyer is found.

All 50 states require real estate agents to be licensed and many have established educational and experience requirements for obtaining that license. States generally have two license classifications: (1) broker and (2) salesperson or sales associate. A broker can perform as an agent for buyers and sellers and receive fees directly from them. If you are a salesperson, you can perform any act performed by a broker, but only if you are associated with a licensed broker. You cannot operate your own firm and can receive compensation only from the broker with whom you are associated. In most states it is necessary to be licensed as a salesperson for a specified period of time before becoming eligible for a broker's license. Real estate brokerage operations and the requirements for becoming licensed are considered in detail in later chapters.

Single Family Residential Markets Single family residential markets in larger cities are organized around a multiple listing service (MLS). In this arrangement, a broker takes a listing from a seller and then, by mutual agreement with other MLS participants, reports the listing to MLS. The broker will prepare an information card reporting the important features of the property. Any MLS member can then attempt to find a buyer for this property. Members of MLS agree to *co-broker,* or split commissions, between the broker listing the property and the broker finding a buyer.

Multiple listing services allow an individual broker or sales associate to have access to a high percentage of all the homes on the market. On a weekly basis MLS members receive a book containing all the current, or active, listings within the area served by the MLS. The book also contains basic information about the property as reported by the listing broker. Much of this information is stored in a computer system and can be accessed by terminals in the broker's office using ordinary telephone lines. So, when you visit a MLS member broker's office as a buyer, the broker or salesperson working with you can quickly and easily identify homes fitting your requirements by using either the MLS book or computer terminals. In this arrangement the brokers are not limited to showing you only homes listed by their office; listings from all brokers belonging to MLS may be shown.

Not all communities are large enough to support an MLS operation for residential markets. In these communities brokers must depend on their own listings for sales. As a seller, you too must depend on the ability of your listing broker to generate potential buyers. As a buyer you may have to work with more than one broker to see all homes that may be of interest to you. Of course, some brokers could agree among themselves to co-broker all or selected properties and eliminate some of these problems.

Income-Producing Property Markets Income property markets generally do not have an MLS. Income property brokers usually work their own listings or they may sell listings of other income property brokers by agreeing on an individual basis to co-broker. Some income property brokers may have standing co-brokerage agreements with selected brokers.

When you deal with an income property real estate broker you should understand that he or she may not have access to all properties that may satisfy your needs. You should also understand that even if a property is not listed with a broker or is not advertised for sale by the owner, a good broker will often contact the owners to ask about their desire to sell. Many transactions result from an owner being approached by a broker capable of explaining market values and the benefits of selling. In spite of these efforts, properties potentially capable of satisfying your needs may go undetected. As a seller, you should also be aware that the broker you list the property with will determine the number and quality of potential buyers made aware that the property is on the market.

Real Estate Rental Markets

Real estate brokers and salespersons also participate in real estate rental markets. For a fee, they attempt to locate individuals and firms to lease space. Additionally, developers and equity investors often have leasing staffs of their own, responsible for performing the same task. Brokers are usually compensated on a percentage commission basis, with the commission being based on the length and rental rate of the lease. The costs of leasing are usually paid for by the lessor.

Markets for various types of rental space are organized differently. For example, apartments are often leased through apartment leasing agencies capable of showing apartments in many complexes throughout the city. Often more than one such agency is authorized to show the same complex. For other types of properties, such as office buildings, a single broker may have the exclusive right to lease the space. Thus, if you are seeking space you may have to visit with more than one broker to be sure you are seeing a fair representation of available space.

Generally, there is no operation similar to a multiple listing service in the office, warehouse, and shopping center rental markets. Even though a multiple listing service is not available, directories for certain types of properties may be available from Chambers of Commerce, the Building Owners and Managers Association International, and others. These directories contain information about the size of the properties and the amenities they offer. However, they usually do not contain current information about the amount of available space in each property or rental rates.

How Well Do Real Estate Equity Markets Work?

How good a job do real estate markets do of balancing supply and demand and determining prices? Are changes affecting real estate supply and demand, such as the interest rate changes mentioned earlier, reflected in prices? If so, how quickly and completely are they reflected? These questions are really another way of asking how well, or how efficiently, do real estate markets operate? While these questions seem simple enough, they really are not. Their answers affect the very existence and success of developers, equity investors, lenders, and all decision support areas. Your successful participation in the real estate business will be vitally affected by the efficiency with which real estate markets operate and your ability to analyze that efficiency.

Fortunes have been made by investors, and those providing services to them, who analyzed markets and spotted trends before they became general knowledge. Anticipating market changes caused by economic and social factors is a useful first step to making good real estate investments. Knowing when the market has become aware of these changes and incorporated them into market values is the other necessary part of this process. The more quickly and completely the market adjusts to such changes, the faster and greater will be the adjustments in market prices. Such adjustments may mean the difference between tremendous profits or tragic losses. In theory it is that simple — anticipate a change and wait for the rest of the market to adjust, and then either sell or buy. In reality it is much more difficult.

To assess the efficiency of real estate markets it may be useful to identify a market generally considered to be very efficient, examine why it works so well, and then compare real estate markets to it. The stock market is such an efficient market (either the New York or American Stock Exchange). It does an excellent job of balancing supply and demand and establishing prices that are easily observed by any interested person. If you own shares of Xerox common stock, information about its price yesterday can be found in *The Wall Street Journal.* Even more current price information is available from your stockbroker, over some cable television systems, and through subscriber computer services. This information is so current that it is a good proxy for the value of your shares. That is, the odds are very good that you can sell your shares for a price very close to the latest available information.

Furthermore, new information is quickly reflected in stock prices and in many instances is anticipated and incorporated into prices before an event occurs or information becomes official. This is simply another way of saying that the stock market moves rapidly toward equilibrium. You have likely heard stock market reports on evening news programs summarizing changes in the stock market and the suspected reasons for those changes. Thus, the stock market does its job efficiently in the same sense that you perform your job efficiently. It balances supply and demand with a minimum amount of wasted motion, and its product, price information, is readily available and useful to anyone as an excellent estimate of the value of individual stocks you own.

Why is the stock market able to function so well? It likely performs so well because of the characteristics of the product being bought and sold, the investors in the market, and the market itself. Consider the following:

1. Every share of stock of a particular company is just like every other share of that company; that is, the product is homogeneous. Every share of Xerox stock is just like every other share of Xerox stock. Because of this, the market is not slowed while buyers examine each share of stock they purchase.

2. Supply and demand are brought together in one place. Since all orders to buy and sell are funneled into one building in New York, imbalances in supply and demand are readily apparent and price adjustments made to move toward a balance once again.

3. It is easy to buy and sell stocks. Once you have established an account with a brokerage firm, you simply call your broker and buy and sell stocks by phone. There are few, if any, legal problems and you seldom have to sign any documents.

4. Brokerage fees are generally small relative to the dollar value of a transaction. This means that the costs associated with the sales transaction for either the buyer or the seller will not discourage a transaction.

5. Plenty of information about prices and the companies whose stock is traded is readily available in newspapers or in publications found in most libraries. Past price information is readily available in *The Wall Street Journal* or in publications found in most libraries. Current price information is available from brokerage offices and many cable television systems. Information about any particular company whose stock is traded in the stock market is available in annual reports published by the company or in reference books published by financial reporting firms such as Standard and Poor's, Dun and Bradstreet, and Moody's. Thus, buyers and sellers should be well informed.

Given these characteristics and their implications, it is not surprising that the stock market is very efficient.

However, you should not think of efficiency as an all-or-nothing situation. A market is not *either* efficient or inefficient; a market's efficiency can be anywhere between these two extremes. For example, an inexperienced mechanic may take longer to make a given repair than a master mechanic, but when he is finished the car may run, perhaps not perfectly but well enough to get you where you want to go. The same situation holds for real estate markets — they are always moving toward equilibrium, that is, a balancing of supply and demand, and they do reflect the impact of events and information in prices. They are *relatively* less efficient than the stock market and do not react as quickly or completely as the stock market.

The relatively less efficient operation of real estate markets is understandable when the same factors that were found to make the stock market efficient are considered for real estate markets. Think about the following characteristics of real estate markets and their likely impact on market efficiency:

1. Each parcel of real estate is unique. This means that a great deal of time and effort must be spent examining properties, thereby slowing the operation of real estate markets.

2. Real estate markets are local in nature. Since values are created by the rents a property can generate, the value of real estate is influenced by local rental levels. Thus, the markets for the same type of real estate may be quite different in two cities only a few miles apart. This also means that there is not a national or regional real estate market for a particular type of property in which supply and demand are balanced. The local nature of markets means that fewer buyers and sellers are in the local market than in a national market and it may be more difficult and time consuming to find a match between buyer and seller.

3. Real estate transactions are often complicated. As you know from Chapters 4–6, real estate transactions take time and are often legally complex. Financing is also somewhat complicated as you will see in later chapters. This complexity causes many persons to avoid frequent transactions and further reduces the number of buyers and sellers in the market at any given time.

4. Because of the greater difficulty of matching buyer and seller and the amount of time involved, real estate sales commissions are generally higher than stock commissions. Higher commission rates reduce the number of transactions. The reduced number of transactions reduces the speed with which supply and demand are balanced and an equilibrium price achieved.

5. There is little published market price information. Real estate transactions are private, and the detailed terms are not published in most cases. Also, most owners do not have to provide public statements about the rents, operating expenses, and financing of investment properties they own. Only corporate owners whose stock is traded by the public must provide such information, and then the results of many properties are often grouped together. This lack of information means that great differences exist in the information used by investors to make investment decisions. The single family residential market often has better information flows than income property markets because of the large number of transactions and the collection of sales data by multiple listing services.

Taken together, these characteristics of real estate markets make them less efficient at balancing supply and demand. The impact of real estate market characteristics on market efficiency can be illustrated using the earlier graphical analysis of supply and demand. In Figure 9.5, the neat lines of the earlier analysis are replaced with bands reflecting

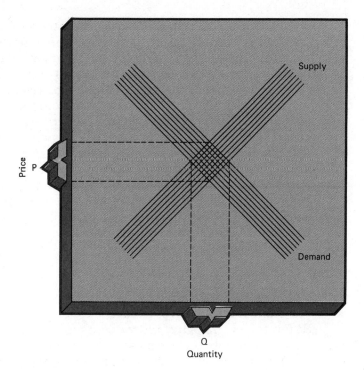

Figure 9.5 Supply and demand bands and range of prices. (Source: Thomas W. Shafer, *Urban Growth and Economics*, Englewood Cliffs, N.J.: Prentice-Hall, 1977, p. 69.)

the uncertainty and lack of consensus created by the characteristics of the real estate markets. These bands intersect to produce an area rather than a point. Notice on the price axis that the "equilibrium" price is actually a range of values rather than a point. An equilibrium point will occur only when markets are efficient enough to produce distinct supply and demand curves. You can see why there is often uncertainty when it comes to analyzing price data and estimating the likely sales price of real estate.

The lesser efficiency of the real estate markets also means that it takes longer for them to adjust to changes in supply and demand. The lack of information, high transactions costs, small number of transactions, and the uniqueness of each parcel translate into a longer time period for changes to be fully reflected in prices. First, it takes longer for events to cause a shift in either band. Then, because the new range of possible prices still likely contains some of the old prices many persons may not realize the range has changed for some period of time. It will take sales at prices outside the old range to help establish the new bounds of the adjusted price range.

Not all real estate markets are equally efficient. The closer the characteristics of a market to those of the stock market, the more efficient it will be. For example, the single family home market has many buyers and sellers, within certain neighborhoods it has a product that is very similar to all others, information about past sales is readily available, and transactions are less complicated than some income property transactions. All of these factors result in a more efficient market than exists for most income properties. The more efficient the market, the narrower the supply and demand bands and range of prices.

Because of this greater efficiency, prices in single family markets more quickly reflect conditions of excess supply or demand. Single family markets also provide buyers and sellers with more reliable and easily observable estimates of worth than less efficient real estate markets. After talking with a broker about recent sales in your neighborhood, you are in a reasonably good position to estimate a range of possible values for your home. A more precise estimate would still likely require professional help. Those persons owning investment properties, where fewer sales occur and less timely and comparable information is available, will have more difficulty estimating the value of their property and will rely on expert assistance even more.

Price and Value — The Need for Real Estate Appraisers

So far, the words **price** and **value** have been used rather loosely. These words have more precise meanings of which you should be aware. Technically, price is an historical number representing the result of a transaction. Value is an estimate of something's worth at a particular time. For example, if you are considering selling your home you will be interested in what it will likely bring in the marketplace — you are interested in its *market value*. Price data on recent sales of similar homes in your neighborhood may be useful in estimating this market value.

However, the lack of reliable price data in adequate quantity or quality often complicates the valuation problem. If you were to gather price data from sales of comparable properties in an attempt to estimate the market value of a particular property, you would, in many instances, observe variations in the prices. These variations exist because the sales of comparable properties occurred at different times and were affected by inflation, differences in the properties, interest rate levels, and, in some cases, incorrect or incomplete information. The difficulties associated with finding and interpreting market data has created a need for professionals specializing in such efforts and, ultimately, estimating market values. These professionals are real estate appraisers.

Real estate appraisers are market experts. Appraisers must apply judgment and analytical techniques to available data to estimate market value. The appraiser's job is to weave art and science into a supportable market value estimate. The actual techniques used by appraisers to estimate market value are considered in more detail in Chapters 23 and 24. However, you should now know that real estate appraisers exist because of real estate market inefficiencies. That is, they are necessary because of the inability of real estate markets to provide adequate quantities of reliable and readily accessible price information.

Market Inefficiencies and Investment Opportunities

You should not criticize real estate markets because they are less efficient than certain other markets. The very inefficiencies that make market value estimation difficult provide you with tremendous opportunities to make exceptional returns from real estate investment and development and providing support services to others developing, lending, and making equity investments. To take advantage of these profit-making opportunities, you need to understand why real estate markets are able to offer them and how to ferret out the excellent opportunities from the many not so good ones.

To say that exceptional returns are available in real estate markets means that it is possible to earn returns that exceed what you expect to earn for the investment risks you are taking. Risk generally involves the possibility that actual returns will not be the same as the returns you expected. It is important to assess the riskiness of investments in considering exceptional investment returns since most investors, if given the choice between two investments promising the same return, would prefer the one with the lesser risk. This is another way of saying that most investors are *risk averse,* that is, they do not like risk and try to avoid it. Another way of stating this concept is to say that investors require a risk premium in the form of higher expected returns for accepting greater risk; the greater the risk, the greater the expected risk premium.

Figure 9.6 illustrates the concept of a trade-off between risk and return required by investors in the real estate market. Any point on the RR line, where R is the expected rate of return required on a real estate

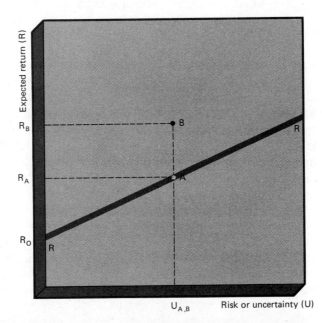

Figure 9.6
Risk-expected return trade-off.

investment with a given level of risk will satisfy the typical market investor. For instance, market investors require an expected return of R_0 on a risk-free investment and an expected return of R_A on an investment with a risk level of A, designated by U_A. Other acceptable combinations of risk and expected return fall on this line. This line reflects the risk premium required by investors for accepting more risk.

To earn a higher return than the market return for a given level of risk, you must find an undervalued investment opportunity. By paying a price lower than would be expected in the market, the returns you earn will represent a higher than market rate of return. For example, investment B represents an investment that provides an expected return, R_B, greater than that justified by its risk, U_B; that is, someone is willing to sell this investment for less than it is really worth in the market. To "beat the market" means to consistently find investments such as Investment B, providing expected returns greater than are justified in the market for that level of risk.

Studies have found that it is virtually impossible to consistently "beat" the stock market. This is because it is difficult to find undervalued assets in an efficient market because buyers and sellers quickly notice an undervalued asset and cause its price to adjust. The availability of good price information also diminishes the opportunity to find undervalued assets. For example, why would you sell your Xerox stock for less than the going price when that price is widely known? Likewise, why would you expect to buy additional shares for less? Fortunately, less efficient markets do not produce easily observable prices and provide you with the opportunity to find undervalued assets and consistently make above normal returns by using thorough analysis.

To illustrate how underpriced properties can be purchased, consider the process you follow in buying a home. Suppose you find a home that you and your spouse really like and the seller tells you that a competent appraiser has estimated the market value of the home to be $135,000, which is also the seller's asking price. You realize that even though you like the home it is not exactly what you are looking for and, also, that you cannot afford to pay $135,000. So, you make an offer of $120,000. The ball is now in the seller's court.

The seller knows that other buyers are in the market, some of whom should be willing to offer more than $120,000 — if they see the home and *if* another home does not represent a better deal. The seller must estimate the likelihood of getting a better offer; unlike the stock market, there is no market price at which the house can always be sold. The seller may feel distressed because he or she did not have one of the buyers willing to pay the asking price come by instead of you. But the decision must be made *now* with a great deal of uncertainty still in the seller's mind. If the seller accepts your offer you have gotten a bargain — a bargain created by market inefficiencies. If the seller had thought the odds of getting a better price were greater, you may not have been able to purchase the home. You could also have gotten a bargain if the seller had not been knowledgeable about market values and had underpriced the property from the beginning.

How Well Do Real Estate Rental Markets Work?

Thus far, the discussion of efficiency has dealt with equity markets. But what about the efficiency of real estate space markets? Like real estate equity markets, and for the same reasons, space markets are not the most efficient markets you can find. There is not a central exchange where all supply and demand for the different types of space are brought together. If you seek an apartment, chances are good you will miss some complexes offering apartments matching your needs. So will other people in the market. Lease terms are often confusing because they will sometimes provide for flat rents, percentage rents, and refurbishing allowances. The net result is the possibility that as a lessor you may be able to lease your space at a premium because of uninformed lessees or may lease it at a discount because of your lack of market knowledge. As a lessee you may pay more than you have to or may be able to quickly spot a bargain. You should make the same efforts to locate underpriced properties before they change as you do to find underpriced properties in equity markets. Not surprisingly, many undervalued equities result from lower than necessary rentals.

ANALYZING EQUITY AND RENTAL MARKETS

If you are going to be making and evaluating offers in a market atmosphere similar to that just described, you must have a thorough understanding of current market conditions to avoid costly mistakes. You can easily pay too much or accept too little for real property by simply not knowing the general supply and demand conditions for equity and leasehold interests in real property. You may never know for sure whether a better offer will come along, but you should at least have some feel for the odds of it happening. If you are acting as a broker, market knowledge is crucial because buyers, sellers, lessees, and lessors depend on you for advice about market conditions. Therefore, the ability to locate reliable data on market conditions and then interpret it are vital real estate survival skills.

Analyzing Single Family Residential Markets

In the single family residential market, some of the most reliable and readily accessible data is available from MLS. In many areas, these organizations issue a new book each week containing all the properties listed in the coverage area. Some MLS organizations maintain the same information in a computer data bank that may be accessed using terminals connected to the computer by using ordinary telephone lines. These computer systems allow you to specify the buyer's requirements such as geographic area, features, and price and have the computer list all the properties meeting those requirements. In addition to current listings, the MLS also prepares "sold books" each quarter showing properties that have sold since the beginning of the year and the features and sales price of each.

By analyzing the information in the MLS publications, you can develop a good feel for types of homes, features, asking prices, selling prices, and the number of days on the market for homes in a given neighborhood. Many brokers use market data for similar homes, called *comparables,* to perform a **competitive market analysis** for a potential seller, with the goal of establishing a reasonable asking price. If comparables are selected carefully, such an analysis can establish upper and lower bounds for pricing and the associated time the property likely will be on the market. Generally, the higher the asking price the longer you would anticipate the time on the market to achieve that price.

Other factors should also be considered in assessing the strength of the single family equity market. Certain demographic data may be useful in developing insights into potential demand for homes. For example, the current and projected rates of employment and population growth and the incomes associated with that growth are important. By combining this information with the location concepts considered in Chapter 7 and an assessment of current subdivision development activity, you may be able to develop a more detailed understanding of single family market activity, now and in the future.

Because most families cannot afford to pay cash for a home, the cost and availability of mortgage financing is one of the strongest factors affecting home equity markets. Higher interest rates mean higher mortgage payments, which in turn, mean that families cannot afford to spend as much for a home. Either the prospect of paying more each month for the same home or buying a smaller home discourages some homebuyers and they drop out of the market. If interest rates increase sharply, market activity can be substantially reduced. As a buyer, seller, or broker you should be aware of changes and possible changes in financial markets affecting home mortgage interest rates. You should, at the very minimum, be aware of mortgage market conditions in your hometown and the likely direction of interest rate movements in order to protect your best interests.

Analyzing Income Property Markets

Analyzing income property markets is often more difficult than single family markets because they are less efficient. Fewer buyers and sellers and fewer transactions of properties that are less comparable than homes make it more difficult to analyze these markets. First of all, MLS sources generally provide little data, which means you must find other data sources. The most common data sources are others in the real estate business such as brokers, appraisers, and lenders. Much information can be gleaned from talking with these professionals and reading the reports they write. Other sources of information are the documents recorded in the county court house, special real estate publications, and the regular daily newspaper.

Interest rates are also important in income property markets, where buyers and sellers depend heavily on borrowed money. An increase in interest rates results in larger payments for principal and interest. These larger payments mean that less profit is left from rents for the equity investor. If interest rates increase enough, buyers cannot afford to pay even the minimum price sellers are willing to accept and the market for income-producing properties becomes very weak. When interest rates fall, exactly the opposite thing happens.

As considered in Chapter 7, an understanding of economic and demographic factors affecting the development of your city is necessary to understand income property markets. Also, as considered in Chapter 8, an understanding of planning efforts and land use controls improves your ability to forecast where future development may occur. Taken together, economic, demographic, and planning considerations can add useful insights into the current and future conditions in income property markets.

There is another intangible factor that can be quite important in analyzing income property markets. This intangible is the general "perception" or "image" of the city or certain sections of it. Cities develop personalties, just as people do. This personality affects the attitude of developers, equity investors, lenders, and those who may ultimately use the space they provide. In cities whose general image is one of prosperity and expansion, you will find more intensive real estate activity, at least in the short run. Perceptions of growth, vigor, and expansion can become self-fulfilling prophecies—essentially enough people thinking something will happen make it happen!

These attitudes toward cities result from many factors. Among them is media coverage; a few positive stories about the vigor and livability of a city in national newspapers, magazines, television, and radio can create a very positive image. Being included or excluded from lists of attractive communities developed by consulting and research groups across the country affects attitudes toward your city. While difficult to evaluate, you should attempt to develop your own idea of how your city is perceived. This may be done by reading magazines and newspapers and listening to radio and television. Your local chamber of commerce and planning and economic development agencies of local government may also be good sources of information about the general "image" of your city.

SUMMARY

In this chapter you have learned about real estate markets. You learned that real estate markets are where everything is tested. A property's ability to generate rents is tested as well as its ability to attract equity investors interested in buying it. Real estate markets are important to everyone in real estate since real estate decision makers are directly affected by the market. You then learned that there are many real estate markets, or submarkets, with the division between equity and space markets being one of the major divisions between markets. Other submarkets exist within the apartment, office, industrial and shopping center markets.

Next, you learned about supply and demand and how they interact to produce a price. Price allocates rental space and equity interests in real estate. Next, you considered the organization and operation of real estate markets. Both single family residential and income property markets are organized around real estate brokers, usually acting on behalf of the seller. In the single family equity market the multiple listing service collects information about all homes on the market and makes those listings and information available to all members. No such service exists in the income property markets.

Real estate markets were found to be relatively less efficient than the stock market. They still move toward balancing supply and demand, although more slowly than less efficient markets. This slower adjustment provides excellent opportunities for you to make exceptional returns on real estate investments. However, to do so requires constant market analysis.

QUICK QUIZ

1. Real estate markets may be classified as either

   I. rental or equity
   II. active or inactive

   a. I only   c. Both I and II
   b. II only   d. Neither I nor II

2. The quantity of a good or service that will be offered in the market at different prices is called

   a. supply   c. equilibrium
   b. demand   d. price

3. The document making the broker an agent and the seller a principal is the

   a. sales contract   c. agreement of sale
   b. option   d. listing contract

4. A market that very quickly and completely reflects any changes affecting prices is said to be

    a. anticipatory   c. efficient
    b. accurate   d. none of the above

5. Investors balance _____ and _____ in making investment decisions.

    a. pricc, cash   c. risk, expected return
    b. expected return, profits   d. tax savings, financing

6. Real estate markets are relatively _____ efficient than the stock market.

7. _____ means that a market has balanced supply and demand and established a market clearing price.

8. Price is a(n) _____ number, while value is an estimate of an asset's worth at a particular time.

9. Beating the market means to earn a return in excess of that justified by its _____ .

10. Market inefficiencies allow you to consistently find _____ properties by using thorough analysis.

QUESTIONS AND EXERCISES

1. Identify as many residential rental submarkets as you can in your town on the basis of geography. On the basis of rent levels.

2. What information would you use to assess the condition of the equity market for expensive single family homes in your town?

3. How does the lack of information in income property markets help create cycles of over and undersupply of various types of space?

4. How are rental and equity markets related?

5. List as many submarkets for retail space as you can find in your town.

6. Do you feel the submarket for homes in the $100,000 to $125,000 price range are in equilibrium in your town? Why? Is there an oversupply or an undersupply?

7. Who owns and runs your local multiple listing service? How often do books listing all properties for sale come out?

8. Do brokers, property managers, or owners do most of the leasing of office space in your community?

9. How would you summarize the need for real estate appraisers?

10. What kinds of opportunities does the inefficiency of the real estate market generate for real estate investors? How do you take advantage of these opportunities?

KEY TERMINOLOGY

agent
competitive market analysis
demand
efficiency
equilibrium
equity market
market
price

principal
quantity demanded
quantity supplied
real estate appraiser
rental market
submarket
supply
value

IF YOU WANT TO READ MORE

American Institute of Real Estate Appraisers, *Readings in Market Research for Real Estate*, (Chicago: American Institute of Real Estate Appraisers, 1985).

JOHN MCMAHAN, *Property Development* (New York: McGraw-Hill Book Company, 1976), Chapters 7–10.

STEPHEN D. MESSNER, BYRL N. BOYCE, HAROLD G. TRIMBLE, and ROBERT L. WARD, *Analyzing Real Estate Opportunities — Market and Feasibility Studies* (Chicago: Realtors National Marketing Institute of the National Association of Realtors, 1977).

STEPHEN A. PYHRR, JAMES R. COOPER, LARRY E. WOFFORD, and STEVEN D. KAPPLIN, *Real Estate Investment: Strategy, Analysis, Decisions* (New York: John Wiley & Sons, 1986), Chapters 10–12.

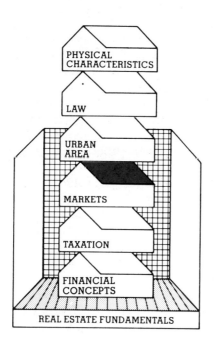

PHYSICAL CHARACTERISTICS

LAW

URBAN AREA

MARKETS

TAXATION

FINANCIAL CONCEPTS

REAL ESTATE FUNDAMENTALS

10
Taxation: real property

PREVIEW

When your grandfather left Blackacre to you, he may have left more than you imagined in the way of financial obligations. Even if Blackacre had no outstanding mortgages against it, you will still be responsible for the payment of its real property taxes. In many areas, these taxes are substantial, not only necessitating immediate cash outlays, but also affecting how Blackacre is used and its market value. In this chapter, the essential elements of property taxation are explained. You will learn:

1. Why we have a property tax and its importance as a revenue source for local government.
2. How your real property is valued for tax purposes.
3. The basic process for appealing the property tax valuation of your real property.
4. How property tax rates and property tax obligations are established.
5. What a special assessment is and why it occurs.
6. How the property tax affects the use and value of your real property.
7. What issues and questions surround the property tax.

The property tax is relatively simple in concept. Its administration, however, is complex and difficult, often embroiled in controversy, and its impacts are far-reaching. It is more than simply a sizable, annual financial burden for you and other landowners and a source of revenue for government. For landowners, it affects the use and value of land and, in turn, their community's development patterns. Thus, you and your town have a big stake in the property tax, especially in how it is administered and its impact on land uses.

If property taxes were optional, there would be no pressing need for you to understand property taxation. Unfortunately, if property taxes are not paid, your real property can be sold at a public sale to satisfy the unpaid tax obligation. Therefore, property taxes represent a real limitation to your ownership rights. With this background, let's consider the property tax and its relationship to you and Blackacre in more detail.

WHY THE PROPERTY TAX?

In feudal England, favored nobles were given the rights of possession and use of land owned by the royal family. In return for these interests in real property, these nobles were expected to be loyal to the Crown and to raise armies to help defend it. In the United States the crown has been replaced by the State, and private ownership rights in land greatly expanded. However, government has maintained the tradition of exacting payments from owners of real property, now in the form of **property taxes.**

Many arguments have been made for why the property tax was initiated and retained until this time. First, it has been, and continues to be, an excellent source of revenue for government, especially local government. Most property tax revenue goes to local government, including school districts and special districts such as those created to provide water, sewerage, and drainage services. Table 10.1 summarizes property tax revenues from 1960 to 1982. Of the $81.9 billion in property taxes collected in 1982, about $79 billion, or about 96 percent, went to finance local government and special districts. This amounted to about 80 percent of all locally generated tax revenue. The remaining $3 billion went to state government, with the federal government receiving no property tax revenues. These are significant amounts of money to these governments.

Other reasons for the taxation of real property include the government's ability to easily identify property owners from the public land records, discussed in Chapter 5. Your ownership of Blackacre is a matter of public record once you file the document transferring ownership to you, and taxing authorities can easily identify you as its present owner. The improvements to land also cannot be hidden easily or moved and are readily available to be valued. If you build a three-story office building on Blackacre, you cannot hide it while your property is being valued for purposes of calculating your tax liability. Other assets such as gold, cash

Table 10.1. Property Tax Revenues 1960–1982

	Total Property Tax (in millions)	State Government		Local Government	
		Total (in millions)	Annual % Change	Total (in millions)	Annual % Change
1960	16,405	607		15,798	
1965	22,583	766	4.8	21,817	6.7
1970	34,054	1092	7.4	32,963	8.6
1975	51,491	1451	5.9	50,050	8.7
1977	62,535	2260	24.8	60,275	9.8
1978	66,422	2364	4.6	64,058	6.3
1979	64,944	2490	5.3	62,453	−2.5
1980	68,499	2892	16.1	65,607	5.0
1981	74,969	2949	2.0	72,020	9.8
1982	81,918	3113	5.6	78,805	9.4

SOURCE: U.S. Bureau of the Census, *Statistical Abstract 1985*, p. 265.

in mattresses and Swiss bank accounts, and securities can be more easily concealed from government. Yet another argument for the property tax is that your real estate benefits from local government services such as water, sewerage, police and fire protection, and so on, making a tax on it reasonable and justifiable.

BASIC PROPERTY TAXATION CONCEPTS

Property taxes are based on the idea that the tax obligation on a given parcel is found by multiplying a **tax base** by a **tax rate,**

$$\text{Tax obligation} = \text{Tax base} \times \text{Tax rate}$$

This equation is called the **basic tax equation.** To be useful, the terms in the basic tax equation must be defined. In property taxation, the tax base is defined as a property's **assessed value,** a measure of the value of a parcel of real property. Tax base has another meaning in property taxation which is discussed later in this chapter. Because property taxes are based on the value of real property, they are sometimes called **ad valorem** taxes, which means "according to value." The property tax rate is a factor indicating the fraction of the tax base that must be paid as taxes.

Tax Base
If property taxes are to be based on the value of your real property, two things must happen. First, the value to be used in calculating your tax obligation must be clearly defined. It is usually current market value, or some percentage of it. Second, someone must accurately estimate the

assessed value of all parcels to be taxed. The estimation of assessed value *begins* with the estimation of the current **market value** of real property.

Market value is considered in more detail in Chapters 23 and 24 on real estate appraisal. For right now, however, you can think of market value as the price a property would likely bring if offered for sale in the marketplace. Put very simply, the market value of Blackacre is what it would bring in the market. You may hear people use phrases like "full market value" and "fair market value" in referring to market value. Except in rare cases, these phrases mean precisely the same thing as market value. The words *full* and *fair* add no meaning, but frequently confuse people.

The person responsible for valuing real property for tax purposes is the **assessor.** Most states have laws requiring assessors to periodically reassess (revalue) every parcel of real property in their jurisdiction. Reassessing an entire city or county is a big job. Every property must be physically inspected to some degree, data about the property gathered, and the data converted into a market value estimate. When you consider the massive problems associated with coordinating such an effort for a county that may have hundreds of thousands of parcels, it is not surprising to find that the computer is being used with increasing frequency to store and retrieve data and to perform the necessary analysis. Some assessors must also reassess properties when they are sold or substantially improved. In these cases, the assessor's office monitors the filing of deeds and the issuance of building permits to identify properties subject to reassessment.

In estimating the market value of a property, say Blackacre, the assessor uses the same approaches as a private appraiser. These approaches to valuation are based on the idea of examining the options open to a potential purchaser of the property being valued. For instance, in valuing Blackacre the assessor knows that a potential buyer of Blackacre could purchase another 30-acre farm with a small home on it instead of Blackacre. This means that data on the recent sales prices of similar properties will be a guide to the value of Blackacre. This approach is called the **sales comparison approach.** The **cost approach** is based on the idea that a similar tract of land could be purchased and any improvements on Blackacre reproduced or replaced by new construction. Thus, the assessor may use land value and building cost data to estimate Blackacre's market value. Finally, perhaps not for Blackacre, but for properties such as office buildings and apartments, the assessor may feel that purchasers would be primarily interested in the income the property produces. In such a situation, an indicator of value would be an estimate of what investors would pay for such an income stream. This is the rationale for the **income capitalization approach** to valuation.

In all the assessor's work, equality in the treatment of owners of properties of equal value is sought. That is, the assessor must try to assure that properties of equal value are assessed at equal value. As a taxpayer, you do not want your home, which has an actual market value of $125,000, valued any higher than other homes worth the same amount. If your home is assessed at a value greater than similar homes, you will pay more property taxes than the owners of those homes. The assessor seeks to eliminate such inequities. This is not an easy task when you consider the number of parcels, in widely differing locations, to be valued. For a subdivision in which properties are quite similar, the job is difficult but more manageable than for an entire city where the differences are greater.

Thus, your real estate will be periodically reassessed, either at intervals specified by state law, say every five years, or when you buy it or make substantial improvements to it. This periodic reassessment provides a mechanism for correcting inequities in tax valuations created by property values changing at different rates. For instance, two homes assessed for $100,000 each in 1984 may be worth $125,000 and $140,000, respectively, today. A reassessment will correct this situation, at least temporarily. Furthermore, new properties assessed for the first time may be valued in current dollars; their values are not usually adjusted back to the date of the last reassessment. This means that in a new subdivision, one home may have been completed and sold in 1984, at which time its market value was estimated to be $100,000 by the assessor. If, in the same subdivision, a similar home was completed in 1986 and its market value assessed at $130,000, the buyer of the second home will have a substantially higher property tax bill than the first, if the first home has not been reassessed. If all properties are reassessed in 1987, the difference in assessment should be corrected.

The market value estimated by the assessor may not be the tax base on which your taxes on Blackacre are calculated. That base is Blackacre's assessed value, and is calculated by multiplying market value by an assessment ratio. The **assessment ratio** is a percentage, either specified by the state or established by local authorities within ranges deemed acceptable by the state, which is used to convert market value into assessed value. Some states define the full market value as the assessed valuation. That is, the assessment ratio is 100 percent. Others use only a fraction of market value. For example, if the assessment ratio for Blackacre is .25, then its $100,000 market value is multiplied by that number to produce a $25,000 assessed value:

$$\text{Assessed value} = \text{Market value} \times \text{Assessment ratio}$$
$$= \$100,000 \times .25$$
$$= \$25,000$$

Your tax bill will be calculated on this $25,000 tax base.

Homestead Exemption Some states allow homeowners to reduce the assessed value of their principal residence (as contrasted to a vacation home) by filing for **homestead exemption.** The amount of the reduction in assessed valuation varies from state to state. If you make your home on Blackacre and your state has a homestead exemption of $3000, then you can reduce Blackacre's assessed value from $25,000 to $22,000 by filing homestead exemption. This can result in a sizable tax savings for you. In some states, if you are a veteran, elderly, or disabled, you may receive additional homestead exemption allowances that further reduce assessed value and property taxes.

Appealing Your Assessed Valuation When your assessor changes the assessed value of Blackacre, you will receive a notice similar to the one in Table 10.2. You have the right to appeal this change. On what

Table 10.2. Notice of Change in Assessed Value

NOTICE OF CHANGE IN ASSESSED VALUE OF REAL ESTATE

OFFICE COPY

Prepared By
Michael Markup, Assessor
Homeowner, U.R.
8905 E. Maplewood
Anytown, Anystate 00000

Sub and Account	Tax Unit	Serial Number
51276-831448540	T-9A	2-80-09765

You are hereby notified that the value of your Property has been affixed by the County Assessor for the current year.

Date Prepared

Feb. 8, 1986

Description & Detail

LAST YEAR

Market/Use Value 1985		ASSESSMENT RATIO	ASSESSED VALUE
LAND	20,000	.15000	3,000
STRUCTURES	85,000	.15000	12,750
TOTAL	105,000		15,750

THIS YEAR

Market/Use Value 1986		ASSESSMENT RATIO	ASSESSED VALUE
LAND	25,000	.15000	3,750
STRUCTURES	95,500	.15000	14,330
TOTAL	120,500		18,080

If you do not approve of this new assessment, you may file a written protest with the County Clerk, who is Secretary of the Equalization Board. This protest must be filed within 30 days from date of the mailing of this notice.

An assessment is a uniform percentage applied to the fair market value of all similar properties.

THIS IS NOT A TAX BILL

If you have any questions call 584-0471. Ask for the Real Estate Department.

grounds can you reasonably file an appeal? Generally, to be successful you must be able to demonstrate that your assessment is not equitable; that is, that Blackacre was valued higher than other properties similar to it. If properties comparable to Blackacre are assessed at about the same level, your appeal will have little chance of succeeding, even if you think its level is generally high.

To find out the assessments of other properties, you can inspect the records at the assessor's office, since they are public documents. The records of all properties in the county are the **assessment rolls.** If after comparing your assessment with comparable properties you still feel your assessment is too high, you may want to file an appeal. This appeal must be filed within a specified number of days to be considered. You may appeal the valuation assigned to either the land or the improvements or both.

Your property tax assessment appeal begins with filing a formal protest form with the assessor's office. Appeals of assessments will ultimately be heard by an appeals review board. At your hearing you will be entitled to present any evidence you may have concerning the value of the land and improvements. Examples from the assessment rolls of assessed valuations lower than yours for comparable homes in your neighborhood represent very good evidence that your assessment is not equitable. After hearing all evidence, the board will decide whether your assessment should be reduced. If you are not satisfied with the board's decision, assessments may be appealed to the courts.

Tax Rate

Once Blackacre's assessed value is known, the only remaining element necessary to calculate your tax obligation is the **tax rate.** The real property tax rate is an expression of the property taxes due for a given amount of assessed valuation. Property tax rates create a great deal of needless confusion. One reason for the confusion is that you will find property tax rates expressed several different ways, even though they all mean exactly the same thing. Ways of expressing property tax rates include:

Mills

Dollars per hundred

Dollars per thousand

Percentage of assessed valuation

A **mill** is one-tenth of a cent, or one-thousandth of a dollar. Tax rates are expressed as so many mills per dollar of assessed value. A rate of 88 mills means that you must pay 88 mills ($.088 or 8.8 cents) per dollar of assessed value. Because of the problems of thinking in terms of mills, the tax rate is often expressed as so much per $100 or $1000 of assessed value. Multiplying the 8.8 cents per dollar rate by 100 produces a rate of

$8.80 per $100, whereas multiplying it by $1000 yields a rate of $88 per $1000. Finally, some people find it easier to simply express the tax rate as a percentage of assessed value. In this case, your property tax obligation is 8.8% of the assessed value.

However expressed, the property tax rate is multiplied by the assessed value of a property to produce the tax bill. You must be careful to match your expression of the assessed value and the rate in calculating the property tax. For example, if you are using the $8.80 per $100 rate, you should express the value of Blackacre in hundreds of dollars. The $25,000 assessed value represents 250 one-hundred-dollar units. This means the tax obligation is calculated as:

$$\text{Tax liability} = \text{Tax base} \times \text{Tax rate}$$
$$= 250 \times \$8.80$$
$$= \$2200$$

If you were using the $88 per $1000 rate, you would multiply 25 by $88 to get the same answer. It seems less confusing to simply use the property tax rate as a percentage of assessed valuation and multiply that rate by the full assessed value:

$$\text{Tax liability} = \$25,000 \times .088$$
$$= \$2200$$

Such an approach lets you avoid converting the assessed value into hundreds or thousands or dealing with mills.

Establishing the Tax Rate To better understand how property tax rates are established, it is helpful to review who receives property tax revenues. In Table 10.1, local government was identified as the primary recipient of property tax revenue. Local government includes cities, counties, school districts, and special districts with property taxing authority. Among these elements of local government, school districts alone often receive over 50 percent of property tax revenue. The remainder is split among water, sewerage, drainage, library, and health districts and city and county governments. Each of these entities generally has a maximum, legally authorized tax rate they can use to generate funds. A county library system, for instance, may be allowed a maximum of 5 mills or $5 per $1000 to raise funds. As the total assessed valuation of the area increases, so do the library's potential tax revenues. In some states, if the library needs more money than the $5 per $1000 can generate, an election must be held for voters to decide whether an increase will be allowed.

Each year, each governmental entity receiving property tax funds prepares a budget. This budget is submitted to a board that must coordinate the property tax, act as a watchdog over its application, and establish property tax rates. This board goes by various names, one of which is the **excise board.** As part of its job, the board reviews all budgets to determine if their request for property tax funds can be satisfied by their maximum allowable tax rate. If it cannot, the budget is sent back for revision. Once satisfied that all budgets are within allowable limits, the excise board is ready to establish property tax rates.

Boards will generally not set one property tax rate for the entire city or county. The reason for this is that some governmental bodies with taxing authority do not have jurisdiction over the entire city or county. School districts, for example, often do not cover entire cities or counties. Your city or county probably has a number of school districts, each with its own budget and tax base within its boundaries to produce the revenues for that budget. (Some states have discontinued this practice, and now depend on statewide school financing.) Consequently, each school district will have its own tax rate. This means that properties in different school districts will have different property tax rates. The tax rate on Blackacre will be the sum of all the different tax rates that apply to it. Consequently, the excise board's first step in setting tax rates is to identify the geographical area from which tax revenue is to be derived by each taxing entity.

Once all taxing entities and their geographical taxing area are determined, the county assessor will provide the board with the total assessed valuation of all properties in each such area. This total assessed valuation is the area's tax base. The board now has two parts of a three-part puzzle; from the budgets supplied by each taxable entity they have the total tax revenues required and from the county assessor they have the tax base available to produce that revenue. All that is missing is the tax rate. You will remember that the revenues produced by a tax is found by:

$$\text{Tax revenues} = \text{Tax base} \times \text{Tax rate}$$

If the tax revenues needed and the base are known, then the rate can be found by:

$$\text{Tax rate} = \frac{\text{Tax revenues needed}}{\text{Tax base}}$$

This procedure is repeated for each taxing entity to determine its tax rate. The total tax rate for any given parcel of property such as Blackacre is found by adding the tax rates for all the taxing entities having property taxing authority over it. When you think about overlaying all the geographical taxing areas on one another, there may be a large number of different tax zones, each with its own tax rate. Thus, tax rates can vary widely within a city or county.

Total Taxes and Effective Tax Rates

Your tax bill on Blackacre, assuming Blackacre has an assessed value of $25,000 and a tax rate of .088, is calculated as follows:

$$\text{Tax liability} = \$25,000 \times .088$$
$$= \$2200$$

Notice that your tax bill depends on the assessed valuation *and* the tax rate. The assessed valuation, in turn, depends on the market value estimate and the assessment ratio. If we assume that the market value of $100,000 is an accurate valuation, your tax bill of $2200 could be the result of countless possible combinations of assessment ratio and tax rates. For example, an assessment ratio of .50 and a tax rate of .044 would have produced the same tax bill. Likewise, with an assessment ratio of .50 and a tax rate of .088, your tax bill would double to $4400. Thus, the *stated,* or *nominal,* tax rate, which is multiplied by the assessed value, is not by itself a reliable indicator of the property tax burden. You must also consider the percentage of market value to which that rate is applied. The lower the assessment ratio for a given **nominal tax rate** the lower the tax obligation.

Did you really pay 8.8 percent of the market value of Blackacre in property taxes? No, if Blackacre's market value is $100,000 and you paid $2200 in property taxes, you only paid 2.2 percent of its market value. This 2.2 percent is your **effective property tax rate.** It takes into account the combination of the assessment ratio and the nominal tax rate. The reason your effective tax rate is only 25 percent of the nominal tax rate is that you paid the 8.8 percent rate on only 25 percent of the market value. Paying 8.8 percent on 25 percent of the estimated market value is the same as paying 2.2 percent on the entire market value. Notice that we could have found the effective rate by multiplying the nominal rate by the assessment ratio:

$$\text{Effective tax rate} = \text{Nominal rate} \times \text{Assessment ratio}$$
$$= 8.8\% \times .25$$
$$= 2.2\%$$

Table 10.3 contains information about the nominal and effective tax rates and the assessment ratios for 30 selected large cities for you to compare.

Tax Levies

After tax rates have been established, the tax obligation of each property owner is calculated. The amount owed is called a **tax levy** and becomes a lien against the property. Tax notices are usually sent annually, although in some areas you will receive a bill quarterly or semiannually. Property taxes can be billed either in arrears or in advance. If billed in arrears, the tax bill you receive will be for the preceding period. If billed in advance, it will be for the coming period. You will have a specified period of time to make payment without interest or penalty and remove the tax lien. If unpaid for a prolonged period of time, the government will seek a court order to have your property sold at a public sale and the proceeds used to satisfy the tax lien. The interesting point about tax liens is that they are legally prior to any other private claims against your property.

Table 10.3. Residential Property Tax Rates in Selected Large Cities: 1982

City	Effective Tax Rate Per $100		Assessment Level (percent)	Nominal Rate per $100
	Rank	Rate		
Boston	1	7.87	34.1	23.09
Newark, NJ	2	5.82	50.0	11.64
Detroit	3	3.94	50.0	7.88
Indianapolis	4	3.78	33.3	11.35
Wilmington	5	3.34	70.0	4.78
Providence	6	3.22	57.2	5.62
Milwaukee	7	2.94	97.5	3.02
Bridgeport	8	2.79	30.0	9.29
Baltimore	9	2.74	44.2	6.20
Philadelphia	10	2.70	40.0	6.75
Manchester	11	2.63	34.0	7.74
Atlanta	12	2.47	40.0	6.17
Des Moines	13	2.46	67.2[a]	3.66
Portland, ME	14	2.44	55.0	4.43
Minneapolis	15	2.27	21.5[b]	10.55
Albuquerque	16	2.16	33.3	6.47
Jackson, MS	17	2.11	26.0	8.10
Omaha	18	2.10	80.0	2.63
Portland, OR	19	2.10	83.8	2.51
Chicago	20	1.99	19.8[c]	10.05
Sioux Falls	21	1.97	29.0	6.80
Houston	22	1.76	100.0	1.76
Memphis	23	1.74	25.0	6.97
Burlington	24	1.66	24.0	6.90
New York City	25	1.66	18.5	8.95
St. Louis	26	1.56	24.9	6.25
Jacksonville	27	1.50	95.6	1.57
Cleveland	28	1.46[d]	35.0	6.85
Oklahoma City	29	1.41	12.0	11.73
Fargo	30	1.33	4.4	30.19

[a] Assessment level of 100% × statewide factor of 67.2223%.

[b] Statutory assessment levels: 16% first $27,000, 22% next $27,000, and 28% over $54,000. Level noted is for $75,000.

[c] Assessment level of 10.25% × statewide equalization factor of 1.9288%.

[d] Effective rate = nominal rate × assessment level (35%) minus residential rollback (30.18%) minus statewide rollback (12.5%).

SOURCE: U.S. Bureau of the Census, *Statistical Abstract 1985*, p. 291.

This means that if a forced sale occurs, the tax obligation is paid in full before any other claim receives a penny. Needless to say, those with other claims on your property, such as mortgage lenders, like to see you pay your property taxes. Lenders feel so strongly about this that they often collect one-twelfth of estimated property taxes with each monthly payment, place this money in an escrow account, arrange to have the tax bill sent to them, and pay it for you (using your money).

The forced sale of real property to satisfy a tax lien deserves some additional attention. While the process varies from state to state, the basic procedure is for government to seek a court judgment authorizing the forced sale of the property. If such a judgment is obtained, the property will be sold in a public sale under the direction of a county official, usually the sheriff. The purchaser at the sale will receive either a tax certificate or a tax deed. A tax certificate does not make the buyer the owner of the property. It does, however, guarantee that if the owner or other interested party does not pay all back taxes, interest, and penalties within a specified period of time, the holder of this certificate will become the owner of the property. In some states, the buyer receives a tax deed conveying ownership to the property.

SPECIAL ASSESSMENTS

As a property owner you may be required to pay **special assessments** in addition to your general property taxes. Special assessments can occur when municipal improvements are made that specifically benefit property owners within a limited distance of the improvements, such as widening a street or installing sewers. For example, in a rapidly developing residential area the increased traffic from development may make it necessary to widen a two-lane arterial street through the area to four lanes. This widening primarily benefits property owners within its immediate vicinity, and it may be appropriate that these property owners pay for the widening rather than requiring all the citizens of the city to pay for it. However, if general growth of the city has made an arterial street near downtown serving commuters from all parts of the city congested, its widening benefits the general population and should be financed using general tax revenue collected from all citizens.

Exactly who pays for a special assessment is determined by the boundaries of the **assessment district.** The assessment district is defined by the governmental entity authorizing the improvement project and represents all those properties receiving direct benefits from the improvement. As you might imagine, not all property benefits to the same extent. In the example above in which a two-lane street was widened to four lanes, property owners farther away from the street may use it less frequently than property owners closer to it. In the interest of fairness, assessments may be made on the basis of benefits received. Sometimes, where all property owners benefit equally, the assessments may be equal.

Special assessments are sometimes paid in one payment and sometimes paid over a period of years with interest. Until fully paid, special assessments represent a lien against the real property. A failure to pay the special assessment on a timely basis can cause a forced sale of the property to satisfy the obligation. In buying real property, therefore, you should find out whether there are any outstanding special assessment liens. An attorney can help you answer questions about such special assessments.

ISSUES, POTENTIAL PROBLEMS, AND PROBLEMS IN PROPERTY TAXATION

The story of real property taxation does not have a storybook ending; everyone does not live happily ever after. As a matter of fact, some people are downright steamed about some aspects of the property tax. Some of the issues and problems creating these debates are now discussed. Hopefully, this discussion will increase your understanding, not only of the present property tax system, but also of any reforms that may occur in the future.

General Level of Property Taxes

One aspect of property taxation that has received much publicity in recent times is the dissatisfaction with the high level of property taxes in some areas. Much of the publicity has centered on California and its passage of Proposition 13 generally limiting property taxes to no more than 1 percent of a property's market value and limiting increases to no more than 2 percent per year. When a property is sold or improved it may be reassessed to the then-current market values. National data on the per capita property tax burden contained in Table 10.4 indicates that this burden has increased from $91 in 1960 to $362 in 1982. You may be

Table 10.4. Per Capita Property Taxes 1960–1982

	Per Capita State and Local (in dollars)
1960	91
1965	117
1970	168
1975	242
1977	289
1978	305
1979	295
1980	302
1981	331
1982	362
Total % Change 1960–1982:	297.8

SOURCE: U.S. Bureau of the Census, *Statistical Abstract 1985*, p. 265.

thinking that *everything* went up in price between 1960 and 1978, perhaps even more on a percentage basis than this increase. So why the interest in property taxes?

The interest comes from the fact that property tax increases hit certain groups particularly hard. Many persons who had spent their lives paying for a home for their retirement found that by the time they retired on a lower, often fixed income, property taxes were so high that they could not afford to keep the home they "owned." Young persons were also having a much harder time affording the inflated monthly tax payments associated with buying a home. Thus, people at both ends of the age spectrum were experiencing problems. Those in the middle, while not affected to the same extent, also felt the pinch of higher property taxes and were having to devote higher percentages of their income to paying property taxes. If property taxes continue to increase, you will likely see property taxes become a major issue in many states.

Property Tax Equity

One of the commonly sought goals of any tax system is **equity.** While economists, sociologists, and philosophers could spend long hours debating what is meant by property tax equity, the gist of it is that a property tax is equitable when the owners of properties of equal market value pay the same tax. That is, you as the owner of Blackacre, with a market value of $100,000, should pay the same property tax as another owner of a real property with a market value of $100,000.

To achieve equity, assessors attempt, with the assistance of taxpayers, to eliminate unintended inequities in assessments. There is rather general agreement that such efforts are desirable. There is also considerable effort at the state level to eliminate differences in assessments between counties. Counties with high assessments will, in some instances, be subsidizing those with low assessments. There will always be concern and debate over the level of equalization efforts. In some instances equity is deliberately set aside through tax abatement, differential rates, and property tax exemptions, the three remaining issues to be discussed.

Property Tax Abatement

To induce development in certain areas of a city or county, property tax obligations for particular properties have been reduced or eliminated for specified periods of time. Such a reduction is called a **tax abatement.** Proponents of tax abatement argue that the economic benefits to the city will make up for any property tax not paid. Often it is contended that initial development will encourage additional development that *will* pay property taxes. Opponents counter that abatement benefits do not exceed their cost to other property owners. The debate over whether this inequity is justified or not occurs anytime it is proposed. You may see it occur in your town, if it has not already.

Properties Exempt From Taxation

Earlier in the chapter we discussed homestead exemption, or the ability to reduce the assessed value of your principal residence. Other groups of properties are routinely **exempt** from all property taxation. In this category is real property owned by government, religious organizations, and not-for-profit organizations such as educational institutions, orphanages, and hospitals. In some cities, especially those with state capitols and military bases, these holdings constitute a significant percentage of total lands. For instance, on Waikiki Beach in Honolulu, the federal government owns a 70-acre parcel of land called Fort DeRussy, with an extensive beachfront and a hotel for military personnel. The value of this parcel is in the hundreds of millions of dollars and it is totally exempt from property taxation. In New York, the landmark World Trade Center with eight million square feet of office space in two 110-story towers is tax exempt because it is owned by the Port Authority of New York. The World Trade Center is of special interest because it competes with privately owned, tax-paying office buildings for tenants.

Differential Assessments

In some areas, different types of real property have different assessments applied to them. For instance, office buildings may have one assessment ratio, apartments another, and so on. One line of reasoning behind this practice is that different types of property make different demands on city services and should pay property taxes accordingly. Opponents argue that the determination of the size of such differences is difficult and the plan invites inequities in property taxation, perhaps even abuse.

In some areas, farmland, ranchland, and other open areas are assessed using a lower assessment ratio than that used for developed areas. The practice has been implemented to reduce the possibility of these land owners being forced to sell their land because of high taxes. This practice directly affects your tax bill on Blackacre.

IMPACT OF THE PROPERTY TAX ON INDIVIDUAL PARCELS AND COMMUNITIES

The property tax has an obvious effect on you as a property owner; you must come up with the necessary annual tax payment. It also has an obvious effect on government, especially local government, which receives these annual tax payments from landowners. However, all of the effects of the property tax are not so simple or obvious. Property taxes have a tremendous impact on individuals and their decisions to own and improve real property, and on the types and timing of development in cities.

Individual Parcels

Perhaps the most direct impact of property taxes on Blackacre is on its value. If you receive word today that the property taxes on Blackacre have been substantially increased, its market value will probably fall. This adjustment will occur because the increased carrying costs associated with owning Blackacre reduce the profit an investor could expect from selling it in the future. If you owned an office building instead of Blackacre, the increase in taxes would increase your operating costs and decrease your annual profits. Potential buyers of the office building realize this and will not pay as much for the reduced income stream. When investors take the change in property taxes into account in deciding how much they can pay, they are said to *capitalize* those taxes into value. **Tax capitalization** is important to property owners faced with substantial changes in property taxes.

If property taxes increase enough, you may be forced to sell Blackacre, especially if you were just using it for a weekend retreat and it was producing no income. Even if you were farming Blackacre, a sharp increase in property taxes might mean the difference between profit and loss. Two situations can produce such a significant increase in Blackacre's taxes. First, the tax rate could be increased. Second, the property could be reassessed and in that reassessment Blackacre could be valued as though it were a site for single family homes or other development, not as a farm. You may argue that you do not intend to sell Blackacre to developers or to develop it yourself. The assessor argues that, by law, the market value of Blackacre must be estimated and that because development is moving your way, the market value is higher than it was before. Thus, the property tax may force you to consider either selling or developing Blackacre before you are ready.

If you owned improved real estate, another aspect of the property tax may affect your plans to remodel or rehabilitate those improvements. If remodeling or rehabilitation results in a reassessment of your property, you may postpone such efforts. Suppose property in your county is reassessed every five years and the last reassessment occurred two years ago. If you remodel and your property is reassessed, that reassessment will take into account two years of value changes since the last assessment *and* the value added by the remodeling. The net result could be a sizable increase in property taxes. As a result, the property tax may discourage the rehabilitation of improvements.

Communities

For your community, the property tax is more than a revenue source, it has strong social and land use planning implications that affect when and how your town develops. For instance, if property taxes are too high relative to the services taxpayers receive, people may consider selling their real property and moving to a town with a more desirable combination of taxes and services. If enough do so, property values will fall and property taxes must then be even higher relative to the market value of the real estate to generate necessary revenues. Such a situation has existed in many large cities during the last 30 years as many people chose to live in suburban communities with lower property taxes and acceptable levels of services. The cities were faced with a shrinking tax base and a population that required more services per capita than before. This situation has now begun to change as cities have started taxing income earned in the city and property values have gotten to the point that they are attractive relative to suburban communities. This is an oversimplification of the problem, but it captures the essence of the situation.

Tax policy also affects the maintenance and rehabilitation of the city by affecting property owner attitudes about spending money on their properties. If, as discussed above for individuals, property owners postpone or simply do not rehabilitate or improve their properties because of possible property tax increases, the community has paid a price for that added tax revenue. The community must evaluate the extent to which tax policy discourages such activity and whether the added revenue from such reassessments outweighs the revenue generated from a generally better maintained stock of real property and possibly higher market values because of that maintenance. These are the same factors that must be considered in deciding tax abatement policies.

One final impact of the property tax is on development at the edge of the urbanized area. For the city, the most economical development will likely be adjacent to already developed land rather than leapfrogging over undeveloped land. If vacant land is valued assuming it can be put to uses other than agricultural ones, then vacant land adjacent to the urbanized area will be valued more highly than land farther out. Such a policy should make more of this land available for development as landowners resist paying higher taxes. However, conflicting with this goal are concerns with the loss of prime farmlands, the preservation of open space, and the forcing of individuals to sell land against their will. Consistent with these goals is the policy of differential assessment for agricultural lands in order to lower the property taxes on them. The costs and benefits of these alternatives must be evaluated.

Unfortunately, tax policy is not under the direction of one unified body. All of the entities receiving a piece of the property tax affect its level and may have opposing views with respect to policy. As a result, overall property tax policy is usually created by accident or simply as a series of unrelated decisions. State government can pass laws within which property taxation must occur, but the ability of state government to produce laws adequate for all of the different situations within its communities is doubtful. As one whose quality of life or livelihood is affected by property tax policy, you should be most interested in how current tax policies were established, how future tax policy will be established, and what the general attitudes are about various aspects of property tax policy in your community.

SUMMARY

This chapter has introduced the important topic of real property taxation. You now should know that property taxes produce revenues primarily for local government, especially school districts. You are also aware of the fact that property taxes represent a growing tax burden for property owners. Property taxes are also called *ad valorem* taxes, meaning "according to value," because they are based on the value of the real property.

The value on which a property owner pays taxes is called the assessed valuation, which is the market value of the property multiplied by a decimal fraction called the assessment ratio. The assessor estimates the market value of the property on a periodic basis. You may appeal the results of the assessor's work. The tax rate is expressed in mills, dollars per hundred, dollars per thousands, or as a percentage of assessed valuation.

The property tax obligation is calculated by multiplying the assessed valuation by the tax rate. Property tax rates are established by a board after consideration of the budgets and assessed valuation of each entity receiving property tax revenues.

Special assessments may be levied against property owners when an improvement benefits a specific group of landowners. These additional property taxes are in addition to regular ones. An attorney can help you determine whether there are any special assessments against a property.

QUICK QUIZ

1. Which one of the following is *not* a reason for having a real property tax?

   a. real property ownership is a matter of public record
   b. improvements cannot be easily concealed
   c. it is a progressive tax
   d. real estate receives many of the benefits produced by the property tax

2. In real property taxation, the assessment ratio is

a. the factor used to convert market value into assessed value
b. the factor used to convert assessed value into market value
c. the ratio of tax exempt to taxable property in a community
d. the percent by which properties are overvalued

3. The phrase *ad valorem* means

a. to the victor go the spoils   c. until reassessed
b. according to value   d. ability to pay

4. Which of the following is not an accepted way to express property taxes?

a. dollars per hundred dollars of assessed valuation
b. dollars per thousand dollars of assessed valuation
c. percentage of assessed valuation
d. dollars per mill of assessed valuation

5. If a property has an assessed valuation of $10,000, and the tax rate is 90 mills, the tax bill for the property would be

a. $900   c. $950
b. $90   d. $95

6. When owners of properties of equal market value pay the same property tax, the tax system is said to be _____.

7. _____ is the process by which investors incorporate changes in property taxes into their estimates of a property's worth.

8. In establishing the property tax rate, the appropriate board will use the formula, _____.

9. The reduction of property tax obligations for specific properties is called _____.

10. _____ provisions allow homeowners in some states to reduce the assessed valuation of their principal residence by a specified amount.

QUESTIONS AND EXERCISES

1. How much would you save in taxes, assuming a property tax rate of $95 per $1000, if you file homestead exemption and reduce your assessed valuation by $3000?

2. Convert a tax rate of 75 mills per dollar to dollars per hundred, dollars per thousand, and a percentage of assessed valuation.

3. If the assessment ratio is .25 and the nominal tax rate $95 per thousand, what is the effective tax rate?

4. Develop arguments, pro and con, for a tax abatement policy in your community.

5. Develop arguments, pro and con, for a system of differential assessment in your community.

KEY TERMINOLOGY

ad valorem
assessed value
assessment district
assessment ratio
assessment rolls
assessor
basic tax equation
cost approach
differential assessment
effective tax rate
equity
excise board
homestead exemption

income approach
market data approach
market value
mill
nominal tax rate
property tax
special assessment
tax abatement
tax base
tax capitalization
tax exempt
tax levy
tax rate

IF YOU WANT TO READ MORE

HENRY J. AARON, *Who Pays the Property Tax* (Washington: The Brookings Institution, 1975).

GAYLON E. GREER and MICHAEL D. FARRELL, *Contemporary Real Estate: Theory and Practice* (Chicago: The Dryden Press, 1983), Chapter 6.

SY NICHOLSON, "Property Taxes: After Proposition 13," *Real Estate Today,* May 1979, pp. 40–48.

SHIRLEY H. OLSEN, "The Economic Effects of Proposition 13," *Journal of Property Management,* September–October 1979, pp. 249–255.

PETER WOLF, *Land In America* (New York: Pantheon Books, 1981), Chapter 4.

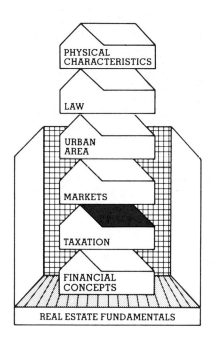

PHYSICAL CHARACTERISTICS

LAW

URBAN AREA

MARKETS

TAXATION

FINANCIAL CONCEPTS

REAL ESTATE FUNDAMENTALS

11

Taxation: basic concepts of federal income taxation

PREVIEW

From time to time you have probably read or heard about people earning very high incomes who pay little or no federal income tax. Your response to this situation may have been one of resentment, envy, or amazement, but probably not indifference. If you had asked friends how such a thing occurs, you probably were told the answer was "tax shelters," without anyone every providing a reasonable explanation of what a "tax shelter" is and how you find them. For that matter, you probably had a difficult time finding anyone who could tell you much about taxes at all, other than giving the universal opinion that they are too high. This chapter tackles the subject of federal income taxation. It introduces some basic taxation concepts including tax shelters and the tax aspects of owning a home. Specifically, it considers:

1. The history of our federal income tax system and how our tax laws are developed.
2. The need for tax planning to minimize income taxes.
3. The fundamentals of our income tax system.
4. What tax shelters are and how they are created.
5. The basic tax consequences of home ownership.

There is a widespread feeling that income taxes are too detailed and complicated to be fully understood. While these charges may be true, the basic concepts of income taxation can be readily understood by almost anyone willing to spend just a little time and effort. If you are planning to enter the real estate business or ever purchase real estate, an understanding of basic income tax concepts is not a luxury; it is a necessity. Income taxes affect your real estate development and equity investment decisions by affecting the income you realize from them. Failure to consider income taxes from an investment will result in either an over- or understatement of income, just as a failure to consider the effects of income taxes on your income from your job will result in a misstatement of that income. Because of their impact on development and investment decisions, taxes consequently affect every other facet of real estate. You cannot take the approach of an ostrich and pretend that by ignoring them, income taxes will go away.

Although generally much less significant than federal income taxes, state income taxes can also have an important impact on real estate investments. However, because state income taxes vary substantially, it is not possible to adequately discuss them here. Suffice it to say that state income taxes should be considered before making any investment decision.

Fortunately, there is no need for you to become an expert on income taxes — tax attorneys and accountants specializing in taxation have invested years of study to spare you that effort. You should be willing to use these professionals and pay them well for their services because you will have peace of mind and be dollars ahead for doing so. However, to make the most of these experts and otherwise avoid obvious mistakes, you need an understanding of basic federal income taxation *concepts*, the subject of this chapter.

THE BIRTH AND DEVELOPMENT
OF THE FEDERAL INCOME TAX

The federal income tax as we know it was born in either 1909, 1913, or 1916 depending on your point of view. In 1909, the Sixteenth Amendment, authorizing the federal government to levy an income tax, was initiated. In 1913, enough states had ratified the amendment to make it a part of the Constitution and in the same year Congress enacted the income tax. In 1916, the Supreme Court upheld the income tax as constitutional, and for the federal government there was no turning back — the income tax was too good a revenue source and tool to control social and economic events to ever be eliminated.

This was not the first attempt at establishing an income tax, nor have things remained the same since. Table 11.1 outlines a brief history of the income tax before and after the 1909 to 1916 period. As you can

Table 11.1. History of Federal Income Tax System

Year	Event
1862	First income tax enacted to finance Civil War. A mildy progressive tax with rates of 1.5 to 5%.
1872	1862 tax eliminated.
1894	Second income tax enacted with a flat tax rate of 2% on individual and corporate incomes.
1895	1894 tax ruled unconstitutional by Supreme Court. Court held that the tax required apportionment among the states on the basis of population.
1909	1% excise tax on corporate income enacted.
1909	Sixteenth Amendment to Constitution initiated. This amendment gives the Congress power to lay and collect taxes on income.
1913	Sixteenth Amendment ratified as part of federal Constitution.
1913	Income tax enacted.
1916	Supreme Court upheld validity of tax.
1939	1913 tax law and its subsequent amendments were brought together under a permanent code.
1954	Internal Revenue Code, which is the present governing tax law with subsequent amendments, was established.
1958, 1962, 1964, 1969, 1971, 1976, 1978	Major revisions in Code were made.
1981	Economic Recovery Tax Act (ERTA)
1982	Tax Equity and Fiscal Reform Act (TEFRA)
1984	1984 Tax Reform Act

SOURCE: From the book, *Tax Planning for Real Estate Investors* by James B. Kau and C. F. Sirmans. Copyright by Prentice-Hall, Incorporated. Updated by author.

see, a number of important events related to the income tax have occurred. In 1939, the first **Internal Revenue Code** (referred to from now on simply as the Code) was developed to organize all tax laws into one coordinated body of law. The Code was rewritten in 1954 and has been revised often, with major revisions being made in the years indicated. The most sweeping reform since 1954 is the **Economic Recovery Tax Act (ERTA)** of 1981. Other changes affecting real estate were made in the Tax Equity and Fiscal Responsibility Act of 1982 (TEFRA) and the Tax Reform Act of 1984. Significant changes are being discussed and will likely be made in the near future.

Tax statutes are a product of the political process, being initiated in Congress and ultimately approved by the executive branch of government. As a result of the process of debate and compromise, and the procedural rules of the Congress, the tax bills that are ultimately passed into law frequently have little resemblance to the original proposals. Often, the logic underlying the proposal becomes twisted or lost. Because of this fact, you should not feel ill at ease if you cannot understand the logic of any particular piece of tax legislation. Trying to consistently apply logic to tax laws, including why the dollar amounts or percentages used throughout the Code are what they are, is often a frustrating and nonproductive exercise. Not all tax law is this way; the logic underlying some tax law is clear. Just don't get discouraged when it is difficult or impossible to understand why certain things are done the way they are. Just remember that the Code is the "Law of the Land" and you must abide by its contents — logical or not!

The basic income tax law today is the 1954 Internal Revenue Code as amended in subsequent years. Tax law is administered by the *Internal Revenue Service* (IRS), created by Congress in 1953 as a part of the Treasury Department. The Code itself, even though quite lengthy, is not detailed enough to cover every possible situation. To remedy this problem, the IRS has developed rules and regulations expanding and clarifying the Code. These **Treasury Regulations,** or *Regs,* represent the official IRS interpretation of the Code, and provide clearer guidelines for taxpayers about how the government will treat certain tax situations.

As a taxpayer you may disagree with the IRS interpretation of a particular part of the tax law. For example, you may feel that a provision of the Code allows you to reduce your tax obligation while the Regs say that such a reduction is not appropriate. Such disputes are settled by the United States Tax Court or other Federal Courts, including the Supreme Court. The decisions of the Courts in such cases often become part of the tax law in the sense that other taxpayers and the IRS rely on them to support a particular position with regard to a specific provision of the Code. All three sources of tax law and their relationship are illustrated in Figure 11.1.

Tax Planning

The Code, Treasury Regs, and court decisions are used by tax professionals to reduce your tax obligation to the lowest possible amount. The use of every legal means to reduce your taxes is called **tax avoidance.**

Figure 11.1
Sources of income tax law.

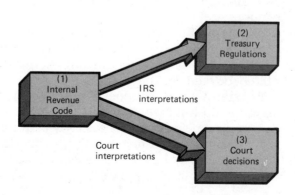

There is nothing patriotic about paying more taxes than required by law and nothing illegal about tax avoidance. **Tax evasion** is another story — it is the illegal avoidance of taxation by concealing income or falsifying other information to reduce your tax obligation. Tax evasion can result in fines and/or prison sentences if you are convicted. By practicing tax avoidance you can reduce the federal government's share of your profits from real estate development or equity investment to a minimum and have more dollars to put into your own bank account. If Uncle Sam is to be a partner in all your income, he should be given as small a portion as legally possible.

Tax avoidance is not a matter of luck. It requires a good bit of planning. Professional tax consultants can help reduce your present and future tax obligations. Such consultants may be either attorneys or accountants. Regardless of which you choose, you will still need the services of a competent accountant to ensure that records conform to accepted accounting principles and are adequate for the IRS.

INCOME TAX FUNDAMENTALS

So far, little has been said about income tax rules themselves. You have been learning about the rulebooks covering the game. It is time you learned about the contents of those books.

Basic Taxation Formula — A Familiar Face

In the last chapter the basic tax equation was presented:

$$\text{Tax liability} = \text{Tax base} \times \text{Tax rate}$$

With one simple modification, this simple equation also holds for income taxes. Your tax obligation for any year can be found by multiplying your tax base by your tax rate and subtracting tax credits:

$$\text{Tax liability} = (\text{Tax base} \times \text{Tax rate}) - \text{Tax credits}$$

The trick now is to define tax base, tax rate, and tax credits.

Tax Base For calculating income tax liabilities the tax base is defined as **taxable income.** Taxable income is what is left of total receipts after all exclusions, exemptions, and deductions have been subtracted. **Total receipts** include *all* the income you received during the period. For example, if you earned $25,000 from your job and had investment income of $7,500, your gross receipts were $32,500. You will receive a W–2 statement of earnings and withholding from employers that tells your earnings from that source. If you are self-employed, as many real estate agents are, you must keep some of your own records.

From total receipts you are allowed to deduct income excluded from taxation, called **exclusions,** such as the interest earned on municipal bonds and death benefits from life insurance. What is left is called *adjusted gross income.* From adjusted gross income you are allowed to subtract **deductions** for certain expenses paid for during the period. The most common personal deductions are medical expenses, interest expenses, property taxes, charitable contributions, and miscellaneous items such as losses to theft.

These deductions may be itemized, or listed, if you have made careful records and have retained receipts. If you have not kept the necessary records, or if your allowable deductions are not that great, then you may deduct an amount allowed all taxpayers who choose not to itemize, the **standard deduction.** Actually, the standard deduction is no longer actually subtracted from gross income, but rather has been included in a series of tax tables that allow you to go directly from gross income to your tax liability. These special tax tables are called **zero-bracket tax tables.**

Another allowable reduction in gross income comes from exemptions. **Exemptions** are reductions in gross income allowed for the taxpayer and each dependent. Presently, each exemption provides a $1000 reduction of gross income. As with the standard deduction, tax tables used to calculate tax liabilities have already considered exemptions. All you have to do is use the table corresponding to the number of exemptions you claim.

If you were to deduct exclusions, exemptions, and deductions from gross receipts, you would have taxable income. So, taxable income may be calculated as follows:

Total receipts
− Exclusions
Adjusted gross income
− Exemptions
− Deductions
Taxable income

For example, suppose you had the $32,500 total receipts above and two dependents (not including yourself). Further, you had no excluded income and itemized deductions of $6000. Your taxable income would be $23,500:

$32,500
− 0   (Income excluded from taxation)
− 3,000   (Exemptions: 3 × $1000 = $3000)
− 6,000   (Deductions)
$23,500   Taxable income

This $23,500 is the amount on which taxes must be paid. It is the tax base.

Tax Rate What was your **tax rate** last year? Chances are you do not know right off, but given time you could drag out your tax return and calculate it. But how would you calculate it? If you think about this question for a moment, you can see that there are several ways to calculate your tax rate.

First you could look in tax tables, such as those in Table 11.2 and see what percentage of an additional dollar of taxable income you would pay in taxes. For example, if in 1984, your taxable income was $23,500, the tax tables reveal that you must pay a lump sum of $2497 plus 22 percent of all income over $20,200 in taxes. This is your marginal tax rate, the tax rate on an additional dollar of income.

You could also calculate your tax rate by simply seeing what percentage of your taxable income you paid in taxes. For the 1984 taxable income of $23,500, you would have paid in taxes:

$$\text{Taxes} = \$2497 + (.22)(\$23,500 - \$20,200)$$
$$= \$2497 + (.22)(3300)$$
$$= \$2497 + \$726$$
$$= \$3223$$

By dividing the $3223 liability by the $23,500 taxable income you find that you paid about 14 percent of each dollar of taxable income in taxes. You have just calculated your **average tax rate,** the percentage of taxable income paid in taxes.

Table 11.2. Tax Rate Schedules for Married Individuals Filing Joint Returns

Taxable Income	1984	
	Pay	+ % on Excess*
0–$ 3,400	0	0
$3,400 – 5,500	0	11
5,500 – 7,600	$231	12
7,600 – 11,900	483	14
11,900 – 16,000	1,085	16
16,000 – 20,200	1,741	18
20,200 – 24,600	2,497	22
24,600 – 29,900	3,465	25
29,900 – 35,200	4,790	28
35,200 – 45,800	6,274	33
45,800 – 60,000	9,772	38
60,000 – 85,600	15,168	42
85,600 – 109,400	25,920	45
109,400 – 162,400	36,630	49
162,400 – 215,400	89,100	50

* The amount by which the taxpayer's taxable income exceeds the base of the bracket.

SOURCE: *1985 U.S. Master Tax Guide,* (Commerce Clearing House, Inc.), p.5.

However, at this point, you may remember that you actually had total receipts of $32,500 during the year. You may want to calculate the percentage of this amount actually paid in taxes. Since you paid $3224 in taxes, you paid about 10 percent ($3224/$32,500) of each dollar of total receipts in taxes. The 10 percent is your **effective tax rate,** the percentage of gross receipts paid in taxes.

At this point you know your marginal tax rate is 22 percent, your average tax rate is 14 percent, and your effective tax rate is 10 percent; a confusing picture at best. The reason your marginal tax rate is higher is because our tax system is designed to be a progressive one; the higher your taxable income, the greater the tax rate on an additional dollar of taxable income.

Some people are confused about what progressive taxation really means. You may have heard someone mistakenly say that they did not want to earn any additional income because it would put them into a higher tax bracket and they would actually pay more in tax than they earned. Such people fail to understand that any additional income they earn will, in the very worst situation, be taxed at a maximum marginal rate of 50 percent and the taxes due on any income they have already earned that year will not be affected. In the worst case, they will be able to keep at least 50 percent of any additional income they earn. Whether what is left after taxes is worth the additional effort necessary to earn it is the pertinent question.

Between the average and effective tax rates, the average tax rate will always be higher. This is because in calculating both rates the numerator is the same but the total receipts used as the denominator to calculate the effective tax rate will always be larger than the taxable income figure used to calculate the average tax rate. This will, of course, produce a lower effective tax rate than average tax rate.

So what is your tax rate? Is it 22 percent, 14 percent or 10 percent? Which is correct depends on what it is to be used for. For the basic tax equation above (Tax = Base × Rate) the average tax rate is the answer. However, if you are thinking about buying a small apartment complex, you will be more interested in how the additional dollars of income will be taxed, since any dollars the apartment produces will be added to your existing income and taxed at the marginal rate. For investment decisions the marginal tax rate is usually the most important one.

Tax Credits After the tax rate is multiplied by the tax base, you may use tax credits to reduce your tax obligation. **Tax credits are** direct reductions in tax liability. You should remember that exclusions, exemptions, and deductions reduce taxable income; they are not subtracted directly from the tax obligation as are tax credits. Tax credits are quite valuable. The most common tax credits affecting real estate are the investment tax credits, which allow credits for investment in certain tangible personal property and the credit for rehabilitating historic structures.

Two Kinds of Income —
Ordinary and Capital Gains

Income and rates considered so far have been ordinary income and ordinary income tax rates. **Ordinary income** generally includes all income you earn from any source other than the sale of certain assets called **capital assets.** Another type of income, called **capital gains,** is defined by the Code. Capital gains (or losses) result from the sale of an asset used in a trade or business or held for investment purposes. Such assets are called capital assets. When the sales price is greater than the value carried for the asset in the seller's accounting records, called the asset's *book value,* a capital gain results. If the sales price is less than the book value of the asset, a capital loss results. For example, if you own an office building that is carried on your books at $250,000 and sell it for $350,000 you will have a $100,000 capital gain.

Your capital gain may be either long-term or short-term in nature. *Short-term capital gains* are added to your ordinary income and taxed as such. *Long-term capital gains* receive preferential treatment since 60 percent of the long-term gain is not taxed. The remaining 40 percent of the long-term gain is added to your other ordinary income and is taxed at ordinary rates. A long-term capital gain occurs when the capital asset has been held for more than one year. In the example just cited, if the sale of the office building produces a long-term capital gain of $100,000, $40,000 (.40 × $100,000) of that gain would be taxed as ordinary income while the other $60,000 is not taxed. It is not surprising that real estate investors seek long-term capital gains treatment.

CORPORATIONS AND PARTNERSHIPS

All the fundamentals considered thus far have dealt with individual, or personal, income taxes. Sometimes people invest in real estate through corporations or partnerships. As discussed in Chapter 4, corporations and partnerships are entities created by law. The Code recognizes their existence and contains rules for taxing them.

Corporate Taxation

The tax code defines two forms of corporate entities and taxes them differently. First, the code recognizes the corporate entity described in Chapter 4 embodying the concept of a corporation being an artificial, legal entity. This type of corporation, called the *C corporation,* is viewed as an entity for tax purposes and pays taxes at the corporate level at the following rates:

TAXABLE INCOME	1985 AND THEREAFTER*
Up to $25,000	15%
$25,001 to $50,000	18%
$50,001 to $75,000	30%
$75,001 to $100,000	40%
$100,001 to $1,000,000	46%
$1,000,001 to $1,405,000	51% (includes 5% add. tax)
Over $1,405,000	46%

* Until changed

C corporation short-term capital gains are taxed as regular income. They may choose either to add long-term capital gains to ordinary income and pay taxes on them at ordinary rates or pay at a flat rate of 28%.

The C corporation is not frequently used for investment real estate because it results in double taxation. First, the C corporation pays taxes on its income when it is earned, and then, when dividends are paid to stockholders, they must pay taxes on them as ordinary income. The net result is that many of the tax advantages of owning real estate are lost.

The second form of corporation, the S *corporation,* is not treated as a legal entity for tax purposes. That is, it does not pay taxes at the corporate level. All income is assumed to be paid to shareholders as dividends and taxed at the personal level. Thus, the S corporation will file an informational tax return informing the IRS as to how income was distributed to shareholders. The S corporation provides many of the advantages of corporate ownership without the burden of double taxation. Recent changes in the tax code have made the S corporation a more attractive option for real estate investment. It will likely become a more widely used ownership form in the future.

Partnership Taxation

The Code also has special provisions for partnerships. Like corporations, partnerships may own property and the income from the partnership is then distributed to the partners. Each year *all* the income generated by the partnership is allocated to the partners whether or not it is distributed. The partnership itself pays no taxes on its income. Instead, a partnership files a return informing the IRS how much ordinary and capital gains income it had during the period and how that income was allocated to the partners. The partners are then responsible for paying personal income taxes on the income distributed to them. When a partnership earns ordinary income, it is allocated on to partners as ordinary income. Likewise, when the partnership earns capital gains income, it is allocated to the partners as capital gains and taxed as such. This means partnerships can pass many tax benefits through to partners and avoid the double taxation of corporations. It is easy to see why, from a tax perspective, partnerships are very popular among those investing in income-producing real estate.

THE CONCEPT OF A TAX SHELTER

We are now ready to answer the question that started this consideration of income taxes, "What is a tax shelter?" A **tax shelter** is a vehicle for postponing and/or permanently avoiding the payment of certain taxes, as shown in Figure 11.2. The most common form of tax shelter provides the investor with a deferral of **tax liability** by lowering present tax obligations and collecting the taxes later, usually when the investment is sold.

Real estate is often considered to be a tax shelter investment. In some cases, real estate benefits from special tax provisions applying only to it or to a limited number of investment types. In other cases, real estate tax shelter results from general provisions applying to virtually everyone. For example, if you own a home, you are allowed to deduct the interest you pay on your home mortgage. This interest is tax deductible, not because of special rules for homeowners, but rather because all interest is generally deductible, including the interest on your Mastercard and your charge account at the local department store. One of the reasons real estate provides good tax shelter benefits is because its characteristics fit provisions of the Code generating tax shelter, not so much because of special provisions applying only to real estate.

Needless to say, tax shelters are in high demand. People will pay for the ability to save on their taxes. The higher their tax rate, the more they will pay. For instance, if you are in the 50 percent **marginal tax rate** bracket, then a tax shelter that reduces your taxable income by $100 will reduce your tax obligation by $50, whereas if you were in the 40

Figure 11.2
Elements of a tax shelter.

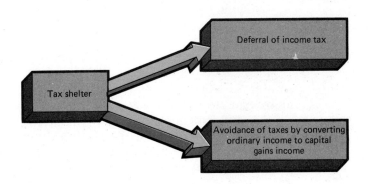

Tax shelter → Deferral of income tax

Avoidance of taxes by converting ordinary income to capital gains income

percent marginal tax bracket, your tax obligation would be reduced by only $40. You need to be very cautious when considering tax shelters and not become overzealous. First, the tax shelter investment is an investment, and like all investments, it may not go as expected. This could cause real cash losses far in excess of any tax savings. Second, you should not let your desire for tax shelter seduce you into paying exorbitant prices for tax shelter. For the $100 reduction in taxable income above, it would not make sense to pay more than the worth of the tax savings it will reasonably produce.

Some tax shelter investments only shelter some or all of the income *they* produce. That is, the amount of taxable income from such an investment is less than the amount of money it puts in your pocket. Other investments not only produce a taxable income lower than the actual cash generated, but actually produce a negative taxable income! Think about a real estate investment such as an apartment building and how the taxable income for a given year is calculated. As the owner, you collect rental income and income from other sources such as washing machines, vending machines, and maybe parking. Like other businesses, you are allowed to subtract operating expenses such as utilities, salaries, repairs, office supplies, and so on. You are also allowed to deduct interest of all types and, as with businesses, you are allowed to deduct depreciation allowance for those assets that eventually wear out. What is left is taxable income, the income you must show on your personal tax return. So far nothing seems out of the ordinary and for good reason — it isn't!

If taxable income from the investment is positive, you simply add that amount to your other taxable income and pay additional taxes. But what if the investment's *taxable income is negative?* If taxable income is negative, it is shown on your tax return as a negative number and reduces your other taxable income. If you had taxable income from all other sources of $23,500 and a real estate investment producing a taxable income of −$4000, your total taxable income for the year is $19,500. By reducing your total taxable income, your real estate investment has saved you tax dollars you would have just learned by putting it into the simple accounting framework of Table 11.3.

Taxable income is not the money you can put in your pocket from your real estate investment. You still must make any principal payments due. Also, one of the items deducted from gross rents did not involve writing a check or paying cash to anyone; that item is cost recovery, also called depreciation. It is discussed in more detail in the next chapter. The Code allows you to deduct a portion of your investment in improvements each year because its purchase represented a business expense, but to deduct it all in the year of purchase would have distorted your income for that year. Deducting the entire cost of the real estate investment in the year of purchase also would not be consistent with the idea that it is not used up in one year like pencils or other business

Table 11.3. After-Tax Cash Flow Framework

Gross Rents
   Less: Operating expenses
Net Operating Income
   Less: Interest
   Less: Cost Recovery
Taxable Income
   Plus: Cost Recovery
   Less: Principal
Before-Tax Cash Flow
   Plus: Tax Savings
   or
   Less: Taxes
After-Tax Cash Flow (Money going into your pocket)

expenses. For this reason, it would not be reasonable to match the entire outlay with one year's income. All that you did to receive the depreciation deduction was to calculate the amount of the deduction according to the provisions of the Code.

Since cost recovery is not paid to anyone, it does not reduce your cash. This is in contrast to other deductions such as interest and operating expenses, which require that cash actually leave your pocket for deductions to exist. Because of this, cost recovery deductions are much sought-after. To compensate for subtracting cost recovery in calculating taxable income, you can now add it back to move closer to the cash produced by the investment that can be put into your bank account. However, you must still account for the cash inflow or outflow caused by taxation. As seen earlier, if taxable income is positive, the impact of taxation on cash flow is negative and if taxable income is negative, cash flow is increased.

Most real estate is purchased using a great deal of borrowed money, so interest deductions are often quite large. Also, in improved real estate the recoverable improvements usually represent a high percentage of the total investment and, therefore, produces relatively large recovery deductions. It is not unusual for taxable income to be negative or relatively small because of the large amount of interest paid and the large noncash deduction for cost recovery in the early years of an investment. However, **after-tax cash flow** is often positive when depreciation and tax savings are added back to taxable income.

By concentrating on taxable income produced each year, only the operations stage of real estate investments has been considered. The disposition of real estate also has some important tax shelter implications. First, the gain can be, at least partially, taxed as a long-term capital gain if the property is held for more than one year. Such treatment means that 60 percent of the gain is excluded from taxation and the remaining 40 percent is taxed as ordinary income. Your gain on the sale of real estate is the difference between the sales price and value at which the real estate is carried on your books at the time of the sale. This book value is also called your **ending basis.** The ending basis is simply the beginning basis, usually the original cost, plus the cost of any improvements made to the property, less the total cost recovery claimed on your income tax forms over the period during which you owned the property. All or part of this gain will be taxed at the preferable long-term capital gains tax rates. This means that to some extent you can defer ordinary income through the use of cost recovery while you own real estate and, when the property is sold, pay only long-term capital gains tax rates on all or a part of the gain. The details of this procedure are considered later in this chapter and in the next chapter.

You now have an overview of real estate as a tax shelter. What has been discussed is *only* the basic concept. Many details must be worked out for real estate to be an effective tax shelter. This discussion has also not considered many additional ways in which real estate acts as a tax shelter, such as tax deferred exchanges and installment sales. The remainder of this chapter is devoted to exploring the tax aspects of home ownership. The next chapter deals with additional tax aspects of income-producing real estate.

FEDERAL INCOME TAXES AFFECTING HOME OWNERSHIP

Home ownership provides some significant tax benefits. These benefits allow a homeowner to reduce taxable income while the home is owned and to postpone, and even sometimes completely avoid, taxes when the home is sold. Like all other areas of taxation, the law changes from time to time, and you should consult a good tax counselor before making any major decisions. However, what follows provides a basic understanding of the taxes affecting home ownership. The discussion considers the acquisition, use, and disposition stages of home ownership.

Acquisition

At the time you acquire your home there are few opportunities to reduce your taxes for that year. In the year of acquisition you may deduct discount points paid to a lender to obtain a loan. A **discount point** is money paid to allow you to get an interest rate below that actually being required by lenders. Each discount point is equal to one percent of the loan amount you are seeking. Discount points are different than the fee you pay, usually called a loan origination fee, to compensate the lender for processing the paperwork involved in borrowing money.

Other costs associated with buying a home are not deductible in the year of purchase. While the other costs are not deductible, they may affect the basis, or investment, you are assumed to have in the property. The basis is used to calculate the gain you must recognize and on which you must pay taxes, when the property is sold. The biggest exceptions to this rule are expenses associated with obtaining financing. Generally, financing expenses, other than discount points, will neither be deducted *nor* added to the basis. Your beginning basis is the price of the home plus allowable closing costs.

Use

While you own the home, certain expenditures are deductible whereas others affect your basis in the property. The cost of routine repairs and maintenance is not deductible; nor is it added to your basis. However, major repairs and improvements may be added to your basis in the property. So, if you add on a gameroom, the cost of that addition will be added to your basis. However, if you repair a broken window, it will not be deductible, nor can it be added to the basis.

Two of the best tax benefits of homeownership are the deductibility of interest and property taxes. Since most homes are financed with borrowed money, the ability to deduct interest results in substantial tax savings. If you are in the 40 percent marginal tax bracket, each dollar of interest reduces your income tax obligation by $.40, making the after-tax cost of that dollar of interest only $.60. Property taxes are also deductible. Thus, the after-tax cost of homeownership can be significantly lower than the before-tax cost. How much lower depends on your marginal tax rate. The higher the marginal tax rate, the greater the impact of savings.

Disposition

Some excellent tax benefits are available when you sell your home. More specifically, these rules apply to your **principal residence,** that is, your main home rather than a vacation home, for example. Under certain conditions, tax law allows you to: (1) defer the payment of taxes resulting from gains from the sale of a home and (2) ultimately exempt from taxation a significant portion of the gains.

Deferring Taxes on Gains If you sell your principal residence for a gain, you may not have to **recognize** and pay taxes on any of that gain at that time. The Code provides that if you purchase another home of equal or greater cost within a specified period of time, none of the gain on the sale must be recognized. Thus, you may **realize** a gain in the form of cash, but in the eyes of the IRS, no gain occurred at this time. If you fail to purchase another home of equal or greater price, you will have to recognize part or all of any gain on the sale of your home. If taxes must be paid, they will be long-term capital gains taxes if you have owned the home for more than six months or ordinary income if you have not. Losses on the sale of your principal residence are not deductible.

As you can imagine, the process is not as simple as it may sound. Certain terms must be defined and certain provisions of the tax law made more explicit in order to determine whether a gain must be recognized. What follows is a brief look at some of these items. It is intended to give you a basic understanding of the process, not answer every possible question that may arise in tax planning for the sale of a principal residence. For that, expert professional help should be used.

Let's start by looking at some details. First, the tax provisions apply to your principal residence, the residence that constitutes your main home. It does not apply to vacation homes or homes owned and rented to others. The principal residence may be any form of home: a detached single family home, a condominium, or even a cooperative. The sale of cooperative stock is treated the same as the sale of a single family home if the owner of the stock occupies the unit as his or her principal residence.

Tax provisions also place time limits within which another home must be purchased to qualify for this special treatment. The replacement home may be purchased any time within a period beginning two years before the date of the sale of your home to two years after that date. That is, you have a 48-month period in which to operate — two years before and two years after the sale of your home.

In determining whether a taxable gain has occurred, the cost of the new residence is compared to the adjusted sales price of the old home. **Adjusted sales price** is the sales price of your old home less fix-up costs and selling expenses. **Fix-up costs** are those costs incurred to prepare the property for sale and must occur within a 90-day period ending the day the sales contract is signed and paid within 30 days after the date of sale. Major **improvements,** such as having a whirlpool spa installed, are not considered fix-up expenses. However, painting the house, replacing missing shingles, replacing cracked windows, and similar items are considered fix-up costs. **Selling expenses** include those outlays associated with selling the property, such as brokerage and attorney's fees.

The *cost* of the new home is the contract purchase price plus allowable costs associated with purchasing the home. The allowable costs include brokerage commissions, attorney's fees, and other direct costs, with the exception of loan origination fees paid to lenders for obtaining financing. Thus, if you are purchasing a home for $95,000 and have $2000 of allowable closing costs, the cost of the new home is $97,000.

Whether a taxable gain is recognized or not depends on whether the cost of the new home equals or exceeds the adjusted sales price of the old home. If it does, no gain must be recognized. If the cost is less than the adjusted sales price, a gain may be recognized and taxes paid. For example, if the adjusted sales price of your home is $90,000 and the cost of your new home is the $97,000 above, no gain must be recognized on the sale of the old residence, no matter what you originally paid for it. However, if the adjusted sales price of the old home was $100,000, you possibly must recognize a gain up to the amount by which the adjusted sales price exceeds the cost of your new home. In this case, that amount is $3000. Whether or not you must pay taxes on the entire $3000 depends on whether you realized a gain of $3000 or more.

To determine your gain on the sale of the old home requires a look at your cost to acquire it and any additional investment in it. All of this poking into the past is concerned with establishing your basis, or net investment in the home. It is the difference between your basis and the adjusted sales price that determines the amount of gain that could be subject to taxation.

Your basis in your first home is its cost, defined as purchase price plus allowable closing costs, as discussed earlier. If your first home had a purchase price of $70,000 and allowable closing costs of $2000, your basis in it is $72,000. This is true even though you may have borrowed a high percentage of the purchase price. Any improvements you may make to the home, as contrasted to maintenance and repairs, increase your basis. For example, if you add a swimming pool at a cost of $18,000, this amount will be added to your $72,000 basis, making it $90,000. The $90,000 is called your *adjusted basis* in the property. If you sell this home for more than the $90,000 adjusted basis, you will realize a gain equal to the difference between the adjusted sales price and the adjusted basis.

However, that gain will be recognized for tax purposes only if you fail to purchase a home with a cost equal to or greater than the first home's adjusted sales price. Thus, if you sell the first home for an adjusted sales price of $100,000, you will realize a $10,000 gain. If you purchase a home with a cost, as defined earlier, of $100,000 or more, no gain will be recognized for tax purposes. However, if a home costing $97,000 is purchased, $3000 of the $10,000 gain must be recognized. If a home costing $88,000 is purchased, the entire $10,000 gain must be recognized and taxes paid. Notice that the maximum taxable gain is limited to the difference between your adjusted basis and the adjusted sales price, regardless of the cost of the new home.

Now, what is your basis in a new home you may purchase after selling your present house? Continuing with the example above, assume you sold your home for $100,000 and purchased a home costing $105,000, producing no taxable gain. This means that you realized a $10,000 gain, but recognized a taxable gain of $0. In other words, you deferred taxation of a $10,000 gain. The basis in your new home will reflect this fact by being reduced by the $10,000 deferred gain. Thus, your adjusted basis in your new home will be $95,000 ($105,000 − $10,000). If you had purchased a home costing $97,000 you would have recognized $3000 of gain and deferred $7000 of gain. Your basis in that home would be $90,000 ($97,000 − $7000). Since the $3000 gain is a long-term capital gain, you will pay ordinary income taxes on only 40 percent of it, or $1200. This $1200 will be added to your other ordinary income at the end of the year.

If you later sell the home costing $105,000 for an adjusted sales price of $125,000 two years from now, you will realize a gain of $30,000. This is the difference between the $95,000 basis and the adjusted sales price of $125,000. Whether or not any of this gain is taxable depends on whether you purchase a home costing $125,000 or more. If, for instance, you purchase a home costing $130,000, you will pay no tax on the sale and your new home will have a basis of $100,000 ($130,000 − $30,000). This deferral process continues throughout your life.

Must the Piper Ever be Paid?

There comes a time for many families when a smaller home is desired or when home ownership itself is undesirable. As children go off to school, find permanent jobs, or marry, a husband and wife may desire less room and less of the upkeep associated with a larger home. At this point, the chain of more expensive homes meeting the tax-deferring criteria of the Code may be broken and taxes must be paid. The size of the tax liability depends on the gain and the age of the taxpayer. With proper planning, you can exempt all or a substantial portion of the gain you have deferred throughout your life!

Specifically, the Code allows you a once-in-a-lifetime exemption of up to $125,000 of gain on your principal residence if you are age 55 or over and have owned and occupied the home for at least three of the last five years. This means that if your gain, adjusted sales price less basis, is $125,000 or less, you can avoid paying all taxes on it if you are 55 or over and you or your spouse have not used this exemption before. For example, if you have a basis of $75,000 in your home, sell it for an adjusted sales price of $200,000, and meet the necessary requirements, you may exercise this option and pay no taxes on your gain. If your gain exceeds $125,000, you must pay taxes only on the excess.

SUMMARY

You should now have a better understanding of the basic concepts of federal income taxation. The basic sources of tax law are the Internal Revenue Code, Treasury Regulations, and court decisions. The current Code was written in 1954 but has been revised many times. As a taxpayer you are within your legal rights to minimize your tax obligation using every legal means. Such activity is called tax avoidance and should not be confused with tax evasion, the use of illegal means to reduce your tax obligation. Professional tax consultants can help you legally minimize your tax obligation.

Income taxes, like other taxes, are based on the familiar concept of your tax liability being the product of your tax base times your tax rate minus tax credits. For income taxes, the base is taxable income. Taxable income is found by subtracting all exemptions, exclusions, and deductions from your total receipts. The tax rate may be either the marginal, average, or effective tax rate. For the fundamental income tax concept of base times rate, the rate is the average rate. However, for making investment decisions, the marginal tax rate should be used. Federal income taxes are designed to be progressive; marginal tax rates increase as taxable income increases. Your tax liability can also be reduced by tax credits, direct reductions from your tax liability.

Income can be categorized as either ordinary income or capital gains income. Capital gains income can be either short-term or long-term in nature. For individual taxpayers, short-term capital gains are taxed the same as ordinary income. Sixty percent of the long-term gains is not taxed and the remaining 40 percent is taxed as ordinary income. For this reason, long-term capital gains are highly prized.

Corporations have a different set of tax rates than individuals. Taxes must be payed on the taxable income of the corporation and shareholders must pay taxes on dividends received. This is called double taxation. Partnerships do not pay taxes on their income. Instead, the income is allocated to the partners and they must pay all taxes. Double taxation is avoided in partnerships.

Tax shelters were seen as ways of deferring or reducing your tax obligation. Income-producing real estate is often an effective tax shelter since it can produce a small or negative income while producing positive after-tax cash flow to you. It also may receive long-term capital gains treatment when sold. Tax shelters can be quite valuable to investors with other income to offset, but only if the underlying investment is economically sound.

Home ownership has many tax implications associated with it. While only limited costs associated with acquiring a home are deductible, owning a home provides some significant tax benefits. Mortgage interest and property taxes are deductible each year. When your principal residence is sold, you can defer the taxation of any gain under certain circumstances. Persons 55 years old or older may receive up to $125,000 in gain without being taxed. Any amount over $125,000 will be taxed.

QUICK QUIZ

1. The rules developed by the IRS that outline how they interpret tax law are called:

   a. Tax Code
   b. Treasury Proclamations
   c. Treasury Decisions
   d. Treasury Regulations

2. Income, for purposes of calculating your tax liability, is defined as:

    a. total receipts   c. cash income
    b. net income   d. taxable income

3. Reductions in taxable income allowed for the taxpayer and each dependent are called

    a. exclusions   c. deductions
    b. exemptions   d. standard deduction

4. A taxpayer who is 55 years old or over may exempt up to _____ of gain from the sale of their principal residence.

    a. $75,000   c. $150,000
    b. $125,000   d. $100,000

5. The deduction for _____ is generally considered to be the key to creating tax shelters in the operation stage of a real estate investment.

    a. cost recovery   c. operating expenses
    b. interest   d. insurance

6. Your _____ in a home is its purchase price plus allowable closing costs.

7. If you sell your home and must recognize a gain, that gain will be taxed as _____ .

8. To avoid paying taxes on the gain from the sale of your home, you must purchase another home of equal or greater value within a _____ month period beginning _____ months before the sale and extending _____ months beyond the date of sale.

9. The tax rate you would pay on an additional dollar of taxable income is your _____ tax rate.

10. _____ is the use of every legal means to reduce your tax obligation.

**QUESTIONS
AND
EXERCISES**

1. If your basis in a home is $80,000 and you sell that home for $100,000 and purchase another home a month later for $105,000, how much of the gain will be taxable and why?

2. For the sale in Question 1, what is the taxable gain if another home is not purchased? What if a home costing $92,000 is purchased within the required time period?

3. What is your basis in a home if you bought it for $67,000, had $1500 of allowable closing costs, added a room costing $12,000, and repainted the home for $1000?

4. A taxpayer had total receipts of $37,000 and paid taxes of $2497 on a taxable income of $20,200. What are his or her average and effective tax rates? From Table 11.2, what is his or her marginal tax rate?

5. Explain what a tax shelter is and how real estate investments create them.

KEY TERMINOLOGY

adjusted gross income
adjusted sales price
after-tax cash flow
average tax rate
capital asset
capital gain
deductions
discount point
double taxation
Economic Recovery Tax Act (ERTA)
effective tax rate
ending basis
exclusions
exemptions
fix-up costs
improvements
Internal Revenue Code

marginal tax rate
ordinary income
principal residence
realize
recognize
selling expenses
standard deduction
tax avoidance
tax credit
tax evasion
tax liability
tax rate
tax shelter
taxable income
total receipts
Treasury Regulations
zero-bracket tax tables

IF YOU WANT TO READ MORE

Commerce Clearing House, *198x Federal Tax Course* (revised annually) (Chicago: Commerce Clearing House).

DONALD R. EPLEY and JAMES A. MILLAR, *Basic Real Estate Finance and Investments, second edition* (New York: John Wiley & Sons, 1984).

JAMES B. KAU and C. F. SIRMANS, *Tax Planning for Real Estate Investors, Second Edition* (Englewood Cliffs, N.J.: Prentice-Hall, Inc., 1982).

STEPHEN A. PYHRR, JAMES R. COOPER, LARRY E. WOFFORD, and STEVEN D. KAPPLIN, *Real Estate Investment: Strategy, Analysis, Decisions, Second Edition* (New York: John Wiley & Sons, Inc., 1986).

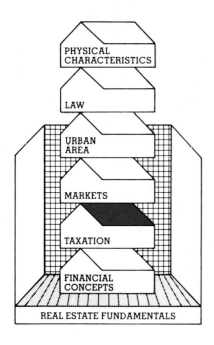

PHYSICAL CHARACTERISTICS

LAW

URBAN AREA

MARKETS

TAXATION

FINANCIAL CONCEPTS

REAL ESTATE FUNDAMENTALS

12

Taxation: federal income taxes and investment real estate

PREVIEW

With Uncle Sam as a partner (through the income tax) in every business venture you undertake, it is not surprising to learn that if you decide to invest in real estate, the federal income tax laws will affect your investment decisions. Real estate is considered to be a tax shelter investment, that is, one in which Uncle Sam's share is less than other investments. Needless to say, these tax shelter benefits are actively sought after by investors and affect the price you will be asked to pay for real estate investments. In order to assess how much the tax shelter aspects of a real estate investment are worth, you must have an understanding of the fundamentals of how taxation affects income-producing real estate. This chapter expands some of the basic concepts of tax shelter considered in the preceding chapter. After reading and studying it you will have a better grasp of:

1. Why you need tax planning over the entire life cycle of a real estate investment.
2. The tax consequences of acquiring real estate.
3. The tax shelter aspects of operating income-producing real estate.
4. The role of cost recovery in tax shelters.
5. The tax effects of disposing of real estate by sale, exchange, or installment sale.

Investment in income-producing real estate is affected by income taxes from the time it is purchased until it is sold. Tax planning for a real estate investment must begin before the real estate is acquired and continue throughout the entire period of time the property is held. Many decisions must be made along the way to assure that you are getting the maximum tax benefits from the investment. To simplify things, the life of a real estate investment and the corresponding decisions that must be made can be divided into three areas: acquiring the property, operating the property, and disposing of the property. The discussion that follows is intended only to highlight some important concepts and considerations and not to take the place of a good tax adviser.

ACQUIRING THE PROPERTY

The first thing you must decide is whether you are going to acquire the property as an individual, partnership, or corporation. The form of organization affects many tax factors once the property is acquired. In Chapter 4, the nonincome tax implications of the form of ownership were discussed, and in Chapter 11 their tax implications were discussed. You should choose the form of ownership that provides you with the best combination of tax characteristics and other considerations.

Once the ownership form is decided, your attention may be devoted to the tax consequences of acquiring the property. Your basic objective is quite simple; you want to deduct the expenditures associated with acquisition as soon as you can. Prior to the latter part of the 1970s, many acquisition expenses were deductible in the year of acquisition. Many investors stretched this allowance to the maximum by prepaying some expenses and deducting the total outlay in the year of acquisition. For a taxpayer with a large income in the year of acquisition, such practices allowed him or her to take maximum advantage of this tax law. However, in the latter part of the 1970s, these excesses led to tax reforms that have severely limited the ability of investors to deduct anything other than the actual expenses incurred in *and* applicable to the year of acquisition. Any additional amount paid in that year must be capitalized (apportioned) over the period during which benefits are received. To make this clearer, if you prepaid three years of property insurance at the time you purchased an office building, only the actual cost of insurance for the year of acquisition may be deducted. If you only owned the building for three months of your tax year, then only three months of insurance costs may be deducted. The remainder of the prepaid premiums must be deducted as the expense is incurred. Given the cost of borrowing money or, conversely, your ability to invest your funds elsewhere, to have prepaid this insurance and not to be able to deduct it until well into the future is a costly mistake unless you received a sizable discount on the premiums for paying in advance.

Other expenses associated with acquiring real estate must also be deducted over some period of time and not in the year they were paid. For example, if you are involved in a partnership, chances are good that some expenses were involved in organizing the partnership. Such costs must be spread over the first 60 months of the partnership. Costs associated with obtaining financing on income properties must usually be allocated over the life of the loan. Because of these limitations on deducting acquisition items, attention has shifted to the two other stages in the life cycle of a real estate investment.

TAX CONSIDERATIONS IN OPERATING A REAL ESTATE INVESTMENT

Operating an income-producing property requires a number of tax decisions. In Chapter 11 you saw the basic accounting framework for calculating the after-tax cash flow for a given period of an investment. This framework is reproduced here as Table 12.1. Essentially, the tax laws and decisions made with respect to operating an income-producing property deal with all of the items between gross income and after-tax cash flow. Your tax shelter strategy is to try to make taxable income as small a positive amount or as large a negative amount as possible while making after-tax cash flow as large as possible. This approach assumes that you have other ordinary income that can be sheltered by the negative taxable income from the real estate investment to produce tax savings.

From the accounting framework in Table 12.1, you can see that only operating expenses, interest, and depreciation are subtracted from gross income to calculate taxable income. Current tax law allows you to deduct all operating expenses involved in operating the property. Some of the items included in operating expenses are property taxes, mainte-

Table 12.1. After-Tax Cash Flow Framework

Gross Rents
   Less: Operating Expenses
Net Operating Income
   Less: Interest
   Less: Cost Recovery
Taxable Income
   Plus: Cost Recovery
   Less: Principal
Before-Tax Cash Flow
    Plus: Tax Savings
    or
    Less: Taxes
After-Tax Cash Flow (Money going into your pocket)

nance expenses, utilities, office supplies, and management expenses. Interest on borrowed money is also tax deductible. Both operating expenses and interest *require cash payments* to get the deduction. This means that to produce a negative taxable income using only operating expenses and interest would require making cash payments *in excess* of the income generated by the property and create real financial losses — not a desirable situation. You are seeking tax losses created by taking deductions not requiring the payment of cash. Such a deduction is cost recovery, or depreciation.

Cost Recovery (Depreciation) — The Key to Tax Shelters

Technically, the Economic Recovery Tax Act (ERTA) (1981) replaced depreciation with "cost recovery." This change is welcomed since the word *depreciation* is loaded with possible meanings, making it very confusing. ERTA created the Accelerated Cost Recovery System (ACRS), which applies to properties acquired in 1981 and thereafter. The term *cost recovery* more accurately describes what is really happening. Certainly, the use of the word depreciation will likely continue out of habit. In the remainder of this chapter the phrase cost recovery is used. The basics of cost recovery are now considered.

Cost recovery, a deduction that does not require a cash payment, is the key to reducing taxable income without making cash payments. After expenses and interest are subtracted from gross income, cost recovery further reduces taxable income, often until it becomes negative. If cost recovery expenses are large enough, a negative taxable income will be produced. As an investor you will want cost recovery deductions to be as large as possible, especially in the early years of an investment. Larger deductions mean smaller taxable incomes and greater tax shelter. The emphasis on early years is due to the fact that a dollar of tax savings today is worth more than a dollar of tax savings in the future.

Cost recovery for tax purposes is the allowable deduction of a portion of the cost of wasting assets with lives longer than one year in arriving at taxable income. Cost recovery deductions were created by Congress for a number of reasons. First, it was thought that such deductions would allow firms to accumulate funds to replace assets that wear out. Next, since business expenses, such as pencils, raw materials, and wages, are tax deductible, it seemed reasonable that expenditures on assets lasting for more than one year should be deductible. The problem was the timing and size of deductions. Since many of the expenditures for such assets were quite large, to allow an investor to deduct the entire cost of such an asset in the year of purchase would distort the investor's income in that year. Also, since the asset would be producing income over its useful life, it seems reasonable that the cost of the asset should be apportioned over its life and, therefore, better matched with the income it produces as illustrated in Figure 12.1. Out of this reasoning came

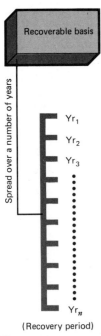

Figure 12.1 Cost recovery (depreciation).

the cost recovery laws in the Code and subsequent Treasury Regs outlining what portion of the cost of an asset can be taken as a deduction each year.

With this historical insight, you realize that cost recovery for tax purposes is often related to the actual wearing out of the asset. As a matter of fact, a building does not actually have to be deteriorating or decreasing in market value at all for you to take cost recovery deductions. It can even be increasing in value and you can still take cost recovery deductions. However, there are limitations on what real property is recoverable and how it can be recovered. Depreciation also has tax implications when the property is sold.

Prior to the Economic Recovery Tax Act of 1981 (ERTA), cost recovery and its application to real estate investments were a constant source of debate and disagreement between taxpayers and the IRS. Disputes arose over virtually every possible aspect of cost recovery. Many of these disputes arose because the cost recovery system allowed taxpayers a great deal of flexibility in arriving at cost recovery deductions. ERTA streamlined the area of cost recovery by eliminating much of this flexibility and, hence, many grounds for possible disagreements. ERTA provisions have since been modified by the Tax Reform Act of 1984.

What Real Estate Qualifies for Cost Recovery?

Virtually any real estate held for the production of income may qualify for cost recovery. Actually, only the portion of the real estate composed of **wasting assets,** assets that wear out over some period of time may be recovered. Since improvements wear out and land does not, only investment in improvements may be recovered. Personal property that wears out, such as furniture, is also recoverable using a different set of rules to be discussed later. The total dollar amount that may be recovered over the life of the real estate is called the beginning recoverable basis. If you buy an apartment building for $1,000,000 and the improvements represent 80 percent of the total cost, then your beginning basis will be $800,000. In order to maximize recovery deductions, you will generally want to maximize the percentage of the total property investment that is recoverable. In the $1,000,000 property above, you would *like* to allocate $999,999 to the improvements and $1 to the land. Offsetting this desire are tax laws requiring that the cost allocation between improvements and land be *reasonable.* The split between land and building used by the county assessor or by a professional appraiser is often used to determine the split between land and buildings.

Salvage Value

Another aspect of cost recovery, salvage value, was simplified by ERTA. Prior to ERTA, investors were required to estimate the value of a depreciable property at the end of its useful life. In some methods of calculating depreciation, the beginning depreciable basis was reduced by the salvage value. ERTA specifies that salvage value not be considered in calculating cost recovery.

Over What Period Are Costs Recovered?

The period over which costs are recovered affects the recovery rate and annual deductions. The shorter the recovery period for a given property, the higher your recovery deduction. The period over which costs are recovered is called the **useful life** or **recovery period.** You are not free to set any recovery period you wish. The ACRS establishes the recovery period to be used on real property. The appropriate recovery period depends on the recovery method used. According to the Tax Reform Act of 1984, if you use the accelerated method you must use an 18-year recovery period. If you use the straight-line method you may choose an 18-, 35-, or 45-year life. These are your only options with respect to recovery period.

Since you will not always purchase real estate at the beginning of your tax year, you may wonder how much of the first year is recoverable. You are allowed to deduct one-half month's cost recovery for the month in which you become owner and all of the remaining months in the first tax year. So if you are operating on a calendar year and purchase an apartment building on October 10, you will be able to take cost recovery for one-half of October and all of November and December.

Cost Recovery Methods

Two methods exist for calculating cost recovery deductions. One approach is to take the same deduction each year of the asset's recovery period. This type of cost recovery is called **straight-line cost recovery.** However, an argument could be made that for some assets, most of the deterioration or decrease in value or usefulness occurs in the property's early years and cost recovery should reflect this pattern by allowing larger cost recovery deductions in early years than in later ones. Cost recovery following this pattern is called **accelerated cost recovery.** Large deductions in early years are usually sought by real estate investors, as discussed earlier.

Straight-Line Cost Recovery Finding the annual deduction allowed using straight-line cost recovery is straightforward. It makes sense that if you are going to recover all of the recoverable basis over a given period, say 18 years, that you will take 1/18th of the basis each year. The percentage of the recoverable basis you take each year is called the *straight-line recovery rate* and is found by dividing the asset's useful life into one:

$$\text{Straight-line recovery rate} = 1/\text{Useful life}$$

For the 18 year example,

$$\text{Straight-line recovery rate} = 1/18$$
$$= .0556$$

The longer the useful life, the lower the straight-line rate. A 35-year useful life produces a .0286 straight-line recovery rate (1/35 = .0286).

Annual cost recovery deductions are found by multiplying the straight-line recovery rate by the beginning recoverable basis. Using the earlier $1,000,000 office building as an example, with an 18-year useful life the cost recovery deduction for each year is found by:

$$\text{Annual cost recovery deduction} = \$800,000 \times .0556$$
$$= \$ \ 44,480$$

Accelerated Cost Recovery If you want to use accelerated cost recovery, you have little flexibility under the ACRS. The cost recovery period is set at 18 years and the annual cost recovery deduction is found by multiplying the beginning cost recovery basis by a factor from a table prepared

Table 12.2. 18–Year Accelerated Cost Recovery Tables for Real Estate (Other than Low-Income Housing)

Year	\multicolumn{12}{c}{Month Placed in Service}											
	1	2	3	4	5	6	7	8	9	10	11	12
	\multicolumn{12}{c}{The Applicable Percentage Is:}											
1	9	9	8	7	6	5	4	4	3	2	1	0.4
2	9	9	9	9	9	9	9	9	9	10	10	10.0
3	8	8	8	8	8	8	8	8	9	9	9	9.0
4	7	7	7	7	7	8	8	8	8	8	8	8.0
5	7	7	7	7	7	7	7	7	7	7	7	7.0
6	6	6	6	6	6	6	6	6	6	6	6	6.0
7	5	5	5	5	6	6	6	6	6	6	6	6.0
8	5	5	5	5	5	5	5	5	5	5	5	5.0
9	5	5	5	5	5	5	5	5	5	5	5	5.0
10-	5	5	5	5	5	5	5	5	5	5	5	5.0
11-	5	5	5	5	5	5	5	5	5	5	5	5.0
12-	5	5	5	5	5	5	5	5	5	5	5	5.0
13-	4	4	4	5	4	4	5	4	4	4	5	5.0
14-	4	4	4	4	4	4	4	4	4	4	4	4.0
15-	4	4	4	4	4	4	4	4	4	4	4	4.0
16-	4	4	4	4	4	4	4	4	4	4	4	4.0
17-	4	4	4	4	4	4	4	4	4	4	4	4.0
18-	4	3	4	4	4	4	4	4	4	4	4	4.0
19-		1	1	1	2	2	2	3	3	3	3	3.6

SOURCE: *1985 U.S. Master Tax Guide*, Commerce Clearing House, Inc.), p. 433.

by the IRS. The IRS table of accelerated factors for all real property except low-income housing is contained in Table 12.2. For the office building with a beginning basis of $800,000, the first year factors range from 9 to .4 percent depending on the month in which the building is purchased. As you can see, the percentages for years 2 through 18 steadily decline, resulting in declining annual cost recovery deductions. If we assume the building is purchased in January, the deduction for the first year is

$$\text{Cost recovery deduction yr 1} = \text{Beginning basis} \times \text{yr 1 factor}$$
$$= \$800,000 \times .09$$
$$= \$\ 72,000$$

By the tenth year, the cost recovery deduction has decreased to $40,000,

$$\text{Cost recovery deduction yr 10} = \text{Beginning basis} \times \text{yr 10 factor}$$
$$= \$800,000 \times .05$$
$$= \$\ 40,000$$

Table 12.3. Comparing Straight Line and Accelerated Cost Recovery

Property: $1,000,000 (Improvements $800,000, Land $200,000)
(Purchased in January)
(18 Year Useful Life)

	Accelerated Cost Recovery Method			Straight-Line Cost Recovery Method		
	Yearly Deduction	Cost Recovery Basis at End of Year	Total Property Basis at End of Year	Yearly Deduction	Cost Recovery Basis at End of Year	Total Property Basis at End of Year
1	72,000	728,000	928,000	44,444	755,556	955,556
2	72,000	656,000	856,000	44,444	711,112	911,112
3	64,000	592,000	792,000	44,444	666,668	866,668
4	56,000	536,000	736,000	44,444	622,224	822,224
5	56,000	480,000	680,000	44,444	577,780	777,780
6	48,000	432,000	632,000	44,444	533,336	733,336
7	40,000	392,000	592,000	44,444	488,892	688,892
8	40,000	352,000	552,000	44,444	444,448	644,482
9	40,000	312,000	512,000	44,444	400,004	600,004
10	40,000	272,000	472,000	44,444	355,560	555,560
11	40,000	232,000	432,000	44,444	311,116	511,116
12	40,000	192,000	392,000	44,444	266,672	466,672
13	32,000	160,000	360,000	44,444	222,228	422,228
14	32,000	128,000	328,000	44,444	177,784	377,784
15	32,000	96,000	296,000	44,444	133,340	333,340
16	32,000	64,000	264,000	44,444	88,896	288,896
17	32,000	32,000	232,000	44,444	44,452	244,452
18	32,000	0	200,000	44,452	0	200,000
Total	800,000			800,000		

Table 12.3 contains the cost recovery deduction for each year of the office building's useful life using straight-line and accelerated cost recovery. This table illustrates several useful points. First, it allows a comparison between the annual deductions generated by the straight-line and accelerated cost recovery methods. As you can see, use of the accelerated method produces higher early deductions and smaller later deductions than the straight-line method. This fact partially explains why many investors using accelerated cost recovery sell their real estate investments after five to 10 years.

The table also highlights the concept that cost recovery deductions reduce your basis in the property. As you remember from the last chapter, your basis is your net investment in a property. When you claim a cost recovery deduction, it is assumed you did just that — you recovered a portion of the cost of the property. Thus, it is assumed that your net investment in the property is reduced by an amount equal to your cost recovery deduction. If your net investment in the office building is initially $1,000,000, then after the first year cost recovery deduction of $72,000, your net investment, or basis, is assumed to have been reduced by $72,000 to $928,000. This reduction in your basis is important, because when you sell the office building, your gain or loss is the difference between the sales price and your basis in the property at the time it is sold. This idea is discussed again later in the chapter.

Another aspect of ACRS illustrated in Table 12.3 is your ability to switch from the accelerated method to the straight-line method at any time in the recovery period. You will make such a switch when it will allow you to take larger deductions than you could take under accelerated deductions. To calculate the straight-line deductions that you will take each year of the remaining useful life, you simply allocate the remaining basis evenly over the remaining years. In our example, after the first year, the remaining recoverable basis is $928,000 and the remaining useful life is 17 years. If you switch to straight-line cost recovery in the second year, the deductions from then on would be $54,588 per year,

$$
\begin{aligned}
\text{Annual cost recovery deduction} &= \text{Recoverable basis} \times 1/17 \\
&= \$928,000 \times .059 \\
&= \$\ 54,588
\end{aligned}
$$

To switch from the straight-line method to the accelerated method requires the approval of the IRS.

Composite and Component Depreciation

When the entire property is depreciated as one unit, as above, it is called **composite depreciation,** "composite" meaning the sum of all the parts. As you can imagine, not all parts of a building wear out at the same rate: roofs may last for 10 years whereas the interior walls may last 20 years. Prior to 1981 it was possible to depreciate the components of real property separately and simply add the depreciation of the components together to calculate total depreciation. Such a practice was called **component depreciation** and was widely used because it produced depreciation deductions larger than those of composite depreciation. ERTA eliminated this possibility by disallowing the use of component depreciation on real property purchased in 1981 or thereafter.

TAXES AFFECTING THE DISPOSITION OF REAL ESTATE

At some point you will choose to dispose of a real estate investment. The reasons underlying your decision may vary from purely economic to purely personal ones. In disposing of an income property you may sell it, trade it, or give it to someone else. The most common method is, of course, selling the property to another investor and receiving all of the sales price at closing. Also popular is the alternative of receiving only a portion of the sales price at closing and receiving the balance over a period of time. All of these choices affect the taxation of any gain you may have on the sale.

Earlier you learned that the sale of income-producing real estate can result in a taxable gain. Part of that gain may receive capital gains treatment and part may be treated as ordinary income. You would prefer to have as much of the gain as possible taxed as long-term capital gains since that tax rate is much lower than ordinary income tax rates. How much of the gain is taxable as long-term capital gains depends on the cost recovery method you chose to use while you owned the property.

Your *total taxable gain* is very easy to calculate. It is the difference between your adjusted basis, what you paid for the property adjusted for the cost recovery deductions you have taken, and its adjusted sales price. The adjusted basis you have in the property at the time of sale is called your ending basis.

Taxable gain from sale of real property = Adjusted sales price − Ending basis

Adjusted sales price is the sales price minus allowable sales costs such as brokerage fees and attorney's fees. If you purchased an apartment building for $500,000, took $150,000 in cost recovery deductions, and sold it five years later for an adjusted sales price of $750,000, your taxable gain from that sale is $400,000. This is so because your basis in the property is not $500,000, but rather the $500,000 less the total cost recovery deductions you have taken. Since you have taken $150,000 in such deductions, your basis in the property at the time of sale is $350,000. This means that your gain is $400,000, the difference between your basis and the $750,000 sales price.

How this total taxable gain of $400,000 is taxed depends on the cost recovery method used and whether the property is used for residential rental purposes or some other use. A **residential rental property** is one from which at least 80 percent of gross rental income is derived from long-term, as compared to transient, residential units. Obviously, hotels and motels are not residential rental properties. The other uses include every other type of improved space that is rented: office, shopping, industrial, hotel, and so on. This category is generally summarized as **commercial property.** ERTA continues the practice of encouraging investment in residential rental properties, started by changes in tax law in 1969, by providing favorable tax treatment to gains from the sale of such properties.

Tax treatment of gains also depends on whether you used accelerated or straight-line cost recovery. Tax law provides favorable gains treatment for those using straight-line cost recovery. The logic of Congress seems to be that they are willing to allow you greater tax shelter while the property is owned through the use of accelerated cost recovery, but when the property is sold, some of those extra tax shelter benefits must be given back. The cost recovery deductions you receive from the accelerated method that exceed what you would have taken using the straight-line method are called **excess cost recovery.** To accomplish this, the tax treatment of gains when accelerated cost recovery was used is more severe than when straight-line cost recovery is employed.

Thus, the taxation of gains favors residential rental properties and the use of straight-line cost recovery. The rules are discussed here and illustrated in Figure 12.2. For residential rental properties when the

Figure 12.2
Taxation of total gain from sale of real property. (Source: Stephen A. Pyhrr and James R. Cooper, *Real Estate Investment: Strategy, Analysis, Decisions,* New York: John Wiley & Sons, Inc., 1982, p. 353, adapted to fit example.)

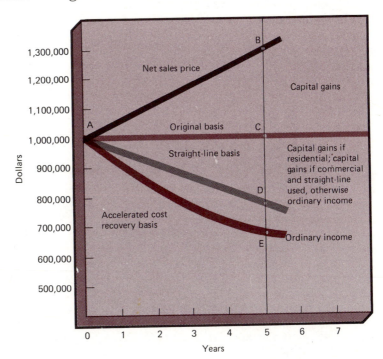

straight-line method is used, the total gain is taxed as a capital gain. When the accelerated method is used, the total gain is divided into two portions, which are taxed differently. One portion is the part of the gain represented by the difference between the adjusted sales price and what your ending basis *would have been* had you used the straight-line method. This portion of the gain is taxed as a capital gain. The remaining portion of the gain is the excess cost recovery and is taxed as ordinary income.

To illustrate, let's assume you purchase an apartment complex for $1,000,000, hold it for five years while using accelerated cost recovery, and then sell it for an adjusted sales price of $1,300,000. Further, assume that the improvements are valued at $800,000 and the land at $200,000. What is the total taxable gain and how will it be taxed? Fortunately, Table 12.3 contains a complete set of cost recovery deductions and the remaining basis for such a property. The relevant portions of that table are contained in Table 12.4. The total taxable gain is the difference between the adjusted sales price and your ending basis. With an adjusted sales price of $1,300,000 and an ending basis of $680,000 (from Table 12.3), the total gain that will be taxed in some manner is $620,000. Of this $620,000 gain, $522,220 of it will be taxed as a capital

Table 12.4. Taxation of Gain on Residential Rental Property

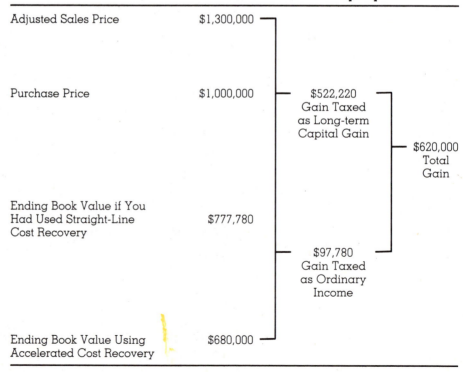

Adjusted Sales Price	$1,300,000	
Purchase Price	$1,000,000	$522,220 Gain Taxed as Long-term Capital Gain
		$620,000 Total Gain
Ending Book Value if You Had Used Straight-Line Cost Recovery	$777,780	
		$97,780 Gain Taxed as Ordinary Income
Ending Book Value Using Accelerated Cost Recovery	$680,000	

gain. This $522,220 is the difference between the adjusted sales price and the ending straight-line basis. The remainder of the gain, the excess cost recovery of $97,780, is taxed as ordinary income. By being taxed as ordinary income, the excess cost recovery is said to be *recaptured*. The net effect of being able to use accelerated cost recovery was only to defer the payment of taxes until the property was sold. The net effect of straight-line cost recovery is to defer taxation and then convert what would have been ordinary income into capital gains income.

For commercial properties, the rules are the same if the straight-line method is used. However, when the accelerated method is used, the gains taxation rules are different than for residential rental properties. If you use the accelerated method on a commercial property, all of the cost recovered will be taxed as ordinary income. Only the difference between the beginning basis and the adjusted sales price will be taxed as a capital gain. If the property just considered above was an office building, the gain would be taxed as illustrated in Table 12.5. In that table, you can see that the total gain is the same, but only $300,000 of the gain is capital gain, while $320,000 of it will be taxed as ordinary income.

To summarize, when accelerated cost recovery is used, residential

Table 12.5. Taxation of Gain on Commercial Property

Adjusted Sales Price	$1,300,000	
		$300,000 Gain Taxed as Long-term Capital Gain
Purchase Price	$1,000,000	
		$620,000 Total Gain
		$320,000 Gain Taxed as Ordinary Income
Ending Book Value Using Accelerated Cost Recovery	$680,000	

rental properties receive favorable gains treatment, relative to commercial properties. For residential rental properties, the portion of cost recovery represented by the straight-line cost recovery that could have been taken is treated as a capital gain. For commercial properties, that amount is treated as ordinary income.

You know how taxes on gains are computed. Consider the office building example above that produced a $300,000 long-term gain and $320,000 of ordinary income. If this was the only transaction you had all year, you would take 40 percent of the $300,000 long-term gain and add it and the $320,000 of ordinary income to your other income for the year.

If the adjusted sales price is less than the ending basis, you have incurred a capital loss. Capital losses are also classified as long- or short-term, exactly as with gains. Long-term capital losses may be used to offset other ordinary taxable income at the rate of $1 of ordinary income for $2 of long-term capital loss. You may offset no more than $3000 of ordinary income per year with long-term losses. Given the two-for-one rate of offset, this means you can use up to $6000 of long-term loss per year. Any unused long-term capital loss may be carried forward indefinitely and used to reduce ordinary income in future years. Short-term capital losses may be used to reduce other ordinary taxable income on a one-for-one basis. Such deductions are limited only by available income to offset. Short-term losses may also be carried forward indefinitely.

Postponing Taxes from Disposing of Real Estate

Installment Sale If you do not need all the cash from the sale of real estate and if you plan properly, you can spread the tax liability resulting from the sale over a number of years as payments are received from the buyer. Such a procedure is called an **installment sale.** The Installment Revision Act of 1980 made some important simplifying changes in claiming installment sale treatment. For example, you used to have to meet a series of requirements, such as receiving less than 30 percent of the sales price in the year of the sale. The 1980 Act eliminated this requirement and made virtually any sale of real property in which the sales price is to be received over time, with interest being paid on the unpaid balance, acceptable for installment sale treatment. As with other tax-related activities, a tax consultant should be used in an installment sale to assure that it is properly structured and that you pay no more tax than necessary.

Tax-Deferred Exchange By trading real estate with another investor instead of selling it, you may be able to postpone taxes until the property traded for is sold. The Code allows, under the appropriate conditions, real estate to be traded and have no taxes due in the year of the trade. Such a procedure is called a **tax-deferred exchange.** For example, if you and another real estate investor successfully create a tax-deferred exchange, you will become the owner of a new property while keeping your basis in your old property. If all conditions are met, you will have no taxable gain in the year of the exchange. However, when the property is ultimately sold, the gain will be taxed just like any other sale of investment real estate. As you can see, taxes are deferred by using tax-deferred exchanges. For such exchanges to occur you must find another investor willing to accept your property while you are willing to accept his or hers. A successful exchange involves a number of complex steps and must be carefully planned.

Miscellaneous Tax Provisions
Affecting Income Property

Income tax provisions affecting income-producing real estate are numerous. Among them are the minimum tax and tax credits for rehabilitating older structures. Once again, professional tax assistance should be consulted before estimating the effects of either of these provisions on you.

Essentially, under pressure to eliminate some of the tax shelter advantages of real estate investment, Congress instituted the **minimum tax** on certain tax preference items such as excess depreciation and the 60 percent of capital gains that are not taxed. If these items exceed a specified amount in a given year, the amount by which they exceed it will be taxed at a rate of 15 percent. This tax is in addition to the regular taxes paid by the taxpayer.

The tax credits for rehabilitating older structures were instituted to encourage the renovation of such structures, rather than destroying them. The investor receives a tax credit of 15 percent of rehabilitation expenditures for qualified structures at least 30 years old, a 20 percent credit for structures at least 40 years old, and a 25 percent credit for those structures that are certified historical structures. These tax measures have been successful. Developers have been very active in buying and renovating many older structures.

SUMMARY

This chapter extended some of the basic concepts of taxation developed in the preceding chapter by discussing selected tax aspects of income-producing real estate. The need for tax planning over the entire life of the investment was emphasized. An investment has three stages in its life: acquisition, operation, and disposition.

In the acquisition stage the ownership form must be selected. Sole ownership and partnerships are generally favored over corporations because corporations face double taxation. In addition, you will attempt to maximize the deductions associated with acquiring the property, even though recent tax law changes have eliminated many of these possibilities. Most of these expenditures must now be capitalized over their useful lives.

The operation stage was seen to be one of prime tax shelter opportunities. By being able to deduct operating expenses, interest, and depreciation it is often possible to create very small or negative taxable income while producing positive after-tax cash flows. Depreciation, because it is a non-cash item, is considered the key to producing tax shelter in the operations stage of a real estate investment.

Depreciation was significantly simplified by ERTA in 1981. That legislation changed the name from depreciation to cost recovery. You may now use either accelerated or straight-line cost recovery on all investment real estate. The IRS has produced tables for calculating your accelerated cost recovery deductions. However, whether the property is residential rental or commercial, the selection of cost recovery methods affects the taxation of gains when the property is sold.

When income-producing real estate is sold for a gain, tax liability results. For residential rental property, any increase in value and cost recovery that would have been taken using the straight-line method is taxed as a capital gain. Excess cost recovery is taxed as ordinary income. For commercial investment properties, any increase in value is taxed as a capital gain, and if straight-line cost recovery is used, all cost recovery is taxed as capital gain. However, if accelerated cost recovery is used, all cost recovery is recaptured as ordinary income.

Not all real estate transactions result in the total gain being taxed in the year of sale. Under proper circumstances, real estate can be exchanged and the gain deferred. Also, real estate may be sold using an installment sale and recognition of gain deferred until the income is actually received.

Real estate also has some miscellaneous tax provisions applying to it. One is the minimum tax, which requires that at least some income tax be paid on certain tax preference items exceeding specified amounts. Another important tax provision is the tax credit for rehabilitating older buildings.

QUICK QUIZ

1. The tax stages in the life of a real estate investment include all of the following except:

   a. acquisition   c. disposition
   b. profit taking   d. operation

2. The form of ownership that involves double taxation of income is the

   a. partnership   c. sole proprietorship
   b. corporation   d. limited partnership

3. In the 1981 Economic Recovery Tax Act, depreciation was replaced by

   a. cost recovery   c. expenditure accounting
   b. capitalization   d. depletion

4. The total gain on the sale of investment real estate that is taxable in some way is the difference between the _____ and the _____ .

5. The _____ portion of the total gain from the sale of investment real estate is always taxed as ordinary income.

6. When real estate is depreciated as one unit, such depreciation is called _____ depreciation.

QUESTIONS
AND
EXERCISES

1. Explain the role of depreciation in creating tax shelters.

2. Why does "cost recovery" more accurately reflect what is happening to income-producing real estate than "depreciation?"

3. Calculate the cost recovery deductions using both accelerated and straight-line recovery methods for the first three years of ownership of an office building costing $600,000 with the improvements being worth $500,000. Assume an 18-year life.

4. How could you estimate a reasonable allocation between land and improvements if you had just bought an existing shopping center?

5. If the property in Question 3 was sold after five years for $800,000, how much of the gain would be taxed as a long-term capital gain using straight-line and accelerated cost recovery? How much would be taxed as ordinary income? Answer the same questions assuming the property is an apartment complex.

6. Why do many investors prefer to use accelerated cost recovery rather that straight-line cost recovery?

KEY TERMINOLOGY

accelerated cost recovery
commercial property
component depreciation
composite depreciation
ending book value
excess cost recovery
excess depreciation
installment sale
minimum tax

recapture
recovery period
rehabilitation tax credits
residential rental property
straight-line cost recovery
tax-deferred exchange
useful life
wasting asset

IF YOU WANT TO READ MORE

Commerce Clearing House, *198x Federal Tax Course* (revised annually) (Chicago: Commerce Clearing House).

DONALD R. EPLEY and JAMES A. MILLER, *Basic Real Estate Finance and Investments*, second edition (New York: John Wiley & Sons, 1984).

JAMES B. KAU and C. F. SIRMANS, *Tax Planning for Real Estate Investors*, second edition (Englewood Cliffs, N.J.: Prentice-Hall, Inc. 1982).

STEPHEN A. PYHRR, JAMES R. COOPER, LARRY E. WOFFORD, and STEVEN D. KAPPLIN, *Real Estate Investment: Strategy, Analysis, Decision* (Boston: Warren, Gorham, & Lamont, 1986).

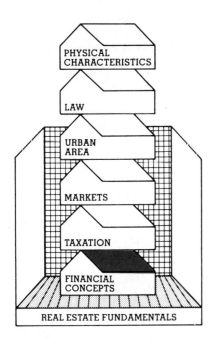

PHYSICAL CHARACTERISTICS

LAW

URBAN AREA

MARKETS

TAXATION

FINANCIAL CONCEPTS

REAL ESTATE FUNDAMENTALS

13

Fundamental Financial Concepts and Applications

PREVIEW   Finance permeates every aspect of real estate. If you borrow money on Blackacre you will come face to face with it. Financial considerations arise again when you invest in real estate either as a lender, equity investor, or developer. Finance is not important just for your personal involvement in real estate, but also when you are assisting others making lending, investment, or development decisions. Finance may be a confusing mix of jargon, vague concepts, and complicated calculations to you. Consequently, the prospect of repeated encounters with finance, either in your personal affairs or in the affairs of others you are assisting, may be quite grim. By the time you finish this chapter you will not feel this way any longer. You will understand many of the "mysteries" of finance and, like other mysteries, you will find the solutions to be quite reasonable and logical. Think of this chapter, then, as a financial tranquilizer to reduce your anxiety about finance. More good news; it is not a tough pill to swallow! After reading this chapter you will understand:

1. That a dollar today is worth more than a dollar tomorrow and how to calculate how much more it is worth.
2. How the use of borrowed money can magnify the gains and losses from an investment.
3. That risk and return are the two most critical factors in making investment decisions.

4. The mechanics of mortgage loans and how to calculate payments and outstanding balances.
5. The concept of yield and its use in making investment decisions.

The field of finance deals with money, something near and dear to the hearts of most people. Because it involves money, people tend to take finance seriously as evidenced by the pomp, ceremony, and general air of formality surrounding financial institutions, financial documents, and financial transactions. Also, people rightly require a high degree of accuracy in financial calculations. People who are generally quite congenial often become very testy, upset, and irrational over financial matters, many times over relatively insignificant amounts of money. Many real estate transactions fall apart because of discussions, negotiations, debates, and downright arguments over such small sums. A mistake in a calculation or a misunderstanding of a basic financial concept can create problems in an otherwise smooth situation.

As either a participant or a third party in a financial transaction, you will want to minimize misunderstandings and irrational thinking and behavior by checking and rechecking all calculations, and studying all necessary financial concepts. In addition to this desire for smooth transactions, you also have a legal and ethical obligation to exercise due care in presenting complete and accurate information to those in a transaction. All of this implies a knowledge of basic financial concepts and calculations.

A rote memorization of selected rules and formulas is not enough. You also need to understand the financial concepts underlying those calculations. Such an understanding will give you a perspective for making sense out of what calculations must be made and why. Even if you cannot solve a particular problem, you will be better able to seek help if you have even a faint idea of the concepts involved in the problem. This chapter's approach is one of developing that perspective and understanding basic calculations. Accordingly, basic financial concepts are considered first in this chapter. Basic financial concepts are then applied to mortgage lending and investment. The concepts and arithmetic are presented in as straightforward a manner as possible with a minimum of complexity. The emphasis is on being able to identify the underlying financial concept, organize the problem, and solve it using readily available financial tables and a bare bones calculator.

You may feel that a reliance on tables is not necessary in an age of inexpensive computers and programmable calculators. In a sense you are right; many calculators and computers have sets of instructions, called programs, available for performing most of the more common financial calculations. To use these devices requires no knowledge of electronics or computer programming. All you need to do is turn the machine on, select and load the proper program, and supply the necessary data. Computers are not going to go away; the trend is in the other direction, especially with the development of smaller and less expensive systems. These units have already gone from novelty to accepted working tools. You should use these electronic wonders whenever possible to save time and reduce the possibility of mistakes in calculations due to human error. The potential for improving your productivity by having the computer perform repetitive operations and calculations at speeds approaching that of light cannot be ignored.

Think about the role you play in using a computer—you must decide the concepts involved, select the correct program (if it exists), and supply the necessary data. The process of defining and formulating the problem and matching that problem with a program requires the ability to "think," a power not possessed by the computer. If you incorrectly define and formulate the problem or select the wrong program, the computer will still perform its computations as quickly and accurately as ever, even though they are completely wrong for the problem at hand! You must be able to correctly channel the efforts of any aid you use, whether that aid is human or electronic in nature. An understanding of financial concepts and accompanying arithmetic can maximize your abilities to solve problems involving financial arithmetic. In this chapter, all problems are presented as though you have access to financial tables and a standard calculator; all under the assumption that if you can solve problems in this manner, you can certainly solve them using a more sophisticated calculator.

A handful of basic concepts form the foundation for much of finance. The solutions to many financial problems you will encounter in real estate are founded on these relatively simple concepts. In what follows, the concepts are presented, including any basic financial arithmetic associated with them. Following the section discussing the concepts, their application to mortgage lending and real estate investment and the additional arithmetic involved are considered in the next two sections of the chapter. In all that follows in this chapter, your learning will be improved if you have a calculator handy to replicate the calculations in the examples. You should also use the tables reproduced in the chapter, and the more complete set of tables in Appendix A.2. at the end of the book, to look up the various factors used in the chapter examples. In other words, participate in this chapter rather than simply being a spectator.

CONCEPT 1: THE TIME VALUE OF MONEY

You have undoubtedly noticed that if you want to use someone else's money today and pay them back at a later time, you must pay back more than you borrowed. This situation occurs because most people do not view having a given amount of money today, say $100, to be the same as having $100 tomorrow, next month, next year, 10 years from now, or any time in the future. All other things being equal, a rational person will prefer to have the $100 in his pocket today at noon than a promise, or even a guarantee, of receiving the same $100 tomorrow at noon. In other words, money has time value.

Compounding

Since financial instruments and investments usually involve the flow of dollars in different time periods, time value takes on a real importance. For instance, when you borrow money on Blackacre, you receive money now in return for your promise to repay it in the future, usually in a series of payments over an extended period of years. Likewise, if you purchase an apartment building, you pay cash now in return for possible income from rents and the sale of the building in the future. The lender lending you money and you in investing, both must decide if the future cash inflows justify the number of dollars you must give up right now. The problem is one of comparing "dollars" that are not all worth the same amount. It is similar to the problem of deciding how many Swiss francs a given number of U.S. dollars are worth. To solve either of these problems you must know the "exchange rate."

For converting Swiss francs to U.S. dollars the exchange rate is stated in so many francs per dollar. Given this rate and the number of U.S. dollars to be exchanged the number of francs can be calculated easily. The exchange rate between present dollars and dollars in the future is stated in percentage rates. For instance, if you lend your brother-in-law $100 for one year, you may want 10 percent more returned to you than you lent. This means that at the end of one year, your brother-in-law must pay you $110, $100 times the exchange rate of 110 percent per year,

$$\$110 = \$100 \times 1.10$$

In your mind, the $110 one year from now produces as much satisfaction as $100 right now. The level of the exchange rate is not as important right now as the idea that once established, it determines the future sum you consider equal to a given number of dollars today.

To summarize, if you require a 10 percent premium, your brother-in-law must pay you 110 percent (1.10) of the original $100 for you to be satisfied. The "1" portion of the 1.10 factor brings the original $100 forward to the end of the first year, while the .10 produces the premium. Put in arithmetic terms, the amount you want in one year is

$$
\begin{array}{lll}
\text{Amount} & \text{Amount} & \text{Amount} \\
\text{owed 1 year} = \text{invested} \times 1 + \text{invested} \times .10 \\
\text{from now} & \text{now} & \text{now}
\end{array}
$$

$$
\begin{aligned}
&= (\$100 \times 1) + (100 \times .10) \\
&= \$100 + \$10 \\
&= \$110
\end{aligned}
$$

Now, if at the end of one year, your brother-in-law is unemployed and can't pay you back, what do you do? You decide to tell him that he can pay you one year later, but you want another 10 percent premium on the entire $110 now due. At the end of this second year, how much will he owe you? Applying the same 110 percent approach used earlier, we find that he owes you $121,

$$\begin{array}{l}\text{Amount} \qquad \text{Amount at} \qquad \text{Amount at} \\ \text{owed at end} = \text{beginning} \times 1 + \text{beginning} \times .10 \\ \text{of 2nd year} \qquad \text{of year 2} \qquad \text{of year 2} \\ \qquad = (\$110 \times 1) + (\$110 \times .10) \\ \qquad = \$110 + \$11 \\ \qquad = \$121 \end{array}$$

Notice that in the second year you are charging a premium on the original amount and the premium earned in the first year. The 10 percent per year premium you are charging is usually called an interest rate or required rate of return. Lending your brother-in-law money for two years at a 10 percent annual interest rate is similar to placing money in a savings account earning 10 percent per year and leaving it there for two years. If the financial institution credits your account with 10 percent interest at the end of the first year, and then pays you interest on the total during the second year, you will have $121 in your account at the end of the second year. Using the logic just discussed above, the balance in the account can be calculated as follows:

```
 YEAR           YEAR           YEAR
 0              1              2
 $100
        × 1   = 100
        × .10 =  10
                110
                       × 1   =  110
                       × .10 =   11
                                $121
```

To find the amount in the account at the end of each year, the amount at the beginning of the period is multiplied by 1 and .10, or, more simply, 1.10. This means that the balance in the account at the end of year 1 is found by:

Balance year 1 = Balance at beginning of year 1 × 1.10

The balance at the end of year 2 is found accordingly,

Balance year 2 = Balance at beginning of year 2 × 1.10

Thus, if today you put $100 into an account earning 10 percent interest per year, you can calculate how much you will have in the account at the end of two years by calculating how much is in the account at the end of year one and multiplying that by 1.10. You can repeat this process to find the balance in the account at the end of any given year. This process can become quite tiresome for years some distance in the future. A more efficient process is readily available. From above, you know that the balance at the end of year 2 was found by multiplying the balance at the end of year 1 by 1.10. Now, you also know that the balance at the end of year 1 is equal to the original balance times 1.10. By substituting this known fact into the equation for finding the balance at the end of year 2, you have:

Balance year 2 = (Balance at beginning year 1 $\times$ 1.10) $\times$ 1.10

This equation can be rearranged to:

Balance year 2 = Balance at beginning year 1 + (1.10 $\times$ 1.10)
= Balance at beginning year 1 $\times$ $(1.10)^2$

If the money is left in the account for a third year, the balance is found the same way,

Balance year 3 = Balance at beginning year 3 $\times$ (1.10)

The balance at the beginning of year 3 is equal to,

Beginning balance year 1 $\times$ $(1.10)^2$

This means that the balance at the end of year 3 can be found by:

Balance year 3 = (Beginning balance year 1 $\times$ $(1.10)^2$ $\times$ 1.10

Which, when rearranged, equals:

Balance year 3 = Beginning balance year 1 $\times$ $(1.10)^3$

You may see a pattern emerging in which the 1.10 factor is multiplied by itself the number of times corresponding to the number of years money has been in the account. This pattern holds for any number of periods, and provides a shortcut for finding the amount to which an initial investment has grown over a given number of years. In general terms, the equation is

Compound value = Present value $\times$ $(1 + i)^n$

where:

Present value = an amount of money at the present time

i = interest rate or compound rate at which compounding occurs

n = the number of years over which the investment has been allowed to earn interest

Compound value = the amount to which an investment has grown in n years

$(1 + i)$ = compound value factor for interest rate i and n periods.

The entire process of transforming or moving an amount of money forward in time, assuming that all interest earned remains in the investment and earns interest in future periods, is called **compounding.** Compounding is a time machine that allows you to see what an amount of money in any period will look like in any future period. All you need is the proper code to use the time machine. That code is the exchange rate between dollars in one period and the next period. Given this code, tables such as Table 13.1 for 10 percent may be used to perform the necessary calculations to compute compound values. Column 1 of Table 13.1 contains the compound value factors for the 10 percent interest rate for one to 50 years. These factors allow you to move sums of money forward in time along curves like those in Figure 13.1. The curve in this figure depicts the compound value of a $100 present value at varying interest rates and periods of time.

Before analyzing Figure 13.1, the use of Table 13.1 in calculating compound values merits explanation. To find the compound value of any amount of money in a future period, multiply the present value by the factor labeled, "Amount of 1 at Compound Interest," for the appropriate period in column 1 of the tables for the current interest rate. For instance, the compound factor for 10 percent and eight years is 2.1436. That is, the value of $(1.10)^8$ is 2.1436. The compound value of $100 compounded at 10 percent for eight years is $214.36,

$$
\begin{aligned}
\text{Compound value} &= \text{Present value} \times \text{Compound factor} \\
&= \$100 \times 2.1436 \\
&= \$214.36
\end{aligned}
$$

To provide another illustration, suppose you are considering purchasing a home for $80,000 and expect it to increase in value at a compound rate of 10 percent for 5 years. What is the value of the home at the end of that period? The solution is $128,840,

$$
\begin{aligned}
\text{Compound value} &= \$80,000 \times 1.6105 \\
&= \$128,840
\end{aligned}
$$

Tables such as Table 13.1 for different compound rates were used to calculate the values shown in Figure 13.1. Tables for other compound rates are contained in Appendix A.2 in the back of the book.

Before continuing, the difference between simple and compound interest should be clarified. In simple interest, it is assumed that any earnings from an investment are withdrawn at the end of each period. This means that the beginning balance is the same for each period and, consequently, so is the interest earned. For instance, $100 invested at 10 percent simple interest for three years will earn $10 of interest each year. The amount of money in the account at the end of the third year will be $100, assuming the $10 interest for the last year has been removed. The total interest earned over the three-year period is $30, compared to $33.10 (from Table 13.1) that would have been earned if the interest had been left in the account to compound.

Table 13.1. 10% Annual Compound Interest Tables

10% = Annual Rate Compound Interest Tables Annual Rate = 10%
Nominal Annual Interest Rate = 10% Compound Frequency (Per Year) = 1

Year	Amount of 1 at Compound Interest (Col. 1)	Accum of 1 Per Period (Col. 2)	Sinking Fund Factor (Col. 3)	Present Value Reversn of 1 (Col. 4)	Present Value Ord Ann 1 Per Period (Col. 5)	Install To Amort 1 (Col. 6)	Period
1	1.1000	1.0000	1.000000	0.9091	0.9091	1.1000000	1
2	1.2100	2.1000	0.476190	0.8264	1.7355	0.5761905	2
3	1.3310	3.3100	0.302115	0.7513	2.4869	0.4021148	3
4	1.4641	4.6410	0.215471	0.6830	3.1699	0.3154708	4
5	1.6105	6.1051	0.163797	0.6209	3.7908	0.2637975	5
6	1.7716	7.7156	0.129607	0.5645	4.3553	0.2296074	6
7	1.9487	9.4872	0.105405	0.5132	4.8684	0.2054055	7
8	2.1436	11.4359	0.087444	0.4665	5.3349	0.1874440	8
9	2.3579	13.5795	0.073641	0.4241	5.7590	0.1736405	9
10	2.5937	15.9374	0.062745	0.3855	6.1446	0.1627454	10
11	2.8531	18.5312	0.053963	0.3505	6.4951	0.1539631	11
12	3.1384	21.3843	0.046763	0.3186	6.8137	0.1467633	12
13	3.4523	24.5227	0.040779	0.2897	7.1034	0.1407785	13
14	3.7975	27.9750	0.035746	0.2633	7.3667	0.1357462	14
15	4.1772	31.7725	0.031474	0.2394	7.6061	0.1314738	15
16	4.5950	35.9497	0.027817	0.2176	7.8237	0.1278166	16
17	5.0545	40.5447	0.024664	0.1978	8.0216	0.1246641	17
18	5.5599	45.5992	0.021930	0.1799	8.2014	0.1219302	18
19	6.1159	51.1591	0.019547	0.1635	8.3649	0.1195469	19
20	6.7275	57.2750	0.017460	0.1486	8.5136	0.1174596	20
21	7.4003	64.0025	0.015642	0.1351	8.6487	0.1156244	21
22	8.1403	71.4028	0.014005	0.1288	8.7715	0.1140051	22
23	8.9543	79.5430	0.012572	0.1117	8.8832	0.1125718	23
24	9.8497	88.4973	0.011300	0.1015	8.9847	0.1112998	24
25	10.8347	98.3471	0.010168	0.0923	9.0770	0.1101681	25
26	11.9182	109.1818	0.009159	0.0839	9.1609	0.1091590	26
27	13.1100	121.0999	0.008258	0.0763	9.2372	0.1082576	27
28	14.4210	134.2099	0.007451	0.0693	9.3066	0.1074510	28
29	15.8631	148.6309	0.006728	0.0630	9.3696	0.1067281	29
30	17.4494	164.4940	0.006079	0.0573	9.4269	0.1060792	30
31	19.1943	181.9434	0.005496	0.0521	9.4790	0.1054962	31
32	21.1138	201.1378	0.004972	0.0474	9.5264	0.1049717	32
33	23.2252	222.2516	0.004499	0.0431	9.5694	0.1044994	33
34	25.5477	245.4767	0.004974	0.0391	9.6086	0.1040737	34
35	28.1024	271.0244	0.003690	0.0356	9.6442	0.1036897	35
36	30.9127	299.1268	0.003343	0.0323	9.6765	0.1033431	36
37	34.0040	330.0395	0.003030	0.0294	9.7059	0.1030299	37
38	37.4043	364.0434	0.002747	0.0267	9.7327	0.1027469	38
39	41.1448	401.4478	0.002491	0.0243	9.7570	0.1024910	39
40	45.2593	442.5926	0.002259	0.0221	9.7791	0.1022594	40
41	49.7852	487.8518	0.002050	0.0201	9.7991	0.1020498	41
42	54.7637	537.6370	0.001860	0.0183	9.8174	0.1018600	42
43	60.2401	592.4007	0.001688	0.0166	9.8340	0.1016880	43

Table 13.1. (Continued)

10% = Annual Rate Compound Interest Tables Annual Rate = 10%
Nominal Annual Interest Rate = 10% Compound Frequency (Per Year) = 1

Year	Amount of 1 at Compound Interest (Col. 1)	Accum of 1 Per Period (Col. 2)	Sinking Fund Factor (Col. 3)	Present Value Reversn of 1 (Col. 4)	Present Value Ord Ann 1 Per Period (Col. 5)	Install To Amort 1 (Col. 6)	Period
44	66.2641	652.6408	0.001532	0.0151	9.8491	0.1015322	44
45	72.8905	718.9049	0.001391	0.0137	9.8628	0.1013910	45
46	80.1795	791.7954	0.001263	0.0125	9.8753	0.1012630	46
47	88.1975	871.9749	0.001041	0.0113	9.8866	0.1011468	47
48	97.0172	960.1724	0.001041	0.0103	9.8969	0.1010415	48
49	106.7190	1057.1896	0.000946	0.0094	9.9063	0.1009459	49
50	117.3909	1163.9086	0.000859	0.0085	9.9148	0.1008592	50

SOURCE: Texas Real Estate Research Center, Texas A & M University.

Figure 13.1
Compound value
curves.

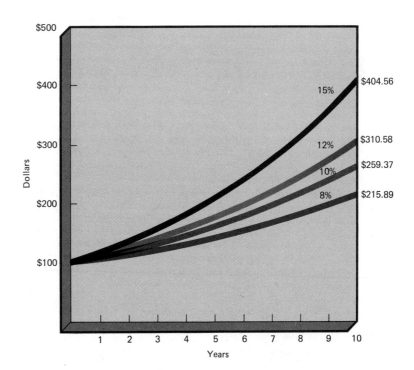

Note that in Figure 13.1, the annual increases in the compound values for any given compound rate get larger as time progresses. This is because the beginning balances for each year get larger and larger. The ability of compound interest to produce very large compound values over long periods of time is an important observation for your personal investment decisions. Even a modest amount of money earning a reasonable rate of return can produce large compound values later in your life. For instance, many families with farms and ranches have been pleasantly surprised by the change in the value of their land, which has been growing in a compound fashion, during their period of ownership. Other families have had similar experiences with their homes.

Another important, while somewhat obvious, observation is that for a given period of time, the higher the compound rate, the higher the compound value. Also, with the passing of time, the differences in compound value become greater. Thus, relatively small differences in compound rates can make substantial differences in compound values.

To complicate your life just a little, assume that you plan to deposit $100 right now in an account earning at the compound rate of 10 percent for 5 years. Further, assume that at the end of the second year you plan to make another deposit of $150 with the intent of leaving it in the account until the end of the original five-year period. What will your balance in the account be at the end of the fifth year? To answer this question you must know that sums of money in the same year can be added and subtracted. Thus, you can calculate the compound value of $100 compounded at 10 percent for five years and add to it the compound value of $150 compounded at 10 percent for three years,

$$\text{Total compound value} = (\$100 \times 1.6105) + (\$150 \times 1.3310)$$
$$= \$161.05 + \$199.65$$
$$= \$360.70$$

The same process would have worked if you had made deposits at the end of any number of years. You must carefully identify the number of periods each deposit will earn interest and use the corresponding compound factor.

Annuities In some situations, you will want to calculate the compound value of equal deposits made at the end of each period. To illustrate, suppose you plan to deposit $2000 at the end of each of the next three years in order to build a down payment for a home. If you can deposit this money in an account earning 10 percent interest, how much money will you have in the account after making the third deposit at the end of the third year? First, such a stream of regular, equal cash flows is called an **annuity.** When the cash flows occur at the end of the periods the annuity is called an ordinary annuity. When they occur at the beginning of each period it is called an annuity due. For the ordinary annuity above, you could calculate the compound value as follows:

$$\text{Compound value of annuity} = (\$2000 \times 1.21) + (\$2000 \times 1.10) + (\$2000 \times 1.00)$$
$$= \$2420 + \$2200 + \$2000$$
$$= \$6620$$

Notice that the **compound factor** for the last year is 1.00, since that deposit is made at the end of the year and earns no interest. Notice also that $2000 is multiplied by each factor. In such a situation, the $2000 can be factored and multiplied by the sum of the compound factors to calculate the same compound value,

$$\text{Compound value of annuity} = \$2000 \, (1.21 + 1.10 + 1.00)$$
$$= \$2000 \, (3.31)$$
$$= \$6620$$

Column 2 of Table 13.1 contains factors for the 10 percent compound rate and different periods of time. These factors are called accumulation of 1 per period factors or annuity compound value factors. Note that the factor for three years is 3.31, the factor we just used. To find the compound value of any annuity, multiply the annuity amount by the appropriate factor. To illustrate, the compound value of a $1000 five-year annuity earning a 10 percent compound rate is $6105.10,

$$\text{Compound value} = \text{Annuity} \times \text{Compound annuity factor}$$
$$= \$1000 \times 6.1051$$
$$= \$6105.10$$

Sinking Fund Suppose that instead of depositing $2000 at the end of each year for three years, you want to make three equal deposits that will produce the $8000 you need to purchase a home at the end of three years. How much must you deposit at the end of each year if those deposits can earn a 10 percent compound rate? In this problem the compound value and the annuity compound value factor can be found in Table 13.1, but the annuity is not known. By analyzing the compound value of an annuity equation above, you can determine how to calculate the annuity. That equation is

$$\text{Compound value} = \text{Annuity} \times \text{Annuity compound factor}$$

By dividing both sides by the **annuity compound factor,** the equation for calculating the annuity can be found,

$$\frac{\text{Compound value}}{\text{Annuity compound factor}} = \frac{\text{Annuity} \times \text{Annuity compound factor}}{\text{Annuity compound factor}}$$

Since the compound annuity factor terms in the numerator and denominator of the right side of the equation cancel, the equation is

$$\frac{\text{Compound value}}{\text{Compound annuity factor}} = \text{Annuity}$$

By moving the compound value expression out of the numerator, you have:

$$\text{Compound value} \times \frac{1}{\text{Compound annuity factor}} = \text{Annuity}$$

The expression in parenthesis is called the sinking fund factor and is found by dividing 1 by the compound annuity factor for the proper number of years and interest rate. Column 3 of Table 13.1 lists sinking fund factors for the 10 percent compound rate.

You can now calculate how much you must deposit at the end of each year to accumulate $8000 at the end of three years by substituting in the last equation,

$$\$8000 \times .302115 = \text{Annuity}$$
$$= 2416.92$$

Thus, if you deposit $2416.92 at the end of each year in an account earning 10 percent, you will have $8000 at the end of three years. To check this, let's use the equation for the compound value of an annuity and Table 13.1,

$$\text{Compound value of annuity} = \$2416.92 \times 3.3100$$
$$= \$8000.01$$

The penny difference is due to the rounding of the annuity compound factors.

Discounting

The compounding process can be reversed. The time machine can also operate to move sums of money back in time along the very curves used to move them forward in time. The process of moving sums of money back in time is called **discounting** and allows you to see what a sum of money looked like in a prior period. Usually, the time period that sums of money are moved back to is the present time. For instance, you may have the opportunity to purchase land today that will be worth $150,000 in five years. In this situation, the critical question is how much is that $150,000 cash flow to be received five years from now worth today? The current equivalent of a future sum of money is called its **present value.** In learning about discounting you will learn about the last three columns in Table 13.1 and how they perform just the opposite functions of the first three columns of that table.

To get a better understanding of discounting, consider the earlier situation in which you were lending your brother-in-law $100. At a 10 percent interest rate, it was easy to see that the exchange rate, or compound factor, for the first year was 1.10. But what is the exchange rate, or discount factor, for an amount to be received in one year? Suppose your brother-in-law came to you and, instead of asking for $100 right now, offers to pay you $110 one year from now in return for you giving him cash right now. If you wanted a 10 percent return on your investment, how much would you give your brother-in-law right now? In this simple example it is easy to see that if you invest $100 now, and receive $110 a year later, you will have received a 10 percent return. In this situation, the exchange rate must be a factor that when multiplied by $110, will produce a $100 present value. Since $100 is less than $110, the factor must be less than one. We can solve this problem as follows:

$$\$100 = \$110 \times \text{Discount factor}$$

$$\frac{\$100}{\$110} = \frac{\$110 \times \text{Discount factor}}{\$110}$$

$$\frac{\$100}{\$110} = \text{Discount factor}$$

$$.909 = \text{Discount factor}$$

Notice that .909 is also equal to the compound factor of 1.10 divided into 1,

$$\frac{1}{1.10} = .909$$

In other words, to find the factor that undoes what compounding does, you simply divide that compound factor for that rate and number of time periods into 1.

You can find the appropriate discounting factors for different interest rates and time periods by consulting tables such as those in column 4 of Table 13.1. The factors in column 4 are called present value reversion of 1 factors, or simply, the present value of 1 factors. Using your calculator you can see that the factors in column 4 are simply the factors in column 1 divided into 1.

To find the present value of an amount of money to be received in the future, you multiply the future amount of money by the factor corresponding to the appropriate rate and time period. For example, if you have an investment that will produce a single cash flow of $200 two years from now, and the **discount rate** is 10 percent, the present value is $165.28,

$$\text{Present value} = \text{Future amount} \times \text{Present value factor}$$
$$= \$200 \times .8264$$
$$= \$165.28$$

If you have a situation in which you are to receive more than one payment in the future, you can find the present value by calculating the present value of each future receipt and adding them together, as you did in finding compound values. Consider finding the present value of an apartment investment that you think will produce receipts as follows:

YEAR	1	2	3
Amount	$120	$175	$340

The present value of this investment, assuming a discount rate of 10 percent, is found by:

$$\text{Total present value} = (\$120 \times .9091) + (\$175 \times .8264) + (\$340 \times .7513)$$
$$= 109.09 + 144.62 + 255.44$$
$$= \$509.15$$

Annuities If all the cash flows had been in the form of an annuity, your problem would have been simpler. You could have used the same approach that was used to find the compound value of an annuity. That approach was to add all the factors and multiply the sum by the annuity. Say all three cash flows had been $120. The problem would have become:

$$\text{Total present value} = \$120 \,(.9091 + .8264 + .7513)$$
$$= \$120 \times 2.4868$$
$$= \$298.42$$

If you look in the row for year 3 of column 5 of Table 13.1, you will find the factor, 2.4869. This number differs very slightly from the number we found by adding the yearly factors due to the rounding off of the factors. The difference is not significant. The factors in column 5 are called present value of an ordinary annuity of 1 per period factors, or simply, **annuity present value factors.** To find the present value of an annuity you multiply the annuity by the annuity present value factor for the appropriate discount rate and time period.

Constants The final factors in Table 13.1 are the installment to amortize 1 factors in column 6. These factors, like the sinking fund factors, are used to find an annuity that satisfies a specific purpose. They are used to find an annuity that, when discounted at a stated discount rate, has a specified present value. That is, if you know the present value of an annuity and the discount rate used to find that present value, what is the annuity? For example, if you know the present value of a three-year annuity is $100 if the annuity is discounted at 10 percent, what is the annuity? It may seem that such a question is absurd. When would you ever know the present value of an annuity and not know the annuity? Actually, this situation occurs every time a loan is made that is to be paid back in equal installments.

If you borrow money on a home, you receive the loan proceeds right now, at the present time, but your payments are made in future time periods. The payments you make must be sufficient to repay the original debt (principal) and provide the lender with interest at the specified rate on the unpaid balance each year (or month). Earlier, when you lent your brother-in-law $100 in return for a payment of $110 one year later, that $110 payment provided for the return of your principal and the 10 percent interest that you demanded on your invested funds. How was the $110 payment calculated? First, you could have calculated the compound value of $100 compounded at 10 percent for one year, since that is what you wanted from the investment. The logic behind this approach is that you could have invested your funds elsewhere at 10 percent and had $110 at the end of the year. Next, since discounting simply undoes the effects of compounding, you could take the opposite approach and calculate the amount of money one year from now that has a present value of $100 when discounted at 10 percent. Either approach produces an answer of $110.

Because it is easier to use in situations involving numerous payments, the present value method is generally used. The method is based on the general principle just discussed, that the proper payment or payments for a loan will have a present value equal to the original loan amount when discounted at the interest rate. Such a stream of payments will repay the principal and provide the lender with the stated rate of interest on the unpaid balance each year. In most real estate lending, the payments are calculated as level payments.

How does the present value approach work? To begin, you know that to find the present value of an annuity you can use the following equation,

$$\text{Present value annuity} = \text{Annuity} \times \text{Present value ordinary annuity factor}$$

You can solve for the annuity by dividing both sides of the equation by the annuity factor,

$$\frac{\text{Present value}}{\text{Present value factor}} = \frac{\text{Annuity} \times \text{Present value factor}}{\text{Present value factor}}$$

Canceling, this leaves

$$\frac{\text{Present value}}{\text{Present value factor}} = \text{Annuity}$$

Which, in turn, is equal to

$$\text{Present value} \times \frac{1}{\text{Present value factor}} = \text{Annuity}$$

The expression, $\dfrac{1}{\text{Present value factor}}$, is the installment to amortize 1 factor, also called the **mortgage constant** or, simply, the **constant.**

To calculate the payments for a level-payment amortizing mortgage, you multiply the loan amount by the constant. For example, the annual payments necessary to repay a $50,000, 10 percent, 30-year mortgage are $5303.96,

$$\text{Payments} = \text{Loan amount} \times \text{Constant}$$
$$= \$50,000 \times .1060792$$
$$= \$5303.96$$

Periods Other Than One Year

You may have heard advertisements claiming quarterly, monthly, or daily compounding. And, of course, most real estate loans have monthly payments, rather than annual ones. How can all the concepts discussed in this chapter be adapted to compounding and discounting periods other than a year? The answer is quite simple.

First, the calculations start with an annual rate. For instance, you are considering depositing $100 in a savings account paying a stated, or nominal, 12 percent annual interest rate, compounded monthly. How much will you have in the account at the end of one year? Monthly compounding means that your account is credited with accrued interest each month, and that accrued interest begins earning interest itself. Thus, at the end of the first month, you will have more than $100 in the account, and that total amount will be earning interest in the second month. There will be 12 compounding periods each year with monthly compounding. If compounding were quarterly, there would be four compounding periods per year. The compound rate applied to each period is the annual rate divided by the number of periods per year. In our example, the 12 percent annual rate is divided by 12 to produce a monthly compounding rate of 1 percent. Thus, at the end of the first month, you will have $101 in your account, composed of the original $100 and $1 of interest. In the second month you will earn $1.01 in interest and so on each period. At the end of one year the $100 will have compounded for 12 periods at the 1 percent rate as compared to having compounded one period at a 12 percent rate with annual compounding.

Put in terms of the basic compounding equation, your $100 has experienced the following,

$$\text{Compound value} = \text{Present value} \times \text{Compound factor}$$
$$= \$100 \, (1.01)^{12}$$
$$= \$100 \times 1.1268$$
$$= \$112.68$$

Because $(1.01)^{12}$ is greater than $(1.12)^1$, you have more money in the account than with annual compounding. Not surprisingly, discounting with monthly factors will produce smaller present values than annual discounting. Tables of factors for daily, weekly, monthly, and semiannual compounding have been developed. Such a set of factors for a 10 percent annual rate and monthly compounding are found in Table 13-1.

CONCEPT 2: FINANCIAL LEVERAGE

You know that by using a long bar as a lever you can effectively magnify the force you can apply to an object. The longer the bar between you and the pivot point relative to its length from the pivot point to the object being moved, the greater the magnification in the force you can apply. The process works in reverse when you are on the short end. If your end of the lever is shorter than the object's end, the force you apply is reduced. This concept has a parallel in the area of finance, called **financial leverage.** However, instead of increasing or decreasing physical force, financial leverage increases or decreases the returns received on your equity investment.

To illustrate the concept of financial leverage, consider a property that presently produces a **net operating income** of $2000, where net operating income is defined as gross rents minus operating expenses. If you purchased this property for $20,000 using only your own equity capital, you would receive the entire $2000 as your return. The $2000 represents a 10 percent simple return on your invested capital ($2000/ $20,000 = .10). Now if you borrow $12,000 at 9 percent interest, the mortgage payments will reduce the amount of money you receive, but at the same time the borrowed funds reduce the amount of your money you must invest. Specifically, if the mortgage payments are $1080, you will receive only the $920 that remains of the $2000. However, since you invested only $8000 in equity, the $920 represents an 11.5 percent simple rate of return on your equity.

By investing in an investment producing income at an overall rate of 10 percent and then borrowing at a 9 percent rate, you were able to achieve a higher return on your equity. In essence, by finding an investor, the lender in this case, willing to accept a return lower than that being generated by the property, you were able to pay the lender and still earn a return on his or her capital. Your return from this investment consists of a 10 percent return on your actual equity plus the difference between the interest rate and the overall rate of return on the borrowed capital. Thus, your total return is

$$
\begin{array}{r}
.10 \times \$8000 = \$800 \\
+ .01 \times \$12,000 = \underline{120} \\
\$920
\end{array}
$$

The lender receives the remainder of the $2000 of net operating income,

$$.09 \times \$12,000 = \$1080$$

This example illustrates some important points. First, it illustrates that the income from a property can be divided between a number of parties. Next, it illustrates that in borrowing, fixed costs are incurred. By incurring these fixed costs, an investor has increased the risk of negative cash flows in future periods. In our example, if net operating income drops below $1080, the equity investor will suffer negative cash flows. Without borrowing, the net operating income could dip to zero before the equity investor is in the same situation. The greater the fixed costs incurred, the greater the risk of negative cash flows. Possibly offsetting this risk is an increase in the **equity rate of return.**

To tell if leverage is increasing or decreasing your equity return, you can compare the rate of return on your equity assuming no borrowing to the interest rate on the borrowed funds. If the investment is producing income at a rate greater than the cost of debt, leverage will increase your equity return, a situation called favorable leverage. If the debt-free return on your equity is greater than the interest rate, leverage is working against you, also called unfavorable leverage. This concept is illustrated in Table 13.2. Favorable leverage is highlighted in Part (a) using three loan-to-value ratios, for a property costing $1000 and producing a net operating income (income after operating expenses but before interest)

Table 13.2.

	(a) Favorable Leverage Interest Rate = 12%		
	Plan		
	1	2	3
Total Cost	$1000	$1000	$1000
Equity	1000	500	250
Debt (12%)	0	500	750
Gross Income	200	200	200
Operating Expense	60	60	60
Net Operating Income	140	140	140
Interest	0	−60	−90
Income after Interest	140	80	50
Return on Equity	14%	16%	20%

	(b) Unfavorable Leverage Interest = 16%		
	Plan		
	1	2	3
Total Cost	$1000	$1000	$1000
Equity	1000	500	250
Debt (16%)	0	500	750
Gross Income	200	200	200
Operating Expense	60	60	60
Net Operating Income	140	140	140
Interest	0	−80	−120
Income after Interest	140	60	20
Return on Equity	14%	12%	8%

of $140. In financing Plan 1, you purchase the apartment using all equity money. On your investment of $1000 you will receive $140, a return on your equity of 14 percent. In Plan 2 you borrow $500 at 12 percent, an interest rate that is lower than the rate of **return on total capital.** As a result, you now have an interest payment of $60 and an income after interest of $80. This $80 represents a 16 percent return on your $500 of equity. This is an increase over the 14 percent you earned if you invested all equity. Plan 3 simply illustrates more extensive use of leverage and the resulting increase in the return on equity.

Part (b) illustrates a situation in which the interest rate exceeds the return on total capital, and the resulting unfavorable leverage. Notice that as the debt ratio increases, the rate of return on equity falls.

CONCEPT 3: RISK, RETURN, AND INVESTMENT DECISIONS

Think back to an important investment decision you have made and the factors you considered in making it. Do not limit investment to stocks, bonds, real estate, and the like, also consider automobiles, electronic equipment, and other major assets. One consideration was probably the benefits the asset would provide. Benefits such as regular income, increase in value, entertainment, pride of ownership, and possibly others may come to mind. You probably visualized a series of events that would most likely occur if you purchased the asset. However, you were also probably aware of a range of outcomes other than those you expected that could occur. For example, in deciding to buy a home you think that realistically the home will provide safe, comfortable, relatively maintenance free shelter while appreciating in value and costing only a moderate amount of money each month. But, you know that major structural defects could surface, that the neighborhood could deteriorate, and that a whole list of other possible problems could upset your expectations. What you have just considered are the return and risk associated with the purchase.

Return

With respect to return, investors establish a minimum acceptable return from the investments they consider. In establishing this required return, investors take into account all returns, financial and nonfinancial. For instance, if pride of ownership is very important to you, then you may be willing to accept a lower financial return on a property that provides a great deal of such pride. Investors prefer more returns to less returns.

Measures of return fall into two general categories: nondiscounted and discounted. Nondiscounted measures do not take the time value of money into account, whereas discounted measures do. Nondiscounted return measures usually are ratios of some measure of income for a given year to some level of investment. The most popular nondiscounted measures are the rate of return on total capital (ROR) and the rate of return on equity (ROE). The rate of return on **total capital invested** is calculated as follows,

$$\text{Rate of return on total capital (ROR)} = \frac{\text{Net operating income}}{\text{Total capital invested}}$$

where:

Net operating income = All the rents the property could produce less a vacancy allowance and operating expenses.

Total capital invested = The total amount of funds invested, debt and equity, in the property.

So, if you are considering an apartment investment, the ROR is simply all the rents the apartments could produce if every unit were rented at the rental rates you are projecting, minus your estimate of vacancy losses and operating expenses, expressed as a percentage of the total cost of the property. This is the same measure of return used earlier to determine if leverage was favorable or unfavorable.

The rate of return on equity is

$$\text{Rate of return on equity} = \frac{\text{Cash flow before tax}}{\text{Equity investment}}$$

where:

Cash flow before tax = Net operating income minus principal and interest.

Equity investment = Cost of the property minus borrowed funds.

The ROE provides a measure of return on the funds you have invested in the property. As the equity investor, your return depends on what is left after all expenses have been paid. This measure expresses what is left as a percentage of your equity funds.

Discounted Return Measures

Discounted return measures take the time value of money into account. There are two types of discounted measures: net present value and internal rate of return. Let's begin with the present value method.

Present Value After reading the first portion of this chapter, the present value method is quite simple. It is the method you used to determine how much to lend your brother-in-law when he said he would pay you $110 at the end of one year. You discounted that $110 to the present time using your required rate of return of 10 percent and found the $110 to have a present value of $100. Once you had done this, your investment decision was simple — if your brother-in-law demanded more than $100 right now you turned down his offer, while if he wanted $100 or less you accepted his offer. Since the $110 payment has a present value of $100, you know that if you invest exactly $100 you will get a 10 percent return. If you invest less than $100 you will get more than a 10 percent return. This same present value approach can be used for all types of investments.

The steps in the present value approach are simple. First, estimate the cash flows in each period including the one at the present time. Next, discount them to the present time using your required rate of return as the discount rate and total the present values. Finally, compare that total to the cost of the investment and accept the investment if the present value is equal to, or greater than, the cost. Otherwise, reject the investment. An alternative to comparing the present value to the cost is to simply total all the present values, including the current cost of the investment that is also a present value, and check to see if the total is negative, positive, or zero. The total is called the **net present value (NPV).** If NPV is positive or zero, the present value of the inflows exceeds or equals the present value of the outflows, and the investment provides acceptable returns. If net present value is negative, the investment does not provide acceptable returns.

Internal Rate of Return It is easy to see that if you invest $100 today and receive $110 one year from now, that you have received a 10 percent return. Given what you now know, it is also easy to see that if you invest $100 and receive $121 two years from now, you have also received a 10 percent compound rate of return. Mechanically, if you discount the $121 two years from now at 10 percent, the present value is $100. If as we have assumed, the investment cost $100, the net present value is zero. To summarize what we know: an investment with a known discounted rate of return of 10 percent has a net present value of $0 when discounted at 10 percent. This coincidence of the net present value equaling zero when cash flows are discounted at the discounted rate of return is valuable because it provides of a method for calculating the discounted rate of return for investments with less obvious rates of return. For instance, in an investment with five cash flows the discounted rate of return is not obvious. However, you now know that the discount rate that creates a net present value of zero is the discounted rate of return. This discounted rate of return is commonly called the **internal rate of return.**

Unfortunately, the internal rate of return must usually be calculated by trial and error, unless you have a calculator or computer that can calculate it for you. However, even these devices use a trial and error approach to its calculation. The actual process of calculating the internal rate of return (IRR) is simple. Select a discount rate, calculate the net present value, and check to see if it is zero. If not, select another discount rate and repeat until you find the discount rate that creates a net present value of zero.

Just because the process involves trial and error does not mean that there is no systematic way to conduct your search for the IRR. Your search can be simplified by considering Figure 13.2 which illustrates the net present value of the $121 to be received two years from now costing $100 using different discount rates. Notice that the discount rate that causes the net present value to equal zero is 10 percent. Also notice that as the discount rate increases, the net present value decreases. This makes sense since the higher the rate, the less we would have to invest now to have $121 two years from now. If you had tried the 12 percent discount rate first, you would have gotten a negative net present value. Because the net present value is negative, you know that the IRR must be less than 12 percent. So perhaps you try 9 percent, which produces a positive net present value. This tells you that the IRR is greater than 9 percent, and from your first calculation, you know it is less than 12 percent. You can then try other discount rates to narrow down the range.

Once you have narrowed the range containing the IRR to one or two percent, you can approximate the IRR using a procedure called interpolation. Suppose you had calculated the net present values associated with 9 percent and 11 percent and found them to be $101.85 and $98.20, respectively. Table 13.3 summarizes the known information and the estimation of the IRR. First, we know the IRR produces a NPV of

Figure 13.2 Net present value and the discount rate.

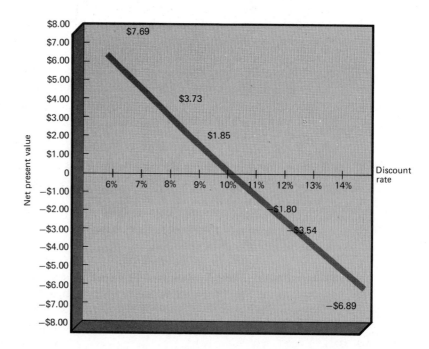

Table 13.3. Interpolating for IRR

Discount Rate			Net Present Value			
		9%	$1.85			
				$1.85 = .5068		
2%		?% = 10.01%	-0-			$3.65
				$1.80 = .4932		
		11%	−$1.80			

zero, so our objective is to estimate where between 9 percent and 11 percent is the discount rate producing an NPV of zero. The assumption is that we must move a distance from either 9 percent or 11 percent that is proportional to the extent the NPVs associated with the rates vary from zero.

In Table 13.3 you can see that the total difference between the two NPVs is $3.65. You can also see that an NPV of zero is $1.85 from the 9 percent NPV and $1.80 from the 11 percent NPV. These numbers amount to 50.68 percent and 49.32 percent of the total difference respectively. Thus, if we start at 9 percent, we can say that the IRR is 50.68 percent of the way to 11 percent. Or, starting with 11 percent, we can say that the IRR is 49.32 percent of the way to 9 percent. Since the difference between 9 percent and 11 percent is 2 percent, the IRR is equal to,

$$IRR = .09 + (.5068 \times .02)$$
$$= .09 + .0101$$
$$= .1001 \text{ or } 10.01\%$$

We get the same answer starting with 11 percent,

$$IRR = .11 - (.4932 \times .02)$$
$$= .11 - .0099$$
$$= .1001 \text{ or } 10.01\%$$

Of course, from earlier in the chapter, you know the IRR is 10 percent. Our approximation is reasonably close. The greater the difference between the two discount rates being interpolated, the greater the difference between the estimated IRR and the actual IRR.

One way to look at the IRR is as the rate at which your initial investment will grow over the life of your investment. You would be in the same financial condition at the end of two years with the example investment with an IRR of 10 percent as with depositing $100 in a savings account paying 10 percent interest for two years.

Risk

If you put any moral objections to gambling aside for a moment, would you take a gamble in which you have a 50 percent chance of losing $1000 and a 50 percent chance of winning $1000? You probably wouldn't. Why? First, $1000 probably represents a significant amount of money to you, so you wouldn't take on the gamble just for the fun of "playing" the game. Second, the pleasure you expect to receive from winning is less than the pain associated with losing. This is an important point, because people make decisions based on what outcomes they think may occur and their assessment of how those outcomes would affect their happiness. If, on balance, the outcomes producing decreases in happiness outweigh those producing increases in happiness, you will decide not to participate.

Because of the tendency of most people to associate a greater loss in happiness with losing a given amount of money than increase in happiness with winning the same amount they are called risk averse, meaning they do not like **risk.** Thus, any time the outcome of a gamble or an investment is now known, investors want to evaluate the possible outcomes and how likely they are to occur. This information is then evaluated by the individual to see if the outcomes and their probability of occurring produce an expectation of being happier or less happy if they make the investment. As you saw above, an even bet will not be taken; investors want to receive a premium for accepting uncertainty, or risk. For example, if the odds on the gamble above were changed so that you had an 80 percent chance of winning $1000 and only a 20 percent chance of losing the same amount, you may take the gamble. The payoffs could also be changed and influence your decision. A 50-50 chance of winning $10,000 and losing only $1000 may induce you to accept the gamble. While most of us are risk averse, we are not all risk averse to the same extent. Some are extremely risk averse while others are only mildly risk averse and will take chances others will not. Of course, there are some people who actually enjoy risk. The thrill of the game makes these risk seekers take chances and make investments that others will not.

All of this means that investors consider all the possible outcomes from an investment, not just the one they expect to receive. Not only do they try to estimate what outcomes are possible, they also try to evaluate the probability each outcome has of occurring. With this information they are better able to assess how, on balance, the investment will likely affect their happiness. Since you are probably not able to foresee the future with unerring accuracy, you do not know what is going to happen. This means that evaluating the possible outcomes from an investment and their probabilities of occurring usually involves a great deal of educated guesses, best estimates, and subjective evaluation. This may sound like a bunch of bunk, but it certainly is not. It is one thing to consider all the facts, make an educated estimate of what may happen, and base a decision on this reasoning, and quite another to simply ignore the future and be surprised by anything that happens. Chapter 18 discusses ways of estimating the riskiness of an investment.

APPLYING BASIC FINANCIAL CONCEPTS TO REAL ESTATE LENDING

Some of the more common uses of basic financial concepts are in real estate lending. Calculating mortgage constants, payments, remaining balances, yields, and other information are common real estate lending problems.

Constants and Payments

You learned how to calculate mortgage payments earlier in the chapter. By looking in the appropriate tables you can find the factor called the mortgage constant which, when multiplied by the original loan amount, produces the payments necessary to amortize the mortgage. Not all tables are in the form of those seen thus far in the chapter and in the back of the book. However, they will all contain factors that can be used to calculate payments. The payments they calculate are for mortgages with interest rates and payments that do not change. Each payment contains interest and principal that gradually pay off, or amortize, the mortgage over its term. Such a mortgage is called a **fixed rate, fixed payment (FRFP) mortgage.**

A different type of loan, one in which the interest rate and payments do not change for a stated period, but are then adjusted, is being made today. For example, a loan may have a 13 percent interest rate for the first three years, with the rate and corresponding payments to be adjusted in some fashion at the end of the third year. If the loan is for $80,000 and a 30-year term, the debt service payments are $884.96. The new payments at the end of the third year calculated by assuming that a new mortgage equal in amount to the outstanding balance, with a term equal to the remaining years of the term, is being made. If a $79,200 balance remains at the end of the third year and the rate is increased to 15 percent, what are the new payments? They will be found by looking up the payments on a $79,200, 15 percent, 27-year mortgage. Using the tables in the back of the book you find the constant to be .01272738, and the payments to be $1008 per month. These payments will continue until another change occurs. These mortgages are called adjustable rate mortgages.

Loan Balance

How was the $79,200 balance at the end of the third year calculated in the example above? The solution to this problem is found back in the discussion of calculating the mortgage constant. At that time it was noted that the present value of all the payments of a mortgage, discounted at the interest rate, is equal to the original loan amount.

Put another way, the original loan amount is equal to the present value of all remaining loan payments at the time the loan is made. This concept holds for any other period as well. The outstanding loan balance is equal to the present value of the remaining payments discounted at the interest rate. The $79,200 balance represents the present value of 27 years of payments of $884.96 discounted at 13 percent. The annuity present value factor for monthly discounting at an annual rate of 13 percent is 89.4954, which when multiplied by the monthly payment of $884.96 equals $79,200. Tables are also available which list the percentage of the original loan outstanding at the end of each period. Figure 13.3 illustrates the outstanding balance of a $100,000, 13 percent, 30-year mortgage over its lifetime.

Mortgage Yield

Investors in mortgages measure their return on the basis of **yield.** Yield is the internal rate of return on their investment in a mortgage. You may be thinking that yield will always be equal to the interest rate, but this is not true. For instance, throughout the chapter, your brother-in-law has been borrowing $100 from you and paying you back $110 at the end of

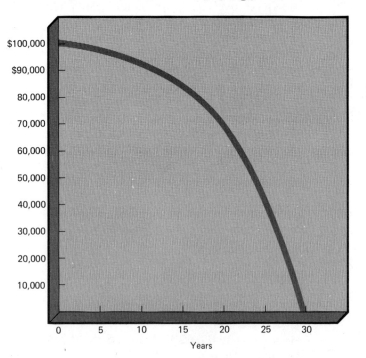

Figure 13.3
Outstanding balance
$100,000, 13%,
30-year loan.

one year. Now suppose that five minutes after you lend the money to your brother-in-law you remember an obligation that needs to be paid and you try to find someone who wants to purchase your brother-in-law's promise to pay you $110 one year from now. You find such a person, but he or she will only pay you $98 for the promise. At the end of the year, they will receive the $110, as promised. What is their yield? They earned $12 on a $98 investment in one year. This represents a return of 12.25 percent (12/98 = .1225). Clearly this is greater than the 10 percent you would have received on your investment of $100. If they had paid you $100, the investors would have received a 10 percent yield and, if they had paid more than $100, they would have received less than a 10 percent yield. The same concept holds true for longer term real estate loans; the yield depends on whether the loan is purchased for less than, more than, or an amount equal to the face amount of the loan. When a loan is purchased at face value it is said to be purchased at par. When purchased at less than face value it is purchased at a discount, and when purchased for more than face value it is purchased at a premium.

Yield is calculated as discussed earlier in the section on IRRs. The cash flows the investor receives are the periodic payments and the ultimate payoff of the loan. Based on experience, it is usually assumed that the loan will be paid off in 10 to 12 years. The greater the discount or premium the more yield is affected. Table 13.4 is a table of yields associated with different discounts, premiums, and loan payoff periods for a mortgage with a face, or nominal, interest rate of 10 percent. The column labeled, "to maturity," simply means the loan is paid over its entire life with normal payments.

Discount Points

Real estate loans are sometimes made at below market interest rates. Loans are made at such rates because lenders feel that borrowers are very sensitive to the stated interest rate. In other situations, such as VA loans (to be discussed in a later chapter), below market rate loans are made because the Veteran's Administration establishes the maximum interest rate that can be charged, and often, that rate is below market levels. Since lenders could invest in loans at the market rate, why are they willing to make below market rate loans? The answer is that at the time of origination they will charge a fee, in the form of **discount points,** for making the loan. Each discount point is one percent of the original loan amount. If you borrow $50,000 and have to pay two discount points, you will pay 2 percent, or $1000, in addition to all other fees, just to get your loan. This means that you have borrowed, and will pay interest on, $50,000, but have received only a net amount of $49,000 ($50,000 − $1000 = $49,000). The lender has parted with a net of $49,000 but will earn interest on the entire $50,000. Just as in the discussion of yield

Table 13.4. Yields and Discounts For a 12% Loan

	15-Year Mortgage				20-Year Mortgage			
	Prepaid In				Prepaid In			
Price	8 Years	10 Years	12 Years	To Maturity	8 Years	10 Years	12 Years	To Maturity
92	13.86	13.70	13.63	13.59	13.75	13.57	13.47	13.35
½	13.73	13.59	13.52	13.49	13.63	13.47	13.37	13.26
93	13.61	13.48	13.41	13.38	13.52	13.37	13.28	13.17
½	13.49	13.37	13.31	13.28	13.40	13.26	13.18	13.09
94	13.37	13.26	13.20	13.18	13.29	13.16	13.09	13.00
½	13.25	13.15	13.10	13.07	13.18	13.06	12.99	12.91
95	13.13	13.04	12.99	12.97	13.07	12.96	12.90	12.82
½	13.02	12.93	12.89	12.87	12.96	12.86	12.81	12.74
96	12.90	12.83	12.79	12.77	12.85	12.76	12.71	12.65
½	12.79	12.72	12.69	12.67	12.74	12.67	12.62	12.57
97	12.67	12.62	12.59	12.57	12.63	12.57	12.53	12.49
½	12.56	12.51	12.49	12.48	12.53	12.47	12.44	12.40
98	12.44	12.41	12.39	12.38	12.42	12.38	12.35	12.32
½	12.33	12.30	12.29	12.28	12.31	12.28	12.26	12.24
99	12.22	12.20	12.19	12.19	12.21	12.19	12.17	12.16
½	12.11	12.10	12.10	12.09	12.10	12.09	12.09	12.08
100	12.00	12.00	12.00	12.00	12.00	12.00	12.00	12.00
½	11.89	11.90	11.91	11.91	11.90	11.91	11.91	11.92
101	11.78	11.80	11.81	11.82	11.80	11.82	11.83	11.84
½	11.68	11.70	11.72	11.72	11.69	11.73	11.74	11.77
102	11.57	11.61	11.62	11.63	11.59	11.63	11.66	11.69

	25-Year Mortgage				30-Year Mortgage			
	Prepaid In				Prepaid In			
Price	8 Years	10 Years	12 Years	To Maturity	8 Years	10 Years	12 Years	To Maturity
92	13.70	13.52	13.41	13.23	13.68	13.49	13.38	13.15
½	13.59	13.42	13.31	13.14	13.57	13.39	13.28	13.07
93	13.48	13.32	13.22	13.06	13.46	13.29	13.19	13.00
½	13.37	13.22	13.13	12.98	13.35	13.20	13.10	12.92
94	13.26	13.12	13.04	12.90	13.24	13.10	13.02	12.85
½	13.15	13.02	12.95	12.82	13.13	13.01	12.93	12.77
95	13.04	12.93	12.86	12.75	13.03	12.91	12.84	12.70
½	12.93	12.83	12.77	12.67	12.92	12.82	12.75	12.63
96	12.83	12.74	12.68	12.59	12.81	12.72	12.67	12.55
½	12.72	12.64	12.59	12.51	12.71	12.63	12.58	12.48
97	12.62	12.55	12.51	12.44	12.61	12.54	12.50	12.41
½	12.51	12.46	12.42	12.36	12.50	12.45	12.41	12.34
98	12.41	12.36	12.34	12.29	12.40	12.36	12.33	12.27
½	12.30	12.27	12.25	12.22	12.30	12.27	12.25	12.20
99	12.20	12.18	12.17	12.14	12.20	12.18	12.16	12.14
½	12.10	12.09	12.08	12.07	12.10	12.09	12.08	12.07
100	12.00	12.00	12.00	12.00	12.00	12.00	12.00	12.00
½	11.90	11.91	11.92	11.93	11.90	11.91	11.92	11.93
101	11.80	11.82	11.84	11.86	11.80	11.83	11.84	11.87
½	11.70	11.73	11.76	11.79	11.71	11.74	11.76	11.80
102	11.60	11.65	11.67	11.72	11.61	11.65	11.68	11.74

SOURCE: Publication #387. *Commercial Loan and Constant Tables.* © 1980, p. 162, Financial Publishing Co. Boston, MA.

above, the discount in this example increases the yield to the lender and the effective cost of the loan to the borrower.

How many discount points are charged varies directly with the difference between the stated interest rate and the market rate. Discount points are frequently charged when the lender is going to sell the mortgage to another party called an investor. In such situations, the investor buys on the basis of yield, with the price paid for the mortgage varying based on the stated interest rate. If the lender knows the yield the investor desires, then the number of points necessary to avoid a loss from selling the mortgage can be calculated. It can be calculated by finding the present value of the mortgage payments and expected prepayment using the investor's required yield as the discount rate. The result can be converted to discount points and passed on to borrowers as the market permits. Actually, the lender could increase the interest rate and reduce the number of points.

Instead of using present value techniques, the lender could use tables such as Table 13.4 to estimate the discount required by selling a mortgage. If a lender had recently made a $50,000, 12 percent, 30-year mortgage and wants to sell it to an investor wanting a 12.75 percent yield, and assuming the mortgage will be prepaid in 12 years, the investor will be willing to pay a price of 95½. This means the investor will pay 95½ percent of par, or face, value of the mortgage. This is a price of $47,750. To break-even, the lender must collect 4½ discount points. You can see that if a lender makes loans not knowing to whom they are going to be sold, possible increases in market interest rates and investors' required yields between when the loan is made and when it is sold can create substantial losses.

SUMMARY

Financial considerations play an important role in all aspects of real estate. In this chapter, certain basic financial concepts and calculations were explained. The idea was not to make you a financial expert, but to provide you with a firm foundation of understanding for dealing with financial matters. Throughout the chapter, the emphasis was on using tables and a simple calculator. Of course, a more sophisticated calculator or computer may be used, but the logic underlying the solution of financial problems remains the same.

Time value of money was the first financial concept presented in the chapter. This basic concept was then expanded through the development of six factors for handling compounding and discounting. Compounding is the process of moving a sum of money into the future. Discounting is just the opposite: the moving of a sum of money back to earlier periods. The six factors developed include: compound value of 1, compound value of an annuity of 1, sinking fund, present value of 1, present value of an annuity of 1, and the constant.

The second concept considered was leverage. Leverage is the use of borrowed funds to create a situation in which a given percentage change in net operating income creates a greater percentage change in equity income. Leverage works to magnify either increases or decreases in equity returns.

Next, risk and return were said to be the critical factors in making investment decisions. Investors establish minimum acceptable levels of return from the investments they consider. Return is measured using nondiscounted and discounted measures. Nondiscounted measures do not take the time value of money into account, and are usually expressed as ratios of a given year's income to an initial investment. Two nondiscounted measures were discussed in the chapter: the rate of return on investment and the rate of return on equity. Discounted measures take the time value of money into account. The two discounted approaches are the internal rate of return and the net present value.

People are generally risk averse. This means they prefer less risk to more risk, all other things being equal. Risk was defined as the possibility of outcomes other than that expected occurring. Because people are risk averse, they require a risk premium for accepting an investment with uncertain outcomes. Techniques for dealing with risk are considered in Chapter 18 dealing with real estate investments.

Next, the basic financial concepts were applied to real estate lending to calculate debt service payments and loan balances. Yields on mortgages were shown to simply be the internal rates of return on such investments. Yield and the stated interest rate of a mortgage will be the same only if the loan is purchased for par. If the loan is purchased at a discount, yield will be greater than the interest rate. If purchased at a premium, yield will be less than the interest rate. Finally, discount points were found to be necessary because stated interest rates were less than market interest rates. The number of discount points necessary to produce a given yield can be calculated using present value techniques.

QUICK QUIZ

1. The process of moving a sum of money forward in time by assuming that all interest earned remains in the investment and also earns interest in future periods is called _____ .

    a. discounting   c. an annuity
    b. compounding   d. present value

2. If an investment offers one cash flow of $200, to be received two

years from now, what is its present value if the discount rate is 10 percent?

a. $163.48   c. $242.00
b. $165.28   d. $200.00

3. In discounting a given sum of money to be received in a given year back to the present time, the _____ .

a. higher the discount rate, the lower the present value
b. lower the discount rate, the lower the present value
c. higher the discount rate, the higher the present value
d. lower the discount rate, the higher the present value

4. Financial leverage magnifies _____ in rates of return on equity.

a. only decreases   c. increases and decreases
b. only increases   d. errors

5. The outstanding balance of a loan at any point in time is the _____ .

a. compound value of all remaining payments
b. original loan amount minus all interest paid
c. original loan minus total debt service
d. present value of all remaining payments

6. Because people associate a greater loss in happiness with losing a given amount of money than gain in happiness from winning the same amount, they are considered to be _____ .

7. The discount rate that causes the net present value to equal zero is the _____ .

8. Cash flow before tax divided by your equity investment is defined as the _____ .

9. Yield on a mortgage is defined as the _____ on that mortgage.

10. An equal amount of money received each year is a(n) _____ .

QUESTIONS AND EXERCISES

1. Write a convincing argument for money having time value.

2. Explain in your own words why discounting and compounding simply reverse what the other does.

3. Calculate the compound value of $500 at the end of 1 year, 5 years, and 10 years, using a compound rate of 12 percent. With time on the horizontal axis and dollars on the vertical axis, plot the results and join them to form a curve. Explain why this curve is shaped the way it is.

4. How much must you place in an account at the end of each year for the next seven years to amass $10,000 at the end of the seventh year assuming the deposits earn 10 percent interest? Show your calculations.

5. What is the compound value of an annuity of $1000 received at the end of each of the next five years if they compound at a 12 percent rate? Is there another way to calculate the answer to this problem? If so, what is it? Show your calculations.

6. You have the opportunity to purchase an investment with cash flows of $111, $123, and $137 in years 1, 2, and 3, respectively, for $300. What is the present value of the cash flows using a 14 percent discount rate? What is the investment's net present value? Show all work.

7. What is the internal rate of return for the investment in question 6? Show all work.

8. Are you risk averse? How does this affect your consideration of an investment opportunity?

9. What would an investor pay for a $50,000, 12 percent, 30-year mortgage made today, if the investor wants a 13 percent return? Assume monthly payments and that the loan will be outstanding the entire 30 years. About how many discount points would the firm making the loan have to charge the borrower to break-even on the loan?

10. How would you determine your required rate of return on an investment?

KEY TERMINOLOGY	annuity	discount rate
	annuity present value factor	discounting
	cash flow before tax	fixed rate, fixed payment mortgage
	compound annuity factor	internal rate of return
	compound factor	leverage
	compounding	mortgage constant
	discount point	net operating income

net present value   risk
present value   time value
return on equity   total capital invested
return on total capital   yield

IF YOU WANT   DONALD R. EPLEY and JAMES A. MILLAR, *Basic Real Estate Finance*
TO READ MORE *and Investments,* second edition (New York: John Wiley & Sons, 1984).

STEPHEN A. PYIIRR, ''Mathematics of Real Estate Finance,'' Chapter 28
in James A. Britton, Jr. and Lewis O. Kerwood, editors, *Financing Income-Producing Real Estate* (New York: McGraw-Hill Book Company,
1977).

C. F. SIRMANS, *Real Estate Finance* (New York: McGraw-Hill Book
Company, 1985), Chapter 2.

J. FRED WESTON and EUGENE F. BRIGHAM, *Essentials of Managerial
Finance,* 5th ed. (Hinsdale, Ill.: The Dryden Press, 1979), Chapters 11
and 12.

PART THREE

REAL ESTATE DECISION AREAS

In this part of the book you will learn about lending, equity investment, and development decisions. These decisions, and those who make them, are the catalysts of the real estate business. They create the need for all the decision support areas. Thus, even though you may not be preparing for a career in lending, investment, or development, an understanding of what decisions must be made and how they are made will enhance your opportunities to provide services and improve your financial well-being.

Your analysis of the decision areas begins with real estate lending. Lending is directly related to development and investment — when money is available at reasonable rates of interest, development and investment thrive; when it is not, they struggle. Three chapters are devoted to lending to help you understand the legal aspects of lending, the financial system, and lenders' decision-making processes.

Next is a chapter on real estate development. From it you will develop a good understanding of how projects ranging in size from small apartments to skyscrapers are "put together." You will also understand the decisions developers must make and how they make them. In short, you will know the how and why of projects in your town and, perhaps, discover a career! The final two chapters consider investing in income-producing real estate such as apartments, office buildings, and industrial buildings. Here you will develop an understanding of investor motivations, the types of real estate investments available, and how to make investment decisions.

14
Real Estate Lending: legal considerations

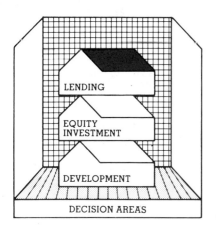

LENDING

EQUITY INVESTMENT

DEVELOPMENT

DECISION AREAS

PREVIEW   Real estate lending carries with it a body of basic law relating to the rights of borrowers and lenders. This body of law is important because it determines the ease with which real estate may be used as collateral and the degree of certainty the lender may place in that use. A clear definition of these rights is necessary for our capital markets to work most efficiently. In this chapter you will learn about the legal characteristics of real estate lending. Specifically you will learn:

1. The legal concept behind the most common financing method—the real estate mortgage.
2. The documents used to finance a real estate transaction.
3. The seller's ability to provide mortgage financing and the legal status accorded such financing.
4. The methods by which a mortgage can be assigned.
5. The methods by which a mortgage can be terminated.
6. The chief alternative to the use of a mortgage as a financing device—the deed of trust.
7. Federal regulation of lending activity.

The development of the modern mortgage has been more evolutionary than revolutionary. That is, the modern concept of mortgages did not emerge fully developed from a legal theorist's mind in a single moment of heightened awareness. Rather, it has evolved from lending law based on practical necessity and much fine tuning over the years. The legal underpinnings of mortgages continue to evolve even today. To understand fully the basics of modern law relating to real estate lending requires an appreciation of the evolution of mortgages and the forces at work causing changes to occur.

HISTORICAL CONCEPT OF MORTGAGE

The mortgage concept appeared in England hundreds of years ago at a time when many landowners were "land rich but money poor." They had vast land holdings but little liquid capital. At this same time the Catholic Church did not allow the loaning of money at interest, considering such practice immoral. So, when a landowner needed to borrow money from a moneylender, he would convey title to a tract of land to the lender to secure repayment of the principal and to provide for interest. The lender would take possession, using the profits of the land as his "interest." The borrower still had to pay back the principal. If the borrower repaid the loan as agreed on a specified day (called the "law day"), he had the right to reacquire title; otherwise, the lender's title became absolute.

Over a period of time it became apparent that this practice of conveying title to the lender, subject to the borrower's reacquiring title if he repaid the loan, took away too much from the borrower and gave too much to the lender. Gradually, modifications were made that transformed the mortgage into its present role — one of giving a lender security for the repayment of a debt by the borrower.

The first modification was to allow the borrower an extended time after "law day" in which to reacquire, or redeem, the title by repaying the debt. This right of the borrower became known as **equity of redemption.** Because the borrower's equity of redemption cast doubt on the lender's title, the lender sought, and was given, the right to demand that the borrower redeem the title within a stated period of time or be barred (foreclosed) from doing so. This right of the lender became known as the **right of foreclosure.** Notice that if the borrower failed to redeem the title by paying the debt within the time specified in the lender's foreclosure lawsuit, the lender acquired full title to the property. This often amounted to a windfall profit to the lender because the property would be much more valuable than the debt. To correct this inequity, the law transformed the foreclosure process into a sale in which, upon default by the borrower, the lender would foreclose by requiring a public sale of the property, with the proceeds first being used to satisfy the debt, and any balance going to the borrower. This process protects the lender by giving adequate security on the debt, yet also protects the borrower by protecting for him or her the value of the property in excess of the amount of the debt. This is the process followed today throughout the United States.

Modern Mortgage Concept

The mortgage as a financing device has been down a long historical road from its origin as a conveyance of an estate in land to the lender, with the borrower being able to reacquire title upon payment of the debt, to its present destination as a security device to secure the payment of a debt between lender and borrower. Some states, mostly in the Northeast, still adhere in theory to the old concept of a mortgage as transferring title to the lender. This theory is known as the **title theory** and these states are called *title theory states*. But most states recognize a mortgage for what it truly is — a collateral device that gives security to the basic obligation of the borrower to repay the debt to the lender. The borrower is viewed as having title to the property, with the lender having only a security interest in the property, giving the lender the right to foreclose and cause the property to be sold in payment of the debt upon the borrower's default in paying the debt. The lender's security interest is considered a *lien* on the title in the eyes of the law. A lien is a claim by someone (the lender, here) that can be enforced under certain circumstances (the borrower's default on the debt). This theory of mortgages is known as the **lien theory** and states following it are known as *lien theory states*.

MORTGAGE DOCUMENTATION

The fact that the modern mortgage is a security device to protect the financial position of a lender who has loaned money to a borrower indicates that there are two aspects to the loan transaction: (1) the debt of the borrower to the lender and (2) the security for the debt. These two aspects of the transaction are evidenced by two separate documents: (1) the debt is evidenced by a **promissory note,** and (2) the security for the debt is evidenced by a **mortgage.** The mortgage document has completely overshadowed the promissory note and given its name to the entire transaction. However, in truth, the mortgage is merely added security for the *personal obligation* of the borrower to repay the debt evidenced by the promissory note. These two documents are now examined in more detail.

Promissory Note

The promissory note, commonly referred to as simply the note, is a document containing the express promise of the borrower(s) to pay a specified person or institution a definite sum of money at a specified time. In some states, this promise to pay is called a **bond.** Since there is little or no difference between a bond and a note, the following discussion applies to both. In order for a note to be valid it must:

Be in writing

Be an agreement between a borrower and lender, each of whom has the capacity to contract

Contain an express promise to pay a specified sum of money

Indicate the terms of payment

Be signed by the borrower(s)

Be delivered by the borrower and accepted by the lender

The promissory note in Table 14.1 contains the most commonly found terms. Take a minute and read through the note to get a feel for its basic contents and to develop an understanding about what it is trying to do for the lender and borrower.

Now that you have read the note, we will take you on a guided tour of its main features. Item (1) identifies the document as the evidence of a

Table 14.1. (1) Promissory Note

(2) US $ _____   (3) _____
                                                          City   State

(4) FOR VALUE RECEIVED, the undersigned ("Borrower") promise(s) to pay (5) _____, (6) or order, the principal sum of (2) _____ Dollars, with interest on the unpaid principal balance from the date of this Note, until paid, at the rate of ___(7)___ percent per annum. Principal and interest shall be payable at _____(8)_____ in consecutive monthly installments of _____(9)_____ Dollars (US $ _____), on the _____(10)_____ day of each month beginning _____, 19 _____, and continuing until the entire debt is fully paid. Any remaining debt, if not sooner paid, shall be due and payable on _____(11)_____.

(12) Borrower may repay the principal amount outstanding in whole or in part.

(13) Borrower shall pay to the note holder a late charge of _____ percent of any monthly installment not received by the note holder within _____ days after the installment is due.

(14) If any monthly installment under this Note is not paid when due, the entire principal amount outstanding and accrued interest thereon shall at once become due and payable at the option of the note holder.

(15) If suit is brought to collect this Note, the Note holder shall be entitled to collect all reasonable costs and expenses of suit.

(16) This Note shall be the joint and several obligation of all makers and sureties, and shall be binding upon them and their successors and assigns.

(17) The debt evidenced by this Note is secured by a Mortgage bearing the same date as this Note and made in favor of _____.

(19)   (18) _____
(This space for witnesses   Borrower
and/or acknowledgments
as required by state law)   _____
                                            Borrower

debt that the borrower owes to the lender. (2) states the amount of the note. (3) identifies the location where the note is executed. (4) states that the borrower has received something of value and, in turn, promises to pay the debt described in the note. (5) identifies the lender. (6) indicates that the lender can require the borrower to repay the debt to a designated third person. The words "or order" mean that the lender may require the borrower to repay someone else specified by the lender. This will occur if the lender sells the note to someone else. (7) identifies the interest rate on the debt. (8) identifies the place where the debt is to be repaid. Normally, this will be the business office of the lender. (9) identifies the monthly payments to be made on the debt. (10) states when the first payment and subsequent payments are due. (11) states when the last payment is due. This enables one to easily determine the length of the loan, that is, whether it is for 10 years, 30 years, and so on.

(12) provides that the borrower may repay all or any part of the debt at any time before the due date of the last payment, without any penalty being charged. Other notes may allow the lender to charge a **prepayment penalty** if the borrower wants to repay the loan before a specified period of time has passed. Usually prepayment penalties apply not only to early prepayment of the complete debt, but also to a significant partial prepayment. Also, prepayments often apply only when the money for the prepayment is borrowed from another lender. The purpose of such a clause is to discourage the borrower from renegotiating the loan with another lender if the interest rate on this type of loan drops. (13) allows the lender to charge another kind of fee, called a *late payment fee*. This fee is collected if the borrower fails to make a payment within a specified number of days of its due date. (14) is the acceleration clause giving the lender the right to make the entire loan balance due and payable if the borrower defaults on installment payments. This acceleration of the date, which is optional with the lender, sets the stage for the foreclosure process, which was mentioned briefly in the historical section above and which is discussed in more detail later. Without this provision the lender could only seek the missed payments and not the entire remaining principal if a borrower was late with payments. (15) requires the borrower to pay all costs and expenses arising from the lender's collection of the debt upon the borrower's default.

(16) makes all the signers of the note *jointly and severally liable*. This means that they are all liable to repay the debt both as a group and individually. The lender can enforce his or her rights against all of them or any one of them individually.

(17) indicates that the debt evidenced by this note is secured by another document — a mortgage. The mortgage gives the lender a property interest in the mortgaged property. Without such a clause, the debt would be a personal debt without any specific property to secure it.

(18) contains the spaces for each borrower, often called the *maker*, to sign the note. This creates the joint and several liability of each maker.

If the borrower is married, the lender will usually require the borrower's spouse to join in the note and sign it.

(19) provides space for any formalities that the state may require. Formalities, such as witnesses' signatures and the acknowledgment of the maker(s), may be necessary for validity or in order for the note to be recordable in the public land records. Normally, however, acknowledgment will not be necessary because it will be the mortgage, rather than the note, which is recorded.

Mortgage

The mortgage is a separate document from the promissory note and is used to give the lender added ability to collect the debt from the borrower in case of default. This added ability is in the form of a property interest in the land used as collateral. The property interest is a lien that can be enforced by a process resulting in a public sale of the property, with the proceeds of the sale being used to satisfy the debt. Pledging property as security for debt, without giving up possession, is called **hypothecation.** The land used as collateral can be the property being purchased *or* other property owned by the borrower.

Essential Elements Because a mortgage is a conveyance of an interest in land, it must have the same basic elements that any conveyance of land must have. You may want to reread the chapter on deeds for a thorough review of these elements. Briefly, the mortgage must:

Adequately identify the grantor (borrower-mortgagor) and grantee (lender-mortgagee)

Adequately identify the property in which the security interest is granted

Use words of conveyance sufficient to show the grantor's intent to presently convey a security interest to the grantee

Contain the grantee's signature

Be delivered by the grantor and accepted by the grantee

See Table 14.2 for a summary of the note and mortgage instruments.

Covenants Because the mortgage's function is to convey a property interest that gives the lender protection in the financing transaction, the mortgage also contains a number of covenants (promises) by the borrower designed to protect the lender's position. In general, these promises fall into three categories:

1. Promises related to repayment of the debt.
2. Promises related to the financial responsibilities connected with the ownership of the property.
3. Promises related to the legal status of the title to the property.

Table 14.2. Mortgage Documentation Summary

Document	Effect	Items Necessary to Be Valid
Promissory note (Bond)	Creates a personal obligation to repay debt (Contractual right)	Must be in writing Agreement between borrower and lender, each having capacity to contract An express promise to repay a specified sum of money Terms of payment Signed by borrower and lender Delivered by borrower and accepted by lender
Mortgage	Creates an interest in the subject property, called a lien, for the lender (Property right)	Adequately identify the grantor and grantee Adequately identify the property Proper words to show intent to convey security interest Grantor's signature Delivered by grantor and accepted by grantee

All of these promises are calculated to protect the lender's security interest and allow the lender to foreclose the mortgage if they are breached.

The simplified mortgage contained in Table 14.3 illustrates the essential elements of a mortgage and many of the elements commonly found in them. Most mortgages contain more complicated legal language than this sample does. The more complicated versions can be defended as necessary to precisely define the legal rights and obligations of the parties. But they can be criticized as obscuring the meaning and nature of the document to the average person. This criticism has led to the suggestion of language reform and the creation of "plain language" instruments more easily understood by the average person. This applies not just to mortgages but all legal instruments.

In Table 14.3, item (1) identifies the date of execution, plus the borrower (mortgagor) and lender (mortgagee). Item (2) describes the amount of the debt and identifies the note evidencing the debt. (3) conveys a security interest in the real property to the lender thereby creating a lien. (4) describes the real property on which the lien has been created. (5) contains title covenants similar to the ones found in the sample deed in Chapter 5.

(6) introduces the promises, called covenants, that the borrower is

Table 14.3. Mortgage

---

(1) THIS MORTGAGE is made this _____ day of _____ between the mortgagor, _____ (herein "Borrower") and the mortgagee, _____ (herein "Lender").

(2) Whereas, Borrower is indebted to Lender in the principal sum of _____ Dollars, which debt is evidenced by Borrower's Note of the same date as this mortgage.

(3) TO SECURE the Lender the repayment of the debt evidenced by the Note, with interest thereon, and the covenants of the Borrower herein contained, Borrower does hereby mortgage, grant and convey to Lender the following described property in the County of _____, State of _____.

(4) (Property Description)
together with all the improvements thereon and all the rights pertaining hereto.

(5) Borrower covenants that Borrower is seized of the estate hereby conveyed and has the right to mortgage the property, and that the borrower will warrant and defend generally the title to the property against all claims.

(6) Covenants. Borrower and Lender covenant as follows:

(7) 1. Borrower shall promptly pay the principal and interest on the debt evidenced by this note when due.

(8) 2. Borrower agrees to pay all taxes, assessments or other charges against the property which could result in the creation of liens having priority over this mortgage.

(9) 3. Borrower agrees to maintain hazard insurance on the property.

(10) 4. Borrower shall keep the property in good repair and shall not permit waste or permit deterioration of the property.

(11) 5. If Borrower fails to perform the covenants contained in this Mortgage, the Lender may make such performance. Any amounts disbursed by the Lender under this paragraph shall become additional debt of Borrower secured by this mortgage.

(12) 6. Lender may make reasonable entries upon and inspections of the Property upon giving prior notice to Borrower.

(13) 7. Any award in connection with the condemnation of the Property is hereby assigned to Lender and shall be applied to the sums secured by this Mortgage, with any excess paid to Borrower.

(14) 8. If all or any part of the Property is sold by Borrower without Lender's prior written consent, the Lender may declare all the sums secured by this Mortgage to be immediately due and payable.

(15) 9. Upon Borrower's breach of any covenant in this Mortgage, except as provided in paragraph 8 hereof, Lender may, after notifying Borrower of breach and giving Borrower not less than 30 days to cure the breach, declare all the sums secured by this Mortgage to be immediately due and payable and may foreclose this Mortgage.

(16) 10. The covenants contained herein shall bind and the rights contained herein shall inure to the successors and assigns of Lender and Borrower.

(17) IN WITNESS HEREOF, Borrower has executed this mortgage.

_____
Borrower

(18) (This space for witnesses
and/or acknowledgments as
required by state law.)

_____
Borrower

agreeing to perform. These covenants should be read in conjunction with (15), which is an acceleration clause. This clause provides that a breach of any of the covenants by the borrower gives the lender the option to accelerate the debt and make it immediately due and payable and, if it is not paid, to foreclose on the mortgage. This is the legal "big stick" that the lender carries that enables him or her to protect both financial and property interests in the transaction. The financial interest is the loan, that is, the debt owed by the borrower. The property interest is the lien that gives security for the debt.

(7) is the debt repayment covenant, obligating the borrower to repay the debt according to the conditions stipulated in the note. (8) is the tax covenant, obligating the borrower to pay all taxes arising against the property. The purpose of this clause is to prevent the creation of a lien for unpaid taxes, which would gain superiority over the lender's lien. (9) is the insurance covenant, obligating the borrower to maintain hazard insurance on the real property. The purpose of this clause is to protect the value of the real property serving as collateral for the debt, in the event buildings or other structures are damaged by fire or other hazard. Without such insurance, the value of the real property might fall below the amount of the debt owed, thereby endangering the lender's security. Any monies collected under the policy could be used to repair or replace damaged or destroyed improvements, thus keeping the value of the collateral sufficient to protect the lender's lien. Many mortgages give the lender the ability to require that any proceeds received for a substantial loss be applied to the outstanding mortgage. Such a provision is called a *mortgage assignment clause.*

(10) is the repair covenant, obligating the borrower to maintain the real property so that it does not deteriorate. It also obligates him or her not to commit any affirmative act, such as removing buildings or natural resources, that would decrease the value of the real property. Such an act is called *waste.* The function of this covenant is similar to the insurance covenant — to prevent a loss in value of the real property that would jeopardize the value of the lender's lien.

(11) is a self-help clause that allows the lender to perform any obligation defaulted on by the borrower. For example, if the borrower fails to pay taxes or insurance premiums, the lender can do so, thereby protecting the lien from impairment. Since these obligations are the borrower's, the lender can pass the cost of meeting them on to the borrower.

(12) is the entry clause that allows the lender to enter the premises under reasonable conditions in order to inspect them. The concept here is that knowledge by the lender of what is happening on the property is necessary to adequately protect the lien. This clause also illustrates the fact that since the borrower still has title and possession, the lender has no right to go on the property without agreement.

(13) is the condemnation clause, stipulating how the proceeds of any award upon state condemnation of the real property are to be divided

between the parties. Since the property can.no longer serve as security for the debt, the award is used to pay off the debt.

(14) is the **due on sale clause,** obligating the borrower to secure the written consent of the lender to the sale or other transfer of the property, or the lender may accelerate the debt and make the entire balance due and payable. This clause has two purposes. First, it allows the lender to consider the credit-worthiness of any buyer who, after the sale, will be making the mortgage payments. Second, if the necessary wording is present, the clause allows the lender to require that the interest rate on the mortgage be adjusted to the current rate or within so many percentage points of the existing rate. In periods of increasing interest rates, this allows the lender to avoid being stuck with a low interest loan that is passed from buyer to buyer. The first purpose is uniformly recognized as a legitimate use of the clause. A recent Supreme Court decision confirmed the second purpose is legitimate. Assuming the validity of the clause, a breach of it by the borrower allows the lender to accelerate the mortgage debt and, if it is unpaid, foreclose on the property.

Item (15) was considered with item (6) earlier.

(16) makes the rights and responsibilities of the covenants flow to any transferee of the lender's interest or the borrower's interest. It is quite possible that the lender can transfer the note and mortgage to an investor interested in owning the mortgage and receiving the payments. Transfers of the borrower's interest are considered in the next section of this chapter.

(17) is the signature clause where the borrower, as grantor, executes the document. As with the note, if the borrower is married and the spouse has an interest in the property, the lender will require the borrower's spouse to join in the mortgage and sign it.

(18) provides space for any formalities that the state may require. Formalities such as the witnesses' signatures and the acknowledgment of the borrower may be necessary for validity or in order for the mortgage to be recordable in public land records. In contrast to the note, some or all of these formalities will normally be followed with a mortgage because it creates an interest in real property and will therefore be recorded.

Subsequent Mortgages

Because a mortgage is merely a lien on the title with the borrower continuing to hold title, it is possible for the borrower to give additional mortgages to secure additional debts. For example, a home purchaser will typically give a mortgage to the lending institution financing the transaction. Later, the same purchaser may decide to add a room to the house and borrow the money from another lending institution to do so. He or she will give another mortgage to this lender as security for the loan.

Where there are two or more mortgages encumbering the title to a property, the relative priority of these mortgages becomes important. The legal rule applied is that the time when mortgages are recorded determines priority, that is, "prior in time is prior in right." Here is an area where the recording system considered in Chapter 5 plays an important role in determining property rights. The first mortgage is often referred to as the senior mortgage and later mortgages are referred to as junior mortgages. Also, the word *senior* is used to describe all mortgages prior to a given mortgage and *junior* is used to describe all mortgages over which the given mortgage has priority. For example, a second mortgage is senior to a third mortgage and junior to a first mortgage. Obviously, no mortgage can be senior to the first mortgage.

So long as all mortgages are paid according to schedule, their priority is not critical. When a senior mortgage is paid off, all junior mortgages are moved up in priority. Upon default of one mortgage, however, the relative priority of all mortgages becomes critical. If the borrower defaults on a junior mortgage and the lender elects to foreclose, senior mortgages are not affected. But if a senior mortgage is defaulted on and the lender forecloses, all junior mortgages are extinguished. If the junior mortgages cannot be satisfied out of the proceeds of the foreclosure sale, the former junior mortgagees hold only unsecured obligations against the borrower. Where the senior mortgage is foreclosed, the order of payment of the sale proceeds follows the priority of the mortgages. That is, the first mortgage is fully satisfied, then the second mortgage is fully satisfied, then the third.

The principal exception to this scheme of priorities relates to **subordination agreements.** These are agreements whereby a senior mortgagee voluntarily gives a junior mortgagee priority. For example, a lender with a first mortgage may, using a subordination agreement, switch priority with the lender holding the second mortgage. Your first impression may be one of astonishment; why would anyone do such an apparently foolish thing? Suppose an owner of land on the edge of town sold 40 acres to a shopping center developer and financed the sale by lending the developer the purchase price and accepting a mortgage. When recorded, this mortgage will be the first mortgage. Now the developer is ready to start building the shopping center and needs to borrow money for the construction. Chances are good the construction lender will require a mortgage, probably a first mortgage, in order to make the loan. If the developer and original landowner had anticipated this situation they could have agreed that the landowner would execute a subordination agreement giving the construction lender a first mortgage position instead of a second mortgage position. The landowner may agree to this because this is the only way the land can be sold at a reasonable price. After all, who would want to buy land on which they cannot finance necessary improvements?

Another reason a senior mortgagee may choose to subordinate is to increase the value of the pledged parcel or remaining lands. In the example in the preceding paragraph, the improvements to the land may dramatically increase the value of the parcel. Such an increase in value may improve the security the property provides for the mortgagees. Likewise, if the person selling the land and taking back a subordinated mortgage owns additional lands adjacent to the parcel, the improvements financed by the new senior mortgage may cause surrounding lands to be more valuable.

Transfer of Borrower's Interest

In considering the characteristics surrounding the borrower's transfer of interest in the real property, it is important to keep in mind the nature of each party's property interest. The borrower owns the fee simple estate in the property, subject to the mortgage lien. The lender has a dual set of rights: (1) a contractual right based on the promissory note, and (2) a property right based on the lien created by the mortgage securing the contractual right.

Transfer Rights and Limitations By owning the fee simple estate, the borrower has the legal right to transfer this interest to another. The lender cannot prevent him or her from doing so. This right of transfer is subject to certain consequences, however.

First, a transfer does not diminish the borrower's continuing liability on the promissory note. Personal contractual liability is completely separate from the property interests each party has in the real property. Thus, if the new buyer takes over the mortgage, the seller is not relieved from personal obligation unless the lender chooses to release him or her.

Second, because the borrower owns the fee simple estate subject to the mortgage lien, this type of estate is all he or she can convey to a buyer unless the note and mortgage are satisfied. The transfer cannot affect the lien and the lender continues to have a property interest that can be enforced under the appropriate circumstances. This is just the familiar idea that you cannot convey a better title than you own. If the borrower pays off the note, the lender should issue a mortgage release that terminates the lender's interest in the property.

Third, if the mortgage contains a due on sale clause, which allows the lender to accelerate the debt unless the borrower secures the lender's prior written consent to the transfer, the lender may have the practical ability to prevent a transfer by the borrower. It is important to realize that this clause does not affect the legal ability of the borrower to transfer, but only the financial obligations between the parties. However, to the extent a potential transferee wants to utilize the existing mortgage in a subject to or assumption transaction, as explained below, rather than paying off the existing mortgage, the due on sale clause results in a practical restraint on the ability of the borrower to sell.

Some states have barred the use of the due on sale clause. Attempts to enforce the due on sale clause in court have met with mixed results. However, the U.S. Supreme Court recently upheld the validity of the due on sale clause.

Types of Transfers

With this background in place, let's examine the four basic types of transfers of the borrower's interest:

1. The new loan transfer
2. The subject to transfer
3. The assumption transfer
4. The novation transfer

It should be emphasized that in each case, the actual transfer of the property interest of the borrower is identical. If the concept of transferring ownership is hazy, you should review Chapter 5, dealing with transfers. The differences lie in the varying financial rights and obligations of the three parties (seller-transferor, buyer-transferee, and lender) and the impact of these rights on the mortgage lien. (Table 14.4).

New Loan In this type of transfer, the transferee obtains new financing in order to purchase the property. This financing may come from the same lender or a new lender. In either case, however, it is used to pay the purchase price. Since there are two parties with an interest in the property, the seller and the lender, the purchase price is split between them. The remaining loan balance of the promissory note secured by the mortgage is paid to the original lender, and the balance of the purchase price, representing the seller's equity, is paid to the seller. The result of the transaction is to terminate the existing note and mortgage. The seller drops out of the picture, having had any obligations on the note and mortgage satisfied. The original lender also drops out of the picture, as do the old note and mortgage, both having been extinguished in the trans-

Table 14.4. Transfers of Borrower Interest

Type of Transfer	Seller Still Obligated to Lender?	Buyer Obligated to Lender?	In Case of Default, Lender May Sue
New loan	No (Old loan paid off and released)	No (Obligated to new lender)	Buyer
Subject to	Yes	No (Obligated to seller)	Seller
Assumption	Yes	Yes	Seller and Buyer
Novation	No	Yes	Buyer

action. Evidence of the seller's satisfaction of the lien should be in the form of a document called the **mortgage release,** which should be recorded. The transferee now owns the fee simple estate subject to whatever new lien was created by the new financing arrangement.

Subject to In this type of transfer, the buyer uses the existing mortgage as a financing tool. This is done by paying the seller the value of his or her equity, but not paying off the mortgage at the time of purchase. The buyer takes title **subject to** the mortgage and *does not* personally assume any obligation to pay off the note and mortgage. This transaction does not terminate the existing note and mortgage. The seller has transferred his or her property interest, but is still personally obligated on the note, although the basic agreement between seller and buyer is that the buyer will now pay off the note and mortgage in installments just as the transferor has been doing. If the buyer defaults on this agreement and the seller must pay off the note and mortgage, the seller can attempt to recover against the buyer.

The lender still has a lien on the property, which can be enforced by the foreclosure process if the mortgage debt is not paid off on schedule. In addition, as just indicated, the lender has the legal right to collect the mortgage debt from the seller if it is unpaid. The buyer now owns the fee simple estate. He or she has no personal obligation to pay off the mortgage note, but has a strong practical reason for doing so because the title is *subject to* the mortgage lien. Failure to pay off the mortgage debt on schedule subjects him or her to the likelihood of losing title through the foreclosure process.

Assumption The assumption is similar to the subject to transfer, with the added provision that the transferee personally assumes the obligation to repay the note and mortgage. This assumption will normally be found in the buyer's deed, although it can be placed in a separate document. The position of the seller is similar to that which he or she occupies in the subject to transaction. The lender's position has been enhanced because he or she not only has the right to foreclose on the property in case of default, but also has the right to sue both the seller and buyer on the mortgage debt. For this reason, lenders prefer assumptions to subject to transactions. The buyer's position has correspondingly changed in that he or she is personally liable on the mortgage debt, as well as holding title subject to the mortgage.

Novation This type of transfer is a modification of the assumption transaction. Here the lender agrees to release the seller from personal liability on the mortgage debt and look solely to the buyer for repayment. Novation, then, is the substitution of one debtor for another. The seller drops out of the picture, as in the refinancing transaction, while the rights and responsibilities of the lender and buyer toward each other are the same as in the assumption transaction.

TERMINATING THE MORTGAGE

There can be what might be described as a successful or an unsuccessful conclusion to the mortgage transaction. The successful conclusion results in the note and mortgage being paid off (satisfied). Happily, an overwhelming majority of mortgage transactions end this way. Unfortunately, a few transactions end unsuccessfully with the borrower or a later buyer, acquiring the property either through assumption or subject to, defaulting on the mortgage debt. Let's now look at what occurs in each event.

Satisfaction — The Successful Conclusion

Most mortgages are paid off, on or before their scheduled due date. This occurs when the borrower pays the debt over its lifetime as stipulated in the note and mortgage. Often, however, it occurs upon the sale of the property, as discussed above. In any event, once the note is paid, the lender will (1) return the note, marked "paid," to the borrower, and (2) execute a release of the mortgage. The *release* is a written document extinguishing the mortgage lien held by the lender. Because the mortgage is a property interest that will have been recorded in the public land records, the release of his property interest should also be recorded in order to clear the title for the current and future fee simple owners.

Normally, the release is not given until the entire debt is paid. This means that as time passes and the debt is paid down, the recorded mortgage, which indicates on its face what the original amount of the debt was, will not be an accurate indication of the current amount of the debt. When it becomes important for the borrower to show exactly what the current amount of the debt is, as when he or she is selling to someone buying under an assumption or subject to, an **estoppel certificate** can be requested from the lender. Estoppel certificates are also often required by investors buying mortgages to assure the outstanding balance. This certificate issued by the lender shows the current balance of the loan and the rate of interest.

Sometimes the borrower and lender will agree that, upon a certain reduction in the amount of the mortgage debt, the mortgage will be released on a portion of the property. This results in the lender giving a partial release to the borrower periodically when the debt has been reduced to a predetermined level. This type of arrangement often occurs where the lender has taken a *blanket mortgage* on a large tract of undeveloped land and the borrower subdivides the land and secures a partial release on a subdivided part at the time it is sold and a portion of the mortgage is paid off.

Default — Prelude to the Unsuccessful Conclusion

A few mortgage transactions do end unsuccessfully. The prelude to this is the borrower's **default** in paying the debt or in meeting some other obligation imposed by the note and mortgage, such as the payment of taxes and insurance or maintenance of the property. Before pursuing legal remedies, however, the lender will often work with the borrower to solve the problem causing the default. The lender is just as anxious that the transaction end successfully as the borrower. For example, if default is occurring because of financial difficulties encountered by the borrower, the lender who is made aware of this fact may be willing to temporarily lower the monthly payments, lengthen the payoff time, or make other *forebearance* arrangements to help solve the default. If no satisfactory nonlegal solutions to the default can be found, then the lender will pursue one of two legal courses of action — foreclosure or deed in lieu of foreclosure.

What constitutes default on a mortgage is frequently misunderstood. Default is important because when it occurs the lender has the legal right to start foreclosure proceedings. Technically, when a borrower fails to meet *any* obligation created by the note or mortgage, he is in default. Default is not limited to a failure to make monthly payment of principal and interest, but monthly payments are the usual source of defaults. With respect to these payments, most notes and mortgages will contain the date when these payments are due, usually the first of the month, and the date when these payments are payable, or late, usually the fifth of the month. If you have not made the payment by the fifth, you are in default. Confusing the issue is another date in the note and mortgage, the date on which late payment fees are charged. This date is usually between the tenth and fifteenth of the month. The fact that a borrower has not had to pay any late payment fees does not mean that he or she has never been in default. Some borrowers who have never been charged a late fee are surprised to learn that their credit report has a number of late mortgage payments listed on it.

Foreclosure — One Remedy
for the Unsuccessful Conclusion

The purpose of a foreclosure action by the lender is to generate the funds necessary to satisfy the mortgage debt when the borrower has failed to meet the terms of the mortgage. At any time before foreclosure is completed, the borrower can end the proceeding by remedying the defect, that is, paying the debt defaulted upon plus accrued interest. This right is the borrower's equity of redemption. However, if the equity of redemption is not exercised, the effect of the foreclosure action is to terminate the interest of the borrower and all junior lienholders.

The method used to generate these funds is a sale of the mortgaged property. Here we see the essence of the mortgage. Its function is to give the lender the ability to require a sale of the property if the borrower defaults on his or her obligations. This is the "security" that the mortgage gives the lender. The sale can be one of two varieties — a judicially supervised sale or an unsupervised sale. Which is used depends on which type the statutes of the jurisdiction and the mortgage itself allow.

Judicially Supervised Sale If the sale must be supervised by some court, the lender must begin the process by filing a foreclosure lawsuit in that court. This lawsuit will have all the legal trappings of any lawsuit. The lender, as plaintiff, will file a petition (1) stating the default of the borrower, now the defendant in the lawsuit, (2) asking the court to foreclose (end) the borrower's equity of redemption and the interests of junior lienholders, and (3) asking the court to order a sale of the property and payment of the debt out of the proceeds of sale.

In order to protect his or her right in the property against third persons who may acquire some interest during the foreclosure action, the lender will normally file a **lis pendens** (lawsuit pending) notice in the public land records. Most states require that such notice be filed by the lender if he or she wants to make a purchaser of any interest in the property take the property subject to the foreclosure action.

At the hearing on the lender's foreclosure action, if the court determines the issues favorably to the lender, it will order a sale of the property by public auction conducted by a designated public official such as a sheriff or referee. The lender must publicize the pending sale. Most states require the placing of sale notices in local newspapers, often "legal newspapers" published for this purpose, or the posting of notices at designated public locations such as the county courthouse.

The sale of the property is by public auction on the theory that such an auction will bring the highest possible price. It is usually held at the courthouse or on the property. Any person can bid at the auction — the borrower, the lender, a junior lienholder, or any third person. The lender has an innate advantage, however, in that he or she can bid up to the full amount of the mortgage debt without having to pay cash. A successful bidder, other than the lender, must normally make a cash down payment immediately upon the conclusion of the sale and pay the balance a short time later when the transaction is closed.

Upon the closing of the transaction, the purchaser pays the balance of the purchase price and receives a sheriff's deed or referee's deed from the public official who conducted the sale. This deed conveys to the purchaser the title of the borrower in its condition immediately prior to the giving of the mortgage being foreclosed. Thus, all later claims are eliminated.

The court having jurisdiction over the foreclosure process must confirm the sale. The only circumstances that will normally prevent confirmation will be fraud by the lender or failure to follow the prescribed procedures. Alleged inadequacy of the sales price will normally not be a basis for refusing to confirm the sale. Although some states require that, in order to be confirmed, a sale bring a designated percentage of the appraised value of the property, mortgage documents routinely waive the appraisal requirement. There may be other protections given to the borrower, however. These protections will be discussed later.

The proceeds of the sale are distributed as follows: (1) the costs of the sale are paid; (2) the senior mortgage being foreclosed is satisfied as fully as possible; (3) if funds exist after the senior mortgage is satisfied, junior lienholders are satisfied in the order of their priority, that is, the second lienholder is satisfied as fully as possible, then, if additional funds exist, the third is paid, and so on; and (4) any excess is paid to the borrower. This order of distribution assumes that the sale brings a sufficient amount to pay all claims and results in an excess. If the amount brought by the sale is not sufficient to satisfy the senior mortgage, there is a **deficiency.** In such a situation the lender may have the right to ask the court for a deficiency judgment against the borrower. This right is based on the borrower's personal liability on the promissory note. If granted, the *deficiency judgment* is an unsecured personal judgment against the borrower, enforceable against any nonexempt property he or she owns.

Out of the massive numbers of foreclosures during the depression of the 1930s arose debtor-oriented legislation in many states that protects the borrower from a deficiency judgment. One form of state statute totally abolishes the deficiency judgment and forces the lender to seek recovery solely from the foreclosure sale. Another form of legislation limits any deficiency judgment to the amount by which the debt exceeds the fair market value of the property (rather than the amount by which the debt exceeds the foreclosure sales price). Given the increasing values of most real estate in our inflationary economy, this latter law virtually eliminates the chances of a deficiency occurring in those states.

Unsupervised Sales In some states a foreclosure sale can be conducted without court supervision. In order for this type of foreclosure to be conducted in such a state, the mortgage must contain a power-of-sale clause giving the lender the authority to conduct a sale upon the default of the borrower. These states require some minimum waiting period between the time of default and the sale in order to give the borrower some reasonable time within which to exercise his or her equity of redemption. The notice and sale procedures discussed above apply to this type of sale.

In one situation, however, a court may become involved. If the sale results in a deficiency, the lender must bring a lawsuit against the borrower to obtain a deficiency judgment, if such a judgment is allowed in the state. The advantages of the unsupervised sale are its greater speed and lower cost. The mortgage with a power-of-sale clause has a great similarity to the more commonly used deed of trust, which is described later in this chapter.

Statutory Redemption Regardless of which type of foreclosure sale occurs, many states give the borrower yet another type of protection, called the **statutory right of redemption.** The purpose of this right is to protect the borrower against a low foreclosure sales price by allowing the borrower to redeem the title from the purchaser at the foreclosure sale. This right arises *after* foreclosure and runs for a specified time period. Be careful to distinguish statutory redemption from the equity of redemption, which arises upon default and continues until it is extinguished by foreclosure.

The borrower can exercise his or her statutory right of redemption by paying to the purchaser the amount paid at the foreclosure sale. If the borrower exercises this right, the effect is to annul the sale. In states recognizing statutory redemption rights, the purchaser at the foreclosure sale receives a certificate of sale (rather than a sheriff's or master's deed), entitling him or her to a sheriff's or master's deed at the end of the statutory redemption period, if the borrower does not exercise the statutory right of redemption. Although these statutes are designed to protect the borrower against low foreclosure sales prices, the practical effect in many situations has been to help ensure a low sales price because of the uncertainties it builds into the title purchased by the successful bidder.

Deed in Lieu of Foreclosure — An Alternative Remedy for the Unsuccessful Conclusion

As an alternative to the lender pursuing a foreclosure remedy upon default, the parties can agree that the borrower will convey title to the property involved to the lender using a deed. This conveyance will be held by the parties to completely satisfy the debt. This optional approach has advantages for both the borrower and the lender. For the borrower it has the advantage of preventing the possibility of a deficiency judgment and a foreclosure on his or her credit record. For the lender it has the advantage of being more expeditious and inexpensive than foreclosure, especially the judicially supervised foreclosure. The disadvantage of this approach, especially from the lender's viewpoint, is that it potentially lacks the conclusiveness of the foreclosure, especially the judicially supervised foreclosure, because the lender still must dispose of the property.

TRUST DEED FINANCING

One mortgage alternative used in a number of states is the **deed of trust.** Its purpose is the same as that of the mortgage — to provide security for the repayment of a debt. However, the method by which the security is created is quite different in concept. Instead of being a two-party agreement between the lender and borrower, the deed of trust is a three-party agreement among the lender, borrower, and trustee. The borrower gives a promissory note to the lender as evidence of the debt, just as in the mortgage transaction. However, instead of conveying a mortgage lien to the lender using a mortgage, the borrower conveys title to the property to a third-party trustee. The trustee holds title in "trust," with an expense obligation to either (1) reconvey title to the borrower in the event the borrower repays the debt, or (2) sell the property at a foreclosure sale and transfer title to the purchaser in the event the borrower defaults on the debt. The foreclosure sale aspect of the deed of trust is substantially similar to that of the mortgage with a power of sale attached.

In many ways the deed of trust is similar to a mortgage. For example, before default, the borrower is entitled to possession of the property, has the ability to give subsequent deeds of trust or mortgages in the property, and has the ability to convey legal title to a purchaser, subject to the deed of trust. In other words, the trustee acquires a bare legal title, with the substantive characteristics of ownership remaining with the owner.

Also, after default, the borrower has an equity of redemption, which he or she can exercise until the trustee sells the property, and has a right to have the foreclosure sale proceeds be distributed in the same order as in a mortgage foreclosure sale. Are there, then, any substantive differences between a deed of trust and a mortgage with power of sale? Some states say no, treating the two identically. In these states there is no advantage to the lender in utilizing a deed of trust.

However, other states recognize substantive differences between a deed of trust and a mortgage. In California, for example, a deed of trust is viewed as actually transferring title to the trustee, while the mortgage gives only a lien to the lender. This difference allows the lender or trustee under the deed of trust to immediately take possession of the property upon default, a right not accorded a mortgagee (lender) without specific agreement.

Also, in California, because the trustee has actual title, he or she can convey that title to a purchaser at the foreclosure sale and the borrower will not have a statutory redemption right against the purchaser, a right sometimes given to the borrower against the purchaser at the mortgage foreclosure sale. It is in states like California, which recognize substantive differences between deeds of trust and mortgages, that deeds of trust are most advantageous to lenders and are used most often.

REGULATION OF LENDING ACTIVITY

Our discussion so far has focused on the financial transaction as a private activity between the lender and the borrower. However, there is government involvement and regulation of this activity at numerous points. At this point we should consider three federal acts that regulate the lender's conduct toward the borrower.

Equal Credit Opportunity Act (ECOA)

This Act is an antidiscrimination act, passed by Congress in 1974, which applies broadly to all lenders involved in extending credit in many areas, including mortgage lending. The Act's purpose is to require lenders to extend credit equally to all credit-worthy applicants, without regard to race, color, religion, national origin, sex, marital status, or age. These factors may not be taken into consideration in determining the credit-worthiness of an applicant; only individual factors affecting the applicant's credit-worthiness may be considered. For example, a woman, otherwise credit-worthy according to the lender's general credit standards, cannot be denied credit or offered harsher terms because of her sex. Thus, the lender may not inquire into her contraceptive practices or childbearing intentions or ability.

ECOA operates by requiring the lender to notify the applicant of its action on the application within 30 days of its receipt. If the action is adverse to the applicant, the applicant must be given a written statement of the reasons. Violations of ECOA can subject the lender to both civil and criminal penalties.

Truth-in-Lending Law (Regulation Z)

This law is a part of the Consumer Credit Protection Act passed by Congress in 1969. It is important to you because it applies not only to lenders, but to virtually anyone who ever advertises consumer credit. The law is often referred to as Regulation Z, the name of the regulation adopted by the Federal Reserve System to implement the Act. The law is designed to provide consumers with adequate information for comparing loan terms and to prevent misleading advertising of financial terms. Both of these objectives are achieved by requiring full disclosure involving financial terms. Additionally, the law provides a three-day recision period for financing involving a consumer's principal residence.

Full disclosure of financial terms includes all the items in Table 14.5. Of particular importance is the annual percentage rate (APR). As you learned in the last chapter, the APR is the cost of debt when discount points, financing charges, and interest charges are considered. All of these items must be disclosed to a prospective borrower. With respect to advertising, any specific financing terms other than the APR will trigger full disclosure. A specific statement is one such as, "Only five percent down." Thus, the advertiser cannot provide only selected favorable terms in advertising.

Table 14.5. Elements of Full Financial Disclosure

Finance charges expressed as an annual percentage rate.
Date finance charges will begin.
Due dates of payments.
Default or delinquency charges.
Payoff penalties.
Balloon penalties.
Total amount of credit that will be made available to the borrower.
Method of computing credits for early payment.
Composition of finance charges.
Total finance charge.
Total of all payments including principal.
Description of any property used as collateral for loan.
PLUS THE FOLLOWING FOR FINANCING CONNECTED WITH A SALE
Cash price.
Down payment.

Real Estate Settlement Procedures Act (RESPA)

RESPA, passed by Congress in 1974 and extensively amended in 1976, complements Regulation Z. While Regulation Z requires the disclosure of factors that affect the annual cost of the loan throughout its life, RESPA requires the disclosure of settlement, or closing, costs that must be paid by the borrower at the time the loan is made. In addition, RESPA contains substantive restrictions on the kinds of costs chargeable to the borrower at closing.

RESPA applies to "federally regulated" first mortgage loans on one-to-four family residences, including condominiums, cooperatives, and mobile homes. "Federally regulated" loans are broadly defined to include (1) FHA and VA loans and (2) conventional loans made by institutions insured by the Federal Deposit Insurance Corporation (FDIC), Federal Savings and Loan Insurance Corporation (FSLIC), or other federal agencies *or* institutions making loans totaling over one million dollars annually. These categories cover a large majority of all residential mortgage loans made.

The first purpose of RESPA mentioned above, that of advance disclosure of settlement practices and costs, is accomplished by the following methods. First, at the time of loan application or within three business days thereafter, the lender must provide the applicant (1) an informational booklet prepared by the Department of Housing and Urban Development (HUD) entitled "Settlement Costs and You" and (2) a good-faith estimate of all charges likely to be imposed at the settlement of the loan. Second, at or before closing, the lender must provide both the borrower and the seller a completed HUD Uniform Settlement Statement Form, indicating the precise amount of all closing costs.

The second purpose of RESPA, that of restricting practices that potentially increase settlement costs, is accomplished by three methods.

First, the Act prohibits referral fees or kickbacks from being paid to or received from anyone except one who actually provides a service. For example, if an attorney splits a portion of a fee with a real estate agent whose only service was to refer a prospective client to the attorney, *both* the attorney and the agent have violated the Act. The Act makes major exceptions for payments made pursuant to cooperative brokerage or referral agreements (MLS) and agreements between real estate agents and brokers.

Second, the Act prohibits a lender from requiring that a buyer purchase title insurance from a particular title insurance company. However, the lender is not prohibited from requiring the utilization of a particular title company or other service providers, such as title examiners or appraisers.

Third, RESPA limits the amount that lenders can require borrowers to place in property tax and insurance escrow accounts. Escrow accounts as used here are accounts containing the borrower's money maintained by the lender, who will pay property taxes and insurance premiums when they come due. Typically, a portion of each monthly payment is put into these accounts. The lender collects these funds to make sure that tax liens are satisfied. Funds are also collected to make certain that adequate hazard insurance is in force to pay off the mortgage should the improvements be damaged or destroyed. The amount that can be required to be placed in escrow at settlement is limited to the borrower's share of property taxes and insurance accruing prior to settlement, plus one-sixth of the estimated amount that will come due in the following year. After settlement, there is a monthly limit on the amount that the lender can require the borrower to place in the escrow account equal to one-twelfth of the estimated annual amount of property taxes and insurance charges.

For example, if the seller of a home had purchased insurance for the year on January for $360 and the buyer wishes to continue that policy after purchase, then the buyer is responsible for paying the seller for the unused insurance. If the transaction closes on July 1, the buyer must pay the seller for the one-half year's insurance, or $180, at closing. The same thing holds for property taxes. In addition to any amounts already due, the lender may require the buyer to place up to two months of future property taxes and insurance costs in escrow at closing. Two months of insurance would be $60 in this example.

SUMMARY

You now know that a mortgage is an interest in land used to secure a personal obligation between the borrower and the lender. Although the historical mortgage actually conveyed title, the modern mortgage merely creates a lien that gives the lender the right to foreclose and require a sale of the property upon the borrower's default. Two documents are used in the financing transaction—(1) a promissory note, which is used to evidence the personal obligation of the borrower, and (2) a mortgage, which is used to secure that personal obligation by giving the lender a property interest in the land that allows the sale of the property upon the borrower's default for the purpose of paying off the obligation. Since the borrower continues to own the fee simple title, he or she can give subsequent mortgages, each having priority according to the date given, assuming they are recorded. The borrower can convey the fee simple title by one of four different types of transfers: (1) the new loan transfer, (2) the subject to transfer, (3) the assumption transfer, and (4) the novation transfer.

A mortgage can be terminated successfully through satisfaction of the debt or unsuccessfully through the foreclosure process or the deed in lieu of foreclosure process. The foreclosure process can be judicially supervised or unsupervised, depending on the state law and the terms of the mortgage. The chief alternative security document to the mortgage is the deed of trust, which theoretically conveys title to a third-party trustee. How literally a state interprets this conveyance of title from the borrower to the trustee determines its usefulness to the lender.

Public law, as well as private agreement, controls the nature of the lending transaction. Three federal laws regulate the lender's conduct toward the borrower. The Equal Credit Opportunity Act prohibits lender discrimination against borrowers on the basis of race, color, religion, national origin, sex, marital status, or age. Regulation Z is a disclosure law requiring lenders to disclose the annual cost of credit by use of the annual percentage rate (APR). The Real Estate Settlement Procedures Act (RESPA) is partly a disclosure law, requiring lenders to disclose to borrowers the costs of settling a loan, and partly a regulatory law, prohibiting certain settlement practices that potentially increase closing costs for borrowers.

QUICK QUIZ

1. Our concept of a mortgage came from _____.

    a. France   c. Spain
    b. Italy   d. England

2. States in which a mortgage does not convey title are called _____.

    a. title theory states   c. assumptive states
    b. common property states d. lien theory states

3. The document containing the express promise of a person to pay a specified person a definite sum of money is the _____.

a. promissory note   c. hypothecation

b. mortgage   d. novation

4. The priority of a mortgage is determined by _____.

     a. the time it is signed by borrower

     b. the time it is recorded

     c. the intention of the borrower and lender

     d. the number printed on the mortgage document

5. The type of transfer in which the new buyer accepts responsibility for an existing mortgage on the property being purchased is the _____.

     a. assumption transfer   c. subject to transfer

     b. novation transfer   d. forebearance transfer

6. *Lis pendens* means _____.

7. Pledging property as collateral without giving up possession is called _____.

8. The provision of a mortgage that makes the entire balance due and payable in case the borrower defaults is the _____.

9. An _____ is issued by the lender and shows the current balance of a loan and the rate of interest.

10. The right of the borrower to end a foreclosure proceeding by paying the debt defaulted plus accrued interest any time before foreclosure is completed is called _____.

QUESTIONS AND EXERCISES

1. Find out whether your state is a lien theory or title theory state.

2. Obtain a specimen copy of a promissory note document from a local lender and examine it to see if it contains:

     a. a prepayment penalty   b. a late payment fee

     If it does, what are the terms of the provisions?

3. A property has the following mortgages outstanding:

     1st Mortgage $100,000   2nd Mortgage $20,000

    a. If the holder of the first mortgage forecloses and the public sale produces $110,000, how will the money be apportioned among the lienholders?

    b. What legal recourse do the lienholders not fully satisfied from sale proceeds have available?

4. Do lenders in your area enforce due on sale clauses? How would this affect you as a borrower?

5. If you sell your home and the buyer assumes your mortgage and later defaults, and the foreclosure sale does not produce enough cash to satisfy the lien, who can the lender sue for the deficiency? What if the buyer had purchased the home subject to the existing mortgage?

6. How does a trust deed expedite the settlement of an unsuccessful conclusion to a mortgage?

KEY TERMINOLOGY

acceleration clause
assumption
bond
covenant
deed in lieu of foreclosure
deed of trust
default
deficiency
due on sale clause
Equal Credit Opportunity Act
equity of redemption
estoppel certificate
foreclosure
hypothecation
lien theory

lis pendens
mortgage
novation
prepayment penalty
priority
promissory note
Real Estate Settlement
    Procedures Act (RESPA)
Regulation Z
statutory right of redemption
subject to
subordination agreement
title theory
Truth in Lending Law

IF YOU WANT TO READ MORE

ROBERT N. CORLEY, PETER J. SHEDD, and CHARLES F. FLOYD, *Real Estate and the Law* (New York: Random House, 1982), Chapter 14.

DONALD R. EPLEY and JAMES A. MILLAR, *Basic Real Estate Finance and Investments* (New York: John Wiley & Sons, 1980), Chapters 8 and 9.

ALFRED A. RING and JEROME DASSO, *Real Estate Principles and Practices, 9th ed.* (Englewood Cliffs, N.J.: Prentice-Hall, Inc., 1981), pp. 303–306.

WILLIAM M. SHENKEL, *Modern Real Estate Principles, rev. ed.*

15

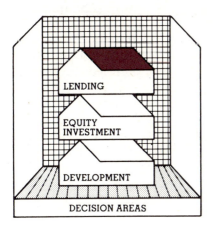

LENDING

EQUITY INVESTMENT

DEVELOPMENT

DECISION AREAS

Real Estate Lending: sources of funds, interest rates, and loan types

PREVIEW

Real estate lending provides much of the money driving the real estate business. The availability and cost of funds affect all real estate decisions and, ultimately, all areas of real estate activity. This chapter introduces real estate lending by considering how money finds its way into real estate, who lends, what types of loans are available, and how interest rates are determined in our economy. Specifically, you will learn:

1. Who invests in real estate loans and why.
2. How money finds its way into real estate loans and how interest rates are determined.
3. What the secondary mortgage market does, what institutions are in it, and how they operate.
4. What a mortgage banker is and does.
5. What types of single family home loans are available.
6. How the income property financing process operates, including what basic types of financing exist.

About two out of every three families in the United States live in homes they own. This does not mean that two out of every three families owe nothing on their homes. Quite the contrary, most homeowners borrowed, and still owe, a great deal of the original purchase price of their homes. Borrowing on real estate has become an accepted way of living. Homeowners do not have a corner on real estate borrowing; a high percentage of the purchase price of most investment properties is also financed with borrowed money.

In 1985 there were more than $1.4 trillion ($1,400,000,000,000) of home mortgage loans outstanding in the United States. In addition, there are more than $560 billion ($560,000,000,000) in outstanding mortgage loans on income-producing real estate such as apartments, office buildings, shopping centers and warehouses. Farm mortgages totaled about $111 billion ($111,000,000,000). For every dollar borrowed on real estate, there must be a lender who is willing to lend it. Who lends this money and why? Where does the money come from in the first place? How are interest rates determined in our economy? What types of loans are available? This chapter starts with an analysis of who lends and how money finds its way into real estate loans. Next, the types of single family home loans are introduced and examined, including the new alternative mortgage financing instruments. The chapter concludes with an overview of the financing of income-producing real estate.

MORTGAGE INVESTORS AND THEIR SPECIALTIES

Money flows into real estate loans primarily from financial institutions, as you can see in Table 15.1. Financial institutions account for about 65 percent of all mortgage debt outstanding. The remainder comes from the federal government, mortgage pools (discussed later), and individuals and others. The financial institutions active in real estate lending are commercial banks, savings and loan associations, mutual savings banks, and life insurance companies. Credit unions have become increasingly active in real estate lending in recent times. Pension funds also have invested in mortgage loans.

Savings and loan associations have more dollars invested in mortgages than any other single type of lender. At present they have over $550 billion of mortgage loans outstanding. This is significantly more than the next largest lender, commercial banks. Mutual savings banks, limited mainly to New England, have a substantial investment in mortgage loans—over $160 billion. Life insurance companies have also passed the $160 billion plateau in mortgage lending.

Other large mortgage investors include the federal government and related agencies such as the Federal National Mortgage Association, or "Fannie Mae," as it is called. Mortgage pools that allow investors to invest in a group, or pool, of mortgages, instead of buying individual mortgages have generated a growing percentage of the money going into single family loans. The final category, individuals and others, accounts for almost $300 billion of outstanding loans.

Table 15.1. Summary of Outstanding Mortgage Debt

Holders	1972 Dollars Outstanding in Millions	1972 % of Total Outstanding	1983 Dollars Outstanding in Millions	1983 % of Total Outstanding	1984 Dollars Outstanding in Millions	1984 % of Total Outstanding
Commercial Banks	301,272	18.3	328,323	18.2	374,186	18.8
Mutual Savings Banks	97,805	5.9	136,054	7.5	160,761	8.1
Savings and Loan Associations	483,614	29.4	494,789	27.5	554,868	27.9
Life Insurance Companies	141,989	8.6	150,999	8.4	157,291	7.9
Government National Mortgage Association	4,227	.3	3,395	.2	2,500	.1
Farmers Home Administration	1,786	.1	2,141	.1	1,800	.1
Federal Housing and Veterans Administrations	5,228	.3	4,894	.3	n.a.	n.a.
Federal National Mortgage Association	71,814	4.4	78,256	4.3	87,940	4.4
Federal Land Banks	50,350	3.1	51,052	2.8	50,679	2.5
Federal Home Loan Mortgage Corporation	4,733	.3	7,632	.4	10,125	.5
Government National Mortgage Association Pools	118,940	7.2	159,850	8.9	179,873	9.0
Federal Home Loan Mortgage Corporation Pools	42,964	2.6	57,895	3.2	70,417	3.5
Farmers Home Administration Pools	40,300	2.5	42,207	2.3	44,514	2.2
Individuals and Others	278,978	17.0	284,955	15.8	294,979	14.8
Totals	1,644,040		1,802,442		1,989,933	

SOURCE: *Federal Reserve Bulletin* and author's calculations.

Table 15.2 makes the lending specialties of different lenders more apparent. For example, savings and loan associations have concentrated in single family (1 – 4 units) lending. Commercial banks, mutual savings banks, government, and individuals and others have also concentrated on single family lending, but to a lesser degree than savings and loan associations. Life insurance companies have specialized in multifamily (more than 4 units) housing and commercial, with the latter category including office buildings, shopping centers, warehouses, hotels and motels, and other income-producing real estate.

There are good reasons for these investment patterns. For savings and loan associations (S&Ls), the basic reason for their involvement in

Table 15.2. Real Estate Lending Activity By Type of Loan 1984

Holder	1 – 4 Family		Multifamily		Commercial		Farm	
	Dollars in Millions	% of Total	Dollars in Millions	% of Total	Dollars in Millions	% of Total	Dollars in Millions	% of Total
Commercial Banks	197,944	15.1	21,142	13.1	144,623	35.6	10,477	9.5
Mutual Savings Bank	114,364	8.7	20,191	12.5	26,176	6.4	31	.1
Savings and Loan Associations	431,132	32.9	48,274	30.0	75,462	18.6	0	0
Life Insurance Companies	14,218	1.1	18,881	11.7	111,692	27.5	12,500	11.3
Government National Mortgage Association	597	.1	1,903	1.2	0	0	0	0
Farmers Home Administration	449	.1	124	.1	652	.2	575	.5
Federal Housing and Veterans Administrations	0	0	0	0	0	0	0	0
Federal National Mortgage Association	82,175	6.3	5,765	3.6	0	0	0	0
Federal Land Banks	2,948	.2	0	0	0	0	47,731	43.1
Federal Home Loan Mortgage Corporation	9,425	.7	700	.4	0	0	0	0
Government National Mortgage Association Pools	175,089	13.3	4,784	3.0	0	0	0	0
Farmers Home Loan Mortgage Corporation Pools	69,817	5.3	600	.4	0	0	0	0
Farmers Home Administration Pools	21,578	1.6	5,835	3.6	7,403	1.8	9,698	8.7
Individuals and Others	192,243	14.7	32,754	20.4	40,131	9.9	29,851	26.9
Totals	1,311,979		160,953		406,139		110,863	

SOURCE: *Federal Reserve Bulletin* and author's calculations.

single family home finance is history. Early savings and loan associations were formed with the express intent of helping people finance homes. Through the years, this mission has stuck with them and has been reinforced by the body regulating most savings and loans in the United States, the **Federal Home Loan Bank Board** (FHLBB). However, S&Ls have recently been given expanded authority to make loans other than real estate mortgage loans.

The Federal Home Loan Bank Board establishes and administers rules and regulations for all federally chartered savings and loan associations and state chartered institutions choosing to become associated with it. You can identify a federally chartered savings and loan by the word "federal" in its name. Institutions regulated by the FHLBB control a high percentage of savings and loan association deposits and loans in the United States.

Commercial banks are regulated by the **Federal Reserve System,** often simply called the "Fed" for short. The Fed has also developed a set of rules and regulations for all federally chartered (national) banks and those state chartered banks who wish to meet its requirements. Fed rules and regulations, while allowing real estate mortgage lending, have tended to discourage extensive mortgage lending by commercial banks. For this reason, and others that will be considered shortly, the commercial banking system, with deposits exceeding those of the savings and loan system, have not invested as heavily in real estate loans as the S&Ls. Federal policies on real estate lending are changing in such a way that savings and loans and commercial banks will compete more directly with one another.

Life insurance companies and mutual savings banks are regulated by the states in which they are chartered. These two institutions operate under different sets of rules within the same state. Such regulations differ substantially from state to state and the investments of the institutions reflect these differences. Generally, life insurance companies and mutual savings banks have been given more investment freedom than commercial banks and savings and loan associations.

HOW DOES MONEY FIND ITS WAY INTO REAL ESTATE LOANS AND HOW ARE INTEREST RATES DETERMINED?

You should think of money as a product—just like food, automobiles, clothing, and homes. And, just like other products, there are times when the demand for money exceeds the supply and, conversely, when supply exceeds demand. You may have observed that when the demand for a product exceeds the supply of that product, its price tends to increase. You can see this same effect in the clothing business where styles change quickly and a particular type of apparel, such as urban cowboy attire, is the "in" thing for a while and then dies out. Usually, this "in" product experiences a sharp increase in price. Designer jeans come to mind as another product that experienced tremendous price increases because of increases in demand. The price of money, called the interest rate, is affected by market supply and demand conditions in exactly the same way.

For some reason, the supply and demand relationships for money are not as apparent to most of us as those for certain other products. Maybe it is easier to see the demand for jeans because the results of that demand are more visible in daily living than the demand for money. It could be that the reason for this obscurity is the complexity of our financial system. You are probably just as confused as many others by the specialized terminology, complicated products, and number of institutions in the financial system. Perhaps another major cause of the inability of many people to be aware of supply and demand considerations for money is that they are not frequently involved with the money markets. This lack of familiarity causes some to feel that the supply of and demand for money, and the interest rate, are controlled by a mysterious "they." "They" made the interest rate go up or "they" made it go down.

The mysterious "they" is never identified, and probably for good reason — it would be difficult to find any individual, body, or group that can *control* interest rates. Certainly, the Fed can *influence* the direction of movement of interest rates, but probably cannot arbitrarily *set* the majority of interest rates in the country. The ability of the Fed to influence interest rates was seen in 1981 and 1982, when its tight money policy kept interest rates at high levels. In the final analysis, interest rates are established by supply and demand factors in the **capital markets.**

Supply and Demand for Money

You should not feel detached from the capital markets — that capital markets involve others, but not you. Each of us affects the supply of and demand for money. Every day you have a demand for money to handle your routine purchases such as lunch, gasoline, and dry cleaning. Business and government have a similar demand for money to handle their daily operations. These are short-term demands, but not all of the demand for money is short-term. You may wish to buy a home someday and chances are good you will have to borrow a substantial portion of the purchase price on a long-term basis. In that particular year, your demand for money will be quite high. Business and government also have years in which their current cash flow is inadequate to cover all of their expenditures, and they too must borrow the difference.

Most of the money you need is supplied by your job and perhaps some investments. When you spend more in a given year than you make, the difference is taken from savings or supplied by lenders and creditors ranging from savings and loan associations to MasterCard and Visa.

Business and government also receive some of the funds they need from income, basically sales revenues and taxes, respectively. But they, too, must be supplied with loans when their outlays exceed their inflows for a given period of time. If in a given period of time, let's say a year, your income exceeds your outlays, that is, your supply of money exceeds your demand for money, you have saved. The income you do not spend is considered to be savings.

The concept of how money finds its way to individuals, businesses, and governments needing it is critical to understanding how the supply and demand for funds are balanced. To understand how this process works, imagine that the economy of the United States has only three major sectors: households, business, and government. Now ask the question, "In a given year will each of these sectors spend more or less than they earn?" Budget balancing attempts aside, government spends more than it receives. Business will generally spend more than they earn. Unless they have adequate reserves from past surpluses or earnings, business and government must borrow the difference between what they take in and whay they spend in a given year.

Within the entire economy, everyone cannot spend more than they earn or have saved, so households, the only remaining sector, must generally spend less than they earn for the system to work. Believe it or not, households do generally spend less than they earn, and represent the ultimate source of much of the money available for lending in our economy. Even so, in a given year, many households will spend more than they earn, as you will do when you purchase a home and must borrow. However, in total, households are net savers.

Flow of Funds

How does money get from households to those needing it? First, many households lend directly by buying corporate and government bonds (bonds are a form of debt as illustrated in Figure 15.1). Households also invest by making deposits in financial institutions. These institutions use these deposits to make loans to those needing money. Included in the financial institutions sector are pension and retirement funds and insurance companies, which also use money contributed by households to lend to others.

The amount of money supplied by households is affected by at least two major factors. First, economic conditions impact the amount of savings available by affecting the ability of households to produce and keep income. For example, high unemployment reduces household income. Also, when the inflation rate exceeds the growth rate in household income, households must spend a higher percentage of their income for essentials and are able to save less. Second, the quantity of savings supplied increases as the interest rate rises. Higher interest rates cause

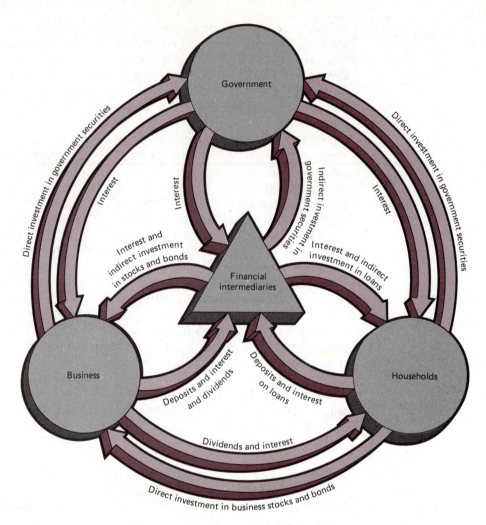

Figure 15.1 Flow of investment funds and returns.

some households to postpone spending money in order to invest and earn the higher rate of interest.

While households provide the capital necessary to satisfy business, government, and households, this capital finds its way into the hands of these different users in a variety of ways. Corporations and government obtain a high percentage of all their capital by direct investment, that is, investors investing directly in them, by buying bonds or stock. When Kodak Corporation needs capital, it will arrange with an investment banking company to issue bonds or stock. Whichever they choose, the instruments will be sold directly to investors. The federal government also sells bonds directly to investors. Business and government will also borrow from financial institutions through lines of credit or by selling bonds to them.

Households, like yours, depend on financial institutions rather than direct investment for capital. Just think about where you and your friends have borrowed money for cars, furniture, and homes. Chances are good that banks, savings and loan associations, and credit unions account for a high percentage of all your loans. Very few of your loans were made directly by individual investors. This dependence on institutions for home financing has subjected borrowers to periods of very high interest rates and, in some cases, virtually no available money.

The reason for this situation can be explained using Figure 15.1. In this figure, the arrows indicate that households invest savings directly and indirectly through financial institutions, in all three sectors. The amounts of money invested directly or indirectly vary with the interest rates. For instance, as interest rates rise, people reduce the flow of funds into financial institutions, or actually withdraw their funds, to invest directly in investments with higher returns. This is to be expected since investors attempt to find those investments paying the highest return while maintaining an acceptable level of risk. While institutions are very safe, they pay a relatively low rate of return. You, for example, are probably quite willing to earn a lower return for the convenience and safety of a savings account as compared to the risk and bother of managing your own direct investments. However, as the difference between the return you earn on your savings account and what you could earn on other investments increases, you will be tempted to invest directly.

This happened in early 1980 and 1981 when the return on treasury bills (13- or 26- week federal government obligations) and money market certificates rose to record levels, causing savings and loan associations to suffer a reduction in deposits. This reduction in deposits, or flow of funds out of financial institutions, is called **disintermediation.** Institutions are unable to raise their interest rates sufficiently to stop disintermediation because of regulations imposed by the Fed and the FHLBB placing a ceiling on the interest rate they may pay on savings accounts. Further, institutions are not financially able to raise interest rates on new savings (passbook) accounts because the higher rate of interest must be paid on existing accounts as well as new ones. To pay all this additional interest, the savings inflows created would often have to be invested at interest rates higher than can be obtained in the market. Thus, even in the absence of regulation, passbook accounts probably could not be made competitive.

To correct this situation, institutions have been allowed to issue certificates of deposit (CDs) paying high rates of interest but requiring a minimum deposit and substantial reductions in interest if the money is withdrawn before a specified time. The interest rate offered on new CDs may change without changing the rate on existing ones. Another attempt to help institutions was the "All Savers Certificate" authorized in the Economic Recovery Tax Act of 1981. All Savers Certificates allowed taxpayers to avoid paying taxes on the interest earned on these accounts. This helped the institutions to some extent. Insurance companies depend on premium income and are not affected to the same extent by people terminating policies because of high interest rates. People are more reluctant to cancel life insurance policies than to take money out of savings. They are affected, however, by the ability of policyholders to borrow at very low rates on the cash value of their policies. Many sharp policyholders borrow at these low rates and invest at the higher market rates.

Because of disintermediation, institutions have not been able to generate enough funds to satisfy the demand for loans in periods of high interest rates. Even though the institutions would have liked to lend, they simply did not have the money. As a result, the purchases of new and existing homes severely decreased during such periods. For example, starts on new homes in 1981 hit the lowest level in decades, about 1.1 million. In the past, the housing markets have experienced downturns while the rest of the economy was booming and borrowing capital. Likewise, when the economy cooled and interest rates fell, the housing markets were quite healthy. For this reason, housing markets have sometimes been called *countercyclical,* and the cycles have been quite pronounced.

To reduce this roller coaster pattern of the housing industry, it was necessary to find new ways to make money available, even at high interest rates, to those making real estate loans. The problem, direct investment in bonds, stocks, and other investments, also became the solution. Why not borrow money in the capital markets at one interest rate and buy mortgages paying a higher rate of interest and thus make a profit on the difference in interest rates? Another possible solution is to simply let investors buy a piece of a package of mortgages made by a loan originator. In either case the originator receives money from the sale of the mortgages with which to make new loans. The concept just described is that of the secondary mortgage market.

THE SECONDARY MORTGAGE MARKET

The market in which mortgage loans are originated is called the **primary mortgage market.** When you borrow money to buy a home you are participating in this market. However, the lender originating the loan and providing the money to you may not want to tie up its funds for the 20 to 30 year term of the loan. If this is so, the lender may sell the mortgage to an investor. These investors are the holders of mortgages in Table 15.1. Existing mortgages are bought and sold in the **secondary mortgage market.** As a borrower, you are not affected by who owns your mortgage since you have signed agreements concerning your interest rate and payments and they cannot be changed by its sale. Thus, none of the terms of your mortgage will be affected by its sale, and any investor buying it must abide by the conditions contained in the original loan documents.

What the investor, or party buying the mortgage, gets is the right to receive all future payments. But what does the originator get? That originator gets the sales price and a servicing contract. Most mortgages are sold at a discount, that is, for less than the face amount. To make a profit on the entire process the lender will sign a servicing contract with the investor to become the servicing agent. Servicing consists of collecting principal and interest payments and forwarding them to the investor, collecting funds from the borrower for the payment of hazard insurance and property taxes on the property, and keeping the lender informed of any problems with delinquent accounts. For this service the servicing agent receives between one-fourth and one-half of 1 percent of the average outstanding loan balance each year, as a fee. For example, for a loan with an average balance of $100,000 and a servicing fee of one-half of 1 percent, the servicing agent will receive $500 ($100,000 × .005 = $500).

You need to become acquainted with three institutions active in secondary mortgage markets. They are the **Federal National Mortgage Association,** the **Government National Mortgage Association,** and **Federal Home Loan Mortgage Corporation.** Obviously, these names alone are enough to confuse almost everyone, so it is not surprising that these institutions have shorter, more popular names. The Federal National Mortgage Association is called *Fannie Mae,* the Government National Mortgage Association is called *Ginnie Mae,* and the Federal Home Loan Mortgage Corporation is commonly called *Freddie Mac* even though the company prefers the name "the Mortgage Corporation."

Fannie Mae

Fannie Mae was started during the Depression as part of President Roosevelt's plan to stimulate the housing industry. At that time it was a government agency designed to create a secondary market for the federally sponsored FHA mortgage program. (Fannie Mae also later became a purchaser of VA loans.) As the federal government became more involved in housing and made it a top priority, Fannie Mae was also given the task of creating a secondary market for special mortgage loan programs, such as low-interest-rate or low-income loans. Trying to act as a secondary market for regular FHA and VA loans and special loan programs created problems for Fannie Mae. Just when it needed funds for performing its secondary market function for regular FHA and VA loans, Fannie Mae also needed funds to perform as a secondary market for special loans.

In 1968, partly as a result of this conflict of interest, Fannie Mae was divided into two entities. Fannie Mae continued as a secondary mortgage market institution for FHA and VA loans and Ginnie Mae was created to handle special mortgage loan programs. Fannie Mae was removed from the Department of Housing and Urban Development (HUD), while Ginnie Mae was added to HUD's list of agencies. In 1970, Fannie Mae started purchasing conventional mortgages in addition to FHA and VA loans.

Who Owns and Runs Fannie Mae? Fannie Mae is considered a semi-private corporation because private citizens own all the company's common stock but the federal government has maintained an interest in and some control over it. Of the 15 directors of the company, ten are elected by shareholders and five are appointed by the President of the United States. Fannie Mae also has a line of credit with the U.S. Treasury if it should be needed. Fannie Mae is a unique combination of private business working in partnership with government.

Fannie Mae has been very active in secondary markets with current investments in mortgage loans exceeding $51 billion. It is the largest single private holder of home mortgages. The income produced by this investment is used to pay for the costs of obtaining money in the capital markets. Fannie Mae relies primarily on long-term bonds to raise capital, although it has issued some short-term notes. It makes a profit by earning more on its investments than it must pay for its funds, a not too startling concept.

Fannie Mae money finds its way to lenders by way of commitments. A **commitment** is a promise by Fannie Mae to purchase a certain dollar amount of loans, over a certain period of time, at a specified price, if asked to do so by the lender. For example, suppose you are a lender and have just obtained a four-month Fannie Mae commitment of $2 million. This means that during the next four months you may sell and deliver to Fannie Mae $2 million worth of mortgages. You are not required to deliver the mortgages to Fannie Mae; the commitment represents an insurance policy guaranteeing that you will be able to sell the mortgages if you wish. To compensate Fannie Mae for standing by to purchase your mortgages you will pay a commitment fee of one-half of 1 percent of the amount of the commitment. For the $2,000,000 commitment you will pay $10,000 (.005 × $2,000,000). You will also pay a delivery fee of one-half of 1 percent of the amount of any loans you deliver.

You likely competed in an auction with other lenders for the Fannie Mae commitment. If you are an approved seller of loans to Fannie Mae, you will periodically receive notices of **Free Market System** auctions. This notice tells you the total amount of money Fannie Mae is making available for commitments and the maximum any one lender can request. On the day of the auction, you will call Fannie Mae, specify the amount of commitment you want, and bid on the basis of the rate of return, or yield, Fannie Mae will receive from the mortgages you would like to sell. At the designated time, the auction will end and Fannie Mae will decide which bids it is accepting. You may also get a commitment, usually for a smaller amount of money, by agreeing to give Fannie Mae the average yield of all loan commitments accepted in that particular auction.

Fannie Mae buys on the basis of yield. That is, Fannie Mae does not care what the interest rate is on a mortgage, just so it provides them with the yield they want. Furthermore, Fannie Mae assumes that all loans it buys will be paid off at the end of the twelfth year. For example, if you had just made a 13 percent loan and now wanted to deliver it to Fannie Mae so that Fannie Mae would get a yield of 13.25 percent, you must sell it for a price such that Fannie Mae would expect a yield of 13.25 percent, assuming the mortgage will be paid off at the end of 12 years. In this case you would be selling the mortgage for a discount, that is, for less than face value. Depending on the movement of interest rates, the lender may be selling mortgages to Fannie Mae at a discount or a premium, although selling them for a discount is more common.

If, as a lender, you had some advance idea of the loss you may incur in selling a mortgage, you could possibly pass this loss on to borrowers. Actually, if you knew you had to sell loans to Fannie Mae at prices giving Fannie Mae a 13.25 percent yield and want to break even on the origination and sale, you have three options: make loans at 13.25 percent and sell them at face value; make loans at over 13.25 percent and sell them for a premium; or make loans at less than 13.25 percent and sell them for a discount. Given a choice, you would choose to make loans at over 13.25 percent and sell them for a premium. However, competition in local financial markets will usually force you to choose one of the other options. Usually the option chosen is to make loans at less than 13.25 percent and sell them at a discount, charging fees, called discount points, to make up your loss. Each *discount point* is one percent of the original loan amount.

As a lender you are indifferent about whether you sell loans to Fannie Mae at face value or selling them to Fannie Mae at a loss and charging borrowers points on the front end. You break even in either case and obtain a profitable servicing contract that authorizes you to collect payments, handle escrow accounts for property taxes and hazard insurance, and forward payments to lenders in return for receiving a servicing fee ranging from one-fourth to one-half of one percent of the average outstanding balance each year.

Ginnie Mae

The Government National Mortgage Association (Ginnie Mae) was created in 1968 as part of HUD. One task given Ginnie Mae was the "special assistance function'' that had previously belonged to Fannie Mae. Ginnie Mae is reponsible for creating a secondary mortgage market for those special mortgage loan programs created by the President or Congress. Special assistance programs may serve two purposes. First, they may seek to provide mortgage loans for a specified segment of the economy, such as those with lower incomes. Second, they may be used to provide mortgage funds when the supply of mortgage money is very limited, such as in the credit crunch of 1974–1975.

Another task, or power, given Ginnie Mae was that of guaranteeing the payment of principal and interest on securities having FHA and VA mortgages as collateral. These securities are commonly called mortgage-backed securities, Ginnie Maes, or mortgage pools. They have become very popular as evidenced by Table 15.1 illustrating the rapid growth in the dollar value of such securities outstanding. Mortgage-backed securities can be easily purchased through ordinary securities dealers, the same people you would call to buy and sell stocks and bonds. Their popularity is good news for real estate finance since they provide another method for attracting direct investment in real estate mortgages and reducing the dependence on deposits in financial institutions.

Mortgage-backed securities are easy to understand in principle. An originator, now called the *issuer,* makes a number of FHA and VA loans and places them into a pool. This lender then makes application to Ginnie Mae outlining the mortgages in the pool, the intent to issue mortgage-backed securities, and the details of that issue. Ginnie Mae then analyzes the pool and will decide whether to issue a guarantee, for which it charges a fee. Ginnie Mae is guaranteeing that investors will not lose money due to the failure of a borrower to make principal and interest payments. The securities are then sold by investment banking and brokerage firms to investors. The issuer services the mortgages for a fee and makes payments to the investors based on the percentage of the pool each investor owns. These securities are sometimes called **pass-through securities** because the issuer simply passes whatever principal and interest is received through to the investors.

Freddie Mac

The Federal Home Loan Mortgage Corporation, alias Freddie Mac, is owned by and under the direction of the Federal Home Loan Bank Board. Freddie Mac purchases FHA, VA, and conventional mortgages from savings and loan associations, mutual savings banks, and commercial banks. Freddie Mac will purchase whole loans on a competitive and non-competitive bid basis, similar to Fannie Mae. Also, Freddie Mac will purchase **participations,** or partial interests, in mortgage loans. The originating institution retains a percentage interest and services the mortgages.

Mortgage Insurance — The Lubricant of Secondary Mortgage Markets

Federal Housing Administration The secondary mortgage market, as you now know it, could not exist if investors did not have faith in the quality of the loans they purchased. You can imagine the problems faced by an investor purchasing many mortgages originated by many different lenders throughout the country in assessing mortgage quality. However, a program started by the federal government provided the answer to the question of mortgage loan quality. That program was the Federal Housing Administration (FHA) mortgage insurance program started in 1934 as part of the New Deal. An investor in an FHA insured mortgage is protected against loss in case of borrower default and foreclosure. Essentially, in case of a default, FHA would either pay off the remaining balance plus accrued interest and take over the mortgage or ask the lender to foreclose and pay any deficiency resulting from the sale of the property. FHA insured loans are low-risk investments and quite attractive to investors.

FHA made tremendous contributions to financing single family homes. First is the obvious contribution of making mortgage investment attractive to investors and, thereby, increasing the flow of funds into mortgage loans. Next, since FHA had to administer a program all over the nation, they had to develop criteria of acceptance for borrowers and properties. These criteria helped standardize mortgage loan evaluation nationwide. Next, FHA changed the thinking about mortgage lending by instituting high-ratio, amortizing mortgage loans. Prior to FHA, the typical borrower could only borrow 50 to 75 percent of a home's purchase price on an interest-only basis for ten to 15 years, and then pay the mortgage off in one large payment called a balloon payment. By insuring mortgage loans that represented a higher ratio of the purchase price, and allowing the borrower to pay the loan off over 20 to 30 years, FHA made housing affordable to a larger segment of the population. FHA has made a permanent mark on home financing.

Over the years the FHA program has been expanded into a number of new mortgage insurance programs covering loans for special groups, such as those with low incomes, and other than fixed-rate, fixed-payment mortgages. However, the basic FHA insurance program, called the FHA 203(b) program, is still in effect. FHA has certain rules that must be followed. For instance, there is a maximum loan amount they will insure. Currently, the maximum single family home loan FHA will insure is $82,500, except in certain high cost housing markets where it is greater. FHA also prohibits the borrower from paying discount points, which means that the seller usually must pay them. The borrower is allowed to, and usually does, pay any other loan costs. All FHA loans have no prepayment penalties and are assumable.

Veterans Administration During World War II a program was initiated that provided mortgage guarantees for qualified veterans. This program is a *guarantee program,* rather than an insurance program, because the veteran does not pay premiums for the mortgage protection. It is part of their veterans' benefit package, administered by the Veterans Administration (VA). The VA loan program has been continued and is available for a wide range of individuals who have served in the armed forces. Qualified veterans are given an *entitlement,* which is the maximum amount the VA will pay a lender if the veteran defaults on the mortgage. Many VA loans are for 100 percent of the purchase price or an appraiser's estimate of value. The entitlement has been increased from time to time to allow for increases in housing costs. Presently, the maximum entitlement is $27,500. Since many lenders consider a real estate loan of 75 percent of the value of the real estate a very safe one, they look to this $27,500 guarantee as protection for the remaining 25 percent of the loan. The maximum 100 percent loan for which the $27,500 guarantee will provide protection on this remaining 25 percent is $110,000. For this reason, even though the VA has established no maximum VA loan amount, the effective limit is usually $110,000. To be eligible for a VA loan, the veteran must be certified by the VA. Veterans Administration loans are assumable by anyone, whether a veteran or not.

Private Mortgage Insurance In 1957, the Mortgage Guaranty Insurance Corporation offered the first private mortgage insurance (PMI) plan. Several other companies have since entered the PMI business. The PMI concept is the same of FHA insurance considered above—it provides coverage for possible losses on a default. PMI covers only the top 20 to 25 percent of the loan that lenders consider to be at risk. Usually, the lender will foreclose and the insurance company will cover any loss up to the maximum amount specified in the policy. On fixed-rate mortgages, borrowers usually pay a PMI fee at closing of about 1 percent of the loan amount and about one-fourth of 1 percent of the outstanding loan balance each year thereafter. Fees are higher for adjustable rate mortgages. Private insurance companies have established standards for borrowers and properties to be insured.

Summary Overview of Mortgage Markets

Figure 15.2 provides a summary of the mortgage markets you have been studying. At the bottom of the figure are the borrowers who sign notes and mortgages given to institutions and others originating lending arrangements. In return, the borrowers receive money. All of this activity takes place in primary mortgage markets. If the originator chooses to hold the mortgage and collect the payments until it is paid off, the secondary mortgage market does not come into play. However, if the originator chooses to sell the mortgage, that sale will take place in the second-

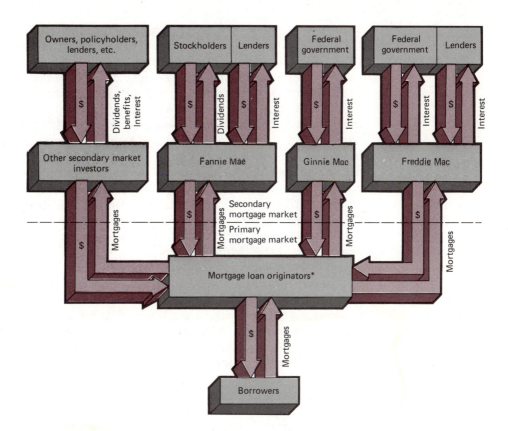

Figure 15.2
Overview of mortgage markets.

ary mortgage market. The originator will transfer the right to receive the principal and interest payments to the investor in return for a cash payment. Originators will also often service the mortgage for the investor for an agreed-upon fee. From the payments it receives from the borrower, the investor will make payments to its owners, those who have lent them money, and anyone else who may receive benefits from the income generated by the mortgages, such as insurance policyholders.

MORTGAGE BANKING

Think for just a moment and then name as many mortgage banking firms in your town as you can. If you have not bought a home or been associated with the real estate business in some way, you may have a great deal of difficulty thinking of a single one. While not particularly well known to the public, **mortgage bankers** have originated, and continue to originate, a significant percentage of all real estate loans. Mortgage bankers are real estate financing specialists. They arrange financing on single family homes and investment properties, although their activities in these two types of lending differ significantly. Because of these differences in activities, some firms specialize in either single family or investment property lending.

Mortgage banking firms are not "banks" in the sense of accepting deposits and then investing these funds in loans and other assets. Thus, they do not have large amounts of money with which to make long-term investments in mortgages. In single family lending, mortgage bankers borrow money and make mortgage loans with the intent of selling these mortgages in the secondary mortgage market to recover their funds. In income property lending, mortgage bankers usually try to match up borrowers and lenders, rather than lending their own funds. In either situation, they are mortgage originators, not long-term investors. Their activities in single family lending are discussed here in a little more detail, while their activities in income property lending are considered again later in the chapter.

The mortgage banker's activities in single family lending include originating, warehousing, and servicing loans. Mortgage bankers originate loans by taking applications, deciding whether the loan should be made, and then actually lending the money. Once an application is approved, the mortgage banker uses a line of credit at a commercial bank to borrow the loan amount. The mortgage that is about to be made is pledged as security for the bank loan. The mortgage loan is then closed, with the mortgage banker receiving a note and mortgage, and the borrower receiving the loan proceeds.

From the time the loan is closed until it is sold to an investor, the mortgage banker warehouses the loan. **Warehousing,** then, refers to the period during which the mortgage banker owns the mortgage. During this period, the mortgage banker is receiving payments from the borrower, but is also having to pay interest to the commercial bank on the money borrowed to make the real estate loan. This bank loan is a short-term loan, which means the mortgage banker must either have enough cash to pay it off or be able to sell the mortgage to an investor and use the proceeds to pay the bank. If an advance commitment has been obtained, say from Fannie Mae or a life insurance company, the mortgage banker may simply sell the mortgage to that investor. However, if an advance commitment does not exist, the mortgage banker will seek an investor to buy the mortgage, or place it in a pool that will serve as the basis for issuing mortgage-backed securities.

When mortgages are sold, the mortgage banker usually executes a servicing agreement with the investor. Servicing involves collecting the monthly payments, taking care of problems with delinquencies, and making sure that the property is insured and property taxes are paid and that principal and interest payments are forwarded to the investor. Monthly mortgage payments include not only principal and interest payments, but also one-twelfth of the annual property insurance premium and property taxes. The mortgage banker places the insurance and property tax funds into an escrow account and pays these items when they come due. For servicing the mortgage, mortgage bankers receive from one-fourth to one-half of 1 percent of the total annual payments collected.

Because of economies of scale, mortgage bankers are able to make a profit on loan servicing. As a matter of fact, mortgage banking firms depend on servicing for the continuing, predictable portion of their income. This is so because originating loans is not always profitable, nor is the level of such activity predictable. The origination fee of about one percent of the loan amount—which is supposed to cover the costs of handling all the paper work, analyzing the property and borrower, and closing the loan—does not always produce a profit. Thus, servicing is the mainstay of mortgage banking profitability.

TYPES OF SINGLE FAMILY LOANS

Single family residential lending has never offered more diversity in the types of mortgage instruments available than at present. If you have had any contact with real estate lending, you probably encountered loan plans that sounded like alphabet soup—GRMs, ARMs, AMLs, SAMs, and so on. Much of this diversity is of recent vintage. Prior to 1979, a homebuyer had essentially one financing option, the fixed-rate, fixed-payment, amortizing loan. Fixed rate and fixed payments meant that the interest rate and payments did not change over the life of the loan. There was some variety with respect to who insured or guaranteed the loan, but real estate loans were about as uniform as Model–Ts. Of course, there were second mortgages and mortgages that also covered personal property, but only one payment plan was regularly offered. In this section of the chapter, the various types of loans are categorized in several ways, corresponding to how you will likely hear them described. As you read this section, please keep in mind that tremendous changes are still occurring and that loans listed here may have been changed or modified and new loan types introduced.

Type of Mortgage Insurance or Guarantee

Loans are often classified on the basis of whether they are insured by FHA, guaranteed by VA, or made under some other arrangement. Loans insured by FHA or guaranteed by VA are called **FHA** and **VA loans,** respectively. All other loans, including those involving PMI, are commonly called **conventional loans.**

Type of Lien

Mortgages are often classified by the priority of the lien associated with them. A first mortgage refers to a first lien, a second mortgage to a second lien, and so on. While all of this is quite clear, there is one type of junior mortgage, usually a second mortgage, that often causes confusion. The source of the confusion is the wraparound mortgage. To understand a wraparound mortgage, it is useful to consider the actions of the lender and borrower. First, the lender actually disburses a specified amount of new money to the borrower and agrees to make the payments on an existing first mortgage. For instance, a lender may agree to lend $10,000 in new money and make the payments on an existing $40,000, 10 percent first mortgage. In turn, the borrower agrees to sign a note for the total of the new money and the existing first mortgage at an interest rate higher than the 10 percent rate on the first mortgage. Thus, a **wraparound mortgage** may be defined as a junior mortgage in which the lender agrees to lend new funds and make payments on an existing senior mortgage in return for the borrower paying a rate of interest on the total indebtedness that is greater than the interest rate on the senior mortgage.

In our example, if the rate on the new note is 13 percent, then the lender receives debt service payments calculated at that rate on the entire $50,000, makes payments on the $40,000, 10 percent mortgage, and pockets the difference. The lender earns 13 percent interest on the $10,000 of new money *plus* 3 percent on the $40,000 first mortgage. Thus, the lender's yield on the $10,000 actually invested is substantially above the stated 13 percent interest rate. The same yield could have been achieved by simply charging the higher interest rate on the $10,000 of new money. However, some borrowers may object to borrowing at those rates, even though they know that they are still paying that rate in a wraparound mortgage.

Type and Quantity of Property

A mortgage loan that covers real and personal property is called a **package mortgage.** A package mortgage may be used to finance a home that includes appliances and other personal property the lender is willing to include in calculating the amount he or she is willing to lend. A **blanket mortgage** is one secured by two or more parcels of real property. For example, you may want to purchase a farm a mile from Blackacre and obtain a new mortgage on both of them. In this case you will pledge both properties as security for a single blanket mortgage.

Alternative Mortgage Instruments

Perhaps the most widely used method of classifying mortgages today is the alternative mortgage instrument. These are called alternatives because they are different from the standard fixed-rate, fixed-payment mortgage that has already been discussed. Alternative mortgages usually have names that attempt to convey how they differ from the fixed-rate, fixed-payment mortgage. For example, the **graduated-pay-**

ment mortgage involves payments that increase over time. The **adjustable-rate mortgage** involves an interest rate that can change from time to time, and so on. The "Inside Real Estate" feature provides important detail on 12 types of mortgages classified as alternative mortgage instruments.

Seller Financing

The increase in housing prices of the 1960s and 1970s and the high interest rates of the early 1980s created a situation that is likely to continue for some time. That situation is the extensive involvement of the seller in home finance. For many buyers, the only way they can afford a home is for the seller to help them reduce the overall interest rate they must pay and the equity they must put into a home by financing all or a part of the purchase price. These financing arrangements take several forms and range from financing the entire purchase to only a small part of it. They are made possible to a large extent by the very growth in value and equity that create the need for such arrangements.

Seller financing arrangements range from lease-purchase contracts to regular second mortgages. The *lease-purchase* method of financing allows the potential buyer to live in the home for some period of time and then decide whether to purchase the home or not at either a previously agreed-upon price or at a price determined by a method previously specified. Other methods used include the contract for deed and the second mortgage. When the seller lends the buyer part of the purchase price under a mortgage arrangement, regardless of the priority of that mortgage, the mortgage is called a **purchase money mortgage.** By combining a second mortgage, contract for deed, or wraparound mortgage with the assumption of an existing mortgage with a rate below current market rates, a buyer and seller can create a financing package that is much more attractive than financing the property completely with a new mortgage. These instruments are often set up such that payments are computed on a 15- to 30-year term with the entire balance coming due in the form of a balloon payment in only one to five years. Such balloon payments often create problems for the buyer and, subsequently, the lender.

Interest Rate Buydowns

Many lenders now allow buyers and sellers to reduce the interest rate on a mortgage by paying fees when the loan is originated, an arrangement called a buydown. Usually the lower interest rate only applies to the first one to five years of the mortgage. The amount that must be paid the lender for the buydown is calculated using the time value of money concepts as illustrated in Chapter 13.

INSIDE REAL ESTATE

ALTERNATIVE MORTGAGE INSTRUMENTS (AMIs)

The long-term, fixed-rate mortgage has for many years been the staple of the mortgage lending industry. Accelerating interest rates and volatile economic conditions, however, have brought about radical changes in mortgage lending practices. Buyers, faced with prohibitive mortgage payments, and lenders, faced with rising costs of funds and deteriorating earnings, are moving beyond the standard fixed-rate mortgage into various alternative mortgage instruments (AMIs). A primary objective of many AMIs is to increase the supply of loanable funds by transferring from the lender to the borrower some of the risks associated with a volatile economy.

The Federal Home Loan Bank Board (FHLBB), recognizing the financial plight of lenders, has been instrumental in developing and implementing many of these innovative mortgage instruments. While the FHLBB governs the lending practices of federally chartered savings and loan associations, the Comptroller of the Currency and the National Credit Union Administration also have taken steps to provide increased lending flexibility to nationally chartered commercial banks and federally chartered credit unions. This report provides a synopis of the principal types of AMIs presently in use and their regulatory restrictions.

Shared Appreciation Mortgage (SAM)

A shared appreciation mortgage, by way of a below-market fixed interest rate, allows lower monthly payments than a standard mortgage. Most SAMs are amortized over a range of 25 to 40 years, although the specified term of the loan is for a shorter duration (e.g., 10 years). In exchange for this below-market rate, the borrower shares with the lender an agreed-upon percentage of the secured property's net appreciation from the time of the loan's origination to the maturity or termination of the loan. The lender's share, referred to as contingent interest, is an amount sufficient to provide the lender an effective yield at least equivalent to that of a mortgage bearing a market rate of interest. The amount the lender receives is calculated from an appraisal made at the time of loan maturity or prepayment, or the home's price at the time of resale, whichever occurs first. If the property is sold during the loan term, or if the loan is prepaid, the borrower must pay the contingent interest in a lump sum. In the event the property is not sold by the end of the term, the lender usually guarantees to refinance the outstanding loan balance along with the contingent interest.

The SAM is receiving increased attention from some lenders, although federal lending institutions are not yet authorized to make this type of loan. The FHLBB, in 1980, issued proposed regulations for such loans, but final approval has been slow in coming.

Because the amount of appreciation is unknown at the time of loan origination, a SAM involves risk for both borrower and lender. If a home appreciates substantially and the borrower is faced with refinancing at the end of the specified term, the increased loan amount (the unpaid contingent interest is now included) and, in all probability, a higher interest rate (now the market rate), may make prohibitive the cost of continuing to own the property. On the other hand, if housing prices increase slowly or remain stable, lenders may receive less than their desired yields.

Deferred Payment Mortgage (DPM)

A deferred payment mortgage is a long-term, fixed-rate mortgage with monthly payments reduced by an arrangement similar to that of a SAM. Under a DPM, a borrower defers payment of an agreed-upon percentage of the total loan amount. The period of deferment may be, for example, ten years. At the end of this period, or upon sale of the secured property, the deferred portion of the loan, plus accrued interest, is due. In this respect, a DPM operates similarly to a balloon payment mortgage; however, if the borrower desires, the lender would be obliged to refinance the outstanding loan balance and the amount deferred.

To illustrate, suppose that a DPM lender makes an $80,000 loan, 20 percent of which is deferred. The borrower's payment would be based on a $64,000 loan amortized over 30 years. At the end of the deferral period, or resale of the property, the deferred $16,000, plus interest, would be due. The borrower then could pay the deferred payment in a lump sum, or refinance the entire outstanding obligation.

Shared Equity Purchase (SEP)

Shared equity purchase plans provide funds for home buyers who are unable to accumulate down payments sufficient to keep their monthly mortgage payments affordable. Whereas several variations of shared equity, or equity participation, loans exist, the shared equity concept is essentially a partnership or joint venture between a buyer and a lender or an investor. The investor may be an individual, corporation, pension fund, etc. Funding for the mortgage may be provided by the investor or by a conventional lender.

A substantial portion, usually greater than 50 percent, of the buyer's down payment is provided by an investor; the investor then holds an equity share in the property equal to an agreed-upon percentage. The investor also pays a set percentage of the loan's closing costs and mortgage expenses, including principal, interest, taxes, and insurance. The buyer provides the remaining portion of the down payment and mortgage expenses. In addition to being a part-owner of the house the buyer is also a tenant, and, in effect, rents the investor's share.

As an illustration, assume that a buyer locates an investor willing to provide 75 percent of the total down payment and 50 percent of the closing costs. The investor further agrees to pay half of the monthly expenses for mortgage, taxes and insurance, and takes title as a 50 percent tenant in common with the new owner. The owner makes monthly payments to the investor sufficient to cover the owner's half of the monthly expenses, plus a payment, equivalent to rent, for use of the investor's share of the home. This rental payment covers the investor's liability for principal, interest, taxes and insurance, plus an additional amount to provide a small return on the investor's capital. The homeowner may remain the investor's partner for any agreed-upon time period, but whenever the home is sold the investor will receive 50 percent of the accumulated equity.

Adjustable Rate Mortgage (ARM)

The adjustable rate mortgage, also known as an adjustable mortgage loan, is becoming the predominant mortgage lending instrument in use today. Regulations have recently been issued which authorize savings and loan associations, commercial banks, and credit unions to make ARMs. FHLBB adjustable rate mortgage regulations, in effect, liberalize prior variable rate and renegotiable rate mortgage regulations.

An ARM permits an upward or downward adjustment of the loan's interest rate, based upon a change in an agreed-upon interest rate index. Rate adjustments may be implemented through changes in the payment amount, in the outstanding loan balance, in the term of the loan, or through combined changes in these variables. Savings and loan associations and credit unions have greater freedom in structuring ARMs than do banks. Whereas banks may peg rate adjustments to one of three approved indices, savings and loan associations and credit unions may choose any index that is beyond their control and that is easily verifiable by the borrower. Savings and loan associations and credit unions may adjust the interest rate as often as monthly, and there are no restrictions on the amount by which the rate may be adjusted up or down at any one time. Banks may adjust the rate only at regular intervals of not less than six months; the maximum change may not exceed 1 percentage point for each six-month period between rate adjustments, and a single rate adjustment may never exceed 5 percentage points. No restrictions exist for any lenders on the amount by which the rate may be adjusted up or down over the life of the loan, and rate decreases are mandatory if the index declines.

Interest rate adjustments on ARMs may not always be reflected in a payment change. All lenders are able to structure an ARM so that a change in the loan's outstanding balance and/or term may prevent, or minimize, an increased payment.

Renegotiable Rate Mortgage (RRM)

The renegotiable rate mortgage, also known as a rollover mortgage, originated in Canada, and in 1980 the FHLBB authorized its use in the United States. An RRM essentially is a series of short-term loans secured by a long-term mortgage. Each short-term loan is issued for a term of three, four, or five years, and is automatically renewable over the life of the mortgage, with adjustments in the interest rate at each renewal. Interest rate adjustments are made in accordance with movements of the FHLBB's index of the national average contract interest rate on the purchase of previously occupied homes. The maximum rate increase or decrease allowed at any renewal is 0.5 percent multiplied by the number of years of the loan term. The maximum increase or decrease over the life of the mortgage, however, is limited to 5 percentage points, allowing the interest rate to vary over a 10 percentage point spread.

Because an RRM is a series of short-term loans, FHLBB regulations prohibit lenders from assessing any fees or charges in connection with the regular renewals, and all conditions of the loan at the time of renewal, other than the interest rate, must be the same as those contained in the original loan. (FHLBB adjustable rate mortgage regulations now replace RRM regulations, although RRM regulations apply to outstanding loans.)

Variable Rate Mortgage (VRM)

A variable rate mortgage is a long-term mortgage on which the interest rate is adjusted to reflect a lender's cost of loanable funds. VRMs have been used extensively in California since 1975, and in 1979 the FHLBB authorized their use by savings and loan associations nationwide.

According to FHLBB regulations, interest rate adjustments may not be made more than once a year; adjustment periods may exceed one year provided that they are multiples of 12 months. The maximum change for any adjustment period is 0.5 percent per year with a maximum net increase of 2.5 percent over the life of the loan. Rate adjustments must reflect the movement of the FHLBB's index of the national cost of funds to federally insured savings institutions.

Interest rate decreases are mandatory if the index declines, although increases are at the lender's option. Upon notification of a rate adjustment, the borrower has the option of changing the payment amount to reflect the new rate or of keeping the payment constant and extending the loan term up to a maximum of one-third of the original term. (FHLBB adjustable rate mortgage regulations now replace VRM regulations, although VRM regulations apply to outstanding loans.)

Graduated Payment Mortgage (GPM)

A graduated payment mortgage is a long-term, fixed-rate mortgage, the payments on which are scaled to match the income expectations of a borrower. Authorized in 1978, the GPM was the FHLBB's initial alternative mortgage instrument, although the FHA Section 245 program is the most widely used GPM.

Monthly payments during the early years of a GPM are lower than for a standard mortgage, and rise in later years to a level sufficient to fully amortize the loan over the remaining term. Initial payments may be inadequate to cover the interest due, thus producing negative amortization and an increased outstanding loan balance.

Under the FHA 245 GPM program, five different payment plans are available with graduation periods of either five or ten years. If a borrower chooses a five-year graduation period, his payments can increase by 2.5, 5.0, or 7.5 percent per year during this period; with a ten-year graduation period, payments can increase by 2 or 3 percent per year. After the initial graduation period, payments remain constant for the remaining term of the loan.

FHLBB regulations allow greater flexibility in the selection of graduation periods and payment increases. Annual increases, however, are limited to a maximum of 7.5 percent for a GPM with a

graduation period of five or fewer years, and decline to a maximum of 3 percent for a GPM with a ten-year graduation period. Borrowers have the option of converting GPMs to other mortgage instruments at any time.

Graduated Payment Adjustable Mortgage (GPAM)

A graduated payment adjustable mortgage, as authorized by the FHLBB, combines the graduated payment feature of a GPM and the adjustable interest rate feature of an ARM. Not only does the GPAM provide borrowers with a mortgage instrument that allows their payments to rise as their incomes rise, but it also enables lenders to maintain their mortgage portfolios near current market rates of interest.

A GPAM, like a GPM, initially has lower monthly payments than either a standard mortgage or an ARM. The lender gradually increases the payment amount during the initial term of the loan, not to exceed ten years, to an amount sufficient to fully amortize the loan over the remaining term. In contrast to a GPM, there are no restrictions on the rate of increase in the payment amount during the graduation period. In addition, the interest rate on a GPAM may be adjusted up or down based upon movement of an agreed-upon interest rate index. In this respect, a GPAM operates the same as an ARM: interest rate adjustments may be made as often as monthly, and may be implemented through changes in the payment amount, in the outstanding loan balance, in the term of the loan, or by any combination of these variables.

Pledged Account Mortgage (PAM)

A pledged account mortgage, or Flexible Loan Insurance Program (FLIP) as it is also known, is a variation of a fixed-rate graduated payment mortgage, providing a first-time buyer with lower initial payments. FHLBB regulations permit limited use of PAMs.

Under a PAM, a lender establishes an interest-bearing savings account using all, or a substantial portion, of the borrower's down payment. This account is pledged as additional security for the loan and serves to supplement loan payments during the initial years of the loan. The borrower's initial payments are lower than required to fully amortize the loan. Each month, however, the lender withdraws from the account an amount that, when added to the borrower's payment, equals the loan's required payment. The borrower's share of the total payment gradually increases, while the supplemental payment from the account decreases. The life of the pledged account is usually three to five years, after which time the full payment is paid by the borrower.

Reverse Annuity Mortgage (RAM)

Reverse annuity mortgages allow homeowners to use their home's equity as supplemental income while still owing and living in the property. The intent is to assist older homeowners on fixed incomes to meet rising costs of living.

FHLBB regulations allow lenders to make loans to homeowners borrowing against the equity in their homes. A lender makes periodic payments in a fixed amount to a homeowner, or purchases shares of an annuity from an insurance company, using a RAM on the home as security. Thus, cash inflows and outflows under a RAM are the reverse of those under a standard mortgage. The owner agrees to repay the amount loaned, plus interest, and the loan becomes due on either a specific date, a specific event such as sale of the property, or the death of the homeowner. A RAM may have an adjustable interest rate, although rate adjustments must comply

with the FHLBB's adjustable-rate mortgage provisions.

Price Level Adjusted Mortgage (PLAM)

A price level adjusted mortgage is a long-term, fixed-rate mortgage on which the outstanding loan balance, rather than interest rate, is variable. At the end of each year the loan balance is adjusted by an inflation factor. This factor may be the percentage change in a selected price index, such as the consumer price index. The loan's interest rate is a real rate of interest; i.e., a rate that would exist if there were no inflation. In this respect, the interest rate on a PLAM is lower than on a standard mortgage because the lender does not need to charge an inflation premium. Instead, the lender annually accounts for the actual level of inflation by adjusting the loan balance. Monthly payments are based on the real rate of interest and the adjusted outstanding loan balance.

Initial payments on a PLAM are lower than on a standard mortgage, and increase at a rate equal to the increase in the general level of prices. Thus, a PLAM may involve substantial risk if the borrower's income fails to keep pace with inflation. Furthermore, the loan may not be fully secured if the appreciation rate of the secured property is less than the general rate of inflation.

Growing Equity Mortgage (GEM)

A growing equity mortgage is a long-term, fixed-rate mortgage, payments on which are tied to a measure of a borrower's ability to pay. The rate of interest on a GEM is usually several percentage points below the current market rate. The unique features of a GEM are its varying payments and the capability to be completely paid off in a fraction of the original loan term.

Monthly payments are adjusted

annually to reflect 75 percent of the rate of change in a national index of per capital disposable personal income, an index which reflects the average borrower's ability to meet rising mortgage payments. The annual adjustment factor is applied to the previous year's monthly payment to determine the payments for the coming 12 months. The increase above the loan's initial payment goes entirely to repay principal. Thus the lender benefits from an increasing cash flow, and the borrower quickly accumulates equity in his property, thereby shortening the life of the loan.

SOURCE: Robert E. Spoerl, *KRERC Real Estate Comments*, Kentucky Real Estate Research Center, University of Kentucky, April 1982, no. 9, pp. 1–4.

FINANCING INCOME PRODUCING REAL ESTATE

With respect to debt financing, income-producing real estate (called commercial or income properties) and single family residences have at least one thing in common — they both require a great deal of it. It is easy to understand why families borrow to purchase a home, but it is not quite so apparent why seemingly wealthy investors would need or want to borrow large sums of money to build or invest in income-producing real estate. In reality not all real estate investors are wealthy, but even those that are may not have the ready cash necessary for large real estate investments or may simply prefer to play the game with someone else's money.

Most of the income properties you see in your town were financed, at least in part, with borrowed money. Presently, over $560 billion of mortgage debt is outstanding on income-producing properties. It is not unusual for 75 to 80 percent of the purchase price of income-producing real estate to be borrowed. This means that the "owners," or equity investors, usually have contributed only a relatively small percentage of the total purchase price. Developers are able to borrow even a higher percentage of the cost of erecting improvements. It is fair to say that developers and equity investors are very sensitive to, even dependent on, the availability and cost of debt financing for their existence. When debt financing is available at reasonable interest rates, development and equity investment occur; when it is not available, they do not.

Types of Income Property Financing

Long-term mortgages are called *permanent loans* or *permanent financing*. Such financing satisfies only one of a number of income property financing situations (Figure 15.3). If you wanted to purchase an existing parcel of improved real estate, it is probably the only debt financing you would need. However, since permanent financing involves improved real estate, if you wanted to erect new improvements, you would likely need financing to pay for the land and constructing the improvement.

Figure 15.3
Income property financing.

Every development starts from one of two points: either a site looking for an idea or an idea looking for a site. Suppose that you think that a site close to the downtown area is suitable for a luxury high-rise apartment complex. If your preliminary research indicates this project may be feasible, then your first problem is controlling the site; following this you must worry about permanent and construction financing.

Land Financing — Controlling the Site

Institutional lenders are hesitant to lend on most unimproved real estate because land prices are quite volatile and it generally produces little or no rental income. Because of this reluctance of institutions to become involved with the risky area of land financing, sellers are forced to provide much of the financing for buyers. The techniques used include loans, options, and leases.

Purchase with Seller Financing One alternative is to simply approach the owner and try to purchase the site. This may not be too difficult if the owner has already decided to sell, but may be more of a problem if that is not the case. As the developer, you do not want to tie up a great deal of the cash in the land at the very start of the project. So if the owner is willing to sell, you will try to get the owner to accept a minimum down payment and allow you to pay off the balance over time. Often, to minimize your cash outlays you will try to get the owner to accept payments of interest only for some period of time, usually until the project can be completed and sold.

Options Often you have not conducted all the necessary research before you talk with the landowner. You need time to complete estimates of costs, rents, and other critical factors before you make a final decision about whether to continue with the project. In this case, if the landowner is willing, you may choose to purchase an option on the site. An **option** gives you the exclusive right to purchase the property at an agreed-upon price for a specified period of time. For example, you may negotiate an option that allows you to purchase the property for $500,000 anytime within the next 180 days. What you will pay for this option is purely a matter of negotiation, but generally if the option is exercised (you buy the land), the option price is applied to purchase price. If you do not exercise the option you generally lose the entire option amount at the end of the option period.

Ground Leases If the owner does not want to sell, then you may be able to persuade him or her to lease the site to you for an extremely long period of time, say for a minimum of 30 years. It is not uncommon for landowners in places with very high land values, such as Waikiki Beach in Honolulu and Manhattan in New York to be reluctant to sell. Even in areas where land values are not so high, some landowners simply do not want to sell their land. Not wanting to sell land, but needing and wanting income from it, often leads landowners to lease their land to others. Lenders are willing to make permanent loans for improvements on leased property if the lease term exceeds the term of the loan by a minimum of about 20 percent. For example, 25-year permanent financing may be available on land leased for 30 years.

Permanent Financing

After you have gained control of the site, you can start more detailed planning. You can analyze markets in more detail to help you decide how much space should be built and what rental rates it will command. You can engage land and site planners and architects to help decide where buildings should be placed on the site and to design them. All of this activity takes a lot of money, and there is no guarantee the buildings will ever be built. One thing that stands between you and the completion of the project is money. Chances are good that you and others involved in the project do *not* have the money necessary to pay for all the costs of planning and construction.

It would seem that the next step would be to find someone to lend you money for construction. This logic is correct, but financial realities make it necessary to do something else before seeking construction financing. That something else is arranging permanent financing. Permanent financing is necessary at this stage because construction loans are short-term loans paid off when construction is completed, and construction lenders are very concerned about where you are going to get the money to pay them. If you cannot show a construction lender that you and others involved in the project have sufficient cash, or other assets that can be converted to cash, to pay off the loan, you must be able to show another source of money in order to get the construction loan. Since permanent lenders give you the proceeds of the permanent loan only when the project is completed, a promise to make a permanent loan from a respectable lender, called a commitment, is often used as the source of funds to satisfy the construction lender.

Permanent income property loan terms are completely negotiable. Some loans have level, unchanging payments calculated over a 25 – to 30 – year term, with the outstanding balance being due at the end of a designated year, such as year 10 or 15. Provisions making the entire balance due at the end of a particular year are *call provisions,* and the loan is said to be *callable* in the designated year. The larger payment made in the call year is called a *balloon payment.* In addition to interest, income property loans may also provide for the lender to participate in the income the property produces. Such a participation, or *kicker,* may substantially increase the payments the lender receives. Participations are extensively used in periods of high interest rates.

If you are buying an existing improved property, such as an office building, permanent financing will be the only form of debt financing necessary; unless you plan to remodel the property and need to borrow for the remodeling. You will add the money you are investing to the amount you are borrowing to fund the purchase. Just as in a single family transaction, the lender will actually write a check for the loan amount at the closing of the transaction. If you are developing a project, you will not receive the permanent loan proceeds until construction is completed and the city or county certifies that it is ready for occupancy.

Getting the Permanent Loan Permanent income property loans are made by life insurance companies, pension funds, and other financial institutions. Life insurance companies are the largest income property lenders. Since the loan volume in most cities does not merit income property lenders maintaining a large number of loan offices, they arrange for mortgage bankers to act as representatives, or *correspondents,* for them. As correspondents they take applications from prospective borrowers, and, if the investment is acceptable, attempt to find a lender interested in making a loan of this type. They then act as an intermediary in the negotiations and ultimately the close of the loan.

Your first step in getting a permanent loan will be a visit to a mortgage banker. In income property lending, mortgage bankers act as intermediaries who bring potential borrowers and lenders together rather than lending their own funds. When a potential borrower comes to a mortgage banker seeking an income property loan, the mortgage banker makes a preliminary assessment of the borrower and the property and decides whether to pursue the loan. If pursued, the mortgage banker will contact lenders with which the firm has a correspondent relationship until a lender interested in the property is found.

Once a potential lender is found, the mortgage banker will start assembling the necessary paperwork to make formal application with the potential lender. The lender will analyze the proposed loan and, usually without personally seeing the property, make a decision. The mortgage banker will also help with any negotiations between the borrower and lender. For this assistance, the mortgage banker receives a fee. The mortgage banker will also service the mortgage for a fee.

In the first meeting with the mortgage banker, you will discuss the property, your experience in real estate, and the terms of the loan you want. The mortgage banker can offer advice as to the reasonableness of your loan request and the likelihood of getting what you want. He or she may suggest financing alternatives to help you obtain more suitable financing. Factors considered in underwriting (analyzing a loan application and deciding whether the loan should be made) are considered in Chapter 16.

If you and a lender reach an agreement on the loan amount, interest rate, and term of the loan, then a *commitment letter* is issued by the lender outlining these points. This letter commits the lender to make the loan on the terms outlined in it. Such a letter will state the period of time for which the commitment is valid. For example, the letter may state that the loan must be closed (documents signed and money disbursed to you) within six months of its date. To indicate your acceptance of the commitment as outlined in the letter, you will sign it and pay a commitment fee.

Construction Loans

Once you have a permanent commitment from a reputable lender you are ready to work on construction financing, often called *interim financing.* It is called interim financing because it covers the interim between the start of construction and when the permanent loan proceeds are disbursed upon completion. Construction financing is short-to-intermediate-term financing, with a term usually equal to the construction period plus some period for leasing the property. Even very large projects will seldom take over three years per phase to complete.

Because of its short-term nature, construction lending appeals to lenders desiring short-term investments. It is not surprising that commercial banks are very active in construction lending since the short life and the safety provided by the permanent commitment produce exactly the kind of investment they like. You may have noticed signs on construction sites with phrases like "Interim financing supplied by First National Bank." If you have not, look for these signs and see who is making construction loans in your area. Developers may approach construction lenders directly or use the services of a mortgage banker in obtaining a construction loan.

When a construction loan is made to a developer, the entire loan amount is not given to the developer at one time. Experience has shown that construction lenders need to monitor the progress of the project and disburse funds as work on the project is completed. Failure to do this in the past has resulted in projects in which 100 percent of the construction money had been spent and only 75 percent of the project completed. This is known in the real estate lending business as "an embarrassing situation."

Obviously, it would not be fair to require the developer to pay interest on the entire amount of money over the entire loan period if the lender disburses it a piece at a time. So developers pay interest only on the amount of money actually disbursed by the lender. Interest is calculated on a daily basis and the interest rate may change at agreed-upon intervals, sometimes as short as one day. The interest rate is based on the lender's prime rate, with construction loans generally carrying interest rates 1 1/2 to 4 percent above the prime rate. Developers must be concerned with changes in interest rates since a project that is profitable at one interest rate may become a disaster at a higher one. In early 1980, the prime rate went from about 12 percent to 20 percent very quickly, forcing many developers with projects in progress to pay interest rates up to 24 percent. These added interest costs played havoc with the profitability of many projects and caused the bankruptcy of many developers.

SUMMARY

In this chapter you learned that money for real estate loans comes primarily from financial institutions and that of those institutions, savings and loan associations are the largest single lender. Mortgage pools, groups of mortgages in which shares are sold, are supplying a growing percentage of new funds being lent on real estate. Lenders have lending specialties, with savings and loan associations investing heavily in housing and life insurance companies concentrating on income-producing real estate loans. Institutional lenders are regulated by a number of different agencies such as the Federal Home Loan Bank Board, Federal Reserve System, and state insurance commissions.

Real estate must compete with all other investments for capital. There is not a pool of funds somewhere in our economy just waiting to be invested in real estate. If other investments provide more attractive combinations of risk and return, investors will choose to invest in them. Because of the importance of financial institutions in real estate finance, real estate lending suffers when these institutions have difficulty in attracting capital. Such a situation occurs when the rates of return on stocks, bonds, and other investments increase to the point that households reduce their institutional savings and invest directly in these instruments.

Interest rates are the result of the supply and demand for capital. Business and government often use more capital than they produce in a given period of time. Households spend less than they produce and supply much of the capital other households, business, and government need to borrow. For this reason, changes in household saving patterns are important to the economy and real estate lending. The secondary mortgage market, in which existing mortgages are bought and sold, plays an important role in providing funds for real estate lending. Institutions such as Fannie Mae and Freddie Mac sell bonds to direct investors and purchase mortgages with the proceeds. They make a profit by earning higher returns on the mortgages than they pay for their funds. Ginnie Mae is a federal government agency creating a market for special mortgages and operating a mortgage-backed securities program that has provided substantial amounts of capital for mortgage markets.

Mortgage banking firms have a prominent place in real estate lending. These firms originate single family mortgages and then either sell them to secondary mortgage market institutions or form mortgage pools and issue mortgage-backed securities. They then service these loans on a fee basis for the owner. In income property lending they act as correspondents for major lenders. As such, they prepare submission packages for lenders, facilitate negotiations, handle the loan closing, and service the mortgage for their lenders. Income property lending incorporates at least three types of lending: land financing, construction financing, and permanent financing.

QUICK QUIZ

1. The largest overall real estate lender is the _____ .

    a. savings and loan association   c. commercial bank
    b. mutual savings bank   d. life insurance company

2. The largest lender on income properties is the _____ .

    a. commercial bank   c. life insurance company
    b. mutual savings bank   d. savings and loan association

3. Households depend principally on _____ for their capital needs.

    a. direct investment   c. tax loopholes
    b. financial institutions   d. all of the above

4. Institutions active in the secondary mortgage markets include _____ .

    a. Fannie Mae   c. Ginnie Mae
    b. Freddie Mac   d. all of the above

5. A discount point is _____ .

    a. a special, reduced price a borrower pays for a loan
    b. a one percent reduction in the interest rate
    c. paid by the lender when a loan is made
    d. one percent of the original loan amount

6. Savings and loan associations are regulated by the _____ .

7. The sector of the economy that traditionally spends less than it earns is the _____ sector.

8. The flow of funds out of financial institutions is called _____ .

9. Mortgage bankers expect to consistently make a profit on _____ .

10. The three types of income property lending are _____, _____, and _____.

**QUESTIONS
AND
EXERCISES**

1. In a popular magazine such as *Time, Business Week, Newsweek,* or *U.S. News and World Report,* find and read a forecast about financial conditions and interest rates. Does this forecast discuss any of the factors affecting interest rates discussed in this chapter? If so, which factors?

2. Call a mortgage lender and find out the current conventional and FHA mortgage terms they are offering. Be sure to find out about interest rates and discount points and how these differ for different loan-to-value ratio loans.

3. From your contact with lenders, determine if there is a difference between the interest rate on fixed-rate and variable-rate mortgages. Should there be a difference? Why?

4. What factors affect the percentage of income households save?

5. Discuss the concept of disintermediation and how it affects the availability and cost of real estate loans.

6. If you were a real estate loan originator, how would yield demands of secondary mortgage market institutions affect your loan terms and lending activity in the primary market?

7. Why are Ginnie Mae mortgage-backed securities so popular with investors?

**KEY
TERMINOLOGY**

adjustable rate mortgage
blanket mortgage
capital markets
commitment
construction financing
conventional loans
deferred-payment mortgage
disintermediation
Federal Home Loan Bank Board
Federal Home Loan Mortgage
  Corporation
Federal Housing Administration
Federal National Mortgage
  Association

Federal Reserve System
FHA loan
financial intermediary
Free Market System
Government National Mortgage
  Association
graduated payment adjustable
  mortgage
graduated payment mortgage
growing equity mortgage
mortgage-backed securities
mortgage banker
option
package mortgage

participations
pass-through securities
pledged-account mortgage
price-level-adjusted mortgage
primary mortgage market
purchase money mortgage

secondary mortgage market
VA loan
variable rate mortgage
Veterans Administration
warehousing
wraparound mortgage

IF YOU WANT TO READ MORE

JAMES A. BRITTON, JR. and LEWIS O. KERWOOD, eds., *Financing Income Producing Real Estate — A Theory and Casebook* (New York: McGraw-Hill, 1977).

WILLIAM B. BRUEGGEMAN and LEO D. STONE, *Real Estate Finance*, 7th ed. (Homewood, IL: Richard E. Irwin, Inc., 1981).

JEROME DASSO and GERALD KUHN, *Real Estate Finance* (Englewood Cliffs, NJ: Prentice-Hall, Inc., 1983).

DONALD R. EPLEY and JAMES A. MILLER, *Basic Real Estate Finance and Investments*, 2nd ed. (New York: John Wiley & Sons, 1984).

C. F. SIRMANS, *Real Estate Finance* (New York: McGraw-Hill, Inc., 1985).

16

Real Estate Lending: decision making

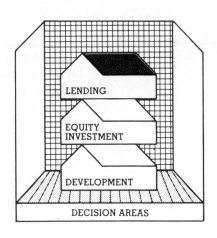

LENDING

EQUITY INVESTMENT

DEVELOPMENT

DECISION AREAS

PREVIEW
Someone once said that what is called "gambling" in Las Vegas and Atlantic City is called "business" in other parts of the country. This statement simply implies that all business carries with it some uncertainty. For many persons, real estate lending decisions involve a great deal of uncertainty. One of the reasons for this feeling is a lack of understanding of the processes real estate lenders follow in making lending decisions. This chapter seeks to remove some of that uncertainty by helping you understand:

1. What underwriting involves and how lending decisions are made.
2. How lenders assess the ability and desire of borrowers to repay a single family loan.
3. How lenders assess a property's desirability as security for a real estate loan.
4. The basic financing process for permanent income property loans.
5. How income property lending decisions are made.

If you perceive real estate lenders as "magic black boxes" that process loan information and mysteriously produce lending decisions, you have added an unnecessary source of uncertainty to the real estate business.

An understanding of the processes lenders follow and the factors they consider in making real estate lending decisions is easy to acquire and a necessary part of maximizing your chances of success in the real estate business. It also reduces unnecessary uncertainty, allowing you to concentrate on the many other sources of uncertainty.

At the outset, you should clearly understand that *lenders want to make loans.* Lenders' very business existence depends on making loans. Savings and loan associations and commercial banks want and need to lend, to put that money to work earning interest in order to pay interest on the money they have borrowed from depositors. Mortgage bankers want to lend in order to increase their income from loan servicing. Life insurance companies look to interest income to pay the claims of policyholders. When a loan application is turned down, it is a waste of everyone's time and energy — lenders, borrowers, and real estate agents. Therefore, lenders should be approached with the idea that a good loan benefits everyone connected with the transaction and that a solid, qualified applicant will likely be approved. You should know when a potential borrower is likely to be favorably considered and why.

OVERVIEW OF SINGLE FAMILY
LENDING DECISION MAKING

Single family real estate loans are *credit loans.* They are called credit loans because lending decisions are based on the credit worthiness of the borrower(s). The process of making single family lending decisions is based on analyzing the borrower's *ability* and *desire* to repay the loan and the appropriateness of the property as security for the loan. Both of these components must be adequate in the underwriter's mind for the loan to be acceptable.

Property

Since the property acts as security for the mortgage loan, it is important that the lender be satisfied that should it become necessary, it can be sold for enough to pay off any remaining loan balance. The long life of real estate mortgages means the lender must be concerned with the present *and* future value of the property. A substantial decline in the value of the property over time may exceed the amortization of the loan and reduce the lender's security.

It may seem strange, but most lenders will not personally visit and inspect the property acting as security, but they will likely see a photo. They depend almost entirely on real estate appraisers to analyze the property and estimate what it would likely sell for in the marketplace, that is, its market value. If the loan being considered is an FHA or VA loan, the property must meet certain minimum property standards established by the federal government. One of the costs you as the borrower usually must bear is the cost of an appraisal of the property. Your maximum loan amount will be based on the lower of the purchase price in the sales contract or the appraised market value. If you are seeking a 95 percent loan on a home with a contract price of $60,000, you are trying to borrow $57,000 (.95 × $60,000). If the home appraises for only $58,000, your maximum loan will be 95 percent of $58,000, or $55,100, not the $57,000 you are seeking.

Borrower

Lenders must assess the ability and desire of borrowers to make payments over the life of a 30-year mortgage. Obviously, nobody knows what is going to happen to a borrower financially, emotionally, and physically over that long a period of time. Nothing indicates that lenders have greater abilities to foresee the future than any other group of people, and they generally do not have budgets large enough to hire a staff soothsayer. Lenders have responded to this situation by using a two-stage approach. First, they assess the present ability of the borrower to make the necessary loan payments and the likelihood of the borrower being able to make these payments in the future. Next, the desire to pay is assessed on the basis of the borrower's past credit performance.

Armed with current information about the ability to pay and a credit history to get an idea of the desire to pay, a lender is in a position to make a judgment about the overall creditworthiness of a borrower for a particular loan. Much of this judgment is developed from past lending experience. Lenders know that a loan that is too great a financial burden for the borrower is likely to be a problem for the lender and certainly is not a favor to the borrower. Therefore, lenders will attempt to obtain and verify information relating to the ability and desire of the borrower to repay the loan.

GATHERING INFORMATION
ON SINGLE FAMILY BORROWERS

Potential lenders and borrowers do not have to wait for formal loan application to exchange information. A preapplication conference can be a useful way to gather and transmit information about one another and to evaluate the likelihood of a successful credit transaction. At this conference the potential lender can find out the amount of money and terms the borrower is seeking. The lender can also find out valuable information about the property under consideration. The borrower can gain insights into the loan terms the lender is seeking as well as limits on loan amounts, the steps the lender will follow in processing the loan application, and the time required to do so. The borrower can also find out what information the lender needs for formal application. As you can see, these conferences are useful in establishing whether a sufficient mutual interest exists to merit a formal loan application.

Loan Application

Applying for a loan is more than a formality. If you are the borrower, it provides the opportunity to relate your qualifications to the lender and to maximize your chances of getting a loan approved. As the lender, the application is your opportunity to gather much-needed employment and financial information for making the loan decision. In addition, the meeting with the lender affords the borrower the opportunity to explain any past or present situations that may affect the loan decision. For example, if your spouse had emergency surgery three years ago and the costs of this medical care severely affected your financial condition, you would want to relay this information to the lender so that your present financial condition can be properly interpreted. In the absence of this information the lender may assume that you simply have not managed your financial affairs satisfactorily and deny the application. Thus, as a borrower you should be prepared to provide the information necessary for an informed lending decision. As you saw above, the lender seeks information about your ability and desire to pay off the loan if it is made. It is in your best interest to be as complete and accurate in your portrayal of your financial position as possible.

A typical loan application form is shown in Table 16.1. The first page of the application requests information on the property and the amount and source of the borrower's income. Page two asks the borrower to provide information about the type and value of assets owned and any outstanding debts. By subtracting the amount of outstanding debts from the value of assets, the net worth of the borrower can be computed. **Net worth** is an estimate of what the borrower could "cash out" for at the time of the application. Page two also requests information on credit references.

When you apply for a loan you will be asked to sign verification requests allowing the lender to verify your deposits in financial institutions and your employment. This is done by mail. If you are self-employed, say as a real estate broker, you will be asked to provide income tax returns for the last two years or financial statements prepared by a certified public accountant as evidence of your income history. If you are applying a significant period of time after the last financial statement or tax return was prepared, you may be asked to provide a profit and loss statement showing your business operations since the last tax return or financial statement. You will also sign a document authorizing the lender to obtain a credit report showing your past credit experiences.

At application you will also be given certain materials outlining your rights, as borrower, under federal Truth-In-Lending laws. Also,

Table 16.1. Residential Loan Application

RESIDENTIAL LOAN APPLICATION

Table 16.1. Residential Loan Application

FHLMC 65 Rev 8/78   FOR LENDERS SUBJECT ONLY TO FEDERAL RESERVE SYSTEM REGULATION B   FNMA 1003 Rev 8/78

Table 16.1. (Continued)

This Statement and any applicable supporting schedules may be completed jointly by both married and unmarried co-borrowers if their assets and liabilities are sufficiently joined so that the Statement can be meaningfully and fairly presented on a combined basis; otherwise separate Statements and schedules are required (FHLMC 65A/FNMA 1003A). If the co-borrower section was completed about a spouse, this Statement and supporting schedules must be completed about that spouse also.

☐ Completed Jointly   ☐ Not Completed Jointly

ASSETS		LIABILITIES AND PLEDGED ASSETS			
Indicate by (*) those liabilities or pledged assets which will be satisfied upon sale of real estate owned or upon refinancing of subject property					
Description	Cash or Market Value	Creditors' Name, Address and Account Number	Acct. Name if Not Borrower's	Mo. Pmt. and Mos. left to pay	Unpaid Balance
Cash Deposit Toward Purchase Held By	$	Installment Debts (include 'revolving' charge accts)		$ Pmt./Mos.	$
Checking and Savings Accounts (Show Names of Institutions/Acct. Nos.)					
Stocks and Bonds (No./Description)					
Life Insurance Net Cash Value Face Amount ($		Other Debts Including Stock Pledges			
SUBTOTAL LIQUID ASSETS	$				
Real Estate Owned (Enter Market Value from Schedule of Real Estate Owned)		Real Estate Loans			
Vested Interest in Retirement Fund					
Net Worth of Business Owned (ATTACH FINANCIAL STATEMENT)					
Automobiles (Make and Year)		Automobile Loans			
Furniture and Personal Property		Alimony, Child Support and Separate Maintenance Payments Owed To			
Other Assets (Itemize)					
		TOTAL MONTHLY PAYMENTS		$	
TOTAL ASSETS	A $	NET WORTH (A minus B) $		TOTAL LIABILITIES	B $

SCHEDULE OF REAL ESTATE OWNED (If Additional Properties Owned Attach Separate Schedule)

Address of Property (Indicate S if Sold, PS if Pending Sale or R if Rental being held for income)	Type of Property	Present Market Value	Amount of Mortgages & Liens	Gross Rental Income	Mortgage Payments	Taxes, Ins. Maintenance and Misc.	Net Rental Income
		$	$	$	$	$	$
TOTALS →		$	$	$	$	$	$

LIST PREVIOUS CREDIT REFERENCES

B—Borrower C Co Borrower	Creditor's Name and Address	Account Number	Purpose	Highest Balance	Date Paid
				$	

List any additional names under which credit has previously been received _____

AGREEMENT The undersigned applies for the loan indicated in this application to be secured by a first mortgage or deed of trust on the property described herein, and represents that the property will not be used for any illegal or restricted purpose, and that all statements made in this application are true and are made for the purpose of obtaining the loan. Verification may be obtained from any source named in this application. The original or a copy of this application will be retained by the lender even if the loan is not granted. The undersigned ☐ intend or ☐ do not intend to occupy the property as their primary residence.

I/we fully understand that it is a federal crime punishable by fine or imprisonment, or both, to knowingly make any false statements concerning any of the above facts as applicable under the provisions of Title 18, United States Code, Section 1014.

_____ Date _____   _____ Date _____
Borrower's Signature   Co-Borrower's Signature

INFORMATION FOR GOVERNMENT MONITORING PURPOSES

If this loan is for purchase or construction of a home, the following information is requested by the Federal Government to monitor this lender's compliance with Equal Credit Opportunity and Fair Housing Laws. The law provides that a lender may neither discriminate on the basis of this information nor on whether or not it is furnished. Furnishing this information is optional. If you do not wish to furnish the following information, please initial below.

BORROWER: I do not wish to furnish this information (initials) _____
RACE / ☐ American Indian, Alaskan Native   ☐ Asian, Pacific Islander
NATIONAL   ☐ Black   ☐ Hispanic   ☐ White   SEX: ☐ Female ☐ Male
ORIGIN ☐ Other (specify) _____

CO-BORROWER: I do not wish to furnish this information (initials) _____
RACE / ☐ American Indian, Alaskan Native   ☐ Asian, Pacific Islander
NATIONAL   ☐ Black   ☐ Hispanic   ☐ White   SEX: ☐ Female ☐ Male
ORIGIN ☐ Other (specify) _____

FOR LENDER'S USE ONLY

(FNMA REQUIREMENT ONLY) _____

_____   _____
                         Name of Employer or Interviewer

REVERSE

FNMA 1003 Rev. 8/78

within three working days of the date of application, the lender must supply you with an itemized good-faith estimate of closing costs. The lender giveth and the lender also taketh at application. You should take your checkbook to application since you will also be asked to pay certain fees. Generally, the fees collected at the time of application are those out-of-pocket costs the lender is going to make on your behalf for a survey and an appraisal.

Property

Gathering information on the property generally consists of arranging for an appraisal. After obtaining the legal description of the property from the borrower, an appraiser, either employed by the lender or with an independent appraisal firm, will be assigned to estimate the market value of the property. The appraiser will inspect the property and the neighborhood, gather necessary market data, estimate market value, and then prepare an appraisal report.

ASSESSING THE ABILITY TO PAY

Once all the information is gathered, the job of the underwriter begins. It is the underwriter's job to organize and analyze available information and make a loan decision. Underwriting is a combination of art and science requiring not only the ability to analyze the numbers from the application and elsewhere, but to also use judgment about the quality of the information and any special conditions such as the medical emergency referred to above.

It doesn't take too much reflection to realize that income is excellent evidence of the ability to pay for a loan. If a family has adequate dependable income, then the loan can usually be paid off. For this reason, the underwriter places a great deal of importance on income. Essentially, the underwriter is trying to determine the level of income that is going to be dependable and continuing. For example, suppose the manager of a clothing store came to your office and applied for a mortgage loan. She tells you that her salary is $40,000 per year and that last year for the first time she received a bonus, based on sales in the store, of $10,000. What income would you be willing to bet on as dependable, continuing income? The answer is not really clear at this point; you would need more information about the conditions under which the bonus was paid and whether or not it is likely to occur again. Only then could you make a determination of whether that income should be considered dependable enough to use in underwriting the loan. Self-employed persons and those in sales present particular challenges.

As a lender, you are interested in determining the amount of **qualified income,** the income you are willing to accept as being available to make payments on the mortgage loan. Generally, most lenders are willing to accept income that has been received for at least two years. Self-employed persons are usually requested to present financial statements or tax returns showing income for the last two years. If you are a college student, this does not mean that you have to work for two years before applying for a mortgage loan. Most lenders will consider your college years to some extent in qualifying your income. Obviously, if you should take seven years as a full-time student to complete a four-year degree program, the lender may not be very sympathetic.

In the past, the sex of the applicant had a bearing on qualifying income. Some lenders used to count the income of a female only if she was employed in certain occupations, such as nursing or teaching. Federal law and common sense have ended this practice. A woman's income is now qualified in exactly the same manner as a man's. Also, with respect to women, lenders cannot ask questions about the plans for children or whether the couple is practicing any form of birth control. Thus, if a woman is now working and has a work history, the fact that she may become pregnant cannot be considered in the loan decision. The marital status of the applicant(s) also is not considered any longer. That is, a single person receives the same consideration as a married couple with all other things being equal. Unrelated persons living together can now pool their incomes, apply for a loan, and receive the same consideration as a married couple. Thus, if you and a friend decide that renting is not desirable any longer, you can jointly apply for a mortgage loan and have both your incomes considered by the lender.

Income Ratios

Once qualified income has been determined, the lender will consider the amount of loan it will support. If the income will support a loan amount greater than or equal to that which is being sought, then this portion of the underwriting is satisfactory. To get a "ballpark" idea of the amount of loan any given amount of qualified income will support, lenders frequently use some ratios developed out of lending experience and the demands of secondary mortgage market investors. These ratios are the mortgage debt service ratio and the fixed obligation ratio.

Mortgage Debt Service Ratio The **mortgage debt service ratio** indicates the percentage the mortgage payment represents of the monthly gross income. Most lenders require a monthly payment consisting of principal and interest (the actual payment on the loan), one-twelfth of the estimated annual property taxes, and one-twelfth of the annual hazard insurance premium (insurance for fire, wind, etc.). Property taxes are estimated from past taxes or by contacting the appropriate government office and finding out the tax bill for the coming year. Hazard insurance costs are estimated from information provided by insurance companies. Monthly gross income is defined as qualified income before taxes.

After these items have been estimated, the ratio can be calculated as follows:

$$\text{Mortgage debt service ratio} = \frac{\text{Principal} + \text{Interest} + \text{Taxes} + \text{Insurance}}{\text{Gross monthly income}}$$

Lenders have traditionally wanted this ratio to be .25 or less. That is, they have wanted the monthly payment to be 25 percent or less of the gross monthly income. However, for fixed rate, fixed payment mortgages, the acceptable level for this ratio has increased to about .28 to reflect rising housing costs and the willingness of borrowers to sacrifice to purchase a home. The ratio remains .25 for adjustable rate mortgages. At this time, great concern exists over underwriting practices for the many types of loans being originated. As a result, the appropriate levels for the mortgage debt service ratio and the fixed obligation ratio (to follow) vary substantially between lenders and are changing frequently.

It is easy to see that as interest rates and principal and interest payments increase, the amount of loan a given gross monthly income will support decreases. In periods of extremely high interest rates, as in 1981 and 1982, families find it very difficult to buy more expensive housing or to simply replace their existing homes if they are forced to move. Table 16.2 highlights the maximum loan you could qualify for at various interest rates using this ratio with a gross income of $3,000 per month.

Fixed Obligation Ratio The **fixed obligation ratio** is simply an extension of the debt service ratio. It considers other fixed, or long-term, obligations of the borrower. Obligations such as car payments, furniture payments, MasterCard payments, or any obligation with more than six to ten monthly payments remaining will be included, depending on the lender. It is calculated as follows:

$$\text{Fixed obligation ratio} = \frac{\text{Principal} + \text{Interest} + \text{Taxes} + \text{Insurance} + \text{Other fixed obligations}}{\text{Gross monthly income}}$$

Lenders want this ratio to be no greater than .36 for fixed rate mortgages and .33 for adjustable rate mortgages.

Interpreting the Ratios Borrowers must comply with *both* ratios. This means that some trade-offs may exist between your mortgage debt and your other fixed obligations. If you just meet the mortgage debt service ratio, that is, the mortgage payment represents 28 percent of your gross income, then if you are to comply with the fixed obligation ratio of 36 percent, your other fixed obligations cannot exceed 8 percent of your gross monthly income (36% − 28% = 8%). To the extent these obligations exceed 8 percent, you will exceed the lender's desired fixed obligation ratio. For example, suppose that you have gross monthly income of $3000. The maximum monthly mortgage payments and fixed obligation payments allowed by the lender are $840 and $1080, respectively,

$$\text{Maximum mortgage payment} = \$3000 \times .28 = \$840$$

$$\text{Maximum fixed obligation payment} = \$3000 \times .36 = \$1080$$

The difference between these two numbers is $240, which is equal to 8 percent of your gross income ($3000 × .08 = $240). If your other fixed obligations exceed $240, you will exceed the fixed obligation ratio. Since both ratios must be satisfied, you must either reduce your long-term obligations by paying something off or reduce the amount of the mortgage loan you are seeking.

Lenders do not view these ratios as absolutes. A value of .29 on the debt service ratio does not mean an automatic rejection. Here, the art of underwriting comes into play. "Significant" deviations from these values raise questions about whether the loan should be made. What is significant depends on the underwriter and whether the loan is going to be sold or kept by the underwriter's firm. In many instances, the balance sheet information will be very useful in making decisions on marginal loans. Naturally, the underwriter has more flexibility on loans the institution is going to keep than on loans that will be sold in secondary markets. Today, with all the uncertainty in the capital markets, most loans are underwritten as if they are to be sold, since the underwriter often does not know whether they eventually will be sold or not. This means the criteria established by secondary market institutions are being followed very closely.

The FHA and VA have each developed their own guidelines for lending. Mortgage bankers and savings and loan associations making FHA and VA loans maintain and update extensive files on the latest FHA and VA rules and regulations. In making an FHA loan, lenders prepare

Table 16.2. Maximum Loans Justified by a Mortgage Debt Service Ratio of 28% and a Monthly Income of $3000*

Interest Rate (%)	Maximum Loan
8	$102,180
10	$ 85,421
12	$ 72,886
14	$ 63,291
16	$ 55,762

* Assuming monthly property taxes and insurance to be $90, and a 30-year term.

all the necessary documents and forward the completed file to the local FHA office, where a decision is made about insuring the loan. If the FHA decides to insure, the loan is made. In VA lending, lenders also prepare a file on the loan but can make the guarantee decision themselves, according to VA guidelines. If there is any question about whether the loan should be made, the file will be sent to the local or regional VA office for a decision.

Balance Sheet

The two income ratios are probably the most important aspect of the underwriting process with respect to estimating the ability to pay. However, they are not the only things underwriters will analyze. Balance sheet information also plays an important role in the underwriting process. The first use of the balance sheet information is to determine the source of down payment and loan fee money. When the borrower cannot demonstrate a source for these funds, it is difficult for a lender to approve the loan application. In such situations, gift letters are often used to provide evidence of the ability to make the necessary down payment. A **gift letter** is a document stating that one person is giving a sum of money to another without any expectation of being repaid. For instance, your parents may give you the money for the down payment on a home. Lenders, except in unusual cases, require that the person signing the gift letter have reasonable cause for making such a gift.

The second use of the balance sheet is to examine the trend of the borrower in amassing assets that may provide a cushion for the loan. For example, suppose you are underwriting an application from an individual who has been out of college working as an accountant for ten years earning a good salary and has been able to amass a net worth of only $5,000. If this person is asking for a loan that will increase his mortgage payments from an existing level of $300 to a new level of $600 per month, you may have reservations about his ability to manage the higher payments since he has shown little ability to accumulate assets. If his income ratios are strong, you may not worry about this facet of the balance sheet, but if they are marginal, it may become an important consideration. In this particular instance, the balance sheet casts doubts on the borrower's ability to generate necessary cash should emergencies arise in the future.

ASSESSING THE DESIRE TO PAY

The ability to pay, by itself, is not enough to ensure the lender that a loan is a good one. The lender also wants to know that the borrower has the desire to repay the loan. Since lenders do not have a device that measures desire to pay, they must rely on other indicators. Generally, they fall back to a very practical approach to the problem: find out how the borrower has dealt with debt obligations in the past and assume debt obligations will be treated the same in the future. Credit reports showing past financial performance are used to assess this past performance.

Credit reports are supplied by credit reporting agencies to lenders, employers, and others for a fee. Credit reporting agencies develop credit files on almost everyone who has ever had credit. Many credit agencies maintain computer files that are updated monthly using computer tapes from creditors. For example, if you have a MasterCard, the bank that issued it and bills you each month may supply a computer tape of the month's transactions to the credit reporting agency on a certain day each month. Information about your account — how much you owe, whether your last payment was on time, the amount of your last payment, and so on — is taken from the MasterCard tape and matched with your credit record at the credit reporting agency. You probably authorized creditors to provide information about your account to these agencies when you signed papers opening the account. Credit agencies also examine local newspapers for deaths, marriages, divorces, and lawsuits affecting persons in their files. This information is also entered into computerized records.

When a request is received from a lender for a mortgage credit report, the credit reporting agency pulls information from your computer file, contacts others who may have recently requested your file to see if any new obligations should be entered, and checks the courthouse to see if any judgments are outstanding. Each credit reporting agency prepares reports in its own format to comply with the desires of report users and applicable law.

ASSESSING THE PROPERTY

The underwriter will use the appraisal report to evaluate the security the property offers for the loan. Appraisal reports on single family homes are normally prepared on forms like the one shown in Table 16.3, and are approved by Freddie Mac and Fannie Mae. The appraisal report contains information about the neighborhood and the subject property. The appraiser assesses the present condition of homes in the neighborhood and whether or not their conditions are improving or declining. Your home will be compared to other homes in the neighborhood with respect to size, condition, and special features like swimming pools, hot tubs, and fireplaces. The appraiser then estimates the market value of your home — the price it would likely bring if offered for sale. For the moment, do not worry about how the appraiser estimates market value; you will learn more about this process in later chapters devoted to appraisal.

In addition to the market value, lenders are also interested in the condition of the property. Since real estate loans have long terms, the

Table 16.3. Residential Appraisal Report

RESIDENTIAL APPRAISAL REPORT   File No.

Borrower	Census Tract Map Reference
Property Address	
City County State Zip Code	
Legal Description	
Sale Price $ Date of Sale Loan Term yrs Property Rights Appraised ☐ Fee ☐ Leasehold ☐ DeMinimis PUD	
Actual Real Estate Taxes $ (yr) Loan charges to be paid by seller $ Other sales concessions	
Lender/Client Address	
Occupant Appraiser Instructions to Appraiser	

NEIGHBORHOOD

	Urban	Suburban	Rural		Good	Avg.	Fair	Poor
Location				Employment Stability	☐	☐	☐	☐
Built Up	Over 75%	25% to 75%	Under 25%	Convenience to Employment	☐	☐	☐	☐
Growth Rate Fully Dev.	Rapid	Steady	Slow	Convenience to Shopping	☐	☐	☐	☐
Property Values	Increasing	Stable	Declining	Convenience to Schools	☐	☐	☐	☐
Demand/Supply	Shortage	In Balance	Over Supply	Adequacy of Public Transportation	☐	☐	☐	☐
Marketing Time	Under 3 Mos	4-6 Mos	Over 6 Mos	Recreational Facilities	☐	☐	☐	☐
Present Land Use __ % 1 Family __ % 2-4 Family __ % Apts __ % Condo __ % Commercial				Adequacy of Utilities	☐	☐	☐	☐
__ % Industrial __ % Vacant __ %				Property Compatibility	☐	☐	☐	☐
Change in Present Land Use Not Likely Likely (*) Taking Place (*)				Protection from Detrimental Conditions	☐	☐	☐	☐
(*) From To				Police and Fire Protection	☐	☐	☐	☐
Predominant Occupancy Owner Tenant % Vacant				General Appearance of Properties	☐	☐	☐	☐
Single Family Price Range $ to $ Predominant Value $				Appeal to Market	☐	☐	☐	☐
Single Family Age yrs Predominant Age yrs								

Note: FHLMC/FNMA do not consider race or the racial composition of the neighborhood to be reliable appraisal factors.

Comments including those factors, favorable or unfavorable, affecting marketability (e.g. public parks, schools, view, noise)

SITE

Dimensions   Sq Ft or Acres   ☐ Corner Lot
Zoning classification   Present improvements ☐ do ☐ do not conform to zoning regulations
Highest and best use Present use Other (specify)

	Public	Other (Describe)	OFF SITE IMPROVEMENTS			Topo
Elec			Street Access	Public	Private	Size
Gas			Surface			Shape
Water			Maintenance	Public	Private	View
San. Sewer			Storm Sewer	Curb/Gutter		Drainage
☐ Underground Elect. & Tel.			Sidewalk	Street Lights		Is the property located in a HUD Identified Special Flood Hazard Area? ☐ No ☐ Yes

Comments (favorable or unfavorable including any apparent adverse easements, encroachments or other adverse conditions)

IMPROVEMENTS

☐ Existing ☐ Proposed ☐ Under Constr.   No. Units   Type (det, duplex, semi-det, etc.)   Design (rambler, split level, etc.)   Exterior Walls
Yrs. Age: Actual   Effective   to   No. Stories
Roof Material   Gutters & Downspouts None Window (Type)   Insulation ☐ None ☐ Floor
Storm Sash Screens Combination   ☐ Ceiling ☐ Roof ☐ Walls
☐ Manufactured Housing   % Basement Floor Drain Finished Ceiling
Foundation Walls   Outside Entrance Sump Pump Finished Walls
Concrete Floor % Finished Finished Floor
☐ Slab on Grade ☐ Crawl Space   Evidence of Dampness Termites Settlement
Comments

BSMT.

ROOM LIST

Room List	Foyer	Living	Dining	Kitchen	Den	Family Rm	Rec Rm	Bedrooms	No. Baths	Laundry	Other
Basement											
1st Level											
2nd Level											

Finished area above grade contains a total of __ rooms __ bedrooms __ baths. Gross Living Area __ sq. ft. Bsmt Area __ sq. ft.

INTERIOR FINISH & EQUIPMENT

Kitchen Equipment: Refrigerator Range/Oven Disposal Dishwasher Fan/Hood Compactor Washer Dryer
HEAT: Type   Fuel   Cond.   AIR COND ☐ Central ☐ Other   ☐ Adequate ☐ Inadequate

Floors	Hardwood	Carpet Over	
Walls	Drywall	Plaster	
Trim/Finish	Good	Average Fair Poor	
Bath Floor	Ceramic		
Bath Wainscot	Ceramic		

Special Features (including energy efficient items)

PROPERTY RATING

	Good	Avg.	Fair	Poor
Quality of Construction (Materials & Finish)	☐	☐	☐	☐
Condition of Improvements	☐	☐	☐	☐
Room sizes and layout	☐	☐	☐	☐
Closets and Storage	☐	☐	☐	☐
Insulation – adequacy	☐	☐	☐	☐
Plumbing – adequacy and condition	☐	☐	☐	☐
Electrical – adequacy and condition	☐	☐	☐	☐
Kitchen Cabinets – adequacy and condition	☐	☐	☐	☐
Compatibility to Neighborhood	☐	☐	☐	☐
Overall Livability	☐	☐	☐	☐
Appeal and Marketability	☐	☐	☐	☐

ATTIC ☐ Yes ☐ No Stairway Drop stair Scuttle Floored
Finished (Describe)   Heated
CAR STORAGE Garage Built in Attached Detached Car Port
No. Cars   Adequate Inadequate Condition
Yrs Est Remaining Economic Life   to   Explain if less than Loan Term

FIREPLACES, PATIOS, POOL, FENCES, etc. (describe)

COMMENTS (including functional or physical inadequacies, repairs needed, modernization, etc.)

Table 16.3. (Continued)

VALUATION SECTION

Purpose of Appraisal is to estimate Market Value as defined in Certification & Statement of Limiting Conditions (FHLMC Form 439/FNMA Form 1004B). If submitted for FNMA, the appraiser must attach (1) sketch or map showing location of subject, street names, distance from nearest intersection, and any detrimental conditions and (2) exterior building sketch of improvements showing dimensions

Measurements		No. Stories		Sq. Ft.		ESTIMATED REPRODUCTION COST – NEW – OF IMPROVEMENTS
x ____	x ____	____	=	____		Dwelling ____ Sq. Ft. @ $ ____ = $ ____

Total Gross Living Area (List in Market Data Analysis below) ____

Comment on functional and economic obsolescence: ____

ESTIMATED REPRODUCTION COST – NEW – OF IMPROVEMENTS:
Dwelling ____ Sq. Ft. @ $ ____ = $ ____
____ Sq. Ft. @ $ ____ = $ ____
Extras ____
Special Energy Efficient Items ____
Porches, Patios, etc. ____
Garage/Car Port ____ Sq. Ft. @ $ ____ =
Site Improvements (driveway, landscaping, etc.)
Total Estimated Cost New ____ = $ ____

Less | Physical | Functional | Economic
Depreciation $ ____ | $ | $ | = $ ( )
Depreciated value of improvements ____ = $ ____
ESTIMATED LAND VALUE ____ = $ ____
(If leasehold, show only leasehold value)
INDICATED VALUE BY COST APPROACH ____ $ ____

The undersigned has recited three recent sales of properties most similar and proximate to subject and has considered these in the market analysis. The description includes a dollar adjustment, reflecting market reaction to those items of significant variation between the subject and comparable properties. If a significant item in the comparable property is superior to, or more favorable than, the subject property, a minus (-) adjustment is made, thus reducing the indicated value of subject; if a significant item in the comparable is inferior to, or less favorable than, the subject property, a plus (+) adjustment is made, thus increasing the indicated value of the subject.

ITEM	Subject Property	COMPARABLE NO. 1		COMPARABLE NO. 2		COMPARABLE NO. 3	
Address							
Proximity to Subj.							
Sales Price	$	$		$		$	
Price/Living area	$	$		$		$	
Data Source							
Date of Sale and Time Adjustment	DESCRIPTION	DESCRIPTION	+(-)$ Adjustment	DESCRIPTION	+(-)$ Adjustment	DESCRIPTION	+(-)$ Adjustment
Location							
Site/View							
Design and Appeal							
Quality of Const.							
Age							
Condition							
Living Area Room Count and Total	Total Br-ms Baths	Total Br-ms Baths		Total Br-ms Baths		Total Br-ms Baths	
Gross Living Area	Sq.Ft.	Sq.Ft.		Sq.Ft.		Sq.Ft.	
Basement & Bsmt. Finished Rooms							
Functional Utility							
Air Conditioning							
Garage/Car Port							
Porches, Patio, Pools, etc.							
Special Energy Efficient Items							
Other (e.g. fire-places, kitchen equip., remodeling)							
Sales or Financing Concessions							
Net Adj. (Total)		☐ Plus; ☐ Minus $		☐ Plus; ☐ Minus $		☐ Plus; ☐ Minus $	
Indicated Value of Subject		$		$		$	

Comments on Market Data ____

INDICATED VALUE BY MARKET DATA APPROACH ____ $ ____

INDICATED VALUE BY INCOME APPROACH ____ (If applicable) Economic Market Rent $ ____ /Mo. x Gross Rent Multiplier ____ = $ ____

This appraisal is made ☐ "as is" ☐ subject to the repairs, alterations, or conditions listed below ☐ completion per plans and specifications:

Comments and Conditions of Appraisal: ____

Final Reconciliation: ____

Construction Warranty ☐ Yes ☐ No Name of Warranty Program ____ Warranty Coverage Expires ____

This appraisal is based upon the above requirements, the certification, contingent and limiting conditions, and Market Value definition that are stated in

☐ FHLMC Form 439 (Rev. 10/78)/FNMA Form 1004B (Rev. 10/78) filed with client ____ 19 ____ ☐ attached.

I ESTIMATE THE MARKET VALUE, AS DEFINED, OF SUBJECT PROPERTY AS OF ____ 19 ____ to be $ ____

Appraiser(s) ____ Review Appraiser (If applicable) ____ ☐ Did ☐ Did Not Physically Inspect Property

underwriter must be careful not to lend on a property that is deteriorating. Such a property may be good security now, but will not be good security in the future. The appraisal report will be used to assess this condition.

The Lending Decision and Loan Closing

After analyzing all of the above factors, the underwriter makes the lending decision. In many instances, the underwriter will submit his or her recommendation to a loan committee made up of designated officers of the institution or firm. That committee can either approve or override the underwriter's decision. The majority of loan decisions are fairly clear-cut to an experienced underwriter; either the borrower clearly meets all the requirements or does not. Marginal cases provide the real tests for the underwriter. What weight should be given certain strengths and weaknesses of an applicant? Resolving problems is not easy and requires all the skills of the underwriter to make sure that reasonable loans are made and unreasonable ones that would work a hardship on the borrower and the lender are not. Single family underwriting remains a combination of art and science.

If the loan is approved, a date will ultimately be established for closing the loan, the final event in the loan origination process of Table 16.4. Closing refers to the signing of the lending documents and the disbursement of the loan proceeds. If a purchase is involved, the loan will usually be closed at the same time the transaction is closed. As the borrower, you can obtain advance copies of all documents you will be asked to sign at closing. You should read these documents carefully, seeking legal counsel if you have any questions about the meaning of any provision. If you have points of disagreement with the lender, you should

Table 16.4. Summary of Single Family Residential Loan Origination Process

Event	Action
Pre-application conference	Discuss needs, terms, necessary information, and processing time.
Application	Information gathered on borrower and property, requests for verifications and credit report signed, fees collected.
Data collection	Verifications, appraisal, and credit report obtained.
Decision	Information processed and underwriter's decision passed to loan committee for action.
	If Approved
Closing	Loan documents signed and loan proceeds disbursed.

contact him or her and either resolve these issues or agree to disagree and terminate the lending transaction. By the time the closing date arrives, both parties should be satisfied with the details of the transaction. For this reason, most loan closings are, thankfully, uneventful.

OVERVIEW OF THE PERMANENT INCOME PROPERTY LENDING PROCESS

As you will recall from Chapter 15, income property financing involves permanent, construction, and land financing. This section considers the one you are most likely to be concerned with, permanent financing. For anything to happen, borrowers must want to borrow and lenders must want to lend. Therefore, the motivations of borrowers and lenders are first reviewed.

Borrower Motivation

Borrowers borrow for all kinds of reasons, including need, leverage, inflation, and taxes. Need is an important motivator since few investors have the cash necessary to purchase or develop real estate without borrowing. Favorable leverage, the ability to potentially increase the return on a good investment by borrowing is another motivating factor. The fact that interest is tax deductible is another factor contributing to borrower's desires to borrow. Finally, inflation motivates borrowers because they can pay off a loan with less valuable dollars. For example, if you borrow money for a small warehouse today, the dollars you make payments with one year from now will likely be worth less than the dollars you received today.

Lender Motivation

Institutional lenders, such as savings and loan associations, insurance companies, and so on, are interested in two things: safety and return. Because they handle other people's money and are placed in a position of trust, these institutions must be concerned with the risk involved in any investment they undertake. They must take only the reasonable risks of a "prudent man." Given a maximum level of acceptable risk, these investors try to find investments from which they expect to earn the maximum level of return. Such a level of expected return allows them to give their investors, depositors, or policyholders the highest return while also maximizing the institution's profits.

The long terms of income property loans, usually 25 to 30 years, also appeal to lenders. Such terms allow them to lock in a return and plan their cash inflows and outflows to meet their obligations. In reality, most loans are paid off much earlier, usually when the property is sold. Lenders take this into account when planning cash inflows and out-flows. Many lenders prefer to make large loans because it costs as much to put a small loan on the books as a large one. Thus, a lender can underwrite a $10 million loan for only a nominal amount more than a $1 million one. In this regard, many income property real estate loans offer adequate size to make them attractive. Large institutions often will not consider real estate loans of less than $750,000 to $1 million.

Desired Loan Terms

Borrowers Borrowers will usually try to borrow the maximum amount possible at the lowest interest rate for the longest period of time. Borrow-ing the largest amount possible minimizes the necessary equity cash to get into a real estate deal. It also may allow the borrower to get into two or more real estate investments rather than a single one. The lowest inter-est rate and longest term minimize the payments for a loan of a given amount. Generally, borrowers are not concerned about paying off the loan through payments because they know they will likely sell the prop-erty well before the loan is paid off. Proceeds from the sale will then be used to pay off the loan.

Lenders Not surprisingly, lenders desire some slightly different loan terms than borrowers. Lenders seek an interest rate as high as competi-tion will allow to increase their return on the loan. With respect to the term of the loan, lenders want long-term investments but not so long that amortization of the loan does not provide protection for possible decreases in property values. Lenders look to the gradual paying off of the loan to provide a safety factor against property value decline in case of a default. Accordingly, lenders have sought terms of from 20 to 30 years. Lenders want to lend the maximum amount that can be safely lent. Since lenders are interested in making low-risk loans, the maxi-mum they are willing to lend may be lower than that sought by an optimistic borrower more willing to take risk and anxious to put a deal together.

Underwriting the Permanent Loan

Suppose you are interested in buying a small office building. Where do you go to find a permanent loan? Looking back at Chapter 15, the logical place to go would be to those investing in such loans, the largest investor being life insurance companies. Chances are, unless you live in a very large city, you will have little success in finding life insurance company loan offices in your hometown. Loan volume in most cities simply is not large enough and is too cyclical to justify having company loan representatives there. The costs of such operations simply outweigh the income they produce.

As an alternative, life insurance companies depend on mortgage bankers to locate and submit promising loan requests to them. A mortgage banker performing this service for a life insurance company is said to be a **loan correspondent.** Both parties benefit from the correspondent relationship; the mortgage banker has a lender to make loans and provide loans to service, and the lender has a source of borrowers. A mortgage banker will generally act as correspondent for more than one lender. Likewise, life insurance companies may have more than one correspondent in a given city.

Your first step will be to visit a mortgage banker with staff members specializing in income property lending. You will discuss the property, the terms under which you are buying it, your background in real estate, your plans for the property, and the general terms of the financing you are seeking. The mortgage banker can answer questions you may have about financing and may make suggestions about the property and financing terms generally available in the market. At this stage you may want to visit more than one mortgage banker to compare terms and find the mortgage banker with whom you feel most comfortable.

After you leave the mortgage banker's office, you and the mortgage banker have decisions to make. You must decide whether the financing terms generally available in the market are acceptable. Is the project going to be profitable at the present interest rates? Do you have the equity money necessary to cover the difference between the loan amount and the purchase price? The mortgage banker must decide whether the price you are paying is a reasonable one, whether you have enough experience and skill to successfully operate a real estate investment, and whether the property will produce enough income to support the loan you are seeking. He will also contact certain lenders by telephone to see if they have an interest in making a loan of this type.

If both parties feel the project is worthwhile, you will again visit the mortgage banker and make formal application for a loan. The formal application requires that you provide a good deal of information. The facts and figures required by one mortgage banker are listed in Table 16.5. Examination of this table shows that everything from the audited financial statements of the borrowers to building plans are required. It is also necessary to specify precisely the terms of the financing you are seeking. In addition to information, you will also be asked to sign a contract authorizing the mortgage banker to seek financing for you for a specified fee.

Once all the information is provided to the mortgage banker, he or she will prepare a **loan submission package** containing all the information about the property, city, and borrower that the lender may need to make a lending decision. When you consider that the lender is miles away in another city and may have little knowledge of your city and its

Table 16.5. Checklist of Information Typically Required
for Income Property Loan Application

Thank you for your mortgage loan inquiry. This "Checklist" is designed to remind you of certain exhibits and documents usually required by our lenders.

The items "x'd" are applicable; other items may be required at a later date. Omission of any item requested will tend to delay processing. *Original or good copies* will enhance your loan possibilities.

<u>Items Required</u>   <u>Items Received to Date</u>

(1) <u>Re Sponsor:</u>

——— Brief but comprehensive biographical sketch re: Business back-   ———
ground, experience, etc. Current signed financial statements.

——— Will borrower be a Corporation? ——— Partnership? ———   ———
Individual? ——— If so, who are the principal officers and shareholders and what is the percentage of ownership of each? Will they
personally endorse the Note and Mortgage?

——— Preliminary Partnership Agreement.   ———

——— Operating Statements (Statements of Income and Expense) last five   ———
years or since formed.

——— List of Clients: (Confidential Information)   ———

——— Bank References   ———

——— Complete formal loan application   ———

Disbursement Date Desired ——————, 19———.

(2) <u>Re Site:</u>

——— (a) Complete plot plan (showing location of proposed improve-   ———
ments, property lines, any easements restricting use of the property, streets abutting the property, ingress and egress, etc.).

(b) Correct legal description of the property to be mortgaged.

(c) Two city street maps (one should indicate location of subject
site.).

(d) Local Chamber of Commerce literature, including "written support" from same for your project (if available).

(e) Evidence of proper zoning.

(f) Evidence of ownership (warranty deed or option).

Applicant shall have full land control, valid deed or option to purchase, purchase agreement and be in compliance with any and all
applicable laws, regulations, zoning requirements. Failure to
comply will not affect the validity of an application.

Name and Address of Interim Construction Lender.

(3) <u>Re Improvements:</u>

——— (a) Preliminary Building Plans (and, eventually, final building   ———
plans). Show <u>Net</u> and <u>Gross</u> square footages (2 sets).

(b) Outline building specifications (and eventually final building
specifications) (2 sets).

(c) Elevation–Concept of Building Design.

(d) Owner's Income and Expense Projection.

(e) Owner's and Architect's and/or Builder's cost Estimate (including all direct, indirect costs, plus land cost and/or value).

(f) List of all chattels, where applicable. Separately financed?

(g) List and copies of all valid leases, lease intents, and correspon-
dence relating thereto, if applicable.

Table 16.5. (Continued)

_____ Copy of Signed Builder's Contract. _____

_____ Franchise Agreement: or intent from Franchisor (Hotels, Restau- _____
rants, etc.).

_____ _____

_____ _____

_____ Furnish an M.A.I. Appraisal Report satisfactory _____ to _____
_____ if required.

_____ Copy of First Mortgage with Note.

(4) Applicant(s) Agree To:

    (a) Deposit a nonrefundable loan processing fee to an amount equal
to 1/10 of 1% of loan application or $350, whichever is greater. $_____

    (b) If project is beyond 50 miles from the city a travel allowance in
the amount of. . . . . $_____

    (c) TOTAL Nonrefundable Deposit required with application. $_____

*If project is ultimately approved and accepted, the above charges shall be credited to
borrowers _____% earned loan placement fee due.

(5) Good Faith Deposit:

    (100% Refundable) Prior to acceptance of a formal loan application,
a _____% or $_____ "good faith deposit" shall have been
tendered to _____ (Escrow Account). Said deposit shall be returned when the loan is completed or disapproved. If a commitment
is accepted but not closed for reasons of the borrower and not the
lender, said deposits shall be forefeited to the lender as liquidated
damages for services performed.

    The Checklist is designed to assist you in our preparation of docu-
ments/exhibits to the best of your ability, permitting our firm to better
serve you. Sketchy information is difficult to service.

    If a loan, or commitment for a loan, is accepted, it shall be a first lien
upon the property above described, free from unpaid taxes, general
and special, judgments, transcripts of judgments, and mechanics' or
materialmens' liens. A loan is not applied for to take up a foreclosed
loan.

Date: _____, 19___

SOURCE: Robert W. Sligar, Mortgage Broker.

real estate markets and, certainly, no knowledge of your project, you can
see why the loan submission package must be very complete. Therefore,
the mortgage banker should know the items each lender likes to see in
such a package. Preparing this package is a time-consuming task but
will spell the difference between whether the loan is made or not. It is not
surprising that loan submission packages for some properties will often
contain 75 pages or more.

Income Property Loan Decision

Underwriters will examine the submission package and call the mortgage banker for any additional information they need. In underwriting
income property loans the income produced by the property, not the
income of the borrower, is the most critical factor. Of course, the bor-

rower's balance sheet and income are considered, but the property must be able to pay its own way. Other factors considered are the real estate experience of the borrower, the mortgage banker's analysis of the local real estate market and this project, and the estimated market value of the property.

In analyzing the income produced by a property, lenders frequently use two ratios. One involves the gross possible income the property is expected to produce. Gross possible income is income from all sources before any reductions for expenses. The other ratio uses net operating income, defined as gross possible income minus a vacancy allowance and expected operating expenses. Gross possible income is used to calculate the breakeven point for the property. The breakeven point is the percentage of gross possible income that must be produced to cover all operating expenses and the debt service payments of principal and interest. It is calculated as follows:

$$\text{Breakeven point} = \frac{\text{Operating expenses} + \text{Debt service}}{\text{Gross possible income}}$$

For a property with operating expenses of $40,000 per year, debt service (principal and interest) on the loan being sought of $45,000, and gross possible income of $100,000, the breakeven point is 85 percent:

$$\text{Breakeven point} = \frac{\$40,000 + \$45,000}{\$100,000}$$

$$\text{Breakeven point} = \frac{\$85,000}{\$100,000}$$

$$= .85 \text{ or } 85\%$$

This ratio indicates that the subject property must generate 85 percent of its gross possible rents just to cover all costs. Obviously, the lower the ratio the less likely the property is to fall short of breakeven.

The second ratio is the debt coverage ratio (DCR), designed to measure the number of times net operating income covers the debt service required on the loan being sought.

$$\text{Debt coverage ratio} = \frac{\text{Net operating income}}{\text{Debt service}}$$

If the property above is expected to have a net operating income of $55,000, then with debt service of $45,000, the DCR is 1.22.

$$\text{Debt coverage ratio} = \frac{\$55,000}{\$45,000}$$

$$= 1.22$$

The larger this ratio, the more secure a lender feels about a property's ability to generate the income necessary to repay a loan.

Both the default point and the DCR are calculated using information supplied by the mortgage banker tempered by the lender's experience and judgment. Values used in the calculations usually represent a typical or normal year of operation. However, in some cases, default points and DCRs are calculated for several years based on forecasts to evaluate the property's long-term ability to generate income to repay the loan. Each lender uses experience to develop maximum allowable values for the default point and minimum allowable values for the DCR they consider acceptable.

From the analysis of these ratios and other factors, the lender decides to either make the loan exactly as requested, make a loan subject to changes in the request, or not make a loan at all. If the lender seeks changes in the requested loan, either the amount, interest rate, or length, you will be contacted by the mortgage banker. You and the lender will then negotiate using the mortgage banker as an intermediary. This negotiation is often a difficult process as you and the lender seek to achieve your goals and structure a loan package with which you both can live.

Once agreement is reached on the terms of the loan, the lender will issue a **commitment letter.** The commitment letter states that the lender is willing to make a loan, the terms of the loan, the fee for the commitment, and the period of time within which the loan must be closed. As the borrower, you will be asked to sign the commitment letter signifying your acceptance of its provisions. When signed, the commitment letter acts as a contract; you have agreed to borrow and the lender has agreed to lend. Money will be disbursed and the note and mortgage signed at closing, the same as in single family lending. Once made, the mortgage banker will service the loan for a fee.

SUMMARY

This chapter has considered the decision-making processes of real estate lenders. Starting with the premise that lenders want to make loans in order to produce income necessary to pay depositors and policyholders, we have discussed the underwriting procedures associated with single family and income property loans.

Single family loans are regarded as credit loans because they are based on the credit worthiness of the borrower. For a loan to be made, the lender must be convinced that the borrower has the ability and desire to repay it. Additionally, the property must provide adequate security for the loan in case the borrower defaults. Property analysis is accomplished using an appraisal performed by a professional appraiser, rather than the lender's personal visit to the property. Neighborhood characteristics and subject property characteristics are considered in estimating the market value of the property.

Assessing the ability to pay involves using information from the application and from verification responses. Income is qualified based on its quality and likely duration. The mortgage debt service and fixed obligation ratios are used to estimate the loan amount the qualified income can likely support at present interest rates. The balance sheet is used to determine from where money for the down payment and any financial emergencies will come.

The desire to pay is estimated using a credit report. Information about past credit performance is considered the best evidence of likely future behavior. Credit reporting agencies supply these reports to lenders for a fee. Lenders look for patterns of poor credit management by the borrower. Some of these problems may be adequately explained away by the borrower.

Permanent income property lending may also be advantageous to borrowers and lenders if the loan is a good one. Loan decisions are based on the ability of the property to produce enough income to repay the loan rather than depending on the credit of the borrower. Many income property loans are originated through mortgage bankers acting as loan correspondents for large lenders such as life insurance companies. After initial screening, the mortgage banker prepares a loan submission package and forwards it to the lender. Usually a period of negotiations follows in which the mortgage banker plays the role of mediator. When, and if, agreement is reached, the lender will issue a letter of commitment outlining the details of the lending arrangements. A closing date is established, and on that date, the loan papers are signed and funds disbursed.

QUICK QUIZ

1. Which of the following types of information will *not* be a part of the loan application?

a. income
b. marital status of applicant(s)
c. employment history
d. assets

2. An appraisal contains information about the

I. property and neighborhood
II. market value of the property

a. I only
b. II only
c. Both I and II
d. Neither I nor II

3. The mortgage debt service ratio considers all of the following except:

a. other financial obligations
b. property taxes
c. hazard insurance premiums
d. principal and interest payments

4. In making income property loans, the mortgage banker acts as a(n) _____ for the lender.

    a. pen pal   c. decision maker
    b. accountant   d. correspondent

5. The best evidence of a potential borrower's desire to pay is the _____ .

    a. credit report   c. income statement
    b. balance sheet   d. gift letter

6. In underwriting a loan application, the lender must assess the _____ and _____ of the borrower to repay the loan.

7. Your net worth may be found by subtracting your _____ from your _____ .

8. In reviewing the income statement, lenders look for income that is _____ and _____ .

9. In underwriting a permanent loan for income producing real estate, _____ is the most critical factor.

10. The _____ letter states that the lender is willing to make a loan, the terms of that loan, the fee the borrower is charged for the promise to lend and the period of time within which the loan must be closed.

QUESTIONS AND EXERCISES

1. If a family with monthly income of $2000 per month and long-term monthly obligations of $350 per month wants to purchase a home with insurance premiums and property taxes of $150 per month, what is the maximum loan they are likely to qualify for at a 10 percent interest rate using the two income ratios considered in the chapter? At 12 percent and 14 percent interest rates?

2. If a loan applicant with ten years experience as an electrical engineer was to apply for a loan and discloses that he or she has net worth of only $10,000 despite earning a high salary, what would you think? List the possible circumstances creating this situation which would make you more favorably inclined toward the applicant. Less favorably inclined.

3. For the applicant in Question 2, would the balance sheet matter at all if income was more than adequate?

4. How would you analyze the balance sheet of a loan applicant?

5. Contact a credit reporting agency in your community and ask them to outline the steps necessary to review your credit report. Also, have them outline the steps necessary to correct a mistake on your credit report. Summarize your findings.

KEY TERMINOLOGY

ability to pay	loan closing
balance sheet	loan correspondent
breakeven point	loan submission package
commitment letter	mortgage debt service ratio
debt coverage ratio	net worth
desire to pay	qualified income
fixed obligation ratio	underwriting
gift letter	verification

IF YOU WANT TO READ MORE

JAMES A. BRITTON, JR. and LEWIS O. KERWOOD, eds., *Financing Income Producing Real Estate — A Theory and Casebook* (New York: McGraw-Hill, 1977).

JEROME DASSO and GERALD KUHN, *Real Estate Finance* (Englewood Cliffs, NJ: Prentice-Hall, Inc., 1983).

DONALD R. EPLEY and JAMES A. MILLER, *Basic Real Estate Finance and Investments,* 2nd ed. (New York: John Wiley & Sons, 1984).

C. F. SIRMANS, *Real Estate Finance* (New York: McGraw-Hill, Inc., 1985).

JOHN P. WIEDEMER, *Real Estate Finance,* 4th ed. (Reston, VA: Reston Publishing Company, Inc., 1983).

17

Real Estate Development

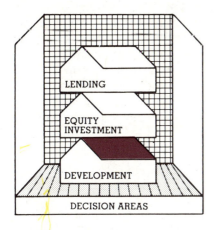

LENDING

EQUITY INVESTMENT

DEVELOPMENT

DECISION AREAS

PREVIEW

Probably few aspects of real estate capture the imagination as much as development. Who hasn't marveled at a tall building or watched the progress of a construction project with some fascination? There is something inside us that marvels at the process of taking a parcel of undeveloped land and turning it into a finished product that is attractive and functional. That is what real estate development is all about. It is the process of providing space for people — space for people to work, shop, and entertain themselves. If you decide to construct apartments or an office building on Blackacre, you must either act as the developer or find someone willing to do so. This chapter provides you with an understanding of:

1. Who develops and why.
2. The development process.
3. The decisions that must be made.
4. New and emerging forms of development.

Real estate development requires a great deal of imagination, planning, management ability, money, patience, and good fortune, all of which are in short supply. Development successes, such as Walt Disney World in

Florida, provide excellent financial rewards for the developer and interesting and useful places for people. Development failures provide potentially staggering financial losses and may not provide the type and quality of space people need. The buildings you see around you were developed by either the government or the private sector. Some developments are made on a grand scale and capture the imagination with their scale or with their dramatic design, such as the Renaissance Center in Detroit, some of the hotels in Las Vegas, Epcot Center, and some of the office buildings of New York and Chicago. Other developments try to combine the buildings and land in such a way as to provide a very natural, unobtrusive feeling. The new towns of Reston, Virginia, and Columbia, Maryland, and probably some residential subdivisions in your own city are examples of such developments. Whatever the development scheme, all buildings share one feature; they were developed to provide space for people.

OVERVIEW OF REAL ESTATE DEVELOPMENT

Development is the process of combining land, labor, capital, and entrepreneurial ability to produce improvements to land. Development is not limited to erecting buildings. It also includes installing streets, water facilities, sewers, electrical lines, and natural gas lines and performing the necessary survey work to create building lots for single family residences. What is important is the activity of adding man-made features to land. Development is concerned with the creation of space: space in which to play, live, work, and build. Today, with the push to restore older structures, development should also include the redevelopment of existing buildings as well as the erection of new ones.

Profit is the primary motivator of developers. They seek to make a profit by producing a product and selling it for more than it cost to produce. That is, a developer who estimates that an office building development will cost a total of $4 million hopes to make a profit by selling the project for more than $4 million. The amount above $4 million is profit and an addition to the developer's wealth. In other words, developers seek to create wealth. If the expected wealth added by the project is not great enough, the developer will not undertake the project.

In this regard, a developer attempts to produce the type, quality, and quantity of space on a particular site that maximizes profits. A developer realizes that the costs of producing space increase with the size and the quality of the space. Further, different types of space such as apartments and office buildings simply do not cost the same to produce. On the value side, a developer knows that the value of the completed project is dependent on the rental income it will produce. That rental income is a function of the condition of real estate rental markets. Thus, the developer attempts to evaluate the costs and values associated with different development concepts in order to choose the most profitable one. This most profitable concept is the highest and best use discussed earlier in the book.

This idea of profit maximization is illustrated in Figure 17.1, which illustrates the relationship between the quantity of space, development costs, value, and developer's profit for a particular type of space. In the upper graph, development costs are seen to increase at an increasing rate as more space is produced on the site. This reflects the higher costs

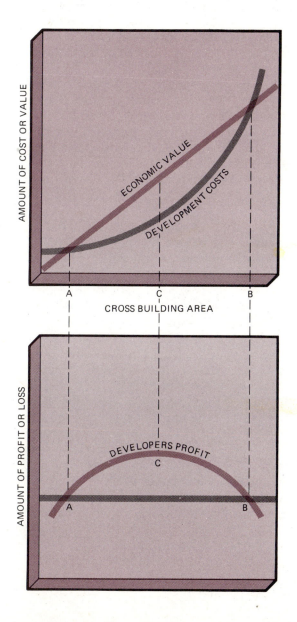

Figure 17.1
Relationship between development costs, economic value, and developer's profit. Source: Bruce Singer, "Determining Optimum Developmental Intensity," *Readings in Real Estate Investment Analysis*, American Institute of Real Estate Appraisers, 1977, p. 223.

associated with building taller, more complex buildings. The economic value curve reflects the assumption that each square foot of additional space adds the same amount of value. This simplifying assumption may not always be true, but is helpful here to illustrate the concept without doing any damage. The lower graph maps the difference between value and costs, which is profit. In this example, profit is greatest at point C. Thus, C is the optimum developmental intensity for this use.

Not all developers plan on selling their projects as soon as they are completed but want to assume the role of equity investor and operate the property. Nevertheless, while the project was being translated from idea to reality, they act as developer. Profit is not the only motivator for developers; many are also motivated by the desire to improve their community and other factors.

For the developer interested in selling the project when it is completed, development is usually a shorter term situation than equity investment. The word *usually* is used because some equity investments are very short-term while some large development projects require a rather long planning and construction period, especially those developed in phases. Thus, developers must always be aware of their next project or, as many developers do, have more than one project going at a time to avoid periods of inactivity.

Development Risks

Development always carries with it the risk of loss. Cost overruns created by high interest rates, poor estimates, labor problems, or bad weather can destroy a project's profitability even if it satisfies the demand for space. Likewise, if the market demand for the type of space being developed is satisfied before the project is completed, the developer may not be able to sell it for as much as anticipated. A combination of cost overruns and changes in markets can be particularly devastating to the developer. These risks are now considered in a little more detail.

Legal Risk From Chapter 8 you know that land use controls, such as zoning, restrict the kinds of space and how much of it may be built on a site. Public services such as water and sewerage may also be used to discourage development by either not allowing a developer to use the system or forcing the developer to pay for extending these services. These regulations create risk for the real estate developer in that he or she may spend a good bit of money in planning a project and making necessary applications for government approval only to be turned down. If denied, the costs associated with planning and application are lost and, if the land is owned, its value may decrease. The costs associated with planning and obtaining legal approval should not be underestimated. Architectural fees, attorney's fees, soil analyses, and so on are terribly expensive.

Because of the expense involved, estimating the legal risk for a project is an important aspect of the developer's feasibility analysis. Public opinion, especially the sentiment of those near the project, should be carefully evaluated to determine what objections may be raised to the project. Often, meetings with future neighbors of the project may be used to communicate the true nature of the project and answer questions about the impact of the development. Likewise, research should be conducted into recent decisions on similar projects to see whether precedents exist. Finally, the availability of utilities should be explored to determine whether they represent a potential problem for the development.

One option available to minimize legal risk is to purchase land already zoned for the intended use. However, much undeveloped land was zoned years ago and that zoning may not reflect current market demands for space. Many developers seek to purchase land subject to necessary approvals, zoning and otherwise. Then, if the necessary approvals cannot be obtained, the developer does not have to purchase. There is still a financial loss since the developer probably incurred expenses in the application process, but at least the developer does not have to hold a parcel of land until it can be sold.

Market Risk Real estate markets create additional risks for developers. In Chapter 9 you learned that there are two general types of markets: rental and equity. You also learned that these two markets are interrelated and that conditions in them are constantly changing. Since the developer will likely want to sell the project either during construction or shortly after completion, and since its value is related to the rents it will produce, along with other factors, these markets are of prime interest to the developer. A real estate developer must assess current conditions in both markets and possible changes in them during the development period. An inability to rent the space being constructed, or having to rent it at reduced rates, will affect the value of the project. Likewise, changes in interest rates and other factors may increase or decrease the desirability of the project as an equity investment.

Market risk can be reduced by solid market research. Specifically, what the developer needs is a **marketability study,** a study of the ability of a type, quality, and quantity of space at a specific location to be rented or sold at varying prices. A marketability study will include a **market study,** which is an analysis of the general supply and demand situation for a particular type of space. Thus, you may perform a market study on the supply of and demand for suburban office buildings in your community. In performing a marketability study for a proposed suburban office building, you will use that market study as the basis for estimating the likelihood of that particular space being rented and the appropriate rental rates, given the characteristics of the building.

Obviously, before the likelihood of renting the space at various prices is estimated, the present quantity of available space, and possible changes in that quantity during development, must be estimated. Once the quantity of space likely to be demanded and the quantity likely to be available are estimated, rents for the proposed building can be estimated based on its location and amenities relative to other buildings and their rents.

Many market studies rely on the development of **absorption rates,** the annual rate at which additional space is being utilized. For instance, research may indicate that, on average, 500,000 square feet of suburban office space has been needed each year for the past five years. Some developers take this to mean that 500,000 additional square feet will be needed next year. This may or may not be true. Absorption rates may provide a clue to possible needs in coming years, but the critical factors are those underlying the creation of a need for 500,000 square feet each year. Another possible problem with absorption rates is that they are often averages, with the actual amount of space absorbed each period varying widely. While the average absorption may be acceptable for the developer, a below-average year may spell disaster. Thus, the importance of analyzing the factors affecting supply and demand to reduce market risk cannot be overemphasized.

In estimating the supply and demand situation in equity markets, attention should be given to interest rate levels and possible changes in those levels. Changes in interest rates affect the income a property can generate for its owner. With all other things staying the same, an increase in interest rates will reduce the market value of a property. Likewise, possible changes in income tax laws that may affect the property, and their impact on the property, should be considered. For instance, when the Economic Recovery Tax Act was passed, certain tax shelter benefits associated with real property ownership were enhanced. Informed developers converted these increased benefits for equity investors into higher prices for their projects. The subject development should also be compared to other properties on the market, or likely to be on the market. Physical condition, amenities, and location, among other factors, should be considered in its analysis. The result of this analysis is an estimate of the project's competitive position in the equity markets.

The possibility of market change during development forces the developer to make decisions about when to sell the project. That is, the earlier the developer sells the venture, the sooner one source of risk is eliminated. This decision is not that simple, because usually the earlier the project is sold, the lower the price. This is true because buyers also know that markets may change and the more time before occupancy, the greater the possibility of adverse market changes occurring and the less the buyer is willing to pay. In some instances, the developer will complete the improvement and lease all or part of it in order to get the maximum price. Figure 17.2 illustrates the trade-off between project value

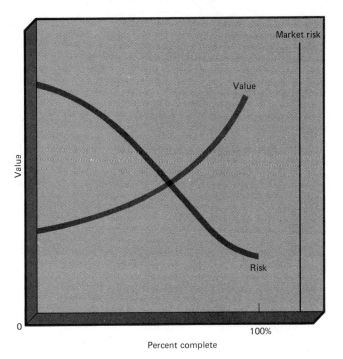

Figure 17.2
Typical pattern of market risk and value during development period. (Value and risk will not increase and decrease exactly as shown; however, the figure illustrates the general trends of increasing value and decreasing risk.)

and market risk. So, the developer must decide when to sell the project and concentrate on the next general source of risk, cost risk.

Cost Risk Even if a developer correctly assesses demand, rents, and the market value of the space being produced, making a profit is dependent on the cost of producing the space. Estimating this cost is no small matter. In times of inflation, costs frequently change during the course of development. Under cost plus contracts with general contractors, the developer pays all costs plus a fee to the contractor. The longer the development period, the greater this risk.

Developers can protect themselves by having the buildings constructed under contracts that fix a maximum price for the construction. Such contracts are called **guaranteed maximum price contracts.** Again, a trade-off exists because contractors agreeing to a fixed contract price will build a cushion to cover possible cost overruns into their cost quote. This means you will not likely get the lowest possible construction cost, but you will have limited your risk. This risk can also be reduced by dealing with **general contractors,** those in charge of the overall construction effort, who are reputable and bonded. One type of bond, called the **completion bond,** guarantees that the project will be completed for the agreed price even if it actually costs more than that amount or the general contractor has financial difficulties. Not only will developers want this protection, but many construction lenders will require that contractors obtain bonds.

Types of Development

You can think of development in terms of two general types. First is development activity involving improvements to land to get it ready for building activity. This area of development includes producing building lots of all types, such as for single family homes and industrial buildings. It is easy to forget that many industrial parks are created by developers who get the individual lots ready and then sell them to business firms or other developers wanting to build on them. The same is true for some office parks.

The second general type of development involves erecting some type of space that is usable by people. These improvements can range from parking lots to shopping centers and multiple use structures like the Omni International complex in Atlanta. Some developers will perform both types of development by developing lots and also building the houses or other buildings.

Who Develops?

Developers come in all sizes and forms, ranging from the part-time builder producing one speculative home per year to large corporate developers undertaking many large projects each year. Gerald Hines, one of the more active developers, may start hundreds of millions of dollars worth of new projects in some years. Developers are organized as sole proprietorships, corporations, and partnerships. Sometimes a project is undertaken as a team effort between two entities in the form of a **joint venture.** The term joint venture is used to describe virtually any cooperative arrangement between two or more parties undertaking a development project. The joint venture participants may be two developers or a developer and a lender or any other combination of skills and interests. In periods of high interest rates, it is quite common for developers and lenders to form joint ventures.

THE DEVELOPMENT PROCESS

Development requires a number of steps; a developer does not simply decide to develop and instantly produce a finished product. The major steps in the development process are illustrated in Figure 17.3. Each step requires the developer to make decisions about whether to continue the project or whether any changes should be made in it. The developer does not have the luxury of performing each step in isolation; many

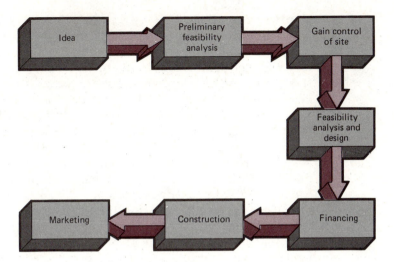

Figure 17.3 The development process.

things are going on at the same time. So in looking at Figure 17.3, keep in mind that the steps are not as distinct and orderly as they may appear.

Idea Stage

Every real estate development starts with an idea. You should not downplay the ability to generate ideas as part of the development process. Many of the now accepted concepts, such as enclosed mall shopping centers, multiple use buildings, exciting new hotels with open lobbies 20 to 30 stories tall, and mini-warehouses, all started out as ideas. Many of the more successful developers are quite good at visualizing what types of space are needed and where they should be located.

In the idea stage, the developer is faced with one of two problems. Either he or she has an existing site and must decide what to do with it or he or she has an idea and must find a site for it. For example, the Marriott hotel chain may feel that St. Louis needs more first class hotel space in the downtown area. They have an idea in search of a site, and must now try to locate the best possible site for their hotel project. In another case, a developer may own a site in downtown Seattle and be seeking the best use for the site.

In the idea phase very little is definite. Marriott may be interested in developing a hotel in downtown St. Louis, but the size, design, and features of that hotel are considered in only very general terms. For instance, they may think the hotel should have a minimum of 600 rooms, good meeting and banquet facilities, and first-class dining facilities. The details of the project are refined throughout the entire development process as more information about market demand, room rates, and land and construction costs become available.

Preliminary Feasibility Stage

Next, the developer will make a "rough-cut" analysis of whether the project is feasible. Feasibility is generally measured in economic terms: Is the project worth a sufficient amount more than it costs to produce? At this point, the developer must settle for rough estimates of the cost of development, the rents it can produce, and the resulting market value. For example, at this point Marriott is interested in whether its profits from room rentals and food and beverage sales will provide an adequate return on its estimated investment. Another developer interested in selling a project when it is completed may estimate the cost of construction, the rents it will produce, and what investors will pay for those rents (the market value of the project).

If the expected profit, the difference between the project's value and its cost, is great enough, the developer will continue with the project. Put another way, if the developer feels the profits provide enough cushion for possible cost overruns or lower than expected rents and market values, then the project will continue. If not, it will be dropped.

Gaining Control of the Site

If the developer does not yet control the site, it must be controlled at this time. It must be controlled, because the same improvements at a different site may not be feasible and the feasibility would have to be redone because of the new economics of the different site. The word *control* is used because the developer will not necessarily purchase the site. The site may be leased on a long-term *ground lease.* If the developer needs more time either for analysis or to arrange financing, he or she may try to buy an option from the landowner. An **option** gives the developer the exclusive right to buy the site at an agreed-upon price for a specified period of time, usually in return for a fee. Frequently, purchase contracts with provisions allowing the contract to be canceled if financing, zoning, or some other factor, cannot be worked out are used by developers.

Feasibility Analysis and Design

Once the site has been selected, more feasibility work can begin. How detailed the feasibility study is depends on the project and the developer. A complete feasibility study will analyze the legal, site, market, and financial aspects of the proposed development as outlined in Table 17.1. Legal analysis will tell the developer how much and what kind of space can legally be developed. Site analysis will provide information about the ability of the soil to support structures and any special problems for construction. Market research will help answer questions about how many square feet, rooms, or units to develop, what rents can be expected, and what features tenants want. Architectural and design work provides alternative designs and different locations on the site, as well as cost estimates. Financial analysis is then used to determine the size and

Table 17.1. Elements of Feasibility Analysis

1. **Objectives of the enterprise for whom the feasibility study is performed*:**
   A. Strategic objectives and priorities.
   B. Tactical alternatives acceptable to the enterprise.
   C. Decision rules or policies ultimately to make a selection from alternatives.
   * Reports dealing with these problems are properly termed *strategy studies.*

2. **Market trends to identify opportunity areas consistent with objectives*:**
   A. Aggregate data on population, employment, and income, for the appropriate area.
   B. National economic and political factors affecting priorities, incentive, timing, etc.
   C. Significant trends in public attitudes and mores that create or delineate sub-market motivations.
   D. Economic innovation relevant to the client.
   * Market analysis reports would include economic base studies, trade area delineation, or broad statistical surveys.

3. **Market segmentation for merchandising targets*:**
   A. Selection of special micromarkets with unmet space needs.
   B. Consumer profile analysis to determine product, price, and motivation.
   C. Determination of capture rates required as a ratio of total micromarket effective demand to achieve required levels of absorption.
   D. Preferred merchandising methods.
   * Merchandising studies include competitive property analysis, consumer surveys, product mix determination, and amenity product and pricing, as well as retail volume projections and formulas.

4. **Legal-political constraints*:**
   A. Regulatory constraints on the decision maker.
   B. Regulatory controls on site and space development.
   C. Regulatory controls on space users and managers.
   D. Regulatory constraints on those who supply capital.
   E. Outside political forces influencing administration of discretionary regulations.
   * These studies include legal opinions, statutes, corporate charters and bylaws, administrative rulings of various agencies, and political briefs.

5. **Aesthetic-ethical constraints*:**
   A. Environmental impact on the physical qualities of the land.
   B. Project impact on the general plans and values of the immediate community.
   C. Project obligations to future space users.
   D. Project influence on prime contractor-subcontractor relationships.
   E. Project relationship to priorities and self-image of the decision maker.
   * Reports on these aspects are generally called *impact* or *compatibility* studies.

6. **Physical-technical constraints and alternatives*:**
   A. Design to fit space user requirements as to location and improvements.
   B. Static and dynamic attributes of the site.
   C. All other space-product engineering considerations.
   * These aspects are treated in engineering studies, architectural schematics, and land suitability reports.

7. **Financial synthesis of proposed enterprise form*:**
   A. Specification of selected profit centers.
   B. Definition of time-line for the enterprise forecast.
   C. Capital budget estimate and schedule of outlays.
   D. Pattern of operating revenues and outlays.
   E. Financing plan for source and application of funds.
   F. Tax strategy.
   G. Selected measures of profitability.
   H. Selected indices of risk.
   * Financial studies may be termed financial feasibility, economic modeling, appraisals, sensitivity studies, cash flow forecasts, or income tax impact analyses.

SOURCE: James A. Graaskamp, "A Rational Approach to Feasibility Analysis," *Readings in Real Estate Investment Analysis,* American Institute of Real Estate Appraisers, 1977, pp. 210, 211.

design providing the best profitability. If these more detailed analyses indicate the project should not be undertaken, it can be dropped at this point.

What constitutes an acceptable or unacceptable project, at this point, depends on the objectives of the developer and the ability of the project to satisfy them. That is, the same results from a feasibility study may lead one developer to consider the project acceptable while another would find it unacceptable. So, you cannot say that a proposed project is acceptable without considering the specific developer. The developer provides the context within which a certain set of findings may be considered feasible or infeasible.

Financing Stage

During the feasibility analysis and design phase, preliminary discussions were started with construction and permanent lenders. Now that these plans are completed and the project has been determined to be feasible, negotiations on financing will be finalized. First, permanent financing will be arranged following the steps considered in Chapters 15 and 16. When the permanent financing has been arranged, the construction financing is then sought. The construction lender will want to see a firm commitment from a reputable permanent lender before considering your request for construction financing. Any difference between the construction loan amount and the cost of the project represents the required equity investment in the development of the project. You may want to review Chapter 16, dealing with real estate lending decisions, to review the general criteria lenders and borrowers may use in assessing a financing arrangement.

Construction Stage

While the activities described earlier are going on, the developer also considers the construction of the improvements. Construction is critical to the success of the entire project. If actual costs exceed the estimates used in the feasibility study, the project may turn from a winner to a loser. If the project is not completed on schedule, extra interest costs and lost rents could hurt profitability. If any of the parties involved in construction run into financial difficulties, the project could be held up by legal proceedings. The developer must decide who is to implement the architectural plans and under what conditions. The person or firm actually performing this task is either the **general contractor** or the **construction manager.**

Some developers may act as their own general contractor, or have someone on staff who can do so. Other developers will hire construction firms to act as the general contractor. In either case, the general contractor may or may not perform all of the construction tasks. In most cases, the general contractor will use subcontractors to perform certain tasks. For example, an electrical company may be used to perform all of the electrical work on a project, a plumbing company for all the plumbing, and a heating company for all the air conditioning and heating work. General contractors use subcontractors because it is not economical for them to have the large number of skilled workers and expensive equipment necessary to perform all facets of construction jobs.

The general contractor acts as the overall coordinator of the project, scheduling the subcontractors and making sure their work conforms to the plans and specifications of the developer. Subcontractors look to the general contractor for payment. The general contractor, in turn, looks to the developer for payment. Since the developer usually does not have either the time or the ability to supervise the actual construction, he or she will usually depend on either the architect or a construction management firm to act as construction manager and assure that the project is built according to agreed-on specifications and timetable. A fee will be paid to the construction manager for his or her services.

General contractors should be selected with care. The contractor should be financially sound, have a good track record in projects similar to the one planned, and be bondable. Bonding companies issue bonds for a fee guaranteeing that should the developer have financial difficulties the project will be completed for the agreed-upon price. Obviously, bonding companies issue bonds only on contractors they feel are good risks. Construction lenders often require that the general contractor obtain a bond.

Marketing Stage

The ultimate success of a development project depends on its marketability. Two types of marketing may accompany a development project. First, the space in the development must be leased. Second, if the project is to be sold, a buyer must be found. These two areas of marketing activity are closely related to one another since the ability to lease the space being produced is a prime determinant of the ability to find a buyer and the price that buyer is willing to pay. A project that has been leased to good tenants at competitive rental rates is attractive to potential equity investors and can command a top dollar price.

Leasing Leasing activity begins as early in the life of the project as possible in an attempt to get tenants into the building and paying rent as soon as the project is completed. Generating cash as early as possible is critical to the success of a project because the entire construction period is one of cash outflows. Often developers underestimate or simply fail to consider the cash necessary to operate the property after construction is completed and before the project is producing enough rents to cover costs. Some projects require years to reach this breakeven point. Many projects ultimately fail during this period, making the rent-up period one of the most dangerous periods in development.

When leasing activity begins varies from one type of property to another. For example, developers of large regional shopping centers usually must have secured the large department stores to serve as anchor tenants before they can even secure financing. Other tenants will usually be secured later in the development process. In contrast, apartment developers find it difficult to lease apartments years in advance and must depend on leasing activities during and after construction. Regardless of when leasing actually occurs, the developer must give considerable attention to developing a marketing plan that maximizes the chances of successfully leasing the space being developed to produce rents sufficient to cover operating expenses.

While leasing is considered in more detail in Chapter 22, dealing with property management, certain aspects of leasing need to be emphasized here as well. First, market research is critical in the leasing process. Knowledge of the market is valuable in determining what features are most important to potential tenants and what pricing structure should be established for the space. Second, you should realize that deciding when to lease space is sometimes not an easy one. If space is leased too early in the development process, it may be leased for rates that are below the going market rate when the project is completed. On the other hand, the opposite situation can occur and the developer may have been able to lock in prime lease rates because of tight market conditions at the time the space was originally leased. Once again, knowledge of the market is of great value in this decision. Another factor affecting when to implement a leasing program is the phase in the development when the project is to be sold.

Sale of Project If the developer does not wish to operate the property when it is completed, then a buyer must be found. The developer must make some important decisions relating to this sale such as when to sell and at what price. The developer realizes that the project is worth more when finished and fully leased than when it is simply an idea and a set of blueprints. The choice is not so simple as whether to sell for less now or more later. It is complicated by uncertainty about future market conditions for leasing the space and the availability and cost of capital now versus later.

If interest rates rise, then the price a buyer will pay, assuming all other items remain the same, will decrease. This is true because an increase in interest rates will increase mortgage payments and leave the investor fewer dollars as a return on invested equity capital. The only way the buyer can increase that equity return is by investing fewer equity dollars. If interest rates increase too much, it may be impossible for an equity investor to pay a price adequate for the developer to sell and make a profit. For this reason, developers must be aware of circumstances in the financial markets. If interest rate increases appear imminent, the developer may move to sell the project as soon as possible rather than risk lower profits, or even losses!

Developers play a risky game in which many of the factors affecting the ultimate profitability of a project are beyond their control. However, just because these factors are out of the developer's control doesn't mean the developer should simply ignore them. It is imperative that the developer closely monitor them and incorporate this information into the many decisions that must be made throughout the life of a project. A good feasibility study will identify these critical variables and provide some initial information about how sensitive the returns from the project are to changes in these variables.

REDEVELOPMENT

Not all development involves the construction of brand new improvements. Because of high construction costs, federal income tax incentives, and a renewed interest in preserving the past, older buildings are being either renovated and modernized or restored to their old elegance. In some cases these properties are also being expanded. Developers and creative architects have produced some startling and beautiful mixtures of old and new. For example, in San Francisco, the old Ghirardelli Chocolate Factory was renovated and expanded into a marvelous shopping area. In Chattanooga, Tennessee, the old train station has been renovated and is now used for a restaurant named The Chattanooga Choo-Choo. Chances are good that your city has some redevelopment projects that have involved older schools, warehouses, offices, and stores. A developer faces many of the same problems and decisions in redevelopment as in developing new space.

TRENDS IN DEVELOPMENT

As the markets for space have changed, development has changed in an attempt to provide the type and quality of space, in the locations demanded, by those needing it. Evidence of these changes is not difficult to find. Take shopping, for example. Once most major shopping was found in the downtown areas of cities. As people moved to the suburbs, farther from the downtown areas, shopping followed them in the form of strips of stores fronting streets with customer parking along the streets. Then the concept of the shopping center with off-street parking was introduced with the development of Country Club Plaza in Kansas City. Later, the concept of the shopping center would go from the long, rambling strips of stores popular in the 1940s and 1950s to open-air malls in which stores were no longer simply lined up but were wrapped around a central mall area. Later, the enclosed, air conditioned mall, introduced in 1956 by Dayton – Hudson Development Company in the Southfield Mall in Edina, Minnesota, would become the prototype for shopping center development. Today, super regional, multilevel enclosed malls, with over 1,000,000 square feet of space are the state-of-the-art in shopping center development.

MUDs and PUDs Patterns of change could also be traced for office buildings, apartments, homes and condominiums, hotels and motels, industrial buildings, resort developments, and any other type of space. While small developments will continue to be needed and developed, the average size of development projects is increasing. Not only is the size increasing, but so is the complexity. Realizing that people do not always neatly compartmentalize their activities into work, shopping, recreation, and relaxation, developers have sought to develop various types of space in a single development to maximize convenience. These developments are called **mixed-use developments (MUDs).** Such an approach compounds the problems of design, zoning, marketing research, construction, financing, and other development activities.

The Galleria built in Houston in the early 1970s provides a three-level mall featuring an ice rink in the center of the first level, first-class office space, and a luxury hotel in one large complex. It has since been enlarged with more shopping, offices, and hotel space. The Crown Center complex in Kansas City is another MUD combining a large tract of land and several different property types on top of one another. Water Tower Place in Chicago is a 70-story structure containing a multilevel shopping arcade, hotel space, and residential condominiums. The John Hancock Building next door has 100 stories divided between shopping space, office space, and residential condominiums.

The desire to create a controlled, planned environment has also led to the development of residential areas containing apartments, detached single family residences, condominiums of various types, and, in some cases, shopping and recreation facilities. These developments are sometimes called **planned-unit developments (PUDs).** The term planned unit development comes from zoning codes that have special provisions for PUDs allowing more land use flexibility to a single developer with a cohesive plan than if each different land use was being developed separately in the usual manner. The term is used very loosely to describe virtually any development containing elements beyond the normal residential subdivision. Therefore, you should be careful not to assume that a given PUD contains any specific land uses.

New Towns Perhaps the ultimate real estate development is the **new town.** Several new towns have been started including Reston, Virginia; Columbia, Maryland; The Woodlands, Texas; Las Colinas, Texas; and Jonathan, Minnesota. Attempts have been made in all of these communities to provide an integrated approach to living by providing residential, shopping, and working areas in close proximity to each other. The federal government provided some financial assistance for new town developers in the late 1960s and early 1970s but has since withdrawn financial support for additional new towns. Given the large financial requirements and the long development period, new town development requires strong financial backing.

Conclusions It is important for you to know that development must constantly change to satisfy the demand for different kinds of space. For long-range success, a developer must be an adaptable creature, able to read and anticipate change as well as design space to serve changing tastes and preferences. Those who can will prosper, while those who cannot will not. This is yet another of the risks associated with development.

SUMMARY

Real estate development is the process of combining land, labor, capital, and entrepreneurial ability to produce improvements to land. Development involves any improvements added to land, including sewer lines, electricity, and other items necessary for erecting space. Developers are motivated primarily by the chance to make a profit, although other motivations are also present. While the profit potential is often great, the risks associated with development are often substantial. These risks include legal risk, the possibility that the developer will not be able to construct the type or size of project desired; market risk, the possibility that the market for the space being produced has changed; and cost risk, the inability of the developer to forecast with certainty the cost of a project.

Development is a complex activity involving a number of steps. All projects begin as an idea. These ideas solve the problem of what to build and where to build it. Ideas are followed by a preliminary feasibility analysis in which the rough idea is tested using some rather coarse cost and income figures. Either before or at roughly the same time as the preliminary feasibility study, the site must be controlled. A site may be controlled by purchase, lease, or option. If the project is still alive, it enters the feasibility and design stage, in which a more detailed analysis is performed and the design of the project is established. Next, the project is financed, followed by construction and marketing. Certainly, these steps are only an approximation of the stages in the development process and are not necessarily followed in all projects.

Development activity is not limited to building totally new improvements. Because of high construction costs, income tax incentives, and a renewed interest in preserving the past, many existing buildings are being renovated. This activity is called redevelopment.

Through time, developments have had to adapt to changing demands for space. Mixed-use developments and planned-unit developments represent attempts to deal with change. Complete new towns have been developed, although this type of development has seen reduced activity in recent times. This adaptive process continues, with developers who correctly anticipate the future prospering.

QUICK QUIZ

1. Which of the following is *not* a development risk?

a. market risk   c. legal risk
b. property risk   d. cost risk

2. Legal, site, market, and financial aspects of a proposed development are analyzed in the _____ stage.

a. idea   c. feasibility analysis and design
b. construction   d. marketing

3. A development containing more than one use in a single building is an example of a:

a. MUD   c. redevelopment
b. PUD   d. CUD

4. When a project is developed jointly by two or more parties who have agreed to cooperate on the project, it is called a _____ .

5. Control of a site may be gained by _____ , _____ , or _____ .

6. General contractors generally work under _____ or _____ contracts.

QUESTIONS AND EXERCISES

1. Find a vacant parcel of land in your town and suggest what kind of space should be developed on it and why.

2. How can a developer reduce cost risk in a project?

3. Why would a developer sometimes prefer to lease land rather than buy it?

4. What are the advantages and disadvantages for a developer going into a joint venture with a large lender?

5. Why would a large retailer, such as Sears, become involved in shopping center development?

6. What characteristics of a site are critical to its development?

KEY TERMINOLOGY

absorption rate
completion bond
construction manager
cost plus
cost risk
development
general contractor
guaranteed maximum price
joint venture
legal risk

market risk
market study
marketability study
MUD
new town
option
PUD
redevelopment
subcontractor

IF YOU WANT TO READ MORE

G. VINCENT BARRETT and JOHN P. BLAIR, *How to Conduct and Analyze Real Estate Market and Feasibility Studies* (New York: Van Nostrand, 1982).

JAMES A. GRAASKAMP, "A Rational Approach to Feasibility Analysis," *Readings in Real Estate Investment Analysis,* American Institute of Real Estate Appraisers, 1977.

JOHN MCMAHAN, *Property Development* (New York: McGraw-Hill Book Company, 1976).

RICHARD H. SWESNIK, *Acquiring and Developing Income Producing Real Estate* (Reston, VA: Reston Publishing Company, Inc., 1979).

18

Equity Investment: basic concepts of income property investment

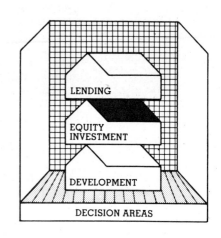

LENDING

EQUITY INVESTMENT

DEVELOPMENT

DECISION AREAS

PREVIEW

If you have browsed through a bookstore, newsstand, paperback bookrack in the supermarket, or any place books are sold lately, you have probably noticed the large number of books dealing with real estate investments. You may already be a real estate investor or have thought of investing in income properties. You may want to sell Blackacre, the 40-acre farm left to you by your grandfather, and invest in a small apartment complex in town. But what are the advantages and disadvantages of investment in real estate? What are your investment options? Do you purchase as a sole proprietor, partnership, or corporation? This chapter considers the basic concepts of investing in income producing real estate. After reading and studying it you should know:

1. The advantages and disadvantages of investing in income producing real estate.
2. Why you need to consider many return and risk factors before you buy property for investment purposes.
3. How you can affect the risks and returns associated with a real estate investment.
4. The various property types and ownership forms that are available to the investor and some of the advantages and disadvantages of each.

5. How to develop an investment strategy.

6. The need to use professional help in analyzing a real estate investment.

Many of the titles of real estate investment books lead you to believe that you can quickly and easily make a fortune by investing in real estate. Much of this get-rich-quick image has been adopted by the public. And, while real estate has, on the average, been a very good investment during the recent past, it is not a foolproof one. Many investors have lost money investing in real estate because of a lack of knowledge about real estate principles and real estate investment analysis in particular. Others have invested only to find that real estate required more time and energy than other investments and quickly sold their interests.

This chapter introduces real estate investment to you, not with the idea that you can become a millionaire within the next 18 months, but rather with the idea that real estate can be an important part of your investment portfolio or the portfolio of your clients once you enter the real estate business. The emphasis in this chapter is on the characteristics of real estate, the motivation of investors and, ultimately, an understanding of how to determine if real estate is an appropriate investment for you. With luck and dedication, you have a chance to become wealthy from your real estate investments.

INVESTOR MOTIVATION

What motivates you, as an investor, to make the investments you do? There are probably many reasons why you may choose to purchase income property, and many ways these motivations can be classified. In the final analysis, these varying motivations can be boiled down to a desire for returns and an avoidance of risk. One of the best ways to view these motivations is to realize that your primary goal as an investor is to achieve a high level of returns relative to the risks that are associated with investments. Of course, returns may be either monetary or nonmonetary in nature. By doing this, you will maximize your chances of success in accumulating substantial amounts of wealth over your lifetime, and also, achieving other nonfinancial objectives important to you. Real estate investment may or may not satisfy your investment motivations. You must evaluate its advantages and disadvantages relative to your investment goals and objectives. Some of the advantages and disadvantages of real estate investment are now considered. How important each is to you is purely a private and personal judgment.

Real Estate Investment Advantages

Pride of Ownership Pride of ownership is a paramount consideration for an individual or family buying a home; it is also important to most investors. For many investors, owning real estate is an expression of one's personality or a measure of greatness, importance, and success. However, this motive can also create trouble for an investor. The desire to own the most prestigious office building or apartment complex, regardless of cost and income factors, has driven many an investor and developer into insolvency or bankruptcy.

Personal Control Unlike investments in stocks and bonds, real estate affords an investor the opportunity to have personal control over the asset and its management. Many investors prefer to be able to make the important decisions regarding purchase price and terms, leverage, form of ownership, property management, and when to sell or refinance.

Self-use and Occupancy Many professionals, such as doctors, dentists, architects, engineers, and Realtors ® prefer to own the building in which they work. By owning rather than renting, you receive the tax shelter and appreciation benefits of the property. In addition, you have the opportunity to design and furnish your offices in any manner that fits your particular needs.

Estate Building Real estate is a popular investment medium for building a large personal estate or portfolio. You can build a substantial estate by buying leveraged properties and periodically selling or refinancing them to realize equity build-up from loan amortization and property appreciation. These funds can then be used to buy larger properties and other types of properties, eventually creating a large diversified portfolio for the investor.

Security of Capital Compared to other investments, real estate is generally believed to rank very high in terms of security of capital. Rarely does a real estate investment go down in value if it is well located and well built. In fact, in the past, most types of real estate kept up with or exceeded inflation.

Operating Cash Flows One of the primary benefits you will seek from an income property is cash flow from operating the property successfully. A good apartment or office building investment can generate substantial rental income that exceeds the actual costs to operate the property, leaving the investor a substantial operating income that can be used to pay debt service (if the property is leveraged) or to reinvest in other properties.

Leverage Traditionally, investors have been able to control a large real estate asset with a small amount of equity capital. While most large manufacturing companies have a leverage ratio (debt/total assets) of only 50 to 60 percent, most equity investors in real estate seek leverage ratios of 75 to 95 percent. By using a high degree of leverage, you hope to use other people's money (OPM) to control more real estate and parlay your returns to much higher levels.

Tax Shelter Factors As discussed in Chapter 12, you would like to structure a real estate investment so as to shelter from income taxes all cash flows produced by the property, and to generate tax losses, which can be used to shelter other income earned in your regular business or income earned on your other investments. Later on, when you sell the property you would like to defer taxes as long as possible and have all or most of your gains taxed at the favorable long-term capital gains rates. Under the Tax Reform Act of 1984, as well as previous tax law, real estate investments receive some favorable tax treatment.

Capital Appreciation and Inflation Protection In addition to getting cash flow from operations, tax shelter benefits, and equity build-up through loan amortization, you hope to receive a return from increases in property value. During the last decade, significant returns have come from appreciation of property value. This appreciation has been caused primarily by inflationary pressures, but also by the increase in demand for real estate relative to supply. Numerous studies have shown that real estate has been a better inflation hedge than stocks and most other types of equity investments.

Investment Disadvantages and Risks

Many investors emphasize the advantages and benefits of real estate ownership and tend to forget or overlook the risks and pitfalls associated with such ownership. As a result, many investors have experienced poor investment results or have gone bankrupt with their real estate investments. You should be aware of the significant disadvantages, risks, and uncertainties associated with real estate investments, such as the following, before you commit your money and time.

Illiquidity Real estate is difficult to quickly convert into cash. Unlike stocks or bonds, real estate is not standardized or traded on an exchange, and the time required for an investor to analyze the possible purchase is quite long. Many times financing is not readily available or interest rates are too high, resulting in profits that are too low— therefore making a proposed investment infeasible. Even after a buyer has reached a decision, much must be done before the transaction is complete—including negotiation of the sale, title search, preparing all the necessary legal papers, and arranging financing.

Required Equity Capital Real estate investments are considered to be capital intensive. This means that it takes a relatively large amount of financial capital to purchase a stream of rental income. While most of the financial capital needed can be raised through some form of debt financing, substantial amounts of equity capital are usually required to purchase real estate. Since most equity investors have limited equity capital, they must tailor their real estate investment purchases to those sizes and types of properties that fit their equity capital resources and constraints. This constraint will significantly limit the growth of your real estate portfolio.

Management Burden Broken leases, busted water pipes, middle-of-the-night calls from disgruntled tenants, and complex financial and tax reports are all part of real estate investment. Most real estate investments require a significant and constant amount of personal attention if their income and property values are to rise. If you do not perform your own property management functions, then you must hire a professional property manager to perform them, or rent to a tenant that takes care of the property (for example, by signing a "new" lease). Many investors find property management to be an unpalatable or frustrating aspect of real estate investment and one that can cause severe mental and physical stress.

Depreciation of Value It is true that price inflation in general tends to raise the monetary value of real estate. However, as discussed in later chapters on appraisal, real depreciation does occur over time and can be caused by physical, functional, and locational factors. Periodically, you will have to take care of physical and functional depreciation through major repairs, refurbishing, and renovating your properties. Locational problems are more difficult to solve and can cause serious cash flow problems for a person owning an apartment or shopping center in a declining part of town. You should be aware of these depreciation factors and not assume that every property automatically goes up in value over time.

Government Controls In recent years, the government has become increasingly involved in regulating and controlling the activities of real estate investors. Some examples are rent controls, controls on foreign investment and ownership, land use and land density controls, flood plain and water runoff controls, and anti-pollution and other environmental controls, all of which impose constraints on the use of your property. With multifamily and commercial income property, as well as single family housing, government controls add thousands of dollars to the cost of buying and operating a property. New laws and ordinances can quickly reduce cash flow and create severe financial problems for you as an owner.

Real Estate Cycles Almost all real estate activities and profits run in cycles. If you buy at the bottom of a cycle and ride it up you can make handsome profits. On the other hand, if you buy at the top of a real estate cycle and must survive two years of economic bad weather, you could go broke. As a real estate investor you must carefully study real estate cycles and learn to time your investments correctly. The most important cycles that create problems for the investor are: construction cycles, real estate financing cycles, and inflation cycles.

Legal Complexity As you saw earlier in the book, the contracts between buyers, sellers, and lenders are very complex, and are complicated by many government regulations that govern real estate transactions. Dealing with these legal technicalities effectively can make or break your transaction. Unfortunately, the rules of the game, such as tax laws, change frequently and unpredictably. In general, and as Murphy's Law predicts, these changes are usually for the worse and adversely affect your property.

Lack of Information and Education The information you need to make an investment decision is hard to find, disorganized, and often neither accurate nor reliable. This makes the investment analysis you wish to perform very difficult indeed. Also, many investors lack the interdisciplinary education needed to make sound investment decisions.

Weighing Advantages and Disadvantages

You should be motivated to carefully analyze the risks as well as the returns that are associated with a real estate investment. Furthermore, you should be careful to identify the financial and non-financial dimensions that are important to you. Table 18.1 summarizes the various risk and return factors as we have discussed them to this point. While this is not a complete checklist, it does itemize the important return and risk factors. You will want to add to this list as you gain experience in real estate investing. A successful investor will consider many investment alternatives, then choose the best one and negotiate the best deal possible. In order to do this you must be able to analyze the basic advantages of each investment and then translate these into a forecast of returns and risks for each investment. Whenever you can, you will develop plans to control or minimize the risks and consequences of incorrect judgment. In the final analysis, you must weight the returns and risks according to your personal preferences.

Table 18.1. Identification of Return and Risk Factors

Investment Advantages and Returns

Financial	Nonfinancial
Estate building	Pride of ownership
Security of capital	Personal control
High operating yield	Self-use and occupancy
Leverage	
Tax Shelter	
Capital appreciation	

Investment Disadvantages and Risks

Financial	Nonfinancial
Illiquidity	Management burden
Required equity capital	Government controls
Depreciation of values	Legal complexity
Real estate cycles	Lack of information and education

Using the above framework for return and risk factors, you would rate each of the factors on some scale according to how important they are to you. Most sophisticated investors place the heaviest weights on the financial factors. Then you would compare the characteristics of each possible investment to see how well it scored on each of the return and risk factors. The investment that best fits your return and risk preferences would be the most desirable. Other investments could be ranked second, third, fourth, etc., based on the same procedure.

Risk-Return Trade-off

As we stated previously, your goal as an investor is to purchase properties that produce a high level of returns relative to risks. In financial management parlance, when you accomplish this you are said to be optimizing your investment. When considering an investment, you must first define your objective in terms of risk and expected return. Then you analyze the project and estimate the amount of expected return and risk, as best you can. Again keep in mind that expected return and risk factors may include some nonfinancial, as well as financial, factors.

Next, you will need to evaluate the expected return and risk of a proposed investment by comparing it to other investments and to your own personal return and risk preferences. This concept is illustrated in Figure 18.1. In this exhibit each dot represents one investment being considered, and each is placed on the graph according to its level of expected return and risk. Ideally, you have analyzed numerous investments and can compare them in this manner. Your indifference curve represents what you feel is the minimal acceptable tradeoff between

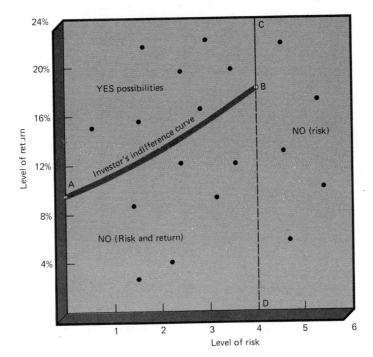

Figure 18.1 Return and risk evaluation. (Source: J. Thomas Montgomery, "Real Estate Investment Risk — Basic Concepts," *Appraisal Journal*, January 1976, p. 20.)

expected return and risk. In general, rational investors who are said to be risk averse demand higher expected returns if they must take higher risks. Consequently, their indifference curve slopes upward to the right, as shown (line AB). However, at some point the risk level gets too great (point B in the exhibit) and the investor chooses not to consider any investments past this point.

To summarize, a rational investor will reject all investments below line AB and to the right of line DC. The acceptable projects ("yes" possibilities) appear above line AB and to the left of line BC. The best projects are the ones that have the highest rates of return relative to the risks — and appear as the highest dots above and to the left of line ABC.

You should be aware that the marketplace tends to work in such a way that, on average, investors must accept higher risks in order to achieve higher returns. This relationship has been proven in many studies of investors in the stock and bond markets (e.g., you receive a higher return on a hotel mortgage loan, historically one of the riskier mortgages, than a CD from a commercial bank because the mortgage is more risky). However, remember that this relationship is only true in "efficient" marketplaces, where the products are homogeneous, information is readily available, and investors are rational. These conditions are not as universal in the real estate investment marketplace. This means that the greater competition for investments in securities markets makes it more difficult for you to find good deals there than in real estate markets.

Ability of Investor to Control Returns and Risks

As an astute real estate investor, you exert considerable control over the projects you purchase—and by doing so, can influence the types and levels of returns and risks that they achieve in their investment portfolio. This is accomplished through careful analysis and negotiation of the financial and nonfinancial investment variables, such as the following:

1. Purchase price and terms of purchase
2. Form of ownership structure and agreements
3. Financing amounts, rates, and terms
4. Tax structure and planning
5. Property management expertise
6. Property location
7. Tenants and lease rates and terms

To the extent that you can acquire greater expertise in the areas of market and marketability analysis, tax planning, financial analysis, property management, and risk management techniques, you will be able to structure real estate investments consistently so as to increase your returns relative to risks. Successful investors have learned to do this consistently and build substantial real estate portfolios over their lifetime.

PROPERTY TYPES

One of the major decisions you face as an investor is determining the types of properties that should be purchased. There is a wide variety of investment property types to consider and each has special characteristics that affect its returns and risks. Table 18.2 illustrates the many individual property types that you might consider as you build a portfolio. We will briefly consider here only the major property types that are commonly found in many portfolios, including raw land, residential rental property, office buildings, industrial property, and shopping centers. Many of the property types listed in Table 18.2 are considered special use properties and have characteristics that make them too risky and too management-intensive for many investors. We will consider these property types only briefly.

Raw Land

Of all the types of real estate investments you might own, **raw land** investments will usually be the most risky. Here, a raw land investment refers to the purchase of undeveloped acreage on the fringe of a city that is expected to be ready for development sometime in the future. Conse-

Table 18.2. Different Property Types

1. Land
   - Raw acreage
   - Recreational acreage
   - Subdivided lots
   - Farms, ranches, and groves
   - Oil and timber lands
2. Residential Permanent Facilities
   - Houses
   - Apartments
   - Townhouses
   - Condominiums
   - Cooperatives
   - Mobile homes
   - Nursing homes
3. Residential Transient Facilities
   - Motels
   - Hotels
   - Resorts
   - Spas
   - Recreational condominiums
   - Convalescent homes
4. Office Property
   - General use buildings
   - Office parks
   - Professional buildings
   - Trade centers
   - Condominiums
5. Retail and Shopping Centers
   - Stores
   - Restaurants
   - Fast food franchises
   - Gas stations
   - Supermarkets
   - Strip centers
   - Neighborhood, community, regional centers
   - Merchandise markets
   - Airport concessions
   - Parking lots and garages
   - Car washes
   - Laundry facilities
6. Industrial
   - Warehouses and mini-warehouses
   - Factories
   - Industrial parks
7. Entertainment and Recreational
   - Theaters
   - Bowling alleys
   - Golf courses
   - Golf driving ranges
   - Miniature golf courses
   - Arenas
   - Museums
   - Convention centers
   - Marinas
   - Target practice ranges
   - Baseball batting ranges
   - Tennis clubs
   - Racquetball clubs
   - Massage parlors
   - Gymnasiums
   - Health spas
8. Comprehensive Development
   - Subdivisions
   - Skiing facilities
   - Amusement parks
   - Retirement communities
   - Urban redevelopments
   - Rehabilitating existing projects
   - New communities
   - New towns
9. Public Service
   - Hospitals
   - Schools
   - Public buildings
10. Other
    - Churches
    - Islands
    - Foreign investments
    - Exotic properties

quently, the investor must be sure that the land is in the future path of growth and that it will be desirable for development. Successful raw land investors must understand market factors such as the dynamics of urban and regional growth and what makes developers do the things they do. If the raw land investor does not understand this process or is wrong in the timing of development activity, the land investment can turn into a financial disaster.

A number of important physical, legal, and political factors must be considered when you are evaluating a raw land investment: (1) access of the property to public roads, (2) slope of the land and the type of soils present, (3) present zoning of the land and the probability that it can be rezoned for a higher and better use, (4) availability of utilities such as water and sewer, electricity, gas, and telephone, and (5) future availability of public services such as fire, police, and sanitation. Problems in any of these areas can substantially affect the rate of return on the land investment.

Raw land is not a very attractive type of investment from the point of view of cash flow or tax shelter. Most raw land investments experience negative cash flows each year (they have to be "fed") because the owner must pay interest, taxes, and insurance — while the property produces no rental income unless it is put to an interim land use such as farming or ranching. Tax shelter is poor because land cannot be depreciated for tax purposes. Consequently, an investor who seeks tax shelter or positive cash flow as an objective would not be very interested in raw land investments. Partly because of the lack of cash flow and partly because of the volatile nature of land values, institutional financing is usually not available for raw land. You will probably have to depend on the seller financing the transaction.

The key factor to financial success is appreciation of property value. Only if the land value rises quickly can you cover the costs of holding the property, make a substantial investment profit, and justify the risks associated with raw land investment. One rule of thumb used by many investors is that land value must increase a minimum of 20 to 30 percent annually for such an investment to be financially attractive. While many millionaires have made their millions in raw land (such as Gene Autry and Roy Rogers) due to such rapid appreciation, many other investors have gone broke because land values did not increase at rapid rates. Novice investors should not venture into this arena.

Residential Rental Property

A popular starting point for many beginning real estate investors is a small residential rental property — such as a house, duplex, fourplex, or small apartment building. One possible strategy as a beginning investor is to turn your house into a rental property (instead of selling it) when ready to move into your second home. Also included in the residential rental property category would be large apartment complexes, mobile home parks, and nursing homes. Often, the last two — mobile home parks and nursing homes — are considered special use properties and are considered risky investments as compared to houses and apartments.

Small residential properties are popular for the beginning investor because most investors are familiar with the operation of a single family home or apartment. Furthermore, during the past 10 years these properties, especially single family homes, have experienced high property value growth rates — sometimes as much as 12 to 20 percent per year or more in the case of single family rental houses.

For both small and large residential properties, location and physical condition are important factors affecting property returns and risks. You should carefully analyze the neighborhood in which the property is located and seek good proximity with respect to transportation to work, school, and shopping. The better the neighborhood the higher the rents you can charge your tenants. Also, the physical condition should be carefully checked to ascertain the level of operating expenses necessary to maintain the property in good operating condition. There are firms that will inspect the mechanical, electrical, plumbing, and general physical condition of the property for a fee.

A critical factor affecting property performance is property management. Residential properties are said to be management intensive — they take a great amount of time, care, and effort, and can often prove to be frustrating when tenants complain or violate lease provisions, as they often do. Calls in the middle of the night from irate tenants are not unusual. With small properties the owner usually cannot afford professional property management and must perform all the management duties himself or herself. With larger properties the owner must interview management firms and choose one that is likely to do the best job. Even in such a case, constant monitoring of the property and meetings with the professional managers are necessary if good performance is to be expected. Many investors avoid investments in apartments and other residential properties because of this intense management requirement.

Some advantages of residential properties are (1) good financing generally is available since such properties normally maintain their value and provide good collateral for a loan and (2) tax shelter is excellent because accelerated cost recovery methods apply, short recovery periods can be used (18 years for real property, five years for furniture and other personal property), and when the property is sold only excess cost recovery over straight-line is recaptured and taxed as ordinary income. With small properties, the cash flow from operations is minimal and often negative in periods of high interest rates and mortgage constants. However, larger properties obtain economies of scale and can generally be purchased at lower prices per unit and per square foot, and therefore produce more before-tax cash flow. In recent years, investors have bid up the prices of most types of residential properties; as a result the cash flow yields on their equity investments have fallen and investors have relied more on tax shelter and appreciation to achieve their rate of return.

Property value appreciation is a prime objective of residential property investors, although not the only objective as it usually is with raw land investors. In general, the value of a residential rental property is a function of the rental income and cash flow it produces and is expected to produce. If a property is well-located and well-maintained, the value of the property should increase in line with the income generated by the property. If rents and cash flow can be raised in line with the inflation rate, property values will tend to increase accordingly. Many investors have been successful at finding properties either poorly managed or maintained, purchasing them and taking corrective action, increasing rents and then selling the property for a handsome gain.

Office Buildings

After you have gained a considerable amount of experience in residential income property investments, you will want to consider diversifying into commercial investments such as office buildings and shopping centers. Office buildings, in general, are considered to be more risky than residential properties and require more knowledge with regard to property management and leasing, but at the same time they offer greater possible returns to the investor than residential property. Two general types of office buildings to consider are medium-rise and high-rise buildings, usually found in downtown areas of a city, and garden (low-rise) office buildings, usually found in suburban areas. A new investor in office buildings will often want to focus on the purchase of suburban low-rise buildings since these more closely resemble the ownership and operation of apartment buildings.

Good location is essential for office buildings because of the elements of prestige and convenience. For suburban office buildings, good location means good access to major highways, near high-income residential areas where property values are growing, and in good proximity to restaurants and shopping facilities. Successful office buildings are frequently found near major highway intersections and adjacent to community and regional shopping centers. The prestige of an office building is directly related to the quality of its tenants. An owner of an office building may want to attract a prestigious tenant, and name the building after that tenant, in order to create a prestigious image for the building and thereby attract other high quality tenants to the project.

The purchase price (per square foot) for an office building is substantially greater than a similar size apartment property, primarily due to higher land cost and better construction quality. On the other hand, well-located office buildings are attractive investments for lenders and represent good collateral for high loan-to-value ratios. As compared with apartment properties, office properties tend to attract more stable tenants, have lower tenant turnover ratios, are less subject to rent controls, and are increasingly characterized by "net leases" that shift many operating expense uncertainties directly to tenants.

Office buildings generally produce a lower degree of tax shelter than apartments due to a higher land to improvement ratio and because most investors choose to use the straight-line cost recovery method because of the less attractive recapture rules that apply to commercial property. On the other hand, the cash flow from operations will usually be higher in a successful office building than a successful apartment building, thus tending to offset the lower tax shelter.

The value of a well-located and well-maintained office building is likely to increase as fast as the rate of inflation and, during periods of strong demand, considerably faster. However, many poorly maintained and built buildings are unable to attract and keep good tenants and end up in bankruptcy. Also, office building markets have a more dramatic boom-and-bust cycle than that of any other real estate sector.

Shopping Centers

Of all the property types discussed so far, the shopping center is the most sophisticated and complex type of property and requires the most management and investor expertise. Lease arrangements tend to be complex, and tenant mix and property management sophistication is essential for success. As a result, the risks tend to be greater, but also the potential rewards are greater. They are highly desirable properties for mortgage lenders because few have been foreclosed in years past, and are generally owned by sophisticated and wealthy investors who have the cash resources to hold a project through adverse economic periods.

There are four basic types of shopping centers:

Neighborhood Centers A neighborhood center is often referred to as a strip center and provides for the sale of convenience goods and services (food, drugs, dry cleaning, laundry, barbering, etc.). It is usually built around a supermarket or drugstore as the principal tenant, and averages about 50,000 square feet of gross leasable area (GLA). It is the smallest type of shopping center.

Community Centers These centers will include the convenience goods found in neighborhood centers plus clothing, furniture, banking, professional offices, and possibly recreational facilities. It is usually built around a junior department store, variety store, or discount department store. A typical size for such a center would be about 150,000 square feet (GLA).

Regional Centers A regional center is built around one or two full-line department stores (e.g. Sears, Ward's) of generally not less than 100,000 square feet each. A typical size is about 400,000 square feet (GLA). These department stores are the "anchors" and act as traffic generators for the many smaller retail outlets in the center. They have been extremely successful in most cities and have been an excellent investment for individuals and institutional equity investors such as REIT's and life insurance companies.

Super Regional Centers This center is found only in major metropolitan areas and is built around at least three major department stores. Its size is usually one million square feet and larger. A super regional center might be anchored by Sears, Ward's, and Penney's as the major national tenants, plus two large regional-chain department stores, in addition to 100 to 200 individual stores and restaurants, providing complete lines of goods.

The success of each of these centers depends on important factors such as the size of the market area, the level and growth rate of family income in the market area, and the number of competitors in the area. Also, income generated by a center will depend on specific project factors such as tenant mix, length of leases, and lease terms. The ideal situation would be a growing and affluent market where:

> Nonanchor tenants are selected to achieve high sales volumes and pay percentage (percent of sales) rents.
>
> Lease terms permit periodic escalation of base rents and raise the guaranteed base rents.
>
> Lease terms provide that all tenants pay a percent of operating expenses of the center and these contributions increase as the owner's operating expenses increase, thus providing an inflation hedge for the owner.

Most investors seek to cover basic operating expenses and debt service through the base (guaranteed) rents collected from the tenants, then make their profits (cash flow before tax) through percentage rents that are tied directly to the sales volumes of the individual anchor and mall tenants. As the sales volumes of the tenants rise because of inflation and growth in the retail demand in the area, the investor's cash flow rises accordingly.

Investors do not usually look to shopping centers to produce substantial tax shelter, because land typically represents a high percentage of total value. Also, as you remember from Chapter 12, if accelerated cost recovery is used, all excess cost recovery is recaptured as ordinary income. Investors in shopping centers are more interested in substantial amounts of cash flow from operations, the automatic rise in cash flow when sales volume of the center rises, and the increase in property value that occurs when sales volumes and cash flows increase.

Shopping centers would be good alternatives to consider once the investor has gained investment experience with other less complicated properties. You should, however, keep in mind that the smaller centers are more risky than the larger ones because they are more subject to competition from new strip centers and retail areas and thus are subject to more economic obsolescence.

Industrial Buildings

Industrial property includes warehouses and mini-warehouses, factories, and industrial parks. Factories are special use properties and are not easily converted to other uses. Therefore, factories tend to be risky properties for the average investor and are avoided except by those who specialize in such investments. We will address various types of special use properties in the following section. Also, the industrial park—a large tract of land containing many compatible buildings that are used for a variety of light industrial uses—is a complex investment alternative that should be considered only by a more sophisticated and wealthy investor. However, if you buy a partnership interest and leave the management and ownership problems to a managing or general partner with a good track record, this alternative may be a viable one for you.

The most popular type of industrial property investment is the warehouse. Warehouses are really nothing more than boxes of space for the temporary storage of goods for businesses and people who will be transporting them to another location in the future. There are small warehouses, known as mini-warehouses, that are used by families and small businesses, and are arranged in one- or two-story buildings that have been subdivided into many small cubicles. Also, there is the traditional warehouse facility that is used by every major business and is a large building with special loading and unloading facilities designed for the businesses who lease space.

As you might guess, the critical factor for good warehouses is access to key transportation arteries. Warehouses are simple construction facilities, have a very long economic life, require little management effort as compared with other income properties, and are popular investments for individuals who wish to avoid management hassles. Many investors seek to lease their warehouse buildings to major industrial companies under long-term net leases (tenant pays most or all of the operating expenses) and then sit back and collect their monthly cash flow. Such investments tend to be long-term, low-return, and low-risk in nature. On the other hand, if you seek higher returns, but with associated higher risks, you can lease out warehouse space at a higher rent per square foot to several smaller, lower credit tenants under short-term leases. While this means higher risk because of the possibility of vacancies, you can charge a higher rent from the start, plus raise rents each time the leases expire. This strategy, of course, means that you must expend a more intensive management effort.

Fully leased warehouses provide good collateral for a loan and are desirable properties for lenders. Consequently, good long-term financing at favorable rates is often available to investors. The cash flow from the property will be stable at a moderate rate if a long-term lease is present. Tax shelter is not a prime motive of the investor because of a high land ratio and relatively low improvement cost of warehouses, in addition to the presence of adverse recapture provisions if an accelerated cost recovery method is used. Also, very few components qualify for investment tax credits, unless the investor plans to buy warehouse equipment and lease it to the business tenant.

The key to increasing property value in a warehouse investment is cash flow. Actually, this is true for all income property. If the leases are structured so as to lock in fixed rental rates for long periods of time, there is little hope of property value appreciation during the term of the lease. However, if leases are short-term and rents can be raised periodically, or if long-term lease rates are indexed to inflation rates, then cash flows can rise and property values will increase to reflect this. Also, it would be advantageous for the investor to structure net leases to pass on expense increases directly to tenants, so as to decrease operating expense risks for the investor.

Special Use Properties

Special use properties include properties such as motels and hotels, nursing homes, hospitals, theaters, recreational facilities, fast food franchises, and auto service stations. Consequently, they include most of the property types listed in Table 18.2 under the headings residential transient facilities, entertainment and recreational, public service, and other.

The unique characteristic of special use properties is that two investment elements are involved: (1) the real estate itself, and (2) the specialized business for which the property is used. When you buy a special use property, you buy both and assume the risks of both. Thus, you should consider these properties only if you are a relatively sophisticated investor and wish to specialize in analyzing and managing the unique business situation created by the special use property. Alternatively, you must have blind faith and trust in others who will perform these functions for you.

However, if you would like to become involved in these types of properties once you have gained considerable experience in other types of properties, you should consider the following factors in your approach to special use investments:

1. They tend to be very risky ventures. Be sure you can manage these risks and bear the possible losses that might occur.
2. Become a serious student in the business that occupies the real estate. If the business is not successful, be ready to substitute another in the real estate you own. Be sure you know the alternative uses for your real estate.

3. Lenders are hard to find and require high interest rates and large equity contributions. Lenders for special use properties are difficult to find and are tough negotiators. They almost always require personal loan guarantees and often demand that you pledge other collateral (e.g., CDs) to guarantee that loan payments will be made.

4. Be prepared to allocate a considerable amount of time to such projects. These are the most management-intensive properties of all we have discussed. Unless you plan to delegate most of these responsibilities and totally trust others, or net lease your property to a good credit business (e.g., Pizza Hut), you will end up devoting much time to managing the affairs of the business and must be prepared to do so. If you do not have the time to devote, despite the promises of extraordinary cash flow returns from such properties, pass up these opportunities.

SELECTING AN OWNERSHIP ENTITY

In every new real estate venture, one of the critical decisions that will confront you is the form of ownership entity that should be used. Should you acquire and own the property individually, through some type of partnership, or a corporation or trust? This decision is extremely important because it directly affects your ability to achieve your objectives. The type of entity chosen and the way it is structured affects your rate of return and risk, and it often defines the nature of your involvement in a project and the degree of control you can exercise over the property.

In Chapters 4 and 11 we described the basic legal ownership forms and their tax treatment, so you should be familiar with this material. Here we will try to reorient our focus to a decision-making framework, and look more at the return and risk characteristics of ownership forms. In the final analysis, you should always seek to choose that ownership form that best fits your specific return and risk criteria.

The ownership forms that we will consider, and the return/risk selection criteria that should be analyzed are shown in Table 18.3. While there are numerous other organizational forms and selection criteria that you might also consider, these are the major ones among which most investors choose.

Of all the forms of ownership used in real estate investments in recent years, the limited partnership form is the most popular because it offers investors the limited liability that a corporation offers, and it achieves the favorable tax treatment (by allowing a pass-through of tax losses and capital gains directly to the investor) that a general partnership offers. However, each ownership form has its advantages and disadvantages and is the best form in certain situations, as we will see. Keep in mind that no single type of entity is best in every investor's situation.

Table 18.3. Ownership Alternatives and Decision Criteria

Ownership Forms to Consider	Ownership Decision Criteria to Consider
1. Individual	1. Favorable Tax Treatment
2. Partnership	a. Avoid double taxation
a. General partnership	b. Pass-through losses
b. Limited partnership	c. Income tax deductions
c. Joint venture	d. Capital gains treatment
3. Corporation	2. Limited liability
a. Regular corporation	3. Marketability and transferability
b. Subchapter S	4. Continuity of life
4. Trust	5. Management control and expertise
a. REIT	6. Degree of privacy
b. Pension trust	7. Required capital
c. Family	8. Other

Evaluating Ownership Criteria and Entity Forms

The importance of the numerous return/risk ownership criteria (Table 18.3) should be defined carefully by the investor. Once these are defined, the investor can select the best form of organization that fits these criteria.

Tax Considerations Tax considerations are usually critical in determining the best form of ownership for a real estate venture. The most important factor is that of double taxation of income. The individual and partnership forms of ownership involve only a single tax on income. In a partnership, the partnership itself is not recognized for tax purposes, but rather, all income and losses are passed through to the individual and reported on his or her tax return. In contrast, a corporation is taxed once at the corporate level, then again at the stockholder level when dividends are paid. Other important tax considerations that you should evaluate are the following:

1. Ability to pass through tax losses. With some forms of organizations, such as partnerships, you can pass through tax losses directly to the individual investor and these can be used to shelter his or her other income. With other forms of organization, such as a corporation, this ability is limited or does not exist.
2. Maximum income tax deductions. With some forms of ownership you can be more aggressive and take more expense deductions, without being challenged by the IRS. For example, you are allowed to deduct for tax purposes liberal amounts of medical and dental expenses for officers in a corporation. On the other hand, such

expenses cannot be deducted by partners in a general or limited partnership.

3. **Favorable capital gains treatment.** With some forms of organization, it is easier to achieve favorable capital gains treatment when a property is sold. When a corporation sells a property and then immediately distributes the sale proceeds to the investors, the IRS will first tax the corporation on the capital gains at the corporate level, at the corporate capital gains rate. Then, when the sale proceeds are distributed to the shareholders, the IRS taxes the amount received as a dividend at the ordinary income tax rates of the individual stockholders.

In analyzing ownership forms, you should be careful not to place too much emphasis on tax considerations. There are many other business and practical considerations to look at when making this decision.

Limited Liability Here you are concerned with the extent and probability of exposure to personal liability that you accept when you set up your ownership entity. If you wish to limit your personal liability significantly, you would prefer a corporation or limited partnership interest. It should be noted that for many small real estate corporations, lenders will demand that borrowers accept personal liability for monies loaned to the corporation. In each of these forms of ownership, if they are structured carefully, you can limit your liability to the amount of equity capital invested. On the other hand, with the individual (and joint tenancy and tenancy in common) and general partnership forms you will assume personal liability for many of the debts of the entity—that are usually far beyond the amount of equity capital contributed.

Marketability and Transferability of Interest You may be concerned with your ability to sell your partial interest in a real estate investment if your goals change or if a liquidity need arises. Two related questions should be addressed here: (1) In a market sense, how difficult will it be to sell your share to another investor?, and (2) In a legal sense, how difficult will it be to transfer your legal interest in a property to another individual? With a corporation, the provision to sell shares and the legalities involved are more clearly spelled out in the law than is true for shares of a partnership.

Partnership agreements are often very restrictive with respect to the individual's ability to sell and transfer legal ownership interests. Also, with pension trusts, your ability to sell and reinvest your investment funds is very limited under the current pension laws if you wish to maintain your tax-preferred status.

Continuity of Life Some ventures are organized with a relatively short holding period in mind and would cease to exist if any of the key investors died. This is often true of a joint venture or general partnership. On the other hand, ventures can be set up to span the lifetimes of many projects and many investors. If a high degree of continuity is desired, you should consider a corporate form of organization, or a trust. Also, you can structure a limited partnership entity to have a high degree of continuity, if this is an important goal.

Management Control and Expertise The number of people required to run an entity, the type of management and expertise required, and the degree of control exercised by the investor over the property will vary for each of the ownership forms. A substantial number of experienced people will be required to organize and operate a large real estate partnership, where the investor-shareholder has no direct control over the properties bought. On the other hand, a general partnership may consist of only a few investors who each choose to exert considerable control over the operations of the property and all partnership matters. If complete control is desired, the individual form of ownership is usually preferred.

Degree of Privacy Some investors seek privacy in their real estate activities and do not wish to have their name appear in public records, such as on recorded partnership agreements, deeds, mortgages, and so on. Using various types of trust devices or specialized partnership agreements can easily accommodate an investor who wishes to operate in such a manner. For example, politicians and public officials often wish to keep their private lives out of the public eye.

Required Capital Some forms of organization are much more costly to organize and operate than others. It is not uncommon, for example, for a limited partnership to spend 20 to 30 percent of the total equity raised on organizational expenses, promotion and legal fees. In contrast, a joint venture, general partnership, or tenancy in common might limit such expenses to five to 10 percent of equity raised — thus allowing more capital to be used for the actual purchase of real estate. Also, the amount of capital needed to purchase a real estate investment may influence the ownership choice. If the equity requirement is modest, you may choose to own and control the property yourself. If you do not have the required equity, or do not choose to invest all your cash in one property, you might choose to use a general partnership form of organization. If many partners are required, and the individual partners have no management expertise and are unrelated, you may choose to use the limited partnership form, establish yourself as the general partner, and sell limited partnership shares to inexperienced investors.

Other Selection Criteria There are many other criteria that may become important in individual situations. For example, if you are in the real estate business and seek to avoid double taxation and generate fringe benefits for your family, you may choose an S corporation form of organization. If you seek to create a retirement fund and wish to have your retirement contributions deducted each year from your taxable income, you might choose to use one of the available qualified pension trust options, such as a Keogh or Individual Retirement Account (IRA) plan — both of which have become very popular in recent years.

Use of Professional Help

The tax laws are complicated and ownership decisions are complex. In assigning weights to the various criteria discussed above, you must analyze the dynamic interactions between legal, tax, business, and practical factors. You are responsible for making the business and practical decisions, but probably cannot hope to have the expertise or knowledge to evaluate all the legal and tax implications of alternative ownership forms. Therefore, you should seek professional help in these two areas. Ideally, you should seek out a qualified tax attorney — one who has been educated in both taxation and law and has considerable experience working for successful real estate investors. Such a person would often be a CPA specializing in tax or an attorney specializing in property law and real estate transactions. Their legal and tax assistance will be expensive in the short run, yet an excellent investment to assure long-run profitability and control downside risks.

SUMMARY

You now have a better understanding of the basic concepts of real estate investments. You know that people invest because investments satisfy motivations. For any investment, real estate included, to be a good one, it must satisfy the investor's needs. Along these lines real estate generally is capable of satisfying the needs of pride of ownership, personal control, self-use and occupancy, estate building, security of capital, operating cash flows, leverage, and tax shelter. It also has the disadvantages of illiquidity, often large equity investment, management burden, possible depreciation, may be subject to government controls, sensitive to real estate cycles, and legal complexity. You must weigh the advantages and disadvantages of real estate investment before making your investment decision. Investments should be evaluated and ranked according to their desirability.

Especially critical to your decision is the tradeoff between risk and return. Since you will likely be risk averse, you must decide what minimal level of return is acceptable for each level of risk and, in so doing, develop your indifference curve. You will then reject any investment opportunity offering a combination deemed unacceptable by your indifference curve. You will attempt to find investments that provide rates of return higher than you require for the associated level of risk. You can control the risk in a real estate investment to some extent by analyzing and negotiating key financial and nonfinancial variables such as: purchase price and terms of purchase, form of ownership, financing, tax structure, property management, location, and tenants and lease terms.

You learned that there are many different types of investment properties, each with different characteristics. These property types include raw land, residential rental, office buildings, shopping centers, industrial buildings, and special use properties. The characteristics of these different property types dramatically affect their risk and return characteristics.

Ownership form also has an important impact on your real estate investment. As you learned in earlier chapters, the ownership form affects your ability to control an investment, your liability to cover any losses, and your income tax situation. This chapter presented a list of criteria to consider in selecting an ownership vehicle. These criteria included tax considerations, extent of liability, continuity of life, management control and expertise, degree of privacy, required capital, and other selection criteria.

Finally, it was suggested that you may need to use various professionals in making investment decisions and operating the investment once acquired. Professionals such as CPAs, attorneys, property managers, and other real estate counselors may be able to provide valuable assistance to you.

QUICK QUIZ

1. Which one of the following factors is *not* usually an advantage of real estate investment?

   a. pride of ownership   c. tax shelter
   b. security of capital   d. required equity capital

2. The minimal acceptable tradeoff between risk and expected return is depicted by the

   a. discounted cash flow curve   c. coefficient of reversion
   b. indifference curve   d. leverage curve

3. Probably the most popular form of investment for beginning real estate investors is

   a. residential rental property   c. raw land
   b. office buildings   d. shopping centers

4. A shopping center having over one million square feet of space, 100 to 200 stores, and anchored by at least three major department stores is called a _____ .

a. regional center   c. community center
b. super regional center d. convenience center

5. The most popular type of industrial property investment is the _____ .

a. factory   c. warehouse
b. industrial park d. large chemical plant

6. Properties that combine real estate and a specialized business for which the property is used are called _____ .

7. The major factors you should consider in choosing the form of ownership for real property include _____ , _____ , _____ , and _____ .

8. Real estate investment decisions require a balancing of _____ and _____ .

9. As an investor, you can control your investment risks and returns by careful analysis and negotiation of variables such as _____ , _____ , _____ , and _____ .

10. Two general types of office buildings are _____ and _____ .

QUESTIONS AND EXERCISES

1. Assess the relative importance to you of each of the investment advantages of real estate discussed in the chapter.

2. Are you risk averse? If so, how risk averse would you say you are? What evidence can you generate to support your contention?

3. Using the 20 to 30 percent annual appreciation rule in the chapter, if you were to purchase a parcel of raw land for $100,000 today, at what price would you have to sell it in three years to make adequate profit? Does this rate of appreciation seem reasonable in your community? Why?

4. What ownership entity would be most appealing to you if you were going to invest in real estate? Why?

5. Why are residential properties generally the most popular form of investment for beginning investors?

KEY TERMINOLOGY		
community center	operating cash flows
continuity of life	personal control
estate building	pride of ownership
expected return	raw land
illiquidity	regional center
indifference curve	residential rental property
limited liability	risk averse
marketability of interest	special use properties
mini-warehouse	super regional center
neighborhood center	

IF YOU WANT TO READ MORE

FRED E. CASE, *Investing in Real Estate* (Englewood Cliffs: Prentice-Hall, 1978).

DONALD R. EPLEY and JAMES A. MILLAR, *Basic Real Estate Finance and Investments* (New York: John Wiley & Sons, 1980).

AUSTIN JAFFE and C. F. SIRMANS, *Real Estate Investment Decision Making* (Englewood Cliffs: Prentice-Hall, Inc., 1982).

JACK KUSNET and LEE J. HOLZMAN, *How to Choose a Form of Ownership for Real Estate, Part 1, Explanation and Practical Guide* (Boston: Warren, Gorham, & Lamont, 1977).

STEPHEN A. PYHRR, JAMES R. COOPER, LARRY E. WOFFORD, and STEVEN D. KAPPLIN, *Real Estate Investment: Strategy, Analysis, Decisions,* second edition (New York: John Wiley & Sons, Inc., 1986).

MAURY SELDIN and RICHARD H. SWESNIK, *Real Estate Investment Strategy,* second edition. (New York: Wiley-Interscience, 1979).

RICHARD H. SWESNIK, *Acquiring and Developing Income Producing Real Estate* (Reston, Va.: Reston Publishing Company, Inc., 1979).

19

Equity Investment: making the investment decision

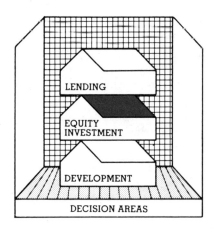

LENDING

EQUITY INVESTMENT

DEVELOPMENT

DECISION AREAS

PREVIEW

You have decided to invest in real estate and now must decide which investment opportunity to accept. An office building near your home looks promising, but so does a small apartment near the college. From the sale of Blackacre you have the money to purchase either, but not both. How do you go about making the investment decision? This chapter explains the essentials of how to make such a decision. It covers:

1. The 10-step investment analysis process.
2. The basic measures of risk and expected return and restructuring an investment to achieve an acceptable risk/expected return level.
3. Possible criticisms of the basic risk and return measures.
4. The logic and concept of discounted cash flow analysis designed to overcome the criticisms of the basic risk and return measures.
5. The details of discounted cash flow analysis in the appendix to the chapter.

For many people a real estate investment decision is too complicated, too uncertain, and too subject to change to deal with in a rational manner. It is perceived to be similar to the once popular and maddening Rubik's Cube puzzle — seemingly without a solution. Like the Rubik's Cube,

there are a few annoying people who can make consistently good investment decisions without any visible calculations or any appreciable
amount of time. Those investors with this ability were naturally gifted or
have a great deal of experience with real estate investment decision
making. Given the rarity of such people, it would not be wise for you to
depend on being naturally gifted in this way.

If you are not so gifted, the only practical way to solve the investment problem is to break it down into a series of smaller, comprehensi-
ble, and solvable problem segments. This technique of atomization has
worked on countless other problems, including the Rubik's Cube, and
will work here. Fitting the problem to the bounds of your rational abilities makes the real estate investment problem manageable. Once all the
pieces are solved, they are put back together to reconstruct the overall
investment problem and make the final decision. This approach also has
the advantage of allowing you to take maximum advantage of investment experience, good and bad, by fitting that experience into the appropriate segment and seeing how it affects that segment and, in turn, how
that segment affects the overall decision. With some experience, you too
may be able to make good investment decisions without breaking them
into smaller pieces. Until then, the less comprehensive approach, as
embodied in the investment analysis process, provides a workable approach to a solution.

THE INVESTMENT ANALYSIS PROCESS

The investment decision can best be described as a *series* of decisions
relating to the acquisition, operation, and termination of a property. It is
not a single decision, but rather a series of decisions that you make as
you proceed through your investment analysis process. You can view the
investment analysis process as ten sequential stages, as shown in Figure 19.1. This particular model was developed for investors seeking to
purchase properties using debt financing who are concerned about
achieving the maximum returns possible with a minimum commitment
of time and other resources. Thus, the investor wants to allocate his or
her *human capital* effectively, as well as his or her *financial capital*.
The investor is interested in achieving different degrees of return from
each of the possible cash flow sources:

1. cash flow from operations (called cash flow before-tax)
2. tax savings
3. equity build-up from loan amortization
4. loan refinancing proceeds
5. appreciation of property value

As we saw previously, the investor may also have other financial as well

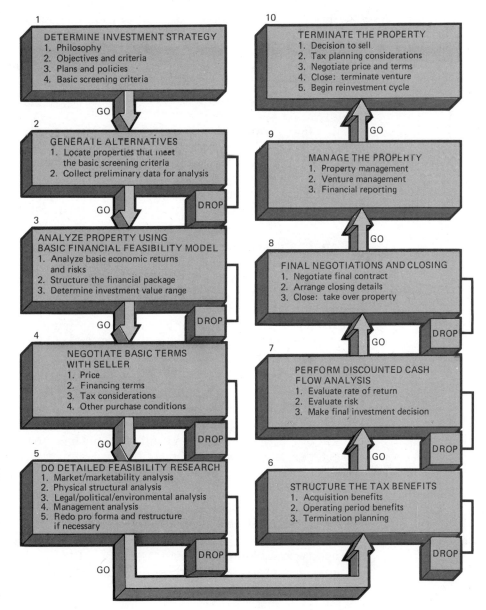

Figure 19.1 A model of the investment analysis process. (Source: Stephen A. Pyhrr and James R. Cooper, *Real Estate Investment: Strategy, Analysis, Decisions.* Boston: Warren, Gorham & Lamont, 1982, p. 192.)

as nonfinancial objectives that should be considered as the investor goes through the process.

The model covers the period from your initial interest in a real estate investment through the purchase, operation, and termination of a property. Each step is interrelated and at each you must make a decision as to whether you will go on or drop the project and look for another. Also, at each step you apply more stringent investment criteria — you begin with simple investment criteria and proceed to more demanding ones later in the process. Only if you make favorable decisions through Step 8 do you end up owning the property. While this may seem like a long and laborious process, it is necessary to go through all these steps in order to analyze accurately the expected returns and risks of a property. If you make serious mistakes at any of these steps, you will probably regret it later.

There is nothing magic about this 10-step process, and it can easily be altered to fit your own particular investment situation. Successful and experienced investors perform many of these steps intuitively, as they have learned to do after many years of investing and making mistakes. Nevertheless, you should understand the importance of each step as it relates to your investment situation in the future.

Step 1: Determine an Investment Strategy You must determine your overall investment philosophy, your specific return and risk investment objectives, and the plans and policies you will follow as you try to locate and analyze properties. From the complete list of investment objectives you will want to define some basic screening criteria that will be used in Step 2 to disqualify properties for which there is little hope of their meeting your more demanding investment objectives. Many investors will make their form-of-ownership decision at this stage, once they have defined their return and risk objectives.

Step 2: Generate Alternatives In this step you must locate properties that meet your basic screening criteria. Plan to spend a lot of time looking at properties, because you will probably have to look at many properties for each one you buy. One of the easiest methods of finding properties is to work with experienced brokers who are familiar with the type of properties you are considering for your investment program.

Step 3: Analyze the Property Using a Basic Financial Feasibility Model At this step you analyze the basic return and risk parameters of a property on a before-tax basis. Also, you will analyze the ways you can finance the property and do some preliminary calculations to measure its economic value. Methods for performing these analyses are discussed later. If a property does not meet these basic financial tests, you will drop the property from further consideration or attempt to negotiate a better deal with the seller. Keep in mind that every property has a *price* or set of purchase terms that will make it attractive to you. You need to estimate these terms and negotiate to achieve them.

Step 4: Negotiate Basic Terms with the Seller You will want to negotiate the basic terms of purchase with the seller before spending a lot of time and money on detailed feasibility research. You want to achieve a meeting of the minds with the seller regarding purchase price, financing terms, tax considerations, and other purchase conditions. At this point, you may want to tie up the property with a conditional contract of purchase that allows you to finish your research and analysis before it becomes binding and yet prevents the owner from selling to someone else.

Step 5: Do Detailed Feasibility Research In this step you collect and analyze information in four areas: (1) market and marketability factors affecting the property, (2) the physical and structural condition of the property, (3) legal, political, and environmental considerations, and (4) how the property will be managed and operated once it is purchased. After you gather this information, along with your estimates of inflation in the future, you can begin to make cash flow forecasts over the contemplated holding period of the investment. In many cases, at this stage you obtain adverse information about the property and either drop it or go back and reanalyze the property (Step 3) and renegotiate the deal with the seller (Step 4).

Step 6: Structure the Tax Benefits Before you can do an after-tax cash flow analysis, you need to make decisions about the tax structure of the property, including cost recovery basis, methods, useful life, and so on. You also need to project your ordinary and capital gains tax rates over the expected holding period of the investment. This information will be used as input data into your after-tax cash flow analysis.

Step 7: Perform a Discounted Cash Flow Analysis You combine all the tax information in Step 6 with the other information from previous steps and estimate after-tax cash flow each year over the holding period. You do a thorough analysis and evaluation of the investment's expected rate of return and risk at this point, using internal rate of return, sensitivity and ratio analysis, and various risk analysis techniques. You then compare the cash flow results with the most stringent investment criteria developed in Step 1. At this point the property has successfully passed all of the tests you have imposed at each step of the investment process. You make a final decision to go or not go. If you decide to go, there will be additional details you will need to negotiate with the seller.

Step 8: Final Negotiations and Closing Both buyer and seller at this point will need to agree on any terms of the purchase that have not yet been covered in a contract. Closing arrangements will be made, legal documents drawn up, contingencies removed from the contract, and a closing time and place established. The buyer, the seller, and their attorneys go to a closing, review the final documents, and sign the necessary papers. Deeds are recorded and monies are disbursed. If the process goes smoothly, the investor has legally acquired the property. Often, however, complications or disputes arise at the closing table, and the closing is delayed or the deal falls through.

Step 9: Manage the Property Unfortunately, your job as an investor has just begun when a closing takes place. You must now make some critical decisions about property management and managing the affairs of the legal entity that owns the property. This latter job is called **venture management** and includes communicating with partners, preparing financial and tax reports on the property, hiring and firing the resident and professional property managers, and monitoring the performance of the property and making decisions regarding cash flow distributions, capital expenditures, refinancing, and selling the property. When you first begin investing, you may perform all of the property management and venture management functions yourself. As your portfolio grows and the properties you purchase are larger, you will probably delegate many if not all of the property management duties to others.

Step 10: Terminate the Property Eventually you will want to dispose of the property in some manner — through sale, exchange, or gift. Now you are on the other side of the negotiating table — trying to sell and close a property you own. You will be seeking to turn most of your gain into a long-term capital gain for tax purposes and defer the payment of taxes as long as possible. You will also need to consider how you will reinvest any cash received from a sale. When you have completed this ten-step process, you have completed the ownership life cycle.

This 10-step process just described emphasizes the many complex and interrelated decisions that an investor must make correctly if long-run investment success is to be achieved. Although the procedure should be modified to fit your particular situation, it provides a checklist of considerations important in most investment situations. In the following sections we will take a close look at the techniques of return and risk analysis, which are the essence of the investment process just described. We will look at some basic measures of return and risk (Step 3) and then proceed to the more sophisticated measures of return and risk using discounted cash flow (DCF) techniques (Step 7).

BASIC MEASURES OF RETURN AND RISK

Step 3 of the investment analysis involves performing a basic financial feasibility analysis of a possible investment's risk and return. Measures of risk and return that can be used at this stage are now considered. To illustrate the basic measures of return and risk that are important, let's consider the purchase of an eight-unit apartment building. The present owner's asking price for the property is $180,000. In checking with local lenders and mortgage bankers, you determine that you could finance the property with a $140,000 loan at an interest rate of 11.5 percent and a term of 30 years. Using financial tables, as discussed in Chapter 13, you determine the annual constant to be 11.89 percent. You will need to

Table 19.1. Cash Flow Pro-Forma for Eight-Unit Apartment Building

Gross possible rental income forecast

Type	Size (square feet)	Number	Per Unit Monthly Rent	Total Monthly Rent
One-bedroom	500	4	$250	$1,000
Two-bedroom	900	4	$450	$1,800
		8		$2,800
			Times 12 months	12
		Gross possible rental income		$33,600

First year cash flow forecast

Gross possible rental income	$33,600
Other income: Vending machines	400
GROSS POSSIBLE INCOME (GPI)	34,000
Less: Vacancy expense (5% of GPI)	1,700
GROSS EFFECTIVE INCOME (GEI)	$32,300
Less: Operating expenses (40% of GPI)	13,600
NET OPERATING INCOME (NOI)	$18,700
Less: Debt service (11.89% × $140,000)	16,646
CASH FLOW BEFORE TAX	$ 2,054

invest $40,000 of equity to buy the property ($180,000 − $140,000). Table 19.1 shows *your* estimates of gross possible income, effective gross income, net operating income, and cash flow before-tax in the form of a pro-forma, or projected, cash flow statement for the first year of ownership.

Return Measures

There are two basic rate of return measures often used to evaluate the property at this early stage of analysis. The first is called the **rate of return on total capital (ROR)** and is computed as follows:

$$\text{Rate of return on total capital (ROR)} = \frac{\text{Net operating income}}{\text{Total capital invested}}$$

This rate of return measures the productivity of your total capital invested ($180,000) before any consideration is given to the way you have financed the property. This return measure is also called the free-and-clear return by some investors.

The second important rate of return measure is the **rate of return on equity (ROE),** and is calculated as follows:

$$\text{Rate of return on equity (ROE)} = \frac{\text{Cash flow before tax}}{\text{Equity investment}}$$

This basic rate of return measure is the most important one to most equity investors because it measures the productivity of their own in-vested dollars. In this case, you will need to invest $40,000 to acquire the property if you pay the full asking price.

Using our eight-unit apartment example, in which the net operat-ing income is $18,700, cash flow before tax is $2054, the total capital investment (asking price) is $180,000, and the equity investment is $40,000, we can compute ROR and ROE as follows:

$$ROR = \frac{\$18,700}{\$180,000} = 10.39\%$$

$$ROE = \frac{\$2054}{\$40,000} = 5.14\%$$

This situation might seem undesirable to many investors because the total capital is earning at a rate greater than that received by the equity investor (10.39 percent compared to 5.14 percent). The problem is that the mortgage constant (K) is 11.80 percent and requires most of the net operating income to pay the debt service, principal and interest, of $16,646. This situation is called **unfavorable leverage,** and exists whenever:

$$ROE < ROR$$

Many investors find this situation to be quite acceptable because they expect to increase rents each year, thus increasing the net operating income and cash flow each year. After a few years, the property is ex-pected to achieve a **favorable leverage** situation where:

$$ROE > ROR$$

If you are not happy with a unfavorable leverage situation and an ROE of only 5.14 percent the first year, you have a number of options:

1. Don't buy the property; stop your analysis and go on to the next potential investment.
2. Reduce the price of the property and the equity invested until an acceptable ROE is reached.
3. Decrease the mortgage loan constant by lowering the interest rate or increasing the loan term. This will decrease the debt service and raise the cash flow and ROE.
4. Raise the net operating income by raising rents or reducing vacan-cies and operating expenses. This will raise the ROR and ROE.
5. Do a combination of the above to achieve an acceptable solution.

As you can see, there are numerous negotiation options if you cannot "make the numbers work" at first.

Risk Measures

Two popular risk measures used by investors are the debt coverage ratio and the breakeven ratio (also called the default point). They can be computed as follows:

$$\text{Debt coverage ratio} = \frac{\text{Net operating income (NOI)}}{\text{Debt service}}$$

$$\text{Breakeven point} = \frac{\text{Operating expense} + \text{Debt service}}{\text{Gross possible income}}$$

Debt service is comprised of payments for principal and interest. In this case, they are the *annual payments*. The *debt coverage ratio* tells the investor how much cushion he or she has before the net income is not sufficient to pay debt service. The higher the ratio, the greater the cushion, and the less risky the investment. On the other hand, if NOI falls or debt service increases, the debt coverage ratio falls and the risk increases. Conservative investors seek to maintain minimum debt coverage ratios of 1.2 to 1.3.

The *breakeven ratio* tells the investor what occupancy must be achieved to "break even"—that is, to be able to pay all operating expenses and debt service with the rental income generated by the property. A breakeven point of 80 percent means that the property must be generating 80 percent of gross possible income in order to pay all the bills. The investor can control this risk factor by not allowing a project to be purchased and financed in such a way that the breakeven point is above a certain level. For example, a conservative investor might set a maximum breakeven ratio at 85 percent and reject all projects or financing alternatives that result in a ratio greater than this.

In our example, the debt coverage ratio and breakeven point can be calculated as follows:

$$\text{Debt coverage ratio} = \frac{\$18,700}{\$16,646} = 1.12$$

$$\text{Breakeven point} = \frac{\$13,600 + \$16,646}{\$34,000} = 88.96\%$$

For the conservative investor, both ratios indicate too much risk. The debt coverage ratio is too low and the breakeven point is too high. The project would be dropped from consideration or must be restructured in order to raise the debt coverage ratio and reduce the breakeven ratio to levels acceptable to the investor.

Restructuring to Achieve an Acceptable Return/Risk Level

The investor can restructure the property by changing the loan amount and terms or the purchase price. For example, if you decide that you could live with the debt coverage ratio of 1.12 (relatively high risk) *if* you were compensated for it by a higher rate of return on equity (ROE) of 11 percent (instead of 5.14 percent), you can restructure the property by lowering the purchase price. To do this, you must determine the equity value by dividing the projected cash flow by the required rate of return on equity (ROE). This process is called **equity capitalization analysis.** The results are as follows:

$$\text{Equity value} = \frac{\text{Cash flow before tax}}{\text{Required ROE}} = \frac{\$2054}{.11} = \$18{,}673$$

This calculation shows that the value of the equity, if you want an 11 percent ROE, is $18,673, not the asking price for the equity of $40,000. If this is true then the investor can pay only $158,673 for the property, not the asking price of $180,000:

Equity value	$ 18,673
Plus: Mortgage amount	140,000
Total property value (Justified purchase price)	$158,673

Thus, if you pay *no more than* $158,673 for the property, assuming everything else is unchanged, you will achieve your required ROE of 11 percent, with a debt coverage ratio of 1.12. You have achieved an acceptable return/risk ratio and are now willing to go on to the next step of your analysis.

Criticism of the Basic Return and Risk Measures

The measures of return and risk presented above can be used in the early stages of your analysis to test the *basic economics* of a property and determine its approximate value based on a one year cash flow projection. However, they ignore many variables that influence a property's total return and risk, and thus its true value to the investor. Specifically, they ignore the following factors:

1. Changes in rents, expenses, and property value each year after the first year.
2. Equity build-up over time through loan amortization.
3. The expected holding period of the investment — how long you will own it.
4. The impact of income tax factors.
5. Start-up and transactions costs, such as brokerage fees and closing costs.
6. The erratic and uneven nature of NOI and cash flows from year to year, thus the true riskiness of the investment. Debt coverage ratios

and breakeven points are only crude measures of the riskiness of an investment.

7. The time value of money—the fact that a dollar promised in the future is worth less than a dollar today.

8. Innovations in the mortgage markets, such as variable rate and renegotiable rate mortgages and other new financing instruments that are products of our current inflationary environment.

These shortcomings can be overcome through the use of discounted cash flow (DCF) techniques and the use of sensitivity analysis and other risk-estimation procedures. While the methods just described are useful in the early stages of your analysis and negotiations, you should use the more sophisticated DCF techniques to analyze return and risk before you make the final investment decision.

DISCOUNTED CASH FLOW ANALYSIS AND RELATED RISK ESTIMATION TECHNIQUES: OVERVIEW

Overcoming the criticisms of the basic return and risk measures just considered requires an approach that incorporates *all* of the after-tax cash flows a real estate investment will produce while you own it. Also, the time value of these cash flows must be considered by using the discounting concepts discussed in Chapter 13. To do this requires that you develop estimates of after-tax cash flow for each year you anticipate owning the property and also an estimate of the after-tax cash you will receive from the sale of the asset. By making these estimates, you will have an idea of the actual after-tax dollars that you expect to go into your pocket each year from operating the property and from selling it at the end of your holding period. If you calculate these cash flows, your problem then becomes one of deciding whether they are adequate.

You can use the time value of money concepts considered in Chapter 13 to assess whether the cash flows justify the price you must pay to receive them. Specifically, you can use the internal rate of return and net present value techniques for this task. Based on the idea that you prefer, and value more highly, dollars today than anytime in the future, these techniques allow you to convert dollars received in different time periods into rates of return or dollar amounts that may be used to decide whether the investment meets your return requirements.

The entire process of calculating all after-tax cash flows and then using time value of money concepts to assess their adequacy is called **discounted cash flow (DCF) analysis.** Do not worry if the details of how the after-tax cash flows, the internal rate of return, and the net present value are not clear to you. The discussion that follows is designed to give you only an overview of DCF analysis with the goal of providing a base on which to build, not to make you a DCF expert. If you want more detail, the appendix to this chapter walks you through the steps required to produce the summary analysis you are about to see.

Discounted cash flow analysis requires a large number of calculations. Not surprisingly, calculators and computers are used extensively to reduce both the required time and likelihood of making an error in arithmetic. Especially useful are many of the small business and personal computers now available that have programs for performing DCF analysis. These computers are fast, fairly inexpensive, and easy to use. Many investors and consultants use them regularly.

However, DCF analysis is a combination of art and science. The art of DCF analysis involves making a number of projections, forecasts, and assumptions on which to base all of your calculations. For instance, you must estimate beginning rents and how they are likely to change over the years. Likewise, you must estimate beginning operating expenses and the change in them, vacancies, and so on. These projections, forecasts, and assumptions are at the heart of discounted cash flow analysis, because once they are made, the mechanics of calculating after-tax cash flows are just that — mechanics. All of these items should be based on the best available judgment about the future. If done with care, the result is a statement showing the expected after-tax cash flows, the money you can actually put in your pocket, for each year and also the after-tax proceeds from the sale of the property — in short, all of the cash flows you can expect from your investment.

The results of DCF analysis performed on the eight-unit apartment considered earlier are summarized in Table 19.2. In this table, it has been assumed the investment is to be held for three years and then sold. Many other assumptions have been made about rents, expenses, growth in value, and so on. The assumptions in this sample analysis represent the most likely value for each variable. As you see, DCF analysis provides a complete picture of what you are buying in this investment.

Not surprisingly, since you are making forecasts, you will not be certain about many of the numbers in your discounted cash flow analysis, even though they represent your best estimate of the most likely outcome. Rents, expenses, taxes, or other variables could have different values than estimated in any year. This means after-tax cash flow could be different than estimated and so could the after-tax proceeds from the property's sale; so could the present value and internal rate of return. All of this potential variability creates risk, the possibility that an outcome other than the expected one may occur.

In Step 3 of the investment process, you analyzed risk by calculating the debt coverage ratio and breakeven point using the most likely values for the variables involved. How much effort you put into risk analysis depends on the size of the investment, how much uncertainty you have about the project, how much time you have, how much money

Table 19.2. Discounted Cash Flow Analysis

(a)
After-tax Cash Flow for Each Year

	1	2	3
A. Gross Possible Income	$ 34,000	$ 36,720	$ 39,658
B. Less: Vacancy	− 1,700	− 1,836	− 1,983
C. Gross Effective Income	$ 32,300	$ 34,884	$ 37,675
D. Less: Operating Expenses	− 13,600	− 14,960	− 16,456
E. NET OPERATING INCOME	$ 18,700	$ 19,924	$ 21,219
F. Less: Interest	− 16,110	− 16,037	− 15,967
G. Cost Recovery	− 14,400	− 14,400	− 12,800
H. TAXABLE INCOME (LOSS)	$ − 11,810	− 10,513	− 7,548
I. Plus: Cost Recovery	14,400	14,400	12,800
J. Less: Principal	− 536	− 608	− 678
K. CASH FLOW BEFORE TAX	$ 2,054	$ 3,279	$ 4,574
L. Plus: Tax Savings (40% × H)	4,724	4,205	3,019
M. CASH FLOW AFTER TAX	$ 6,778	$ 7,484	$ 7,593

(b)
Net Sales Proceeds

Gross Sales price	$ 214,383
Less: Selling Expenses	− 12,833
Net Sales Price	$ 201,550
Less: Mortgage Balance	− 138,178
Taxes	− 13,688
NET SALES PROCEEDS	$ 49,684

(c)
Summary of Cash Flows over Holding Period

	0	1	2	3
Equity Investment	$ 40,000			
Annual Cash Flow After Tax		$6,778	$7,484	$ 7,593
Net Sale Proceeds				49,684
Total Cash Flows	$ − 40,000	$6,778	$7,484	$57,277

(d)
Internal Rate of Return, Net Present Value and Total Project Value

Internal Rate of Return = 24%
Net Present Value   = $3,992
Total Project Value:

Present Value of Equity	$ 43,992
Original Loan Amount	140,000
Total Project Value	$183,992

you want to spend, and the extent to which you are risk averse. There are four levels of risk analysis you can undertake for this three-year investment. They are:

1. *Ratio analysis of the most likely cash flow forecast.* You compute debt coverage ratios and breakeven points each year for three years, using the numbers in the cash flow analysis.
2. *Sensitivity analysis of uncertain variables.* You analyze which variables are subject to uncertainty and determine how their values might fluctuate over the next three years. You redo your DCF analysis using these new numbers and test the impact of changes in these variables on the investor's IRR, or other return measures (ROE, ROR, etc.). You are testing to see how sensitive your rate of return is to different economic and market conditions.
3. *Optimistic/pessimistic/most likely analysis.* You decide what values to place on all your DCF input data to reflect optimistic and pessimistic economic conditions. You already have your most likely cash flow data. You redo your DCF analysis using the pessimistic and optimistic data and compute the impact on IRR and NPV, or other measures of return that are important to you. This analysis produces some variability measures that are good indicators of the range of possible outcomes.
4. *Computer-assisted analysis.* The computer can be used to do all of the analysis described above. In addition, there are models available, known as Monte Carlo risk simulation models, which allow you to do a complete risk analysis by inputting probability distributions for each of the uncertain variables. The computer model simulates possible combinations of market and economic conditions and their impact on the investor's rate of return. Only sophisticated investors, however, can attempt to use such a complete risk analysis model.

Once all the risk data is generated, you are ready to make a final investment decision.

The Final Investment Decision

If the return and risk measures you have calculated meet your minimum levels of acceptability (Step 1 of the investment process), then you are ready to invest. If not, you will need to either modify and renegotiate your deal or drop it and move on to the next potential investment. You should purchase a property only if its short- and long-term expected returns and risks match your needs.

USING PROFESSIONAL HELP

The procedures just described are not easy, nor can they be mastered in a short time. It will take much concentrated effort, education and training, and time to become an expert in the field of investment. It would be foolish for you to try to do it alone; in fact, it would probably be impossible. The smart approach is to assemble a team of advisors to help you with the various facets of project analysis and evaluation when your expertise is lacking. For example, you may want to develop a working relationship with each of the following types of experts:

1. *Real estate brokers.* Use brokers to assist in locating desirable properties and to assist in the mechanics of the purchase. Also, when you are ready to sell a property you own, they can locate buyers and assist in the mechanics of the sale. Brokers who are investment specialists are also a ready source of information on market conditions and trends.

2. *Appraisers and counselors.* Some are professionally trained to help you do the investment analysis using DCF techniques and arrive at a sound investment decision. Find one who specializes in investments of the type you are interested in, and preferably one who has good computer capabilities, to generate the cash flow data for your analysis.

3. *Property managers.* Property managers can provide useful information about rental rates, features desired by tenants, and operating expenses. They can also help you establish and implement a plan for managing the property once acquired.

4. *Mortgage bankers.* Mortgage bankers are mortgage market experts and have the training to assist you in determining the various financing alternatives that are available to you and for any specific property you are analyzing.

5. *Tax advisors and attorneys.* The importance of using these experts in the investment process was discussed earlier.

6. *Others.* Commercial bankers, engineers, architects, and contractors may also be able to add important expertise to your analysis to solve problems or answer questions that you cannot.

Don't expect these professionals to make your decisions for you. Only you can do that. Do expect them, however, to provide specific input on areas they are qualified to discuss. You are responsible for defining what specific information you need from the expert. Be sure you define what the nature and scope of services you require from each, and determine what the cost will be. In most cases you "get what you pay for," so don't plan to get good advice without adequate compensation.

Develop the team of specialists you will need, get to know them well, pay them well, and be sure that you use them effectively at various steps in the investment process when their input is critical. This is one of the keys to successfully managing the investment process and creating a substantial amount of wealth over your lifetime.

SUMMARY

You now have a better understanding of how to make real estate investment decisions. By breaking the problem down into smaller pieces in a systematic fashion, solving the pieces, and then putting them back together, you can solve the investment problem more easily. You found that in reality the investment decision is a series of decisions rather than one big decision. The investment analysis process was discussed as an organized framework you can use in analyzing investments.

Basic measures of risk and return to be used early in the investment analysis process were introduced. Basic return measures include the rate of return on total capital and rate of return on equity. Risk measures introduced at this point were the debt coverage ratio and the breakeven point. It was also demonstrated that the expected return and risk of the investment could be adjusted by restructuring the financing or terms of purchase. Finally, criticisms of the basic risk and return measures were discussed and they were found to be less than perfect.

You were then introduced to discounted cash flow analysis, a more comprehensive approach to analysis that overcomes many of the problems of the basic return measures. It is better because it considers the entire life of the investment. Risk measures that could be used with the DCF analysis included ratio analysis, sensitivity analysis, optimistic/pessimistic/most likely analysis, and computer-assisted analysis.

Becoming good at real estate investment analysis requires professional assistance. You will likely need help from experts such as brokers, appraisers, counselors, property managers, mortgage bankers, tax advisors, and attorneys. In addition, you may need help from engineers, architects, and contractors. These people must be paid well, but are invaluable in making consistently good real estate decisions.

QUICK QUIZ

1. The second step in the investment analysis process is _____.

    a. negotiate basic terms with seller   c. terminate the property
    b. manage the property   d. generate alternatives

2. Which of the following is *not* a way of terminating an investment?

    a. sale   c. refinance
    b. exchange   d. gift

3. Which of the following is *not* a basic risk or return measure?

   a. rate of return on total capital   c. rate of return on equity
   b. internal rate of return   d. debt coverage ratio

4. Dividing projected cash flow before tax by the required rate of return on equity to determine equity value is called _____.

   a. equity capitalization analysis   c. internal rate of return
   b. net present value   d. sensitivity analysis

5. Risk analysis involving the use of the debt coverage ratio and the breakeven point is called _____.

   a. sensitivity analysis
   b. computer-assisted analysis
   c. optimistic/pessimistic/most likely analysis
   d. ratio analysis

6. Three real estate experts you may use to analyze an investment include _____, _____, and _____.

7. Analysis that involves calculating after-tax cash flows and then using the internal rate of return and net present value techniques is called _____.

8. Detailed feasibility research involves collecting and analyzing information in the four general areas of _____, _____, _____, and _____.

9. Four of the criticisms of the basic risk and return measures are _____, _____, _____, and _____.

10. The _____ tells the investor the occupancy that must be achieved to be able to pay all operating expenses and debt service from rental income.

QUESTIONS AND EXERCISES

1. What is the debt coverage ratio for an office building with net operating income of $130,000 and debt service of $100,000?

2. What is the default point for an apartment complex with debt service of $100,000 per year, operating expenses of $90,000, and gross possible rents of $230,000?

3. You have an opportunity to purchase a 10-unit apartment complex for $210,000. If you estimate gross possible income to be $35,000 per year, vacancies to be 5 percent of that amount, operating expenses to be 40 percent of gross possible income, and debt service to be $17,000 per year, what is your rate of return on total capital (ROR)? If you had borrowed $150,000, what is the rate of return on equity (ROE)?

4. Is the investment in Question 3 an example of favorable or unfavorable leverage? Why?

5. Find a home for sale in the classified ads in a neighborhood you know and check with a lender to find out current interest rates. If you could borrow 80 percent of the purchase price, would the investment provide an ROR and ROE that you would find acceptable? Why?

6. Why is real estate investment analysis called a combination of art and science?

7. If you were contemplating purchasing a small shopping center, what experts might you consult and what would you ask each to do?

8. Price is one very important purchase term. What are some others and why are they important?

9. How can you affect the risk and return characteristics of a piece of real estate you are trying to purchase?

10. What factors do the one year basic return and risk measures fail to consider?

KEY TERMINOLOGY

basic financial feasibility model
cash flow before-tax
discounted cash flow analysis
equity capitalization analysis
negative leverage
optimistic/pessimistic/most likely analysis

positive leverage
rate of return on equity
rate of return on total capital
sensitivity analysis
venture management

IF YOU WANT TO READ MORE

G. VINCENT BARRETT and JOHN P. BLAIR, *How to Conduct and Analyze Real Estate Market and Feasibility Studies* (New York: Van Nostrand, 1982).

[Handwritten margin notes: Rent $700/mo; Price $60,000; Int ~ 10%; Loan To Value 80%; Vac 5%; Op Exp $1500/yr; OP]

FRED E. CASE, *Investing in Real Estate* (Englewood Cliffs, N.J.: Prentice-Hall, 1978).

DONALD R. EPLEY and JAMES A. MILLAR, *Basic Real Estate Finance and Investments* (New York: John Wiley & Sons, Inc. 1980).

JAMES A. GRAASKAMP, "A Rational Approach to Feasibility Analysis," in *Readings in Real Estate Investment Analysis*, Vol. 1 (Cambridge: Ballinger Publishing Company, 1977), pp. 207–215.

AUSTIN JAFFE and C. F. SIRMANS, *Real Estate Investment Decision Making* (Englewood Cliffs: Prentice-Hall, Inc., 1982).

STEPHEN A. PYHRR, JAMES R. COOPER, LARRY E. WOFFORD, and STEVEN D. KAPPLIN, *Real Estate Investment: Strategy, Analysis, Decisions,* second edition (New York: John Wiley & Sons, Inc., 1986).

MAURY SELDIN and RICHARD H. SWESNIK, *Real Estate Investment Strategy,* second edition (New York: Wiley-Interscience, 1979).

APPENDIX:
DISCOUNTED CASH FLOW ANALYSIS EXAMPLE

Discounted cash flow analysis (DCF) is based on the idea of considering all the after-tax cash flows an investor will receive from a real estate investment. Once estimated, all cash flows are evaluated using either the internal rate of return or present value technique. In this appendix you are walked through an example of a DCF analysis for the eight-unit apartment building you are considering as an investment.

To begin with, assume that you plan to hold your apartment building for three years, at the end of which time you will sell it. After you do a careful market study, you decide that the following assumptions would be appropriate for your DCF analysis — that is, they represent the *most likely* conditions that you expect over the next three years:

1. Gross possible income in the first year of $34,000 will increase each year by 8 percent; operating expenses of $13,600 will increase by 10 percent; and property value of $180,000 by 6 percent. The vacancy rate will remain constant at 5 percent.
2. Your ordinary income tax bracket is 40 percent and your capital gains tax bracket is 16 percent. Recall that your effective capital gains rate is 40 percent of your ordinary rate (40% × 40% = 16%).
3. The land value is $20,000; therefore, you can depreciate $160,000 of the total purchase price of the property. You assume that you, in fact, must pay the full asking price of $180,000 for the property.
4. Cost recovery will be calculated using the accelerated cost recovery tables in Chapter 12, assuming the property is purchased in January.

Table 19.3. Mortgage Schedule

	1	2	3
Loan amount	$140,000	$139,464	$138,856
Interest rate	× .115	× .115	× .115
Interest amount	16,110	16,038	15,968
Principal amount	+ 536	+ 608	+ 678
Debt service	$ 16,646	$ 16,646	$ 16,646

Balance at End of Year 3 = $138,856 − $678 = $138,178

5. Selling expenses will be 6 percent of the projected sales price, including brokerage fees and closing costs.
6. Your minimum acceptable after-tax internal rate of return is 20 percent. You will not invest in a project of this type unless you can expect to achieve *at least* this IRR.

In the following sections we will generate all the schedules necessary to complete the DCF analysis.

Mortgage Schedule The first schedule to be calculated is the mortgage schedule, which shows the breakdown between interest and principal. Recall that our original loan amount is $140,000; the debt service is $16,646 annually and reflects an interest rate of 11.5 percent for 30 years. Given these factors, we can calculate the mortgage schedule as in Table 19.3.

Each year the interest rate is multiplied by the remaining loan amount to calculate the interest amount. The difference between the amount of interest and the total debt service is the principal amount (e.g., $16,646 − $16,110 = $536 for year 1). To find the balance of the loan the following year (beginning of year 2), the amount of principal is subtracted from the previous year's loan balance (e.g., $140,000 − $536 = $139,464). At the *end of year 3*, the loan balance is $138,856 − $678, or $138,178. When the property is sold at the end of year 3 you will have to pay off the remaining loan balance of $138,178. Actually, the easiest way to arrive at a mortgage schedule is to buy a calculator that is

Table 19.4. Cost Recovery

	1	2	3
Recoverable basis	$160,000	$160,000	$160,000
Recovery factor (from Table 12.2)	.09	.09	.08
Recovery deduction	$ 14,400	$ 14,400	$ 12,800

Total Cost Recovery Deductions = $14,400 + $14,400 + $12,800 = $41,600

Table 19.5. Property Value at End of Each Year

	1	2	3
Property value, beginning of year	$180,000	$190,800	$202,248
Rate of appreciation	1.06	1.06	1.06
Property value, end of year	$190,800	$202,248	$214,383

preprogrammed to generate these numbers or a computer with a program to generate them.

Cost Recovery Schedule As discussed in Chapter 12, the cost recovery schedule is calculated as in Table 19.4.

Property Value Schedule You assumed that the property is increasing in value at an annual (compound) rate of 6 percent, starting from an initial property value (purchase price of $180,000). You calculate the property value at the end of each year as in Table 19.5. Therefore, it is assumed that the property can be sold at the end of year 3 for $214,383.

Annual Cash Flow Before-Tax and After-Tax You are now ready to calculate the cash flows for each year of the holding period. These cash flows are calculated in Table 19.6. Each year the gross possible income increases by 8 percent, while expenses grow at 10 percent. Gross possible income is the total dollars the property would generate if every unit were occupied every day of the year at the rental rates you have projected. Gross possible income also includes any income from parking, vending machines, washers and dryers, and so on. Obviously, you will have some vacant units, units rented for less than you had planned, and

Table 19.6. After-tax Cash Flow for Each Year

	1	2	3
A. Gross Possible Income	$ 34,000	$ 36,720	$ 39,658
B. Less: Vacancy	− 1,700	− 1,836	− 1,983
C. Gross Effective Income	$ 32,300	$ 34,884	$ 37,675
D. Less: Operating Expenses	− 13,600	− 14,960	− 16,456
E. NET OPERATING INCOME	$ 18,700	$ 19,924	$ 21,219
F. Less: Interest	− 16,110	− 16,037	− 15,967
G. Cost Recovery	− 14,400	− 14,400	− 12,800
H. TAXABLE INCOME	$ − 11,810	$ − 10,513	$ − 7,548
I. Plus: Cost Recovery	14,400	14,400	12,800
J. Less: Principal	− 536	− 608	− 678
K. CASH FLOW BEFORE TAX	$ 2,054	$ 3,279	$ 4,574
L. Plus: Tax Savings (40% × H)	4,724	4,205	3,019
M. CASH FLOW AFTER TAX	$ 6,778	$ 7,484	$ 7,593

some bad debts, which add up to your not actually receiving the amount represented by gross possible rents. Because of this, you will build in a vacancy allowance. What is left of gross possible rents after the vacancy allowance is called effective gross rents. This is the amount of money you actually plan on receiving. Operating expenses are all the expenses associated with the apartments, except for debt service. The net operating income, the difference between effective gross rents and operating expenses, increases from $18,700 in year 1 to $21,219 in year 3.

Net operating income is not the amount that you must report on your income tax return. Mortgage interest and cost recovery can both be deducted from net operating income in arriving at taxable income. Taxable income is the amount that is carried to your tax return. Taxable income for the apartment starts at −$11,810 and increases to −$7548 in year 3. Accordingly, the tax savings on other income decreases over the same period from $4724 to $3019. This decrease in tax shelter occurs because interest and cost recovery are decreasing and net operating income is increasing, causing taxable income to increase. You should note that tax savings occur because you have assumed that you have other income to offset with the negative taxable income generated by the apartment investment.

Taxable income is an important number, but it is not the amount of money from the apartment you can put into your pocket. So far, the principal that you paid during each period has not been considered because it was not tax deductible. However, it does represent a drain of cash and can now be subtracted from taxable income. Also, cost recovery deductions did not involve a payment of cash to anyone. At this point, cost recovery deductions have been deducted to arrive at taxable income. Thus, the actual amount of cash from the investment is now understated by the amount of that deduction. To eliminate this situation, cost recovery is now added back to taxable income. When principal is subtracted from and cost recovery added to taxable income, before-tax cash flow results. By considering the impact of taxes, after-tax cash flow is produced. If taxable income is positive, taxes must be paid and those taxes are subtracted from before-tax cash flow. If taxable income is negative, a tax savings results, which is added to before-tax cash flow. For the apartment, the after-tax cash flow increases from $6778 in year 1 to $7593 in year 3. In effect, the loss of tax shelter each year is roughly offset by rising net operating income.

Taxes on the Sale of the Property at End of Holding Period At the end of year 3, the property is sold for $214,383. Selling expenses of 6 percent of the sales price are paid:

Sales Price	$214,383
Selling Expense Rate	× .06
Selling Expenses	$ 12,833

Table 19.7. Taxes on Sale of Property

Gross sales price	$214,383
Less: Selling expenses	− 12,833
Net sales price	$201,550
Less: Ending basis ($180,000 − $41,600)	−138,400
TOTAL TAXABLE GAIN	$ 63,150
Less: Amount of excess depreciation	$ 14,833
CAPITAL GAIN	$ 48,217
Tax on: Capital gain (.16 × $48,217)	$ 7,715
Excess depreciation (.40 × 14,933)	5,973
TOTAL TAX LIABILITY	$ 13,688

Also, recall that the accelerated cost recovery method was used and resulted in total cost recovery over three years of $41,600 ($14,400 + $14,400 + $12,800). If the straight-line method had been used, the total amount of cost recovery claimed would have been $26,667 (1/18 of $160,000 each year for three years). Therefore, the excess cost recovery on the property is $14,933 ($41,600 − $26,667), which will be taxed at the ordinary income tax rate.

We can now calculate the taxes on the sale of the property as in Table 19.7. The tax liability includes the capital gains taxes (at the 16 percent tax rate) plus the ordinary income tax (at the 40 percent tax rate) on the amount of excess cost recovery claimed. Notice that all the capital gains income is taxed at the same rate. This is a simplifying assumption that was made to make the explanation clearer. In reality, 40 percent of the capital gain would be added to your other taxable income and taxes paid at the ordinary rate. By adding this income to your other income, your marginal tax rate would actually increase, not stay constant. However, the simplifying assumption of unchanging tax rates makes the example easier to follow. The total taxes to be paid when the property is sold are $13,688.

Net Sales Proceeds The after-tax cash flow resulting from the sale of the property at the end of year 3 can be calculated as in Table 19.8. After paying all selling expenses and repaying the mortgage loan balance of $138,178 and the capital gain tax and recapture tax on excess cost recovery, you are left with $49,684 in your pocket. This is your net after-tax cash flow resulting from the sale of your property.

Table 19.8. Net Sales Proceeds

Gross sales price	$214,383
Less: Selling expenses	− 12,833
Net sales price	$201,550
Less: Mortgage balance	−138,178
Taxes	− 13,688
NET SALES PROCEEDS	$ 49,684

Summary of Cash Flows over Holding Period Over the 3-year holding period, your cash flows after-tax are those calculated in the previous sections, as shown in Table 19.9. The year of sale results in a total cash flow from operations and sale proceeds of $57,277. It is important to realize that these cash flows are *equity* cash flows. That is, they accrue to the equity investor because all operating expenses and mortgage payments have already been deducted. What is left belongs to you, the owner of the apartment complex. You are now ready to calculate the internal rate of return and the net present value of the apartment investment.

Internal Rate of Return The internal rate of return (IRR) defined in Chapter 13 is the discount rate that causes the present value of an investment's outflows to equal the present value of its inflows. Put another way, it is the discount rate that causes the net present value to be zero. The internal rate of return is found by trial and error. (For a review of IRR calculation, see Chapter 13). In this case

$$\text{NPV} = 0 = \frac{-\$40,000}{(1 + .24)^0} + \frac{\$6778}{(1 + .24)^1} + \frac{\$7484}{(1 + .24)^2} + \frac{\$57,277}{(1 + .24)^3}$$

Because the calculated IRR, 24 percent, is greater than the required IRR of 20 percent, the project should be undertaken. It meets your IRR criterion.

Present Value The present value of the equity is calculated by discounting the equity after tax cash flows by the 20 percent required rate of return:

$$\$43,992 = \frac{\$6778}{(1 + .20)^1} + \frac{\$7484}{(1 + .20)^2} + \frac{\$57,277}{(1 + .20)^3}$$

The present value of the equity is $43,992. This means that under the assumptions used in the DCF analysis, including a $140,000, 11.5 percent mortgage, the equity is worth $43,992 to you. Since the apartment requires an equity investment of only $40,000, it is worth more than its cost and should be acceptable to you on the basis of return.

The total present value of the property is the equity value plus the

Table 19.9. Summary of Cash Flows over Holding Period

	0	1	2	3
Equity investment	$ 40,000			
Annual cash flow after tax		$6,778	$7,484	$ 7,593
Net sale proceeds				49,684
Total cash flows	$ −40,000	$6,778	$7,484	$57,277

mortgage loan value, as follows:

Equity Value	$ 43,992
Original Loan Amount	140,000
Total Project Value	$183,992

Again we see that the project is acceptable because it is worth $183,992 but only cost you $180,000. Thus, it has a net present value (NPV) of $3,992. This means you could pay up to $183,992 for the apartment and still receive your required rate of return.

PART FOUR

REAL ESTATE DECISION SUPPORT AREAS

Real estate is far too complex for most persons to become experts in all facets of activity. These limitations are especially critical to real estate decision makers, who must deal with many areas involving specialized expertise. As a result, there are numerous opportunities to provide specialized support services for real estate decision makers either directly or indirectly through another person or firm providing such support services.

Real estate decision support areas include marketing, property management, appraisal, and counseling. Each of these areas provides a different service to decision makers and each requires specialized knowledge. Compensation comes in different forms, ranging from commissions to professional fees. Many people have found satisfying and rewarding careers in the decision support areas. Whether you make a career out of one of them or not, you need a working knowledge of the nature and scope of the activities of each area, should it become necessary to use such services.

This part of the book, containing six chapters, is designed to give you that working knowledge. The first two chapters deal with marketing and the role brokers and salespersons play in real estate. The next chapter examines the activities associated with property management. Two chapters then introduce and explain the specialty that deals with estimating the market value of real estate, appraisal. The final chapter outlines the emerging field of real estate counseling.

The chapters in Part Four only introduce the decision support areas. However, they should round out your knowledge of real estate and convey the flavor of each activity area in sufficient detail for you to form some impressions of them. The chapters also provide a solid base on which to build a more exhaustive study of any decision support area or areas you find interesting.

20

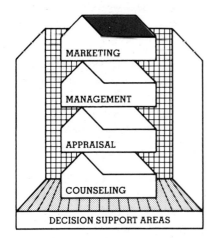

MARKETING

MANAGEMENT

APPRAISAL

COUNSELING

DECISION SUPPORT AREAS

Marketing: overview — the brokerage business and the real estate transaction

PREVIEW

As either developer or equity investor, your ability to realize profits will depend on your ability to market your space either to renters or buyers. Finding firms and individuals to lease space or purchase property is not easy. Likewise, if you are in the market to buy property or find space to lease, you may not have an easy time of it. Real estate marketing services offered by brokers may provide valuable assistance to your marketing efforts. This chapter provides you with information about real estate marketing. Specifically, it explains:

1. What real estate marketing is and how it is accomplished.
2. The basic activities associated with marketing real estate.
3. The role of real estate brokerage in real estate marketing.
4. How brokerage firms are compensated and, in turn, how they compensate those in the firm.
5. The basic steps in a real estate sales transaction.
6. How real estate marketing is likely to change in the future.

Marketing either rental space or equity interests in real estate requires a large number of decisions, and these decisions require an understanding of real estate markets. If you are a developer, you must decide when and how to lease the space you are building. Decisions must be made on pricing and other possible negotiating points in finding tenants. As an equity investor you must decide when to sell, how much to ask, and who likely purchasers may be. Another decision must be made as to whether you are going to use in-house personnel to perform the marketing or contract with an outside party to find tenants or sell the equity interest. If you contract with an outside party to assist you, that outside party will be in the real estate brokerage business. The word *broker* is used in this chapter to describe anyone performing these services.

For example, suppose that you own a home and have decided to sell it. What would you do? (Don't forget that if you have read all the material up to this chapter you are much more knowledgeable about real estate than most people.) You would probably want to estimate what your home is worth, find out what kind of financing is available, find out whether it is a buyers' or sellers' market, and generally obtain information affecting the transaction. If you are not actively involved in the real estate market, you may not know how to assess these factors, or if you know how, it may take a good bit of time. Once these questions are answered, another set of questions will occupy your time. You will want to know how best to advertise your home, how best to show it, and how to handle the paperwork connected with the sale. If you feel comfortable with these details and believe that sufficient interest can be generated by your own efforts, you probably will choose to sell your home without using a broker. If you are uncomfortable with these details or feel that you need other people to direct potential buyers to and through your home, then you will likely use the services of a broker.

You probably already have a good idea of how real estate brokerage basically works: a broker tries to find a ready, willing, and able buyer for the seller's real property in return for a fee, usually paid by the seller. The same concept applies to leasing space: brokers locate tenants willing to meet terms established by the owner in return for a fee. Beyond this basic understanding, the details of brokerage probably become somewhat hazy.

This chapter seeks to improve your understanding of what brokerage is all about. The emphasis on brokerage is not intended to suggest that using brokers is always better than using expertise and resources within a developer's or equity investor's own organization. However, once the decision has been made either to use or not to use a broker, the activities involved are the same whether performed by a broker or another person.

This chapter considers the activities of brokers in the real estate transaction, not what requirements you must meet to legally enter the brokerage business. The next chapter addresses the question of how the brokerage business is regulated by the states.

OVERVIEW OF REAL ESTATE BROKERAGE BUSINESS

Real estate brokerage is a service business. Brokers provide services in return for a fee. That fee, called a commission, is usually paid by the seller and is often stated as a percentage of the sales price. Sometimes buyers will engage a broker to find a property and pay a commission, but this is rare. For example, a large pension fund interested in purchasing investment real estate throughout the country may engage a broker to locate attractive properties because such a search would be too costly or difficult for the pension fund operators to undertake themselves. Regardless of who is paying the commission, it is a matter of negotiation between the broker and the potential client.

The commission percentage and other information important to the relationship between the broker and seller are contained in a document called the listing agreement. **Listing agreements** are contracts between broker and seller creating an agency relationship and defining the duties and obligations of each party. The listing agreement identifies the broker as the **agent** and the seller as the **principal.** An agent is one who acts on behalf of the principal in dealing with third parties. Agents receive power, or authority, from the principal to perform certain acts and must not exceed that authority. Real estate brokers are usually given the authority to seek a buyer for the seller's real property. Agents are also occasionally given authority by buyers to seek properties for purchase. An agent has a number of duties to the principal, which are covered in more detail in the next chapter. It is sufficient at this time to know that legally the agent is considered to be in a position of trust and must act accordingly by keeping the principal's interests foremost at all times.

Not just anyone can hold himself out as a real estate agent and attempt to perform brokerage services for a fee. All fifty states require that you obtain a **real estate license** to act as a real estate agent. Each state has developed their own requirements for obtaining such a license. Requirements often include satisfactory completion of certain real estate courses (perhaps the one you are now taking) and passing an examination. Real estate licenses come in two varieties — the *broker's license* and the *salesperson's* or *sales associate's license.* The license type has nothing to do with the type of real estate you may sell, but rather affects your ability to operate your own firm and take listings in your own name. Only brokers can own and operate real estate firms and take listings in their own name; salespersons must be affiliated with a broker in order to be active in the real estate business.

For example, if you obtain a salesperson's license after completing this course, you must find a brokerage firm willing to let you affiliate before you may practice real estate. You would not be able to simply hang out your shingle and start taking listings in your own name. Any listings you take as a salesperson will be in the name of the firm with which you have affiliated. Likewise, any compensation you receive will come from the firm. Once you get your broker's license you may open your own company if you wish, or continue to affiliate with a brokerage firm. If you choose to remain affiliated with a firm, you still must take listings in that firm's name and receive your compensation from that firm and not directly from sellers. Thus, inside a real estate brokerage firm, you will find brokers *and* salespeople. Unlicensed people also work for real estate firms performing tasks such as preparing necessary paperwork, planning advertising, and performing the accounting and other necessary business functions associated with any business. Licensing laws are considered in more detail in the next chapter.

Primary Brokerage Functions (Actually Producing Income!)

How does the brokerage firm make money? How do you as a salesperson or broker associated with a firm make money? The answer is quite simple — you make money by obtaining listings (sellers making you their agent) and finding ready, willing, and able buyers for those listings. Obviously, listings are an essential part of the lifeblood of a brokerage firm since they represent the firm's inventory. However, listings give the firm only the *potential* to earn an income. And until a ready, willing, and able buyer is found, listings produce only cash outlays for advertising and showing the property, among other expenses. Listings produce income for the firm and the brokers and salespeople involved only when the property is sold and the commission received.

When a firm gets a listing and the property is sold, the seller will pay the entire commission *to the firm.* The firm will then pay the brokers and salespersons in the company who obtained the listing and found the buyer. For example, if you obtained the listing, you may receive a percentage of the commission received by the firm, while the sales associate who found the buyer may also get a percentage. The actual percentages received by a sales associate for listing or selling a property vary from broker to broker. The firm makes a profit only if what is left over is sufficient to pay all operating expenses and provide a profit.

Salespersons — Employees Or Independent Contractors?

Salespersons and brokers associated with a brokerage firm as **independent contractors** also make a profit only if something is left over after expenses. This is because they must pay for their own costs associated with selling properties and obtaining listings from the income they earn. The brokerage firm will normally maintain an office with a staff for handling much of the paperwork, provide some form of in-house training, and be available to answer questions and help you solve problems. As an independent contractor you contract with the brokerage firm to provide them with your services as a salesperson. You are paid for your services just as any other contractor is paid, with no withholding for social security and federal and state income taxes. Other fringe benefits associated with employee status such as company-provided medical insurance and pension plans are also missing. You must provide these items for yourself.

Another aspect of being an independent contractor is that you can, technically, work the hours you wish, and are not subject to direction and control from the brokerage firm. However, you are still likely to have certain obligations, and you must follow the rules established by your brokerage firm for professional conduct. As an employee of the brokerage firm, you would be subject to a much greater degree of direction and control. Employee and independent contractor status are contrasted in Table 20.1.

Being an independent contractor has both positive and negative aspects for you. Some people are not able to cope with the personal freedom and lack of direction real estate brokerage offers. As a result, they waste a good deal of productive time. Others, perhaps more motivated and disciplined, find that they can be very productive and enjoy the freedom from day-to-day scrutiny of their activities. To thrive as an independent contractor, you must develop good work habits and deal effectively with personal and financial matters. For example, you must be able to juggle the time spent in leisure or with your family with the sometimes strange schedules of potential buyers and sellers. Odd hours can often be a source of aggravation to you and your family. On the financial side, since you earn income only when you sell a property or a property you have listed is sold, income is neither regular nor predictable. You must be able to budget funds to avoid financial problems. More than one real estate broker or salesperson with a seemingly good income has gotten into financial problems by incurring excessive fixed pay-

Table 20.1. Employee and Independent Contractor Status

	Control	Business Costs	Benefits	Income Taxes
Employee	Direct control by employer	Generally paid by employer	Vary, but may be provided by employer	Income taxes withheld; employer portion of social security paid
Independent contractor	No direct control by broker; must conduct by accepted practices	Paid by independent contractor	None	No withholding; independent contractor must pay all social security

ments and not saving enough money to cover living expenses during slack periods in the market.

Most licensees associated with brokerage firms are independent contractors, not employees. However, some brokerage firms have employment relationships with their licensees. These firms have found that the greater control and increased productivity of employees more than offsets any additional cost. The Internal Revenue Service continues to monitor the brokerage business to assure that the independent contractor status is not violated. Should the IRS determine that independent contractors are actually employees subject to withholding and social security payments, the brokerage business may be altered. The likely result will be fewer salespersons, with only the more productive licensees finding employment opportunities.

Brokerage Specialties

As a broker or salesperson you will probably specialize in either single family residential properties or commercial properties. It simply takes too long to keep up with market changes in several markets. Even within the broad areas of single family residential and commercial brokerage, you will find other specializations. For instance, many single family brokers specialize by area of town, by type of property, such as condominiums, or by price range. In Beverly Hills and other exclusive areas, there are brokerage firms catering to the "carriage trade" wanting very expensive homes. In commercial brokerage, it is not unusual to find brokers specializing by property type, such as office buildings, shopping centers, industrial properties, or apartments. By specializing, these brokers can become experts and provide better services to sellers and buyers while earning greater incomes.

Summary of Brokerage Overview

You should now have a better idea of what the real estate brokerage business is all about. It involves providing a service to those trying to buy, sell, and lease real property. Income is produced by commissions, usually expressed as a percentage of the sales price or lease payments. Those providing this service for a fee must be licensed by the state as either a broker or a salesperson (sales associate). Only licensed brokers may operate brokerage firms and take listings in their own names. Commissions are paid to the brokerage firm, which in turn compensates the individuals listing and selling the property. Brokers and salespersons tend to specialize in order to increase their ability to stay current, provide the best possible service, and maximize their earnings.

OVERVIEW OF THE REAL ESTATE
SALES TRANSACTION

Now that you have a general feel for the brokerage business, you can concentrate on understanding the steps in a real estate transaction. You should approach the following discussion of the real estate transaction with the objective of learning not only the steps in the transaction, but also the roles played by sellers, buyers, brokers, and others in completing the transaction. Throughout the discussion of the transaction, it is assumed that a broker is used. This assumption is made for two reasons. First, it allows the role of the real estate agent to be considered in the remainder of the chapter. Second, most transactions involve agents, as indicated in Table 20.2 which displays the results of a recent national study of those who had recently bought or sold homes. Notice that 82 percent of the buyers used the services of an agent and 85 percent of the sellers sold their homes through an agent. Only 12 percent of the sellers sold their homes themselves without ever using an agent. However, if a broker is not used the basic steps are the same, but *someone* must perform the functions performed by the broker.

Suppose that you wish to sell Blackacre, the farm left to you by your grandfather in an earlier chapter. How does the transaction proceed? Technically, the sales transaction of Blackacre began the instant you decided to sell. However, unless you seek a buyer yourself, the first step involving any real action is the **listing** of the property with a broker. The listing gets the ball rolling on finding a ready, willing, and able buyer. **Prospecting,** trying to find an interested buyer, is the second step in the transaction. Once an interested buyer is found, *negotiations* can begin, and if they are successful, agreement is reached that the buyer is going to buy and the seller is going to sell according to some mutually acceptable

Table 20.2. Use of Real Estate Professionals
(Percentage Distribution)

	Percent of Total
Buying	
Purchased through an agent	82
Direct from owner	10
Direct from builder	8
Total	100%
Selling	
Used only an agent and agent sold home	77
First tried to sell themselves but then used an agent	8
Sold themselves without ever using agent	12
First listed with an agent but then sold themselves	3
Total	100%

SOURCE: "National Homebuying Survey," The Economics and Research Division, *National Association of Realtors,* 1981, p. 17.

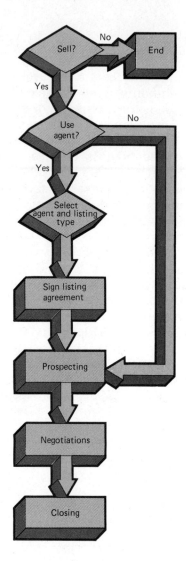

Figure 20.1
Overview of sales
transaction.

terms. Following this agreement, numerous *details* must be attended to before the transfer of ownership can actually occur. Ultimately, the transaction concludes with the *closing*. Each of these major steps is illustrated in Figure 20.1.

CHOOSING A BROKER AND LISTING THE PROPERTY

Choosing your broker is an important decision because the broker will assist you, as a seller, in setting your asking price, seeking qualified buyers, and giving you other important advice throughout the entire sales transaction. Thus, you should feel that the individual and firm you choose can provide you with reliable information for decision making, as well as locating a ready, willing, and able buyer. As the one paying the commission, you must know that the firm will look out for your best interest at all times.

If you are familiar with the market in your area, you probably have some idea of which brokerage firms have been around for some time and enjoy a good reputation. Perhaps you have had dealings with a specific broker or sales associate or brokerage firm and have been satisfied with the results. If new to an area, you may depend on friends and relatives living in the area for advice. In some instances, the brokers in your old hometown may be able to recommend an individual or firm to you in your new city. When more than one firm has been recommended to you, it may be advisable to talk with each one and see what kind of gut feel you develop; it could be that one of the choices appears much easier to work with or more competent.

Once you have decided on the broker, a listing agreement will be completed and signed by the seller and listing broker. The listing agreement is a contract establishing the employment of the broker by the seller. It creates the agency relationship referred to so often in this book. A listing agreement must contain all of the elements of any valid contract. A complete sample listing agreement is contained in Table 20.3. Listing agreements differ from one place to another, but the sample listing agreement contains the critical elements found in most of them. It contains provisions that:

1. Create the agency relationship
2. Describe the terms of the agency relationship
3. Describe the listed property
4. Describe the sales terms acceptable to the seller

Not all states require that listing agreements be in writing, but for your own protection as a broker or seller you should insist on having a written listing agreement.

Creating the Agency

The first sentence of text material in the sample listing agreement contains the basic language creating the employment, or agency, relationship. Notice the phrase ". . . grants to Realtor the exclusive right to sell the property . . ." in the second line. This phrase is important because it creates what is called an **exclusive right to sell listing,** which means the broker is to receive a commission regardless of who finds a buyer during the term of the listing. For example, if you list Blackacre using an exclusive right to sell listing and later find a potential buyer yourself during the listing period, show the property, and negotiate the sale, you

Table 20.3. Sample Listing Agreement

COPYRIGHT 1981 – METROPOLITAN TULSA BOARD OF REALTORS

Price *	Comp. to Selling Broker *	How Shown *	FZD *	D-4 *
$				

Special Photo Instructions:

_____

_____

Addr. *			Area:	Zone:
Brms. *	ESK	Story *	Yr Blt	
Baths *	R & O	Ext *	C. Water	
Club	D Wash	Gar *	Sewer *	
LR	Util Rm	Roof	Septic *	
Combo	Heat *	Floor *	Spl. Ftrs.	
FP	A/C	Bsmt	Corp. Acct.	
DR	Fence	Lot Size:		
Lender:	Loan Bal:		LN #:	
As of:	Int Rate +	Adj.	Type:	Yrs Left
Paymt:	Taxes: *	Yr:	HS:	Poss:
Schl: Gr.	Jr.		Sr.	
Legal: *				
Remarks:				

Owner:		Ph:
Associate:		Ph:
Realtor:	No:	Ph:

Disclosures (see Paragraph 4 below):

4a. The Property (has) (has not) been damaged or affected by water or flooding.

If "Has", explain: _____

_____

_____

4b. The Property (has) (has no) material defects.

If "Has", explain: _____

_____

_____

_____

_____

Seller's Initials: _____

This is a legally binding contract; if not understood seek advice from an attorney.

In consideration of the services to be rendered by the undersigned Realtor, the undersigned ("Seller") hereby exclusively lists with Realtor the property described above (the "Property"), and grants to Realtor the exclusive right to sell the Property and to accept a deposit thereon, within the term of this listing, at the price and on the terms herein stated, or at such other price and terms as shall be acceptable to Seller. This listing shall be subject to the following:

1. This Agreement shall be for a term of _____, terminating (except for the provisions of paragraph 2) at midnight on_____ 19____.

2. Seller agrees to pay a commission equal to _____% of the total sale price of the Property herein described, as and for the compensation of Realtor, in any of the following events:
   (a) The sale or exchange of the Property during the term of this Agreement, whether procured by Realtor, Seller or a third person;
   (b) The sale or exchange of the Property within _____ days after the termination of this Agreement, if with any one to whom Realtor has shown the Property, or with whom the Realtor has negotiated concerning the Property prior to the termination of this Agreement; provided that this clause shall not apply if Seller re-lists the Property at the termination of this Agreement with another Licensed Real Estate Broker;
   (c) If Realtor procures a buyer who is ready, willing and able to purchase the Property, at the price and on the terms set forth herein, or at such other price and terms as shall be acceptable to Seller;
   (d) The sale or exchange of the Property during or after the term of this Agreement to any party to whom the Property is rented or leased, during the term of this Agreement or within _____ days thereafter.

3. In the event a contract for sale or exchange (a "Contract") is entered into with a buyer, Seller agrees:
   (a) Unless the Contract provides otherwise, Realtor shall receive and hold any earnest money deposit, which may be in the form of the buyer's personal check endorsed for deposit without recourse, in Realtor's trust or escrow account in compliance with the terms of the contract, applicable law, rules and regulations governing funds;
   (b) To furnish a current Uniform Commercial Code Search certificate and an abstract of title certified to date showing merchantable title in Seller, subject only to reasonable utility easements and building restrictions of record and other exceptions specified in the Contract;
   (c) At the time prescribed in the Contract, to convey the Property by warranty deed to buyer, free and clear of all liens and encumbrances, except those specifically reserved in the Contract;
   (d) Unless otherwise provided in the Contract, all ad valorem taxes, interest, rents and other continuing items shall be prorated to the date of transfer, except that personal property taxes for the entire year shall be paid by Seller;
   (e) To pay the necessary discount charged by a lender to place a loan, up to a maximum of _____%, in the event that the loan is an FHA insured or VA guaranteed loan;
   (f) If the Contract, lender or government agency requires: (i) Seller shall furnish a report by a licensed exterminating company showing the Property to be free and clear of visible termites or visible termite damage; and (ii) fixtures and equipment relating to plumbing, heating and cooling, including ducts, electrical systems and built-in appliances will be in normal working order at the closing, ordinary wear and tear excepted, and Seller shall pay the estimated costs of necessary repairs in excess of $100.00 of the total (but not exceeding a maximum amount agreed to by Seller) necessary to meet the foregoing standards.

4. In order to fulfill Seller's and REALTOR'S obligations of disclosure, if the Property has been damaged or affected by water or flooding, or if the Property has any other material defect, Seller has communicated any such defect in the space provided above. REALTOR is authorized to disclose to any potential buyer any such defects and any other material information, including the flood hazard zone status of the Property, known by the REALTOR relating to the Property.

5. All of the information provided herewith or which may be provided to Realtor shall be true and Seller agrees to hold Realtor, Realtor's employees, agents and subagents harmless from any cost, expense or damage due to any information which is withheld by Seller from Realtor or which is incorrect.

6. In connection with this Listing Agreement, Seller authorizes Realtor:
   (a) To place a "For Sale" sign on the Property and to remove all other similar signs;
   (b) At Seller's expense, to turn on, or leave on, all utilities and to authorize service men to do so in order to show the Property to its best advantage or to permit inspection thereof;
   (c) To obtain all information pertaining to any present mortgage on the Property from any mortgage or mortgage service company and to furnish information pertaining to the Property to any prospective lender;
   (d) To obtain a key to the Property, place a key box thereon, and furnish keys to others necessary to show the Property or to carry out the objectives of this Agreement;
   (e) To have access to the Property for the purpose of showing it to prospects at any reasonable hour.

7. Realtor's sole duty shall be to use his best efforts to effect a sale of the Property during the terms of this Agreement, in accordance with the Code of Ethics of the National Association of Realtors. Realtor shall not be charged with the custody of the Property, its management, maintenance or repair.

8. Forfeited earnest money, if any, shall be divided equally between Seller and Realtor, except that Realtor's portion shall in no event exceed the agreed commission; provided, however, that no release of a buyer or waiver of a forfeiture of earnest money after a Contract is executed shall relieve Seller of any obligation to pay a commission.

9. The term "Realtor" herein shall include any sales associate or subagents of the Realtor whose signature appears on this Agreement.

10. This property is offered without regard to sex, race, religion, color, ancestry or national origin.

11. Seller and Realtor agree to the terms herein set forth and understand that this is a binding agreement and that it cannot be cancelled or terminated except upon their mutual written consent.

12. Seller acknowledges that Seller has read this Agreement and has received a copy hereof.

13. The REALTOR® certifies that he is a member of the Multiple Listing Service of Tulsa REALTORS®, Inc. The parties hereto understand and agree that the REALTOR® is hereby authorized to file: (i) the above listing information; (ii) timely notice of all changes in the above information as approved by seller and (iii) upon the closing of a sale, sales information including sales price, with the MLS for processing and dissemination to MLS participants.

ACCEPTED THIS _____ DAY OF _____ , 19 _____

_____   _____
REALTOR   NUMBER   SELLER - OWNER

PHONE NO. _____   _____
                                        SELLER - OWNER

By _____   _____
                                        MAILING ADDRESS OF SELLER - OWNER

Source: Metropolitan Tulsa Board of Realtors.

still must pay the broker a commission, just as if the broker had found the buyer. The same thing is true if another broker drops by with a buyer for Blackacre.

The exclusive right to sell is not the only possible listing arrangement. You may want to reserve the right to sell the property yourself without paying a commission. In this case you would like to execute an **exclusive agency listing** that provides that the principal may personally find a buyer and not pay a commission. However, in an exclusive agency listing, if another broker finds the buyer, you still must pay a commission to the broker with the exclusive agency listing. Thus, you are limited in your ability to list the property with more than one broker by contract and by virtue of possibly having to pay more than one commission.

If you wish to list Blackacre with more than one broker and not pay multiple commissions if one of them produces a ready, willing, and able buyer, you should try to get an **open listing.** In an open listing, the principal reserves the right to list the property with other brokers or find a buyer without being responsible for a commission to the listing broker. For example, if you sign an open listing with Broker A and two days later Broker B produces a buyer willing to make an attractive offer for Blackacre, you may accept the offer and not be responsible to Broker A for a commission. An open listing also allows you to personally find a buyer without paying a commission to a listing broker.

There are two other "types" of listings that need explanation. First is the net listing. A net listing does not deal with the conditions under which a commission is due the broker, but rather deals with the amount of the commission. In a **net listing,** the principal specifies the amount of money he or she wants to receive from the sale of the property after any commission has been paid, with the broker receiving any difference between that specified amount and the sales price. Net listings are full of potential problems for the broker and principal. If the sales price is not significantly greater than the net amount desired by the principal, the broker receives a very small commission. If the sales price is significantly greater than the specified amount, the principal may contend that the broker failed to adequately advise him or her as to the value of the property. Either way, an unhappy situation may develop and serve to discourage the use of net listing. Net listings are illegal in many states.

Second is the **multiple listing,** which is not really a type of listing at all, since it does not deal with the conditions under which a commission is payable to the broker or the amount of the commission. A multiple listing is an exclusive right to sell listing that the listing broker has agreed to co-broker with other members of a multiple listing service. *Co-brokering* means that other brokers may try to find a buyer for the listed property and, if successful, receive part of the commission from the listing broker.

Choosing the Listing Type

Selecting the type of listing is usually a simple matter. It is simple because many brokers insist on exclusive right to sell listings. This is understandable since a broker may be reluctant to spend a great deal of money and effort advertising and otherwise promoting a property if that money and effort could result in a commission for someone else! From the seller's perspective, an exclusive right to sell ties him or her to one broker, but also provides the greatest incentive for the broker to perform. Further, if the property is placed on the multiple listing service, the listing must be an exclusive right to sell to protect the listing broker's right to a commission. If you have good reasons, say a potential buyer in mind, then you may negotiate something other than an exclusive right to sell listing. However, you should carefully evaluate the possible advantages and disadvantages of each type of listing.

Terms of the Agency Relationship

The listing agreement not only creates the agency relationship but also contains provisions that clarify the terms of the relationship and more clearly define the responsibilities of the principal and agent. The provisions numbered 1 and 2 detail the term of the listing agreement, the commission to be paid, and the conditions under which the broker is entitled to a commission. Provisions 3 through 12 deal with the duties, obligations, and authority of the principal and agent. You should read these stipulations to get a feel for the scope of the listing agreement.

Describing the Listed Property

The upper portion of the listing agreement contains a legal description of the property, financial and tax information, school district information, and physical characteristics of the property. This information is put into the listing to provide as complete and accurate information as possible for those trying to find a buyer for the property. Those trying to sell the property will depend on the information on the listing sheet in dealing with potential buyers. With this information available, salespersons in the listing firm or other multiple listing brokers and salespersons will have a consistent base of information and avoid misrepresenting the property.

Sales Terms

The upper portion of the listing agreement also contains the terms of the sale acceptable to the seller. It contains the asking price, when the buyer may take possession of the property, and the type of financing the seller is willing to accept. All of these terms are important and require good advice from the broker and good decisions by the seller.

Establishing the Asking Price

One of the important decisions to be made during a transaction is the asking price. It is also often an emotional one and requires some very delicate handling by the broker. To illustrate, let's return to your decision to sell Blackacre and consider your objectives in setting an asking price for it. You probably want to get the highest possible price for Blackacre both to feel that you have done the best by your late grandfather and to maximize the dollars going into your bank account. However, you may also have time constraints on the sale because you want to use the profits to purchase a home that other buyers are also considering or to pay inheritance taxes. You are now in a dilemma because you realize that a higher asking price may discourage some people who may potentially have some interest in Blackacre and it is likely to take longer to sell. Even if you are willing to negotiate down to a lower price, some potential buyers will simply not make the effort, sensing that the difference between the maximum price they are willing to pay and the asking price is just too great. Many sellers do not realize that this trade-off exists and concentrate on establishing a relatively high asking price only to be disappointed later by the time required to sell their property.

Now assume that you are a broker trying to list Blackacre. You want the seller to get the highest possible price but you also know that the seller may not be aware that setting too high an asking price may reduce the market for Blackacre. You also know that the seller may have an unrealistic opinion of Blackacre's value because of incomplete or inaccurate market information and a tendency to incorporate certain personal experiences associated with the property into its value. A reasonable asking price also reduces the time the property is on the market and the difference between the sales price and the asking price, both of which tend to make your job easier and the seller happier.

Competitive Market Analysis All of this means that you must assist the seller in fixing the asking price. As a real estate expert, your knowledge of the market and data on recent sales provide the seller with useful pricing information. Many brokers perform a competitive market analysis in which comparative recent sales are presented and analyzed to establish the range, or ballpark, within which the asking price should be established. Establishing this range is useful because you can then point out that the higher the asking price chosen from this range, the longer, on average, it will take to sell the property, and vice versa. In this way, you have established the fact that there is not *one* best asking price in case you later feel an adjustment in asking price is necessary and when negotiations begin. You have also made the seller aware of the trade-off between asking price and sales time. Of course, terms other than price affect the time a property is on the market.

The competitive market analysis is an excellent listing tool but requires care and effort to prepare. To prepare one, you must identify properties comparable to the subject property that are for sale now or have sold in the recent past and listings that have expired in the recent past. The properties currently for sale provide a feel for present market competition. Properties that have sold give insight into terms agreeable to both buyers and sellers. You must be careful not to include properties that were sold using financing arrangements significantly different from those likely for the subject property since such financing may have affected the sales price. Expired listings provide evidence on the impact of overpriced properties and the level of prices where overpricing occurs. Data for these properties may be found from personal or company records, as well as multiple listing records.

Also, in the course of an analysis, you must rate the appeal of the property to buyers and the ability of the sellers to expedite the transaction. Area market conditions affecting the sale must also be evaluated. Finally, the selling costs are estimated and combined with the estimated probable sales price to produce an estimate of the net proceeds from the sale of the property.

Net to Seller Analysis A variation of the final sections of the competitive market analysis, which may be used as a supplement to it or alone, is the **net to seller analysis.** Many firms and local real estate boards have prepared forms, similar to the one in Table 20.4, which aid this analysis. As you can see, this form's function is to provide information about the net proceeds the seller should receive if his or her home is sold for a particular price. By preparing a number of analyses for alternative financing arrangements, you can give the seller a good idea of the desirability of each alternative. This is useful information for the seller and allows him or her to make the best possible decisions. Much of the information for the analysis can be obtained from lenders.

Other Terms

Terms other than price are important. Favorable financing can make a home that is too expensive at a higher interest rate affordable. The seller has the right to choose whether or not he or she will allow the purchaser to use FHA or VA financing since such financing requires that the seller pay any discount points associated with originating the loan. If the home qualifies, these forms of financing can be quite attractive and enhance the marketability of the property. Assumable mortgages may also be attractive, especially when combined with seller financing for a portion of the equity.

Servicing the Listing

Once the broker gets the listing, the work has just begun. It is important that as the work of trying to find a buyer continues, the broker provides

Table 20.4. Net to Seller Form

```
                        ESTIMATED                          [R]
                      NET TO SELLER                      REALTOR®


  Sales Price . . . . . . . . . . . . . . .              _____
  Less Existing 1st Mortgage . . . . . . . _____
  Less Existing 2nd Mortgage . . . . . . . _____

      SUB TOTAL . . . . . .  . . . . . . . . . . . . . .  _____

      SELLING EXPENSES
  a. Abstracting. . . . . . . . . . . . . _____
  b. Documentary Stamps . . . . . . . . . _____
  c. Recording Fees . . . . . . . . . . . _____
  d. Discount Points. . . . . . . . . . . _____
  e. Special Assessments . . . . . . . . . _____
  f. Prepayment Penalty . . . . . . . . . _____
  g. Termite (inspection only). . . . . . _____
  h. EMP Repairs. . . . . . . . . . . . . _____
  i. Requirements . . . . . . . . . . . . _____
  j. Interest Adjustment . . . . . . . . . _____
  k. Taxes . . . . . . . . . . . . . . . . _____
  l. Realtor's Fee . . . . . . . . . . . . _____
  m. Other items _____
     _____
     _____
     _____
     _____


      ESTIMATED EXPENSES . . . . . . . . . . . . . . . =  _____

      ESTIMATED NET TO SELLER . . . . . . . . . . . .     _____


  IT IS UNDERSTOOD THAT THESE FIGURES ARE APPROXIMATE, FUR-
  NISHED AT DATE OF CONTRACT AND MAY VARY FROM THOSE AT
  TRANSFER OF DEED.

  Seller's Acknowledgment:


  _____ Date: _____

  Realtor's Acknowledgment:


  _____ By: _____ Date: _____
```

Source: Metropolitan Tulsa Board of Realtors.

periodic updates of activity on the listing to the principal. Advertising efforts, results of open houses and showings, and assessments of current market conditions should be regularly communicated to keep the seller informed and to generally maintain good relations.

PROSPECTING—FINDING A QUALIFIED BUYER

The ultimate happiness of the seller and the broker depends on finding a qualified buyer who is ready, willing, and able to purchase the listed property under terms acceptable to the seller. Finding such a buyer requires that the broker attract a potential buyer, assess that buyer's preferences and purchasing power and match them with the proper set of properties on the market, and, finally, show the properties and generate interest in one or more of them. At that point, negotiations can begin with the owner of the property selected by the buyer.

Attracting Potential Buyers

You are bombarded daily by people trying to get your attention. Signs, television and radio commercials, newspaper ads, and blimps are all used to get you to notice a particular product, service, or cause. Brokers use yard signs, newspaper ads, open houses, and television commercials to attract potential buyers to particular properties or to the firm in general. They also depend on referrals, repeat buyers and sellers, and personal contacts to generate potential buyers. Often a call about a particular property will allow the broker to suggest and possibly to show a number of other listings. Finding a potential buyer is the necessary first step to selling any listing. The more potential buyers, the better the chance of selling the property quickly at a reasonable price.

Qualifying the Buyer

Suppose you are a salesperson for the Success Real Estate Company. One morning you receive a call from a Mrs. Smith, who tells you that she and her husband are interested in buying a new home. A friend had referred them to you. What would you do? How would you decide whether you are wasting your time and that of the Smiths by showing them homes they cannot afford? What information would you want to get from the Smiths in order to locate homes that may interest them?

Probably the first thing you would do is arrange a meeting in your office with the Smiths. This meeting will allow you to establish rapport and build their confidence in your ability to help them locate a suitable home. It also gives you the chance to find out the type of home they are seeking, the features they desire, and the area of the city they like best. Since most of us would like to own a mansion but cannot afford it, this meeting also gives you an opportunity to assess the Smiths' financial ability to purchase the home they have described to you, or any home for that matter. This process is called *qualifying the buyer.*

Assessing financial ability must be done with some delicacy. Some brokers will occasionally ask the buyers to complete a questionnaire concerning preferences, employment, and so on. Many buyers do not like to disclose such information and will respond negatively to direct questions about personal items. Other buyers are open and ask you how much home they can afford on their income. A good broker can ask a number of indirect questions about their present home and its estimated value and Mr. and Mrs. Smith's employment to get a feel for the ability to make a down payment and monthly payments.

In virtually every case, you will want to examine alternative and seller financing arrangements, as discussed in Chapter 15, to see how they affect the buyer's ability to purchase housing. Many firms have developed forms that allow you to provide the buyer with estimates of the cost of alternative financing arrangements. One such *cost to buyer* form, as they are commonly called, is illustrated in Table 20.5. The broker or sales associate will prepare a copy of this form for any financial alternatives deemed suitable and then go over them with the buyer to illustrate how the financing alternatives affect required front-end money and monthly payments. The cost to buyer form provides a convenient and effective way to aid the buyer in comparing financial alternatives.

Showing Properties

Once you have a good feel for the general price range and style of properties for which the buyers are likely candidates, you can start assessing the available alternatives. Those properties finally selected will be shown to the buyer. Brokers take various approaches to showing properties, ranging from a very casual one in which the buyers simply look through the house on their own to a more structured approach in which the broker carefully guides the buyer through the home. A skilled broker can show a home to its best advantage regardless of the type of potential buyer involved. Whatever approach is used, the buyers need time to fully consider the home and reexamine any portion of it they wish.

In showing homes, you can more clearly establish what it is the buyers are really looking for than you can in the office. More than once, a broker has found the home that has *everything* the buyers have requested, and more, only to have them look at the home and not like it! Of course, the reverse also happens; a broker shows a contemporary home to people who have expressed an interest only in traditional homes and they love it. The feedback from showings provides you with the opportunity to zero in on buyer preferences.

Liking a home is often not enough for many buyers. They need

Table 20.5. Cost to Buyer Form

NEW LOAN
ESTIMATED COST TO BUYER

R REALTOR®

SALES PRICE . . . . _____

LESS NEW LOAN . . . . _____

CASH DOWN PAYMENT . . . . _____

Expenses . . . . _____

   a. Loan Fee_____%. . . . . . . _____

   b. Attorney Fee (Title Opinion). . _____

   c. Private Mortage Insurance. . . _____

   d. Tax Escrow. . . . . _____

   e. Interest Paid in Advance . . . _____

   f. EMP Inspection Fee . . . . . _____

   g. EMP Repair Cost . . . . . . _____

   h. Survey with stake (without stake) _____

   i. Title Insurance . . . . . . _____

   j. Flood Insurance . . . . . . _____

   k. Hazard Insurance . . . . . _____

   l. Approximate Closing Costs . _____
     (includes Appraisal Fee, Credit Report Fee,
     VA FHA Photos, Mutual Mortgage Insurance,
     Amortization Tables, Recording Fees,
     Abstracting after closing)

   m. Other Items - _____

_____

_____

   ESTIMATED "EXPENSES" . . . . + _____

ESTIMATED TOTAL COST. . . . . _____

Monthly Payment (Estimated) Interest Rate . . . . . _____ %

   Principal & Interest . . . . _____

   Ad. Val. Taxes . . . . _____

   Hazard Insurance . . . . _____

   Flood Insurance . . . . _____

   Mtg. Insurance . . . . _____

   Total Monthly Payment (Estimated) . . . . _____

IT IS UNDERSTOOD THAT THESE FIGURES ARE APPROXIMATE, FUR-
NISHED AT DATE OF CONTRACT AND MAY VARY FROM THOSE AT
TRANSFER OF DEED.

Buyers Acknowledgement:

_____ Date _____

Realtors Acknowledgement

_____ By: _____ Date _____

Source: Metropolitan Tulsa Board of Realtors.

encouragement to make that final commitment to make an offer on the property. Some buyers simply would not make a purchase decision unless someone reinforced the fact that they are making a good choice. As a broker, you need to develop a feel for people and be able to establish when and how much encouragement any particular buyer may need to make a commitment to purchase.

NEGOTIATIONS AND AGREEMENT

Once the decision to make an offer is made, the broker will prepare the offer and the buyer will sign it. The offer is actually made in the form of a real estate sales contract, which, when signed by the seller, states that the buyer has agreed to buy and the seller has agreed to sell according to specified terms. The problem is that the buyer and seller rarely agree to the terms of the original offer. What results is a period of negotiation during which buyer and seller attempt to reach mutually acceptable terms (Figure 20.2).

Mechanically, the negotiating process is somewhat clumsy since the listing broker generally presents all offers to the seller. Thus, the original offer goes from the selling broker to the listing broker, who then presents it to the seller. Once the seller, with any desired advice from the listing broker, has considered the offer and decided what changes would make it acceptable, the revised offer goes from the listing broker to the selling broker to the buyer. This process is repeated until the parties agree to the transaction or agree to disagree and end the negotiations. A good bit of time may pass from the time the original offer is made until the negotiations are completed. Notice that buyer and seller do not sit down at a negotiating table and remain there conducting "arms length" negotiations until an agreement or an impasse is reached.

While this process is clumsy, it is not without merit. Many buyers and sellers are not accustomed to negotiating, and face-to-face sessions may degenerate into destructive arguing sessions. Under the existing arrangement, each party has time to mull over the other party's offer, seek clarification, discuss it with his or her spouse, and develop a response in a lower pressure atmosphere than in face-to-face negotiations. The arrangement also allows the broker to provide pertinent information and suggestions. Obviously, there are some situations in which everyone would be better off using more direct face-to-face negotiations.

For the broker, the negotiating process can be very stressful. By the time negotiations start, you have probably put a good deal of time into the

Figure 20.2
Typical real estate
negotiating process.

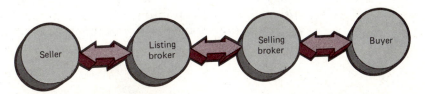

transaction. If you are both the listing and selling broker, you have gotten to know both the buyer and seller fairly well and do not want to see either party disappointed. You will be placed on the spot about your opinion of certain sales terms. You may have to explain to the buyer or the seller why certain terms are actually good for them even though they do not like them. In short, the broker has all the problems of someone caught in the middle, an experience we have all had at one time or another.

The broker must walk a tightrope in the negotiation process. The present agency relationship with the seller must be honored, but at the same time the buyer must be dealt with fairly. Ideally, both the buyer and seller will be pleased with the transaction. Pleased buyers and sellers represent future brokerage business. Even if the final terms are not what was expected by either party, they will both appreciate being treated fairly by the broker. The negotiating process described above is essentially the same for income-producing properties and single family homes, with face-to-face negotiations more common for income-producing properties.

Details

Just because a sales contract has been signed does not mean the transaction is complete. As you learned in Chapter 6, the sales contract simply means that the buyer and seller have agreed that a transaction will occur according to a specific set of terms. Among the terms in a typical sales contract are those dealing with the buyer obtaining financing, having the title examined, and inspecting the property. Sellers are generally required to provide an abstract of title and make certain repairs. These tasks must be accomplished within a certain period of time so that closing can occur. Usually the contract will specify that closing is to take place within a certain number of days from the contract signing date. As a broker you must check on the progress of the transaction to make sure everything is going smoothly and on schedule. Where problems develop, you may have to solve them to preserve the transaction. Where one party or both are procrastinating, you must encourage them to act. In some states, **escrow companies** handle many of these details after the sales contract is signed. For this service they receive an *escrow fee*.

In addition to the contractual details, you, as the selling broker, may want to reassure the buyer that he or she did the right thing. Telephone calls and visits may be used to accomplish this task. It is normal for a letdown to occur after the contract is signed and doubts about the transaction to creep into the buyer's mind. Marketing people call this process of questioning and doubting the decision *cognitive dissonance*. Reassurance is the best way to reduce cognitive dissonance.

Closing

After all details have been handled, the transfer of title is made. The actual transaction occurs at a closing, sometimes called escrow or **settlement** in various parts of the country. Closings are usually talked about in hushed tones, partly because many people view the closing process as a mystery with the truth unraveling at the last minute, just as in a Sherlock Holmes novel. This is unfortunate since the basic concept of closing is very simple and all problems should have been solved by the time the transaction reaches the closing. The essential concept of closing is that it is where the seller receives anything due him or her and the buyer receives title to the property.

While the essential concept of closing is the same everywhere, local differences exist with respect to how closing details are handled. Differences occur even within a state; one metropolitan area may handle closings in one way while local custom in another metropolitan area may be different. For this reason, this section considered two of the general approaches to closing: the closing meeting and escrows. These two general closing types should cover the majority of closing situations. However, keep in mind that in your area certain details may be handled differently. After reading this section you should make a thorough study of how closings are accomplished in your area.

Closing Meeting In closing meetings, all parties meet at an appointed time and conduct all the business associated with closing. The meeting may be held at the listing broker's office, the lender's office, the office of either party's attorney, or any other mutually agreeable location, depending on local custom. The parties at the closing will include buyer and seller (or their representatives), listing and selling brokers, attorneys for buyer and seller (optional), the lender, and probably a person skilled in conducting the closing, such as a closer for the lender. Certainly, one or more of these parties, including buyer and seller, may not be present at any particular closing meeting. If the buyer or seller are not present, they may be represented by their attorneys or other designated persons at the closing.

Prior to closing, someone should have been responsible for making sure that all necessary details were completed and all documents are ready for closing. The listing broker often assumes this responsibility, even if the actual documents are prepared by others. For example, the seller will usually be responsible for preparing the deed and obtaining a termite certificate guaranteeing that the property has been inspected for termite infestation as well as any other documents required by the sales contract. The buyer must have a check prepared for the seller and lender. Lenders must have all the paperwork associated with closing the loan transaction as considered in Chapter 16. Usually, both the lender and the listing broker will have closing statements ready for the buyer and seller showing who is supplying and receiving all funds involved in the transaction. In practice, many of these duties and documents are handled by the listing broker and lender, with the buyer and seller providing information and agreeing to pay fees.

Escrow Closing Some states, such as California, make use of escrow agents to handle closings. In these states, the buyer and seller agree on an escrow agent at the time the sales contract is signed. They then execute an *escrow agreement* with the escrow agent outlining the services the agent is to perform in handling the transaction. The agreement will clarify such things as who will arrange for having the abstract of title brought up to date, examined, and so on. Documents outlining these duties are also called the *escrow instructions*. The buyer and seller must also agree on whom is to pay for the escrow services. Naturally, the expense can be apportioned in any manner agreeable to both parties, although usually the expense is shared in some manner. In an escrow, there may or may not be a meeting of buyer and seller for closing. The parties may sign the documents at different times with the transaction being concluded when both have signed the necessary papers. Conceptually, the very same things are happening in an escrow closing as in a closing meeting; the mechanism is just a little different.

The Moment of Truth —
The Routine Transaction

If the person in charge of organizing the closing has done a good job, the transaction should be routine and contain no surprises. A routine closing involves the buyer signing all the necessary papers to close the mortgage loan, the lender and the buyer giving the seller the balance of the sales price remaining after the initial down payment, the seller giving the buyer a deed to transfer title, and the buyer or the seller paying all necessary fees, including the real estate commission. The entire routine closing transaction will probably require less than one hour.

As the buyer at a closing, you have a number of very important duties. For example, you are probably bound by the sales contract to have arranged your financing according to agreed-on terms. The lender, and your own best interest, will cause you to obtain hazard insurance to provide the lender with financial protection should the property be damaged or destroyed. You should also have made sure that the title you are going to receive at the closing is a good one by having either a title examination performed by an attorney or a title insurance policy issued or, in some cases, both. Likewise, you have the right, and should exercise it, to inspect the property just prior to closing. If you do not feel competent to inspect all parts of the home, use a professional inspection service.

The broker plays a role that is a combination of nursemaid and ramrod. As the broker, you know that preparation is the key to a smooth, routine closing. The role played by the broker at closing depends on who is conducting it. If the closing is being handled by an escrow company or mortgage lender, the broker's role at closing is minimized. If the closing is being conducted in the broker's office, staff closers will conduct the closing, but the broker may take a more active role than in the offices of others.

CLOSING STATEMENTS

Both the buyer and the seller should receive a closing statement (also called a settlement statement) showing their financial responsibilities in the transaction. This statement is prepared by the party conducting the closing. Even if the listing broker is not conducting the closing, he will still prepare closing statements for each party because most states re-

Table 20.6. Information for Preparing Closing Statements

Closing date is November 13, 1985.

Transaction Item	Amount	Responsible Party
Terms of Purchase		
Purchase price	$124,500	Buyer
New loan amount	80,000	
Earnest money	2,000	
Existing loan	95,132	Seller
Transaction Expenses		
Loan origination fee (1% of loan)	800	Buyer
Discount points (½% of loan)	400	Buyer
Appraisal fee	95	Buyer
Credit report	25	Buyer
Photos and amortization schedule	15	Buyer
Interest from closing date to 1st of following month		
(18 days @$25.00)	450	Buyer
Hazard insurance for one year	497	Buyer
Title search	112	Seller
Title examination (attorney's opinion)	75	Buyer
Title insurance policies	389	Buyer
Recording fees (deed and mortgage)	13	Buyer
State documentary stamps	187	Seller
Survey	55	Buyer
Closing fee	25	Seller
Real estate commission (6% of $124,500)	7,470	Seller
Termite inspection	45	Seller
Prorated and Escrow Items		
Hazard insurance escrow (2 months)	83	Buyer
Property taxes for year of sale (1986)	1,565	Seller
(Paid in arrears)	235	Buyer
Property taxes for next year (1986) 2 months at $150	300	Buyer

quire the listing broker to do so. These statements perform a double duty. First, they make the financial consequences of the transaction clear to the parties involved. Second, they demonstrate that the broker or escrow agent has performed his or her duties as prescribed and that all monies have been properly handled. Closing statements are not difficult to prepare, but require a great deal of care to make sure that all details are included.

To better understand the closing statement, consider the example transaction and the associated activities and costs in Table 20.6. Who is responsible for each item is determined by the sales contract and local custom. Of course, the buyer and seller can agree to override local custom on who is to pay for any cost item.

The closing statements for the buyer and seller contained in Tables 20.7 and 20.8 were prepared from the information in Table 20.6. Notice that these statements have columns labeled debits and credits. For the buyer, debits represent the items for which he or she is financially responsible. The credits represent the source of the funds necessary to pay for those items. For each party, the total debits must equal the total credits. However, the total debits and credits for the buyer will not necessarily equal the total debits and credits for the seller. In Table 20.7, you can see that the buyer's total financial obligation is $127,932. Since the buyer has arranged to borrow $80,000, and has already paid $2000 as earnest money, the difference between that $82,000 and the necessary $127,932 must be paid by the buyer at closing. For the seller, debits also

Table 20.7. Buyer's Closing Statement

Item	Debits	Credits
Purchase price	$124,500	
Mortgage loan		$ 80,000
Earnest money		2,000
Loan origination fee	800	
Appraisal fee	95	
Credit report	25	
Discount points	400	
Photos and amortization schedule	15	
Interest from Nov. 13 to Dec. 1	450	
Hazard insurance	497	
Title examination	75	
Title insurance policies	389	
Recording fees	13	
Survey	55	
Hazard insurance escrow	83	
Property tax proration	235	
Property tax escrow	300	
Net due from buyer at closing		45,932
	$127,932	$127,932

Table 20.8. Seller's Closing Statement

Item	Debits	Credits
Sales price		$124,500
Mortgage loan payoff (existing loan)	$ 95,132	
Title search	112	
State documentary stamps	187	
Termite inspection	45	
Closing fee	25	
Prorated property taxes	1,565	
Real estate commission (6% of $124,500)	7,470	
Total debits	$104,536	
Cash due seller at closing	19,964	
	$124,500	$124,500

represent items of financial responsibility. Credits again represent sources of funds, usually the sales price of the property. In Table 20.8, the seller has total debits of $104,536 compared to credits of $124,500. This means the difference of $19,964 will be paid to the seller in cash at closing.

Table 20.9 is the Department of Housing and Urban Development settlement statement form, which, according to the Real Estate Settlement Procedures Act (RESPA), must be given to all parties in a single family transaction. To reduce confusion and time, money does not change hands for each expense item on the closing statement, but, rather, debits and credits are totaled and then compared to determine the net amount each party is to receive or pay at closing.

In more general terms, you will find that closing statements have three categories of items that produce either debits or credits for the buyer and seller. First are the terms of purchase and financing such as the price, earnest money required, and loan amount. Second are the expenses incurred in the transaction such as loan origination fees, credit reports, termite inspections, title insurance, and so on. Finally, there are items paid for either in advance or in arrears, such as property taxes. If annual property taxes are paid in arrears in January, a buyer taking title in November would expect the seller to pay the taxes for the portion of the year he or she owned the home. Accordingly, property taxes and other such items are usually prorated at closing. Proration is the allocation of cost, usually on the basis of each party's period of ownership. In addition to prorations, this closing expense category contains the amounts of money that must be placed in lender's property tax and hazard insurance escrow accounts. Lenders often require that one or two months of each expense be placed in the escrow account at closing.

Table 20.9. HUD Settlement Statement

HUD-1 Rev. 5/76

Form Approved
OMB No. 63-R1501

A.		B. TYPE OF LOAN:
U.S. DEPARTMENT OF HOUSING AND URBAN DEVELOPMENT **SETTLEMENT STATEMENT**		1. ☐ FHA 2. ☐ FmHA 3. ☐ CONV. UNINS. 4. ☐ VA 5. ☐ CONV. INS. 6. FILE NUMBER: 7. LOAN NUMBER: 8. MORTGAGE INSURANCE CASE NUMBER:

C. **NOTE:** *This form is furnished to give you a statement of actual settlement costs. Amounts paid to and by the settlement agent are shown. Items marked "(p.o.c.)" were paid outside the closing; they are shown here for informational purposes and are not included in the totals.*

D. NAME OF BORROWER:	E. NAME OF SELLER:	F. NAME OF LENDER.
G. PROPERTY LOCATION:	H. SETTLEMENT AGENT: PLACE OF SETTLEMENT:	I. SETTLEMENT DATE:

J. SUMMARY OF BORROWER'S TRANSACTION		K. SUMMARY OF SELLER'S TRANSACTION	
100. GROSS AMOUNT DUE FROM BORROWER:		**400. GROSS AMOUNT DUE TO SELLER:**	
101. Contract sales price		401. Contract sales price	
102. Personal property		402. Personal property	
103. Settlement charges to borrower (line 1400)		403.	
104.		404.	
105.		405.	
Adjustments for items paid by seller in advance		*Adjustments for items paid by seller in advance*	
106. City/town taxes to		406. City/town taxes to	
107. County taxes to		407. County taxes to	
108. Assessments to		408. Assessments to	
109.		409.	
110.		410.	
111.		411.	
112.		412.	
120. **GROSS AMOUNT DUE FROM BORROWER**		420. **GROSS AMOUNT DUE TO SELLER**	
200. AMOUNTS PAID BY OR IN BEHALF OF BORROWER:		**500. REDUCTIONS IN AMOUNT DUE TO SELLER:**	
201. Deposit or earnest money		501. Excess deposit (see instructions)	
202. Principal amount of new loan(s)		502. Settlement charges to seller (line 1400)	
203. Existing loan(s) taken subject to		503. Existing loan(s) taken subject to	
204.		504. Payoff of first mortgage loan	
205.		505. Payoff of second mortgage loan	
206.		506.	
207.		507.	
208.		508.	
209.		509.	
Adjustments for items unpaid by seller		*Adjustments for items unpaid by seller*	
210. City/town taxes to		510. City/town taxes to	
211. County taxes to		511. County taxes to	
212. Assessments to		512. Assessments to	
213.		513.	
214.		514.	
215.		515.	
216.		516.	
217.		517.	
218.		518.	
219.		519.	
220. **TOTAL PAID BY/FOR BORROWER**		520. **TOTAL REDUCTION AMOUNT DUE SELLER**	
300. CASH AT SETTLEMENT FROM/TO BORROWER		**600. CASH AT SETTLEMENT TO/FROM SELLER**	
301. Gross amount due from borrower (line 120)		601. Gross amount due to seller (line 420)	
302. Less amounts paid by/for borrower (line 220) (	)	602. Less reductions in amount due seller (line 520) (	)
303. CASH (☐ FROM) (☐ TO) BORROWER		603. CASH (☐ TO) (☐ FROM) SELLER	

483

Table 20.9. (Continued)

–2–

L. SETTLEMENT CHARGES	PAID FROM BORROWER'S FUNDS AT SETTLEMENT	PAID FROM SELLER'S FUNDS AT SETTLEMENT
700. TOTAL SALES/BROKER'S COMMISSION based on price $ @ % =		
Division of Commission (line 700) as follows:		
701. $ to		
702. $ to		
703. Commission paid at Settlement		
704.		
800. ITEMS PAYABLE IN CONNECTION WITH LOAN		
801. Loan Origination Fee %		
802. Loan Discount %		
803. Appraisal Fee to		
804. Credit Report to		
805. Lender's Inspection Fee		
806. Mortgage Insurance Application Fee to		
807. Assumption Fee		
808.		
809.		
810.		
811.		
900. ITEMS REQUIRED BY LENDER TO BE PAID IN ADVANCE		
901. Interest from to @ $ /day		
902. Mortgage Insurance Premium for months to		
903. Hazard Insurance Premium for years to		
904. years to		
905.		
1000. RESERVES DEPOSITED WITH LENDER		
1001. Hazard insurance months @ $ per month		
1002. Mortgage insurance months @ $ per month		
1003. City property taxes months @ $ per month		
1004. County property taxes months @ $ per month		
1005. Annual assessments months @ $ per month		
1006. months @ $ per month		
1007. months @ $ per month		
1008. months @ $ per month		
1100. TITLE CHARGES		
1101. Settlement or closing fee to		
1102. Abstract or title search to		
1103. Title examination to		
1104. Title insurance binder to		
1105. Document preparation to		
1106. Notary fees to		
1107. Attorney's fees to		
(includes above items numbers;)		
1108. Title insurance to		
(includes above items numbers;)		
1109. Lender's coverage $		
1110. Owner's coverage $		
1111.		
1112.		
1113.		
1200. GOVERNMENT RECORDING AND TRANSFER CHARGES		
1201. Recording fees: Deed $; Mortgage $; Releases $		
1202. City/county tax/stamps: Deed $; Mortgage $		
1203. State tax/stamps: Deed $; Mortgage $		
1204.		
1205.		
1300. ADDITIONAL SETTLEMENT CHARGES		
1301. Survey to		
1302. Pest inspection to		
1303.		
1304.		
1305.		
1400. TOTAL SETTLEMENT CHARGES (enter on lines 103, Section J and 502, Section K)		

HUD-1 Rev. 5/76

We the undersigned, have this day executed our note for $_____ Payable to Charles F. Curry Company secured by the above property and hereby authorize Charles F. Curry Company to pay proceeds of our loan. This being the balance we owe on the purchase of the above property.

THE UNDERSIGNED hereby acknowledge receipt of a copy of this statement; and, in addition, have reviewed and accepted as final all settlement charges.

_____ _____
SELLER   BUYER/BORROWER

Date:_____ Date:_____

SUMMARY

In this chapter you studied real estate marketing, particularly the brokerage business, the role it plays in a real estate transaction, and the basic steps in a real estate sales transaction. You learned that the brokerage business is a service business with the seller usually paying the commission. Brokers act as agents, with the principal being the person contracting with the broker and paying the commission. The contract creating the agency relationship is the listing agreement. Generally, with the seller as principal, the agent has earned a commission when a buyer, ready, willing, and able to purchase on terms acceptable to the seller, is found.

All 50 states require real estate agents to be licensed. Two types of licenses exist in most states: the broker's license and the salesperson's or sales associate's license. Salespersons and brokers associated with a brokerage firm usually act as independent contractors, not employees. Most real estate agents tend to specialize in either single family homes or income-producing properties. Within these general categories many agents will further specialize in particular types of properties or areas of the city.

The general steps in selling real estate are: listing, prospecting, negotiating, detail work, and closing. Property may be listed using an open, exclusive agency, or exclusive right to sell listing. Exclusive right to sell listings are the most common type of listing because they afford the agent the most protection from losing the commission if a buyer is found elsewhere; these listings also help insure a maximum effort. Competitive market analysis and net to seller forms were shown to be useful listing devices and to provide information for properties already listed.

To find buyers, agents depend on advertising, referrals, and repeat business. These buyers are qualified and shown the properties. This is followed by a period of negotiations, and finally, agreement. Details are then handled and the transaction closed. Closing statements are prepared and given to the buyer and seller. These statements summarize the financial responsibilities of these parties.

QUICK QUIZ

1. Legally, the seller and the real estate agent have a(n) _____ relationship.

    a. agency   c. fiduciary
    b. contractual   d. all of the above

2. Usually a salesperson's relationship with a broker is as a(n) _____.

    a. independent contractor   c. legal guardian
    b. employee   d. trustee

3. The listing arrangement that requires the seller to pay the broker a commission regardless of who finds a buyer is the _____.

a. open listing   c. exclusive agency listing
b. net listing   d. exclusive right to sell listing

4. The document that outlines for each party to a transaction the financial consequences of the transaction is the _____.

a. listing agreement   c. final accounting
b. closing statement   d. debit and credit statement

5. A competitive market analysis provides sellers with information about _____.

a. the net cash he or she will receive from a sale at a specified price
b. market activity in the neighborhood
c. likely sales price of their home
d. all of the above

real estate liscence

6. Every state requires real estate agents to obtain _____ before entering business.

7. A real estate agent has earned a commission when he or she finds *a* _____.

8. The process of evaluating the ability of a potential buyer to purchase a home is called _____. *qualifying the buyer*

9. Offers are usually presented to the seller by the ~~buyers~~ *listing* agent.

10. Development of doubt by a buyer after a major purchase is called _____. *cognitive dissonance*

QUESTIONS AND EXERCISES

1. Call a local broker and find out about his or her fees. What would the fee be for selling a $125,000 home?

2. Why do brokers and salespersons tend to specialize?

3. How would you go about prospecting to sell a single family house? An office building?

4. Explain how you would use the competitive market analysis and net to seller forms to obtain listings.

5. What advantages can you identify to working the single family home market in a particular area of the city?

6. What basic provisions should a listing agreement contain?

7. Why is the listing agreement so important to the seller and agent?

8. Why is it important to establish reasonable sales terms in the listing agreement?

9. What is involved in servicing a listing?

10. What is the agent's role in the closing of a transaction?

11. Summarize the closing practices in your town.

12. How can you, as an agent, minimize the problems associated with escrow?

KEY TERMINOLOGY

agent
cost to buyer
escrow companies
exclusive agency listing
exclusive right to sell listing
independent contractor
listing
listing agreement

multiple listing
net listing
net to seller analysis
open listing
principal
prospecting
real estate license
settlement

IF YOU WANT TO READ MORE

GEORGE F. BLOOM, ARTHUR M. WEIMER, and JEFFREY D. FISHER, *Real Estate*, 8th ed. (New York: John Wiley & Sons, 1982).

FREDERICK E. CASE, *Real Estate Brokerage* (Englewood Cliffs: Prentice Hall, Inc., 1965).

JACK L. GALE, *Commercial/Investment Brokerage: An Introduction with Case Studies* (Chicago: Realtors National Marketing Institute, 1979).

BRUCE LINDEMAN, *Real Estate Brokerage Management* (Reston Publishing Company, Inc., 1981).

WILLIAM M. SHENKEL, *Marketing Real Estate* (Englewood Cliffs: Prentice-Hall, Inc., 1980).

21

Marketing: public regulation of the brokerage business

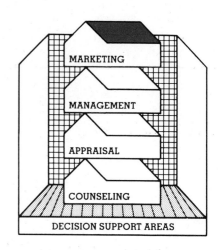

MARKETING

MANAGEMENT

APPRAISAL

COUNSELING

DECISION SUPPORT AREAS

PREVIEW

Every state has real estate licensing laws on the books requiring that anyone acting as a real estate agent be licensed. This is a relatively new situation, with the first license law being established in 1919. These laws were passed to protect the public, and that concept has lead to increasingly more stringent licensing requirements. The federal government has also passed legislation affecting the brokerage business, although not involving licensing. Together, these state and federal regulations represent the minimum standards you must meet to enter and remain in the brokerage business. If you have any interest in marketing real estate, these laws vitally affect you. In this chapter you will learn about how government regulates the brokerage business, including:

1. Why public regulation of the brokerage business is necessary.
2. What agency law is and what it has to do with real estate brokerage.
3. How agency relationships are created and terminated.
4. The basic concepts of state licensing laws.
5. Who implements and enforces state licensing laws.
6. What basic federal laws affect real estate brokerage.

Many people equate getting a real estate license with entering the real estate business. If you plan on entering the brokerage business, obtaining this license is, indeed, a necessity. You may be reading this book as part of a course to satisfy your state's license law. It is important that you understand license laws and the roles they play in the real estate business.

License laws are enacted by the states and vary substantially. These laws also change from time to time, and ignorance of these changes is not a useful defense in case of a violation. Every state makes copies of its license law available to the public. Some states even have manuals containing the license law and other useful information for those wanting to practice in the state. These publications are generally available through the body responsible for administering the license law, usually called the real estate commission.

PUBLIC REGULATION IN PERSPECTIVE

Throughout history, mankind has adopted formal and informal rules of behavior reflecting beliefs about what is right and wrong. Depending on the nature of the rules, a violation, if detected, results in varying responses. In the United States, when society, acting through its elected representatives, perceives certain behavior to be important enough, public regulation, in the form of laws, will be enacted. Laws represent a code of behavior, violations of which will be punished. In real estate agency, for example, a violation of real estate licensing laws may result in your license being suspended or revoked. Society has decided that behavior in violation of these laws is against the public interest and the elimination of your right (or privilege) to act as a real estate agent is an acceptable punishment. In other words, your individual rights or privileges are subordinate to the public interest.

You should remember that the law represents the *minimum standard* for remaining in the real estate business. Therefore, it is in your best interest to be aware of all the provisions of the licensing laws in order to avoid violations. Society has dictated that certain behavior is not acceptable and you must live by that decision, whether you agree with it or not. If you disagree, you may work to have it changed within the legislative system by lobbying efforts, supporting alternative candidates, or running for office yourself.

Public regulation of brokerage involves three basic areas of law. First, brokerage as an agency relationship comes under the state's common law of agency. Because of its specialized nature, real estate brokerage also comes under the provisions of special laws passed dealing specifically with real estate agencies. These are the licensing laws passed by every state and the District of Columbia. These first two bodies of law are state laws. The federal government also has laws affecting real estate brokerage in the areas of discrimination, disclosure, and the availability of credit.

AGENCY LAW

Real estate agents, like all other agents, are within the scope of the law in each state that covers the actions of all types of agents. Agency law defines agency relationships, their creation, and the duties the parties in an agency relationship have to one another.

Agency — Creation and Types

When you engage a real estate broker to act as your agent, what have you really done? You have entered into an agency relationship in which you have authorized your agent, the broker, to represent you and act in your behalf in dealing with third parties. You are called the principal. To summarize, an agent is one authorized to act for another, called the principal, in dealing with third parties.

If you create the agency by actually discussing the agency with the potential agent and then agreeing that the agency will be created and defining exactly what the agent is to do for you, you have created an **actual agency.** If, on the other hand, you have not created an actual agency relationship, but you give third parties reason to believe that someone is your agent, you have created an **ostensible agency.** For example, if someone knocks on your door and asks if your home is for sale and you answer that it is but they should visit the Sunshine Real Estate Company, you have created an ostensible agency with the Sunshine Real Estate Company, even if you did not have an existing agency relationship with Sunshine. This agency may occur whether you intentionally or unintentionally gave the third party reason to believe the agency existed. In real estate, most agencies are actual agencies created using a written listing agreement. (Listing agreements were discussed in the previous chapter.)

Agents may be classified according to the scope of authority given them by the principal. If you authorize an agent to perform each and every act that can legally be delegated, then your agent is a **universal agent.** For example, if you authorize an agent to conduct all of your affairs while you take an around-the-world cruise, that agent is a universal agent. This agent is acting as an **attorney-in-fact** under a power of attorney granted by you. The word *attorney* does not mean that this individual must be a lawyer; he or she may be anyone capable of becoming an agent. To be an agent you must have reached your majority, that is, be considered an adult in the eyes of the law, and otherwise be able to contract. This means you must not be insane or otherwise incapable of entering into a legal agreement.

If you give the agent more limited authority, such as running your dry cleaning business, then the agent is a **general agent.** For example, if you own an apartment complex and hire a manager to operate it and give that manager the authority to hire and fire employees, contract for goods and services, and generally conduct the business of running the complex, that manager is a general agent. Real estate salespersons associated with a brokerage firm are often considered general agents of the firm. Their principal is the real estate firm. We will come back to this point later in this chapter and again in the next chapter.

If the authority given the agent is even more specific and limited, such that the agent is authorized to conduct a particular piece of business for you, the agent is a **special agent.** If you authorize a real estate broker to find a ready, willing, and able buyer for a particular property, he or she is a special agent. Usually real estate agents act as special agents, with the seller being the principal.

Agent's Authority

An agent receives authority from the principal. In dealing with third parties, the agent must act within the authority given by the principal. If an agent represents to a third party that he or she has greater authority than he or she actually does, the third party may sue if damaged by actions based on this claim of authority. An agent's authority may be categorized into actual and apparent authority. **Actual authority** is that authority either expressly given the agent or implied by the principal. Authority specifically given the agent in the agreement creating the agency relationship is called **express authority.** Authority not specifically given the agent but is reasonably necessary for the agent to perform the assigned tasks is called **implied authority.** For example, an agent generally has the implied authority to delegate authority to salespersons associated with the firm. In addition to actual authority granted either expressly or by implication, an agent can receive **apparent authority** through the actions of the principal with third parties. If you, as the principal, cause third parties to believe that your agent has certain authority, those third parties may assume that the agent actually possesses that apparent authority. Thus, an agent can receive authority from the principal without knowing it, through the principal's actions with third parties.

DUTIES ASSOCIATED WITH AGENCY RELATIONSHIPS

An agency relationship creates duties and responsibilities for principal and agent to each other and to third parties. These duties reflect the mutual trust that must characterize an agency relationship, especially the trust of the principal in the agent. Because of this trust and the need to look out for the best interests of the principal, agents are often called **fiduciaries,** meaning one in a trusted position. However, the principal also has some duties to the agent and both have responsibilities to third parties such as buyers.

Duties of Agent to Principal

Agents are in a position of trust and may be able to take advantage of the relationship with the principal to unduly enrich themselves. If the duties that follow are adhered to, the agent will not likely violate this trust.

Loyalty Perhaps the foremost duty of the agent is to remember that his or her loyalty belongs with the principal. This means that in all situations the agent must look out for the principal's best interests. If you have employed an agent to help you sell Blackacre, that agent should not make a profit from the agency, except for the compensation you have agreed to pay. For example, the agent should not make a profit from recommending that you use a particular survey company because the agent receives a referral fee from that company. Loyalty also means that the agent should keep the principal fully informed at all times. For instance, if the real estate broker fails to tell you of a zoning change near Blackacre that may affect its value, and you later sell Blackacre at a price lower than necessary, the broker has not fulfilled the duty of loyalty and risks the possibility of being sued for this shortcoming.

Performance The agent has a duty to perform the tasks of the agency to the best of his or her ability and with due diligence. Further, the agent has a duty to obey all lawful and reasonable instructions given by the principal. Agents are responsible for any losses the principal suffers because of a failure to follow lawful instructions or perform with due diligence. If, as an agent, you feel any instruction is unreasonable, you should discuss the request with your principal to see if agreement can be reached. If it cannot, you must choose between honoring the request or ending the agency relationship.

Cannot Delegate Authority Agency relationships are extremely personal, and agents are often selected because of special skills or feelings of trust between the principal and the agent. Because of this special relationship, the agent cannot delegate authority to others without the permission of the principal. Typically, in real estate brokerage it is assumed that the sales staff of the brokerage firm may seek a buyer for the property without violating this duty. Co-brokerage arrangements are not as clear and, if co-brokerage is to be used to find a buyer, the listing agreement should authorize this activity. If this issue is not clarified in this listing agreement, the principal may contend the agent violated this duty and try to avoid paying a commission.

Not Acting for Both Parties in a Transaction As you read above, the duty of loyalty requires the real estate broker to always keep the principal's interest foremost in mind. It makes sense that it would be more difficult for a broker to keep the principal's interest foremost in mind if he or she was the agent for both the buyer and the seller in a transaction. Certainly, either the buyer or seller, on finding out about such a dual agency, may feel that the agent did not act in their best interest and sue the agent for damages. To avoid inevitable conflicts of interest, the agent should not act as agent for both buyer and seller without informing and getting permission in writing from both parties.

Accounting for Monies and Documents During the course of a transaction, an agent may handle monies and documents belonging to others, a possibly ticklish situation. The agent should provide receipts for all items and store them in a safe place. Monies held in trust should not be mixed, or *commingled*, with the broker's personal or business monies. Most states require that trust, or escrow, accounts be established for depositing all monies belonging to others. You are not required to have a trust account for each transaction but, rather, a single account into which all monies belonging to other people are placed. Receipts should be given to all parties whose property is held. Accurate records must be kept of all deposits and withdrawals since real estate licensing agencies perform unannounced audits of these accounts. Additionally, all property, documents, and monies should be promptly paid or delivered to the appropriate parties. Unreasonable delays may give rise to lawsuits as well as violating license laws.

Reasonable Care You must exercise reasonable care in all your dealings as an agent. *Reasonable care* has many possible meanings, including not committing misrepresentation or fraud, carefully preparing all documents, providing all available information to the principal, and taking care that no damage to the principal's property results because of your negligence. For example, if you prepare a real estate sales contract and omit an important condition of the sale, you have probably not exercised due care. Likewise, if you leave the principal's home unlocked after showing it and damage or theft results, you may be responsible to the principal for those losses. By holding yourself out as a knowledgeable and competent real estate agent you have accepted strong responsibilities to act in a businesslike and professional manner.

Duties of Principal to Agent

Duties are not a one-way street—the principal also has duties to the agent. What kinds of things can you expect of your principal?

Compensation The principal has a legal obligation to pay you the agreed-on compensation when you have fulfilled the terms of your agency. We will discuss the conditions under which real estate agents have earned their compensation later in this chapter.

Performance Real estate is easier to sell when the principal and agent work as a team. This means the principal must do his or her part by cooperating with the sales efforts. Performance means that the principal does everything reasonably possible to achieve the goals of the agency relationship. For example, the principal should keep the property neat and in good repair for showing and should allow showings whenever possible. Principals who do not accept these responsibilities can create frustration for the agent and leave themselves open to the agent ending the agency relationship.

Indemnify for Losses The principal may be responsible for the agent's losses resulting from the agent's improper actions within the scope of the agency, but not the fault of the agent. The most common example of this situation is where the agent unintentionally misrepresents a fact because the principal provided the agent with incorrect information. Of course, the agent may be guilty of not exercising proper diligence in situations where research would have provided correct information. Thus, the line between the duties of the principal and those of the agent is a very fine one.

Reimbursing Agent for Expenses Some agencies provide that the principal shall reimburse the agent for expenses incurred in the course of the agency. Real estate brokerage generally does not abide by this rule. The broker usually must cover his or her own expenses and receive only the compensation agreed to in the listing agreement. However, the principal does have a responsibility to reimburse the agent for expenses not ordinarily related to selling the property. For example, if the principal has moved to another city and *asks* the agent to have a cleaning service clean the home, the principal has a responsibility to reimburse the agent for the cost of cleaning.

DUTIES OF AGENT TO THIRD PARTIES

Dealing with third parties often puts the broker in a difficult situation. Picture yourself as a broker trying to sell a home. You want to sell the home because your principal needs the money from the sale and, of course, you need the money from the commission. Many buyers do not understand that you are not legally employed by them, but rather, are employed by the seller. This does not mean that you may treat the buyer with gay abandon. It simply means that in the final analysis you have certain duties to your principal that cannot be relinquished for the buyer's interests.

Buyers should expect to be treated fairly and honestly. A good agent knows that a truly successful transaction is one in which the buyer and the seller feel that they were treated fairly and their best interests

Table 21.1. Reasons for Choosing Agent/
Broker/Firm (Ranked in Order of Importance)

1. Agent was a friend, relative, or neighbor
2. Used agent before
3. Recommendation of friend
4. Direct contract by agent (personal, mail, or telephone)
5. Newspaper advertisement
6. Signs
7. Magazine advertisements
8. Radio/television advertisements

SOURCE: *National Homebuying Survey*, The Economics and
Research Division, National Association of Realtors, 1981, p. 17.

served. Once again, the Golden Rule serves as an excellent guide to the
agent's actions with both parties. Repeat business and referrals represent two of the surest paths to long-term success in brokerage. This
contention was reinforced in a recent study of homebuyers, as shown in
Table 21.1. Both referrals and repeat business are maximized by fair
treatment of all parties in a transaction. Developing this perception of
fair treatment requires that the broker skillfully handle potential conflicts of interest and turn points of contention into points of agreement.
The old adage, *caveat emptor* — let the buyer beware — has *never* been
particularly appropriate in real estate brokerage. Consumer protection
legislation and court decisions favoring consumer rights have made this
adage even less applicable to all areas of brokerage.

Principals owe third parties the same consideration afforded them
by agents. Honesty and fair treatment by the principal should be expected by all buyers. Principals can be held legally liable for their own
misrepresentations, as well as those made by their agents with their
approval. Too often, greed causes sellers to amend the Golden Rule to
"Do unto others *before* they do unto you." This is a dangerous and
foolish business philosophy.

CREATING AN AGENCY RELATIONSHIP
(LISTING AGREEMENTS)

Some states require listings to be in writing while others allow oral
listings. Because memories and morals are not perfect, it is best to use
written agreements to create real estate agency relationships. This written agreement is called the listing agreement and was considered in the
previous chapter. However, you should remember that a written listing
agreement is essential to your receiving a commission under the laws of
most states. Even in states not requiring that listing agreements be in
writing, your best protection in case of a dispute over a commission is a

written listing agreement. A written listing agreement also protects the principal by making the agency conditions clear and well defined.

TERMINATING AN AGENCY RELATIONSHIP

Once an agency relationship is created, it does not continue forever. In real estate brokerage the agency will probably end with the sale of the property. That is, the agent will have performed the assigned job and be compensated, and the agency will be happily ended. The agency, however, may be terminated in ways other than *performance* (see Table 21.2).

An agency may be terminated by *mutual agreement*. This agreement to end the agency relationship should be put into writing and signed by both parties. Also, if the listing is on the multiple listing service, it may take some period of time to get proper notification of the cancellation to all brokers and sales associations. The listing broker and the principal can be in a ticklish position if before notice of the cancellation is received by all multiple listing brokers another broker produces an offer meeting all of the principal's terms. That broker may legally be entitled to a commission. This situation should be considered in canceling any listing.

An agency may also be terminated by either the principal or agent individually, but only for good cause. Such an ending is called *renunciation.* If the agency is ended by either party, that party may be responsible for expenses and possible breach of contract remedies imposed by courts. In practice, many brokers allow the principal to end the agency without a great deal of difficulty, realizing that selling a property for an owner not wanting to sell is a most difficult task. In some instances, the broker may require the principal to pay for expenses incurred on their behalf. Brokers will usually protect themselves, however, from principals who want to end the agency in order to sell to someone to whom the broker has previously shown the property without having to pay a commission. As protection for the broker, the listing agreement usually provides that if the property is sold to anyone originally interested in the property by the broker within a certain number of days (usually, 30 to 60 days) after the termination of the agency, the broker is to receive a

Table 21.2. Terminating an Agency Relationship

Performance
Mutual agreement
Renunciation by either party
Law
Time

commission. This strategy usually works since few buyers and sellers want to wait 30 to 60 days to sign a sales contract.

Agencies can also be terminated automatically *by law* and by the passage of *time*. In case of the insanity, death, or bankruptcy of either principal or agent, the agency is terminated. The agency also ends by law if the listed property is destroyed by fire, tornado, or other cause. Agencies in real estate are established for some specified period of time, such as three months or six months. If a ready, willing, and able buyer has not been found by that time, the listing agreement automatically ends. Thus, a listing agreement may end by the simple passage of time.

REAL ESTATE LICENSING LAWS

If after finishing this course you want to become a real estate agent, you must obtain a state real estate license. All 50 states and the District of Columbia have passed laws requiring real estate agents to be licensed and have established various qualifications necessary for obtaining such a license. This section provides you with an understanding of present-day licensing laws and some of the changes occurring in them. Since many of the state licensing laws have been based on model legislation developed by the National Association of Realtors, many are quite similar. In spite of significant similarities with other states, your state's licensing law probably has some unique features. What follows is designed to acquaint you with the rationale and general elements of license laws, and not to detail the license law of your state. You should thoroughly study your state's license law before sitting for your license examination. Copies of this law may be obtained from your state licensing agency.

History and Purpose of License Laws

License laws have been with us since California passed the first one that ultimately proved to be Constitutional in 1919. Licensing laws have been created to *protect the public*, which is not involved in real estate transactions on a regular basis, from unscrupulous practices by real estate agents. Originally these laws acted simply as registration devices, forcing agents to publicly declare themselves and provide other information designed to make real estate agency less attractive to dishonest persons. Later, experience and education requirements for licensing were added to these laws. Appendix A.1 at the end of the book summarizes the education and experience requirements of the various states. As you can see, some states are enacting continuing education requirements for licensees, making it necessary for them to complete additional education to retain their licenses. Once again, these changes have been designed to protect the public, not only from dishonest agents, but also from incompetent ones.

Administering License Laws

License laws represent rather general statements of the licensing requirement and require a good bit of detail work before they can be implemented. For example, the law may specify that before a person may take the license examination he or she must satisfactorily complete an approved real estate course. What is satisfactory completion? What is an approved real estate course? Who prepares and grades the license examination? These and many other questions must be answered to implement license laws effectively. To provide these answers, license legislation provides for the creation of an administrative body called a real estate commission or department. The real estate commission may be an independent body or may be a part of a larger state body dealing with all kinds of occupational licenses such as insurance, securities, barbers, beauticians, and the like.

The real estate commission is usually composed of commissioners appointed by the governor. In some states, all commissioners are active in the real estate business, while in other states some commissioners are members of the public and not involved in the real estate business. Commissioners are not full-time state employees and usually receive only expenses and either minimal or no compensation. The commissioners usually meet on a designated day(s) of the month, to consider the business of the commission requiring group decisions. At these meetings the commission will consider and adopt the **rules and regulations** necessary to implement the license law (See Figure 21.1). Rules and regulations provide working definitions and other necessary details. For example, they will decide what constitutes an approved course, which affects your ability to take the license examination after completing that course. They will also answer the other questions asked above and many others.

The commission conducts hearings for licensees accused of violating the license law or the rules and regulations of the commission. When conducting these hearings, the commission is acting under what is called **administrative law.** Commissioners hear any special requests from licensees for exemptions from the license law, extensions of time, and so on. They will also keep the legislature and governor informed as to the need for changes in the license law and the general effectiveness of the license law in protecting the public.

Commission Staff To handle the day-to-day decisions and the tremendous amount of paperwork accompanying a license law, the real estate commission has a staff. Heading that staff will be a full-time employee called the secretary or secretary-treasurer (in some states this person is called the real estate commissioner). The staff will handle the prepara-

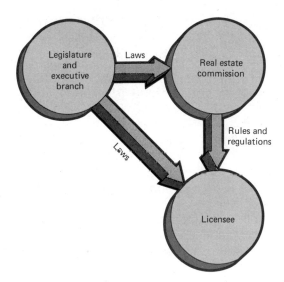

Figure 21.1 Real estate licensing laws, rules, and regulations.

tion and grading of examinations, exam applications and test scheduling, billing for licenses, preparing a newsletter or bulletin, and other necessary recordkeeping functions. Also on staff will be investigators to research complaints concerning licensees filed with the commission. An educational director may be available to provide seminars and other opportunities for licensees to stay informed.

Real estate commissioners and key staff members likely belong to the National Association of Real Estate License Law Officials (NARELLO). NARELLO holds regional and district meetings that allow an opportunity to exchange ideas and discuss licensing problems. NARELLO also gathers and disseminates information about licensing practices.

License Types and Who Must Be Licensed

Most states issue two types of licenses, one for brokers and another for salespersons. The salesperson's license is also called a sales associate's license in some states. As a broker, you may act as an agent and take listings in your name or, if you own a firm, the name of that firm. If you hold a broker's license and are employed by another broker or firm, you will not take listings in your own name but, rather, in the name of your firm. As a salesperson, you *must* be associated with a licensed broker and take all listings in the name of that broker. You cannot open your own firm and you cannot take listings in your own name. You must also work for, and receive compensation from, only one broker.

Technically, most states define a broker similar to the following:

. . . any person, partnership, association, or corporation, foreign or domestic, who for a fee, commission or other valuable

consideration, or with the intention or expectation of receiving or collecting a fee, commission or other valuable consideration, lists, sells or offers to sell, buys or offers to buy, exchanges, rents or leases any real estate, or who negotiates or attempts to negotiate any such activity, or solicits listing of places for rent, or solicits for prospective tenants, or who advertises or holds himself or herself out as engaged in such activities.

Notice that this definition is not limited to individuals. Corporations, partnerships, and associations acting as agents must also be licensed. Also notice that if you do *virtually anything* involving the buying, selling, or renting of real estate for a fee or with the expectation of being paid a fee, whether you are ever actually paid or not, you must obtain a license. Some states also require property managers or appraisers to hold real estate licenses.

A salesperson is defined in license laws in a manner similar to the following:

. . . any person employed or engaged by, or associated as an independent contractor with, or on behalf of, a real estate broker to do or deal in any act, acts, or transactions set out in the definition of a real estate broker.

A salesperson is not a "second-class" license with respect to the properties the salesperson may sell. A salesperson may find a buyer for any property in town, either single family or commercial. However, the listing must be in the name of the brokerage firm with whom he or she is associated or in the name of another broker who has agreed to co-broker with the salesperson's broker.

Who Is Not Required to Have a License?

Most state license laws do not require certain people to obtain a real estate license. Owners of real estate do not have to be licensed to sell their own property. This includes employees of firms selling real estate belonging to the firm. For example, if you work for a fast food chain buying and selling restaurant sites, you would not need a real estate license. People acting in specified legal capacities are not required to be licensed. If you are acting under a *power of attorney* as attorney-in-fact, you do not have to be licensed. Likewise, an attorney-at-law conducting a purchase, sale, or rental as an ordinary part of his or her practice does not have to be licensed. However, an attorney must have a license to open a brokerage office. Finally, any person acting under direction of a court, such as a trustee in bankruptcy, an executor, an administrator or one acting as trustee in a trust deed arrangement generally does not have to be licensed.

Getting a Real Estate License

To get a real estate license, you must meet a series of requirements that vary from state to state. These requirements fall into four general categories:

1. General requirements
2. Education requirements
3. Examination requirements
4. Experience requirements

General requirements often include being of a specified minimum age and being of good moral character. Most states require the successful completion of a prescribed number of hours of approved real estate coursework as an education requirement. As a further test of real estate knowledge, you will be required to pass a written examination with a minimum score of 70 to 75 percent. Finally, to become a broker, many states require that you have a specified amount of experience as a licensed salesperson.

Getting your real estate license is more difficult in some states than others, as indicated by Appendix A.1. It is possible that these requirements may have changed while this book was being prepared and will certainly change over time. Your state real estate commission can supply up-to-the-minute licensing requirements.

Notes on Licensing Examinations The examinations given by your state are prepared by the state real estate commission, the Educational Testing Service (ETS), or the American College Testing Service (ACT), except in South Carolina where they are prepared by the University of South Carolina. Currently, 29 states and the District of Columbia use the services of ETS and 13 states use the services of ACT. The eight remaining commissions prepare their own examinations. Examinations prepared by ETS and ACT contain 100 to 140 multiple choice questions divided into two sections. One section is called the *uniform* or *general section* and contains questions relating to general real estate knowledge. According to their Bulletin of Information for Applicants, the uniform part of the ETS salesperson examination contains 80 questions divided among topics as follows:

Real estate contracts	13%
Financing	24%
Real estate ownership	22%
Real estate brokerage	24%
Real estate valuation	17%

The broker examination has different topics and weightings:

Real estate brokerage	35%
Contracts and other legal aspects	27%
Pricing and valuation	15%
Finance and investment	23%

The second section of these examinations is a state section, containing questions specific to your state. Questions in this section cover real estate license laws, rules, and regulations, other appropriate state law, and relevant aspects of real estate practice particular to your state. This section will typically contain 30 to 50 questions. Usually, minimum passing scores are about 70 to 75 percent.

Broker's License Getting your broker's license will require some combination of additional coursework, another examination, and experience as a licensed salesperson. Experience is difficult to evaluate, so many states simply require some designated period of "active experience." To verify your experience, your employing broker may be required to sign a statement attesting to your activity in the real estate business.

Licenses for Corporations and Partnerships

Corporations may be licensed in most states if the managing officer(s) holds a broker's license. Licenses may be issued to partnerships in which all partners hold broker's licenses. Likewise, you may wish simply to do business as an individual with a company name. For example, you may wish to open a real estate firm named Empire Real Estate. Operating this firm does not require that you get a license for the firm, but you must file the firm name with the real estate commission and the county clerk. This is so any legal documents can be properly delivered to you. Technically, you will be considered as Dale Broker dba (doing business as) Empire Real Estate.

KEEPING YOUR LICENSE

Violations of the license law or the rules and regulations of the real estate commission may result in your license being **suspended** (temporarily withdrawn) or **revoked** (permanently withdrawn). If someone files a complaint about your activities as a licensee, the real estate commission staff will conduct an investigation. Documents and statements from individuals associated with the situation will be gathered and analyzed. Also, the real estate commission may start an investigation of your real estate affairs on its own through the unannounced auditing of trust (escrow) accounts in which monies belonging to others are held. If necessary, a hearing before the commission will be scheduled, at which time you and the plaintiff (person filing the complaint) may be represented by attorneys. All parties may subpeona witnesses and documents. After reviewing the testimony and evidence, the commission makes its decision. Violations may result in suspension or revocation of your license or fines. In some states, jail sentences are also possible if the state decides to prosecute you in the courts. The decision of the commission may be appealed to the court system.

This hearing before the real estate commission may not be the end of your problems since the plaintiff may also file a civil suit in the courts for damages. In some cases, the lawsuit will involve you and your employing broker or you as the employing broker and one of your salespersons. If you lose the case, you or your professional liability insurance company if your actions are covered by the policy, must pay the judgment. As protection for the public, some license laws provide that all licensees must purchase a bond to cover judgments of this type in the event the licensee cannot or does not pay. However, in many cases this bond is for a relatively small amount of money and does not really offer adequate protection. To partially remedy this situation, many states have replaced bonds with a state-run **recovery fund** into which each licensee pays a certain amount each year. This fund is then used, up to established limits, which usually exceed those of previously required bonds, to pay judgments against licensees resulting from violations of the license law or commission rules and regulations.

Causes for Suspension or Revocation

Any violation of the state license law may result in the suspension or revocation of your license. Ignorance is no defense. By virtue of having taken and passed the licensing examination and holding yourself out as a licensed broker or sales associate, you are assumed to know the license law and the rules and regulations of the real estate commission enacted to implement it. Among other things, misrepresentation, acting for more than one party in a transaction without full disclosure and approval, commingling funds belonging to others in your personal or business accounts, failure to pay a salesperson his or her share of a commission, or any other conduct constituting untrustworthy, improper, fraudulent, or dishonest dealings may result in the suspension or revocation of your license. Most states also provide that making false statements on your license application and paying any fees to the real estate commission with a bad check constitute grounds for suspension or revocation.

The relationship between the duties of an agent under agency law and the real estate license law should be clear. Both seek to define agency relationships that are fair and equitable to all parties. A study of the license law and the rules and regulations of your state will reinforce the importance of developing a good sense of right and wrong in agency relationships.

Getting a License In Another State

If you get a license in your present state and later move to another state, what must you do to get a new license? In states having full *reciprocity,* you may be able to get a new license simply by filling out the proper forms and paying the necessary fees. In states with limited reciprocity, you will have to satisfactorily complete at least some of the state's requirements for licensing. You may have to take an examination or a course or perhaps gain some experience in the state to get a broker's license. It is best to contact the **real estate commission** in the state to which you are moving and get the full details of what is required to be licensed there. The same concepts apply to maintaining your residence in your present state but conducting brokerage business in another state.

CHANGES IN LICENSING

Licensing laws have gotten more stringent over the years. From simple registration, some license laws have developed into substantial requirements to obtain a license. The trend continues; virtually every year one or more states will pass new license laws increasing the educational requirements or expanding the experience requirements for becoming licensed.

Certain states have instituted educational requirements for those already having a real estate license. These *continuing education requirements* must be satisfied before a license can be renewed. If not renewed, the license simply lapses and the individual is no longer licensed. The rationale for continuing education requirements is that licensees must keep up with changes in real estate if the public is to be served by competent real estate agents.

FEDERAL LAWS AFFECTING REAL ESTATE BROKERAGE

The federal government has passed a number of laws affecting real estate brokerage. Of special importance to you are laws dealing with equal housing opportunities and the advertising of financing terms. These laws do not affect your ability to get a license and enter the real estate business; however, they do affect how you perform your duties as a real estate agent.

Equal Housing Opportunity

Federal law now mandates that all persons regardless of race, color, religion, sex, or national origin shall have equal opportunity in housing. In short, discrimination against anyone on the basis of any of the factors just mentioned is illegal. The foundation for this strong position goes all the way back to 1866. In that year, Congress passed the *Civil Rights Act of 1866* which states that:

All citizens of the United States shall have the same right, in every State and Territory, as is enjoyed by white citizens thereof to inherit, purchase, lease, sell, hold and convey real and personal property.

In 1968, the U.S. Supreme Court, in a case known as *Jones vs. Mayer*, held that the 1866 law prohibits *all* racial discrimination in the sale or rental of property.

In 1968, Congress passed another law called the **1968 Civil Rights Act** asserting the rights of everyone to purchase property. This law made any discrimination in the sale or rental of housing on the basis of race, color, religion, sex, or national origin illegal. Notice that this law expanded the concept of discrimination beyond racial boundaries. The law demands equal treatment of all persons seeking to rent or purchase housing. Specifically, under the Act, you cannot:

1. Refuse to sell or rent
2. Discriminate on terms, conditions, and the like in sale or rental
3. Advertise a preference, limitation, or discrimination
4. Represent a property as *not* available when in fact it *is*
5. Practice blockbusting or steering

Anyone who feels they have been discriminated against according to the provisions of this law may file a complaint with the local office of the Department of Housing and Urban Development.

The 1968 Civil Rights Act prohibits blockbusting and steering. **Blockbusting** is the act of starting rumors that a minority individual or family is buying a home in a particular neighborhood in an attempt to cause panic selling. The person starting the rumor then buys these properties at depressed prices and resells them later for a substantial gain. **Steering** involves showing minorities only properties in areas populated by members of that minority group. Steering can also occur when members of a nonminority group are systematically guided away from areas inhabited by minorities. The Act also makes it illegal for anyone to threaten or actually harm the property or person of anyone protected by this law because they are attempting to purchase or sell property. The same protection is extended to agents showing property to anyone protected by this law.

Truth-In-Lending

The **Truth-In-Lending Act,** considered in Chapter 14, has provisions that affect the real estate agent in regard to advertising containing any financial terms. The law is intended to reduce misleading or "baiting" type advertisements. This is accomplished by restricting the extent to which anyone can advertise partial financial terms. If an advertisement contains virtually any financial terms other than the APR, then a full disclosure must be made. The APR must be printed in a type that is bolder than the remainder of the advertisement.

You may be wondering what constitutes advertising. Advertising is virtually all information available to the public. This means television, radio, and newspapers, along with posters, billboards, or any information made available to potential buyers. Thus, great care must be exercised to avoid making a disclosure of partial financial terms that may be in violation of the truth-in-lending laws.

Other Federal Laws

You may wish to review other federal laws contained in Chapter 14. Laws such as the Real Estate Settlement Procedures Act (RESPA) and the Equal Credit Opportunity Act (ECOA) may apply to you in certain situations. Certainly if you are ever in the position of being an *arranger of credit,* one who assists those seeking credit as distinguished from actually lending, these acts may be of special significance to you.

As with all other aspects of law, a good attorney can help you avoid problems with federal laws affecting brokerage. Also, you should try to remain aware of changes in federal law affecting your activities as a broker.

SUMMARY

Real estate agents must be licensed in every state and the District of Columbia. License laws were passed to protect the public from incompetent or dishonest agents. In addition to license laws, real estate agents are also subject to state agency laws and certain federal laws.

Agency law identifies the person granting authority to the agent as the principal. Real estate agents are special agents because they are authorized to perform only a specific act for the principal. Agents may have actual authority either given expressly or by implication. Additionally, an agent may have apparent authority if the principal causes others to believe he or she possesses such authority.

Agents and principals owe each other, and third parties, certain duties. Agents owe principals the duties of loyalty, performance, not delegating authority, not acting for both parties in a transaction, accounting for all monies and property, and using reasonable care in performing all dealings. Principals are obligated to compensate the agent, perform certain tasks, indemnify for losses, and reimburse for certain expenses. Both owe third parties fair treatment and honesty.

Agency relationships are created using listing agreements. Many states require that listing agreements be in writing. They may be terminated by performance, mutual agreement, renunciation, law, or by time.

Real estate license laws are administered by real estate commissions or departments, usually made up of appointees and serving with minimal or no pay. In addition to the commission, there are full-time employees who perform the chores of administering the license laws. The commission also enacts rules and regulations to amplify and operationalize the license laws. The commission has the power to conduct hearings and to suspend or revoke real estate licenses for violations of the license law or commission rules and regulations.

Most states have two types of licenses: broker and salesperson. The essential difference is that only brokers may take listings in their own name or the name of their firm and accept commissions from sellers. Salespersons must be associated with a broker and must take listings in the name of that broker. Virtually any activity involving the buying and selling of real estate requires a license. The only persons generally excepted from licensing are property owners or employees of property owners, persons acting under power of attorney, attorneys-at-law acting in their ordinary practice, and persons acting under the direction of a court. Getting a license normally requires meeting specified educational and examination requirements. Brokers often must meet specified experience requirements.

Federal laws affecting real estate do not directly involve licensing. They do affect the manner in which an agent conducts business. These laws include those dealing with equal housing opportunity, Truth-In-Lending Act, Real Estate Settlement Procedures Act, and the Equal Credit Opportunity Act.

QUICK QUIZ

1. An agency created by you giving third parties reason to believe that someone is your agent is a(n) _____.

    a. natural agency   c. apparent agency
    b. ostensible agency   d. actual agency

2. Agents are sometimes called fiduciaries because they _____.

    a. act for more than one party   c. have apparent authority
    b. are in a position of trust   d. are not attorneys

3. Which of the following is *not* a type of authority an agent may have?

a. express authority   c. apparent authority
b. implied authority   d. general authority

4. An agency relationship may be terminated by any of the following except _____ .

a. mutual agreement   c. performance
b. renunciation   d. reciprocity

5. Federal laws affecting real estate include all of the following except _____ .

a. 1968 Civil Rights Act   c. Truth-In-Lending Act
b. Federal Licensing Act   d. Equal Credit Opportunity Act

6. The duty of an agent to look out for the best interests of the principal is the duty of _____

7. Real estate license laws have been enacted for the purpose of _____

8. To implement the license laws, real estate commissions formulate _____ and _____

9. The 1968 Civil Rights Act made discrimination in the sale or rental of housing on the basis of _____ , _____ , or _____ illegal.

10. When a broker places money belonging to others in his or her personal or business account, he or she is guilty of _____ .

QUESTIONS AND EXERCISES

1. What are the requirements for becoming a licensed salesperson in your state?

2. Discuss why *caveat emptor* is not a reasonable attitude for a real estate agent.

3. When did your state first adopt a real estate license law? When was it last changed?

4. For what reasons can real estate licenses typically be suspended or revoked?

5. Do you think more stringent licensing requirements would better protect the public? Why or why not?

6. If your state has an experience requirement for brokers, how is that experience measured? Do you feel this system can be improved? Why or why not?

KEY TERMINOLOGY

actual agency
actual authority
administrative law
apparent authority
attorney-in-fact
blockbusting
express authority
fiduciary
general agent
implied authority
license law

1968 Civil Rights Act
ostensible agency
real estate commission
recovery fund
revocation
rules and regulations
special agent
steering
suspension
Truth-In-Lending Act
universal agent

IF YOU WANT TO READ MORE

GEORGE F. BLOOM, ARTHUR M. WEIMER, and JEFFREY D. FISHER, *Real Estate,* 8th ed. (New York: John Wiley & Sons, 1982).

CHARLES F. FLOYD, *Real Estate Principles* (New York: Random House, Inc., 1981).

National Association of Real Estate License Law Officials, *Guide to Examinations and Careers in Real Estate* (Reston: Reston Publishing Company, Inc., 1979).

22

Property Management

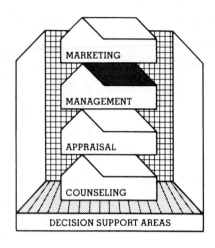

MARKETING

MANAGEMENT

APPRAISAL

COUNSELING

DECISION SUPPORT AREAS

PREVIEW

If there is a real estate support activity that is either ignored, taken for granted, generally minimized, oversimplified, or simply forgotten about, it is likely property management. This is unfortunate because property management is the support area responsible for making the projections of the equity investor or developer a reality. The difference between good and poor management is often the difference between a successful investment and an unsuccessful one. Research has consistently shown that good management is one of the items most highly sought by all types of tenants, whereas bad management is one of the most frequent reasons for leaving a building as a tenant. Less apparent than the turnover of tenants, but still serious, are the numerous other problems created by inept property management. After reading and studying this chapter you will understand:

1. What property management is and why it is necessary.
2. Who manages real property.
3. The pros and cons of managing a property yourself or contracting for professional management.
4. The property manager's role in leasing, collections, maintenance, insurance, and recordkeeping and reporting.
5. How property managers are educated and professional property management designations.

6. Some of the current trends affecting property management such as mixed-use properties and condominium conversions.

Far from being the simple, foolproof activity it is often assumed to be, property management is a complex discipline involving a number of areas of expertise. To understand the decisions the property manager must make, imagine that you have purchased a new office building and have decided to manage it yourself. You first must develop some overall management goals and objectives. One such goal is making a profit from operating the office building. However, you also know that appreciation in the value of the building is very important, and that means the building must be well-maintained to preserve and enhance its rents and values. Thus, you must carefully balance current profit and the potential for future appreciation.

A little more thought will make you aware of other, more specific, activities that must be performed to achieve the overall goals you have just established. For example, you realize that the space in the building will not lease itself and that you need to decide what kinds of tenants you want and how you will attract them, what lease terms are desirable, and who will prepare the necessary lease documents. What you really need is a *marketing plan*. Likewise, decisions must be made about a collections policy, maintenance plan, recordkeeping and reporting plan, insurance coverage plan, and personnel plan for the people necessary to run the building. Each of these plans requires a good bit of time and specialized knowledge to develop.

While considering all of these decisions, it may occur to you that you really do not want to manage the property yourself because of a lack of time or expertise, or both. This means you must decide who will manage the property. You have essentially two options: hire a property manager as an employee or retain an independent management firm on a fee basis to manage the property. There are advantages and disadvantages to each arrangement. Whatever your choice, the manager must perform all of the tasks that are necessary to achieve your goals and objectives. Understanding the scope of the duties and responsibilities of a property manager will make it easier for you to select a manager for your property.

PROPERTY MANAGEMENT ACTIVITIES

Property management is a composite of many areas of business activity. You need to understand the essential nature of these activities if you ever anticipate acting as broker, investor, developer, lender, or appraiser. You also need to understand them to see if property management interests you as a career area. Property management activities can be divided into five areas: leasing, collections, maintenance, insurance, and budgeting and recordkeeping, as illustrated in Figure 22.1.

Leasing

Leasing activity is critical to the risk and returns associated with a property. To see this, simply consider a property leased to a number of financially strong and responsible tenants at premium rental rates that will increase periodically in relation to a price index. Further, the leases have staggered expiration dates and provisions that the tenants pay for all operating expenses. Imagine what this leasing program has done to increase the return and reduce the risk to the owner, while also maximizing the value of the property. The situation just described is not likely to occur by accident. In most instances, such an ideal situation cannot even be created by design; however, progress toward the best possible lease situation can be made if goals are established, plans made, and efforts expended to implement the plan. Whether the property manager or another party actually finds the potential tenants, the property manager is involved in many leasing activities that mean the difference between success and disaster.

Among the leasing activities of the property manager is the formulation of acceptable lease terms. The terms of a lease include much more than the initial rental rate. Other terms include the type of tenancy to be created, as discussed in Chapter 4. Payment type and provisions for future changes in rental levels must also be determined. The basic options in these categories include:

Gross lease. A lease in which the lessee makes a fixed payment from which the lessor must pay all operating expenses.

Net lease. A lease in which the lessee makes a fixed payment and also pays agreed-on operating expenses and property taxes. Sometimes you will hear of a net-net or a net-net-net lease. Generally, the more expenses paid by the lessee, the more nets in the lease. Conceptually, with a net-net-net lease all operating expenses, except mortgage payments, are paid by the lessee. Unfortunately, there are no universally accepted definitions of net, net-net, and net-net-

Figure 22.1 Property management activities.

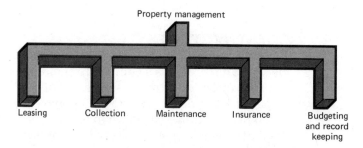

Property management

Leasing   Collection   Maintenance   Insurance   Budgeting and record keeping

net leases. This means you must always determine exactly what another person means when they use these terms.

Percentage lease. A lease in which payments are expressed as an agreed-on percentage of some measure of the lessee's income, usually gross receipts. These leases are used extensively in retail leases.

There are several variations on these basic themes. Among them are:

Percentage lease with base rent. A lease in which the lessee pays a fixed minimum rent and then pays a percentage rent on gross income above an agreed-on amount. For instance, a retail store may pay a fixed rent of $1500 per month and a percentage of gross sales over a specified amount.

Gross lease with graduation. A lease with a payment that remains fixed for a specified period but is then either increased or decreased by agreed-on amounts or an amount determined by changes in some index, such as the Consumer Price Index. For instance, a lease may provide fixed payments for the first 3 years, with an increase in the fourth year. This increase allows the lessor to keep up with escalating costs and also earn a reasonable return on a property with increasing value.

Other terms such as the period of time covered by the lease, renewal options, insurance requirements, restrictions on business hours, deposits, parking, property maintenance, financial standards for lessees, and many others must also be developed. The lease document itself must be drafted. Lease agreements can run many pages in length. Some shopping center leases run 20 to 30 pages. Such long documents are necessary to outline clearly and completely the rights and obligations of the lessee and lessor. Every state has a body of law, usually called landlord-tenant laws, that defines certain rights of the landlord and tenant. Because landlord-tenant laws affect many aspects of property management, they are considered in more detail later in the chapter. The essential legal elements of leases and other contracts were discussed in Chapter 6. You should review that chapter if you have any questions about the lease document.

To effectively perform all the tasks just outlined, the property manager must continually be aware of conditions in the rental markets. This includes knowledge of the terms available in competing buildings, the amenities they offer, potential new space being developed, and when it is likely to become available. In short, the property manager must be aware of the operation and economics of real estate markets as explained in Chapter 9.

The property manager must also screen potential tenants for fit with other tenants and for creditworthiness. For example, in an office building occupied exclusively by physicians, an accounting firm may not fit well and may damage the image of the building as a medical office building. Likewise, the inclusion of a physician may have a negative effect on a building of accountants, especially when the introduction of a physician and the attendant load of patients makes a bad parking situation even worse. Examining the creditworthiness of a tenant may include reviewing credit reports and checking with references to make sure the potential tenant has a history of paying rents, not abusing leased space, and being considerate of other tenants. Credit reports are supplied by numerous credit reporting firms such as Dun and Bradstreet.

The property manager must also plan for lease expirations by keeping track of when leases expire. Lease expirations provide the opportunity to renegotiate lease terms with the present tenant or create the need/opportunity to find new tenants. Lease expiration can be very bothersome if plans have not been made to lease the space so that rental income is not unduly interrupted. A good property manager will perform a lease audit and stay informed as to the amount of space on which leases will expire in any particular period.

Collections

Collections conjures up a picture of a muscular individual "suggesting" that someone pay the money they owe to "the boss." Even when strongarm tactics are not used, collections can create image problems for the property manager and owner. Few people really enjoy being nasty with other human beings, often to the point of tolerating inappropriate and unnecessary abuses. Property managers should not fall prey to this latter situation; tenants have voluntarily signed leases agreeing to pay specified rentals on certain dates. Failure to live up to these agreements is money out of the pocket of the owner, money that was to be paid in return for providing space. A firm collections policy should be developed and communicated to each tenant at the time the space is leased. Such a policy can minimize the possibility of misunderstandings due to a lack of information and understanding.

However, a wishy-washy enforcement policy will undo much of the good a collections policy can serve. In addition to establishing when and how much rental the tenant is to pay, the lease should contain a provision establishing late payment fees and fees for returned checks. Such provisions work to the benefit of all involved. By impressing on the tenant the importance of timely payment, they encourage good payment habits and help avoid creating the habit of late or missed payments, which may lead to real problems for the tenant (and you). These policies help you as the property manager or property owner because they prepare the tenant for any notices he or she may receive from you concerning unpaid rentals. If the situation gets progressively worse, it may be necessary to take legal action to have the tenant evicted for nonpayment of rentals.

Property Maintenance

Even if a building is not used, it deteriorates; paint cracks, peels, and fades, while roofs develop problems from exposure to sun, cold, rain, and snow. When a building is occupied, the normal use will cause wear of some elements of the building in addition to the natural wear and tear created by nature. If you own a home, you are painfully aware of this deterioration. Even if you rent your home, you are probably aware of deterioration and the need either to prevent or repair problems associated with the building simply wearing out, even though you may not make the maintenance decision or pay for it immediately. You *will pay* for it later in your rents.

Not all maintenance around your home or in income-producing real estate is alike. Some maintenance is purely routine and involves relatively simple tasks associated with keeping the real estate livable and functioning as designed. For example, vacuuming the carpeting not only makes it cleaner and nicer looking, but also extends its life by removing dirt, which makes the carpet wear faster. This maintenance is called **routine maintenance.** In addition to routine maintenance, many parts of your home require special attention from time to time. For example, the filters in your air conditioning system and vent hoods require cleaning or replacement and air conditioning units need recharging and lubrication. All of these activities are examples of **preventive maintenance.** Finally, even if you have used preventive maintenance, some things simply stop working. At this point you must perform **corrective maintenance.** When any maintenance is not performed when it should be, it is called **deferred maintenance.**

The property manager must balance a number of factors in developing a maintenance plan and making maintenance decisions. First, the tenants have contracted for a certain level of services that must be provided. Next, the manager must be aware that maintenance affects the rents that can be charged for the space in the building. Thus, good maintenance has a positive impact on attracting and retaining tenants at premium rents. By increasing rents, maintenance also increases the value of the property when it is sold. Not all aspects of maintenance are positive; the manager must consider the cost of performing the maintenance. The manager must also take into account the desires of the owner; some owners may choose to defer maintenance in order to increase the current income from the property. (This may or may not be the smartest thing to do, depending on the condition of the property and the financial condition of the owner.)

The property manager must develop a maintenance plan that reflects the best possible balance of these factors for the owner. This balance will differ from property to property owned by the same person and also from owner to owner. The implementation of the plan requires a manager devoted to making initial and periodic inspections of the property, listing all necessary maintenance, and then following through on those needs. It is possible that in some cases the property manager and the owner will not agree on what maintenance is necessary. This may put the property manager in the uncomfortable position of being between dissatisfied tenants and an owner who will not allow the manager to perform the necessary repairs. If the differences of opinion between the manager and owner cannot be settled, the independent management firm or the manager may choose to protect his or her reputation and end the association with the owner.

Insurance

Insurance is one of those products you buy and hope you never have to use, much along the same lines as automobile jumper cables and burglar alarms. Perhaps because of the negative thoughts the events being insured against bring to mind, many people choose not to give insurance matters the consideration they deserve. Ignorance may be another reason insurance is given little attention. Consider your own insurance situation for a moment. Do you have adequate insurance on your life and your property? What would happen to your income if you became disabled? Are you adequately insured if the mail carrier files a lawsuit against you for injuries suffered from stepping on your garden rake? The phrase "adequate insurance" involves a number of factors such as the amount of insurance, events insured against, special features, and your personal financial situation. These factors mean that adequate insurance for you may not be adequate for someone else.

A good property manager will assist the owner in analyzing the insurance coverage on a property by performing an insurance audit. This means the property manager must have a working knowledge of insurance. He or she does not have to be an insurance expert, but must know enough to identify obvious gaps in coverage and effectively deal with an insurance broker or counselor. The insurance professional will be the expert, but the property manager must be able to act either as a competent adviser to the owner or decision maker if the owner asks him or her to do so.

Insurance does not really insure that certain events will or will not occur; it only guarantees that if the event does occur, you will be **indemnified** (paid) according to the provisions of the policy. The events that lead to *your* receiving payments under the insurance policy are called **perils.** Insurance can protect you financially from virtually anything. For example, actors and actresses have insured various parts of their bodies in case of injury, and in the major league baseball strike of 1981, the club owners were insured by Lloyd's of London for games not played to the tune of $100,000 per missed game. (They were not insured in 1985.) For convenience, insurance for real estate can be divided into two basic categories: casualty and liability.

Casualty Insurance If your property is destroyed by fire or damaged by hail, you have suffered a casualty loss. Casualty losses result from **perils.** Fire insurance is probably the most widely used form of **casualty insurance.** It indemnifies the insured if the property suffers damage from actual flames. It is important to note that smoke and heat damage is not usually covered by fire insurance, unless flames are actually present. Insurance covering all sorts of additional perils such as smoke, heat, hail, wind, and riot, may also be purchased. Often, many of the more common perils are grouped into a single blanket policy for which you pay one premium.

Many other perils may be insured against and often are. These perils include plate glass breakage, boiler explosion, burglary, and water damage from sprinkler malfunctions, among others. Whether or not you need these coverages is a decision you must make with advice from your insurance counselor and property manager.

Decisions must be made in regard to how much insurance is needed and the terms of that insurance, such as the amount of **deductible.** Deductible simply means that you, as the insured, will absorb losses up to a stated amount. For example, if you have $500 deductible fire insurance, you will pay for the first $500 of damage per claim. If the damage from a fire is less than $500, then you will absorb all of the loss; this is a form of self-insurance. Deductibles keep the insurance company from being barraged with relatively small claims, thereby lowering their cost of administration and losses. This, in turn, lowers the insurance premium you have to pay. Thus, the higher your deductible, the lower your premiums will be for a given amount of protection.

In deciding how much casualty insurance you need, you must know the value of the real and personal property being insured. Since land is not likely to be destroyed by any peril, the value of the improvements is of prime concern. There is some tricky language with respect to valuing these improvements that could cost you a great deal of money in case of a loss. **Actual cash value** is a commonly used phrase that means the value of the property today less accrued depreciation. *Accrued depreciation* is a term used to describe the accumulated effects of improvements wearing out. For example, carpeting, elevators, and other items wear out over time. If your building partially burns 5 years into the 10-year expected life of the elevators, the actual cash value will be reduced to reflect this aging of the elevators. The same thing will be true of other building components. Total physical depreciation will be the sum of the depreciation of all components.

If you insure your office building for actual cash value and it is destroyed, you will receive a check for an amount equal to the value of the building less any depreciation caused by aging of the building and any deductible. This is the maximum amount you will receive. This will probably not be enough to restore the building. As an alternative, if you insure your office building for **replacement cost,** the insurance company will pay you enough money to replace your office building with a new one or the maximum amount of the policy, whichever is lower. You must be careful to determine which kind of coverage you have and whether or not it is adequate.

Co-insurance In case a building is only partially damaged, say the roof suffers fire damage, you may find yourself paying for part of the loss even though the face amount of your policy is greater than the amount of the damage. In other words, you may have a $500,000 fire policy and the fire damage is only $200,000, yet you may have to pay for part of the $200,000 loss yourself. The reason for this is the **co-insurance clause** in most policies requiring that insurance coverage be at least some stated percentage of the building value in order for the insurance company to be completely responsible for partial losses. Usually you must carry insurance equal to around 80 to 90 percent of value to avoid co-insurance. To the extent you carry insurance below this required percentage, you are responsible for any loss. For example, if your policy has an 80 percent co-insurance clause and you have a building worth $800,000, you must carry $640,000 of insurance ($640,000 = $800,000 × .8). If you fail to carry this much insurance and sustain a partial loss, you must share in the loss. The percentage of the loss you must pay is equal to the percentage your actual insurance is below the $640,000 of required insurance. For example, if you carry $500,000 of insurance on the above building, the insurance company will pay 78.125 percent of a partial loss since $500,000 is 78.125 percent of the required $640,000 of insurance. Of course, you still must pay any deductible stated in the policy. This calculation is summarized as:

Insurance company responsibility =

$$\text{Insurance required by co-insurance clause} \times \text{Loss}$$

$$= \frac{\$500,000}{\$640,000} \times \text{Loss}$$

$$= .78125 \times \text{Loss}$$

This means you will be co-insuring 21.875 percent of any partial loss.

Most fire insurance policies are fire and extended coverage policies. The policy provides basic coverage for fire and lightning with extended coverage for hail, windstorm, explosion other than boiler equipment, which must be insured separately, riot, aircraft, and smoke. If you want broader coverage, you can purchase *all risk* coverage. This coverage includes collapse, falling objects, water damage, and certain other conditions not covered by the fire and extended coverage policy. There are exclusions from even this coverage and you should consult an insurance professional to determine whether you need additional coverage.

Loss of Rents Associated with a disaster will be a loss of rents while repairs are being made. To protect yourself from a loss of income during this period, you may wish to purchase **loss of rents insurance,** also called business interruption insurance. This insurance may allow you to continue your operations and make necessary payments without getting into credit or legal problems with those to whom you owe money.

Liability Insurance You have probably read of some of the tremendous settlements that have been awarded by the courts for injuries received in accidents. As a building owner or manager, you may be involved in such a suit. The size of these possible judgments means that you will want to protect yourself from the financial ruin that may result from such suits. **Liability insurance** is designed to provide this protection. It will pay up to the policy amount for court awarded or agreed-to damages involving property and people. A standard general liability policy is available to provide you with coverage for bodily injury and property damage protection. You must decide how much liability insurance is needed and the kinds of events from which you need protection.

Selecting an Insurance Professional As a property manager or owner, you need to select and cultivate a relationship with a competent insurance professional. This individual can provide much-needed information and counseling about insurance matters. He or she can find the insurance carriers offering the best protection for the money, to help you get the most for your insurance dollar. This person also facilitates the settlement of any claims and reduces the time required for payment.

Record Keeping, Reporting, and Budgeting

In conducting the business affairs of the owner, the property manager has accepted an implied responsibility to keep detailed records of operations and make timely reports to the owner. The actual recordkeeping and reporting systems will vary greatly, but the basic areas of concern will not. The owner wants to know about the condition of the property, occupancy, rental rates, collections problems, operating expenses, and overall performance of the property. Whether done by hand or computer, reports dealing with each of these areas will be generated for the owner at specified periods of time, usually monthly. Additionally, summaries for quarters and the entire year will be provided as additional information for the owner.

Operating expense data are gathered nationally by the Institute of Real Estate Management for apartments, condominiums, and suburban office buildings. The Building Owners and Managers Association International gathers operating expense data on downtown office buildings. The Urban Land Institute gathers data on shopping centers. Operations data are presented by these organizations in a number of publications providing a good bit of detail. While it is impossible to present a sample of the detailed data provided by all these reports, Figure 22.2 illustrates general, summary-type data for one type of property, garden apartments.

Preparing a **budget** is not a difficult task. Preparing a *realistic* and *useful* budget often is another story. If you put yourself in the position of the property manager whose efforts will be evaluated by comparing actual performance to budgeted figures and whose abilities and capabilities to make and implement decisions are affected by the budget, the importance of the budget becomes apparent. Likewise, the budget is important to the property owner because it translates objectives into dollar amounts and provides guidance and a tool to evaluate the success for the property manager.

Preparing a budget is a joint effort of the property manager and the owner. They must decide what period of time the budget will cover and the level of detail in the budget. The time period covered by the budget should be related to some cycle, such as rental receipts, expense payments, income taxes, calendar year, or fiscal year, if it is to be most meaningful. Usually, budgets are prepared one year in advance on a monthly basis. Sometimes they are prepared for more than 1 year, but forecasting farther than one year in the future is usually done in less detail than month-by-month, 1-year forecasts.

The appropriate level of detail depends on how the budget is to be used. For instance, a less detailed budget affords you as property manager more flexibility in expenditures than a more detailed budget. Through good management you may be able to spend more in some categories and less in others and meet your overall budget. With more detail, you stand a greater chance of having variances between budgeted and actual performance in individual categories, which you may have to explain. As the owner, you may want a more detailed budget for that very reason. However, it may not be the best use of your time to be constantly analyzing all the details of a manager's performance when the overall performance is quite good. The level of detail must be adequate to satisfy the manager's need for guidance and the owner's need for a benchmark for comparing actual performance with the budget without causing undue problems for either party. An experienced property manager can be of great assistance to the owner in designing a useful budget.

The budget should be a realistic estimate of expected operating results. It is easy to be overly optimistic about the future and produce a totally unrealistic budget. Budgets, once neatly typed, often take on an aura of importance and accuracy that was not there when they were being prepared. If the figures are unrealistic, they may lead to needless disappointment for the manager and owner over the actual operations.

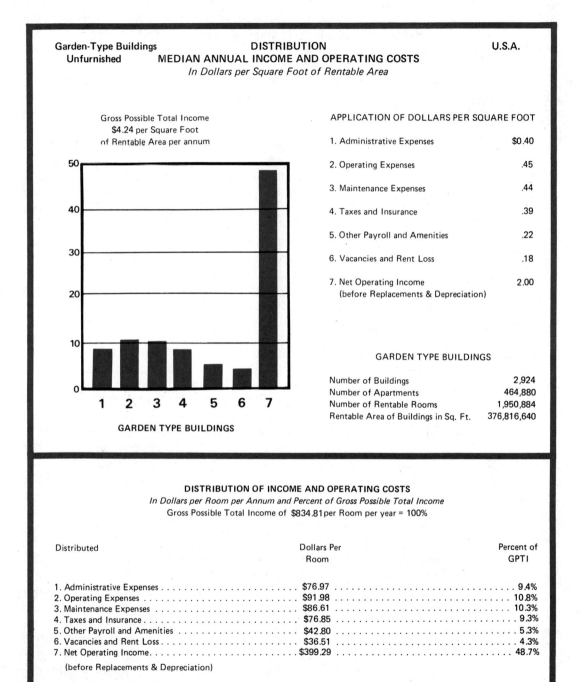

Garden-Type Buildings   **DISTRIBUTION**   U.S.A.
Unfurnished   **MEDIAN ANNUAL INCOME AND OPERATING COSTS**
In Dollars per Square Foot of Rentable Area

Gross Possible Total Income
$4.24 per Square Foot
of Rentable Area per annum

GARDEN TYPE BUILDINGS

APPLICATION OF DOLLARS PER SQUARE FOOT

1. Administrative Expenses	$0.40
2. Operating Expenses	.45
3. Maintenance Expenses	.44
4. Taxes and Insurance	.39
5. Other Payroll and Amenities	.22
6. Vacancies and Rent Loss	.18
7. Net Operating Income (before Replacements & Depreciation)	2.00

GARDEN TYPE BUILDINGS

Number of Buildings	2,924
Number of Apartments	464,880
Number of Rentable Rooms	1,950,884
Rentable Area of Buildings in Sq. Ft.	376,816,640

DISTRIBUTION OF INCOME AND OPERATING COSTS
In Dollars per Room per Annum and Percent of Gross Possible Total Income
Gross Possible Total Income of $834.81 per Room per year = 100%

Distributed	Dollars Per Room	Percent of GPTI
1. Administrative Expenses	$76.97	9.4%
2. Operating Expenses	$91.98	10.8%
3. Maintenance Expenses	$86.61	10.3%
4. Taxes and Insurance	$76.85	9.3%
5. Other Payroll and Amenities	$42.80	5.3%
6. Vacancies and Rent Loss	$36.51	4.3%
7. Net Operating Income	$399.29	48.7%
(before Replacements & Depreciation)		

Figure 22.2   Example of published summary expense data. (Source: *Income/Expense Analysis: Apartments.* Chicago: Institute of Real Estate Management of the National Association of Realtors.)

Along these same lines, the budget should contain footnotes recording all the assumptions underlying its development.

LEGAL ENVIRONMENT OF PROPERTY MANAGEMENT

The property manager's ability to satisfactorily perform necessary tasks is affected by various aspects of law. Perhaps most obvious are the real property and contract law aspects associated with leasing. Earlier in the chapter, the importance of a review of these areas was emphasized. However, less obvious but tremendously important to the property manager are the areas of landlord-tenant laws, rent control, and laws pertaining to limiting residential units to adults only.

Many states have passed landlord-tenant laws that apply to residential leases. The usual reason for passing these laws is to provide greater legal protection to tenants; however, in many instances landlords also benefit from a clearer statement of the rights and obligations of both parties in a residential lease agreement. A model landlord–tenant law, called the Uniform Residential Landlord and Tenant Act, has been developed. This model act, or an amended version of it, has been adopted by several states. While landlord-tenant acts vary from state to state, they all deal with similar issues. Specifically, your state's landlord-tenant act will address such topics as property maintenance, conditions under which rent may be withheld, landlord's right to enter the property, security deposits and their return, and eviction of tenants.

Rent control laws that establish the maximum rental rates for residential rental properties have been enacted by numerous political jurisdictions. The laws have been enacted as an attempt to make rental housing more affordable. A significant amount of controversy has surrounded the enactment and implementation of rent control legislation. Proponents argue that rent controls produce affordable housing for segments of the population needing it. Opponents argue that rent controls fail to provide adequate income for maintenance and rehabilitation and reduce or eliminate the motivation for producing additional rental housing units. Rent control will continue to be an important real estate issue in the 1980s — so important that anyone in real estate should continue to learn about it and its impacts on investment and management.

Yet another area of legal activity is that of whether children can be barred from residential rental properties. Many rental properties are available to adults only. Reasons for this policy include tenant demand for such complexes and the increase in maintenance costs associated with children. However, in some communities it is difficult to find reasonably priced residential rental property that will accept children. This situation creates a hardship on families depending on such housing. Some communities have passed laws eliminating, or limiting in some manner, adults only rental properties. These laws have important ramifications for real estate investment and management.

WHO MANAGES PROPERTY?

If you own a home, you are a property manager. You make many of the same types of decisions as professional property managers, such as what kind of maintenance to perform and when. The difference is that professional managers earn their living managing real estate assets. Who are these people, how did they learn about **property management,** and how do you find good property managers?

If you look in the Yellow Pages under "real estate management," you will find firms that offer management services in addition to brokerage and other real estate services and other firms that are purely real estate management firms. Property managers come from all backgrounds and have found their way into property management by design and by accident. Some got into real estate management out of necessity; properties were not performing well and they were forced to take over management responsibilities. Others simply became interested in property management and joined that profession.

Many firms and individual property managers specialize in a particular type of property. They specialize because it allows them to concentrate on developing the skill and expertise necessary to deal with the subtleties of that particular type of property. This is not to say that managing each type of property is completely different from managing all other types but, rather, that differences do exist in the property management activities discussed earlier, which make specialization useful in some instances. Among the categories of properties in which property managers specialize are

Commercial

Residential (single family, duplex, triplex, and fourplex)

Residential (apartments)

Condominiums

Mobile home parks

Shopping centers

Industrial parks

Property managers have courses available to them for developing skills in virtually all of these areas.

WHO DOES WHAT
IN A PROPERTY MANAGEMENT FIRM?

If you were to start a property management firm tomorrow and perform all of the functions associated with property management, you would perform a variety of activities. These activities would range from handling the routine problems of tenants to preparing and analyzing reports for each property to planning your overall management approach and dealing with property owners. As your firm grows, you would probably find that it pays to have some specialization; you simply cannot do everything.

Other real estate management firms have discovered the same thing and, as a result, three levels of property managers have been identified. Starting with a specific property, the property manager who is in the building handling the day-to-day problems is called a **site manager.** The site manager spends a great deal of time dealing with rather short-term problems and implementing policy established by others rather than policies he established. The site manager will report to a **property manager,** the person actually responsible for the management of a particular property. The property manager is the person who makes the decisions and policies that are implemented on a daily basis by the site manager. Finally, running the property management firm is the **executive property manager.** The executive property manager, in effect, manages the property managers to see that the management services provided are of the quality expected and that management operations are conducted in a way that is profitable for the management firm.

SELECTING A PROPERTY MANAGER

You have essentially three options with respect to obtaining property management services: manage the property yourself, hire a property manager as an employee, or contract with a property manager on a fee basis. Which of these options you choose depends on the size of your building, how much direct control you want over the property manager, and cost.

Managing the Property Yourself

This is the only financially viable option for many smaller properties. These properties simply cannot produce enough income to pay someone for performing the management duties. If you own or are thinking of buying a smaller property, you should carefully estimate the amount of time you will have to devote to management and estimate what your personal management services are worth in dollar terms. You should then include this estimate in operating expenses to assess your investment return. The point is simple: a real estate investment should be more than a part-time job unless you have all kinds of free time that desperately needs to be filled. It could be that you would be financially better off spending the property management time on your regular job to earn extra income and investing the money necessary for the real estate investment in an investment requiring little attention, even if it produces a lower return than the real estate investment.

If the property is still desirable after this test, then you may find personal management an attractive situation. Certainly by managing the property yourself you will have direct control over management and will develop an appreciation for good property management. If the property is an apartment complex, you may be able to hire a resident manager to handle many of the routine problems as well as some of the leasing duties in return for free or reduced rent.

Property Management Education

Property management is based on the same general concepts and activities as any type of management. The basic activities associated with management are planning, organizing, actuating (motivating), and controlling. The property manager must have a thorough understanding of these management activities as well as the real estate commodity and how its characteristics affect the management task. Additionally, the property manager must have certain other specialized knowledge in the areas of accounting, marketing, construction, and finance. Obviously, a good business administration education at a college or university would provide a strong background for anyone interested in property management. However, such a background is not a necessity for getting into property management, and even someone with such a background would likely have to take additional courses dealing specifically with property management.

Property management courses are offered at community colleges and 4-year colleges and universities, and by professional property management organizations. Perhaps the most extensive and intensive property management courses are offered by national organizations of property managers. The Institute of Real Estate Management (IREM), a part of the National Association of Realtors; the Building Owners and Managers Association International (BOMAI); the National Apartment Association (NAA); the National Association of Homebuilders (NAHB); and the International Council of Shopping Centers (ICSC) all offer property management courses relating to their specializations.

Professional Property Management Designations

IREM, BOMAI, NAA, NAHB, and ICSC each offer designation programs to promote education, professionalism, and competence in property management. These programs recognize property managers meeting established education, examination, and experience requirements by awarding them a designation. IREM awards the Certified Property Manager (CPM) to candidates considered competent to manage virtually any type of real property and the Accredited Resident Manager (ARM) designation to those considered competent to be on-site managers. BOMAI awards the Real Property Administrator (RPA) designation to those completing its program. ICSC grants the Certified Shopping Center Manager (CSM) designation, and NAA awards the Certified Apartment Manager (CAM), Certified Apartment Maintenance Technician (CAMT), and Certified Property Supervisor (CPS) designations. The NAHB awards the Registered Apartment Manager (RAM) designation.

You should view these designations not as an absolute guarantee of quality but, rather, a demonstration of the property manager's desire to improve the quality of management services. While there are excellent property managers not possessing any designations, these professional designations provide useful evidence of basic competence at one point in time. If you are searching for a property manager, a designated property manager or a candidate for a designation will likely be worth considering.

An Employee as Property Manager

Hiring a professional to manage your property as an employee provides you with direct control over property management activities. The employee is answerable to you and can make requested adjustments very quickly. By employing your property manager, you can also control who the property manager hires to perform various jobs. If selection and control of management personnel is important to you, then you may want to employ a property manager and maintain this extensive control.

Hiring a property manager requires a substantial recurring expense. Not only must you pay the manager's salary, but you will also have to provide other benefits or sufficient additional salary for the manager to purchase his or her own benefit package, to attract a professional manager. In addition, you will have to provide office space and a support staff ranging from one secretary to many employees. You should carefully consider your present and future scale of real estate investment to see if you want to make the commitment to employing a property manager.

Fee Property Management

Property management firms exist that specialize in managing the properties of others. These firms vary in quality, but if you check out their reputations you can likely find a competent one. Your relationship with these firms is established by a **property management contract.** This contract establishes an agency relationship in which the owner is the principal and the firm is the agent. This contract is somewhat longer and more detailed than the brokerage listing agreements considered in Chapter 20. This is because the scope of property management services includes a larger number of duties for both property manager and owner that need to be clearly specified in the contract. Rather than being a special agent, as are real estate brokers, property managers are often *general agents.* However, just as in brokerage, the management agreement establishes the rules of the game for the agency relationship.

Property management firms are usually compensated on the basis of the income produced by the property, with a minimum fee being guaranteed regardless of rents. Property managers may receive additional compensation for performing special duties. If you own a small property, you may have a difficult time finding a property management firm willing to manage it. The costs associated with smaller projects make the necessary fees prohibitively large. Also, smaller projects usually do not produce the premium rents of larger, more prestigious projects which affects the fees charged by the management firm.

A good property management firm offers you the chance to have professional property managers operating your property. In some cases, you will be able to take advantage of the economies of scale enjoyed by management firms to hire better, more competent management than you can provide yourself or using employees. On the other hand, you lose some of the control over who actually manages the property and which employees are used on the project. Of course, the property manager will listen to your point of view, but you are at least one step removed from directly calling the shots.

PROPERTY MANAGERS AS CONSULTANTS

As a professional property manager, you may be asked to act as consultant in matters not involving the actual operation of property. For example, you may be asked to develop rental rate schedules for a property being purchased or developed. Or, you may be asked to prepare an operating expense schedule for a property before and after certain renovation work is undertaken. In other cases, the property manager may be consulted to inspect a property from the perspective of estimating its condition and the cost of making necessary repairs. In some instances, a property manager will perform complete feasibility studies for clients constructing new improvements or renovating existing ones. Lease provisions, accounting and reporting systems, and maintenance programs represent other areas where you, as a property manager, may provide counseling services on a fee basis.

CHANGES IN PROPERTY MANAGEMENT

Recent trends in real estate development resulting in larger, more complex projects involving more than one type of space have affected real estate management. The skills necessary to manage a single project that may contain office space, hotel space, apartments, and condominiums are varied indeed. Some projects contain mixed uses in a single building while others have several buildings integrated into one development. The larger scale of projects has created a new environment for property managers. The World Trade Center in New York contains over 8 million square feet of office space. If you consider recent projects in your city, you will probably find larger, more elaborate projects than have ever been built before, creating new challenges for the property manager.

The growing number of condominium projects also presents a challenge for the property manager. When managing a condominium, the property manager works for the owners' association, often made up of people inexperienced in real estate ownership and management. Establishing policies and procedures may be more difficult than for a property with a single owner.

SUMMARY

Property management is a real estate support activity involving leasing, collection of rents, maintenance, insurance decisions, and budgeting and recordkeeping. As a property owner, you have the option of managing the property yourself, having an employee manage it for you, or contracting with an independent property manager to act as our general agent in managing the property. Each situation has advantages and disadvantages with respect to the time you must devote to management activities, the amount of control you have over necessary decisions, and cost. In deciding which alternative best fits your needs, an understanding of what property managers do is most beneficial.

Property management is based on the same general concepts and activities as any type of management. In addition to a thorough understanding of these activities, a property manager must have an understanding of the real estate commodity and how its characteristics affect its management.

Property management courses are offered at community colleges, senior colleges, universities, and professional property management organizations. National organizations of property managers offer a wide assortment of courses, usually specializing in a certain type of property. These organizations also offer designations to promote education, competence, and professionalism. When choosing a property manager, these designations provide evidence of basic competence and may prove helpful in the selection of a property manager.

There are three basic levels of property management, beginning with the site manager, who works on the premises of the property, handling the routine operations. These routine activities are determined by the decisions and policies established by the property manager. An executive property manager is responsible for insuring that property managers are providing effective and profitable management operations. In addition to managing properties, professional property managers, because of their experience and expertise, are often hired as consultants. In this role, they develop or evaluate rental rates and operating expenses, report on property condition and its impact on operating expenses, report on the necessary repairs, develop management plans, and provide any number of other valuable services for developers and equity investors.

QUICK QUIZ

1. A plan devised to effectively lease the space available in a structure is called _____ .

   a. a marketing plan   c. a space plan
   b. a business plan   d. none of the above

2. Which of the following is not usually a property management activity?

   a. leasing   c. insurance
   b. collections   d. financing

3. Relatively simple tasks associated with keeping real estate livable and functioning as designed is _____ .

   a. preventive maintenance   c. corrective maintenance
   b. routine maintenance   d. periodic maintenance

4. If an asset is destroyed, actual cash value insurance pays the insured on the basis of the asset's _____ .

   a. value less accrued depreciation
   b. actual cost of replacement
   c. original cost plus an inflation factor
   d. wholesale cost new

5. The person ultimately responsible for managing a particular property is called the _____ .

    a. executive property manager   c. site manager

    b. property manager   d. chief property manager

6. Property managers are often _____ agents rather than _____ agents.

7. Property management has been affected by trends toward _____ and _____ projects.

8. The provision in an insurance policy requiring an insured to carry insurance equal to some specified minimum percentage of an asset's value or share in losses is called the _____ .

9. Preparing a budget for a property is a joint effort of the _____ and _____ .

10. Two of the organizations providing property management education are _____ and _____ .

**QUESTIONS
AND
EXERCISES**

1. Evaluate the property maintenance program for the building in which you work, live, or have class.

2. How would you screen potential tenants for a regional mall shopping center?

3. Prepare a collections policy for an apartment in which rents are due monthly.

4. Why would someone choose to self-insure some risks?

5. If you were a property owner, how would you evaluate the performance of your fee property management firm?

**KEY
TERMINOLOGY**

actual cash value	executive property manager
budget	indemnified
casualty insurance	insurance
co-insurance	leasing
collections	liability insurance
corrective maintenance	loss of rents insurance
deductible	perils
deferred maintenance	preventive maintenance

property management
property management contract
property manager

replacement cost
routine maintenance
site manager

**IF YOU WANT
TO READ MORE**

JAMES C. DOWNS, *Principles of Real Estate Management,* 12th ed. (Chicago: Institute of Real Estate Management, 1980).

ROBERT C. KYLE and ANN M. KENNEHAN, *Property Management* (Chicago: Real Estate Education Company, 1979).

WILLIAM M. SHENKEL, *Modern Real Estate Management* (New York: McGraw-Hill Book Company, 1980).

23
Real Estate Appraisal: basic concepts and the appraisal process

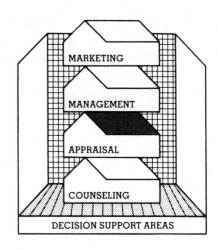

MARKETING

MANAGEMENT

APPRAISAL

COUNSELING

DECISION SUPPORT AREAS

PREVIEW   If there is a central theme underlying your involvement in real estate it is estimating value and the problems associated with that task. You will constantly be interested in what your property or a property you are considering developing or purchasing is worth. In Chapter 18, on equity investment, you learned about one type of value, investment value. This value is what a property is worth to a particular investor. Another critical value concept is **market value.** The market value of Blackacre, undeveloped and developed, affects all of your decisions involving what to do with it. Market value also plays an important role in the decisions made by lenders. Understanding market value, as well as the forces that shape it, and how it is estimated, is an important piece of knowledge affecting your involvement with real estate either as a career or as an investment. Estimating market value is called appraising. This chapter introduces the basic appraisal concepts necessary to understand the estimation of market value. After reading and studying this chapter you will understand:

1. The definition of market value.
2. The basic principles underlying real estate appraisal.
3. Who performs real estate appraisals.
4. That real estate appraisal is a combination of art and science.

5. The appraisal process as a systematic approach to problem solving.
6. The approaches to estimating market value.

Value can be a confusing concept — primarily because there are so many different types of value. Earlier, you learned about investment value, which was defined as the value of an investment to a particular investor. In dealing with the federal income tax, you learned about book value used for calculating gains or losses on the sale of real estate. Other types of value that may come to your mind may include assessed value, insurable value, and market value. It is not surprising that the word *value* creates some confusion in your mind.

However, you cannot ignore value concepts and estimates just because of a little confusion. Value estimates are important to you because they affect decisions and, ultimately, your financial well-being. Market

Table 23.1. Typical Situations Creating a Need for Market Value Estimates

1. Transfer of ownership
   a. To help prospective buyers decide on offering prices
   b. To help prospective sellers determine acceptable selling prices
   c. To establish a basis for exchanges of real property
   d. To establish a basis for reorganization or for merging the ownership of multiple properties
2. Financing and credit.
   a. To arrive at the essential security offered for a proposed mortgage loan
   b. To provide an investor with a sound basis for deciding whether to purchase real estate mortgages, bonds, or other types of securities.
   c. To establish a basis for a decision regarding the insuring or underwriting of a loan on real property
3. Just compensation in condemnation proceedings
   a. To estimate market value of property as a whole — that is, before the taking
   b. To estimate value after the taking
   c. To allocate market values between the part taken and damage to the remainder
4. Realty decision making
   a. To identify and quantify most probable markets and related timing
   b. To determine marketability of a proposed land use
   c. To analyze or compare real estate investment alternatives
   d. To decide feasibility of accomplishing stated investment goals
5. A basis for taxation
   a. To separate assets into depreciable items, such as buildings, and nondepreciable items, such as land, and to estimate applicable depreciation rates
   b. To determine gift or inheritance taxes
6. A basis for rental schedules and lease provisions
7. Feasibility in relation to a renovation program
8. A basis for corporations or third-party companies to purchase homes of transferred employees
9. Other situations in which a decision about real estate is necessary

SOURCE: *What to Look for in an Appraisal*, American Institute of Real Estate Appraisers, 1979.

value is a particularly critical concept because it affects so many important decisions, as indicated in Table 23.1.

This chapter deals with **market value** — its importance, definition, underlying principles, and estimation. All of these topics are grouped under the heading **appraisal,** or the more modern term, **valuation.** You *will not* be a professional appraiser after reading this chapter. You *will* have a sufficient understanding to make better use of appraisal principles in all of your real estate work, as well as making better use of professional real estate appraisals. The following chapter expands these concepts by considering their application in single family and income property appraisal.

WHAT IS MARKET VALUE?

Many people talk about market value as though its definition is clearly understood by all. Unfortunately, market value is clearly understood by few people. Intuitively, market value is the answer to the question, "What is a specific parcel of real estate worth?" Professional appraisers, who sign their name to appraisals and often appear in court to testify as to how market value is defined and estimated, have found a more detailed definition necessary. Actually, two definitions representing two schools of thought have achieved some degree of acceptance among professional appraisers. They will be referred to here as the highest price definition and the most probable selling price definition.

Highest Price Definition

There really isn't an "official" definition of market value. However, the closest thing to it is the definition contained in a book entitled *Real Estate Appraisal Terminology,* published jointly by two leading appraisal organizations, the American Institute of Real Estate Appraisers and the International Society of Real Estate Appraisers. The definition in that book has roots in the courts, which decide what definition of market value will be used in each case before them. For our purposes, this definition is referred to as the highest price definition of market value (HPD). The complete definition as stated in *Real Estate Appraisal Terminology* is given here:

The highest price in terms of money which a property will bring in a competitive and open market under all conditions requisite to a fair sale, the buyer and seller, each acting prudently, knowledgeably, and assuming the price is not affected by undue stimulus.

Implicit in this definition is the consummation of a sale as of a specified date and the passing of title from seller to buyer under conditions whereby:

1. Buyer and seller are typically motivated.
2. Both parties are well informed or well advised, and each is acting in what he considers his own best interest.
3. A reasonable time is allowed for exposure in the open market.
4. Payment is made in cash or its equivalent.
5. Financing, if any, is on terms generally available in the community at the specified date and typical for the property type in its locale.
6. The price represents a normal consideration for the property sold unaffected by special financing amounts or terms, services, fees, costs, or credits incurred in the transaction.

Most Probable Selling Price Definition

There is some question as to whether the HPD and its conditions accurately portray most real estate markets. For instance, consider its second condition. Although it is difficult not to agree that buyers and sellers act in what they consider to be their best interest, it is a little more difficult to accept universally the assumption that in actual real estate markets both parties to a transaction are well informed or well advised. As you read the chapter on real estate markets, you learned that real estate markets are often characterized by poor or costly information which means that many buyers and sellers are not likely to be well informed. Likewise, condition one is difficult to accept without reservation. Many buyers and sellers are likely buying and selling because of some compulsion, such as being transferred to a new job in another city or having financial problems. You can go through the other conditions of the HPD and make similar arguments.

To all of this you may say, "Big deal, what real difference does it make how market value is defined?" The answer to this question is that it can make a great deal of difference or none at all. If the real estate market assumed by the conditions of the HPD has characteristics different from those actually existing, then market value estimates made using that definition represent what market value *should be* if the conditions *were* true, not necessarily what market value is, given the actual characteristics of real estate markets. The greater the difference between the assumed conditions and reality, the greater the possible difference between market value as defined by the HPD and a property's actual worth in the marketplace. The most probable selling price definition of market value is proposed as a means of overcoming this problem. It defines market value as the most probable selling price of a property under conditions prevailing in the market at that time. That is, the real estate market with all its possible problems is considered *as it exists*.

Implications of Different Market Value Definitions

Real estate appraisers should include a definition of market value in appraisal reports. If you have any questions about the definition of market value used in a particular report, you should ask the appraiser whether a significant difference in market value would result from a different definition of market value. Actually, as you know from Chapter 9, on real estate markets, the more efficient the real estate market, the less difference is likely to be created by the use of either definition. This is true because market efficiency is determined by market characteristics, and the more efficient a real estate market, the more closely it resembles the market assumed in the highest price definition. In reality, many appraisers may say they are using the HPD, but are using real estate market data reflecting the actual characteristics of real estate markets to produce a most probable selling price market value.

Market Value and Market Price

You should avoid using the terms market price and market value to mean the same thing. Market price is the result of a transaction. It is an historical number established by negotiation between a buyer and a seller. Market value is an *estimate* of the worth of real estate at a particular point in time. The market price for that real estate will not be known until it is sold. Numerically, market price will equal market value only rarely.

WHO APPRAISES?

Professional appraisers are not the only people who estimate the market value of real estate. If you have bought a home, you probably became skilled at estimating the value of homes in certain parts of your city just from your shopping experiences. Your market value estimating methods may have been very organized or quite random, depending on your nature. Real estate agents also estimate market value (most probable selling price) when they perform a competitive market analysis for a seller, as considered in Chapter 20. In performing this analysis, agents should follow an organized approach using market data and judgment about how comparable the seller's home is to homes for which listing and sales data are available. Professional appraisers represent the next level of appraisal activity. They use a systematic approach to estimating market value, accept a fee for their work, and stake their professional reputation on the estimate by signing their names to the appraisal.

Even professional appraisers, with their market knowledge and systematic approach to valuation, cannot eliminate a subjective element from appraisal. They are dealing in a market environment that often does not provide all the data they need to estimate market value purely on the basis of objective data. They must overcome these deficiencies with judgment and not so common, common sense. You should realize that appraising is a *combination* of art and science involving technical skills and a good sense of the market. Professional appraisers must possess a good bit more of the art *and* the science than others who occasionally "appraise" properties.

Appraisers do not need real estate licenses in most states if their only real estate business is appraisal. If they are involved in other real estate activity, such as brokerage, a license may be required for that activity. As a result, virtually anyone can become a professional appraiser. Reputations are created rather quickly and incompetent appraisers are readily discovered.

WHY DO WE NEED APPRAISERS?

From Chapter 9, you know that real estate markets are not as efficient as some markets, such as securities markets. Because of this inefficiency, it is often difficult to find readily accessible, reliable data for estimating the value of real estate. Therefore, if you want to sell Blackacre and need to estimate its market value, there is usually no easy way to observe price data suitable for estimating market value. Thus, to estimate Blackacre's market value requires that you scrape up any available information and then apply judgment as to how dependable and comparable the information is and how the market may have changed since the transactions occurred. This task could be costly and time consuming, and your judgment may be faulty. Fortunately, there are professional appraisers who will estimate the market value of Blackacre. If real estate markets were efficient enough to provide sufficient amounts of readily obtainable, reliable data, these real estate appraisers would seldom be needed. However, they are not, and appraisers are needed.

SELECTED APPRAISAL PRINCIPLES

Since appraisal is a form of applied economics, it is not surprising to find that it is founded on some basic economic concepts, called appraisal principles. These principles deal with the actions of buyers and sellers, the operations of real estate markets, and their collective impact on market value estimation. What follows is a discussion of *selected* appraisal principles, not a complete listing.

Principle of Highest and Best Use

If you seek to develop Blackacre, the chances are good that you will develop it in what you think is its most profitable use. You will do so because it is in your economic best interest. Likewise, any future owners of Blackacre and owners of different parcels will also tend to do the same thing. This tendency is embodied in the Principle of Highest and Best Use, which states that land tends to be developed with the use and in the quality and intensity which produces the most profit. If you consider that the value of land is directly related to the profitability of any use that can be made of it, the highest and best use is also the use that creates the highest present land value.

From earlier chapters dealing with the physical characteristics of real estate and land use controls, you know that you are not free to do anything you wish with the parcel — physical characteristics and legal limitations effectively eliminate certain development ideas. Thus, you must consider programs of development that readily satisfy these constraints or have a reasonable probability of satisfying them. For instance, if office development is the most profitable use of Blackacre, but zoning allows only single family homes, office development would be the highest and best use only if you feel that a reasonable likelihood exists for rezoning Blackacre. If such a likelihood does not exist, then you would not consider office development to be the highest and best use. You must be concerned not only with obtaining office zoning, but also with the intensity of allowable office development. Obtaining office zoning alone may not be enough, if rather intensive office development must occur for office zoning to be more profitable than single family development. You must be able to obtain the right kind of office zoning.

Another important aspect of highest and best use is that of market demand for the space being developed. When you felt that office space would be more profitable than single family development, you must have sensed that adequate demand existed for office space to justify such development. The income expected from a land use must be sufficient to warrant the expenditures necessary to produce it. That is, the use must be financially feasible to be considered as the highest and best use. If no development program is feasible, then the highest and best use is for the land to be left vacant or, put another way, to simply hold the Earth together.

Thus, the highest and best use of Blackacre, or any site, depends on a number of factors whose values are uncertain. This means that people may disagree on the highest and best use at any point in time. All of this is reflected in the definition of highest and best use contained in *Real Estate Appraisal Terminology:*

. . . that reasonable and probable use that will support the highest present value, as defined, as of the effective date of the appraisal

or

. . . that use, from among reasonable, probable and legal alternative uses, found to be physically possible, appropriately supported, financially feasible, and which results in the highest land value.

Highest and best use is important to you as the owner or appraiser of Blackacre because you will value the land as though it is being employed in its highest and best use. You will do so because a reasonable and prudent potential buyer would be expected to do so. Thus, differences of opinion over the highest and best use may mean a great deal of difference in market value estimates.

Principle of Change

This principle assumes that real estate markets are dynamic and constantly changing. For the appraiser, this means that factors affecting market values, and market values themselves, are always changing. For example, the announcement of a new shopping center at a certain intersection affects the value of all land around that intersection. This principle is the basis for requiring that appraisals be made as of a certain date.

Principle of Substitution

This principle covers a basic concept of consumer behavior. It suggests that when two or more parcels of real estate providing the same utility are available, demand will be greatest for the less expensive parcel. This not too surprising revelation provides the foundation for the three approaches to valuation to be considered later in this chapter.

Principle of Anticipation

The Principle of Anticipation states that value results from expected future benefits. Benefits may be tangible, such as the income a property is expected to produce, or intangible, such as the pride of ownership attached to a property. If the present value of these future benefits can be estimated, it will represent an estimate of the worth of the property. This principle is the basis for the income approach discussed later.

Principle of Increasing and Decreasing Returns

If you choose to develop office space on a portion of Blackacre, say a 4-acre corner, you must decide what quality and quantity of space to develop. With respect to quality, it is fairly easy to see that up to a point, increases in quality will add to the rents and value of the office building. However, beyond a certain point, tenants will not pay for the added luxury, so the increase in value would not offset the increased cost. The same thing holds for increasing the quality of rentable square footage while keeping parking constant and facing the rising construction costs associated with high-rise construction. How much will you develop? Conceptually, the answer is easy; you will develop to the point that an additional dollar of outlay no longer increases value by more than a dollar. At this point you have milked every possible extra dollar from your investment. You can readily see how this concept applies to determining highest and best use.

Principle of Contribution

The Principle of Contribution is a specialized version of the Principle of Increasing and Decreasing Returns. It asserts that the value of a component is equal to its contribution to the overall value of an asset, not the cost of the component. For example, it may cost $10,000 to completely renovate your kitchen, but such a renovation adds only $8000 to the value of your home. Thus, the value of the renovation is $8000, not $10,000. On a purely financial basis, such as selling your home immediately after the renovation, the renovation is a losing proposition. However, if you are going to live in the home for several more years, the investment may be justified in increased personal satisfaction.

HOW IS MARKET VALUE ESTIMATED?

Appraisers are not mysterious black-boxes that produce market value estimates out of thin air. They use one or more basic valuation approaches in every appraisal. What's more, these basic approaches are founded on relatively simple reasoning. If you were asked to estimate the market value of a small apartment complex, do any valuation approaches come to mind intuitively? Perhaps if you consider that the appraiser must be able to simulate the thinking and actions of buyers and sellers in the marketplace, something will come to you. That is, the appraiser should have a feel for the values buyers are likely to impute to a property and the values sellers of competitive properties are likely to think reasonable. Each buyer calculates an investment value he or she feels is reasonable. You may be willing to pay more for an apartment building than another investor and so on. Likewise, the sellers of comparable structures are willing to accept different prices. The appraiser tries to capture, or simulate, as much of this thinking as possible in appraising a property. In other words, the appraiser tries to answer the question, "What are buyers and sellers doing with respect to properties of this type?"

If simulating and capturing the essence of the market is the appraiser's job, doesn't it seem reasonable to consider the options open to a buyer in the market? For example, in appraising the small apartment building mentioned above, the appraiser may feel that all of the prices acceptable to buyers and sellers are as illustrated in Figure 23.1. In this figure, the prices buyers and sellers are willing to pay or accept are indicated on the horizontal axis. On the vertical axis are percentages. The height of each bar represents the percentage of buyers or sellers thinking the apartment complex's value falls in the range indicated on the horizontal axis. For example, the appraiser perceives that 25 percent of all buyers would be willing to spend between $260,000 and $270,000 for the complex. A transaction can occur anywhere in the area where the two distributions overlap, since in this area buyers are willing to pay more than sellers demand. For this property, the price at which a transaction is likely ranges from $260,000 to $290,000. The price at which the transaction occurs depends on which buyer and seller find each other and the relative bargaining strength of each. Usually, the appraiser is asked to estimate the one potential price *most representative* of the market value of the property. That is, the appraiser typically

Figure 23.1 Appraiser's perception of the market.

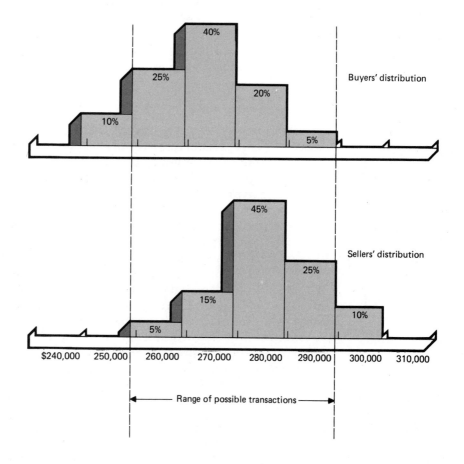

concentrates on the range of possible values in Figure 23.1 and estimates the value that best represents that range, not an easy task.

Conceptually, to estimate this range, the appraiser will consider the options open to buyers and sellers. First, any buyer could buy another property instead of the subject property. Thus, recent sales data on comparable properties may provide clues to this range of possible transactions. Second, any buyer could construct improvements to satisfy his or her needs instead of buying the subject property. This means the appraiser can estimate the cost of such construction, including land costs, to get another piece of evidence about the options available to buyers. Finally, if the property is being purchased for the income it produces, a buyer may purchase another property producing a similar income stream. The appraiser can use knowledge of the rate of return being required on similar properties to value the income stream produced by the subject property.

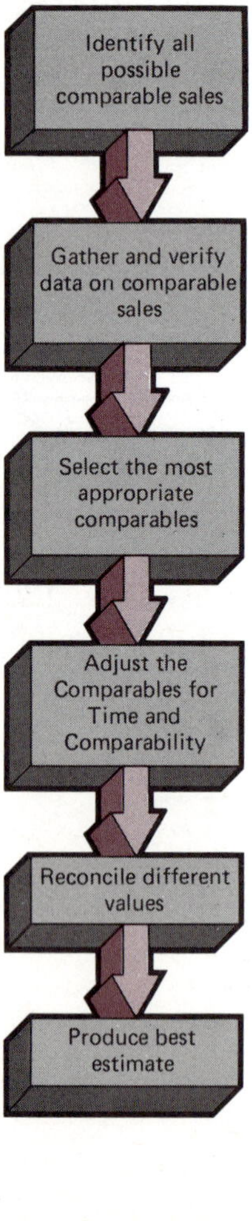

These approaches to valuation are called the sales comparison, cost, and income capitalization approaches, respectively. They are *all* based on the market, but emphasize different aspects of it, corresponding to alternatives available to buyers. As you will see, even the cost approach makes use of market-determined adjustments to arrive at the cost of replacing a property. These approaches to valuation are obviously not as simple as they seem. Each approach involves a number of steps and a good deal of judgment. Each approach also has strengths and weaknesses.

Figure 23.2 Steps in the sales comparison approach.

Identify all possible comparable sales

Gather and verify data on comparable sales

Select the most appropriate comparables

Adjust the Comparables for Time and Comparability

Reconcile different values

Produce best estimate

Sales Comparison Approach

The sales comparison approach relies on finding reliable, recent sales data on properties comparable to the subject property. Such sales are called **comparables,** or simply comps. If many recent, high quality comps are available, the appraiser has strong evidence for estimating market value. In most cases, even the best comps require the appraiser to make some subjective adjustment to the price to offset differences between the comp and the subject property or the effects of time since the comparable sale occurred.

In simplest form, the sales comparison approach involves identifying all possible sales that could act as comps, gathering all possible data about those comps, verifying the data when possible, selecting the most appropriate comps, adjusting the comps for time and comparability to the subject property, and reconciling different indicated values to produce a single best estimate of market value. These steps are summarized in Figure 23.2. As you can see, what seems like a straightforward, reliable, and objective approach to valuation is not necessarily so. Each step in the approach can create problems that may affect the ability of the appraiser to rely on, or even use, this approach. For example, in appraising a church, the appraiser may find that the very first step, identifying

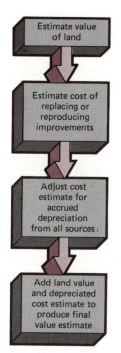

Figure 23.3 Steps in the cost approach.

possible sales, effectively eliminates any chance of relying heavily on this approach because no sales may have been made in the last 5 years.

Cost Approach

In the **cost approach,** you will estimate the value of a subject property by estimating the value of the land and adding to it the cost of reproducing or replacing the improvements. The logic behind this approach is that such an approach is an alternative to a buyer, and a rational person would pay no more for an existing structure than it would cost to buy land and build a structure producing a similar level of satisfaction. Likewise, no rational seller would think they could get more than this price from a buyer willing to wait for such construction. As with the market data approach, the supporting logic is straightforward while the application of the approach requires care and judgment to obtain reliable results.

The cost approach involves four basic steps (Figure 23.3). First, you must estimate the value of the land as though vacant and available for development, using the market data approach. Second, you must estimate today's cost of replacing or reproducing the improvements. Third, you must estimate and reduce this cost estimate for loss in value due to all causes, called **accrued depreciation.** Fourth, you must add the cost, adjusted for depreciation, to the land cost to produce the final value estimate using the cost approach.

Before estimating costs, you must decide whether you are going to estimate replacement cost or reproduction cost. **Reproduction cost** is the current cost of constructing a replica of the subject property using the same or very close to the same materials. **Replacement cost** is the cost of constructing improvements of similar utility using current standards of material, design, and skill. In theory, reproduction cost is the appropriate cost to be estimated. However, if reproduction cost is strictly interpreted, it is rarely estimated in practice. Appraisers generally deviate from an exact replica in some manner, often because of an inability to find reliable cost estimates for certain outmoded materials and skills. Only relatively new improvements readily lend themselves to reproduction cost. In practice, appraisers generally estimate the cost of replacing the subject improvement with one of a design as close as possible to the subject using modern materials and building techniques.

As stated above, **depreciation,** as used in appraisal, is the loss in value from any cause. The sources of depreciation may be categorized into three classifications: physical deterioration, functional obsolescence, and economic obsolescence. **Physical deterioration** is the loss in value due to the actual "wearing out" of the improvements. **Functional obsolescence** is the inability of an improvement to perform the job for which it is designed. For instance, the increased use of computer equipment calls for office buildings with adequate air conditioning and floors strong enough to support the weight of the machines. Buildings built several years ago that do not have these capabilities suffer from depreciation from functional obsolescence. You can probably think of other situations where changes in design and use have created a reduction in value. **Economic obsolescence,** also called locational obsolescence, is the loss in value due to factors outside the property itself. For example, the deterioration of a neighborhood may reduce the value of a home. Likewise, changes in traffic patterns may reduce the value of a retail store. The appraiser must estimate depreciation from each source by carefully analyzing the market and estimating the impact of various types of depreciation on a property's value. This link between the cost approach and the market is often overlooked.

Market value, reproduction or replacement cost, and accrued depreciation are closely related. First, since replacement cost assumes new materials and new standards, all functional obsolescence has been eliminated. Thus, replacement cost is equal to reproduction cost minus functional obsolescence. Next, market value is equal to reproduction cost minus all accrued depreciation, or replacement cost minus physical deterioration and economic obsolescence. The only way reproduction cost, replacement cost, and market value can be equal is for accrued depreciation to be zero. The only time accrued depreciation is likely to equal zero is when a project is brand new.

Figure 23.4 Steps in the income capitalization approach.

Gather market information on rents, operating expenses and capitalization rates

Estimate typical operating expenses

Develop proforma income statement

Estimate capitalization rate

Capitalize income into market value estimate

Income Capitalization Approach

The final approach to estimating market value, the income capitalization approach, is built on the concept that many buyers do not really buy the bricks, steel, wood, and other physical components of a property, but rather they buy the right to receive the income it produces. This is the same reason people buy corporate bonds and stocks. As you learned in Chapters 18 and 19, real estate investments often can provide an attractive expected rate of return relative to the risk an investor must accept. You also know that for a given property, different investors will require different rates of return from that property and also perceive different income streams from the property. Accordingly, different investors will be willing to pay different prices for the right to receive the income from the property. This is another way of saying that the investment value of the property varies from investor to investor. Collectively, all of the potential buyers and sellers of this and competing properties represent the market for this investment. Their collective investment values combine to produce a range of possible market values.

If you were an appraiser, you could estimate the income the property is typically expected to produce and a rate of return representative of that expected by investors, and then apply the same techniques investors use to estimate what a typical investor would be willing to pay (see Figure 23.4). If all of the numbers used are representative of the market and not a particular investor, then the value produced is a market value estimate. For example, if investors want a 10 percent return on their investment and a property will produce $25,000 in income, how much will investors pay for the right to receive that income? Put another way, the $25,000 income represents a 10 percent return on what amount? One possible answer is $250,000, calculated as follows:

$$\text{Value} \times .10 = \$25,000$$

Rearranging,

$$\text{Value} = \frac{\$25,000}{.10}$$

$$\text{Value} = \$250,000.$$

The process of converting an income stream into a value estimate is called **capitalization,** and can be expressed in symbols as:

$$V = \frac{I}{R}$$

where V is the market value, I is the income produced by the property, and R is the rate of return required by market investors, also called the capitalization rate. In traditional appraisal, *income* is defined as net operating income, also called net income. Net operating income is the income left after vacancies and operating expenses are subtracted from gross possible income. The **capitalization rate** is any rate used to convert income into value. In estimating market value, the appraiser derives capitalization rates from the market and uses them to capitalize market-derived estimates of income into market value estimates. It is important that you have a clear understanding of what is meant in appraisal by income and rate of return. Income and capitalization rates used in appraisal are considered in more detail in the next chapter.

THE APPRAISAL PROCESS

If you are an appraiser, every assignment represents a problem to be solved. Someone wants to know something or else you would not have been contacted. While each problem is somewhat unique, your approach to solving it should not be. By developing an approach, or process, for researching and formulating answers to clients' problems, you can save yourself a lot of time. You can also provide your clients with the best possible service since you are less likely to omit something of importance if you are following an established procedure.

Many appraisers have adopted the general guidelines of the **appraisal process,** an organized, step-by-step approach to estimating the market value of a property to solve clients' problems. The appraisal process is illustrated in Figure 23.5. There is nothing revolutionary or

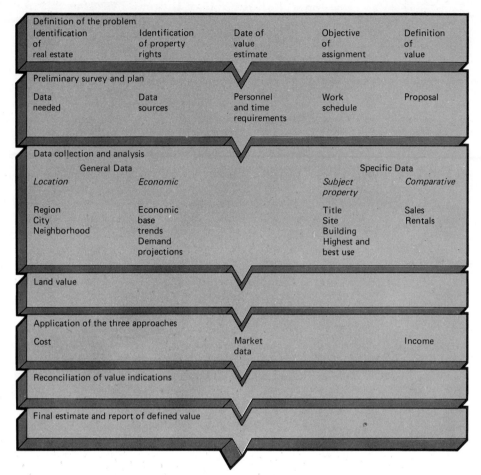

Figure 23.5 The appraisal process. (Reprinted from *What to Look for in an Appraisal*, the "Valuation Process," by permission of AIREA. Copyright AIREA, Chicago, 1979.)

startling about the appraisal process, it is simply an adaptation of the scientific method used in many fields of work to systematize problem solving. We will use the appraisal process not only to see how an appraisal unfolds, but also to see what the appraiser does once market value has been estimated using one, two, or all three of the basic approaches to valuation.

Definition of the Problem

Before a problem can be solved, it must be properly defined. This requires that the appraiser and client clearly communicate exactly what is to be done. A complete legal description of the property must be obtained. The bundle of property rights to be appraised should be identified. For example, is it a leasehold or fee interest? Since values can literally change daily, the date of the appraisal must be established. Every value estimate is made *as of* a specific date. Some very interesting recent appraisal assignments have involved the valuation of real estate interests in the past. In some court cases involving Indian lands, appraisers have been asked to value land as of dates in the 1800s. Since the appraiser is interested in providing the client with the best possible information, the appraiser must know the objective of the appraisal. Finally, the definition of market value should be clearly established, a problem considered earlier in this chapter.

Preliminary Survey and Plan

Once the nature and scope of the problem is known, the ball is squarely in the appraiser's court. The appraiser now must assess the potential assignment with the objectives of planning the appraisal and establishing the fee. To do this, the appraiser determines what data are needed and where they will be obtained, what personnel will be involved, what other resources, such as computer time, will be needed, and when the work will be completed. The result of this effort is a proposal outlining the appraisal and the appraiser's fee. The potential client must then decide whether to continue with the appraisal.

Data Collection and Analysis

Once the client approves the proposal, the appraisal plan is implemented. Data is gathered about the region, city, neighborhood, and subject property. Such data provides the appraiser with insight into the current and expected future condition of the regional, city, and neighborhood economies and how the supply and demand for space of various kinds will be affected. The process also allows the appraiser to gather information about the design and condition of the property and assess the desirability of the site for various uses. Finally, market data is gathered for use in the valuation approaches considered earlier.

Application of the Three Approaches

After data is collected, the appraiser must decide which of the three approaches to valuation to use in the appraisal. If there is a lack of reliable data for any of the approaches, the appraiser may choose not to use that approach. For example, if the subject property is a church, adequate market sales data may be very difficult to find. The appraiser will then value the subject property using the selected approaches.

Reconciliation of the Three Approaches

Theoretically, each approach should produce the same market value estimate. However, in reality, the imperfections in the real estate mar-

Table 23.2. A Form Appraisal Report

RESIDENTIAL APPRAISAL REPORT   File No. _____

To be completed by Lender

Borrower **James W & Debra**   Census Tract **1075.8**   Map Reference _____

Property Address **2634 Keyesport Drive**

City **Cincinnati**   County **Hamilton**   State **Ohio**   Zip Code **45239**

Legal Description **Lot 51 Greenridge Subdivision**

Sale Price $ **60,000**   Date of Sale **10/78**   Loan Term **30** yrs   Property Rights Appraised ☒ Fee ☐ Leasehold ☐ DeMinimis PUD

Actual Real Estate Taxes $ **not ass.** (yr) Loan charges to be paid by seller $ _____   Other sales concessions _____

Lender/Client **First Federal Savings & Loan**   Address **128 E. 6th Street**

Occupant **Vacant**   Appraiser **John Grady**   Instructions to Appraiser _____

NEIGHBORHOOD

					Good	Avg.	Fair	Poor
Location	☐ Urban	☒ Suburban	☐ Rural	Employment Stability	☐	☒	☐	☐
Built Up	☐ Over 75%	☒ 25% to 75%	☐ Under 25%	Convenience to Employment	☐	☒	☐	☐
Growth Rate ☐ Fully Dev.	☒ Rapid	☐ Steady	☐ Slow	Convenience to Shopping	☒	☐	☐	☐
Property Values	☒ Increasing	☐ Stable	☐ Declining	Convenience to Schools	☒	☐	☐	☐
Demand/Supply	☒ Shortage	☐ In Balance	☐ Over Supply	Adequacy of Public Transportation	☐	☒	☐	☐
Marketing Time	☒ Under 3 Mos.	☐ 4–6 Mos.	☐ Over 6 Mos.	Recreational Facilities	☐	☒	☐	☐

Present Land Use **100** % 1 Family ___ % 2–4 Family ___ % Apts. ___ % Condo ___ % Commercial

___ % Industrial ___ % Vacant ___ %

				Good	Avg.	Fair	Poor
Change in Present Land Use ☒ Not Likely	☐ Likely (*)	☐ Taking Place (*)	Adequacy of Utilities	☒	☐	☐	☐
(*) From ___ To ___			Property Compatibility	☒	☐	☐	☐
			Protection from Detrimental Conditions	☒	☐	☐	☐
Predominant Occupancy ☒ Owner	☐ Tenant ___ % Vacant		Police and Fire Protection	☒	☐	☐	☐
Single Family Price Range $ **45000** to $ **75000** Predominant Value $ **60000**			General Appearance of Properties	☒	☐	☐	☐
Single Family Age **new** yrs to **15** yrs Predominant Age **5** yrs			Appeal to Market	☒	☐	☐	☐

Note: FHLMC/FNMA do not consider the racial composition of the neighborhood to be a relevant factor and it must not be considered in the appraisal.

Comments including those factors, favorable or unfavorable, affecting marketability (e.g. public parks, schools, view, noise) _____
Rapidly growing area near I-275

SITE

Dimensions **75 X 300** = **22,500** Sq. Ft. or Acres ☐ Corner Lot

Zoning classification **Residential**   Present improvements ☒ do ☐ do not conform to zoning regulations

Highest and best use: ☒ Present use ☐ Other (specify) _____

Public	Other (Describe)	OFF SITE IMPROVEMENTS	Topo **Level**
Elec. ☒		Street Access: ☒ Public ☐ Private	Size **Average**
Gas ☐		Surface **Macadam**	Shape **Rectangular**
Water ☒		Maintenance: ☒ Public ☐ Private	View **Good**
San.Sewer ☒		☒ Storm Sewer ☐ Curb/Gutter	Drainage **Front to Rear**
	☐ Underground Elect. & Tel	☐ Sidewalk ☐ Street Lights	Is the property located in a HUD Identified Special Flood Hazard Area? ☒ No ☐ Yes

Comments (favorable or unfavorable including any apparent adverse easements, encroachments or other adverse conditions) **None**

IMPROVEMENTS

☒ Existing ☐ Proposed ☐ Under Constr.   No. Units **1**   Type (det, duplex, semi/det, etc.) **Detached**   Design (rambler, split level, etc.) **Rambler**   Exterior Walls **Cedar & Stone**

Yrs. Age: Actual **new** Effective **new**   No. Stories **1**

Roof Material **Shingle**	Gutters & Downspouts ☐ None **Aluminum**	Window (Type) **Aluminum** ☒ Storm Sash ☒ Screens ☒ Combination	Insulation ☐ None ☒ Floor ☐ Ceiling ☒ Roof ☒ Walls

☐ Manufactured Housing	**50** % Basement ☒ Floor Drain Finished Ceiling ___
Foundation Walls	☐ Outside Entrance ☐ Sump Pump Finished Walls ___
Concrete	☒ Concrete Floor ___ % Finished Finished Floor ___
☐ Slab on Grade ☒ Crawl Space	Evidence of: ☐ Dampness ☐ Termites ☐ Settlement

Comments _____

Room List	Foyer	Living	Dining	Kitchen	Den	Family Rm.	Rec. Rm.	Bedrooms	No. Baths	Laundry	Other
Basement											
1st Level	1	1	1	1		1		3	2		
2nd Level											

Finished area above grade contains a total of **7** rooms **3** bedrooms **2** baths. Gross Living Area **272** sq. ft. Bsmt Area **550** sq. ft.

Kitchen Equipment: ☐ Refrigerator ☒ Range/Oven ☒ Disposal ☒ Dishwasher ☒ Fan/Hood ☐ Compactor ☐ Washer ☐ Dryer ☐

HEAT: Type **Electric** Fuel **F/A** Cond. **Good**   AIR COND. ☒ Central ☐ Other   ☐ Adequate ☐ Inadequate

Floors ☐ Hardwood ☒ Carpet Over **plywood**			Good	Avg.	Fair	Poor
Walls ☒ Drywall ☐ Plaster		Quality of Construction (Materials & Finish)	☒	☐	☐	☐
Trim/Finish ☒ Good ☐ Average ☐ Fair ☐ Poor		Condition of Improvements	☒	☐	☐	☐
Bath Floor ☒ Ceramic ☐		Rooms size and layout	☒	☐	☐	☐
Bath Wainscot ☒ Ceramic ☐		Closets and Storage	☒	☐	☐	☐
Special Features (including energy efficient items) ___		Insulation—adequacy	☒	☐	☐	☐
Fireplace		Plumbing—adequacy and condition	☒	☐	☐	☐
		Electrical—adequacy and condition	☒	☐	☐	☐
		Kitchen Cabinets—adequacy and condition	☒	☐	☐	☐
ATTIC: ☐ Yes ☐ No ☐ Stairway ☐ Drop-stair ☐ Scuttle ☐ Floored		Compatibility to Neighborhood	☒	☐	☐	☐
Finished (Describe) ___ ☐ Heated		Overall Livability	☒	☐	☐	☐
CAR STORAGE: ☐ Garage ☐ Built-in ☐ Attached ☐ Detached ☐ Car Port		Appeal and Marketability	☒	☐	☐	☐
No. Cars ___ ☐ Adequate ☐ Inadequate Condition ___		Yrs Est Remaining Economic Life **50** to **60** Explain if less than Loan Term

FIREPLACES, PATIOS, POOL, FENCES, etc. (describe) **Fireplace, Wood Deck**

COMMENTS (including functional or physical inadequacies, repairs needed, modernization, etc.) **None**

FHLMC Form 70 Rev. 10/78   ATTACH DESCRIPTIVE PHOTOGRAPHS OF SUBJECT PROPERTY AND STREET SCENE   FNMA Form 1004 Rev. 10/78

Table 23.2. (continued)

VALUATION SECTION

Purpose of Appraisal is to estimate Market Value as defined in Certification & Statement of Limiting Conditions (FHLMC Form 439/FNMA Form 1004B). If submitted for FNMA, the appraiser must attach (1) sketch or map showing location of subject, street names, distance from nearest intersection, and any detrimental conditions and (2) exterior building sketch of improvements showing dimensions.

Measurements		No. Stories		Sq. Ft.
53	x 24	x 1	=	1272
	x	x	=	
	x	x	=	
	x	x	=	
	x	x	=	

Total Gross Living Area (List in Market Data Analysis below) _____

Comment on functional and economic obsolescence: _____

ESTIMATED REPRODUCTION COST – NEW – OF IMPROVEMENTS:

Dwelling 1272 Sq. Ft. @ $ 30.62 = $ 38,948
_____ Sq. Ft. @ $ _____
Extras Cabinets, heat pump = 5,000
Special Energy Efficient Items _____
Porches, Patios, etc. = 1,000
Garage/Car Port 407 Sq. Ft. @ $ 8.00 = 3,256
Site Improvements (driveway, landscaping, etc.)
Total Estimated Cost New . . . . . . = $ 48,204

Less | Physical | Functional | Economic
Depreciation $ ___ | $ ___ | $ ___ = $ -0-
Depreciated value of improvements . . . = $ 48,204
ESTIMATED LAND VALUE = $ 11,000
(If leasehold, show only leasehold value)
INDICATED VALUE BY COST APPROACH . . . . $ 59,204

The undersigned has recited three recent sales of properties most similar and proximate to subject and has considered these in the market analysis. The description includes a dollar adjustment, reflecting market reaction to those items of significant variation between the subject and comparable properties. If a significant item in the comparable property is superior to, or more favorable than, the subject property, a minus (-) adjustment is made, thus reducing the indicated value of subject; if a significant item in the comparable is inferior to, or less favorable than, the subject property, a plus (+) adjustment is made, thus increasing the indicated value of the subject.

ITEM	Subject Property	COMPARABLE NO. 1	Adjustment	COMPARABLE NO. 2	Adjustment	COMPARABLE NO. 3	Adjustment
Address	2634 Keyesport	2611 Keyesport		2627 Kensport		6109 Greenridge	
Proximity to Subj.		same block		same block		same block	
Sales Price	$60,000	$59,000		$58,000		$60,650	
Price/Living area	$30.62	$31.80		$30.79		$30.95	
Data Source	Contract	Court House		Court House		Court House	
Date of Sale and Time Adjustment	10-78	8-78		4-78		8-78	
Location	Good	Good		Good		Good	
Site/View	Good	Good		Good		Good	
Design and Appeal	Ranch	Ranch		Ranch		Ranch	
Quality of Const.	Cedar/Stone	Same		Same		Same	
Age	New	New		New		New	
Condition	Good	Good		Good		Good	
Living Area Room Count and Total	Total 7 / B-rms 3 / Baths 2	Total 7 / B-rms 3 / Baths 1½		Total 7 / B-rms 3 / Baths 1		Total 7 / B-rms 3 / Baths 2	
Gross Living Area	1272 Sq.Ft.	1170 Sq.Ft.	+1000	1154 Sq.Ft.	+1500	1292 Sq.Ft.	-650
Basement & Bsmt. Finished Rooms	Partial	Partial		Partial		Partial	
Functional Utility	Good	Good		Good		Good	
Air Conditioning	Central	Central		Central		Central	
Garage/Car Port	2 car	2 car		2 car		2 car	
Porches, Patio, Pools, etc.	Rear Deck	Same		None	+500	Same	
Special Energy Efficient Items	Heat Pump	Same		Same		Same	
Other (e.g. fire-places, kitchen equip., remodeling)	Equipped	Same		Same		Same	
Sales or Financing Concessions	Conventional	Conventional		Conventional		Conventional	
Net Adj. (Total)		[X] Plus; [ ] Minus $1,000		[X] Plus; [ ] Minus $ 2,000		[ ] Plus; [X] Minus $ 650	
Indicated Value of Subject		$60,000		$ 60,000		$60,000	

Comments on Market Data All comps. are recent and from the same area. _____

INDICATED VALUE BY MARKET DATA APPROACH . . . . $ 60,000
INDICATED VALUE BY INCOME APPROACH (If applicable) Economic Market Rent $450 /Mo. x Gross Rent Multiplier 130 = $ 58,500
This appraisal is made [X] "as is" [ ] subject to the repairs, alterations, or conditions listed below [ ] completion per plans and specifications.
Comments and Conditions of Appraisal: _____

Final Reconciliation: Most consideration was given to the Market Date Approach _____

Construction Warranty [ ] Yes [ ] No   Name of Warranty Program _____   Warranty Coverage Expires _____
This appraisal is based upon the above requirements, the certification, contingent and limiting conditions, and Market Value definition that are stated in
[ ] FHLMC Form 439 (Rev. 10/78)/FNMA Form 1004B (Rev. 10/78) filed with client _____ 19 ___ [ ] attached.
I ESTIMATE THE MARKET VALUE, AS DEFINED, OF SUBJECT PROPERTY AS OF Oct. 18 1978 to be $ 60,000

Appraiser(s) _____   Review Appraiser (If applicable) _____
[X] Did [ ] Did Not Physically Inspect Property

FHLMC Form 70 Rev. 10/78   REVERSE   FNMA Form 1004 Rev. 10/78

ket, which create the need for the appraiser, almost always result in different value estimates from each approach. Thus, the appraiser may be dealing with three different value estimates, which are usually reconciled into a single "best" estimate for the appraisal report. Before making this **reconciliation,** the appraiser should examine the differences between the value estimates to see whether they are reasonable. If they aren't, then the appraiser may question the data used in the appraisal and seek the source of the differences in indicated values.

If the values are acceptably close in the opinion of the appraiser, they can be reconciled. It may seem that one way to reconcile them is to simply find the mean. The problem with this approach is that the appraiser may think that all approaches are not equally reliable. For example, for a single family home, the appraiser may not feel the income capitalization approach is generally as reliable as the sales comparison approach because homes are seldom purchased based on the rental income they will produce. Reliability problems may also result from a lack of quality data. Ultimately, the appraiser must place a weight on each approach reflecting his subjective assessment of the reliability of that approach. The total weights should add to 100 percent. These weights are then multiplied by the corresponding value estimate and the products totalled to produce a weighted average market value estimate. This weighted average market value is the "reconciled" market value estimate.

Final Estimate and Report of Defined Value

The appraiser now prepares the **appraisal report** according to the specifications of the proposal. This report is the vehicle that will officially convey the results of the appraisal process to the client. It should contain the market value estimate, of course, along with other supporting information showing how the value was estimated. Appraisal reports come in three formats: form, letter, and narrative.

A *form report* is often used on single family home appraisals to provide information to lenders interested in using the subject property as collateral for a mortgage loan. Forms used are generally those approved by Fannie Mae and Freddie Mac. Such a sample form appraisal is contained in Table 23.2. *Narrative appraisals* are in a longer, more detailed format than form appraisals. They detail every step of the appraisal process for the client and can run for more than 100 pages. *Letter reports* contain the market value estimate and refer to supporting documentation retained in the appraiser's file. Just because the report format is brief does not mean the appraiser uses less diligence and care in preparing the report nor that supporting documentation is not available. The appraiser goes through exactly the same appraisal process as in a narrative report, but simply does not organize all the information into a formal narrative report.

Appraisal reports should include information about the data used, the techniques used, and any assumptions or, as they are sometimes called, limiting conditions, inherent in the study, and the final market value estimate. In short, the client should be able to read the report and follow the logical development of the market value estimate. Writing this report can be a very time-consuming element of the appraisal process.

SUMMARY

Estimating market value is an important activity since it affects virtually every real estate decision. Estimating market value is the domain of real estate appraisal, also called real estate valuation.

If you want to appraise a property, you must first define market value. Two definitions have received the widest acceptance: the highest price and the most probable selling price. The highest price definition, often used by courts, defines market value within the context of an assumed real estate market and the participants in it. Many have argued that the real estate market assumed by this definition is unrealistic, and that an alternative definition based on the real estate market as it exists is preferable. Such a definition is the most probable selling price definition. This difference is important to you if the definition of market value selected affects the market value estimate.

Real estate appraisers are needed because real estate markets do not usually provide enough readily accessible, reliable information for market participants to make defensible market value estimates. In short, they are not as efficient as markets in which appraisers are not needed. Virtually everyone associated with real estate acts as an appraiser at various times. Buyers, sellers, brokers, and others in the real estate business estimate market value. However, professional appraisers sign their appraisals and stake their reputations on their work.

Market value is estimated using three approaches, which correspond to alternatives in the marketplace. In short, the appraiser attempts to simulate the market by simulating the actions of those in it. The sales comparison approach is based on the alternative of purchasing another property rather than the subject property. Thus, market value is estimated by examining the price at which comparable properties have recently sold. The cost approach assumes that another option in the market is to construct either a replica of the property or another structure with similar utility. Presumably, no buyer would pay more for the subject property than it costs to replace it. In this approach, the appraiser must estimate the reproduction or replacement cost. The final approach, the income capitalization approach, assumes that buyers are purchasing income and they will pay no more for the income stream produced by the subject property than for another income stream of equal quantity and quality. To estimate market value, the appraiser estimates the income the subject property will produce and capitalizes it at the rate being required for an income stream of that quality.

To solve appraisal problems, the appraiser frequently uses the appraisal process, an organized approach to estimating the market value of real estate. This process divides appraisal into the areas of problem definition, preliminary survey and plan, data collection and analysis, application of the appropriate approaches, reconciliation of these approaches, and final estimate and report preparation. By following this general process, the appraiser is more likely to produce a reliable, defensible market value estimate.

QUICK QUIZ

1. Real estate appraisal is usually concerned with estimating _____.

    a. assessed value   c. liquidation value
    b. market value   d. tax value

2. Market value and market price _____.

    I. mean the same thing
    II. are always numerically equal

    a. I only   c. Both I and II
    b. II only   d. Neither I nor II

3. The three approaches to estimating market value are

    a. cost, market data, and investment
    b. investment, market data, and weighted average
    c. cost, income, and sales comparison
    d. depreciation, income, and market data

4. The first step in the cost approach is to _____.

    a. estimate the value of the land
    b. estimate cost of replacing or reproducing improvements
    c. estimate accrued depreciation
    d. estimate value of any extras in subject property

5. The rate used to convert an income stream into a value estimate is called _____. •

    a. an interest rate   c. a return on investment rate
    b. a recapture rate   d. a capitalization rate

6. The market value definition that uses the real estate market as it actually exists is the _____ definition.

7. _____ is the cost of constructing a replica of the subject property.

8. The basic appraisal principle underlying the income approach is the _____.

9. Real estate appraisal requires technical knowledge and judgment, which is another way of saying that it is a combination of _____ and _____.

10. Recent sales considered similar enough to the subject property to be used in the sales comparison approach are called _____.

QUESTIONS AND EXERCISES

1. Why is the sales comparison approach likely to be given more weight in a single family appraisal than in an office building appraisal?

2. You are the owner of Blackacre. List five situations that may give rise to the need to have it appraised.

3. If you are trying to establish an asking price for Blackacre before putting it on the market, which definition of market value would you ask the appraiser to use?

4. Compare and contrast the conditions of the highest price market value definition with those of efficient markets in Chapter 9. What are the implications of these similarities and differences?

5. Why are professional appraisers different from others who estimate market value?

6. How do appraisers develop a "sense" of the market?

7. The three valuation approaches considered in this chapter correspond to options open to those in the market. What are those options?

8. If you were an appraiser, what factors would you consider in selecting comparables for a subject property?

9. Why is it important to make an appraisal as of a certain date?

10. Why should each of the three approaches theoretically produce the same value indication? Why do they not do so in reality?

KEY TERMINOLOGY

accrued depreciation
appraisal
appraisal process
appraisal report
capitalization
capitalization rate
comparable
cost approach
depreciation
economic obsolescence
functional obsolescence
income capitalization approach
market data approach
market price
market value

net operating income
physical deterioration
Principle of Anticipation
Principle of Change
Principle of Contribution
Principle of Highest and Best Use
Principle of Increasing and
  Decreasing Returns
Principle of Substitution
reconciliation
replacement cost
reproduction cost
sales comparison approach
valuation

IF YOU WANT TO READ MORE

GEORGE F. BLOOM, ARTHUR M. WEIMER, and JEFFREY D. FISHER, *Real Estate*, 8th ed. (New York: John Wiley & Sons, 1982), Chapters 11, 15, and 16.

GEORGE F. BLOOM and HENRY S. HARRISON, *Appraising the Single Family Residence* (Chicago: American Institute of Real Estate Appraisers, 1978).

BYRL N. BOYCE and WILLIAM N. KINNARD, JR., *Appraising Real Property* (Lexington: D.C. Heath and Company, 1984).

WILLIAM M. SHENKEL, *Modern Real Estate Appraisal* (New York: McGraw-Hill Book Company, 1978).

Textbook Revision Subcommittee of the American Institute of Real Estate Appraisers, *The Appraisal of Real Estate*, 8th ed. (Chicago: American Institute of Real Estate Appraisers, 1983).

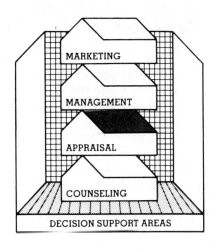

MARKETING

MANAGEMENT

APPRAISAL

COUNSELING

DECISION SUPPORT AREAS

24

Real Estate Appraisal: applying appraisal concepts

PREVIEW

The basic appraisal concepts presented in the preceding chapter form the foundation of good appraisal practice. The three approaches briefly considered in the last chapter are easy to understand conceptually, but somewhat more difficult to apply. You may want a better understanding of the steps involved with each approach to make their application in actual appraisal situations clearer. This chapter extends the discussion of the three valuation approaches to consider the application and problems with each in valuing single family homes and income properties. Specifically, this chapter increases your understanding of real estate appraisal by:

1. Considering the gathering of data for the market data, cost, and income approaches.
2. Examining the use of gathered data to estimate market value for each approach.
3. Discussing the reconciliation of differing value estimates within each approach.

The application of appraisal concepts is critical to understanding the work of appraisers or to act as your own appraiser. How data is gathered and used is an exercise in applied market research, an activity everyone in real estate must perform, even if not to the degree of the professional appraiser. What follows is a brief discussion of the three appraisal approaches described in the last chapter. As you read this chapter, picture yourself as an appraiser facing the problem of valuing a piece of real estate and actively try to imagine gathering and processing market data.

Each valuation approach (just to refresh your memory), represents an alternative course of action for buyers in the market. The sales comparison approach is founded on the concept of the subject property competing with all other existing properties providing similar utility to the buyer. Thus, the prices at which these properties have sold represent

Table 24.1. Summary of Valuation Approaches

Approach	Rationale	Concept	Basic Steps
Sales Comparison	Buyers will pay no more than the cost of purchasing a property with utility equal to the subject's.	Estimate market value by examining recent sales of similar properties.	1. Identify all possible comparable sales. 2. Gather and verify data on comparable sales. 3. Select the most appropriate comparables. 4. Adjust the comparables for time and comparability. 5. Reconcile different values into single estimate.
Cost	Buyers will pay no more than it costs to erect a building with utility equal to the subject's.	Estimate market value by estimating land costs and cost of reproduction or replacement.	1. Estimate value of land. 2. Estimate cost of replacing or reproducing. 3. Adjust cost estimate for accrued depreciation from all sources. 4. Add land value and depreciated cost estimate to produce value estimate.
Income Capitalization	Buyers will pay no more than the cost of purchasing an income stream of equal quality and quantity.	Estimate market value by capitalizing market rents using a market capitalization rate.	1. Gather market information on rents, operating expenses, and capitalization rates. 2. Estimate typical operating expenses. 3. Develop pro forma income statement. 4. Estimate capitalization rate. 5. Capitalize income into market value estimate.

good indications of the likely value of the subject. The cost approach represents the option of constructing an improvement providing similar utility. It is surmised that you would pay no more for the subject than it would cost to produce a building providing similar utility. Finally, the income capitalization approach is premised on the purchase of real property for the production of income. If a property is being purchased for its income, then a buyer would pay no more for it than for an income stream of equal quantity and quality. Table 24.1 provides a summary of the three valuation approaches. With this brief background, each of the approaches can now be considered.

All three of the valuation approaches are market approaches in that they use market data. They simply concentrate on different aspects of activity in the marketplace. All three are market based, and in valuing real estate, you will be going to the market for information for all three approaches.

SALES COMPARISON APPROACH

The sales comparison approach uses direct sales data from the market as the basis of estimating market value. The general steps in the sales comparison approach summarized in Figure 23.1 are now considered in more detail.

Identifying Sales

Your first step is to identify all possible sales that *may* be used as comparables. To do this you will use many sources. You may not wait until you need a specific set of comparables to begin gathering data. As a normal part of your business you will gather and organize all possible market data. This collection of information is sometimes called your **appraisal data plant** or **data base.** Properly developing a data base requires a good bit of time and money, but can pay large dividends in time savings and the ability to produce reliable appraisals. One of the things a client is paying for is your data base and the market knowledge you gain from it. Exactly what data you collect depends on your appraisal practice. You may specialize in one type of property, in which case you will focus your data gathering on that type of property. So, your first source of possible comparables is your own office.

If you cannot identify enough possible comparables from your data base, you may consult an organization that collects data on sales and makes it available either through a computer terminal in your office or at their office for a fee. One such service is the Society of Real Estate Appraisers Market Data Center. Other services are also available to help you.

Public records are also useful. As you remember, most deeds are recorded in the county clerk's office (this office may have a different name in your area). The assessor's office may be a useful source of information since it is likely to have information about properties such as the number of bedrooms, square footage, and other factors useful in assessing the home.

You may also refer to other sources such as lenders, real estate brokers, other real estate appraisers, or anyone else in the real estate business who may have information. One good source is the local multiple listing service. It usually publishes a quarterly summary of all properties sold containing the listing price, sales price, and all listing information. In some cities, weekly or biweekly publications devoted to the real estate market exist. These publications report transactions of all types and contain announcements of development and redevelopment plans.

Obtaining and Verifying Data on Comparables

The keys to obtaining data on comparables are to find a source and to gather data in a consistent manner. Before you start gathering data you should decide what data you need for every property to allow you to make decisions about the comparability of any particular sale with the subject property. Table 24.2 contains a card used by one appraisal firm to gather sales data on each sale. This firm may gather additional data on certain

Table 24.2. Sales Data Gathering Card

Comparable Sales

Property Address: _____ Sale Price: _____
Property Name: _____ Date of Sale: _____
Legal: _____
Book: _____ Page: _____ Inst. No.: _____ Filed: _____ IRS: _____
Grantor: _____ Grantee: _____
Mortgage(s): _____
Verified-Seller ☐ Buyer ☐ Other ☐ Name: _____ Date: _____
LAND: Dimensions: _____ Area: _____
Remarks: _____
IMPROVEMENTS: Type: _____ Age: _____ No. of Main Bldgs.: _____
Stories: _____ Construction: _____ Area-Gross: _____ Net: _____

Analysis

Price: Land: $_____ Bldg.: $_____ Other: $_____
Land Price Per SF: $_____ Bldg. Price Per SF: $_____ Unit: $_____
Est. Replacement Cost: $_____ Indicated Depr.: $_____
Gross Rent: $_____ GRM _____ Vacancy _____
Expenses Reported: $_____ Year: _____ Adjusted: $_____ %
Resales: _____
Comments: _____

appraisal assignments. Other firms may routinely gather more or less data than this firm; the important thing is that data is gathered in a consistent manner.

Data for comparables may be gathered from the varied places where initial information on the sale was gathered. More than one source may be used to gather all the necessary information. Obtaining data can be a time-consuming and expensive affair for certain income properties since so few sales occur and the data are harder to find. Generally, gathering data on single family sales in urban areas is more easily accomplished because of the numerous sources of information.

To reduce the chance of gathering incorrect information, any information gathered should be confirmed by one of the parties involved in the transaction. This could be the buyer, seller, or the broker, and sometimes the lender. This person should be asked to **verify** data gathered from other sources and to provide any additional information about the terms of sale, any extenuating circumstances, description of improvements, condition of property at sale, personal property included in sale, and any assessments or encumbrances against the property at the time of sale.

Selecting the Most Appropriate Comparables

So far, it may appear that you should gather sales data on every property that may remotely be comparable to the property. This is not really the case. You should exercise judgment as to what general area of the city and property type would be likely comparables. For example, if you are appraising a single family home, the immediate neighborhood or subdivision will likely provide the most useful comparables. Only if this area did not produce the necessary comparables would the search be expanded.

Some comparables can be eliminated as not being representative of the market. Sales between relatives, foreclosure and bankruptcy sales, and sales involving government agencies may not be true indicators of the market. Old sales should also be eliminated if you have not already done so. Six months to a year is roughly the limit of the life of most comparables. How old a comparable can be before being out of date depends on the stability of the market. The more stable the market, the longer a comparable may be used. After you have eliminated less comparable properties, the remaining ones provide the pool from which final comparables are selected for use in the appraisal. Usually somewhere from three to five comparables will be used.

Adjusting the Comparables

Even sales in the same neighborhood are often not perfect substitutes for the subject. They may differ from the subject property in size, location,

Table 24.3. Adjusting Comparables to Fit Subject Property

	Comp 1	Comp 2	Comp 3
Sales Price	$115,000	$120,000	$123,000
Adjustments (Relative to Subject)			
Size	+1,000	−1,500	−2,000
Location	− 500	+ 500	− 750
Lot Size	+ 500	−1,000	−1,500
Amenities	+ 750	− 800	−1,250
Style	0	0	0
Date of Sale	0	0	+1,000
Net Adjustment	+1,750	−2,800	−4,500
Indicated Value	$116,750	$117,200	$118,500

lot size, amenities, style, and date of sale. To the extent that these differences affect market value, you must make **adjustments** in the sales price of each comparable. This adjustment is accomplished by adding or subtracting an amount of money sufficient to offset the difference between the comparable and subject property. If you were an appraiser, the amount of each adjustment would be estimated by analyzing market data on sales of properties with differing characteristics. This process is illustrated for a single family home in Table 24.3. The adjustments in this table are based on the appraiser's analysis of the market.

Arriving at the Final Market Value Estimate

After all adjustments, three adjusted market prices remain in Table 24.3 as evidence of market value. You must now *reconcile* these three pieces of evidence into a single market value estimate by evaluating the relative merits of each comparable to determine the weight to be assigned to it. Notice that a simple average is appropriate only if you feel each comparable is an equally good indicator of value. By dividing the possible 100 percent of weight among the comparables, you can then develop a weighted average representing the market value estimate for the property, as in Table 24.4. In this example, Comparable 1 is considered the

Table 24.4. Reconciling Market Values Indicated by Comparables

Comparable	Indicated Value	Weighting		Weighted Value
1	$116,750	.50	=	$ 58,375
2	$117,200	.30	=	$ 35,160
3	$118,500	.20	=	$ 23,700
Total Weighted Value			=	$117,235
				(Say $117,250)

best comparable and is given a weighting of 50 percent. Comparable 2 is second best with a weighting of 30 percent.

COST APPROACH

You may have some difficulty trying to connect the cost approach to the market. For instance, you may be thinking that cost and value are unrelated. After all, a 70-story office building in the middle of the Sahara Desert would cost a fortune to build, but its market value would be minimal. So far your logic is correct, but the cost approach has one very important trick up its sleeve that connects it with the market and overcomes the difficulties you envision. After the cost of construction is estimated, the appraiser must then deduct an allowance for accrued depreciation from all sources. Depreciation is a loss in value from any purpose, one of which could be location, as in the Sahara Desert case. This depreciation adjustment is derived from the market by analyzing market data. Thus, what appears to be an approach divorced from the market is, indeed, closely tied to it. The steps in the cost approach are now considered in more detail.

Estimate Value of Site

The site should be valued as though vacant and ready for development in its highest and best use. The highest and best use of the site assumed vacant may differ from its present use. For example, a site near an expressway with a small warehouse on it may be better suited to high-rise office development, a fairly common phenomenon in many cities. You will value the site according to this highest and best use as if vacant. Since this highest and best use as vacant differs from the present use, you cannot simply add the value of the warehouse to complete the appraisal. For example, if the site is worth $750,000 and the improvements are worth $250,000 you cannot add the two and arrive at a total value estimate of $1,000,000. Because you assumed the site to be vacant, the current improvements actually represent an obstacle to development that must be removed, at some cost, before the office building can be erected. Therefore, the market value of the site is the $750,000 less the cost of clearing the site, say $25,000, $750,000 − $25,000 = $725,000.

Because the site is improved you are not yet through with the land. The highest and best use of the site as improved may be different from the highest and best use as vacant. You must now consider the existing improvements and estimate what alterations or additions can be made to them that will create more value than they cost. That is, if adding a patio increases value by an amount equal to or greater than its cost, it is assumed that such a change will be made. After considering possible additions or repairs to the existing improvements, you must value the property. If its total value exceeds that of the value of the site when assumed vacant, then the current use is the highest and best use. If the vacant site has a greater market value, then the existing use is no longer the highest and best use. Put another way, so long as the present improvements, after considering possible additions, repairs, or renovations, contribute anything above the value of the land assumed vacant, the current use is the highest and best use.

Estimating Construction Costs

Construction costs can be estimated in a number of ways ranging from very simple and easy to use to very detailed and difficult to use. Regardless of which method is used, you should remember that costs can be classified as either direct or indirect. **Direct costs** are those directly associated with the construction of the improvement such as materials, labor, contractor's fees, and so on. **Indirect costs** are those not so directly associated with construction, such as professional fees for appraisers, lawyers, and accountants, and financing fees. Both direct and indirect costs must be included in your cost estimate for a property.

If you are knowledgeable about construction and the subject property, you may choose to estimate the quantity and cost of all materials and labor necessary to construct an improvement. For example, you may estimate the amount of steel necessary for the framework of a building and the cost of erecting it. By adding to this cost estimate similar cost estimates for all other portions of the building, you can estimate the total cost of the improvement. This is called the **quantity survey method.** It is the most detailed of the cost estimation techniques. Because of the detailed information and construction knowledge required, it is not used as frequently as some easier to use techniques.

You may prefer simply to gather information about the cost of putting certain components in place rather than detail each piece of material and labor in that component. For example, drywall may be priced according to square footage of wall to be covered. This price includes materials and labor. To estimate the cost of drywall using this method, you will multiply the square footage of drywall times the cost per square foot. By pricing all of the components in the improvement and totaling them, you can estimate the total cost of construction. This is the **unit-in-place method.** It, too, is a relatively detailed approach to estimating the cost of construction.

Finally, you could simply estimate the cost **per square foot** to build the structure. If different areas of the structure have different construction costs, each such area's construction costs can be estimated separately and added together to estimate total construction costs. For example, in a single family home the garage does not cost as much to build as the heated and cooled living space. You may choose to treat the entire improvement as one unit and use a single average cost per square foot to estimate the market value. The cost per square foot technique is the most widely used one for the cost approach.

Data on per square foot construction costs can be misleading if not properly used. You must make sure the cost figures are based on improvements very similar in quality and amenities to the subject's. If material variations exist, you must make adjustments to take them into account. Suppose you find that construction costs for homes very similar to the subject are running $35 per square foot, but the subject property has a hot tub enclosed in a greenhouse-type room, a feature not possessed by any of the comparable homes. The adjustment to the reproduction cost estimate may be made by adding the cost of the hot tub and greenhouse room to the estimate made from per square foot costs, as in Table 24.5.

Data for estimating construction costs is gathered from contractors, lenders, and others in the real estate business. Such data is also available in **cost manuals** produced by a number of firms, such as Marshall and Swift, McGraw-Hill, and Boeckh. These firms gather cost data from around the country and publish it for appraisers and others to use. This cost information is frequently updated. Whatever source is used to secure cost data, the appraiser must be very careful to compare the subject property's characteristics to those of the improvements used to generate the cost data. The appraiser should be sure that cost data includes all direct and indirect costs and be willing to make adjustments when necessary.

Estimate Accrued Depreciation

As you know from the preceding chapter, reproduction or replacement cost must be adjusted by accrued depreciation in order to estimate market value. Also in that chapter, you learned that accrued depreciation was comprised of three components: physical deterioration, functional obsolescence, and economic obsolescence. Estimating accrued depreciation requires that you either directly estimate overall depreciation or build up such an estimate from individual depreciation components. In

Table 24.5. Example of Cost per Square Foot Technique With Adjustments for Property Differences

Cost using per square foot technique	2700 sq. ft.* × $45/sq. ft. = $121,500
Adjustments:	
Hot tub	$ 3,000
Greenhouse room	$10,000
Total adjustments	$ 13,000
Total estimated cost	$134,500

* This square footage does *not* include the greenhouse room.

either approach, you must analyze the property to determine its characteristics and condition and then analyze the market to estimate how these characteristics and conditions affect value. Such a process requires a good bit of objective and subjective analysis.

Suppose you have been asked to estimate the accrued depreciation for a single family home in a subdivision in your town. How would you go about this task? One approach to estimating accrued depreciation is by comparing market prices to cost. For instance, suppose that you know the following about a home that was recently sold:

Sales Price	$100,000
Value of Land	20,000
Reproduction Cost of Improvements	90,000

What insights about depreciation can you garner from this information? Since the cost of reproducing the improvements is $90,000 and they are worth only $80,000 in the market, they have incurred $10,000 of depreciation. This $10,000 represents 11 percent of the $90,000 reproduction cost,

$$\frac{\$10,000}{\$90,000} = .11$$

If you find that other sales in this neighborhood provide similar depreciation indications, you have a firm foundation for estimating depreciation for the cost approach for your subject property. This **market abstraction method** is often used in estimating accrued depreciation for properties in markets with adequate market information.

Another approach to your problem is called the **effective age method.** This method considers what percentage of its expected life the house has already used up. For instance, if the expected life of the home is 40 years and the home is effectively 10 years old, then it has used 25 percent of its life, and has accrued depreciation equal to 25 percent of its reproduction cost. The expected life of the home is its economic life, not its physical life. **Economic life** for improvements is the period over which they add to the value of the property. At the moment the property is worth the same or less with the improvements than without them, the improvements have reached the end of their economic life. **Physical life** is the period over which the improvements will actually exist, assuming normal maintenance and repairs. These two lives will usually not be equal.

Economic life is constantly changing as the city, neighborhood, and subject property change. For instance, a neighborhood rehabilitation effort may add years to the economic life of a home. Likewise, repairs and modifications to the home itself may change its economic life. In estimating accrued depreciation, you are concerned with estimating the effective age of the improvements, not their chronological age. **Effective age** is the age of the property relative to other properties in the market. It is a function of the property's condition, design and amenities, and location. Thus, a home that is 25 years old chronologically may have an effective age that is less than, more than or equal to 25 years. Estimating effective age requires keen analysis and good judgment.

Effective age represents the number of years that depreciation has accrued for the property. The percentage of the total economic life represented by effective age is the percentage of accrued depreciation for the property. Economic life is the sum of the effective age of the property and the remaining economic life. Thus, if your subject home has an effective age of 20 years and you estimate the remaining economic life to be 30 years, its economic life is 50 years. Further, since the home has already used up 20 years of that life, it has consumed 40 percent,

$$\frac{20 \text{ years}}{50 \text{ years}} = .40$$

of its economic life. That is, it has accrued depreciation equal to 40 percent of its reproduction cost. This number can be used to estimate the dollar amount of accrued depreciation, given the estimated reproduction cost of your subject home. In a less frequently used variation of this method, the effective age of the various components of an improvement and their accrued depreciation are estimated, then totaled to produce an estimate of overall accrued depreciation.

You could also estimate the amount of each of the three types of depreciation and then total them to find overall depreciation. This approach is called the **breakdown method.** This more detailed method requires more time and experienced judgment than the other methods. For this reason, it is used when the other methods do not produce sufficiently reliable estimates of accrued depreciation.

Value Estimate

The final step in the cost approach is a mechanical one. The estimate of reproduction or replacement cost is reduced by the amount of accrued depreciation and added to the estimated land value to produce the market value estimate for the cost approach.

INCOME CAPITALIZATION APPROACH: SINGLE FAMILY HOMES

Earlier you learned that appraisers attempt to simulate the actions of buyers and sellers in the real estate market for the property they are appraising. Since most single family homes are purchased for the amen-

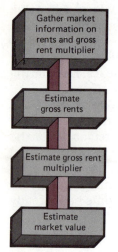

Figure 24.1 Steps in using the gross rent multiplier.

ities they provide, and not for the production of rent, appraisers generally do not depend on the income approach as much as in valuing income-producing real estate. This is not to say they ignore it, but rather they do not weight it as heavily as the sales comparison and cost approaches. Appraisers use a special variation of the income approach, called the **gross rent multiplier** (GRM), outlined in Figure 24.1. The gross rent multiplier is also called the gross income multiplier.

Using the GRM, market value is estimated by multiplying economic gross rents by a market-derived multiplier. If you assume that the monthly multiplier for single family homes in a neighborhood is 125, then a home with an estimated monthly economic rent of $1000 per month would have a market value of $125,000. As you can see, this technique is quick and easy to use, which may explain its popularity with appraisers and investors alike.

Gross rents may be defined as either gross possible rents or effective gross rents. Gross possible rents are the total rents a property will likely generate if no vacancies or bad debts occur. Effective gross rents represent gross possible rents less an allowance for vacancies and bad debts. Whichever you choose to use, you must exercise care to make sure that data is gathered and analyzed consistently. First, you must use economic rents which could be produced by typical management or that are typical for the market, not the actual rents collected for a particular home. Next, you must always compute the gross rent multiplier in a consistent manner, not using gross possible rents one time and effective gross rents the next. The GRM is calculated as the ratio of sales price to gross rents,

$$GRM = \frac{\text{Sales Price}}{\text{Gross Rents}}$$

Consistency also involves making sure the data used to estimate the GRM represents properties comparable to the subject property. Differences in size, amenities, and age between the properties used to develop the multiplier and the subject can cause substantial errors. One reason such differences may cause errors is that they affect the operating expenses associated with a property. If you ignore operating expenses when using the GRM, you are implicitly assuming that operating expenses and other characteristics of properties used to develop the multiplier and the subject are similar. For example, to use a GRM developed from sales of relatively new, large apartment complexes with swimming pools and clubrooms to value a smaller, older complex with fewer amenities is incorrect. Just as in other approaches, good comparables and good judgment in using them is critical to the reliability of the market value estimate.

INCOME CAPITALIZATION APPROACH: INCOME PROPERTIES

In applying the income capitalization approach to income properties, appraisers will generally use the steps as outlined in Table 24.1. However, appraisers often use the GRM at some point in the appraisal. Some appraisers use the GRM to get a "ballpark" estimate of market value either as a check on the other approaches to valuation or as a backup to the income capitalization approach as outlined later. It is applied exactly as described for single family homes earlier. What follows is a discussion of the income capitalization approach as outlined in Table 24.4.

Income

Income in appraisal usually means *net operating income.* Net operating income, also called net income, is the income produced by a property after vacancies and operating expenses are deducted from gross possible income. Net operating income estimated by the appraiser should represent the income this property would generate if it was typical of the market. This means that rents are typical for property of this type, operating expenses are typical, vacancies are typical, *everything* is typical. The use of typical values means that the actual operating experience of a particular property may have to be adjusted by the appraiser to make it reflect the results of typical management and operation. If actual management is particularly good, the net income may be higher than could be expected from typical operation. Thus, the appraiser cannot simply use past accounting records without analyzing them and, if necessary, *reconstructing* them to show the results one could expect if management was typical for the property.

In estimating the gross possible income, the appraiser must use *economic rents,* defined as market rents at the time of the appraisal. The rents actually being collected from a property are called **contract rents** and may not reflect current rental market conditions. For example, an apartment complex may have 35 2-bedroom units actually renting at an average of $325 per month (contract rent) when the current market rental is $375 per month. The appraiser, realizing that typically competent management would be able to increase rents to $375, will use that figure as the economic rents in the appraisal. Also included in gross possible income is income from other sources such as parking fees, vending machines, and washers and dryers.

Vacancies and operating expenses are analyzed in a similar manner. If the actual vacancy loss experienced by the subject property is above or below that for the market, the appraiser must make an adjustment to the loss typical for the market. This vacancy factor will include not only losses from empty units but also losses from bad debts. Actual expense data for the property will be analyzed for possible variations from the typical situation. The appraiser will look for possible under- or overstatements of expenses and expense items that may have been omitted. For example, if you as present owner pay your brother-in-law a well-below-market wage for performing certain maintenance chores, the appraiser must make an adjustment to account for the actual cost of such services in the marketplace.

Developing the Pro Forma Income Statement

After all adjustments have been made in gross possible rents, vacancy allowances, and operating expenses, the appraiser constructs a pro forma income statement. Such a pro forma statement is in Table 24.6. The appraiser will make a final check of the statement to make sure that the numbers are reasonable for a property of this type based on the available data *and* the appraiser's judgment.

Estimating the Capitalization Rate

Capitalization is the process of converting net operating income into an estimate of present value. This is accomplished by studying the relationship between income and value in the market and then applying that relationship to a subject property. The "relationship" between income and value that is sought is the **capitalization rate,** often called simply the *cap rate,* to be used in the basic valuation equation. A capitalization rate is any rate used to capitalize an income stream into a value estimate. The capitalization rate provides for a **return of capital** and a **return on capital** invested in a property. These rates are estimated in various ways.

Overall Rate from Market Suppose you are appraising an office building producing a net operating income of $150,000. By analyzing the ratio of net operating income to sales price for each of four recent sales of comparable buildings, you determine that investors are seemingly satisfied when this ratio is between 9.85 percent and 10.20 percent. You decide that a 10 percent rate of return is representative of the rate of

Table 24.6. Pro Forma Income Statement

Gross potential income	$100,000
Less: Vacancy and collection loss	5,000
Effective gross income	$95,000
Less: Operating expenses	35,000
Net operating income	$60,000
(Also called Net Income)	

return required by the market. By using 10 percent as the capitalization rate, you calculate that the $150,000 net operating income has a market value of $1,500,000,

$$\frac{\$150,000}{.10} = \$1,500,000$$

The 10 percent capitalization rate you used in the above example was derived directly from the market and represents a rate of return sufficient to satisfy all of the financial desires of the typical market investor. In the sense that this rate embodies *all* of the investor's desires, it is called an **overall rate.**

Band of Investment Since the overall rate is the rate found in the market, it must be satisfactory to investors. To be satisfactory to investors, it must be sufficient to cover all of their financial requirements. For instance, it must provide enough income to repay all debt and provide an adequate return on the equity investment. From Chapter 13, dealing with financial concepts, you know that the rate of **required equity return** to repay a mortgage loan is called the **constant.** If a typical buyer could obtain a mortgage loan equalling about 75 percent of the value of the property, then the equity investor has to invest only the remaining 25 percent. By dividing the property interest into financial segments, or bands, you can estimate the return on the total investment required by each financial interest. For example, if the constant is 12 percent and the mortgage represents 75 percent of the total property value, then a 9 percent return on the total property will satisfy the lender's requirements:

$$.75 \times .12 = .09$$

If the equity investor demands a 16 percent return on invested capital, then a 4 percent return on the total investment will provide that return:

$$.25 \times .16 = .04$$

By adding these two financial components, or bands, together, you can estimate the return on the total investment to satisfy both. That is 13 percent (4% + 9% = 13%). Theoretically, this capitalization rate should be equal to the overall rate estimated directly from the market. To see that this process works, assume a property costs $1,000,000. A $750,000 mortgage with a 12 percent constant would require annual payments of $90,000,

$$\$750,000 \times .12 = \$90,000$$

If the equity investor requires a 16 percent return, then to be satisfied, the $250,000 of equity investment must produce $40,000,

$$\$250,000 \times .16 = \$40,000$$

This means a total of $130,000 must be generated to satisfy both parties. This $130,000 is 13 percent of the total $1,000,000 investment.

Capital Market Data Everyone who invests in real estate has other investment opportunities. For investment in real estate to occur, investors must feel that real estate offers returns superior, or at least equal, to other investments of similar risk. Thus, the appraiser must keep abreast of rates of return required on other investments and be able to assess the risk of these investments relative to real estate. For example, if federal government bonds, which are virtually *risk-free,* are providing a return of 9.0 percent, a risky real estate investment logically must provide a return greater than this. How much greater the return must be can sometimes be estimated by analyzing the rates of return being required on a host of security investment opportunities of differing risk and deciding which has a **risk premium** comparable to a particular property. You can then estimate the return required for that level of risk. The attractiveness of this approach is that rate of return data are readily available for all sorts of capital market instruments in *The Wall Street Journal, Federal Reserve Bulletin,* popular business and finance magazines, and numerous other places.

SUMMARY

This chapter has expanded your understanding of the three approaches to real estate valuation used by real estate appraisers. The basic steps associated with each approach were considered. All of the approaches depend on market data and involve the judgment of the appraiser. Because of this, market value is estimated, not determined, by any of the approaches.

The sales comparison approach requires the identification of sales either from the appraiser's data base or other sources. This data is then organized and verified by contacting one of the principals in the transaction. The most appropriate comparables are then selected based on time of sale, property characteristics, and area of town. These comparables are adjusted to compensate for any differences between them and the subject. After these adjustments, the appraiser arrives at the final value estimate by weighting the market value estimates produced by the different comparables.

In the cost approach, you must estimate the value of the site as though vacant and available for development in the highest and best use. The cost of reproducing or replacing the improvements is then estimated and adjusted for any depreciation. This adjusted cost is added to the value of the site to produce a market value estimate. Costs are estimated by using knowledge of local markets or using commercially prepared cost manuals. The quantity survey, unit-in-place, or square foot methods may be used to estimate costs. The square foot method is the most popular.

In the income capitalization approach, the appraiser must estimate the income the subject will produce and then capitalize it at the rate of return required by the market, called the capitalization rate. In the gross rent multiplier method, the income used is gross income. The capitalization rate is replaced by a multiplier that is multiplied by gross rents to estimate market value. The gross rent multiplier is used extensively for valuing single family homes. For valuing income-producing properties, the appraiser uses the subject property's net operating income and a market capitalization rate. Income is defined as the income that typical management would produce. Capitalization rates may be estimated by direct examination of market transactions, by band of investment analysis, or by examining the capital markets. Direct analysis of transactions is the most widely used technique.

QUICK QUIZ

1. Information contained in multiple listing sold entries includes which of the following?

a. sales price
b. listing price

c. date of sale
d. all of the above

2. Depreciation as used in the cost approach includes _____.

I. functional obsolescence, economic obsolescence
II. physical deterioration, economic obsolescence

a. I only
b. II only

c. Both I and II
d. Neither I nor II

3. The GRM is _____.

a. the rate used to capitalize net income into market value
b. the factor used to convert gross income into investment value
c. the ratio of gross income to property value
d. the ratio of sales price to gross income

4. The capitalization rate must provide a return sufficient for all of the following, except _____.

a. return on and return of capital
b. use of debt and equity capital
c. operating expenses and vacancy allowance
d. risk free return plus a risk premium

5. The rents that a property will generate under typical management are called _____ .

    a. contract rents   c. economic rents
    b. legal rents   d. lease rents

6. The process of contacting a participant in a transaction to confirm the terms of that transaction is called _____ .

7. To the extent that differences exist between the subject property and comparables, the comparables must be _____ .

8. Data on construction costs are frequently published in _____ .

9. The cost estimating method in which the cost of all materials and labor are estimated and totaled to estimate reproduction or replacement cost is the _____ method.

10. An _____ is a capitalization rate derived from analysis of sales and income data.

QUESTIONS AND EXERCISES

1. If you were appraising a small suburban office building, where would you seek data for the cost approach?

2. If you, as a professional appraiser, were asked to appraise a building in a city about which you had little knowledge, what would you do? Under what circumstances would you accept the assignment? Reject it?

3. Visit your county assessor's office and list the information you can obtain about a property.

4. For the information in Question 3, how reliable is this information? Would you verify any of it?

5. Once you have determined the comps to be used in the sales comparison approach, how do you determine the amount of adjustments for differences between the subject and the comparable? For example, how do you determine the adjustment necessary when the comparable has 2 1/2 baths and the subject has only 2?

6. Why do appraisers most often use the cost per square foot method to estimate the reproduction or replacement cost of a single family home?

7. Under what conditions is the appraiser likely to estimate reproduction cost?

8. Why does an appraiser using the income approach assume typical management of the subject property? What complications does this assumption create for the appraiser?

9. How does the appraiser estimate the weighting to be assigned each valuation approach?

KEY TERMINOLOGY

adjustment	gross rent multiplier
appraisal data base	indirect costs
appraisal data plant	market abstraction method
band of investment	overall rate
breakdown method	per square foot method
capitalization	physical life
capitalization rate	pro forma income statement
constant	quantity survey method
contract rents	required equity return
cost manuals	return of capital
direct costs	return on capital
economic life	risk free
economic rents	risk premium
effective age	unit-in-place method
effective age method	verify

IF YOU WANT TO READ MORE

GEORGE F. BLOOM, ARTHUR M. WEIMER, and JEFFREY D. FISHER, *Real Estate*, 8th ed. (New York: John Wiley & Sons, 1982), Chapters 11, 15, and 16.

GEORGE F. BLOOM and HENRY S. HARRISON, *Appraising the Single Family Residence* (Chicago: American Institute of Real Estate Appraisers, 1978).

BYRL N. BOYCE and WILLIAM N. KINNARD, JR., *Appraising Real Property* (Lexington: D.C. Heath and Company, 1984).

WILLIAM M. SHENKEL, *Modern Real Estate Appraisal* (New York: McGraw-Hill Book Company, 1978).

Textbook Revision Subcommittee of the American Institute of Real Estate Appraisers, *The Appraisal of Real Estate*, 8th ed. (Chicago: American Institute of Real Estate Appraisers, 1983).

25

Real Estate Counseling

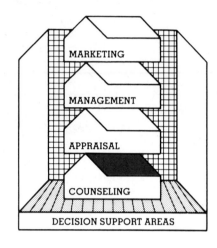

MARKETING

MANAGEMENT

APPRAISAL

COUNSELING

DECISION SUPPORT AREAS

PREVIEW
Many real estate decisions involve questions that you cannot answer without some help from someone specializing in some aspect of real estate. You can either ignore these questions, a very cavalier and often very costly approach, or you can seek out a competent, unbiased person to provide information or expert advice. The subject matter of these questions is without bounds. You may need advice on everything from who will buy or rent the space you are about to develop to what ownership form you should use to purchase a property. All of the professionals who provide you with this kind of decision support for a fee are collectively included in the area of real estate counseling. This chapter provides insights into this general decision support area by providing you with an understanding of:

1. What real estate counseling is and why it is needed.
2. The nature of the counseling process.
3. What specific counseling areas exist and who provides counseling within each.
4. What types of studies answer various questions.
5. How consultants work and what you should consider in selecting and dealing with them.

Real estate **counselors** are involved in all areas of real estate activity and may sometimes wear their counselors' hats and at other times wear another real estate hat. To understand how this on-again, off-again situation can occur, consider the definition of counseling developed by the **American Society of Real Estate Counselors,** a part of the National Association of Realtors. They define **counseling** as:

Providing competent, disinterested and unbiased advice, professional guidance and sound judgment on diversified problems in the broad field of real estate involving any or all segments of the business such as merchandising, leasing, management, planning, financing, appraising, court testimony and other similar services. Counseling may involve the utilization of any or all of these functions.

For example, a broker may be asked to help a buyer analyze a potential real estate investment being offered for sale by another broker. In performing this function, the broker will be providing counseling services as an independent third party. The broker receives only a fee and the amount of compensation is in no way related to whether the investment is found to be good or bad. The broker will prepare and sign a report on which he stakes his professional reputation as a counselor. Likewise, the appraiser who prepares a report containing a financial analysis of an investment opportunity is acting as a counselor. So is the property manager helping a prospective investor estimate the costs of operating an investment property. Thus, counseling is best defined by the nature of the work it involves, not the counselor's specific area of expertise.

Real estate counseling includes areas often thought of as being beyond traditional real estate specialties such as law, accounting, market research, taxation, securities, design, construction, and economics. Specialists in all of these areas can provide you with valuable research and advice when needed. Careerwise, if you are simultaneously interested in one of these areas, as well as a more traditional area of real estate, you may be able to very successfully marry the two by concentrating on becoming a real estate counselor.

HOW DO COUNSELORS WORK?
IS THERE METHOD TO THEIR MADNESS?

To understand how a counselor can help you, you must remember that counselors are usually called on to help solve a problem. For example, suppose you have two real estate investment opportunities and the money to undertake only one of them. You go to a well-known broker to help you perform a financial analysis of the two opportunities. You have a problem, and the counselor's job is to help you solve it. Often the counselor will answer your question in either formal report format or an

Table 25.1. Counseling Questions and Report Forms

Question	Report Form
What is the property worth?	Appraisal
What is the property worth to me?	Appraisal, investment analysis, investment counseling
Should I move or stay where I am?	Property utilization study, market search, appraisal, cost/benefit study
Should I buy (sell) this property?	Appraisal, investment counseling, risk analysis, property utilization study, market search, cost/benefit study
How should I go about acquiring (disposing of) this property?	Market search, negotiation counseling
How can I improve my enjoyment of the property?	Management study, rehabilitation study, operation or use counseling, cost benefit study, optimization
What kind of property do I need?	Operations research, property utilization study, location study
How should I develop my property?	Highest and best use study, management study
Will my plan for the use of the property work?	Feasibility study
How much can I safely lend on the security of the property?	Appraisal, underwriting analysis
How does the property compare as an investment to other investment opportunities?	Investment analysis, market investigation, appraisal
What events are likely to affect my property?	Trend analysis, forecasting, planning study, engineering study
How should I develop my property?	Highest and best use study, development planning, development counseling
Who will be interested in my property?	Market research, market counseling
How long should I hold my property or wait before acquiring it?	Trend analysis, forecasting, tax and investment counseling
How can I best finance an acquisition or disposition of the property?	Financing plan, investment analysis, underwriting analysis, investment counseling
Should the property be divided, and, if so, how?	Highest and best use study, appraisal, marketing study, acquisition plan
How well are my agents performing?	Management study, supervision
How can I get permission to use the property in accordance with my desires?	Zoning study, expert testimony, tactical guidance
How can I best deal with a conflict situation involving the property?	Strategy formulation, tactical support
What can I do about an actual or threatened condemnation?	Appraisal, eminent domain counseling, expert testimony
How should a community area be used?	Zoning study, land use study, redevelopment program
How should property within a given jurisdiction be taxed?	Assessment study or review, real estate tax planning and budgeting

Table 25.1. (continued)

Question	Report Form
What is happening to the tax base?	Economic base study, trend analysis, forecasting
What impact will a given use have on the community?	Environmental impact study, economic impact study
Are the costs of a given policy in proportion to the benefit?	Cost/benefit study

SOURCE: Reprinted with permission from Real Estate Counseling, copyright American Society of Real Estate Counselors, 430 N. Michigan Avenue, Chicago, IL 60611, p. 7.

expanded letter format. Table 25.1 contains some common real estate questions and the general type of report typically developed and used to answer each. Do not be overly concerned if you do not understand all of the report types. Often the same report will be called different things by different people.

A systematic approach is best for solving any kind of problem. The systematic approach adopted by real estate counselors is called the **counseling process** and is outlined in Table 25.2. The counseling process, like the appraisal process you studied in Chapter 23, is a variation of the scientific approach to solving any problem, real estate or otherwise. The counseling approach is of value to you, not only because it helps you understand how counselors work, but also as a plan of attack for any real estate problems you may tackle without counseling help. Although the counseling process is virtually self-explanatory, a little explanation may make it clearer and more meaningful.

Define the Problem

Many problems elude solution because they are never clearly defined. It is natural that the counselor wants to avoid this possibility and spends a good bit of time with the client defining precisely which problems are to be solved. This may be the most valuable service the counselor performs. It seems that often problems are not clearly defined because it is a difficult job — especially when the problems you are facing are amorphous or when emotional involvement is high.

The real estate counselor will also use this initial stage to develop the context of your problem. He or she will try to find out a great deal about you, your goals and aspirations, and your relationship to the problem area to be analyzed (for example, owner, lender). Then the counselor turns to the issues to be addressed to examine the types of real estate involved and special items to be considered. Next, the counselor identifies the specific nature of his or her assignment. The counselor will also make an inventory of the expertise necessary to perform the assignment

Table 25.2. The Counseling Process

This overview of counseling and its characteristics permits a closer look at the counseling *process*, seen as a sequence of tasks carried out for a specific purpose or purposes on behalf of a specific client, dealing with specific subject matter, utilizing specific materials and skills, and couched in a specific and appropriate form. The following statement of these tasks and their sequence constitutes a definition of the counseling process.

After a preliminary review of the problem and a clearing away of extraneous matters, the counselor's steps are ordinarily as follows:

I. Define the problem as to:
   A. Client: nature, relationship to the property, goals and priorities, needs, resources, constraints, attitudes, and position.
   B. Subject matter: kind and type of real estate involved, special characteristics if any.
   C. Purpose: questions to be answered, problems to be solved, goals to be achieved.
   D. Materials and skills required.
   E. Form: kind of report needed.

II. Establish the counseling relationship: confirm the problem definition with the client, define the relationship, and enter into the counseling contract.

III. Plan the assignment:
   A. Establish deadlines.
   B. Review files and library for available data and methodologies.
   C. Establish time budgets.
   D. Establish expense budgets.
   E. Allocate tasks and schedule work, with appropriate points for consultation and review.

IV. Do the work:
   A. Collect preliminary data.
   B. Formulate hypothesis.
   C. Test hypothesis.
   D. Reformulate hypothesis, if required, and follow with additional testing.
   E. Consider and compare alternative hypotheses.
   F. Formulate conclusions and recommendations.

V. Prepare the report: the counseling report may consist of an oral presentation ordinarily supported by a brief memorandum report for record purposes, or of a formal report analogous to an appraisal report. At a minimum, the memorandum report should contain the following items:
   A. Identification of client.
   B. Identification of property as to location, nature, and kind.
   C. Date.
   D. Author.
   E. Purpose.
   F. Sources and methods employed.
   G. Limiting conditions and presumptions.
   H. Statement of findings.

VI. Review the report, check computations; test presumptions where possible.

VII. Present the report: normally done in person, the report presentation helps to prevent misunderstandings and permits clarification of any questions that remain unclear to the client. The report may be presented initially in draft form.

SOURCE: Reprinted with permission from Real Estate Counseling, copyright American Society of Real Estate Counselors, 430 N. Michigan Avenue, Chicago, IL 60611, pp. 8 and 9.

to see whether additional help will be needed. Finally, the report format is considered. Is the report to be essentially oral with only a bare bones letter or memorandum supporting it? Or, should there be a detailed written report prepared with supporting data? At this point, you, your problem, and what the counselor is to do about it are well defined.

Establish the Counseling Relationship

The next step is to formalize your relationship with the counselor. Everything discussed earlier should be reduced to writing and the document signed by both parties. This contract should clearly outline your responsibilities to the counselor and the counselor's responsibilities to you, including the exact questions or issues to be addressed in the report and time schedules for completing the work.

Plan the Assignment

A counselor will now plan the assignment to establish priorities and detail the work schedule. Other experts may be consulted to help in this phase.

Do The Work

The actual work is now performed. In Table 25.2, this step involves formulating an hypothesis. This simply means that some course of action will be assumed to be best for purposes of testing. If the data and analysis do not support the hypothesis, then a new hypothesis will be required. For example, if you are considering investing in an office building, the hypothesis to be tested may be that the investment, exactly as proposed, is a good one. If data and analysis suggest this to be untrue, the hypothesis will be rejected, and a new hypothesis will be developed and tested. It could be that several alternative hypotheses will be tested before an acceptable solution is found and recommendations made.

Preparation, Review, and Presentation of Report

Once the best course of action or best answer is identified, the counselor will prepare the report in the format agreed to by the client. When the report is completed, the counselor will check it for possible errors and then present it to you. The counselor may provide an oral presentation along with the formal report. After the report is presented, you should have the opportunity to ask any questions about the methodology used and conclusions reached.

USING COUNSELORS

Chances are good that you will use a real estate counselor of some sort even if you do not go into the real estate business as a full-time occupation. In buying homes or investing in income properties, you will likely need the services of some sort of counselor. If you enter the real estate business, the chances of using a counselor increase. Counselors are best used to avoid problems rather than solve problems after they arise. Properly used, counselors can not only help you avoid problems but also help maximize the performance of an investment or development opportunity. There is a certain pattern counseling experiences tend to follow. There are also some things you need to know in order to deal more effectively with counselors and to get your money's worth from them.

SELECTING A COUNSELOR

Real estate counselors are a low-profile group. They do not advertise extensively, especially in popular publications read by the general public. Because of this, you may not know where to go when a problem arises. As with many professionals, referrals from trusted persons may prove your best bet for finding a competent counselor. Referrals may come from friends, people in the real estate business, bankers, or any other source you trust. If referrals are not available, the Yellow Pages of the telephone book may provide a place to start. Some counselors may be listed as such; if not, various professional organizations, such as the American Institute of Real Estate Appraisers, have sections in the Yellow Pages in which their members are listed. Some of these individuals may belong to the American Society of Real Estate Counselors (ASREC), and hold the Real Estate Counselor (CRE) designation. Membership in ASREC is by invitation only. ASREC has adopted a code of ethics for its members to follow in providing counseling services.

Initial Meeting

However you choose a counselor, a meeting with the counselor should be arranged to form impressions about the counselor's competence and ability to work constructively with you. You may want to ask for references, and you will certainly want to ask any trusted persons their opinion of the counselor, even if they could not earlier recommend one. You should not be afraid to ask the counselor about qualifications as a counselor and experience in dealing with problems similar to yours. Questions should also be asked about counseling fees and how they are determined. In all fairness, the counselor will also want some information about you and the nature of your problem.

Follow-up Meeting
and Establishing the Counseling Relationship

If you feel comfortable after considering the information you have gathered to this point, you may arrange a second meeting to discuss your problem in more detail. At this meeting, the counselor will probably ask a number of additional questions about you and the problem to be solved and outline some general steps to take. You should ask about alternative approaches to the problem and the costs associated with each. If all is satisfactory, you will ask the counselor to prepare a detailed proposal that reduces your discussion to writing.

You should read the proposal and contract very carefully to make sure you are getting the services you really want. Special care should be taken to insure that you get progress reports and that performance standards are included that tell you exactly what questions are to be answered in the report and what constitutes adequate analysis of each question. For example, if you are interested in the characteristics of potential tenants for an apartment investment, it may be specified that the report contain a profile of likely tenants based on government data and original market research performed by the counselor. The contract should specify that the counselor provide all supporting data for any conclusions reached about the market for those apartments.

Before you give the counselor approval to prepare a detailed proposal, a number of things should be very clear, including exactly what problem the counselor is attacking, how the problem is to be solved, who will do the work, how long the work will take, what kind of report you will get, how much the work will cost, and how performance will be measured. Once you approve the contract, the counselor will begin work. The contract should also specify what payments should be made for expenses incurred by the counselor and when counseling fees are due and payable. For your protection, you should not pay all of the fee until the final report is received and reviewed for completeness and quality.

A Final Word on Using Counselors

Your relationship with the counselor is one of trust. You must trust the counselor to give a best effort to solve your problem. The counselor must trust you to provide all possible information to help solve that problem. A failure to treat the counseling relationship with trust and openness may spell the difference between a satisfying, productive experience and bitter disappointment.

SUMMARY

Real estate counseling involves providing professional real estate problem solving assistance on a fee basis. Counseling services are provided by experts in many traditional fields of real estate specialization, including appraisal, brokerage, and property management. Some counselors are members of the American Society of Real Estate Counselors, a part of the National Association of Realtors.

In solving problems, counselors will often use the counseling process, a variation of the scientific approach to problem solving. This process includes: defining the problem, establishing the counseling relationship, planning the assignment, doing the work, and preparing and presenting the report. Counseling reports can range from brief summaries to lengthy narratives.

The time to use a counselor is before a real problem develops. Counselors are often found by referrals, but the listings of professional organizations in the Yellow Pages may also be a reasonable place to start your search for a counselor. Unless you have had experience with a particular counselor, it may be useful to visit with more than one in order to assess which counselor is best for you. Initial and follow-up meetings with prospective counselors should be used to answer any questions about what the counselor can do for you, the timetable for these services, and the fee. You should be willing to deal openly and honestly with the counselor and to define clearly the problem to be researched.

QUICK QUIZ

1. The organized approach to counseling is called the _____.

    a. work plan   c. business plan
    b. counseling process   d. none of the above

2. "Doing the work" involves all but which one of the following?

    a. preparing the report   c. developing an hypothesis
    b. collecting data   d. testing the hypothesis

3. Selecting a real estate counselor may involve _____.

    I. using the yellow pages
   II. referrals from friends

    a. I only   c. Both I and II
    b. II only   d. Neither I nor II

4. The professional group of counselors that is part of the National Association of Realtors is the _____.

5. Before giving a counselor approval to perform services, the following items should be clear: _____, _____, _____, _____, _____, _____, and _____.

6. The services the counselor will provide are detailed in the _____ and _____.

QUESTIONS AND EXERCISES

1. Look in the Yellow Pages and see how many individuals or firms offer real estate counseling services. What particular areas of expertise (for example, appraising) do these counselors have?

2. For the first eight questions in Table 25.1, identify the areas of real estate expertise of counselors likely to provide assistance in answering them.

3. Why do you think real estate counselors are often not used by persons who could benefit from their services? How can this situation be corrected?

KEY TERMINOLOGY

American Society of Real Estate
  Counselors
counseling
counseling process
counselor

IF YOU WANT TO READ MORE

American Society of Real Estate Counselors, *Real Estate Counseling* (Chicago: American Society of Real Estate Counselors, 1976).

G. VINCENT BARRETT and JOHN P. BLAIR, *How to Conduct and Analyze Real Estate Market and Feasibility Studies* (New York: Van Nostrand, 1982).

PART FIVE

REAL ESTATE OUTLOOK

There is an old adage that states, "Hindsight is more certain, but foresight is more profitable." Although such homilies are seldom correct all the time, this one is often appropriate in the real estate business. In an environment characterized by change, the ability to anticipate and incorporate that change into your activities is a valuable skill. Of course, no one can accurately foresee all possible changes, but being able to identify significant trends is often sufficient to improve your chances of thriving in the real estate business.

This section presents some of the possible areas of change affecting various aspects of real estate. It contains only a single chapter and does not attempt to consider *all* possible courses of events that could affect you. It is intended to point out some possible changes and arouse your interest and creativity in identifying important reasons for change and the impact of evolutionary or revolutionary change on you and your role in the basic real estate activity, providing space.

26

Real Estate Outlook: where do we go from here?

PREVIEW   Not long ago, in the best seller **Future Shock,** Alvin Toffler wrote about change and its impact on all of us. He noted that in recent times the rate of change has been increasing, often making it difficult to cope with continually changing surroundings — a condition he called **future shock.** Real estate is no exception to change. The real estate environment is complex, dynamic, and filled with uncertainty. Although the basic concepts you have learned in this book will likely be valid for some time, much of the environment in which they are used will change — perhaps just a little, perhaps substantially. The point is clear: you cannot stop learning now. This book was designed to be only a beginning. It was intended to provide you with a *perspective* for further learning and for dealing with changes in the real estate environment. These changes make real estate interesting and exciting, and provide tremendous economic opportunities for those anticipating and creating change. This chapter provides a brief look at changes, possible changes, and trends in real estate. After reading this chapter you will understand:

1. Some of the trends creating change in real estate.
2. Some of the possible changes in real estate fundamentals, decision areas, and decision support areas.

The role of change in providing opportunities for exciting and profitable real estate activity cannot be overemphasized. A static, unchanging real estate environment would lack not only excitement, but also the personal and financial potential so many people in the real estate business find exciting. Change creates a set of economic winners and losers. This is true whether the change is economic, social, technological, or legal in nature. For example, changes in the income tax law provide opportunities for knowledgable developers and investors to maximize their economic gains by proper anticipation and planning. Certainly, luck plays a part in who wins and loses. However, it seems that those who are knowledgeable have more good luck than those who aren't.

This chapter is designed to make you aware of the importance of the dynamic nature of real estate and to highlight certain areas of possible change. It is not an attempt to forecast the future, nor is it in any way to be considered a complete discussion of possible areas of change in real estate. The chapter is purposely brief to make you aware of the breadth of change in real estate, but not to appear to cover everything. It is intended to be a gentle nudge to help you understand that each day you fail to study the market or learn new techniques or read about some aspect of real estate is another day you are behind. *You* must keep up with change.

The discussion that follows is organized just like the book. Real estate fundamentals are discussed first, followed by decision areas and decision support areas. As you read about the outlook for real estate, you should keep some basic concepts in mind. First, the basic real estate product is space, either rented or sold for use over time. Space for people to work, live, and play is what real estate is all about. Not surprisingly, demography dramatically affects the future of real estate. Second, the availability and cost of money affects all aspects of the real estate business. Much of the change, and possible change, to be discussed is rooted in demography and/or money.

REAL ESTATE FUNDAMENTALS

Law

Law is a reflection of society. As an issue becomes a matter of concern to society, law will likely be created by either legislation or court cases dealing with that issue. One such issue is land use regulation. In the 1980s and 1990s, private ownership rights, public rights to control land use, and the relationship between the two areas will be subjects of controversy, and possibly change. The trend in recent times has been toward a more malleable definition of private property rights. As a result, land has come to be treated much as a public utility subject to public regulation. Put another way, the bundle of private property rights may be redefined in the coming years. With respect to land use regulation, the

1980s and 1990s will be a period in which the role of federal and state governments in the field will be more clearly defined. At this time, it appears that role will be an increasingly active one.

Other possible areas of change are in the way disputes are settled and the preparation of legal documents. The increased propensity for litigation has created backlogs in courts and tremendous legal expenses. Alternatives to court cases may become more common. Administrative proceedings by professional organizations and arbitration by independent third parties are two possible alternatives. For example, a dispute between third parties and Realtors® may be settled at an administrative proceeding at the local Board of Realtors® more frequently than at present. **Arbitration** involves both parties agreeing to be bound by the decision of an independent third party. The increased tendency to go to court has led to more care in the preparation of legal documents. Not only will legal documents be prepared more carefully, but they may also be prepared in what is called "plain language." More states may pass laws requiring that documents be readable and understandable by those signing them.

Urban Areas

So many changes are possible in urban areas that only a few selected ones will be discussed here. First, the rural to urban movement has ended. It has been replaced in many areas by a return to rural and smaller town areas. During the 1980s, rural and nonmetropolitan areas are projected to grow at faster rates than metropolitan areas. However, because of national population growth, urban populations will continue to increase. And because of flows of people between cities and regions, some cities will grow much faster than others, and some will actually lose population. Second, within many metropolitan areas, there is a renewed interest in the city. Redevelopment and rehabilitation efforts are now gaining momentum. The reasons for this trend include a desire to escape the suburbs, federal income tax benefits, the cost and availability of energy, and the lower cost of rehabilitation as compared to new construction. Whether this trend continues depends on factors such as prices, quality of schools, crime, and the cost of energy.

Property Taxation

Property taxation promises to be a lively topic in coming years. The biggest issue will be the level of property taxes, with many property owners now feeling that property taxes are entirely too high. Proposition 13 in California is an example of this feeling and what it can produce. Similar political movements have arisen in other states and may well spread to even more states. The impact of lower property taxes on property values and the level of public services are two important consequences to consider.

Federal Income Taxation

Pressure to eliminate tax loopholes and the promotion of tax equity will remain strong. Evidence of this pressure is seen in the passage of the Tax Equity and Fiscal Responsibility Act of 1982 and the Tax Reform Act of 1984. Significant legislation designed to reduce the tax shelter aspects of real estate will likely be passed in the next 3 to 5 years. Another issue of potentially major importance is the growing support for a **flat-rate tax** system in which all, or virtually all, deductions are eliminated and all income is taxed at the same flat rate. The impact of such a tax system on real estate would be significant.

DECISION AREAS

Lending

Lending will continue to be an area of substantial change. Single family residential lending, long a straightforward, relatively static field, has experienced tremendous change in the flexibility afforded borrowers and lenders. The immediate future will probably be a period of digesting and refining the many changes of the recent past. New alternative mortgage instruments may be created, but the pace will be slower than in the last 6 years. A trend that is likely to continue is the decreased dependence on thrift institutions for mortgage money. The use of direct investment in mortgages through mortgage-backed securities should increase in the remainder of the 1980s.

In income property lending, the question is whether lenders will continue to become joint venture partners in the projects they choose to fund. The high interest rates of the early and mid-1980s have created a situation in which lenders became joint venture partners with developers and equity investors by participating in the project's income in addition to the collecting interest. It will be interesting to see whether this activity continues when interest rates fall.

Equity Investment

Homeownership is in for a period of adjustment. High prices have taken many families out of the market, either financially or psychologically. Coupled with record high interest rates, high prices have made renters out of many families that in other periods would have been buyers. In an attempt to overcome this problem, some builders are offering smaller, less luxurious homes. A similar situation occurred in the tight money period of the mid-1970s, with the public generally not accepting the scaled-down version of the American Dream. However, housing prices have continued to increase since that period. More families today that already have both spouses working and do not have a readily available source of substantial additional income may accept these smaller homes as their only way of getting into the housing market. On the other hand, some buyers may feel that the reduced rate of appreciation in housing prices in the first half of the 1980s may be the start of a longer period of slower price appreciation. This may cause them to postpone their home purchase even longer. Whether this slowdown in appreciation is long-term or short-term will be an important item to watch in the next few years.

As mentioned earlier, investment in income-producing real estate has changed, with lenders becoming partners with equity investors. In some cases this has reduced the investor's returns and operating freedom. However, few institutional investors are willing to allow a property to fail, and have provided funds to keep a marginal property going until it becomes healthy. This has reduced the equity investor's risk. Additionally, some lenders have become direct investors by purchasing properties themselves. Will these trends continue?

International real estate investing has also become big business. Many foreign investors have purchased virtually every kind of U.S. real estate, including farmland. The stability of our political and economic systems, coupled with favorable income tax situations, have been prime attractions to these investors. In many instances, foreign investors have been willing to pay top prices and accept rates of return lower than their U.S. counterparts. Will this trend continue? Will states enact legislation limiting foreign investment? These and other questions will be answered in the next decade.

Development

Development tends to occur in cycles with periods of overbuilding followed by relatively calm periods in which excess space is absorbed. The early 1980s was a period of overbuilding. How long will it be to the next development cycle? What types of projects will be developed? For instance, will new towns, condominiums, and large regional shopping centers be developed? Who will develop them—developers alone or developers acting as joint venture partners with large institutional investors? What kinds of land use planning and regulation will affect development in the 1980s?

DECISION SUPPORT AREAS

Marketing

There are several issues in marketing that merit consideration. First is the entry of large firms into the brokerage business. Sears, Roebuck & Co. has acquired Coldwell Banker & Co, a brokerage firm with offices around the country. Other firms, such as Merrill Lynch, have gotten into real estate marketing. In addition, franchise firms such as Century 21, Red Carpet, Gallery of Homes, Better Homes and Gardens, and E.R.A. have become active. Will these trends continue and, if so, what impact will they have on real estate marketing? Will these new national firms introduce a wider range of services than presently offered by marketing firms? Will independent firms be able to compete with these firms?

Service packages and compensation may also change in the 1980s. Will brokerage firms break the current complete package of services offered for a commission into individual pieces performed for a fee? For example, will a seller be able to choose the services needed, such as help in establishing an asking price, and pay only for those services? How will these services be priced?

Another area of possible adjustment is in the relationship between sales personnel and the brokerage firm. Specifically, will the independent contractor arrangement, which now accounts for over 90 percent of all sales personnel associated with marketing firms, continue or be replaced by an employee arrangement? There are several reasons why such a change may occur. First, the IRS has had an interest in the independent contractor arrangement for some time. There are indications they would like to see independent contractors treated as employees for tax purposes. This means the brokerage firm would have to withhold income and social security taxes from compensation. They would also have to pay the employer's portion of social security taxes. Second, employee status would give the brokerage firm greater control over their sales personnel. Many brokerage firms find this added control very appealing.

A widespread change to employee status for sales personnel would mean a reduction in the size of the sales force for many firms. The added costs of taxes and benefit programs would force firms to employ only very productive people. Such a situation would result in a reduction in the total number of sales personnel needed. In short, firms would probably be leaner, with greater average productivity per sales associate.

Licensing requirements for brokers and salespersons will continue to evolve in the next decade. The trend toward more stringent educational requirements for obtaining a license will continue throughout the nation. Less certain is the future of educational requirements to renew real estate licenses, called continuing education requirements. The next few years should determine the popularity of continuing education requirements.

Management

Changes to watch in property management include continuing computerization, greater activity as consultants, and the growing importance of the property management function. Computers will be used increasingly to handle accounting, tenant and maintenance information, and report preparation for the property manager. Increased competition for real estate investments and development opportunities will create a need for property managers acting as consultants. The same competition will likely cause investors to pay top dollar for properties, a situation that increases the need for efficient property management. Good property management will allow investors to get the most from their investment and will mean the difference between the success and failure of many investments.

Appraising

In the appraisal area, the introduction of tremendous variations in financing will continue to make it difficult for the appraiser to find truly comparable properties. To overcome this problem and generally improve the quality and efficiency of the appraiser's work, computerized data bases will be expanded and improved. Appraisers will increasingly be performing tasks other than estimating market value. Such work will include market studies, financial analysis, and overall feasibility analysis.

Counseling

Counseling will be a growth industry in the 1980s. In the competitive investment and development arena of the 1980s, counselors will be used frequently to analyze everything from the market to the financial arrangements. Firms of all types may form counseling organizations as part of existing firms or as new firms. There will likely be an increase in the number of full-service firms capable of providing a wide range of counseling and support services. In effect, they will be able to provide turn-key real estate investment, an attractive proposition for those too busy to devote a great deal of time to their investment matters. Professionals from appraising, property management, commercial brokerage, accounting, mortgage banking, law, and other areas will find their way into counseling.

KEEPING CURRENT

Keeping current in real estate requires that you continue to be a student of the field. Being a student means that you never stop trying to learn by reading, listening to others in real estate and related areas, attending courses, and gaining your own experience. You should select a set of periodicals that provide you with up-to-date information about real estate trends and thinking. Two of the best and most readable general real estate publications are *Real Estate Today,* published by the Realtors

National Marketing Institute of the National Association of Realtors, and *Real Estate Review,* published by Warren, Gorham & Lamont. There are also some fine publications and subscription services that provide concise, current information on specific fields, which you may find of interest. Some real estate and real estate–related firms gather and publish current statistics, information, and analyses on matters relating to real estate. In addition, there are specialty journals on everything from appraisal to mortgage banking that you can read and study.

There is a tremendous amount to be learned from others in the real estate business. By listening to the successful people you meet and deal with, you can gain insights into their thinking, knowledge, and personal philosophies. Activity in real estate organizations can provide you with opportunities to meet and visit with others sharing your interests.

Finally, you can attend seminars and courses on real estate offered by your local real estate board; the institutes, societies, and councils of the National Association of Realtors; and local colleges and universities. These courses allow you to learn about new areas of interest or deepen your knowledge of familiar real estate topics.

However you choose to do it, this book has provided you with a firm foundation for continuing your study of real estate. Best of luck to you in your business and learning activities.

SUMMARY

This chapter has provided a brief glimpse at possible changes in real estate in the near future. Change is important because it creates a set of winners and losers. Those who anticipate change and adjust to it are often the winners in such situations. The chapter was not intended as a complete discussion but as a listing of some of the changes that may affect the real estate business. Underlying many of the changes are demography and the availability and cost of money.

Essentially all areas considered in the book are subject to change in the 1980s. Fundamental real estate areas such as law, urban areas, property taxation, and federal income taxation are all dynamic fields that materially affect real estate decisions. Topics of interest there include land use regulation, plain language documents, alternatives to litigation, population growth, migration, redevelopment, property tax limitations, the elimination of tax loopholes, and the flat rate tax plan. The distinctions between lending, equity investment, and development are being blurred by the increased use of joint ventures. Additional issues in the decision areas are the increase in alternative mortgage instruments, foreign investment in U.S. real estate, affordable housing, and adapting development to satisfy the need for space. Finally, in the decision support areas, considerations include the entry of large non-real estate firms in the brokerage business, franchising, independent

contractor arrangements, service packages and fees, licensing requirements, activity as consultants, variations in financing, and the growth
of counseling.

QUICK QUIZ

1. One of the leading legal issues in the 1980s will likely be _____ .

   a. the use of restrictive covenants   c. concurrent ownership
   b. mortgage law   d. land use regulation

2. Two factors described as being critical to many of the changes in
real estate are _____ .

   a. demographics and money
   b. money and law
   c. law and urban development
   d. demographics and urban development

3. Which of the following was *not* cited as a reason for foreign investment in U.S. real estate?

   a. stable economy
   b. favorable currency exchange rates
   c. favorable tax treatment
   d. stable political environment

4. A widespread conversion from independent contractors to employees would cause a(n) _decrease_ in the number of sales associates.

5. When markets for real estate investments are competitive,
managerial professionals are of increased importance.

6. The decision support area identified as a real growth area was
___counselors___

**QUESTIONS
AND
EXERCISES**

1. Why does change create opportunities for you in the real estate
business?

2. What is future shock? Do you see any signs of future shock among
the general public with respect to present conditions in real estate?

3. List and discuss the pros and cons of submitting a real estate disagreement to a system other than the courts for resolution.

4. What impact will the consumerism movement have on real estate brokerage?

5. Do you think the interest in moving back to cities from the suburbs will continue and gain strength? Why?

6. How successfully do you think a brokerage firm can sell individual services instead of a complete package as they now do? How would they establish the prices for these services?

KEY TERMINOLOGY

arbitration
flat rate tax
future shock

IF YOU WANT TO READ MORE

JERRY C. DAVIS, "Big Business Enters Real Estate," *Real Estate Today* (August 1979), pp. 43–48.

NORMAN G. MILLER, "The Changing Nature of Residential Brokerage," *Real Estate Review* (Fall 1978), pp. 46–50.

Real Estate Research Corporation, *Emerging Trends in Real Estate* (Chicago: The First National Bank of Chicago). Updated annually.

Glossary

The number(s) in parentheses after each term indicates the chapter(s) in which the word is discussed.

Absorption rate. (17) A number indicating the average amount of a particular type of new space that has been demanded over some specified period of time.

Abstract company. (5) A firm gathering data on recorded documents affecting real property and producing abstracts of title.

Abstract of title. (5) A chronological collection of all recorded documents affecting title to real property.

Acceleration clause. (14) A mortgage clause that gives the lender the option of making the entire outstanding balance of a mortgage due and payable if the borrower breaches any covenant.

Acceptance. (6) In contracts, agreeing to the terms of a proposed offer.

Accessibility. (7) The time and money cost of getting to and from a site.

Accounting. (4) The process by which rights and responsibilities between concurrent owners are determined and adjusted.

Accretion. (5) An increase in land area caused by a stream gradually building up an area of dry land by depositing dirt and rock.

Accrued depreciation. (23,24) The total loss in the value of a property from all causes.

Acknowledgment. (5) Certification by some designated person, such as a notary public, that the party or parties signing a document did, in fact, appear before him and sign the acknowledged instrument.

Acre. (3) A measure of land area containing 43,560 square feet.

Actual agency. (20,21) An agency relationship created by direct discussion and agreement between the agent and principal.

Actual authority. (20,21) Express or implied authority given the agent by the principal.

Actual cash value. (22) In insurance, the cost of an asset minus accrued depreciation and the maximum amount many policies will pay if an asset is damaged or destroyed.

Adjustable rate mortgage. (15) A mortgage in which changes may be made in the loan's interest rate based on changes in an index.

Ad valorem. (10) According to value.

Ad valorem taxes. (10) Property taxation in which the amount of tax is based on the value of the property.

Adverse possession. (4) The right of an occupant to obtain title to real property by actual, continuous, open, and exclusive possession for a specified period of time.

Agency. (20,21) A relationship in which one party, the agent, is authorized to act on behalf of another party, the principal. In real estate, the most common agency occurs between a seller and a broker.

Agent. (20,21) One authorized to act for another, called the principal.

Air rights. (4) Rights in the air space above the surface of the earth, usually beginning a designated number of feet above the surface or sea level.

Air space. (3) The physical area above the surface of real estate.

Alternative mortgage instruments. (15) Mortgages with features different from the fixed-rate, fixed-payment mortgage.

American Institute of Real Estate Appraisers. (23,24) An institute of the National Association of Realtors composed of those engaged in real estate appraisal and awarding the designations of Residential Member (RM) and Member Appraisal Institute (MAI).

American Society of Real Estate Counselors. (25) A society of the National Association of Realtors composed of those engaged in real estate counseling and invited to hold the CRE designation.

Amortization. (13) The paying off of a loan by regular payments composed of principal and interest.

Annexation. (8) The process of expanding the legal boundaries of a city or town.

Annual percentage rate (APR). (13) An indication of the cost of debt in percentage terms when financing costs are considered. Its disclosure is required by Regulation Z in many situations.

Annuity. (13) A series of equal cash flows each period.

Apparent authority. (21) Authority given an agent by the principal's actions with third parties.

Appraisal. (23) A report containing an estimate of the market value of a parcel of real property.

Appraisal data base. (24) The in-house collection of market data used by the appraiser to estimate market value.

Appraisal plant. (24) See appraisal data base.

Appraisal process. (23) An organized framework for estimating market value patterned after the scientific approach to problem solving.

Appraiser. (23,24) One who estimates the market value of real property for a fee or as part of employment duties. Appraisers also often provide consulting services other than appraisal.

Appurtenance. (4) An asset, interest, or right that passes from one owner to the next with the land.

Appurtenant. (4) The legal terminology for indicating that an asset, interest, or right, called an appurtenance, passes with title to real property.

Assessed value. (10) An estimate of the value of real property used to calculate the property tax liability for that parcel.

Assessment district. (10) The geographical area encompassing all the properties deemed to receive direct benefits from a particular public improvement and the financial responsibilities for a special assessment.

Assessment ratio. (10) The factor, expressed as a percentage, that is used to convert market value into assessed value.

Assessment roll. (10) The public records of the assessed value of each parcel of property within a taxing jurisdiction.

Assessor. (10) A public official responsible for estimating the assessed value of each parcel of real property within a jurisdiction.

Attorney-at-law. (20) One who has passed the bar examination and is authorized to practice law.

Attorney-in-fact. (21) One authorized to act on behalf of another under a power of attorney.

Average tax rate. (11) The ratio of tax liability to taxable income.

Balance sheet. (16) A financial statement showing assets, liabilities, and net worth of an individual or firm.

Balloon payment. (13) The payment required to pay off the remaining balance of an unamortized loan or a loan not completely amortized.

Bargain-and-sale deed. (5) A deed implying that a certain interest is being conveyed but containing no express covenants to that effect.

Base line. (3) The east-west line used in conjunction with a principal meridian to legally describe real property using the rectangular or government survey method.

Basic employment. (7) Employment engaged in producing goods and services sold outside the area under consideration.

Basic tax equation. (10,11) The general formula expressing the relationship between tax liability, tax base, and tax rate: Tax liability = Tax rate × Tax base.

Basis point. (13) One-hundredth of a percent, used to express the difference or change in a rate.

Bearing. (3) The angles used in a metes and bounds description measured in degrees, minutes, and seconds.

Blanket mortgage. (15) A mortgage secured by two or more parcels of real property.

Blockbusting. (21) Starting rumors that a member of a minority group is buying a home in a particular neighborhood in an attempt to cause panic selling.

Breach. (6) The failure of a contracting party to satisfy an obligation that has not been discharged.

Broker. (20,21) Anyone acting as an agent for a fee or the expectation of receiving a fee in the sale, purchase, or rental of real property.

Building code. (8) Laws specifying minimum standards for materials, workmanship, and safety features of improvements to real estate.

Building Owners and Managers Association International. (22) An organization providing educational opportunities and gathering operations data related to office building management.

Bundle of rights. (4) The concept that ownership of real estate involves a group of rights, not a single, all-encompassing right.

Call provisions. (15) Terms in a mortgage that make the entire balance of a loan due at some specified point in time.

Capital gains income. (11) Income from the sale of a capital asset that if long-term in nature is taxed at lower rates than ordinary income and if short-term in nature is taxed the same as ordinary income.

Capitalization. (23,24) The process of converting future cash flow(s) into a present value.

Capitalization rate. (23,24) Any rate used to convert future cash flows into a present value.

Cash flow after tax. (18,19) Cash flow before tax minus tax liability or plus tax savings.

Cash flow before tax. (18,19) Gross possible income minus vacancy allowance, operating expenses, debt service, and cost recovery.

Certificate of occupancy. (8) A document certifying that an improvement has met all building code requirements and may be occupied.

Chain of title. (5) A chronological ordering of all parties ever having an interest in a subject property.

Chattel. (4) Personal property.

Closing. (20) The consummation of a transaction at which title to real property is actually conveyed.

Closing statement. (20) A document showing the financial obligations and inflows of each party in a transaction.

Cloud on the title. (5) An outstanding claim or interest that could adversely affect the quality of a present ownership interest.

Co-insurance. (22) A situation in some insurance policies in which the insured must bear a pro rata share of any losses unless insurance equal to or greater than a specified percentage of the property's value is carried.

Commitment. (16) A promise from a lender that a loan with specified terms will be made.

Community property. (4) A doctrine of some states that presumes all property purchased after marriage is owned jointly by the wife and husband.

Comparable. (23) A property, for which data is available, sufficiently similar to a subject property to be used as an indicator of market value.

Competitive market analysis. (9,20) An analysis of current market offerings and recent sales for pricing, financing, and time on the market for properties similar to a subject property with the goal of establishing an asking price.

Compound interest. (13) Interest calculated on the assumption that all interest earned remains in the investment and earns interest in future periods.

Compounding. (13) The process of converting present dollars into equivalent amounts in future periods.

Concurrent ownership. (4) Simultaneous ownership of a parcel of property by more than one party.

Condemnation. (4) The process of having the courts establish the right of the state to purchase private property along with the amount of just compensation.

Condition precedent. (6) An event that must occur or a condition that must exist before an obligation for one party to a contract is created.

Condominium. (4) A form of ownership in which one has fee simple ownership in a particular unit and an undivided interest as a tenant in common in the shared areas of a building or project.

Consideration. (6) Something of legal value; it may be a promise, money, action, or forebearance from action.

Construction financing. (15) Short-term loans to pay for materials, labor, and indirect costs associated with making improvements to land.

Constructive notice. (5) The legal presumption that any document pertaining to a parcel of real estate that is filed in the appropriate recording office is public knowledge and is, therefore, assumed to be known by any party.

Contingent remainder. (4) A remainder in which the remainderman is not known.

Contract for deed. (14) A financing arrangement in which the seller finances all or part of the purchase price with title not passing to the buyer until the final payment is made.

Conventional mortgage. (15) Any mortgage not insured by FHA or guaranteed by the VA.

Continuing education requirement. (21) A statute enacted by some states making participation in a specified number of hours of real estate education necessary for license renewal.

Conveyance. (5) Transfer of an interest in real property from one owner to another.

Cooperative. (4) A not-for-profit corporation that owns and operates an apartment building and makes ownership of specified amounts of the corporation's stock a requirement for renting a unit.

Corporation. (4) A form of business organization that involves the creation of an entity that acts as a legal person in that the entity may contract, own property, and conduct business as an actual person.

Cost approach. (23,24) A method for estimating the market value of a parcel of real property by estimating and adding together the value of the land and the cost of reproducing or replacing the improvements.

Cost recovery. (11,12) The legal expensing for tax purposes of a portion of the cost of long-lived wasting assets each year of the allowed cost recovery period.

Counseling. (25) Providing disinterested and unbiased advice, analysis, and guidance on virtually any aspect of real estate for a fee.

Counselor. (25) One who provides consulting and advice as a disinterested party for a fee.

Court decree. (4) A legal document signed by the judge presiding at the proceedings, stating the court's decision in a case.

Covenant. (5) A warranty or promise made by one party to another.

Curtesy. (4) The right of a husband to a portion of the family's real property upon the death of his wife. The existence of curtesy and the extent of the husband's rights vary from state to state.

Debt coverage ratio. (16) The ratio of an investment property's net operating income to debt service.

Debt service. (13) The periodic payment on a mortgage loan consisting of principal and interest.

Dedication. (8) The giving of land to a governmental body for a public use, usually involving the development of a subdivision when the developer may give lands for schools and parks.

Deed. (5) A written instrument that conveys title to real property.

Deed in lieu of foreclosure. (14) Satisfying a default through the voluntary transfer of real property to a lender rather than through foreclosure.

Deed of trust. (14) A three-party agreement between the borrower, lender, and trustee used to secure the payment of a debt. Also called a trust deed.

Deed restrictions. (4) See restrictive covenants.

Default. (14) Failure to fulfill any aspect of a debt obligation.

Defects. (5) See cloud on the title.

Deferred maintenance. (22) Postponing maintenance to reduce operating expenses.

Deferred payment mortgage. (15) A long-term, fixed-rate mortgage in which payment of a percentage of the principal is deferred until a specified period, at which time the deferred portion plus accrued interest is due.

Deficiency judgment. (14) An unsecured personal judgment against a borrower obtained when proceeds from the public sale of mortgaged property are insufficient to repay the outstanding balance of the debt.

Demand. (7) A schedule of the quantity of a good or service that will be purchased at various prices.

Demographic characteristic. (7) A feature of a population.

Demography. (7) The study of the characteristics of populations.

Depreciation. (11,12,23,24) For income tax definition see Cost recovery. In appraisal, it is the loss in the value of a property from any cause.

Depreciation recapture. (12) The taxing of all or a portion of excess depreciation as ordinary income instead of as long-term capital gain income.

Development. (17) The process of combining land, labor, capital, and entrepreneurial ability to produce improvements to land.

Differential assessment. (10) A situation in which different types of real property are taxed at different rates or different assessment ratios are used.

Discharge. (6) Ending a contractual relationship by completing all obligations or by the occurrence of certain events specified by law.

Discount. (13) The difference between the face value of a loan and its sale price when it is sold for less than face value.

Discount point. (13) A fee charged when a loan is originated to increase the yield to the investor with each discount point equaling one percent of the original loan amount.

Discount rate. (13) A rate used in converting future sums of money into present values.

Discounted cash flow analysis. (19) The process of calculating all after-tax cash flows and using time value of money concepts to assess their adequacy.

Discounting. (13) The process of converting future sums of money into present values.

Disintermediation. (15) A reduction in the flow of funds into financial intermediaries.

Doctrine of prior appropriation. (4) A doctrine of water usage applied extensively in the western United States in which the first to use water develops a right to continued use even though later users may have more urgent need for the water.

Dower. (4) A wife's legal right to a portion of real property owned by the family in the event of her husband's death. Not all states have dower rights nor are dower rights equal in all states having such statutes.

Downzoning. (8) A change in zoning to a less intensive classification.

Due on sale clause. (14) A provision in a mortgage that obligates the borrower to secure the written consent of the lender for sale or other transfer of the property or the lender may accelerate the debt and make the entire balance due and payable.

Earnest money. (20) A sum of money given to the seller by the buyer to act as a deposit for a real estate purchase.

Easement. (4) A right to make specified use of real property owned by another.

Easement appurtenant. (4) An easement whose benefits attach to a parcel of land and are transferred to subsequent owners.

Easement in gross. (4) An easement benefiting a particular individual and not transferable.

Economic base. (7) Employment in an industry engaged in producing goods and services sold outside the area.

Economic base study. (7) A study of an economy in which economic activity is divided into basic and nonbasic components.

Economic life. (24) The period during which improvements can be expected to add to the value of land.

Economic obsolescence. (23,24) A loss in the value of a property due to factors external to the property itself.

Economic rent. (23,24) Rents justified by the market for the type of space under consideration.

Effective age. (24) The age of an improvement based on a comparison of its condition with other improvements whose ages are known.

Effective tax rate. (10,11) For federal income taxes, the ratio of tax liability to total receipts; for property taxes, the ratio of tax liability to the market value of a property.

Eminent domain. (4) The right of government to take private property for a public purpose in return for payment of just compensation.

Encroachment. (3) A building or other improvement that rests entirely or partially on the land of another.

Encumberance. (5) Any lien, interest, or other claim clouding title to real property.

Enforceable. (6) A term that applies to an agreement that the courts will support if necessary.

Environmental influence area. (7) The area surrounding a site perceived to be influencing the site's character.

Environmental Protection Agency. (8) The federal agency charged with implementing much environmental legislation.

Equal Credit Opportunity Act (ECOA). (14) A federal law requiring lenders to extend credit equally to all creditworthy applicants, without regard to race, color, religion, national origin, sex, marital status, or age.

Equilibrium. (9) A condition in a real estate market in which supply and demand are balanced.

Equity investment. (18,19) The funds invested in real property that are supplied by the owner rather than being borrowed.

Equity right of redemption. (14) In some states, the right of a borrower to retain legal title to property by paying the outstanding balance plus all accrued interest during the period after default and before foreclosure.

Erosion. (5) The gradual loss of land caused by it being washed away.

Escheat. (4) The passing of title to the state of any property no longer having a private owner.

Escrow. (20) The entrusting of money, documents, or other items to a third party along with instructions on the terms and conditions of the disposition of those items. Often used in contractual situations.

Escrow company. (20) One who acts as a disinterested third party in a real estate transaction according to a set of written escrow instructions outlining the conditions that must be met for title to be conveyed.

Estate. (4) Present interests in real property.

Exclusive agency listing. (20,21) A listing in which the agent is entitled to a commission if anyone other than the seller procures a ready, willing, and able buyer during the period of the listing.

Exclusive right to sell listing. (20,21) A listing in which the agent is entitled to a commission if anyone procures a ready, willing, and able buyer during the period of the listing.

Fannie Mae. (15) See Federal National Mortgage Association.

Favorable exposure. (7) Any attribute of the environmental influence area, not related to convenience, that enhances the desirability of a site.

Feasible. (17) A term that refers to a project that has a reasonable likelihood of satisfying the goals and objectives of the developer.

Feasibility analysis. (17) A study that considers the legal, site, market, and financial aspects of a proposed project to determine whether it has a reasonable likelihood of satisfying the goals and objectives of the developer.

Federal Home Loan Bank Board. (15) The body regulating federally chartered savings and loan associations.

Federal Home Loan Mortgage Corporation. (15) A secondary mortgage market institution affiliated with the Federal Home Loan Bank Board that buys mortgages from savings and loan associations. Also called Freddie Mac and The Mortgage Corporation.

Federal Housing Administration (FHA). (15) A federal agency in the Department of Housing and Urban Development that insures mortgage loans.

Federal National Mortgage Association. (15) A privately owned, but government-related secondary mortgage market institution. Also called Fannie Mae.

Federal Reserve System. (15) The body regulating all federally chartered (national) banks.

Fee simple. (4) The freehold estate containing the most complete possible bundle of rights with such rights theoretically continuing forever. Also called fee and fee simple absolute.

FHA. (15) See Federal Housing Administration.

FHA loan. (15) A loan insured by the Federal Housing Administration.

Fiduciary. (21) A person, firm, or institution in a position of trust.

Fixed obligation ratio. (16) A ratio used in mortgage underwriting calculated by dividing the total of monthly expenditures for principal, interest, property taxes, insurance, and other fixed obligations by gross monthly income.

Fixed-rate, fixed-payment mortgage. (13) A loan in which the interest rate and debt service payments do not change over the loan's life.

Fixture. (4) An item that was originally personal property but due to being attached or affixed to real estate has become real property.

Floor area ratio. (8) Calculated as the ratio of square feet of improvements to land area and used in zoning law to determine the maximum square footage of improvements that can be erected on a given parcel.

Forebearance. (14) A nonlegal solution to a default problem involving such activities as temporarily lowering payments or extending the time to pay.

Foreclosure. (14) A legal proceeding to end the borrower's equity of redemption and produce a court ordered sale of the property with the proceeds going to pay off the defaulted sums.

Fractional time period ownership. (4) An interest in a property that covers a specified period of time each year.

Fraud. (6) An intentional misrepresentation of a material fact with the intent of causing another to act.

Freddie Mac. (15) See Federal Home Loan Mortgage Corporation.

Freehold estate. (4) An estate involving the ownership of real property and lasting for an indefinite period of time.

Functional obsolescence. (23,24) A reduction to the reproduction cost of an improvement caused by the inability of the improvement to most efficiently perform the job for which it is intended because of design, structural inadequacies, and so on.

Future interest. (4) An interest in real property that will become possessory at some future date.

General agent. (20,21) One authorized to act on behalf of another, called the principal, in a particular business or at a particular location.

Gift letter. (16) A document stating that one person is giving a sum of money to another without any expectation of being repaid. Often required by lenders when such funds are being used for a down payment.

Ginnie Mae. (15) See Government National Mortgage Association.

Good consideration. (6) Nonmonetary consideration, such as love and affection, considered to have legal value.

Government National Mortgage Association. (15) An agency of the Department of Housing and Urban Development charged with creating a secondary market for special loan programs and guaranteeing the repayment of loans in mortgage pools.

Government survey method. (3) See rectangular survey method.

Graduated payment mortgage. (15) A fixed-rate mortgage in which the payments start at a lower than normal level and increase at specified intervals for a period of time and then become stable for the remainder of the loan term.

Graduated payment adjustable mortgage. (15) A graduated mortgage in which the interest rate is allowed to vary according to a specified index.

Grantee. (5) Person receiving an interest in real property from the grantor.

Grantor. (5) Person giving an interest in real property to the grantee.

Grantor-Grantee Index. (5) A retrieval system used to find recorded documents in which the documents are indexed on the basis of the grantors' or grantees' names.

Gross lease. (22) A lease in which the lessee makes a fixed payment and the lessor is responsible for all property expenses.

Gross rent multiplier. (23,24) The ratio of sale price to gross income that, when derived from the market for properties comparable to a subject property, can be multiplied by the economic gross rents to produce an estimate of market value.

Ground lease. (15) A lease for land.

Growing equity mortgage. (15) A fixed-rate mortgage with gradually increasing payments, the increases in which are applied directly to principal, resulting in a payoff of the loan in a period of time substantially shorter than the stated term.

Growth planning. (8) A blanket term for the process of planning, implementing, and monitoring orderly urban development.

Habendum clause. (14) The element of a deed that describes the estate being conveyed.

Highest and best use. (9,17) That land use creating the highest land value.

Homestead. (4) Real estate occupied by the owner as a principal residence.

Homestead exemption. (10) In some states, the reduction in assessed value of a principal residence upon the filing of proper documents by the owner and also, in some states, the legal protection afforded that homestead from attachment or sale to satisfy debts other than mortgages and taxes.

Hypothecation. (14) Pledging property as security for debt without giving up possession.

Implied authority. (20,21) Authority not explicitly given an agent but reasonably necessary to perform the assigned duties.

Improvement. (3) Man-made addition to land.

Income capitalization approach. (23,24) A technique for estimating the market value of real estate by capitalizing the income it is expected to produce into a present value.

Independent contractor. (20) One associated with a firm, usually a salesperson or broker associated with a brokerage firm, under a contractual arrangement to perform certain tasks at his own expense and not under the direction and control of the firm.

Institute of Real Estate Management (IREM). (22) An affiliate of the National Association of Realtors conducting research and providing education on property management and awarding professional property management designations.

Insurance. (22) A method of shifting risks to a firm by paying premiums in return for a policy guaranteeing indemnification in the event of a loss.

Interest. (13) A charge for the use of money or a right in property.

Interim financing. (15) See construction financing.

Internal rate of return. (13) The discount rate that equates the present value of outflows and the present value of inflows from an investment opportunity.

Internal Revenue Code. (11) All of the statutory law affecting federal income taxation.

International Council of Shopping Centers (ICSC). (22) An organization devoted to research and education on the management of shopping centers.

International Society of Real Estate Appraisers. (23) An organization providing educational opportunities, conducting research, and awarding designations to real estate appraisers.

Intestate. (5) The legal terminology for one who died without a will.

Intestate succession. (5) Laws defining how the property of a person who dies without a will is to be distributed among that person's heirs.

Investment strategy. (19) An investor's overall investment philosophy, objectives, plans, and policies.

Investment theory of urban growth. (7) Suggests that the form of an urban area is the result of many public and private real estate investment decisions.

Investment value. (18,19) The value of an asset to a particular individual given his or her set of assumptions and forecasts.

Joint and severally liable. (14) A situation in which all signers of a note are liable to repay the debt both as a group and individually.

Joint tenancy. (4) A form of concurrent ownership satisfying the unities of time, title, interest, and possession and having the right to survivorship.

Joint venture. (17) The joining of forces of two or more individuals or businesses to undertake real estate investment or development.

Junior mortgage. (14) A mortgage of lower priority than another mortgage.

Just compensation. (4,8) Compensation for private property taken for a public purpose that is reasonable and fair, usually defined as the market value of the property taken.

Land. (3) The crust of the Earth, including minerals and air space to a reasonable altitude.

Land contract. (15) See contract for deed.

Land financing. (15) Arrangements for purchasing land by a method other than an individual's own capital.

Land use. (3) The utilization of land for one or more types of space.

Land use controls. (8) Tools used to regulate the use of land and the intensity, bulk, and other aspects of that use.

Late payment fee. (14) A fee charged the borrower if payments are not made within a specified number of days of the due date.

Lease. (4) A contract that gives the lessee possession of property for a period of time in return for paying rent to the lessor. It establishes a landlord-tenant relationship between the parties.

Leasehold estate. (4) A nonfreehold estate involving the possession and use of space for a specified period of time.

Legal description. (3) The establishment of the boundaries of a parcel of land in a manner complete and precise enough that it cannot be confused with any other parcel in the world and will be accepted by a court of law.

Lessee. (4) The tenant under a lease agreement.

Lessor. (4) The landlord under a lease agreement.

Leverage. (13) The use of borrowed funds to magnify the impact of changes in net operating income on equity returns.

License. (4) A personal and revocable right to use the land of another for a specific purpose.

Lien. (4) A claim against property that, if not satisifed, can be enforced by the courts through a sale of the property.

Lien theory. (13) A doctrine adopted by some states that assumes that the execution of a mortgage does not pass title from the mortgagor to the mortgagee.

Life estate. (4) An interest in real property that lasts until the death of the owner or some other designated person.

Linkage. (7) An origin and destination between which trips are frequently made.

Lis pendens. (13) A notice that a lawsuit affecting real property is pending.

Listing. (20,21) A contractual arrangement between a broker and a property owner creating an agency relationship in which the broker is to attempt to sell or lease real property.

Listing agreement. (20,21) The document creating a listing.

Loan correspondent. (15,16) An individual or firm, usually a mortgage banking firm, with a working relationship with mortgage investors seeking lending opportunities.

Loan submission package. (15,16) The documentation transmitted to an income property lender for consideration in making a lending decision.

Loan-to-value ratio. (13) The amount of loan on real property expressed as a percentage of the property's value.

Location quotient. (7) The ratio of local employment in a particular industry to the national percentage of total employment in that industry; used as a measure of employment concentration.

Lot and block method. (3) A technique for legally describing land by referencing a recorded subdivision plat containing lot and block numbers and the exact dimensions of each lot.

Marginal tax rate. (11) The percentage of an additional dollar of taxable income paid in income taxes.

Market. (9) A mechanism by which the interaction of supply (sellers) and demand (buyers) establishes a price.

Marketable title. (5) A title a reasonable person would accept without a reduction in purchase price or a title that is of such quality that the courts would compel a buyer to accept it.

Market price. (23) An historical number reflecting the result of a completed transaction.

Market value. (23) The highest price in terms of money that a property will bring in a competitive and open market under all conditions requisite to a fair sale, the buyer and seller each acting prudently and knowledgeably, and assuming the price is not affected by undue stimulus; or the most probable selling price of a property under conditions prevailing in the market at that time.

Metes and bounds. (3) A method for legally describing real property by specifying a point of beginning and distances around the boundaries of the property.

Metropolitan Statistical Area (MSA). (7) Areas defined by the Bureau of the Census as a group of counties with a high degree of economic and social integration and must include at least one city with 50,000 or more inhabitants or a Census Bureau defined urbanized area of at least 50,000 inhabitants and a total MSA population of at least 100,000. Current MSA standards were adopted in January, 1980 and the term was officially changed from Standard Metropolitan Statistical Area (SMSA) to MSA in 1983.

Mill. (10) One-thousandth of a dollar or one-tenth of a cent.

Misrepresentation. (6) An innocent or unintentional misstatement of fact.

Mixed-use development (MUD). (17) A real estate development involving several different land uses in a single complex.

Monuments method. (3) A technique for describing land using natural and man-made objects, called monuments, to identify corners and boundary lines of parcels.

Moratorium. (8) A freeze on the extension of public facilities such as water and sewerage service.

Mortgage. (14) A pledge of real property, creating an interest in the lender, as security for a debt; also, the instrument used to make this pledge and create this interest.

Mortgage-backed securities. (15) Securities whose income is derived from a pool of insured mortgages that have been guaranteed by a secondary mortgage market institution such as Ginnie Mae or Freddie Mac.

Mortgage banker. (15) A real estate financing specialist acting as an originator, seller, and servicer of mortgages.

Mortgage constant. (13) The factor that is multiplied by the original loan amount to determine the periodic payments necessary to amortize a mortgage loan.

Mortgage debt service ratio. (16) A ratio used to assess the ability of a borrower to repay a single family home loan. It is the ratio of monthly debt service to the gross income of the borrower.

Mortgage release. (14) A written document extinguishing the mortgage lien held by the lender.

Mortgagee. (14) The party receiving a mortgage interest from a borrower as security for a promissory note.

Mortgagor. (14) The party conveying a mortgage interest to a lender as security for a promissory note.

MSA. (7) See Metropolitan Statistical Area.

Multiple listing. (20,21) An exclusive right to sell listing the broker has agreed to co-broker with other members of a multiple listing service.

National Apartment Association. (22) An organization providing information and education for those owning and managing apartment properties.

National Association of Home Builders. (22) An organization providing information, education, political lobbying, and other services to those in home building and allied fields.

National Association of Realtors. (20) The oldest and largest real estate organization in the United States. Acts as the central coordinating body for numerous societies, institutes, and councils providing educational opportunities, research, political lobbying, and professional designations for its members.

Net lease. (22) A lease in which the lessee makes a rental payment and also pays agreed-upon operating expenses and property taxes.

Net listing. (20,21) A listing in which the broker's compensation is the difference between the sales price and a net amount the seller has requested. This listing is illegal in many states.

Net operating income. (18,19) For income-producing real estate, gross possible income minus a vacancy allowance and operating expenses.

Net present value. (13) The difference between the present value of inflows and the present value of outflows from an investment.

Nonbasic employment. (7) Employment in the production of goods and services sold within a designated area.

Nonconforming use. (8) An existing improvement that no longer is allowed on a particular site because of changes in zoning.

Novation. (14) A situation in which the lender agrees to release the original borrower and substitute the personal liability of the party assuming the loan.

Offer. (6) A promise to do something in return for a requested act or counterpromise.

Offeree. (6) The person receiving an offer.

Offeror. (6) The person making an offer.

Open listing. (20,21) An agency relationship in which the broker is entitled to a commission only if he or she finds a ready, willing, and able buyer.

Option contract. (15) An exclusive right to purchase a property at an agreed-upon price for a specified period of time in return for the payment of a fee.

Ordinary income. (11,12) In income taxation, income derived from sources other than the sale of capital assets and taxed at the regular rates.

Ostensible agency. (20,21) An agency created by a person giving third parties reason to believe that another individual is that person's agent.

Owners association. (4) The organization charged with operating a condominium property through an elected board of directors.

Package mortgage. (15) A mortgage that includes personal and real property.

Participations. (15,16) A financing arrangement in which the lender receives not only interest, but also a portion of the income produced by the income property securing the loan.

Partition. (4) The termination of a concurrent ownership arrangement with each person receiving exclusive ownership of a portion of the property.

Partnership. (4) A form of business organization in which two or more people join together to operate a business, with no income taxes being paid at the partnership level and all profits and losses being allocated as taxable to the partners according to their monetary and nonmonetary contributions.

Pass-through security. (14) A mortgage-backed security in which all principal and interest payments received by the servicing agent are passed along to investors.

Patent. (4) The document used to convey ownership from the state to a private grantee.

Percentage lease. (22) A lease in which payments are expressed as a proportion of some measure of the lessee's income, usually gross receipts.

Performance. (6) The termination of a contract caused by all parties completing their obligations.

Periodic tenancy. (6) A leasehold estate that is automatically extended from period to period unless lessee or lessor gives appropriate notice. Also called a tenancy from period to period.

Permanent financing. (15) Long-term mortgages.

Personal property. (4) Interests in personalty, which are all things other than real property.

Physical deterioration. (23,24) A reduction in value due to the wearing out of improvements.

Physical life. (23,24) The period over which improvements are expected to be standing and capable of functioning as intended.

Planned unit development (PUD). (8,17) A comprehensive development involving a mixture of land uses and densities not available with separate zoning for each land use, but allowed because the entire development is viewed as an integrated single project.

Plat. (3,8) A map showing the details of lots, easements, streets, and other aspects of a subdivision.

Pledged account mortgage. (15) A real estate loan in which the borrower agrees to place an amount of money in an account from which the lender draws money each month to be added to a lower than normal payment from the borrower.

Plottage. (3,9) Combining two or more parcels of land into a single parcel with a value greater than the sum of the individual parcels.

Point of beginning. (3) A readily identifiable point from which a metes and bounds description commences.

Police power. (4) The inherent power of government to limit the activities of private individuals in order to protect certain public interests such as health, safety, and the general welfare.

Premium. (13) An amount paid for an investment, such as a mortgage, in excess of its face value.

Prepayment penalty. (14) A fee charged the borrower for paying off all or a substantial portion of a loan before it is due.

Present value. (13) The worth in current dollars of one or more future receipts.

Price level adjusted mortgage. (15) A loan in which the outstanding balance is adjusted each period according to changes in a price level index.

Primary mortgage market. (15) The market in which real estate loans are orginated.

Principal. (13,20,21) In brokerage, the person giving authority to an agent; in finance, the amount owed on a loan.

Principal residence. (11) A taxpayer's primary home.

Private mortgage insurance. (15) An insurance plan that protects a lender from financial loss in case of default by the borrower. Usually covers only a portion of the total loan amount.

Principal meridian. (3) The north-south reference line used in a rectangular survey description.

Procuring cause. (20,21) A requirement for receiving a commission in an agency relationship consisting of the agent being the immediate and principal reason for a buyer choosing to purchase a home.

Promissory note. (14) A document containing the express promise of the borrower(s) to pay a specified person or institution a definite sum of money at a specified time. Called a bond in some states.

Property. (4) An interest or right or a set of interests or rights in land or personality.

Property management. (22) The process of operating a parcel of real estate.

Prospecting. (20) The act of locating a buyer for a property.

Purchase money mortgage. (15) A mortgage given to the seller by the buyer as payment for all or part of a property's purchase price.

Qualified fee simple. (4) A freehold estate that ends on the occurrence of a specified event.

Qualified income. (16) In single family loan underwriting, the amount of income that is considered dependable and likely enough to continue to be used in underwriting a loan request.

Quit claim deed. (5) A deed containing no warranties of title and providing no definition of what interest is being conveyed. It conveys whatever interest the grantor may have in the property.

Range. (3) A column of townships running parallel to the principal meridian.

Rate of return on equity. (19) The ratio of cash flow before tax to equity investment for a given year of a real estate investment.

Rate of return on total capital. (19) The ratio of net operating income to total capital invested for a given year of a real estate investment.

Real estate. (1) Land and everything, natural and man-made, attached to it.

Real estate commission. (20,21) The body charged with implementing the real estate license laws in most states.

Real estate decision areas. (2) The real estate activity areas concerned with the basic decisions associated with lending, development, and equity investment.

Real estate decision support areas. (2) Real estate activity areas providing support for decision makers. Includes the general activities of marketing, management, appraisal, and counseling.

Real estate investment trust (REIT). (4) A form of business organization in which one party, the trust, holds property for the benefit of another party, called the beneficiary, with a high percentage of all income passed on as taxable income to the beneficiaries and the trust paying no federal income taxes.

Real Estate Settlement Procedures Act

(RESPA). (14,21) A federal law requiring advance disclosure of settlement practices and costs and restricting practices that potentially increase settlement costs.

Real property. (4) Interest(s) or right(s) in land.

Real property tax. (10) A tax paid by landowners that is based on the value of a parcel of real property and that, if unpaid, may lead to a public sale to satisfy the unpaid tax lien.

Reality of assent. (6) A true meeting of the minds between the parties to a contract.

Realtors National Marketing Institute (RNMI). (20) An institute of the National Association of Realtors providing educational opportunities for those in real estate marketing and awarding a number of designations to members meeting specified education and experience requirements.

Reconciliation. (23) Developing a single best estimate of market value from the market value indications produced by different valuation approaches.

Recordation. (5) The process of filing a document with the appropriate public official in order to provide constructive notice.

Rectangular survey method. (3) A method for legally describing land based on reference to a principal meridian and base line and a grid arrangement.

Registered title. (5) See Torrens title.

Regulation Z. (14) Truth-in-lending laws requiring disclosure of complete terms of financing requirements and implemented by the Federal Reserve System.

Remainder. (4) The future possessory interest that remains after a life estate when a remainderman has been established.

Remainderman. (4) A person who holds a future interest, called a remainder.

Renegotiable rate mortgage. (15) A short-term mortgage with payments calculated over a normal 25- to 30-year period but renewed at 3- to 5-year intervals with possible interest rate adjustments.

Rent. (22) The consideration given for a leasehold estate.

Replacement cost. (23,24) The cost of constructing an improvement with utility similar to a subject property.

Reproduction cost. (23,24) The cost of producing a replica of the subject property.

Restrictive covenant. (4) Limitations on the use of real property created by way of the deed at the time the property is conveyed from one owner to another. Also called deed restrictions.

Reverse annuity mortgage. (15) A loan whose proceeds are paid as an annuity to the borrower with interest accumulating on the increasing balance and paid back in a lump sum, usually from the sale of the property acting as security.

Reversion. (4) A future interest held by the grantor or his or her heirs.

Right of survivorship. (4) A situation in which the surviving concurrent owners of land automatically receive the interests of a deceased concurrent owner.

Riparian rights. (4) The right of a landowner to access and use water so long as that use does not significantly reduce the quality or quantity of water available to other riparian owners.

Risk. (13,18,19) In investments, the possibility that an outcome other than the one expected may occur.

Risk averse. (18) A condition descriptive of many investors not liking risk and demanding a risk premium for many risky investments.

Sales comparison approach. (23,24) A technique for estimating the market value of real estate that involves the selection of properties comparable to the subject property and using data from those sales to estimate the market value of the subject.

Sales contract. (6) An agreement between two parties committing one to buy and the other to sell real property and also stipulating the conditions of that sale.

Salesperson. (20) One performing the acts of a broker through an association with a licensed broker.

Secondary mortgage market. (15) The market in which existing mortgages are bought and sold.

Section. (3) An area one mile square containing 640 acres. In the rectangular survey, 36 sections comprise a township.

Senior mortgage. (14) A mortgage legally prior to another mortgage.

Service industry. (7) See nonbasic employment.

Servicing fee. (15,16) The fee received for collecting and forwarding payments to the mortgage investor and maintaining escrow accounts for the payment of property taxes and hazard insurance.

Setback requirement. (8) A part of the zoning code requiring that buildings be built a specified distance from property boundaries.

Settlement. (20,21) See closing.

Share equity purchase. (15) Any arrangement in which a home purchaser receives all or a portion of the equity investment in a home from another party in return for giving that party rent on that portion of the home they own and a pro-rata share of the sales price.

Shared appreciation mortgage. (15) A mortgage loan made at below market rates in return for the lender participating in any appreciation in the property's value when it is sold.

SMSA. (7) See Metropolitan Statistical Area.

Special agent. (20,21) An agent with authority to perform only a specific act on behalf of a principal. Real estate brokers usually act as special agents.

Special assessment. (10) An obligation assigned to a group of properties, called an assessment district, for public improvements considered to directly benefit them. If not paid, the courts force the sale of a property to satisfy the lien.

Standard Metropolitan Statistical Area. (7) See Metropolitan Statistical Area.

Statute of Frauds. (5,6) A statute designed to reduce fraud by requiring that documents involving the sale of real property and leases for more than one year be evidenced by a writing to be enforceable.

Statutes of descent and distribution. (5) Laws determining who receives the property of a deceased person dying intestate.

Statutory right of redemption. (14) The right, in some states, of the mortgagor to redeem the property for a specified period after foreclosure.

Steering. (20) The illegal practice of guiding members of minority or majority groups to particular neighborhoods or areas of town to promote segregation.

Subdivision. (8) A large parcel of real estate that has been divided into a number of smaller parcels.

Subdivision regulations. (8) The requirements that must be met and the approvals that must be obtained by anyone wanting to subdivide land.

Subject to. (14) A financing arrangement in which the purchaser of a property with an existing mortgage agrees to make the payments but does not assume liability for the repayment of the mortgage.

Subordination. (14) A situation in which an individual with a prior interest agrees to a reduction in priority.

Survey. (3) The process of accurately establishing the boundaries of real estate.

Takings issue. (8) The question of how vigorously the police power may be exercised before such activity so reduces the usefulness of the property to the owner that a taking of private property without due process and/or just compensation has occurred.

Tax abatement. (10) A reduction in property tax obligations for particular properties, usually intended to promote development.

Tax avoidance. (11,12) The legal reduction of income taxes through the use of tax planning.

Tax base. (10,11) The measure to which a tax rate is applied to calculate a tax liability.

Tax credit. (11) A direct, dollar-for-dollar reduction in income tax liability.

Tax deferred exchange. (12) A trade of like-kind property that does not trigger a recognition of a taxable gain at the time of the trade.

Tax evasion. (11,12) The illegal reduction of income taxes.

Tax exempt. (10) Properties not required to pay the property tax.

Tax lien. (10) A claim against property for the payment of property taxes that, if unpaid, may result in the forced sale of the property to remove it.

Tax levy. (10) The property tax obligation of a particular property.

Tax shelter investment. (11,12) An investment that allows for postponing or permanently avoiding the payment of taxes.

Tenancy. (4) The right to possession and use of real property and the conditions relating to those rights.

Tenancy at sufferance. (4) The status a tenant occupies when the leasehold no longer exists and the tenant still occupies the property without the owner's permission.

Tenancy at will. (4) A leasehold estate that continues for an indefinite period until notice is given by either lessee or lessor.

Tenancy by the entirety. (4) Concurrent ownership between a husband and wife with right of survivorship and limitations on the ability to dispose of one's interest.

Tenancy for years. (4) A leasehold estate of specified duration that automatically ends at the end of that period.

Tenancy in common. (4) Concurrent ownership in which each tenant in common has an undivided interest in the property and may sell or give that interest away while living, or will it to another upon death.

Tier. (3) A row of townships either north or south of the base line.

Time share. (4) See fractional time period ownership.

Time value of money. (13) The concept

that the value of money depends on when it is received, with money at or nearer the present time worth more than the same sum in a later period.

Title. (4,5) An ownership interest in land. Also, a single document or a series of documents evidencing such ownership.

Title closing. (20) See closing.

Title examination. (5) A thorough review of all recorded documents relating to a particular property by an attorney to determine what interests in the property exist and their nature.

Title insurance. (5) A policy protecting a lender or owner of real property against financial loss due to defects in the title.

Title opinion. (5) An attorney's opinion of the quality of title following a title examination.

Title theory. (14) A doctrine adopted in some states that a mortgage conveys title from the mortgagor to the mortgagee.

Torrens title. (5) A doctrine adopted in some states that a mortgage conveys title from the mortgagor to the mortgagee.

Township. (3) In the rectangular survey method, an area six miles square containing 36 sections. Also, a row of townships either north or south of the base line.

Tract system. (5) A retrieval system for recorded documents in which documents are indexed by the legal description of the property.

Transfer tax. (5) A tax levied on deeds, usually based on the purchase price and payable at the time the deed is recorded.

Treasury regulations (Regs). (11) The official Internal Revenue Service interpretation of the Tax Code explaining how they will treat certain tax situations.

Trust deed. (14) A financing arrangement in which title is transferred to a third party, called a trustee, along with a set of instructions concerning to whom title should be transferred in case of default or payoff. Used in some states instead of a mortgage.

Truth-in-Lending Act. (14) See Regulation Z.

Undivided interest. (4) A situation in which each concurrent owner has an interest in an entire parcel rather than each having an exclusive interest in a particular portion of the parcel.

Unfavorable exposure. (7) Any attribute of the environmental influence area, not related to convenience, that reduces the desirability of a site.

Usury law. (14) In some states, a law limiting the maximum interest rate that can be charged on real estate loans.

VA loan. (15) A loan guaranteed by the Veterans Administration.

Valuable consideration. (6) Consideration in the form of money, promises, or property.

Valuation. (23,24) The process of estimating the market value of real estate.

Variance. (8) Permission to deviate from specific portions of the zoning classification applying to a property.

Vested remainder. (4) A remainder in which the remainderman can be identified.

Warehousing. (15) The activity between the time a mortgage is originated and when it is sold; thus it is the period during which a lender, intending to sell a mortgage, actually owns it.

Warranty deed. (5) A deed containing warranties as to the quality of title being conveyed.

Will. (5) A document executed during a person's lifetime that conveys that person's property at death.

Yield. (13) The internal rate of return on an investment.

Zoning. (8) Laws establishing what can be built on a parcel of land, how much of it can be built, how tall the building can be, and where on the parcel it can be built.

Appendix

Table A.1. Education and Experience Requirements for Licensees*

| | Salesperson's | | Experience Required for Broker's License | Broker's | |
	Prelicensing Education	Continuing Education		Additional Prelicensing Education	Continuing Education
Alabama	45 hours	None	2 years full time	45 hours or 15 semester hours if applicant has less than 2 years experience	None
Alaska	None	None		None	None
Arizona	45 hours	24 hours/every 2 years	3 years	90 hours	24 hours every 2 years
Arkansas	30 hours course must be completed in first year	None	2 years — May be waived for education	90 hours or 2 years as salesman and 30 hours or 6 college credits	None
California	None	45 hours every 4 years	2 years within last 5 years	6 courses	45 hours every 4 years

Table A.1. Education and Experience Requirements for Licensees* (Continued)

| | Salesperson's | | Experience Required for Broker's License | Broker's | |
	Prelicensing Education	Continuing Education		Additional Prelicensing Education	Continuing Education
Colorado	2 courses	None	2 years or equivalent in related field	2 courses	None
Connecticut	30 hours	12 hours within 2 years	2 years	60 hours	12 hours within 2 years
Delaware	126 hours	15 hours per 2 years	5 years and 30 sales	90 hours	15 hours per 2 years
D.C.	45 hours	6 hours per year	2 years	180 hours	6 hours per year
Florida	63 hours	14 hours per 2 years	1 year	72 hours	14 hours per 2 years
Georgia	24 hours	80 hours first 2 years 6 hours every 2 years thereafter	3 years	60 hours	6 hours every 2 years
Hawaii	40 hours or equivalent experience	None	2 years	46 hours or equivalent experience	None
Idaho	45 hours	None	2 years	90 hours	None
Illinois	30 hours	None	1 year	90 hours	None
Indiana	40 hours	None	None	24 hours	None
Iowa	30 hours	36 hours in 3 years	None	None	36 hours in 3 years
Kansas	30 hours	8 hours per 2 years	2 years	None	8 hours per 2 years
Kentucky	96 hours or 6 college credits	None	2 years	96 hours or 12 college credits	None
Louisiana	90 hours	15 hours/2 years	2 years	60 hours	15 hours per 2 years
Maine	None	12 hours per 2 years	None	90 hours	12 hours per 2 years
Maryland	45 hours	12 hours per 2 years	3 years	135 hours	12 hours per 2 years
Massachusetts	24 hours	None	1 year	30 hours	None
Michigan	30 hours if applicant fails first exam, otherwise none	6 hours per year	None	90 hours	6 hours per year

Table A.1. Education and Experience Requirements for Licensees* (Continued)

| | Salesperson's | | Experience Required for Broker's License | Broker's | |
	Prelicensing Education	Continuing Education		Additional Prelicensing Education	Continuing Education
Minnesota	60 hours	45 hours every 3 years	2 years	None	45 hours every 3 years
Mississippi	6 semester hours or 2 GRI credits	None	None	12 semester hours or 9 semester hours plus 1 year experience as salesman	None
Missouri	54 hours	12 hours per 2 years	40 hours or 1 year experience	40 hours or 1 year experience	12 hours per 2 years
Montana	None	None	2 years	None	None
Nebraska	60 hours	None	None	6 courses	None
Nevada	90 hours or 6	20 hours first 2-year period, 10 hours per subsequent 2-year period	2 years	24 semester hours credit	20 hours first 2-year period, 10 hours subsequent 2-year period
New Hampshire	None	3 hours per 2 years	1 year	None	3 hours per 2 years
New Jersey	75 hours	None	2 years	90 hours	None
New Mexico	60 hours	None	None	120 hours or 30 hours plus 2 years experience	None
New York	45 hours	45 hours	Yes	90 hours	Yes
North Carolina	30 hours	None	None	90 hours or 2 years experience	None
North Dakota	None	30 hours within first year and 24 hours every 3 years	2 years	90 hours	24 hours per 3 years
Ohio	60 hours	30 hours every 3 years	2 years	180 hours	30 hours every 3 years
Oklahoma	45 hours	21 hours every 3 years	1 year	45 hours	21 hours every 3 years
Oregon	90 hours	24 hours every 2 years	3 years active within	150 hours	24 hours every 2 years

Table A.1. Education and Experience Requirements for Licensees* (Continued)

| | Salesperson's | | Experience Required for Broker's License | Broker's | |
	Prelicensing Education	Continuing Education		Additional Prelicensing Education	Continuing Education
Pennsylvania	60 hours	None	3 years	180 hours	None
Rhode Island	None	None	None	90 hours or 1 year experience	None
South Carolina	30 hours	30 hours within first year of licensure	See education	90 hours and 3 years experience or 5 years experience	None
South Dakota	30 hours	24 hours per 2 years	2 years	60 hours	24 hours per 2 years
Tennessee	30 hours	3 hours within first 2 years	2 years	60 hours	6 hours within first 2 years
Texas	180 hours	90 hours over first 3 years of licensure	2 years	540 hours	None
Utah	90 hours	None	3 years	120 hours	None
Vermont	None	None	1 year	None	None
Virginia	45 hours	None	3 years	12 semester hours	None
Washington	None	30 hours within first 2 years	2 years	60 hours	None
West Virginia	90 hours	None	2 years	90 hours	None
Wisconsin	30 hours	30 hours within first 2 years and 10 hours per 2 years	None	60 hours or 20 semester hours	10 hours per 2 years
Wyoming	30 hours	None	2 years	30 hours	None

* SOURCE: National Association of Real Estate License Law Officials, *Digest of Real Estate License Laws 1985.*
 Subject to change.

Table A.2. Annual Rate 8%

Nominal Annual Interest Rate = 8%   Compounding Periods per Year = 1

Year	Amount of 1 at Compound Interest (Col. 1)	Accumu-lation of 1 per Period (Col. 2)	Sinking Fund Factor (Col. 3)	Present Value Rever-sion of 1 (Col. 4)	Present Value Ordinary Annuity 1 per Period (Col. 5)	Installment to Amortize 1 (Col. 6)	Period
1	1.0800	1.0000	1.000000	0.9259	0.9259	1.0800000	1
2	1.1664	2.0800	0.480769	0.8573	1.7833	0.5607692	2
3	1.2597	3.2464	0.308034	0.7938	2.5771	0.3880335	3
4	1.3605	4.5061	0.221921	0.7350	3.3121	0.3019208	4
5	1.4693	5.8666	0.170456	0.6806	3.9927	0.2504565	5
6	1.5869	7.3359	0.136315	0.6302	4.6229	0.2163154	6
7	1.7138	8.9228	0.112072	0.5835	5.2064	0.1920724	7
8	1.8509	10.6366	0.094015	0.5403	5.7466	0.1740148	8
9	1.9990	12.4876	0.080080	0.5002	6.2469	0.1600797	9
10	2.1589	14.4866	0.069029	0.4632	6.7101	0.1490295	10
11	2.3316	16.6455	0.060076	0.4289	7.1390	0.1400763	11
12	2.5182	18.9771	0.052695	0.3971	7.5361	0.1326950	12
13	2.7196	21.4953	0.046522	0.3677	7.9038	0.1265218	13
14	2.9372	24.2149	0.041297	0.3405	8.2442	0.1212969	14
15	3.1722	27.1521	0.036830	0.3152	8.5595	0.1168295	15
16	3.4259	30.3243	0.032977	0.2919	8.8514	0.1129769	16
17	3.7000	33.7502	0.029629	0.2703	9.1216	0.1096294	17
18	3.9960	37.4502	0.026702	0.2502	9.3719	0.1067021	18
19	4.3157	41.4463	0.024128	0.2317	9.6036	0.1041276	19
20	4.6610	45.7620	0.021852	0.2145	9.8181	0.1018522	20
21	5.0338	50.4229	0.019832	0.1987	10.0168	0.0998322	21
22	5.4365	55.4568	0.018032	0.1839	10.2007	0.0980321	22
23	5.8715	60.8933	0.016422	0.1703	10.3711	0.0964222	23
24	6.3412	66.7648	0.014978	0.1577	10.5288	0.0949780	24
25	6.8485	73.1059	0.013679	0.1460	10.6748	0.0936788	25
26	7.3964	79.9544	0.012507	0.1352	10.8100	0.0925071	26
27	7.9881	87.3508	0.011448	0.1252	10.9352	0.0914481	27
28	8.6271	95.3388	0.010489	0.1159	11.0511	0.0904889	28
29	9.3173	103.9659	0.009619	0.1073	11.1584	0.0896185	29
30	10.0627	113.2832	0.008827	0.0994	11.2578	0.0888274	30
31	10.8677	123.3459	0.008107	0.0920.	11.3498	0.0881073	31
32	11.7371	134.2135	0.007451	0.0852	11.4350	0.0874508	32
33	12.6760	145.9506	0.006852	0.0789	11.5139	0.0868516	33
34	13.6901	158.6267	0.006304	0.0730	11.5869	0.0863041	34
35	14.7853	172.3168	0.005803	0.0676	11.6546	0.0858033	35
36	15.9682	187.1021	0.005345	0.0626	11.7172	0.0853447	36
37	17.2456	203.0703	0.004924	0.0580	11.7752	0.0849244	37
38	18.6253	220.3159	0.004539	0.0537	11.8289	0.0845389	38
39	20.1153	238.9412	0.004185	0.0497	11.8786	0.0841851	39
40	21.7245	259.0565	0.003860	0.0460	11.9246	0.0838602	40
41	23.4625	280.7810	0.003561	0.0426	11.9672	0.0835615	41
42	25.3395	304.2435	0.003287	0.0395	12.0067	0.0832868	42
43	27.3666	329.5830	0.003034	0.0365	12.0432	0.0830341	43

Table A.2. Annual Rate 8% (Continued)

Nominal Annual Interest Rate = 8%   Compounding Periods per Year = 1

Year	Amount of 1 at Compound Interest (Col. 1)	Accumu- lation of 1 per Period (Col. 2)	Sinking Fund Factor (Col. 3)	Present Value Rever- sion of 1 (Col. 4)	Present Value Ordinary Annuity 1 per Period (Col. 5)	Installment to Amortize 1 (Col. 6)	Period
44	29.5560	356.9496	0.002802	0.0338	12.0771	0.0828015	44
45	31.9204	386.5056	0.002587	0.0313	12.1084	0.0825873	45
46	34.4741	418.4260	0.002390	0.0290	12.1374	0.0823899	46
47	37.2320	452.9001	0.002208	0.0269	12.1643	0.0822080	47
48	40.2106	490.1321	0.002040	0.0249	12.1891	0.0820403	48
49	43.4274	530.3427	0.001886	0.0230	12.2122	0.0818856	49
50	46.9016	573.7701	0.001743	0.0213	12.2335	0.0817429	50

SOURCE: Tables A.2–A.19 from Texas Real Estate Research Center, Texas A & M University.

Table A.3. Annual Rate 9%

Nominal Annual Interest Rate = 9% · Compounding Periods per Year = 1

Year	Amount of 1 at Compound Interest (Col. 1)	Accumulation of 1 per Period (Col. 2)	Sinking Fund Factor (Col. 3)	Present Value Reversion of 1 (Col. 4)	Present Value Ordinary Annuity 1 per Period (Col. 5)	Installment to Amortize 1 (Col. 6)	Period
1	1.0900	1.0000	1.000000	0.9174	0.9174	1.0900000	1
2	1.1881	2.0900	0.478469	0.8417	1.7591	0.5684689	2
3	1.2950	3.2781	0.305055	0.7722	2.5313	0.3950548	3
4	1.4116	4.5731	0.218669	0.7084	3.2397	0.3086687	4
5	1.5386	5.9847	0.167092	0.6499	3.8897	0.2570925	5
6	1.6771	7.5233	0.132920	0.5963	4.4859	0.2229198	6
7	1.8280	9.2004	0.108691	0.5470	5.0330	0.1986905	7
8	1.9926	11.0285	0.090674	0.5019	5.5348	0.1806744	8
9	2.1719	13.0210	0.076799	0.4604	5.9952	0.1667988	9
10	2.3674	15.1929	0.065820	0.4224	6.4177	0.1558201	10
11	2.5804	17.5603	0.056947	0.3875	6.8052	0.1469467	11
12	2.8127	20.1407	0.049651	0.3555	7.1607	0.1396507	12
13	3.0658	22.9534	0.043567	0.3262	7.4869	0.1335666	13
14	3.3417	26.0192	0.038433	0.2992	7.7862	0.1284332	14
15	3.5425	29.3609	0.034059	0.2745	8.0607	0.1240589	15
16	3.9703	33.0034	0.030300	0.2519	8.3126	0.1202999	16
17	4.3276	36.9737	0.027046	0.2311	8.5436	0.1170463	17
18	4.7171	41.3013	0.024212	0.2120	8.7556	0.1142123	18
19	5.1417	46.0185	0.021730	0.1945	8.9501	0.1117304	19
20	5.6044	51.1601	0.019546	0.1784	9.1285	0.1095465	20
21	6.1088	56.7645	0.017617	0.1637	9.2922	0.1076166	21
22	6.6586	62.8733	0.015905	0.1502	9.4424	0.1059050	22
23	7.2579	69.5319	0.014382	0.1378	9.5802	0.1043819	23
24	7.9111	76.7898	0.013023	0.1264	9.7066	0.1030226	24
25	8.6231	84.7009	0.011806	0.1160	9.8226	0.1018063	25
26	9.3992	93.3240	0.010715	0.1064	9.9290	0.1007154	26
27	10.2451	102.7231	0.009735	0.0976	10.0266	0.0997349	27
28	11.1671	112.9682	0.008852	0.0895	10.1161	0.0988521	28
29	12.1722	124.1354	0.008056	0.0822	10.1983	0.0980557	29
30	13.2677	136.3075	0.007336	0.0754	10.2737	0.0973364	30
31	14.4618	149.5752	0.006686	0.0691	10.3428	0.0966856	31
32	15.7633	164.0370	0.006096	0.0634	10.4062	0.0960962	32
33	17.1820	179.8003	0.005562	0.0582	10.4644	0.0955617	33
34	18.7284	196.9824	0.005077	0.0534	10.5178	0.0950766	34
35	20.4140	215.7108	0.004636	0.0490	10.5668	0.0946358	35
36	22.2512	236.1247	0.004235	0.0449	10.6118	0.0942351	36
37	24.2538	258.3760	0.003870	0.0412	10.6530	0.0938703	37
38	26.4367	282.6298	0.003538	0.0378	10.6908	0.0935382	38
39	28.8160	309.0665	0.003236	0.0347	10.7255	0.0932356	39
40	31.4094	337.8825	0.002960	0.0318	10.7574	0.0929596	40
41	34.2363	369.2919	0.002708	0.0292	10.7866	0.0927079	41
42	37.3175	403.5282	0.002478	0.0268	10.8134	0.0924781	42
43	40.6761	440.8457	0.002268	0.0246	10.8380	0.0922684	43

Table A.3. Annual Rate 9% (Continued)

Nominal Annual Interest Rate = 9%   Compounding Periods per Year = 1

Year	Amount of 1 at Compound Interest (Col. 1)	Accumulation of 1 per Period (Col. 2)	Sinking Fund Factor (Col. 3)	Present Value Reversion of 1 (Col. 4)	Present Value Ordinary Annuity 1 per Period (Col. 5)	Installment to Amortize 1 (Col. 6)	Period
44	44.3370	481.5218	0.002077	0.0226	10.8605	0.0920768	44
45	48.3273	525.8588	0.001902	0.0207	10.8812	0.0919017	45
46	52.6767	574.1861	0.001742	0.0190	10.9002	0.0917416	46
47	57.4177	626.8628	0.001595	0.0174	10.9176	0.0915952	47
48	62.5852	684.2805	0.001461	0.0160	10.9336	0.0914614	48
49	68.2179	746.8657	0.001339	0.0147	10.9482	0.0913389	49
50	74.3575	815.0837	0.001227	0.0134	10.9617	0.0912269	50

Table A.4. Annual Rate 10%

Nominal Annual Interest Rate = 10%					Compounding Periods per Year = 1	

Year	Amount of 1 at Compound Interest (Col. 1)	Accumulation of 1 per Period (Col. 2)	Sinking Fund Factor (Col. 3)	Present Value Reversion of 1 (Col. 4)	Present Value Ordinary Annuity 1 per Period (Col. 5)	Installment to Amortize 1 (Col. 6)	Period
1	1.1000	1.0000	1.000000	0.9091	0.9091	1.1000000	1
2	1.2100	2.1000	0.476190	0.8264	1.7355	0.5761905	2
3	1.3310	3.3100	0.302115	0.7513	2.4869	0.4021148	3
4	1.4641	4.6410	0.215471	0.6830	3.1699	0.3154708	4
5	1.6105	6.1051	0.163797	0.6209	3.7908	0.2637975	5
6	1.7716	7.7156	0.129607	0.5645	4.3553	0.2296074	6
7	1.9487	9.4872	0.105405	0.5132	4.8684	0.2054055	7
8	2.1436	11.4359	0.087444	0.4655	5.3349	0.1874440	8
9	2.3579	13.5795	0.073641	0.4241	5.7590	0.1736405	9
10	2.5937	15.9374	0.062745	0.3855	6.1446	0.1627454	10
11	2.8531	18.5312	0.053963	0.3505	6.4951	0.1539631	11
12	3.1384	21.3843	0.046763	0.3186	6.8137	0.1467633	12
13	3.4523	24.5227	0.040779	0.2897	7.1034	0.1407785	13
14	3.7975	27.9750	0.035746	0.2633	7.3667	0.1357462	14
15	4.1772	31.7725	0.031474	0.2394	7.6061	0.1314738	15
16	4.5950	35.9497	0.027817	0.2176	7.8237	0.1278166	16
17	5.0545	40.5447	0.024664	0.1978	8.0216	0.1246641	17
18	5.5599	45.5992	0.021930	0.1799	8.2014	0.1219302	18
19	6.1159	51.1591	0.019547	0.1635	8.3649	0.1195469	19
20	6.7275	57.2750	0.017460	0.1486	8.5136	0.1174596	20
21	7.4003	64.0025	0.015624	0.1351	8.6487	0.1156244	21
22	8.1403	71.4028	0.014005	0.1228	8.7715	0.1140051	22
23	8.9543	79.5430	0.012572	0.1117	8.8832	0.1125718	23
24	9.8497	88.4973	0.011300	0.1015	8.9847	0.1112998	24
25	10.8347	98.3471	0.010168	0.0923	9.0770	0.1101681	25
26	11.9182	109.1818	0.009159	0.0839	9.1609	0.1091590	26
27	13.1100	121.0999	0.008258	0.0763	9.2372	0.1082576	27
28	14.4210	134.2099	0.007451	0.0693	9.3066	0.1074510	28
29	15.8631	148.6309	0.006728	0.0630	9.3696	0.1067281	29
30	17.4494	164.4940	0.006079	0.0573	9.4269	0.1060792	30
31	19.1943	181.9434	0.005496	0.0521	9.4790	0.1054962	31
32	21.1138	201.1378	0.004972	0.0474	9.5264	0.1049717	32
33	23.2252	222.2516	0.004499	0.0431	9.5694	0.1044994	33
34	25.5477	245.4767	0.004074	0.0391	9.6086	0.1040737	34
35	28.1024	271.0244	0.003690	0.0356	9.6442	0.1036897	35
36	30.9127	299.1268	0.003343	0.0323	9.6765	0.1033431	36
37	34.0040	330.0395	0.003030	0.0294	9.7059	0.1030299	37
38	37.4043	364.0434	0.002747	0.0267	9.7327	0.1027469	38
39	41.1448	401.4478	0.002491	0.0243	9.7570	0.1024910	39
40	45.2593	442.5926	0.002259	0.0221	9.7791	0.1022594	40
41	49.7852	487.8518	0.002050	0.0201	9.7991	0.1020498	41
42	54.7637	537.6370	0.001860	0.0183	9.8174	0.1018600	42
43	60.2401	592.4007	0.001688	0.0166	9.8340	0.1016880	43

Table A.4. Annual Rate 10% (Continued)

Nominal Annual Interest Rate = 10%   Compounding Periods per Year = 1

Year	Amount of 1 at Compound Interest (Col. 1)	Accumulation of 1 per Period (Col. 2)	Sinking Fund Factor (Col. 3)	Present Value Reversion of 1 (Col. 4)	Present Value Ordinary Annuity 1 per Period (Col. 5)	Installment to Amortize 1 (Col. 6)	Period
44	66.2641	652.6408	0.001532	0.0151	9.8491	0.1015322	44
45	72.8905	718.9049	0.001391	0.0137	9.8628	0.1013910	45
46	80.1795	791.7954	0.001263	0.0125	9.8753	0.1012630	46
47	88.1975	871.9749	0.001147	0.0113	9.8866	0.1011468	47
48	97.0172	960.1724	0.001041	0.0103	9.8969	0.1010415	48
49	106.7190	1057.1896	0.000946	0.0094	9.9063	0.1009459	49
50	117.3909	1163.9086	0.000859	0.0085	9.9148	0.1008592	50

Table A.5. Annual Rate 11%

| Nominal Annual Interest Rate = 11% | | | | | | Compounding Periods per Year = 1 | |

Year	Amount of 1 at Compound Interest (Col. 1)	Accumu-lation of 1 per Period (Col. 2)	Sinking Fund Factor (Col. 3)	Present Value Rever-sion of 1 (Col. 4)	Present Value Ordinary Annuity 1 per Period (Col. 5)	Installment to Amortize 1 (Col. 6)	Period
1	1.1100	1.0000	1.000000	0.9009	0.9009	1.1100000	1
2	1.2321	2.1100	0.473934	0.8116	1.7125	0.5839336	2
3	1.3676	3.3421	0.299213	0.7312	2.4437	0.4092131	3
4	1.5181	4.7097	0.212326	0.6587	3.1024	0.3223264	4
5	1.6851	6.2278	0.160570	0.5935	3.6959	0.2705703	5
6	1.8704	7.9129	0.126377	0.5346	4.2305	0.2363766	6
7	2.0762	9.7833	0.102215	0.4817	4.7122	0.2122153	7
8	2.3045	11.8594	0.084321	0.4339	5.1461	0.1943211	8
9	2.5580	14.1640	0.070602	0.3909	5.5370	0.1806017	9
10	2.8394	16.7220	0.059801	0.3522	5.8892	0.1698014	10
11	3.1518	19.5614	0.051121	0.3173	6.2065	0.1611210	11
12	3.4985	22.7132	0.044027	0.2858	6.4924	0.1540273	12
13	3.8833	26.2116	0.038151	0.2575	6.7499	0.1481510	13
14	4.3104	30.0949	0.033228	0.2320	6.9819	0.1432282	14
15	4.7846	34.4054	0.029065	0.2090	7.1909	0.1390652	15
16	5.3109	39.1899	0.025517	0.1883	7.3792	0.1355167	16
17	5.8951	44.5008	0.022471	0.1696	7.5488	0.1324715	17
18	6.5436	50.3959	0.019843	0.1528	7.7016	0.1298429	18
19	7.2633	56.9395	0.017563	0.1377	7.8393	0.1275625	19
20	8.0623	64.2028	0.015576	0.1240	7.9633	0.1255756	20
21	8.9492	72.2651	0.013838	0.1117	8.0751	0.1238379	21
22	9.9336	81.2143	0.012313	0.1007	8.1757	0.1223131	22
23	11.0263	91.1479	0.010971	0.0907	8.2664	0.1209712	23
24	12.2392	102.1741	0.009787	0.0817	8.3481	0.1197872	24
25	13.5855	114.4133	0.008740	0.0736	8.4217	0.1187402	25
26	15.0799	127.9988	0.007813	0.0663	8.4881	0.1178126	26
27	16.7386	143.0786	0.006989	0.0597	8.5478	0.1169892	27
28	18.5799	159.8173	0.006257	0.0538	8.6016	0.1162571	28
29	20.6237	178.3972	0.005605	0.0485	8.6501	0.1156055	29
30	22.8923	199.0209	0.005025	0.0437	8.6938	0.1150246	30
31	25.4104	221.9132	0.004506	0.0394	8.7331	0.1145063	31
32	28.2056	247.3236	0.004043	0.0355	8.7686	0.1140433	32
33	31.3082	275.5292	0.003629	0.0319	8.8005	0.1136294	33
34	34.7521	306.8374	0.003259	0.0288	8.8293	0.1132591	34
35	38.5749	341.5896	0.002927	0.0259	8.8552	0.1129275	35
36	42.8181	380.1644	0.002630	0.0234	8.8786	0.1126304	36
37	47.5281	422.9825	0.002364	0.0210	8.8996	0.1123642	37
38	52.7562	470.5106	0.002125	0.0190	8.9186	0.1121254	38
39	58.5593	523.2667	0.001911	0.0171	8.9357	0.1119111	39
40	65.0009	581.8261	0.001719	0.0154	8.9511	0.1117187	40
41	72.1510	646.8269	0.001546	0.0139	8.9649	0.1115460	41
42	80.0876	718.9779	0.001391	0.0125	8.9774	0.1113909	42
43	88.8972	799.0655	0.001251	0.0112	8.9886	0.1112515	43

Table A.5. Annual Rate 11% (Continued)

Nominal Annual Interest Rate = 11%   Compounding Periods per Year = 1

Year	Amount of 1 at Compound Interest (Col. 1)	Accumu- lation of 1 per Period (Col. 2)	Sinking Fund Factor (Col. 3)	Present Value Rever- sion of 1 (Col. 4)	Present Value Ordinary Annuity 1 per Period (Col. 5)	Installment to Amortize 1 (Col. 6)	Period
44	98.6759	887.9626	0.001126	0.0101	8.9988	0.1111262	44
45	109.5302	986.6385	0.001014	0.0091	9.0079	0.1110135	45
46	121.5786	1096.1688	0.000912	0.0082	9.0161	0.1109123	46
47	134.9522	1217.7473	0.000821	0.0074	9.0235	0.1108212	47
48	149.7969	1352.6996	0.000739	0.0067	9.0302	0.1107393	48
49	166.2746	1502.4965	0.000666	0.0060	9.0362	0.1106656	49
50	184.5648	1668.7711	0.000599	0.0054	9.0417	0.1105992	50

Table A.6. Annual Rate 12%

Nominal Annual Interest Rate = 12%					Compounding Periods per Year = 1	
Year	Amount of 1 at Compound Interest (Col. 1)	Accumulation of 1 per Period (Col. 2)	Sinking Fund Factor (Col. 3)	Present Value Reversion of 1 (Col. 4)	Present Value Ordinary Annuity 1 per Period (Col. 5)	Installment to Amortize 1 (Col. 6)	Period
---	---	---	---	---	---	---	---
1	1.1200	1.0000	1.000000	0.8929	0.8929	1.1200000	1
2	1.2544	2.1200	0.471698	0.7972	1.6901	0.5916981	2
3	1.4049	3.3744	0.296349	0.7118	2.4018	0.4163490	3
4	1.5735	4.7793	0.209234	0.6355	3.0373	0.3292344	4
5	1.7623	6.3528	0.157410	0.5674	3.6048	0.2774097	5
6	1.9738	8.1152	0.123226	0.5066	4.1114	0.2432257	6
7	2.2107	10.0890	0.099118	0.4523	4.5638	0.2191177	7
8	2.4760	12.2997	0.081303	0.4039	4.9676	0.2013028	8
9	2.7731	14.7757	0.067679	0.3606	5.3282	0.1876789	9
10	3.1058	17.5487	0.056984	0.3220	5.6502	0.1769842	10
11	3.4785	20.6546	0.048415	0.2875	5.9377	0.1684154	11
12	3.8960	24.1331	0.041437	0.2567	6.1944	0.1614368	12
13	4.3635	28.0291	0.035677	0.2292	6.4235	0.1556772	13
14	4.8871	32.3926	0.030871	0.2046	6.6282	0.1508712	14
15	5.4736	37.2797	0.026824	0.1827	6.8109	0.1468242	15
16	6.1304	42.7533	0.023390	0.1631	6.9740	0.1433900	16
17	6.8660	48.8837	0.020457	0.1456	7.1196	0.1404567	17
18	7.6900	55.7497	0.017937	0.1300	7.2497	0.1379373	18
19	8.6128	63.4397	0.015763	0.1161	7.3658	0.1357630	19
20	9.6463	72.0524	0.013879	0.1037	7.4694	0.1338788	20
21	10.8038	81.6987	0.012240	0.0926	7.5620	0.1322401	21
22	12.1003	92.5026	0.010811	0.0826	7.6446	0.1308105	22
23	13.5523	104.6029	0.009560	0.0738	7.7184	0.1295600	23
24	15.1786	118.1552	0.008463	0.0659	7.7843	0.1284634	24
25	17.0001	133.3339	0.007500	0.0588	7.8431	0.1275000	25
26	19.0401	150.3339	0.006652	0.0525	7.8957	0.1266519	26
27	21.3249	169.3740	0.005904	0.0469	7.9426	0.1259041	27
28	23.8839	190.6989	0.005244	0.0419	7.9844	0.1252439	28
29	26.7499	214.5827	0.004660	0.0374	8.0218	0.1246602	29
30	29.9599	241.3327	0.004144	0.0334	8.0552	0.1241437	30
31	33.5551	271.2926	0.003686	0.0298	8.0850	0.1236861	31
32	37.5817	304.8477	0.003280	0.0266	8.1116	0.1232803	32
33	42.0915	342.4294	0.002920	0.0238	8.1354	0.1229203	33
34	47.1425	384.5210	0.002601	0.0212	8.1566	0.1226006	34
35	52.7996	431.6635	0.002317	0.0189	8.1755	0.1223166	35
36	59.1356	484.4631	0.002064	0.0169	8.1924	0.1220641	36
37	66.2318	543.5987	0.001840	0.0151	8.2075	0.1218396	37
38	74.1797	609.8305	0.001640	0.0135	8.2210	0.1216398	38
39	83.0812	684.0101	0.001462	0.0120	8.2330	0.1214620	39
40	93.0510	767.0914	0.001304	0.0107	8.2438	0.1213036	40
41	104.2171	860.1423	0.001163	0.0096	8.2534	0.1211626	41
42	116.7231	964.3594	0.001037	0.0086	8.2619	0.1210370	42
43	130.7299	1081.0825	0.000925	0.0076	8.2696	0.1209250	43

Table A.6. Annual Rate 12% (Continued)

Nominal Annual Interest Rate = 12%   Compounding Periods per Year = 1

Year	Amount of 1 at Compound Interest (Col. 1)	Accumulation of 1 per Period (Col. 2)	Sinking Fund Factor (Col. 3)	Present Value Reversion of 1 (Col. 4)	Present Value Ordinary Annuity 1 per Period (Col. 5)	Installment to Amortize 1 (Col. 6)	Period
44	146.4175	1211.8124	0.000825	0.0068	8.2764	0.1208252	44
45	163.9876	1358.2299	0.000736	0.0061	8.2825	0.1207362	45
46	183.6661	1522.2175	0.000657	0.0054	8.2880	0.1206569	46
47	205.7060	1705.8836	0.000586	0.0049	8.2928	0.1205862	47
48	230.3907	1911.5896	0.000523	0.0043	8.2972	0.1205231	48
49	258.0376	2141.9804	0.000467	0.0039	8.3010	0.1204669	49
50	289.0022	2400.0180	0.000417	0.0035	8.3045	0.1204167	50

Table A.7. Annual Rate 13%

Nominal Annual Interest Rate = 13%					Compounding Periods per Year = 1	
Year	Amount of 1 at Compound Interest (Col. 1)	Accumulation of 1 per Period (Col. 2)	Sinking Fund Factor (Col. 3)	Present Value Reversion of 1 (Col. 4)	Present Value Ordinary Annuity 1 per Period (Col. 5)	Installment to Amortize 1 (Col. 6)	Period
1	1.1300	1.0000	1.000000	0.8850	0.8850	1.1300000	1
2	1.2769	2.1300	0.469484	0.7831	1.6681	0.5994836	2
3	1.4429	3.4069	0.293522	0.6931	2.3612	0.4235220	3
4	1.6305	4.8498	0.206194	0.6133	2.9745	0.3361942	4
5	1.8424	6.4803	0.154315	0.5428	3.5172	0.2843145	5
6	2.0820	8.3227	0.120153	0.4803	3.9975	0.2501532	6
7	2.3526	10.4047	0.096111	0.4251	4.4226	0.2261108	7
8	2.6584	12.7573	0.078387	0.3762	4.7988	0.2083867	8
9	3.0040	15.4157	0.064869	0.3329	5.1317	0.1948689	9
10	3.3946	18.4197	0.054290	0.2946	5.4262	0.1842896	10
11	3.8359	21.8143	0.045841	0.2607	5.6869	0.1758415	11
12	4.3345	25.6502	0.038986	0.2307	5.9176	0.1689861	12
13	4.8980	29.9847	0.033350	0.2042	6.1218	0.1633503	13
14	5.5348	34.8827	0.028667	0.1807	6.3025	0.1586675	14
15	6.2543	40.4175	0.024742	0.1599	6.4624	0.1547418	15
16	7.0673	46.6717	0.021426	0.1415	6.6039	0.1514262	16
17	7.9861	53.7391	0.018608	0.1252	6.7291	0.1486084	17
18	9.0243	61.7251	0.016201	0.1108	6.8399	0.1462009	18
19	10.1974	70.7494	0.014134	0.0981	6.9380	0.1441344	19
20	11.5231	80.9468	0.012354	0.0868	7.0248	0.1423538	20
21	13.0211	92.4699	0.010814	0.0768	7.1016	0.1408143	21
22	14.7138	105.4910	0.009479	0.0680	7.1695	0.1394795	22
23	16.6266	120.2048	0.008319	0.0601	7.2297	0.1383191	23
24	18.7881	136.8315	0.007308	0.0532	7.2829	0.1373083	24
25	21.2305	155.6195	0.006426	0.0471	7.3300	0.1364259	25
26	23.9905	176.8501	0.005655	0.0417	7.3717	0.1356545	26
27	27.1093	200.8406	0.004979	0.0369	7.4086	0.1349791	27
28	30.6335	227.9499	0.004387	0.0326	7.4412	0.1343869	28
29	34.6158	258.5834	0.003867	0.0289	7.4701	0.1338672	29
30	39.1159	293.1992	0.003411	0.0256	7.4957	0.1334106	30
31	44.2010	332.3151	0.003009	0.0226	7.5183	0.1330092	31
32	49.9471	376.5160	0.002656	0.0200	7.5383	0.1326559	32
33	56.4402	426.4631	0.002345	0.0177	7.5560	0.1323449	33
34	63.7774	482.9033	0.002071	0.0157	7.5717	0.1320708	34
35	72.0685	546.6808	0.001829	0.0139	7.5856	0.1318292	35
36	81.4374	618.7493	0.001616	0.0123	7.5979	0.1316162	36
37	92.0243	700.1867	0.001428	0.0109	7.6087	0.1314282	37
38	103.9874	792.2109	0.001262	0.0096	7.6183	0.1312623	38
39	117.5058	896.1983	0.001116	0.0085	7.6268	0.1311158	39
40	132.7815	1013.7041	0.000986	0.0075	7.6344	0.1309865	40
41	150.0431	1146.4856	0.000872	0.0067	7.6410	0.1308722	41
42	169.5487	1296.5288	0.000771	0.0059	7.6469	0.1307713	42
43	191.5901	1466.0775	0.000682	0.0052	7.6522	0.1306821	43

Table A.7. Annual Rate 13% (Continued)

Nominal Annual Interest Rate = 13%   Compounding Periods per Year = 1

Year	Amount of 1 at Compound Interest (Col. 1)	Accumulation of 1 per Period (Col. 2)	Sinking Fund Factor (Col. 3)	Present Value Reversion of 1 (Col. 4)	Present Value Ordinary Annuity 1 per Period (Col. 5)	Installment to Amortize 1 (Col. 6)	Period
44	216.4968	1657.6676	0.000603	0.0046	7.6568	0.1306033	44
45	244.6414	1874.1643	0.000534	0.0041	7.6609	0.1305336	45
46	276.4447	2118.8057	0.000472	0.0036	7.6645	0.1304720	46
47	312.3825	2395.2504	0.000417	0.0032	7.6677	0.1304175	47
48	352.9923	2707.6330	0.000369	0.0028	7.6705	0.1303693	48
49	398.8813	3060.6252	0.000327	0.0025	7.6730	0.1303267	49
50	450.7358	3459.5065	0.000289	0.0022	7.6752	0.1302891	50

Table A.8. Annual Rate 14%

Nominal Annual Interest Rate = 14%   Compounding Periods per Year = 1

Year	Amount of 1 at Compound Interest (Col. 1)	Accumulation of 1 per Period (Col. 2)	Sinking Fund Factor (Col. 3)	Present Value Reversion of 1 (Col. 4)	Present Value Ordinary Annuity 1 per Period (Col. 5)	Installment to Amortize 1 (Col. 6)	Period
1	1.1400	1.0000	1.000000	0.8772	0.8772	1.1400000	1
2	1.2996	2.1400	0.467290	0.7695	1.6467	0.6072897	2
3	1.4815	3.4396	0.290731	0.6750	2.3216	0.4307315	3
4	1.6890	4.9211	0.203205	0.5921	2.9137	0.3432048	4
5	1.9254	6.6101	0.151284	0.5194	3.4331	0.2912835	5
6	2.1950	8.5355	0.117157	0.4556	3.8887	0.2571575	6
7	2.5023	10.7305	0.093192	0.3996	4.2883	0.2331924	7
8	2.8526	13.2328	0.075570	0.3506	4.6389	0.2155700	8
9	3.2519	16.0853	0.062168	0.3075	4.9464	0.2021684	9
10	3.7072	19.3373	0.051714	0.2697	5.2161	0.1917135	10
11	4.2262	23.0445	0.043394	0.2366	5.4527	0.1833943	11
12	4.8179	27.2707	0.036669	0.2076	5.6603	0.1766693	12
13	5.4924	32.0887	0.031164	0.1821	5.8424	0.1711637	13
14	6.2613	37.5811	0.026609	0.1597	6.0021	0.1666091	14
15	7.1379	43.8424	0.022809	0.1401	6.1422	0.1628090	15
16	8.1372	50.9804	0.019615	0.1229	6.2651	0.1596154	16
17	9.2765	59.1176	0.016915	0.1078	6.3729	0.1569154	17
18	10.5752	68.3941	0.014621	0.0946	6.4674	0.1546212	18
19	12.0557	78.9692	0.012663	0.0829	6.5504	0.1526632	19
20	13.7435	91.0249	0.010986	0.0728	6.6231	0.1509860	20
21	15.6676	104.7684	0.009545	0.0638	6.6870	0.1495449	21
22	17.8610	120.4360	0.008303	0.0560	6.7429	0.1483032	22
23	20.3616	138.2970	0.007231	0.0491	6.7921	0.1472308	23
24	23.2122	158.6586	0.006303	0.0431	6.8351	0.1463028	24
25	26.4619	181.8708	0.005498	0.0378	6.8729	0.1454984	25
26	30.1666	208.3327	0.004800	0.0331	6.9061	0.1448000	26
27	34.3899	238.4993	0.004193	0.0291	6.9352	0.1441929	27
28	39.2045	272.8892	0.003664	0.0255	6.9607	0.1436645	28
29	44.6931	312.0937	0.003204	0.0224	6.9830	0.1432042	29
30	50.9502	356.7869	0.002803	0.0196	7.0027	0.1428028	30
31	58.0832	407.7370	0.002453	0.0172	7.0199	0.1424526	31
32	66.2148	465.8202	0.002147	0.0151	7.0350	0.1421468	32
33	75.4849	532.0350	0.001880	0.0132	7.0482	0.1418796	33
34	86.0528	607.5199	0.001646	0.0116	7.0599	0.1416460	34
35	98.1002	693.5727	0.001442	0.0102	7.0700	0.1414418	35
36	111.8342	791.6729	0.001263	0.0089	7.0790	0.1412631	36
37	127.4910	903.5071	0.001107	0.0078	7.0868	0.1411068	37
38	145.3397	1030.9981	0.000970	0.0069	7.0937	0.1409699	38
39	165.6873	1176.3378	0.000850	0.0060	7.0997	0.1408501	39
40	188.8835	1342.0251	0.000745	0.0053	7.1050	0.1407451	40
41	215.3272	1530.9086	0.000653	0.0046	7.1097	0.1406532	41
42	245.4730	1746.2358	0.000573	0.0041	7.1138	0.1405727	42
43	279.8392	1991.7089	0.000502	0.0036	7.1173	0.1405021	43

Table A.8. Annual Rate 14% (Continued)

Nominal Annual Interest Rate = 14%   Compounding Periods per Year = 1

Year	Amount of 1 at Compound Interest (Col. 1)	Accumulation of 1 per Period (Col. 2)	Sinking Fund Factor (Col. 3)	Present Value Reversion of 1 (Col. 4)	Present Value Ordinary Annuity 1 per Period (Col. 5)	Installment to Amortize 1 (Col. 6)	Period
44	319.0167	2271.5481	0.000440	0.0031	7.1205	0.1404402	44
45	363.6791	2590.5648	0.000386	0.0027	7.1232	0.1403860	45
46	414.5942	2954.2439	0.000338	0.0024	7.1256	0.1403385	46
47	472.6373	3368.8381	0.000297	0.0021	7.1277	0.1402968	47
48	538.8066	3841.4754	0.000260	0.0019	7.1296	0.1402603	48
49	614.2395	4380.2820	0.000228	0.0016	7.1312	0.1402283	49
50	700.2330	4994.5215	0.000200	0.0014	7.1327	0.1402002	50

Table A.9. Annual Rate 15%

Nominal Annual Interest Rate = 15%   Compounding Periods per Year = 1

Year	Amount of 1 at Compound Interest (Col. 1)	Accumu- lation of 1 per Period (Col. 2)	Sinking Fund Factor (Col. 3)	Present Value Rever- sion of 1 (Col. 4)	Present Value Ordinary Annuity 1 per Period (Col. 5)	Installment to Amortize 1 (Col. 6)	Period
1	1.1500	1.0000	1.000000	0.8696	0.8696	1.1500000	1
2	1.3225	2.1500	0.465116	0.7561	1.6257	0.6151163	2
3	1.5209	3.4725	0.287977	0.6575	2.2832	0.4379770	3
4	1.7490	4.9934	0.200265	0.5718	2.8550	0.3502654	4
5	2.0114	6.7424	0.148316	0.4972	3.3522	0.2983156	5
6	2.3131	8.7537	0.114237	0.4323	3.7845	0.2642369	6
7	2.6600	11.0668	0.090360	0.3759	4.1604	0.2403604	7
8	3.0590	13.7268	0.072850	0.3269	4.4873	0.2228501	8
9	3.5179	16.7858	0.059574	0.2843	4.7716	0.2095740	9
10	4.0456	20.3037	0.049252	0.2472	5.0188	0.1992521	10
11	4.6524	24.3493	0.041069	0.2149	5.2337	0.1910690	11
12	5.3503	29.0017	0.034481	0.1869	5.4206	0.1844808	12
13	6.1528	34.3519	0.029110	0.1625	5.5831	0.1791105	13
14	7.0757	40.5047	0.024688	0.1413	5.7245	0.1746885	14
15	8.1371	47.5804	0.021017	0.1229	5.8474	0.1710171	15
16	9.3576	55.7175	0.017948	0.1069	5.9542	0.1679477	16
17	10.7613	65.0751	0.015367	0.0929	6.0472	0.1653669	17
18	12.3755	75.8364	0.013186	0.0808	6.1280	0.1631863	18
19	14.2318	88.2118	0.011336	0.0703	6.1982	0.1613364	19
20	16.3665	102.4436	0.009761	0.0611	6.2593	0.1597615	20
21	18.8215	118.8101	0.008417	0.0531	6.3125	0.1584168	21
22	21.6447	137.6316	0.007266	0.0462	6.3587	0.1572658	22
23	24.8915	159.2764	0.006278	0.0402	6.3988	0.1562784	23
24	28.6252	184.1679	0.005430	0.0349	6.4338	0.1554298	24
25	32.9190	212.7930	0.004699	0.0304	6.4641	0.1546994	25
26	37.8568	245.7120	0.004070	0.0264	6.4906	0.1540698	26
27	43.5353	283.5688	0.003526	0.0230	6.5135	0.1535265	27
28	50.0656	327.1041	0.003057	0.0200	6.5335	0.1530571	28
29	57.5755	377.1697	0.002651	0.0174	6.5509	0.1526513	29
30	66.2118	434.7452	0.002300	0.0151	6.5660	0.1523002	30
31	76.1435	500.9570	0.001996	0.0131	6.5791	0.1519962	31
32	87.5651	577.1005	0.001733	0.0114	6.5905	0.1517328	32
33	100.6998	664.6656	0.001505	0.0099	6.6005	0.1515045	33
34	115.8048	765.3655	0.001307	0.0086	6.6091	0.1513066	34
35	133.1755	881.1703	0.001135	0.0075	6.6166	0.1511349	35
36	153.1519	1014.3458	0.000986	0.0065	6.6231	0.1509859	36
37	176.1247	1167.4977	0.000857	0.0057	6.6288	0.1508565	37
38	202.5434	1343.6224	0.000744	0.0049	6.6338	0.1507443	38
39	232.9249	1546.1657	0.000647	0.0043	6.6380	0.1506468	39
40	267.8636	1779.0906	0.000562	0.0037	6.6418	0.1505621	40

Table A.10. Annual Rate 16%

| Nominal Annual Interest Rate = 16% | | | | | Compounding Periods per Year = 1 | |

Year	Amount of 1 at Compound Interest (Col. 1)	Accumulation of 1 per Period (Col. 2)	Sinking Fund Factor (Col. 3)	Present Value Reversion of 1 (Col. 4)	Present Value Ordinary Annuity 1 per Period (Col. 5)	Installment to Amortize 1 (Col. 6)	Period
1	1.1600	1.0000	1.000000	0.8621	0.8621	1.1600000	1
2	1.3456	2.1600	0.462963	0.7432	1.6052	0.6229630	2
3	1.5609	3.5056	0.285258	0.6407	2.2459	0.4452579	3
4	1.8106	5.0665	0.197375	0.5523	2.7982	0.3573751	4
5	2.1003	6.8771	0.145409	0.4761	3.2743	0.3054094	5
6	2.4364	8.9775	0.111390	0.4104	3.6847	0.2713899	6
7	2.8262	11.4139	0.087613	0.3538	4.0386	0.2476127	7
8	3.2784	14.2401	0.070224	0.3050	4.3436	0.2302243	8
9	3.8030	17.5185	0.057082	0.2630	4.6065	0.2170825	9
10	4.4114	21.3215	0.046901	0.2267	4.8332	0.2069011	10
11	5.1173	25.7329	0.038861	0.1954	5.0286	0.1988607	11
12	5.9360	30.8502	0.032415	0.1685	5.1971	0.1924147	12
13	6.8858	36.7862	0.027184	0.1452	5.3423	0.1871841	13
14	7.9875	43.6720	0.022898	0.1252	5.4675	0.1828980	14
15	9.2655	51.6595	0.019358	0.1079	5.5755	0.1793575	15
16	10.7480	60.9250	0.016414	0.0930	5.6685	0.1764136	16
17	12.4677	71.6730	0.013952	0.0802	5.7487	0.1739522	17
18	14.4625	84.1407	0.011885	0.0691	5.8178	0.1718848	18
19	16.7765	98.6032	0.010142	0.0596	5.8775	0.1701417	19
20	19.4608	115.3797	0.008667	0.0514	5.9288	0.1686670	20
21	24.5745	134.8405	0.007416	0.0443	5.9731	0.1674162	21
22	26.1864	157.4150	0.006353	0.0382	6.0113	0.1663526	22
23	30.3762	183.6014	0.005447	0.0329	6.0442	0.1654466	23
24	35.2364	213.9776	0.004673	0.0284	6.0726	0.1646734	24
25	40.8742	249.2140	0.004013	0.0245	6.0971	0.1640126	25
26	47.4141	290.0883	0.003447	0.0211	6.1182	0.1634472	26
27	55.0004	337.5024	0.002963	0.0182	6.1364	0.1629629	27
28	63.8004	392.5027	0.002548	0.0157	6.1520	0.1625477	28
29	74.0085	456.3032	0.002192	0.0135	6.1656	0.1621915	29
30	85.8499	530.3117	0.001886	0.0116	6.1772	0.1618857	30
31	99.5828	616.1616	0.001623	0.0100	6.1872	0.1616229	31
32	115.5196	715.7474	0.001397	0.0087	6.1959	0.1613971	32
33	134.0027	831.2670	0.001203	0.0075	6.2034	0.1612030	33
34	155.4431	965.2697	0.001036	0.0064	6.2098	0.1610360	34
35	180.3141	1120.7129	0.000892	0.0055	6.2153	0.1608923	35
36	209.1643	1301.0269	0.000769	0.0048	6.2201	0.1607686	36
37	242.6306	1510.1912	0.000662	0.0041	6.2242	0.1606622	37
38	281.4515	1752.8218	0.000571	0.0036	6.2278	0.1605705	38
39	326.4837	2034.2733	0.000492	0.0031	6.2309	0.1604916	39
40	378.7211	2360.7570	0.000424	0.0026	6.2335	0.1604236	40

Table A.11. Annual Rate 20%

Nominal Annual Interest Rate = 20%					Compounding Periods per Year = 1	
Year	Amount of 1 at Compound Interest (Col. 1)	Accumu- lation of 1 per Period (Col. 2)	Sinking Fund Factor (Col. 3)	Present Value Rever- sion of 1 (Col. 4)	Present Value Ordinary Annuity 1 per Period (Col. 5)	Installment to Amortize 1 (Col. 6)	Period
1	1.2000	1.0000	1.000000	0.8333	0.8333	1.2000000	1
2	1.4400	2.2000	0.454545	0.6944	1.5278	0.6545455	2
3	1.7280	3.6400	0.274725	0.5787	2.1065	0.4747253	3
4	2.0736	5.3680	0.186289	0.4823	2.5887	0.3862891	4
5	2.4883	7.4416	0.134380	0.4019	2.9906	0.3343797	5
6	2.9860	9.9299	0.100706	0.3349	3.3255	0.3007057	6
7	3.5832	12.9159	0.077424	0.2791	3.6046	0.2774239	7
8	4.2998	16.4991	0.060609	0.2326	3.8372	0.2606094	8
9	5.1598	20.7989	0.048079	0.1938	4.0310	0.2480795	9
10	6.1917	25.9587	0.038523	0.1615	4.1925	0.2385228	10
11	7.4301	32.1504	0.031104	0.1346	4.3271	0.2311038	11
12	8.9161	39.5805	0.025265	0.1122	4.4392	0.2252650	12
13	10.6993	48.4966	0.020620	0.0935	4.5327	0.2206200	13
14	12.8392	59.1959	0.016893	0.0779	4.6106	0.2168931	14
15	15.4070	72.0351	0.013882	0.0649	4.6755	0.2138821	15
16	18.4884	87.4421	0.011436	0.0541	4.7296	0.2114361	16
17	22.1861	105.9306	0.009440	0.0451	4.7746	0.2094401	17
18	26.6233	128.1167	0.007805	0.0376	4.8122	0.2078054	18
19	31.9480	154.7400	0.006462	0.0313	4.8435	0.2064625	19
20	38.3376	186.6880	0.005357	0.0261	4.8696	0.2053565	20
21	46.0051	225.0256	0.004444	0.0217	4.8913	0.2044439	21
22	55.2061	271.0307	0.003690	0.0181	4.9094	0.2036896	22
23	66.2474	326.2369	0.003065	0.0151	4.9245	0.2030653	23
24	79.4969	392.4843	0.002548	0.0126	4.9371	0.2025479	24
25	95.3962	471.9811	0.002119	0.0105	4.9476	0.2021187	25
26	114.4755	567.3773	0.001762	0.0087	4.9563	0.2017625	26
27	137.3706	681.8528	0.001467	0.0073	4.9636	0.2014666	27
28	164.8447	819.2234	0.001221	0.0061	4.9697	0.2012207	28
29	197.8136	984.0680	0.001016	0.0051	4.9747	0.2010162	29
30	237.3763	1181.8816	0.000846	0.0042	4.9789	0.2008461	30
31	284.8516	1419.2580	0.000705	0.0035	4.9824	0.2007046	31
32	341.8219	1704.1096	0.000587	0.0029	4.9854	0.2005868	32
33	410.1863	2045.9315	0.000489	0.0024	4.9878	0.2004888	33
34	492.2236	2456.1178	0.000407	0.0020	4.9898	0.2004071	34
35.	590.6683	2948.3414	0.000339	0.0017	4.9915	0.2003392	35
36	708.8019	3539.0096	0.000283	0.0014	4.9929	0.2002826	36
37	850.5623	4247.8116	0.000235	0.0012	4.9941	0.2002354	37
38	1020.6748	5098.3739	0.000196	0.0010	4.9951	0.2001961	38
39	1224.8098	6119.0487	0.000163	0.0008	4.9959	0.2001634	39
40	1469.7717	7343.8585	0.000136	0.0007	4.9966	0.2001362	40

Table A.12. Monthly Compounding 8%

Nominal Annual Interest Rate = 8%　　　　　　　　　Compounding Periods per Year = 12

Year	Amount of 1 at Compound Interest (Col. 1)	Accumulation of 1 per Period (Col. 2)	Sinking Fund Factor (Col. 3)	Present Value Reversion of 1 (Col. 4)	Present Value Ordinary Annuity 1 per Period (Col. 5)	Installment to Amortize 1 (Col. 6)	Period
1	1.0830	12.4499	0.080322	0.9234	11.4958	0.08698843	12
2	1.1729	25.9332	0.038561	0.9526	22.1105	0.04522729	24
3	1.2702	40.5356	0.024670	0.7873	31.9118	0.03133637	36
4	1.3757	56.3499	0.017746	0.7269	40.9619	0.02441292	48
5	1.4898	73.4769	0.013610	0.6712	49.3184	0.02027639	60
6	1.6135	92.0253	0.010867	0.6198	57.0345	0.01753324	72
7	1.7474	112.1133	0.008920	0.5723	64.1593	0.01558621	84
8	1.8925	133.8686	0.007470	0.5284	70.7380	0.01413668	96
9	2.0495	157.4295	0.006352	0.4879	76.8125	0.01301871	108
10	2.2196	182.9460	0.005466	0.4505	82.4215	0.01213276	120
11	2.4039	210.5804	0.004749	0.4160	87.6006	0.01141545	132
12	2.6034	240.5084	0.004158	0.3841	92.3828	0.01082453	144
13	2.8195	272.9204	0.003664	0.3547	96.7985	0.01033074	156
14	3.0535	308.0226	0.003247	0.3275	100.8758	0.00991318	168
15	3.3069	346.0382	0.002890	0.3024	104.6406	0.00955652	180
16	3.5814	387.2092	0.002583	0.2792	108.1169	0.00924925	192
17	3.8786	431.7973	0.002316	0.2578	111.3267	0.00898257	204
18	4.2006	480.0861	0.002083	0.2381	114.2906	0.00874963	216
19	4.5492	532.3830	0.001878	0.2198	117.0273	0.00854501	228
20	4.9268	589.0204	0.001698	0.2030	119.5543	0.00836440	240
21	5.3357	650.3588	0.001538	0.1874	121.8876	0.00820428	252
22	5.7786	716.7881	0.001395	0.1731	124.0421	0.00806178	264
23	6.2582	788.7311	0.001268	0.1598	126.0315	0.00793453	276
24	6.7776	866.6454	0.001154	0.1475	127.8684	0.00782054	288
25	7.3402	951.0264	0.001051	0.1362	129.5645	0.00771816	300
26	7.9494	1042.4111	0.000959	0.1258	131.1307	0.00762598	312
27	8.6092	1141.3806	0.000876	0.1162	132.5768	0.00754280	324
28	9.3238	1248.5646	0.000801	0.1073	133.9121	0.00746759	336
29	10.0976	1364.6447	0.000733	0.0990	135.1450	0.00739946	348
30	10.9357	1490.3595	0.000671	0.0914	136.2835	0.00733765	360
31	11.8434	1626.5085	0.000615	0.0844	137.3347	0.00728148	372
32	12.8264	1773.9579	0.000564	0.0780	138.3054	0.00723038	384
33	13.8910	1933.6454	0.000517	0.0720	139.2016	0.00718382	396
34	15.0439	2106.5870	0.000475	0.0665	140.0292	0.00714137	408
35	16.2926	2293.8826	0.000436	0.0614	140.7933	0.00710261	420
36	17.6448	2496.7236	0.000401	0.0567	141.4989	0.00706719	432
37	19.1093	2716.4004	0.000368	0.0523	142.1504	0.00703480	444
38	20.6954	2954.3102	0.000338	0.0483	142.7520	0.00700516	456
39	22.4131	3211.9665	0.000311	0.0446	143.3075	0.00697800	468
40	24.2734	3491.0080	0.000286	0.0412	143.8204	0.00695312	480

Table A.13. Monthly Compounding 10%

Nominal Annual Interest Rate = 10% Compounding Periods per Year = 12

Year	Amount of 1 at Compound Interest (Col. 1)	Accumu- lation of 1 per Period (Col. 2)	Sinking Fund Factor (Col. 3)	Present Value Rever- sion of 1 (Col. 4)	Present Value Ordinary Annuity 1 per Period (Col. 5)	Installment to Amortize 1 (Col. 6)	Period
1	1.1047	12.5656	0.079583	0.9052	11.3745	0.08791589	12
2	1.2204	26.4469	0.037812	0.8194	21.6709	0.04614493	24
3	1.3482	41.7818	0.023934	0.7417	30.9912	0.03226719	36
4	1.4894	58.7225	0.017029	0.6714	39.4282	0.02536258	48
5	1.6453	77.4371	0.012914	0.6078	47.0654	0.02124704	60
6	1.8176	98.1113	0.010193	0.5502	53.9787	0.01852584	72
7	2.0079	120.9504	0.008268	0.4980	60.2367	0.01660118	84
8	2.2182	146.1811	0.006841	0.4508	65.9015	0.01517416	96
9	2.4504	174.0537	0.005745	0.4081	71.0294	0.01407869	108
10	2.7070	204.8450	0.004882	0.3694	75.6712	0.01321507	120
11	2.9905	238.8605	0.004187	0.3344	79.8730	0.01251988	132
12	3.3036	276.4379	0.003617	0.3027	83.6765	0.01195078	144
13	3.6496	317.9501	0.003145	0.2740	87.1195	0.01147848	156
14	4.0317	363.8092	0.002749	0.2480	90.2362	0.01108203	168
15	4.4539	414.4703	0.002413	0.2245	93.0574	0.01074605	180
16	4.9203	470.4363	0.002126	0.2032	95.6113	0.01045902	192
17	5.4355	532.2627	0.001879	0.1840	97.9230	0.01021210	204
18	6.0047	600.5632	0.001665	0.1665	100.0156	0.00999844	216
19	6.6335	676.0156	0.001479	0.1508	101.9099	0.00981259	228
20	7.3281	759.3688	0.001317	0.1365	103.6246	0.00965022	240
21	8.0954	851.4502	0.001174	0.1235	105.1768	0.00950780	252
22	8.9431	953.1737	0.001049	0.1118	106.5819	0.00938246	264
23	9.8796	1065.5490	0.000938	0.1012	107.8537	0.00927182	276
24	10.9141	1189.6915	0.000841	0.0916	109.0050	0.00917389	288
25	12.0569	1326.8333	0.000754	0.0829	110.0472	0.00908701	300
26	13.3195	1478.3356	0.000676	0.0751	110.9906	0.00900977	312
27	14.7142	1645.7022	0.000608	0.0680	111.8446	0.00894098	324
28	16.2550	1830.5946	0.000546	0.0615	112.6176	0.00887960	336
29	17.9571	2034.8470	0.000491	0.0557	113.3174	0.00882477	348
30	19.8374	2260.4876	0.000442	0.0504	113.9508	0.00877572	360
31	21.9146	2509.7558	0.000398	0.0456	114.5242	0.00873178	372
32	24.2094	2785.1256	0.000359	0.0413	115.0433	0.00869238	384
33	26.7444	3089.3302	0.000324	0.0374	115.5131	0.00865703	396
34	29.5449	3425.3889	0.000292	0.0338	115.9384	0.00862527	408
35	32.6386	3796.6375	0.000263	0.0306	116.3234	0.00859672	420
36	36.0563	4206.7606	0.000238	0.0277	116.6719	0.00857105	432
37	39.8319	4659.8289	0.000215	0.0251	116.9873	0.00854793	444
38	44.0028	5160.3394	0.000194	0.0227	117.2729	0.00852712	456
39	48.6105	5713.2599	0.000175	0.0206	117.5314	0.00850836	468
40	53.7007	6324.0784	0.000158	0.0186	117.7654	0.00849146	480

Table A.14. Monthly Compounding 11%

Nominal Annual Interest Rate = 11%   Compounding Periods per Year = 12

Year	Amount of 1 at Compound Interest (Col. 1)	Accumu- lation of 1 per Period (Col. 2)	Sinking Fund Factor (Col. 3)	Present Value Rever- sion of 1 (Col. 4)	Present Value Ordinary Annuity 1 per Period (Col. 5)	Installment to Amortize 1 (Col. 6)	Period
1	1.1157	12.6239	0.079215	0.8963	11.3146	0.08838166	12
2	1.2448	26.7086	0.037441	0.8033	21.4556	0.04660784	24
3	1.3889	42.4231	0.023572	0.7200	30.5449	0.03273872	36
4	1.5496	59.9562	0.016679	0.6453	38.6914	0.02584552	48
5	1.7289	79.5181	0.012576	0.5784	45.9930	0.02174242	60
6	1.9290	101.3437	0.009867	0.5184	52.5373	0.01903408	72
7	2.1522	125.6949	0.007956	0.4646	58.4029	0.01712244	84
8	2.4013	152.8641	0.006542	0.4164	63.6601	0.01570843	96
9	2.6791	183.1772	0.005459	0.3733	68.3720	0.01462586	108
10	2.9891	216.9981	0.004608	0.3345	72.5953	0.01377500	120
11	3.3351	254.7328	0.003926	0.2998	76.3805	0.01309235	132
12	3.7210	296.8341	0.003369	0.2687	79.7731	0.01253555	144
13	4.1516	343.8072	0.002909	0.2409	82.8139	0.01207527	156
14	4.6320	396.2161	0.002524	0.2159	85.5392	0.01169054	168
15	5.1680	454.6896	0.002199	0.1935	87.9819	0.01136597	180
16	5.7660	519.9296	0.001923	0.1734	90.1713	0.01109000	192
17	6.4333	592.7192	0.001687	0.1554	92.1336	0.01085381	204
18	7.1777	673.9318	0.001484	0.1393	93.8923	0.01065050	216
19	8.0083	764.5423	0.001308	0.1249	95.4687	0.01047464	228
20	8.9350	865.6381	0.001155	0.1119	96.8815	0.01032188	240
21	9.9690	978.4326	0.001022	0.1003	98.1479	0.01018871	252
22	11.1226	1104.2796	0.000906	0.0899	99.2828	0.01007223	264
23	12.4097	1244.6894	0.000803	0.0806	100.3001	0.00997008	276
24	13.8457	1401.3473	0.000714	0.0722	101.2118	0.00988027	288
25	15.4479	1576.1335	0.000634	0.0647	102.0290	0.00980113	300
26	17.2355	1771.1457	0.000565	0.0580	102.7615	0.00973127	312
27	19.2300	1988.7245	0.000503	0.0520	103.4179	0.00966950	324
28	21.4552	2231.4813	0.000448	0.0466	104.0063	0.00961480	336
29	23.9380	2502.3296	0.000400	0.0418	104.5337	0.00956629	348
30	26.7081	2804.5202	0.000357	0.0374	105.0063	0.00952323	360
31	29.7987	3141.6799	0.000318	0.0336	105.4300	0.00948497	372
32	33.2470	3517.8553	0.000284	0.0301	105.8097	0.00945093	384
33	37.0943	3937.5613	0.000254	0.0270	106.1500	0.00942063	396
34	41.3868	4405.8352	0.000227	0.0242	106.4550	0.00939364	408
35	46.1761	4928.2973	0.000203	0.0217	106.7284	0.00936958	420
36	51.5195	5511.2180	0.000181	0.0194	106.9734	0.00934812	432
37	57.4813	6161.5936	0.000162	0.0174	107.1931	0.00932896	444
38	64.1329	6887.2300	0.000145	0.0156	107.3899	0.00931186	456
39	71.5543	7696.8362	0.000130	0.0140	107.5663	0.00929659	468
40	79.8345	8600.1290	0.000116	0.0125	107.7244	0.00928294	480

Table A.15. Monthly Compounding 12%

Nominal Annual Interest Rate = 12%   Compounding Periods per Year = 12

Year	Amount of 1 at Compound Interest (Col. 1)	Accumulation of 1 per Period (Col. 2)	Sinking Fund Factor (Col. 3)	Present Value Reversion of 1 (Col. 4)	Present Value Ordinary Annuity 1 per Period (Col. 5)	Installment to Amortize 1 (Col. 6)	Period
1	1.1268	12.6825	0.078849	0.8874	11.2551	0.08884879	12
2	1.2697	26.9735	0.037073	0.7876	21.2434	0.04707347	24
3	1.4308	43.0769	0.023214	0.6989	30.1075	0.03321431	36
4	1.6122	61.2226	0.016334	0.6203	37.9740	0.02633384	48
5	1.8167	81.6697	0.012244	0.5504	44.9550	0.02224445	60
6	2.0471	104.7099	0.009550	0.4885	51.1504	0.01955019	72
7	2.3067	130.6723	0.007653	0.4335	56.6485	0.01765273	84
8	2.5993	159.9273	0.006253	0.3847	61.5277	0.01625284	96
9	2.9289	192.8926	0.005184	0.3414	65.8578	0.01518423	108
10	3.3004	230.0387	0.004347	0.3030	69.7005	0.01434709	120
11	3.7190	271.8959	0.003678	0.2689	73.1108	0.01367788	132
12	4.1906	319.0616	0.003134	0.2386	76.1372	0.01313419	144
13	4.7221	372.2090	0.002687	0.2118	78.8229	0.01268666	156
14	5.3210	432.0970	0.002314	0.1879	81.2064	0.01231430	168
15	5.9958	499.5802	0.002002	0.1668	83.3217	0.01200168	180
16	6.7262	575.6220	0.001737	0.1480	85.1988	0.01173725	192
17	7.6131	661.3077	0.001512	0.1314	86.8647	0.01151216	204
18	8.5786	757.8606	0.001320	0.1166	88.3431	0.01131950	216
19	9.6666	866.6588	0.001154	0.1034	89.6551	0.01115386	228
20	10.8926	989.2553	0.001011	0.0918	90.8194	0.01101086	240
21	12.2740	1127.4002	0.000887	0.0815	91.8527	0.01088700	252
22	13.8307	1283.0652	0.000779	0.0723	92.7697	0.01077938	264
23	15.5847	1458.4725	0.000686	0.0642	93.5835	0.01068565	276
24	17.5613	1656.1258	0.000604	0.0569	94.3056	0.01060382	288
25	19.7885	1878.8465	0.000532	0.0505	94.9466	0.01053224	300
26	22.2981	2129.8138	0.000470	0.0448	95.5153	0.01046952	312
27	25.1261	2412.6100	0.000414	0.0398	96.0201	0.01041449	324
28	28.3127	2731.2718	0.000366	0.0353	96.4680	0.01036613	336
29	31.9035	3090.3480	0.000324	0.0313	96.8655	0.01032359	348
30	35.9496	3494.9639	0.000286	0.0278	97.2183	0.01028613	360
31	40.5090	3950.8953	0.000253	0.0247	97.5314	0.01025311	372
32	45.6465	4464.6502	0.000224	0.0219	97.8093	0.01022398	384
33	51.4356	5043.5621	0.000198	0.0194	98.0558	0.01019827	396
34	57.9589	5695.8945	0.000176	0.0173	98.2746	0.01017556	408
35	65.3096	6430.9590	0.000155	0.0153	98.4688	0.01015550	420
36	73.5925	7259.2481	0.000138	0.0136	98.6412	0.01013776	432
37	82.9258	8192.5849	0.000122	0.0121	98.7941	0.01012206	444
38	93.4429	9244.2922	0.000108	0.0107	98.9298	0.01010817	456
39	105.2938	10429.3823	0.000096	0.0095	99.0503	0.01009588	468
40	118.6477	11764.7715	0.000085	0.0084	99.1572	0.01008500	480

Table A.16. Monthly Compounding 13%

Nominal Annual Interest Rate = 13%   Compounding Periods per Year = 12

Year	Amount of 1 at Compound Interest (Col. 1)	Accumulation of 1 per Period (Col. 2)	Sinking Fund Factor (Col. 3)	Present Value Reversion of 1 (Col. 4)	Present Value Ordinary Annuity 1 per Period (Col. 5)	Installment to Amortize 1 (Col. 6)	Period
1	1.1380	12.7415	0.078484	0.8787	11.1960	0.08931728	12
2	1.2951	27.2417	0.036708	0.7721	21.0341	0.04754182	24
3	1.4739	43.7433	0.022861	0.6785	29.6789	0.03369395	36
4	1.6773	62.5228	0.015994	0.5962	37.2752	0.02682750	48
5	1.9089	83.8945	0.011920	0.5239	43.9501	0.02275307	60
6	2.1723	108.2161	0.009241	0.4603	49.8154	0.02007411	72
7	2.4722	135.8949	0.007359	0.4045	54.9693	0.01819196	84
8	2.8134	167.3942	0.005974	0.3554	59.4981	0.01680726	96
9	3.2018	203.2415	0.004920	0.3123	63.4776	0.01575359	108
10	3.6437	244.0369	0.004098	0.2744	66.9744	0.01493107	120
11	4.1467	290.4634	0.003443	0.2412	70.0471	0.01427611	132
12	4.7191	343.2983	0.002913	0.2119	72.7471	0.01374625	144
13	5.3704	403.4260	0.002479	0.1862	75.1196	0.01331210	156
14	6.1117	471.8534	0.002119	0.1636	77.2044	0.01295264	168
15	6.9554	549.7260	0.001819	0.1438	79.0362	0.01265242	180
16	7.9154	638.3475	0.001567	0.1263	80.6459	0.01239988	192
17	9.0080	739.2016	0.001353	0.1110	82.0604	0.01217615	204
18	10.2514	853.9769	0.001171	0.0975	83.3033	0.01200433	216
19	11.6664	984.5950	0.001016	0.0857	84.3954	0.01184898	228
20	13.2768	1163.2425	0.000882	0.0753	85.3551	0.01171576	240
21	15.1094	1302.4083	0.000768	0.0662	86.1984	0.01160114	252
22	17.1950	1494.9244	0.000669	0.0582	86.9394	0.01150226	264
23	19.5685	1714.0140	0.000583	0.0511	87.5905	0.01141676	276
24	22.2696	1963.3451	0.000509	0.0449	88.1627	0.01134267	288
25	25.3435	2247.0919	0.000445	0.0395	88.6654	0.01127835	300
26	28.8417	2570.0051	0.000389	0.0347	89.1072	0.01122244	312
27	32.8228	2937.4908	0.000340	0.0305	89.4954	0.01117376	324
28	37.3534	3355.7014	0.000298	0.0268	89.8365	0.01113133	336
29	42.5094	3831.6387	0.000261	0.0235	90.1362	0.01109432	348
30	48.3771	4373.2708	0.000229	0.0207	90.3996	0.01106200	360
31	55.0547	4989.6657	0.000200	0.0182	90.6310	0.01103375	372
32	62.6541	5691.1432	0.000176	0.0160	90.8344	0.01100905	384
33	71.3024	6489.4473	0.000154	0.0140	91.0131	0.01098743	396
34	81.1444	7397.9434	0.000135	0.0123	91.1701	0.01096851	408
35	92.3450	8431.8414	0.000119	0.0108	91.3081	0.01095193	420
36	105.0916	9608.4509	0.000104	0.0095	91.4293	0.01093741	432
37	119.5976	10947.4708	0.000091	0.0084	91.5359	0.01092468	444
38	136.1060	12471.3190	0.000080	0.0073	91.6295	0.01091352	456
39	154.8930	14205.5077	0.000070	0.0065	91.7117	0.01090373	468
40	176.2733	16179.0708	0.000062	0.0057	91.7840	0.01089514	480

Table A.17. Monthly Compounding 14%

Nominal Annual Interest Rate = 14%					Compounding Periods per Year = 12	
Year	Amount of 1 at Compound Interest (Col. 1)	Accumu- lation of 1 per Period (Col. 2)	Sinking Fund Factor (Col. 3)	Present Value Rever- sion of 1 (Col. 4)	Present Value Ordinary Annuity 1 per Period (Col. 5)	Installment to Amortize 1 (Col. 6)	Period
1	1.1493	12.8007	0.078120	0.8701	11.1375	0.08978712	12
2	1.3210	27.5132	0.036346	0.7570	20.8277	0.04801288	24
3	1.5183	44.4228	0.022511	0.6586	29.2589	0.03417763	36
4	1.7450	63.8577	0.015660	0.5731	36.5945	0.02732648	48
5	2.0056	86.1951	0.011602	0.4986	42.9770	0.02326825	60
6	2.3051	111.8684	0.008939	0.4338	48.5302	0.02060574	72
7	2.6494	141.3758	0.007073	0.3774	53.3618	0.01874001	84
8	3.0450	175.2899	0.005705	0.3284	57.5655	0.01737150	96
9	3.4998	214.2688	0.004667	0.2857	61.2231	0.01633370	108
10	4.0225	259.0689	0.003860	0.2486	64.4054	0.01552664	120
11	4.6232	310.5595	0.003220	0.2163	67.1742	0.01488666	132
12	5.3136	369.7399	0.002705	0.1882	69.5833	0.01437127	144
13	6.1072	437.7583	0.002284	0.1637	71.6793	0.01395103	156
14	7.0192	515.9348	0.001938	0.1425	73.5029	0.01360490	168
15	8.0675	605.7863	0.001651	0.1240	75.0897	0.01331741	180
16	9.2723	709.0564	0.001410	0.1078	76.4702	0.01307699	192
17	10.6571	827.7490	0.001208	0.0938	77.6713	0.01287476	204
18	12.2486	964.1675	0.001037	0.0816	78.7164	0.01270383	216
19	14.0779	1120.9590	0.000892	0.0710	79.6257	0.01255876	228
20	16.1803	1301.1660	0.000769	0.0618	80.4168	0.01243521	240
21	18.5967	1508.2855	0.000663	0.0538	81.1052	0.01232967	252
22	21.3739	1746.3367	0.000573	0.0468	81.7041	0.01223929	264
23	24.5660	2019.9389	0.000495	0.0407	82.2251	0.01216173	276
24	28.2347	2334.4014	0.000428	0.0354	82.6785	0.01209504	288
25	32.4513	2695.8264	0.000371	0.0308	83.0730	0.01203761	300
26	37.2977	3111.2274	0.000321	0.0268	83.4162	0.01198808	312
27	42.8678	3588.6651	0.000279	0.0233	83.7148	0.01194532	324
28	49.2697	4137.4044	0.000242	0.0203	83.9746	0.01190836	336
29	56.6278	4768.0935	0.000210	0.0177	84.2006	0.01187639	348
30	65.0847	5492.9710	0.000182	0.0154	84.3973	0.01184872	360
31	74.8045	6326.1032	0.000158	0.0134	84.5684	0.01182474	372
32	85.9760	7283.6571	0.000137	0.0116	84.7173	0.01180396	384
33	98.8158	8384.2140	0.000119	0.0101	84.8469	0.01178594	396
34	113.5732	9649.1302	0.000104	0.0088	84.9596	0.01177030	408
35	130.5344	11102.9517	0.000090	0.0077	85.0576	0.01175673	420
36	150.0287	12773.8898	0.000078	0.0067	85.1430	0.01174495	432
37	172.4343	14694.3691	0.000068	0.0058	85.2172	0.01173472	444
38	198.1860	16901.6568	0.000059	0.0050	85.2818	0.01172583	456
39	227.7835	19438.5853	0.000051	0.0044	85.3380	0.01171811	468
40	261.8011	22354.3838	0.000045	0.0038	85.3869	0.01171140	480

Table A.18. Monthly Compounding 15%

Nominal Annual Interest Rate = 15%   Compounding Periods per Year = 12

Year	Amount of 1 at Compound Interest (Col. 1)	Accumu- lation of 1 per Period (Col. 2)	Sinking Fund Factor (Col. 3)	Present Value Rever- sion of 1 (Col. 4)	Present Value Ordinary Annuity 1 per Period (Col. 5)	Installment to Amortize 1 (Col. 6)	Period
1	1.1608	12.8604	0.077758	0.8615	11.0793	0.09025831	12
2	1.3474	27.7881	0.035987	0.7422	20.6242	0.04848665	24
3	1.5639	45.1155	0.022165	0.6394	28.8473	0.03466533	36
4	1.8154	65.2284	0.015331	0.5509	35.9315	0.02783075	48
5	2.1072	88.5745	0.011290	0.4746	42.0346	0.02378993	60
6	2.4459	115.6736	0.008645	0.4088	47.2925	0.02114501	72
7	2.8391	147.1290	0.006797	0.3522	51.8222	0.01929675	84
8	3.2955	183.6411	0.005445	0.3034	55.7246	0.01794541	96
9	3.8253	226.0226	0.004424	0.2614	59.0865	0.01692434	108
10	4.4402	275.2171	0.003633	0.2252	61.9828	0.01613350	120
11	5.1540	332.3198	0.003009	0.1940	64.4781	0.01550915	132
12	5.9825	398.6021	0.002509	0.1672	66.6277	0.01500877	144
13	6.9442	475.5395	0.002103	0.1440	68.4797	0.01460287	156
14	8.0606	564.8450	0.001770	0.1241	70.0751	0.01427040	168
15	9.3563	668.5068	0.001496	0.1069	71.4496	0.01399587	180
16	10.8604	788.8326	0.001268	0.0921	72.6338	0.01376770	192
17	12.6063	928.5014	0.001077	0.0793	73.6539	0.01357700	204
18	14.6328	1090.6225	0.000917	0.0683	74.5328	0.01341691	216
19	16.9851	1278.8054	0.000782	0.0589	75.2900	0.01328198	228
20	19.7155	1497.2395	0.000668	0.0507	75.9423	0.01316790	240
21	22.8848	1750.7879	0.000571	0.0437	76.5042	0.01307117	252
22	26.5637	2045.0953	0.000489	0.0376	76.9884	0.01298897	264
23	30.8339	2386.7140	0.000419	0.0324	77.4055	0.01291899	276
24	35.7906	2783.2495	0.000359	0.0279	77.7648	0.01285929	288
25	41.5441	3243.5298	0.000308	0.0241	78.0743	0.01280831	300
26	48.2225	3777.8022	0.000265	0.0207	78.3410	0.01276470	312
27	55.9745	4397.9613	0.000227	0.0179	78.5708	0.01272738	324
28	64.9727	5117.8138	0.000195	0.0154	78.7687	0.01269540	336
29	75.4173	5953.3859	0.000168	0.0133	78.9392	0.01266797	348
30	87.5410	6923.2800	0.000144	0.0114	79.0861	0.01264444	360
31	101.6136	8049.0889	0.000124	0.0098	79.2127	0.01262424	372
32	117.9485	9355.8767	0.000107	0.0085	79.3217	0.01260688	384
33	136.9092	10872.7365	0.000092	0.0073	79.4157	0.01259197	396
34	158.9180	12633.4384	0.000079	0.0063	79.4966	0.01257916	408
35	184.4648	14677.1811	0.000068	0.0054	79.5663	0.01256813	420
36	214.1183	17049.4647	0.000059	0.0047	79.6264	0.01255865	432
37	248.5388	19803.1035	0.000050	0.0040	79.6781	0.01255050	444
38	288.4925	22999.4023	0.000043	0.0035	79.7227	0.01254348	456
39	334.8690	26709.5205	0.000037	0.0030	79.7611	0.01253744	468
40	388.7007	31016.0571	0.000032	0.0026	79.7942	0.01253224	480

Table A.19. Monthly Compounding 16%

| Nominal Annual Interest Rate = 16% | | | | | Compounding Periods per Year = 12 | |

Year	Amount of 1 at Compound Interest (Col. 1)	Accumu- lation of 1 per Period (Col. 2)	Sinking Fund Factor (Col. 3)	Present Value Rever- sion of 1 (Col. 4)	Present Value Ordinary Annuity 1 per Period (Col. 5)	Installment to Amortize 1 (Col. 6)	Period
1	1.1723	12.9203	0.077398	0.8530	11.0216	0.09073086	12
2	1.3742	28.0664	0.035630	0.7277	20.4235	0.04896311	24
3	1.6110	45.8217	0.021824	0.6207	28.4438	0.03515703	36
4	1.8885	66.6358	0.015007	0.5295	35.2855	0.02834028	48
5	2.2138	91.0355	0.010985	0.4517	41.1217	0.02431806	60
6	2.5952	119.6386	0.008359	0.3853	46.1003	0.02169184	72
7	3.0423	153.1691	0.006529	0.3287	50.3472	0.01986206	84
8	3.5663	192.4760	0.005195	0.2804	53.9701	0.01852879	96
9	4.1807	238.5543	0.004192	0.2392	57.0605	0.01752525	108
10	4.9009	292.5706	0.003418	0.2040	59.6968	0.01675131	120
11	5.7452	355.8923	0.002810	0.1741	61.9457	0.01614317	132
12	6.7350	430.1224	0.002325	0.1485	63.8641	0.01565825	144
13	7.8952	517.1402	0.001934	0.1267	65.5006	0.01526705	156
14	9.2553	619.1487	0.001615	0.1080	66.8965	0.01494845	168
15	10.8497	738.7303	0.001354	0.0922	68.0874	0.01468701	180
16	12.7188	878.9123	0.001138	0.0786	69.1032	0.01447110	192
17	14.9099	1043.2435	0.000959	0.0671	69.9698	0.01429188	204
18	17.4785	1235.8842	0.000809	0.0572	70.7090	0.01414247	216
19	20.4895	1461.7113	0.000684	0.0488	71.3396	0.01401746	228
20	24.0192	1726.4417	0.000579	0.0416	71.8775	0.01391256	240
21	28.1570	2036.7775	0.000491	0.0355	72.3364	0.01382431	252
22	33.0077	2400.5752	0.000417	0.0303	72.7278	0.01374990	264
23	38.6939	2827.0445	0.000354	0.0258	73.0617	0.01368706	276
24	45.3598	3326.9820	0.000301	0.0220	73.3466	0.01363391	288
25	53.1739	3913.0442	0.000256	0.0188	73.5895	0.01358889	300
26	62.3342	4600.0678	0.000217	0.0160	73.7968	0.01355072	312
27	73.0726	5405.4454	0.000185	0.0137	73.9736	0.01351833	324
28	85.6609	6349.5662	0.000157	0.0117	74.1245	0.01349082	336
29	100.4178	7456.3313	0.000134	0.0100	74.2531	0.01346745	348
30	117.7168	8753.7598	0.000114	0.0085	74.3629	0.01344757	360
31	137.9960	10274.6974	0.000097	0.0072	74.4565	0.01343066	372
32	161.7686	12057.6480	0.000083	0.0062	74.5364	0.01341627	384
33	189.6367	14147.7491	0.000071	0.0053	74.6045	0.01340402	396
34	222.3055	16597.9135	0.000060	0.0045	74.6626	0.01339358	408
35	260.6023	19470.1697	0.000051	0.0038	74.7122	0.01338469	420
36	305.4964	22837.2317	0.000044	0.0033	74.7545	0.01337712	432
37	358.1245	26784.3403	0.000037	0.0028	74.7906	0.01337067	444
38	419.8189	31411.4204	0.000032	0.0024	74.8213	0.01336517	456
39	492.1415	36835.6113	0.000027	0.0020	74.8476	0.01336048	468
40	576.9231	43194.2319	0.000023	0.0017	74.8700	0.01335648	480

INDEX